Computational Learning Theory and Natural Learning Systems

Computational Learning Theory and Natural Learning Systems

Volume I: Constraints and Prospects

edited by Stephen José Hanson, George A. Drastal, and Ronald L. Rivest

A Bradford Book
The MIT Press
Cambridge, Massachusetts
London, England

This book was set in Times Roman by Asco Trade Typesetting Ltd., Hong Kong and was printed and bound in the United States of America.

Library of Congress Cataloging-in-Publication Data

Computational learning theory and natural learning systems / edited by Stephen J. Hanson, George A. Drastal, and Ronald L. Rivest.
 p. cm.
"A Bradford Book."
Includes bibliographical references and index.
Contents: Contents: v. 1. Constraints and prospects.
ISBN 0-262-58126-4 (v. 1)
 1. Machine learning—Congresses. I. Hanson, Stephen José. II. Drastal, George A. III. Rivest, Ronald L.
Q325.5.C65   1994
066.3′1—dc20   93-34468
                                                                          CIP

Contents

Preface

This volume is based on a workshop, Computational Learning Theory and "Natural" Learning Systems: Constraints and Prospects, held September 5–6, 1990, in Princeton, New Jersey. This two-day workshop was sponsored by Siemens Corporate Research, MIT, and Princeton University in order to explore the emerging intersection of theoretical learning research and natural learning systems (AI and neural nets). Over 100 participants attended to hear 16 oral presentations and 25 poster presentations. As defined by participants, natural systems could include those that have been successful in a difficult engineering domain or those that represent natural constraints arising from biological or psychological processes and mechanisms. This unusual workshop attracted researchers interested in the intersection of three historically distinct styles of learning research: computational learning theory, which has undergone a renaissance; neural network research, which has seen exponential growth; and symbolic machine learning, which has become a dominant influence in the AI field. Notwithstanding various accidental intersections between these three disparate groups, there has not been a single focused attempt to find common points of influence and interaction. Although there are many possible points of contact, the organizers (Steve Hanson, Siemens and Princeton University; Ron Rivest, MIT; and George Drastal, Siemens) felt that one with many possible long-term implications is the relation between theory and experiment in learning systems.

Some scientific fields are characterized by a wide gulf between theory and practice. Computer science (AI and cognitive science) attacked the practicalities of getting machines to "learn" some decades ago and has made some reasonable beginnings; it acquired some theoretical approaches to the problem from other fields (psychology and biology, among others), but the gulf between theory and practice was huge. Just a few years ago, though, some new work brought the theoretical treatments into the finite domain and reduced the gap between approaches.

Workshop participants were encouraged to explore how general issues in learning systems could provide constraints for theory, while at the same time theoretical results were interpreted in the context of experiments with actual learning systems. Speakers with theoretical topics were juxtaposed with speakers working in experimental domains, maximizing the likelihood of lively discussion and substantive exchange. Invited speakers were Eric B. Baum, NEC Corp.; Tom Mitchell, Carnegie Mellon University; Dave Rumelhart, Stanford University; and Les Valiant, Harvard University.

Introduction

Learning systems research has been growing at a rapid pace in three historically distinct areas: computational learning theory, which has undergone a renaissance in the last few years; connectionist/neural network learning research, which has grown explosively; and symbolic machine learning, which has become a dominant influence in the artificial intelligence (AI) field. All three maintain their separate conferences and activities but overlap in significant ways at the conceptual level, which suggests that unifying these three views of similar phenomena is a worthy, if distant, goal.

Potential barriers to congenial commerce between these three distinct learning areas can be understood better by considering two dimensions of potential interaction. One relevant dimension is experimental versus theoretical approaches to learning systems. In the three areas, theory dominates one area but appears sparingly (usually independently of experiment) in the other areas. A second sort of dimension might be signals versus symbols; continuous variables versus discrete; dynamical systems versus logic; numbers versus words. This is a comparatively older tension arising between traditional computer science or engineering disciplines with AI and neural network approaches. The distinction rests primarily on styles of computation and their relation to developing various kinds of algorithms and their convenience in describing one sort of phenomena versus another.

For example, computational learning theory research has had little or no contact with experiment; research tends to focus on finding guarantees on resource bounds for learning algorithms. This sort of focus tends to limit its contact with experimental work, which focuses on achieving the best possible results in a subspace of typical problems. Computational learning theory has provided for the most part negative results, while the more experimental learning fields have produced positive (but modest) results with many kinds of problem domains. Both neural network learning and symbolic learning have been strongly empirical fields, and many practitioners of empirical learning have responded to this tension by ignoring theory research.

On the other hand, the experimentalists have tried many kinds of algorithms and representations that are blatantly ad hoc. The choice of discrete, separable features that define necessary and sufficient categories (symbols), or continuous, integral features defining fuzzy, probabilistic categories can seem arbitrary to a theorist concerned about more generic learning problems. To the experimentalist such differences loom large since learning may concern human faces, or the verb argument structure of natural language, both of which a theorist reduces to "concept learning." These differences in focus create arbitrary divisions between experimentalists and theorists, which can appear as a huge gulf, leading to further miscommunication and confusion.

We have also seen conflicts between symbolists and connectionists. These could roughly be considered to be different computational styles leading to different sorts of accounts of similar phenomena. At one level, the conflicts are quite real, and yet we see many commonalities and problems. Symbolic approaches have stressed heuristic, deterministic models, whereas connectionist approaches have stressed optimal (sometimes heuristic), stochastic models. Such differences do not hopelessly polarize the camps but can lead to disagreements on the kind of approach that is most likely to work for a given application or problem.

This book is an attempt at examining the state of the learning field based on representative examples taken from each of the three areas. These examples should provide the reader with a rich view of the fields and their potential for integration. Several themes emerge from the joint consideration of these different learning approaches, which we feel are somewhat generic and provide for future directions of learning systems. The following questions arise within the context of this book:

What are natural systems? Alternatively, how can we make learning easy? Does the world conspire to make learning easy for us by providing "good" examples, examples at the right time, or sets of examples that would be unlikely for other kinds of tasks? Are biological systems wired up in a certain way to take advantage of the way the world is structured? Are there simple constraints on classes of functions that make them tractable? Are typical neural net functions thus constrained? How can we characterize these functions and biases in order to construct learning systems that are guaranteed to learn as easily and with the generality of biological systems?

How should learning systems use prior knowledge? Many researchers agree that the trick is to walk a line that we all consider reasonable between "giving away the store" and forcing our systems to restart every new learning task from scratch. Much of the current work in symbolic learning is concerned with extracting an appropriate task-specific inductive bias from a generic prior theory of the task domain. Some researchers have shown that a neural network can converge more rapidly if only some way can be found to translate prior knowledge into an initial set of weights. Researchers have tried to estimate the number of examples equivalent to the prior knowledge a system was given.

What makes a learning problem hard? In characterizing the kinds of learning tasks that are well suited to networks or symbolic algorithms, one possibility is to assume that some algorithms are better with one kind of data versus another. Some learning researchers have argued that the style of computation is critical in this regard. Some problems are better solved with a neural net, while others seem more suited to rule-based symbolic method. What dimensions characterise these biases?

If knowledge is important, can we quantify how important? We know from statistics how the confidence of a hypothesis varies with the amount of data used to support it. But if a picture is worth a thousand words, how much are 1000 examples worth in the form of prior knowledge? An open question is how the confidence of a hypothesis should vary with its interpretation in the prior knowledge that is supported by data, or how strong are the data really, when the hypothesis is seen in the light of what we already knew.

How are neural network learning and symbolic machine learning similar? Techniques in symbolic machine learning like constructive induction create new features that can be likened to the higher-order features developed in the hidden layers of a neural network during training. Constructive induction methods require either some prior knowledge of potentially useful features or ways to build them. This can be a liability if the domain is truly knowledge free but an advantage when we know even a little, because these methods provide the means to encode that knowledge. Many researchers agree that there are important similarities between neural nets and symbolic machine learning methods that need further exploration.

How can we trade off complexity of hypothesis versus fit to data? This is similar in statistics to the notion of trading estimation error for approximation error. Without removing noise or systematic errors, parameter estimation techniques will tend to bias away from the true underlying data model, while those same techniques, given enough resources, will approximate the known data perfectly. Thus, we must strike a balance between accounting for a known data sample and pursuing constraints (e.g., prior knowledge) on the approximate model that better represents the true model. This is also related to learning systems that try to adjust the complexity of their representations while learning from examples.

We believe these questions can help frame the intersection of these three areas and drive them toward some common set methods and views. Further, based on the material in this book and what has been emerging in the field we feel that the current outlook is very favorable and exciting. Research continues to stimulate developments that will increase the intersection of the three fields and lead to methods of learning that are founded in a secure understanding and successful in practice.

I FOUNDATIONS

1 Logic and Learning

Daniel N. Osherson, Michael Stob, and Scott Weinstein

1.1 Introduction

The predicate calculus provides a convenient medium for expressing facts and hypotheses, and it is thus no suprise that numerous systems of machine learning are designed to discover predicate logic sentences that summarize or extend the data presented to them (e.g., [Michalski 1983]). Theoreticians of learning have also found the language of logic to be of central concern, as witnessed by influential studies that bear on the discovery of various kinds of formulas (e.g., [Haussler 1989, Kearns 1987, Shapiro 1981, Laird 1986, Angluin 1987]). In contrast, the theory of the predicate calculus—that is, contemporary Model Theory (see, e.g., [Chang and Keisler 1973])—rarely emerges in theoretical studies of learning, at least within the movement represented by [Haussler and Pitt 1988, Rivest et al. 1989, Fulk and Case 1990]. We may speculate about two reasons for this absence. First, other mathematical theories—notably, the theories of computation, complexity, and probability—have yielded a rich harvest of results, so it is natural that researchers continue to focus on these tools in their analysis of learning. Second, deductive logic seems to be divorced from the inductive processes that lie at the heart of learning, since the inferences involved in empirical discovery are uncertain and subject to retraction, which is quite the opposite of deductive inference.

The purpose of this chapter is to suggest that, appearances notwithstanding, Model Theory is a potentially valuable tool for understanding learning algorithms designed to discover predicate logic sentences. As evidence for this suggestion, we consider the problem of producing necessary and sufficient conditions for a concept whose extension is available in part or in whole. Two model-theoretic perspectives are proposed; the first is related to PAC learning in the sense of [Valiant 1984, Blumer et al. 1989], the second to identification in the limit in the sense of [Gold 1967, Blum and Blum 1975]. As a preliminary, we observe that Model Theory need not be viewed as bearing primarily on deductive implication. Rather, implication may be seen as derivative to the primary concern of the theory, namely, the conditions under which specified sentences are true in given situations (or "models"). It is the concern for truth-in-a-situation that renders the theorems of Model Theory relevant to discovering a true description of one's environment.[1]

theorem says that the class of all first-order concepts can be learned in any model of a strong theory.

THEOREM 3   *Suppose that T is a strong theory. Then $\mathscr{L}(x)$ is learnable in $\{\mathscr{S} | \mathscr{S} \models T\}$.*

Second Finding: Given a set $\Phi \subseteq \mathscr{L}(x)$, we say that a theory T *expresses the learnability of* Φ just in case for all models $\mathscr{S}$, Φ is learnable in $\mathscr{S}$ iff $\mathscr{S} \models T$. Such theories are useful inasmuch as they provide a test for learnability in given situations. Unfortunately, no theory expresses the learnability of even relatively simple subsets of $\mathscr{L}(x)$. This is the content of the next theorem, stated with the following notation. The subset of $\mathscr{L}(x)$ of form $\exists y \forall z \varphi(xyz)$, with φ quantifier-free, is denoted by $\mathscr{L}_{\exists\forall}(x)$.

THEOREM 4   *Suppose that $\mathscr{L}$ contains at least one binary relation symbol. Then there is no theory that expresses the learnability of $\mathscr{L}_{\exists\forall}(x)$.*

1.3   Discovering First-order Intensions in the Limit

1.3.1   Overview

This section is devoted to a paradigm in which the entire extension of a target concept is revealed to the scientist in piecemeal fashion. In response to these data, the scientist advances a succession of first-order formulas in the hope of stabilizing on a necessary and sufficient condition for membership in the concept. For notational convenience we consider only unary concepts; extension to concepts of arbitrary arity is straightforward. The paradigm is formalized in this section. Section 1.4 is devoted to theorems. A related paradigm is studied in [Osherson et al. 1990b], and several proofs below will refer to constructions appearing there. On the other hand, new techniques are used to prove the results of sections 1.4.2 and 1.4.3, and they illustrate the use of model-theoretical constructions in the study of learning.

1.3.2   Paradigm

1.3.2.1   Language and Models   We fix a countable, first-order language $\mathscr{L}$ (with identity) that includes a distinguished, unary predicate C.[2] This predicate represents the target concept for which a first-order intension is sought. We also distinguish a variable x and denote by $\mathscr{L}(x)$ the set of all formulas of $\mathscr{L}$ in which just the variable x occurs free and in which C

does not occur. $\mathscr{L}(x)$ represents the set of potential intensions for the target concept; C is excluded from the vocabulary of $\mathscr{L}(x)$ in order to rule out intensions that are accurate but trivial (e.g., the formula Cx).

A formula φ of $\mathscr{L}$ is *basic* just in case φ is an atomic formula or the negation of such. The set of all basic formulas is denoted BAS.

We conceive of Nature as choosing one member from a class $\mathscr{K}$ of models of $\mathscr{L}$. $\mathscr{K}$ is conceived as representing the class of "possible worlds" known to the scientist to be theoretical alternatives prior to his inquiry. Attention is limited to models with countable domains. Henceforth, by *model* we understand "countable model that interprets $\mathscr{L}$." By a *complete assignment* to a model $\mathscr{S}$ is meant any mapping of the (countable) set of variables of $\mathscr{L}$ onto $|\mathscr{S}|$. Thus, a complete assignment to $\mathscr{S}$ provides every member of its domain with at least one temporary name.

1.3.2.2 The Data Made Available to Scientists An *environment* is any ω-sequence over BAS.[3] The set of formulas appearing in an environment e is denoted by *range(e)*. The initial finite sequence of length $i \in \omega$ in e is denoted $\bar{e}_i$. $A\bar{x} \in range(e)$ [respectively, $\neg A\bar{x} \in range(e)$] may be understood as a message from Nature of the form: "The objects assigned temporary names $\bar{x}$ fall [do not fall] into the set that interprets A." The following definition specifies the sense in which a model underlies an environment.

DEFINITION 5 *Let environment e, model $\mathscr{S}$, and complete assignment g to $\mathscr{S}$ be given. e is for $\mathscr{S}$ via g just in case $range(e) = \{\beta \in BAS | \mathscr{S} \models \beta[g]\}$. e is for $\mathscr{S}$ just in case e is for $\mathscr{S}$ via some complete assignment.*

To illustrate, suppose that the following environment e is for model $\mathscr{S}$.

$$Tx_3 \quad \neg Qx_3x_2 \quad x_4 = x_5 \quad Tx_4 \ldots$$

Then e may be construed as the following, endless message about $\mathscr{S}$ (where we write P^S to denote the set that interprets the predicate P in $\mathscr{S}$).

The object given temporary name x_3 belongs to $T^\mathscr{S}$. The object with temporary name x_3 is such that the pair x_3, x_2 belongs to the complement of $Q^\mathscr{S}$. The objects given temporary names x_4 and x_5 are identical. Object x_4 (and hence object x_5) belongs to $T^\mathscr{S} \ldots$.

Models are determined by their environments. This is the content of the following lemma proved in [Osherson and Weinstein 1986].

LEMMA 6   *Let environment e and models $\mathscr{S}$ and $\mathscr{U}$ be given. If e is for both $\mathscr{S}$ and $\mathscr{U}$ then $\mathscr{S}$ and $\mathscr{U}$ are isomorphic.*

1.3.2.3   Scientists and Success   Scientists are conceived as working in an environment e for a model $\mathscr{S}$ by examining the $\bar{e}_i$ in turn. The scientist announces at each stage some $\varphi \in \mathscr{L}(x)$ to express the hypothesis that $\mathscr{S} \models \forall x(Cx \leftrightarrow \varphi)$.[4] Lemma 6 ensures that no ambiguity arises about the truth of such hypotheses. To proceed formally, let SEQ be the set of all finite sequences over BAS. (Thus, SEQ = $\{\bar{e}_i | i \in \omega$ and e is an environment$\}$). By a (*formal*) *scientist* is meant any function from BAS to $\mathscr{L}(x)$. Note that scientists can be computable or uncomputable, total or partial.

To be successful in a given environment, we stipulate that a scientist's successive conjectures must eventually stabilize to a formula that gives an accurate, necessary, and sufficient condition for membership in the concept expressed by C.

DEFINITION 7   *Let collection $\mathscr{K}$ of models, model $\mathscr{S}$, environment e for $\mathscr{S}$, and scientist Ψ be given.*

(a) Ψ *solves e just in case there is $\varphi \in \mathscr{L}(x)$ such that $\mathscr{S} \models \forall x(Cx \leftrightarrow \varphi)$, and $\Psi(\bar{e}_i) = \varphi$ for all but finitely many $i \in \omega$.*

(b) Ψ *solves $\mathscr{S}$ just in case Ψ solves every environment for $\mathscr{S}$.*

(c) Ψ *solves $\mathscr{K}$ just in case Ψ solves every $\mathscr{S} \in \mathscr{K}$. In this case, $\mathscr{K}$ is solvable.*

1.3.3   Examples

We give an example of solvability followed by an example of unsolvability.

1.3.3.1   Solvability

EXAMPLE 8   *Suppose that $\mathscr{L}$ is limited to the binary relation symbol R plus the distinguished predicate C. Let P be the set of positive integers, and N the set of negative integers. The symbol < denotes the usual ordering on all integers. Let $\mathscr{K}$ consist of all models of either of the forms:*

(a)   (*P*, <, *X*), *where < interprets R, and X is a finite or cofinite subset of P that interprets C;*

(b)   (*N*, <, *X*), *where < interprets R, and X is a finite or cofinite subset of N that interprets C.*

Then $\mathcal{K}$ is solvable.

Proof: We give an informal description of a scientist Ψ that solves $\mathcal{K}$. Ψ is equipped with an enumeration of triples $(y, \mathcal{S}, \varphi)$ such that y is a variable, $\mathcal{S} \in \mathcal{K}$, and $\varphi \in \mathcal{L}(x)$. At each stage in the examination of the environment e, Ψ finds the first triple, $(y, \mathcal{S}, \varphi)$, in the enumeration consistent with the hypotheses:

(a) e is for $\mathcal{S}$,

(b) y is the temporary name of 0 in $\mathcal{S}$, and

(c) $\mathcal{S} \models \forall x(Cx \leftrightarrow \varphi)$.

Ψ then conjectures φ. It is clear that e will cause Ψ to abandon any triple $(y, \mathcal{S}, \varphi)$ such that e is not for $\mathcal{S}$. On the basis of this observation, it is easy to verify that Ψ solves $\mathcal{K}$. ∎

1.3.3.2 Unsolvability Let $\mathcal{S} = (S, r_1, r_2, \ldots, X)$ be a model for $\mathcal{L}$, where X interprets C. If $|\mathcal{S}|$ is infinite then there are uncountably many choices for X. On the other hand, there are only countably many formulas in $\mathcal{L}(x)$. Consequently, for fixed r_1, r_2, ..., the collection $\mathcal{K} = \{(S, r_1, r_2, \ldots, X) | X \subseteq S\}$ is trivially unsolvable inasmuch as necessary and sufficient conditions for membership in C cannot be expressed for some choices of X. A nontrivial example of unsolvability is given next. Its verification depends on the following lemma. The set of variables appearing in a given $\sigma \in \text{SEQ}$ is denoted by $var(\sigma)$, the conjunction of the members of σ is denoted by $\bigwedge \sigma$.

LEMMA 9   *Let scientist Ψ and model $\mathcal{S}$ be given. Suppose that Ψ solves $\mathcal{S}$. Then there is $\sigma \in \text{SEQ}$, $p: var(\sigma) \to |\mathcal{S}|$, and $\varphi \in \mathcal{L}(x)$ such that:*

(a) $\mathcal{S} \models \bigwedge \sigma[p]$;

(b) $\mathcal{S} \models \forall x(Cx \leftrightarrow \varphi)$.

(c)   *for all $\gamma \in \text{SEQ}$, if*

   (i) $\sigma \subseteq \gamma$ *and*

   (ii) $\mathcal{S} \models \exists x_1 \ldots x_k \wedge \gamma[p]$, *where $var(\gamma) - var(\sigma) = \{x_1 \ldots x_k\}$*

   then $\Psi(\gamma) = \varphi$.

The proof of Lemma 9 is easily adapted from a similar result proved in [Osherson et al. 1990b, Lemma 27].[5]

EXAMPLE 10   *Suppose that $\mathscr{L}$ is limited to the binary relation symbol R plus the distinguished predicate C. Let $\omega + \omega$ represent two copies of the natural numbers ordered this way: 0, 1, 2, ..., 0, 1, 2, ... The symbol $<$ denotes the usual ordering on ω or $\omega + \omega$. Let $\mathscr{K}$ consists of all models of either of the forms:*

(a) $(\omega, <, \{i\})$, *where $<$ interprets R, and $i \in \omega$.*

(b) $(\omega + \omega, <, \{\underline{0}\})$, *where $<$ interprets R, and $\underline{0}$ is the second zero in $\omega + \omega$.*

Observe that for every $\mathscr{S} \in \mathscr{K}$ there is $\varphi \in \mathscr{L}(x)$ such that $\mathscr{S} \models \forall x(Cx \leftrightarrow \varphi)$. For example:

(a) $(\omega, <, \{2\}) \models \forall x(Cx \leftrightarrow \exists yz(Ryz \wedge Rzx \wedge \forall w(Rwx \rightarrow w = y \vee w = z)))$.

(b) $(\omega + \omega, <, \{\underline{0}\}) \models \forall x(Cx \leftrightarrow \exists y(Ryx \wedge \forall z(Rzx \rightarrow \exists w(Rzw \wedge Rwx))))$.

Nonetheless, $\mathscr{K}$ is unsolvable.

Proof: Let scientist Ψ solve $\mathcal{O} = (\omega + \omega, <, \{\underline{0}\})$. We show that for some $i \in \omega$, Ψ does not solve $(\omega, <, \{i\})$. But Lemma 9 there is $\sigma \in \text{SEQ}$, $p: var(\sigma) \rightarrow \omega + \omega$, and $\varphi_0 \in \mathscr{L}(x)$ such that:

(a) $\mathcal{O} \models \bigwedge \sigma[p]$;

(b) $\mathcal{O} \models \forall x(Cx \leftrightarrow \varphi_0)$.   (11)

(c)   for all $\gamma \in \text{SEQ}$, if

   (i) $\sigma \subseteq \gamma$ and

   (ii) $\mathcal{O} \models \exists x_1 \ldots x_k \wedge \gamma[p]$, where $var(\gamma) - var(\sigma) = \{x_1 \ldots x_k\}$
   then $\Psi(\gamma) = \varphi_0$.

It is evident that:

For all but at most one $i \in \omega$, $(\omega, <, \{i\}) \not\models \forall x(Cx \leftrightarrow \varphi_0)$.   (12)

It is also easy to verify that there are infinitely many $\ell \in \omega$, complete assignments h to $(\omega, <, \{\ell\})$, and environments e for $(\omega, <, \{\ell\})$ via h such that:

(a) $\sigma \subseteq e$,

(b)   for all $j > length(\sigma)$, $\mathcal{O} \models \exists x_1 \ldots x_k \wedge \bar{e}_j[p]$, where   (13)
$var(\bar{e}_j) - var(\sigma) = \{x_1 \ldots x_k\}$.

By (11)a, c and (13), $\Psi(\bar{e}_j) = \varphi_0$ for cofinitely many $j \in \omega$. So by (12), Ψ does not solve $(\omega, <, \{\ell\})$ for some choice of ℓ.   ■

1.4 Theorems on the Discovery of First-order Intensions

We present four theorems on the solvability of classes of models, in the sense of the paradigm just introduced. Of particular interest are classes that arise from theories in the following way.

DEFINITION 14

(a) *Let* $T \subseteq \mathscr{L}$ *be given. The class* $\{\mathscr{S} | \mathscr{S} \models T\}$ *is denoted by* $\mathrm{MOD}(T)$.

(b) *Let collection* $\mathscr{K}$ *of models be given. If* $\mathscr{K} = \mathrm{MOD}(T)$ *for some* $T \subseteq \mathscr{L}$ *then* $\mathscr{K}$ *is called elementary. If* $\mathscr{K} = \mathrm{MOD}(T)$ *for some recursively enumerable* $T \subseteq \mathscr{L}$ *then* $\mathscr{K}$ *is called recursively axiomatizable.*[6]

For simplicity we limit attention to recursively axiomatizable classes; extension to arbitrary elementary classes is straightforward (see [Osherson et al. 1992. Osherson et al. 1990b] for analogous developments).

1.4.1 A Universal Scientist

It is not difficult to specify recursively axiomatizable classes of models that can be solved neither by computable nor by uncomputable scientist (for example, any recursively axiomatizable class containing the models of example 10). Consequently, no scientist is universal in the sense of solving all such classes. On the other hand, the following theorem shows that there is a mechanical, universal scientist in the weaker sense of solving all recursively axiomatizable classes that are solvable (by machine or nonmachine). To state the theorem, let Turing Machines be conceived as enumerating subsets of $\mathscr{L}$, and let T_i denote the set of sentences enumerated by the ith machine.

THEOREM 15 *There is a computable function* $f: \omega \times \mathrm{SEQ} \to \mathscr{L}(x)$ *such that for all* $i \in \omega$, *if* $\mathrm{MOD}(T_i)$ *is solvable (by either computable or noncomputable scientist), then* $\lambda \sigma f(i, \sigma)$ *solves* $\mathrm{MOD}(T_i)$.

In the theorem, $\lambda \sigma f(i, \sigma)$ represents the computable scientist that results from parameterizing f with an index for theory T_i.

Proof: The function f is computed by a simple modification to the algorithm M presented in [Osherson et al. 1990b, section 3]. Specifically, it suffices to:

(a)   set **P** in M's oracle equal to the class of all sentences of form $\forall x(Cx \leftrightarrow \varphi)$ where $\varphi \in \mathscr{L}(x)$, and

(b)   delete the first clause from the definition of T, **P**-*potential* in the description of M's behavior (thereby allowing M to stabilize on a theory that follows logically from T_i along with the data in the current environment).

Verification of the universality of the resulting algorithm follows essentially the same proof as that given in [Osherson et al. 1990b, theorem 18]. ∎

Theorem 15 shows that noncomputable scientists have no advantage over their computable counterparts when it comes to solving recursively axiomatizable classes of models. This fact may be expressed as follows.

COROLLARY 16   *Let $\mathscr{K}$ be a recursively axiomatizable class of models. If $\mathscr{K}$ is solvable then some computable scientist solves $\mathscr{K}$.*

Corollary 16 has the following practical consequence. Suppose that a software engineer is thinking of writing a program to solve a certain, recursively axiomatizable class $\mathscr{K}$ of models. Before proceeding, she wishes to confirm that the task is possible in principle. For this purpose it is sufficient to conceive of an arbitrary scientist (not necessary computable) that solves $\mathscr{K}$. This guarantees that a program can ultimately be found to solve $\mathscr{K}$.

1.4.2   Nonuniversality for Nonelementary Classes

The validity of theorem 15 hinges on the elementary character of the model-classes in question. Indeed, the next theorem shows that for nonelementary classes, mechanical scientists are neither universal nor in general equivalent to nonmechanical scientists. To state the theorem, we fix the nonlogical vocabulary of $\mathscr{L}$ to be the binary relation symbol R, the constant symbol a, the constant symbol $\underline{0}$, and the unary function symbol S, along with the distinguished predicate C. We also define a collection

$\mathscr{K}_0$ of models as follows. Given $\mathbf{r} \subseteq \omega^2$, we let $p_1(\mathbf{r})$ denote the first projection of $\mathbf{r}$.

DEFINITION 17   *Choose $Z \subset \omega$ to be nonarithmetical.[7] $\mathscr{K}_0$ is the class of all models of either of the following forms (where the nonlogical vocabulary of $\mathscr{L}$ is interpreted in the order $R, a, \underline{0}, S, C$).*

(a)   *$(\omega, \mathbf{r}, i, 0, s, p_1(\mathbf{r}))$, where $i \in Z$, s is successor, and $\mathbf{r}$ is an arbitrary subset of ω.*

(b)   *$(\omega, \mathbf{r}, \mathbf{i}, 0, s, \mathbf{f})$, where $i \notin Z$, s is successor, $\mathbf{r}$ is an arbitrary subset of ω, and $\mathbf{f}$ is an arbitrary, finite subset of ω.*

THEOREM 18

(a)   *$\mathscr{K}_0$ is solvable, but not by computable scientist.*

(b)   *For every computable scientist Ψ there is a computable scientist Φ such that $\{\mathscr{S} \in \mathscr{K}_0 | \Phi \text{ solves } \mathscr{S}\} \supset \{\mathscr{S} \in \mathscr{K}_0 | \Psi \text{ solves } \mathscr{S}\}$.*

Proof: Some notations will be helpful. For the first notation, we observe that for every model in $\mathscr{K}_0$, the interpretation of $\underline{0}$ and S is 0 and successor, respectively. Consequently, for every finite $\mathbf{f} \subseteq \omega$ we may choose C-free $\phi_{\mathbf{f}} \in \mathscr{L}(x)$ such that $\phi_{\mathbf{f}}$ defines $\mathbf{f}$ in every $\mathscr{S} \in \mathscr{K}_0$. As a second notation, we use $\underline{i}$ to denote the term $S \ldots S\underline{0}$ (i occurrences of S). Finally, for $\sigma \in$ SEQ, $range(\sigma)$ denotes the set of formulas appearing in σ.

Proof of Part (a):   We define a (noncomputable) scientist Γ that solves $\mathscr{K}_0$. Let $\sigma \in$ SEQ be given. If $range(\sigma)$ does not contain exactly one formula of form $a = \underline{i}$ then $\Gamma(\sigma) = (x \neq x)$. Otherwise, if σ contains one formula of form $a = \underline{i}$ then:

(a)   if $i \in Z$, $\Gamma(\sigma) = \exists y R x y$;

(b)   if $i \notin Z$, $\Gamma(\sigma) = \phi_{\mathbf{f}}$, where $\mathbf{f} = \{n \in \omega | \sigma \text{ contains a formula of form } C\underline{n}\}$.

It is easy to verify that Γ solves $\mathscr{K}_0$.

To show that no computable scientist solves $\mathscr{K}_0$, we rely on the following definitions and lemmas. Let $\text{VAR} = \{v_i | i \in \omega\}$ be the variables of $\mathscr{L}$, and let $g_0 \colon \text{VAR} \to \omega$ be such that $g_0(v_i) = i$ for all $i \in \omega$. Given $i \in \omega$ and $\gamma \in$ SEQ, γ is called "i-good" just in case there is a model $\mathscr{S}$ of form $(\omega, \mathbf{r}, i, 0, s, p_1(\mathbf{r}))$ such that $\mathscr{S} \models \bigwedge \gamma[g_0]$. The following facts are easy to prove.

(a)   The set $\{(i, \gamma) | i \in \omega$ and γ is i-good$\}$ is recursive.

(b)   For all $i \in \omega$, $\gamma \in$ SEQ, and atomic formulas α of $\mathcal{L}$, if γ is i-good then either $\gamma\alpha$ or $\gamma \neg \alpha$ is i-good (where juxtaposition denotes concatentation).

(19)

LEMMA 20   *Suppose that scientist Ψ solves $\mathcal{K}_0$. Then for all $i \in Z$ there is $\sigma \in$ SEQ such that*:

(a)   *σ is i-good*;

(b)   *for every i-good $\gamma \in$ SEQ, if $\gamma \supseteq \sigma$, then $\Psi(\gamma) = \Psi(\sigma)$*.

Proof of the Lemma: Suppose that scientist Ψ solves $\mathcal{K}_0$, and let $i_0 \in Z$ be given. We prove a contradiction from the hypothesis that the lemma fails for this Ψ and i_0. Falsity of the lemma implies:

For all $\sigma \in$ SEQ, if σ is i_0-good then for some i_0-good $\gamma \in$ SEQ, $\gamma \supseteq \sigma$ and $\Psi(\gamma) \neq \Psi(\sigma)$.

(21)

We shall exhibit an environment for some model in $\mathcal{K}_0$ of form $(\omega, \mathbf{r}, i_0, 0, s, p_1(\mathbf{r}))$ that Ψ does not solve, contradicting our choice of Ψ. The environment to be constructed will be called e, and the model in question will be called $\mathcal{S}$. e will be for $\mathcal{S}$ via g_0. We construct e in stages, the mth stage devoted to $e^m \in$ SEQ. It will be the case that $e^0 \subseteq e^1 \subseteq \cdots$. We take $e = \bigcup_{m \in \omega} e^m$. $\mathcal{S}$ will be defined from e. The construction will ensure that for every $m \geq 0$, for at least m many $i < length(e^m)$, $\Psi(\bar{e}_i) \neq \Psi(\bar{e}_{i+1})$. Consequently, Ψ does not solve e. For the construction, let $\{\alpha_i | i \in \omega\}$ enumerate the atomic formulas of $\mathcal{L}$.

Stage 0:   Set $e^0 = \varnothing$.

Stage $m + 1$:   Suppose that e^m has been defined, and that e^m is i_0-good. By (21) choose i_0-good $\gamma \in$ SEQ such that $\gamma \supseteq \sigma$ and $\Psi(\gamma) \neq \Psi(\sigma)$. Let $j \in \omega$ be least such that $\{\alpha_j, \neg \alpha_j\} \cap range(\gamma) = \varnothing$. If $\gamma\alpha_j$ is i_0-good, let $e^{m+1} = \gamma\alpha_j$; otherwise, let $e^{m+1} = \gamma \neg \alpha_j$. By (19)b, e^{m+1} is well defined (and i_0-good).

   Let $\mathcal{S} = (\omega, \mathbf{r}, i_0, 0, s, p_1(\mathbf{r}))$, where $\mathbf{r} = \{(i, j) \in \omega^2 | R\underline{i}\underline{j} \in e\}$. The construction implies that e is for $\mathcal{S}$ via g_0, and that $\Psi(\bar{e}_i) \neq \Psi(\bar{e}_{i+1})$ for infinitely many $i \in \omega$. However, $\mathcal{S} \in \mathcal{K}_0$.   ∎

LEMMA 22   *Suppose that scientist Ψ solves $\mathcal{K}_0$, and let $i \notin Z$ be given. Then there is no $\sigma \in$ SEQ such that*:

(a) σ is *i-good*;

(b)   for every *i-good* $\gamma \in SEQ$, *if* $\gamma \supseteq \sigma$, *then* $\Psi(\gamma) = \Psi(\sigma)$.

Proof of the Lemma: Suppose that scientist Ψ solves $\mathscr{K}_0$, and let $i_0 \notin Z$ be given. We prove a contradiction from the hypothesis that the lemma fails for this Ψ and i_0. Falsity of the lemma implies:

There is $\sigma \in SEQ$ such that:

(a) σ is i_0-good;

(b)   for every i_0-good $\gamma \in SEQ$ if $\gamma \supseteq \sigma$ then $\Psi(\gamma) = \Psi(\sigma)$.   (23)

Let σ_0 be as specified by (23). Let $\mathscr{S} = (\omega, \mathbf{r}, i_0, 0, s, p_1(\mathbf{r}))$, where $\mathbf{r} = \{(i, j) \in \omega^2 \mid R\underline{ij} \in range(\sigma_0)\}$. $p_1(\mathbf{r})$ is finite, so (since $i_0 \notin Z$) $\mathscr{S} \in \mathscr{K}_0$. Choose $k \in \omega - p_1(\mathbf{r})$, and let $\mathscr{U} = (\omega, \mathbf{r}, i_0, 0, s, p_1(\mathbf{r}) \cup \{k\})$. $\mathscr{U} \in \mathscr{K}_0$. Then:

No $\varphi \in \mathscr{L}(x)$ defines both $p_1(\mathbf{r})$ in $\mathscr{S}$ and $p_1(\mathbf{r}) \cup \{k\}$ in $\mathscr{U}$.   (24)

Let t be an environment for $\mathscr{S}$ via g_0 such that $\sigma_0 \subseteq t$. Let u be an environment for $\mathscr{U}$ via g_0 such that $\sigma_0 \subseteq u$. It is easy to verify the following.

For all $j \in \omega$, both $\bar{t}_j$ and $\bar{u}_j$ are i_0-good.   (25)

From (25) and (23) it follows that for all but finitely many $j \in \omega$, $\Psi(\bar{t}_j) = \Psi(\bar{u}_j) = \Psi(\sigma_0)$. Since $\mathscr{S}, \mathscr{U} \in \mathscr{K}_0$, (24) implies that Ψ does not solve $\{\mathscr{S}, \mathscr{U}\} \subseteq \mathscr{K}_0$, contradicting our choice of Ψ.   ∎

Returning to the proof of part (a) of theorem 18, suppose for a contradiction that computable scientist Ψ solved $\mathscr{K}_0$. Then, by Lemmas 20 and 22:

For all $i \in \omega$, $i \in Z$ if and only if there is $\sigma \in SEQ$ such that:

(a) σ is *i-good*;

(b)   for every *i-good* $\gamma \in SEQ$, if $\gamma \supseteq \sigma$, then $\Psi(\gamma) = \Psi(\sigma)$.   (26)

However, (26), (19)a, and the computability of Ψ exhibit Z as arithmetical, contradicting our choice in Definition (17).   ∎

Proof of Part (b):   Let computable scientist Ψ be given. By part (a) of the theorem, either there is $i_0 \in Z$ such that Ψ does not solve some model of form $(\omega, \mathbf{r}, i_0, 0, s, p_1(\mathbf{r}))$, where $\mathbf{r}$ is an arbitrary subset of ω^2, or there is $i \notin Z$ such that Ψ does not solve some model of form $(\omega, \mathbf{r}, i_0, 0, s, \mathbf{f})$ where $\mathbf{r}$ is an arbitrary subset of ω^2, and $\mathbf{f}$ is an arbitrary, finite subset of ω.

for all $i \in \omega$, $g_0(v_i) = i$, and let $\{\alpha_i | i \in \omega\}$ recursively enumerate the atomic formulas of $\mathscr{L}$. Given $i \in \omega$ and $\mathbf{x} \subseteq \omega$, the *canonical* environment for $\mathscr{S}(i, \mathbf{x})$ is the environment e for $\mathscr{S}(i, \mathbf{x})$ via g_0 such that for all $j \in \omega$, the jth member of e is either α_j or $\neg\alpha_j$. We note:

There is a mechanical procedure that inputs $i \in \omega$ and finite $\mathbf{x} \subseteq \omega$
and outputs the canonical environment for $\mathscr{S}(i, \mathbf{x})$.   (31)

Now let $i_0 \in \omega$ be given, corresponding to scientist Ψ_{i_0}. We define $\mathscr{K}_{i_0}$ by constructing in stages a canonical environment a and a set $A \subseteq \omega$. The result of the mth stage in the construction of a and A will be denoted by a^m and A^m, respectively. If the construction proceeds through infinitely many stages, then $\mathscr{K}_{i_0} = \{\mathscr{S}(i_0, A)\}$, where $A = \{j | Cj \in range(a)\}$ (A may be infinite in this case). If the construction proceeds through only m stages, then $\mathscr{K}_{i_0} = \{\mathscr{S}(i_0, A^m), \mathscr{S}(i_0, A^m \cup \{j_m\})\}$, where $j_m \in \omega - A^m$.

Construction for i_0

Stage 0: $a^0 = \varnothing$. $A^0 = \varnothing$.

Stage $m + 1$:   Suppose that a^m and A^m have been constructed, that $A^m = \{j | Cj \in range(a^m)\}$, and that a^m is an initial segment of the canonical environment for $\mathscr{S}(i_0, A^m)$. Let $j_m \in \omega$ be least such that $j_m \notin A^m$. Let b be the canonical environment for $\mathscr{S}(i_0, A^m)$ and let c be the canonical environment for $\mathscr{S}(i_0, A^m \cup \{j_m\})$ (thus, both b and c begin with a^m). Observe that if $\Psi_{i_0}(\bar{b}_j) = \Psi_{i_0}(\bar{c}_j) = \Psi_{i_0}(a^m)$ for all $j > length(a^m)$, then Ψ_{i_0} fails to solve at least one of $\{\mathscr{S}(i_0, A^m), \mathscr{S}(i_0, A^m \cup \{j_m\})\}$. In this case the construction remains at the present stage, and $\mathscr{K}_{i_0}$ is defined to be $\{\mathscr{S}(i_0, A^m), \mathscr{S}(i_0, A^m \cup \{j_m\})\}$. Let $q \in \omega$ be least such that $q > length(a^m)$ and either:

(a) $\Psi_{i_0}(\bar{b}_q) \neq \Psi_{i_0}(a^m)$ or

(b) $\Psi_{i_0}(\bar{c}_q) \neq \Psi_{i_0}(a^m)$.

In case (a), set $a^{m+1} = \bar{b}_q$; otherwise, set $a^{m+1} = \bar{c}_q$. In either case set $A^{m+1} = \{j | Cj \in range(a^{m+1})\}$.

Observe that for every $m \in \omega$, if a^{m+1} exists, then Ψ_{i_0} changes its conjecture at least m times before reaching the end of a^{m+1}.

In case the construction completes infinitely many stages, we define environment a to be $\bigcup_{m \in \omega} a^m$. In this case define $A = \{j | Cj \in range(a)\}$, and take $\mathscr{K}_{i_0}$ to be $\{\mathscr{S}(i_0, A)\}$. It is easy to see that in this case a is the canonical environment for $\mathscr{S}(i_0, A)$, and that $\Psi_{i_0}(\bar{a}_j) \neq \Psi_{i_0}(\bar{a}_{j+1})$ for infinitely many $j \in \omega$. So in this case Ψ_{i_0} does not solve $\mathcal{K}_{i_0}$. On the other hand, suppose that the construction completes only finitely many stages, and let b, c be the environments created during the last stage entered (say, m). Then b is the canonical environment for $\mathcal{S}(i_0, A^m)$ and c is the canonical environment for $\mathcal{S}(i_0, A^m \cup \{j_m\})$. Take $\mathcal{K}_{i_0} = \{\mathcal{S}(i_0, A^m), \mathcal{S}(i_0, A^m \cup \{j_m\})$. As noted in the construction, Ψ_{i_0} converges on b and c to the same formula and hence fails to solve at least one of them. So in this case too, Ψ_{i_0} does not solve $\mathcal{K}_{i_0}$.

Define $\mathcal{K} = \bigcup_{i \in \omega} \mathcal{K}_i$. Then no computable scientist solves $\mathcal{K}$. It remains to exhibit computable scientist Φ that weakly solves $\mathcal{K}$.

For $i \in \omega$, let A_i be the set defined by the construction for i. This set may be infinite in case the construction completes every stage; otherwise it is finite. In view of (31) it is easy to verify the following about the sets A_i.

There is a computer program P with the following property. For all input $i \in \omega$, P returns $\varphi \in \mathcal{L}(x)$ such that:

(a) φ contains only the vocabulary $\underline{0}$, $\underline{1}$, $\oplus$, $\otimes$;

(b)   for every $\mathcal{S} \in \mathcal{K}$ and $n \in \omega$, $n \in A_i$ iff $\mathcal{S} \models \varphi(\underline{n})$.   (32)

Given $i \in \omega$, let φ_i be as specified in (32). By our definition of $\mathcal{K}$ we have the following fact.

Let $\mathcal{N}$ be the standard model of arithmetic.[9] Then for all $\theta \in \mathcal{L}$ over the vocabulary $\underline{0}$, $\underline{1}$, $\oplus$, $\otimes$, $\mathcal{N} \models \theta$ iff $T(\mathcal{K}) \models \theta$.   (33)

The desired scientist Φ may now be defined. Given $\sigma \in \mathrm{SEQ}$, let $\Gamma(\sigma) \in \mathcal{L}(x)$ be the disjunction of $\{x = \underline{n} \mid C\underline{n} \in range(\sigma)\}$. For all $\sigma \in \mathrm{SEQ}$, $\Phi(\sigma)$ is defined to be $x \neq x$ if $range(\sigma)$ does not include exactly one sentence of the form $a = \underline{i}$. Otherwise, $\Phi(\sigma)$ is $\varphi_i \vee \Gamma(\sigma)$, where $(a = \underline{i}) \in range(\sigma)$.

By (32), Φ is computable. To verify that Φ weakly solves $\mathcal{K}$, let $i \in \omega$ be given and suppose that e is an environment for $\mathcal{S}(i, \mathbf{x}) \in \mathcal{K}$. Then for all but finitely many $j \in \omega$, $\mathcal{S}(i, \mathbf{x}) \models \forall x(Cx \leftrightarrow (\varphi_i \vee \Gamma(\sigma)))$. Moreover, using (33), it is easy to verify that for all but finitely many j, $k \in \omega$, $T(\mathcal{K}) \models \forall x((\varphi_i \vee \Gamma(\bar{e}_j)) \leftrightarrow (\varphi_i \vee \Gamma(\bar{e}_k)))$.   ∎

1.5   Concluding Remarks

The foregoing paradigms and theorems suggest the potential role of contemporary logical theory in the analysis of machine learning. It is evident that research within this perspective is still in its infancy and would profit greatly from interaction with more established theoretical traditions. New techniques from Model Theory may also be required to settle questions that emerge from the framework we have presented. One such question is formulated as follows.

DEFINITION 34   *Let collection $\mathcal{K}$ of models, model $\mathcal{S}$, environment e for $\mathcal{S}$, and scientist Ψ be given.*

(a)   *Ψ BC-solves e just in case for all but finitely many $i \in \omega$ there is $\varphi \in \mathcal{L}(x)$ such that $\mathcal{S} \models \forall x (Cx \leftrightarrow \varphi)$, and $\Psi(\bar{e}_i) = \varphi$.*[10]

(b)   *Ψ BC-solves $\mathcal{S}$ just in case Ψ BC-solves every environment for $\mathcal{S}$.*

(c)   *Ψ BC-solves $\mathcal{K}$ just in case Ψ BC-solves every $\mathcal{S} \in \mathcal{K}$. In this case, $\mathcal{K}$ is BC-solvable.*

OPEN QUESTION 35

(a)   *What is the relation between solvability and BC-solvability among elementary and nonelementary collections of models?*

(b)   *Under what circumstances does BC-solvability imply BC-solvability by computable scientist?*

We conclude on a speculative note. Interaction may well be desirable between a model-theoretic approach to learning, on the one hand, and issues in knowledge representation, on the other. To see what is at stake, consider a sophisticated database, DB. Part of the knowledge stored in DB may consist of well-confirmed statements that serve as the axioms of a class of models. To augment its knowledge, DB can wait for external assistance to augment the axiom set, or it can launch its own investigation via an automated system of scientific discovery. In the latter case, DB would be wise to reflect on the prospects for successful inquiry. What guarantee is there that DB will succeed in any arbitrary model of its axioms, that is, in any situation consistent with what DB knows so far? If DB elects to adopt some version of the "closed world assumption," what guarantee exists that DB's empirical inquiry will succeed even in just the minimal models, those it relies on to extrapolate its data to new, plausible claims? If there is no guarantee of success, can DB at least be certain that it will not stabilize on a false theory, but rather continue endlessly to advance theories, each ultimately perceived to be inaccurate? And suppose that DB's scientific discovery routine asks for an opinion about some sentence that does not follow from the available data, but does follow from some nonmonotone rule of inference. To what extent is the reliability of the routine compromised by supplying it with information of this sort?

Such questions, and many more like them, are crucial to the confidence that DB can place in the results of an empirical investigation that it carries out to some—always incomplete—point. So we would like to equip DB with the mathematical means necessary to determine in advance the feasibility of the empirical inquiry that it contemplates.

Answers to feasibility questions depend on the kind of axioms that DB takes as a scientific starting point—whether they involve more than monadic predicates, second-order quantification, etc. The answers depend as well on the kind of data available to DB, and the criterion of success to which DB aspires. It is not unlikely that progress along these lines would be facilitated by deploying the considerable understanding that has accumulated about logical theory over the last century. This knowledge figures prominently in theoretical studies of knowledge representation.[11] Perhaps it can be deployed, as well, in learning and used as bridge between the two disciplines.

Notes

Research support was provided by the Office of Naval Research under contract No. N00014-87-K-0401 to Osherson and Weinstein, and by a Siemens Corporation grant to Osherson.

1. Formulas of the predicate calculus are often called "first-order" to distinguish them from formulas with more complex kinds of quantification. We sometimes employ this terminology in what follows.

2. The countability of $\mathscr{L}$ means that $\mathscr{L}$'s vocabulary is countable and that $\mathscr{L}$ includes denumerably many individual variables.

3. An ω-sequence over a set X may be conceived as an infinite list $x_1, x_2, \ldots$ of elements drawn from X.

4. Recall that if $\varphi \in \mathscr{L}(x)$, then x is the only variable occurring free in φ.

5. Both results are based on an idea found in [Blum and Blum 1975].

6. A theorem due to Craig [1953] shows that for every recursively enumerable $T \subseteq \mathscr{L}$ there is recursive $T' \subseteq \mathscr{L}$ such that T and T' have the same deductive consequences. Consequently, $\mathscr{K}$ is recursively axiomatizable iff $\mathscr{K} = \text{MOD}(T)$ for some recursive $T \subseteq \mathscr{L}$.

7. For a definition of nonarithmetical sets along with discussion of other technical material figuring in the proofs of this section, see [Rogers 1967].

8. For discussion of acceptable indexings, see [Machtey and Young 1978].

9. For background discussion of the Model Theory of Arithmetic, see [Enderton 1972, chapter 3].

10. BC stands for "behaviorally correct." See [Case and Lynes 1982] for an analogous definition in the recursion-theoretic context.

11. See, for example, [Parikh 1990].

References

[Angluin 1987]   Angluin, D. Learning Propositional Horn Sentences with Hints. Yale University Technical Report, 1987.

[Blum and Blum 1975]   Blum, L. and Blum, M. Toward a mathematical theory of inductive inference. *Information and Control* 28:125–155, 1975.

[Blumer et al. 1989]   Blumer, A., Ehrenfeucht, A., Haussler, D., and Warmuth, M. Learnability and the Vapnik-Chervonenkis Dimension. *Journal of the ACM* 36 (4): 929–965, 1989.

[Case and Lynes 1982]   Case, J., and Lynes, C. Machine inductive inference and language identification. In *Proceedings of the 9th Colloquium on Automata, Languages, and Programming.* Springer-Verlag, Berlin, Lecture Notes in Computer Science 140, pp. 107–115, 1982.

[Chang and Keisler 1973]   Chang, C. C., and Keisler, H. J. *Model Theory.* North Holland, Amsterdam, 1973.

[Craig 1953]   Craig, W. On Axiomatizability Within a System. *Journal of Symbolic Logic* 18:30–32, 1953.

[Ehrenfeucht et al. 1989]   Ehrenfeucht, A., Haussler, D., Kearns, M., and Valiant, L. A General Lower Bound on the Number of Examples Needed for Learning. *Information and Computation* 82:247–261, 1989.

[Enderton 1972]   Enderton, H. *A Mathematical Introduction to Logic.* Academic Press, New York, 1972.

[Fulk and Case 1990]   Fulk, M., and Case, J. (eds.). *Proceedings of the Third Annual Workshop on Computational Learning Theory.* Morgan Kaufmann, San Mateo, 1990.

[Gold 1967]   Gold, E. M. Language Identification in the limit. *Information and Computation* 10:447–474, 1967.

[Haussler 1989]   Haussler, D. Learning conjunctive concepts in structural domains. *Machine Learning* 4:7–40, 1989.

[Haussler and Pitt 1988]   Haussler, D., and Pitt, L. (eds.). *COLT 88: Proceedings of the 1988 Workshop on Computational Learning Theory.* Morgan Kaufmann, San Mateo, 1989.

[Kearns 1987]   Kearns, M., Li, M., Pitt, L., and Valiant, L. On the Learnability of Boolean Formulae. In *Proceedings of the 19th ACM Simposium on Theory of Computation,* New York, 1987.

[Laird 1986]   Laird, P. Inductive Inference by Refinement. In *Proceedings of AAAI-86,* pp. 472–476, Morgan Kaufmanne, Los Altos, 1986.

[Machtey and Young 1978]   Machtey, M., and Young, P. *An Introduction to the General Theory of Algorithms.* North Holland, Amsterdam, 1978.

[Michalski 1983]   Michalski, R., and Stepp, R. Learning from observation: Conceptual clustering. In R. Michalsky, J. Carbonell, and T. Mitchell (eds.), *Machine Learning: An Artificial Intelligence Approach.* Tioga, Palo Alto, 367–404, 1983.

[Osherson and Weinstein 1986]   Osherson, D., and Weinstein, S. Identification in the limit of first-order structures. *Journal of Philosophical Logic* 15:55–81, 1986.

[Osherson et al. 1990a]   Osherson, D., Stob, M., and Weinstein, S. New Directions in Automated Scientific Discovery. *Information Sciences* 57–58: p. 217–230, 1991.

[Osherson et al. 1990b]   Osherson, D., Stob, M., and Weinstein, S. A Mechanical Method of Successful Inquiry. In [Fulk and Case 1990].

[Osherson et al. 1992]   Osherson, D., Stob, M., and Weinstein, S. A universal inductive inference machine. *Journal of Symbolic Logic* 56 (2): 661–672, 1991.

[Parikh 1990]   Parikh, R. (ed.). *Theoretical Aspects of Reasoning about Knowledge.* Morgan Kaufmann, Los Altos, 1990.

[Rivest et al. 1989]   Rivest, R., Haussler, D., and Warmuth, M. (eds.). *COLT 89: Proceedings of the Second Annual Workshop on Computational Learning Theory.* Morgan Kaufmann, San Mateo, 1989.

[Rogers 1967]   Rogers, H. *Theory of Recursive Functions and Effective Computability.* McGraw-Hill, New York, 1967.

[Shapiro 1981]   Shapiro, E. An algorithm that infers theories from facts. *Proceedings of the Seventh International Joint Conference on Artificial Intelligence (IJCAI).* AAAI, 1981.

[Valiant 1984]   Valiant, L. A Theory of the Learnable. *Communications of the ACM* 27:1134–1142, 1984.

2 Learning Theoretical Terms

Ranan B. Banerji

2.1 Introduction

This chapter describes a learning algorithm which learns theories in the limit [3]. The theories which can be learned by this algorithm are different from the ones appearing in Shapiro [1] as well as that of Muggleton [7], but can have models similar to the ones described by some of Shapiro's theories. Also, the hypothesis language includes "Theoretical Terms," i.e. predicates which do not occur in any clause in the observation language. As a result, the algorithm follows the refinement methods [2] only partially.

The work has many similarities with those done by Muggleton [7], Ling [15], and Rouveirol and Puget [17]. We have attempted to describe the relationships to their work at various points in the chapter while describing various aspects of the language and the algorithm. Some of the procedures arise directly out of our previous work with Sammut [18].

The induction algorithm does not start with any initial knowledge of the language. Unlike in Shapiro's system, the algorithm tries to infer the language as well as the theory from the enumeration of facts.

We believe that the main contribution of the chapter is not in the presentation of a different algorithm, but the precision with which the hypothesis and observation languages have been delineated and the care with which the correctness of the algorithm has been proved. The need for the various restrictions on the class of learnable theories has been made clear only because the proofs would not be correct without these restrictions. We could not use Shapiro's results as our proof of correctness since the algorithm is not a refinement algorithm in the sense of Shapiro.

2.2 The Language

The clauses that can occur in a theory which can be learned by this algorithm consist of Horn clauses of a class of polyadic first order theories with

Reprinted, with revisions, from "Learning Theoretical Terms," in *Inductive Logic Programming*, ed. Stephen Muggleton (Academic Press, 1992), by permission of the author and publisher.

monadic function symbols. Constants are not allowed to be terms. Instead, constants are only used in literals of the form "term = constant." We shall call such literals *base atoms*. Clauses whose antecedents consist only of base atoms will be called *base clauses*. Base atoms do not occur in the consequents. In our discussion we shall never call equality a predicate. There is a subset of the predicates in the language called "Theoretical Terms." Clauses having Theoretical Terms as consequents will be called Theoretical Clauses. Base clauses whose consequents do not contain Theoretical Terms are called ground clauses (this causes no conflict with usual nomenclature here; since constants are not called terms, the language contains no ground atoms or ground clauses in the conventional sense). Only variables can occur in the consequent parts of the Horn clauses. A variable occurs in the antecedent if and only if it appears in the consequent. We shall use the ground clauses as our "language of observation," so that by this definition no theoretical term ever occurs in the examples. A ground clause would be in the *model* of a theory if it was implied by the theory and no clause with the same consequent and a subset of its antecedent was implied.

As an example, the definition of natural numbers in this theory would have to take the form

$$nat(X) \leftarrow X = 0$$
$$nat(X) \leftarrow n(pred(X))$$

instead of the usual

$$nat(0)$$
$$nat(succ(X)) \leftarrow n(X).$$

Instead of producing clauses like $nat(succ(succ(0)))$ our form of the theory will produce clauses like

$$nat(X) \leftarrow pred(pred(pred(X))) = 0.$$

In our discussions, we shall consider the antecedents of Horn clauses to be sets of literals rather than conjunctions.

2.2.1 Two Properties of Proofs

Because of the restrictions on the form of the clauses allowed in the language, the proofs take a simplified form. We initially introduce some definitions which we use to describe the way one can take advantage of the simplification in discussing some convenient properties that proofs have in this language.

A clause $A \leftarrow B$ *directly implies* the clause $E \leftarrow F$ and the clause $C \leftarrow D$ *indirectly implies* $E \leftarrow F$ if A is the same as E, there is a substitution σ such that $C\sigma \in B$ and $F = B - \{C\sigma\} \cup D\sigma$. It is to be noted that if $A \leftarrow B$ directly implies $A \leftarrow F$ and $C \leftarrow D$ indirectly implies it, then the set of base atoms of B is a subset of the set of base atoms of F. Also the construction of F is such that for each x_i in C with $x_i\sigma = t_i$, we have t_i occurring in B. If x_i occurs in D, then t_i is a subterm of that term in $D\sigma$. Thus each term occurring in B and in D is of depth no greater than those occurring in F. (We define the *depth* of a term as 0 if it is a variable and the depth of $f(t)$ as one more than the depth of t.) We thus have

LEMMA 2.1   *If a clause X directly or indirectly implies clause Y then the depth of no term in X exceeds the depth of any term in Y.*   ∎

Given a theory T we define a sequence $T(i)(i \geq 0)$ of theories as follows:

$T(0) = T.$

$T(i + 1) = T(i) \cup \{$all clauses directly or indirectly implied
by members of $T(i)\}.$

A clause $A \leftarrow B$ is said to be *implied by* T if there is a clause $A \leftarrow B'$ in $T(i)$ for some i such that $B' \subset B$.

If T is a theory such that the depth of all terms on the antecedents of clauses in T exceed k, then no element of the model of T has antecedents with terms of depth k or less. From this we can readily deduce the following.

PROPOSITION 2.1   *Provability is decidable in these restricted theories.*

Proof: Let S be a clause which has no term of depth greater than k and whose antecedent has l literals. Since the number of variables, constants, functions, and predicates in the theory is finite, the number of predicates with terms of depth k or less is finite. Thus the number of clauses whose terms have depth k or less and which contain no more than l literals is finite. Let P_S be the set of all such clauses. Since P_S is finite, there is an i such that $P_S \cap [T(i + 1) - T(i)]$ is empty. Since all elements of $P_S \cap [T(i + 2) - T(i + 1)]$ must be implied by at least one element of the previous set, one can see by induction that $P_S \cap [T(j) - T(i)]$ is empty for all $j > i$. Hence if S does not occur in $T(i)$ it is not implied by T. ■

Another fact of some importance is brought out by considering a proof tree in this restricted class of theories. Given S in $T(i)$ the *proof tree* for S is defined as follows. If $S \in T$ then the proof tree of S is the single node S. This node is the *main clause* of the proof tree. If S is directly implied by S_1 and indirectly implied by S_2 then the proof tree of S has S as its root and the proof trees of S_1 and S_2 as its *direct subtree* and *indirect subtree* respectively. The main clause of the direct subtree is the main clause of the proof tree. It can be seen that

LEMMA 2.2 *The consequent of the main clause of the proof tree for S is the same as the consequent of S.*

Proof: The consequent of the clause directly implying S is the same as the consequent of S. The rest follows by induction on the depth of the proof tree. ■

The tree obtained by deleting the direct and indirect subtrees of an ancestor S' of the main clause from a proof tree of S is called the *proof tree of S from S'*. Given a proof tree of S from S' we define its *main depth* as 0 if $S = S'$. Else it is one more than the main depth of the proof tree of S from the father of S'.

We can now prove

PROPOSITION 2.2 *Given the proof tree of a base clause S from a clause S' it can always be rewritten in a form where the root of every indirect subtree of every ancestor of S' is a base clause.*

Proof: By induction on the main depth. If the main depth is 0 there is nothing to prove. If the main depth is 1, let $A \leftarrow B$ directly imply the base clause S and let $C \leftarrow D$ indirectly imply S, so that S is

$$A \leftarrow B - \{C\sigma\} \cup D\sigma.$$

Since the antecedent of S only contains base atoms, so does $D\sigma$ and hence also D. Hence the proof tree already has the form described in the theorem.

If the main depth is greater than 1, let the main clause S' be $A \leftarrow B$ and the root of the indirect subtree of its father be $C \leftarrow D$. The proof will be by induction on the number of non-base atoms in D.

If D has only base atoms then there is nothing to prove, since by induction hypothesis on the depth of the tree, the proof of S from the father of S' can be written in the desired form. Else let $M(t_1, \ldots, t_n)$ occur in D. Let us denote this predicate by $M(x_1, \ldots, x_n)\sigma_1$ where σ_1 is a substitution. So D can be written as $Y \cup M(x_1 \ldots x_n)\sigma_1$.

Now $A \leftarrow B$ and $C \leftarrow D$ resolve to $A \leftarrow B - \{C\sigma\} \cup D\sigma$. $D\sigma$ contains the literal $M(x_1, \ldots, x_n)\sigma_1\sigma$. Denote the resolvent by $A \leftarrow X_1 \cup \{M(x_1 \ldots x_n)\sigma_1\sigma\}$. There is a proof of S from this clause of depth 1 less than the depth of the proof of S from S' and hence this proof tree can be rewritten (by induction hypothesis) in the desired form. We can then obtain a new proof of S from S' by attaching the direct and indirect subtrees back as $A \leftarrow B$ and the proof tree of $C \leftarrow D$. The only non-base root of any indirect subtree in this tree is $C \leftarrow D$. This tree can now be modified as follows. One first locates an indirect subtree whose root has the clause $M(x_1 \ldots x_n) \leftarrow N$ at the root. Such a clause must exist since S is a base clause. Also, N consists of base atoms only by induction hypothesis. Let the father of this node occur i steps below S'. The antecedent of each node below S' and up to this node contains $M(x_1 \ldots x_n)\sigma_1\sigma$. Denote these by $A \leftarrow X_1 \cup M(x_1 \ldots x_n)\sigma_1\sigma \ldots A \leftarrow X_i \cup M(x_1 \ldots x_n)\sigma_1\sigma$. To modify the tree one does two things. The proof tree of $C \leftarrow D$ is modified by resolving its root with $M(x_1 \ldots x_n) \leftarrow N$, obtaining a new subtree with $C \leftarrow Y \cup N\sigma_1$ at its root (recall the form of D above). We then use this as the root of the indirect subtree and $A \leftarrow B$ as the trivial direct subtree to obtain at the root $S'' = A \leftarrow B - \{C\sigma\} \cup Y\sigma \cup N\sigma_1\sigma$. If we compare this with $S' = A \leftarrow B - \{C\sigma\} \cup D\sigma$ which we previously wrote as $X_1 \cup \{M(x_1 \ldots x_n)\sigma_1\sigma\}$ and recall that $D = Y \cup \{M(x_1 \ldots x_n)\sigma_1\}$ we see that S'' is obtained by replacing $M(x_1 \ldots x_n)\sigma_1\sigma$ by $N\sigma_1\sigma$ in S'.

Each ancestor of S' is now rewritten, replacing each $X_j \cup \{M(x_1 \ldots x_n)\sigma_1\sigma\}$ by $X_j \cup N\sigma_1\sigma (1 \leq j \leq i)$. The resulting structure is still a proof tree for S from $A \leftarrow B$, but the indirect subtree of the father of the main clause now has one less non-base atom and all the roots of all the other indirect subtrees are base clauses. ∎

It will be noted that all the indirect subtrees are proof trees of base clauses and hence they in their turn can be written in the desired form, leading to

COROLLARY 2.1   *If a base clause S is implied by a theory T, then a proof tree for S exists in which the root of every indirect subtree is a base clause.*

∎

The importance of proposition 2.1 and corollary 2.1 is that they allow one to test a theory to find if it explains all facts and to diagnose its errors. Following Shapiro, a *fact* is defined to be an ordered pair (S, t) where S is a ground clause and t is a truth value. If the truth value is "true" then S is called a true fact: the rest are false facts. A theory for a model is supposed to imply only all the elements of the model and the ground clauses subsumed by them.

Proposition 2.1 tells us that given a ground clause, we can determine whether it is provable. Also, when a clause outside the model is implied by a theory, then an analog of the backtrace algorithm of [1] can be used to locate the false clause in the theory. It will be recalled that in the backtrace algorithm the Oracle needs to be questioned about the truth values of ground clauses only. The structure of the special proof trees in corollary 2.1 allows us to do this in a manner somewhat different from Shapiro's in that when a base clause (including the proven ground clause) is known to be false in the model, then either the direct or indirect subtree must have a false root. The indirect subtree has a base clause in its root. If it is a ground clause, the Oracle can tell whether the fact is true or false. If it is not a ground clause, then its consequent is a Theoretical Term, so since it leads to a proof of a false ground clause, the direct subtree (whose root has that Theoretical Term in its antecedent) is to be taken to be false.

2.3   The Induction Process

An *enumeration* is a sequence of facts in which every ground clause of the language occurs as the first component of some fact in the sequence. It will be noted that given a model and an enumeration, the set of true facts coincides with the model and those that subsume elements of the model.

A major difference between this program and those used by authors of related programs is in the fact that true sentences need not be sentences in the model but also those that subsume sentences in the model. The extraneous predicates which are not essential for the theory need to be weeded out. Some of the definitions and lemmata that follow are introduced specifically to discuss this weeding process.

The program constructs two structures, the theory and the *language conjecture*. The former has been discussed already, except for some further restrictions that we shall discuss later. The language conjecture L associates with each predicate letter a set of base atoms. The set of atoms associated with the predicate P will be denoted by $L(P)$ in the following discussion.

In what follows, when we say that a clause S is *bound* by a language conjecture L, we shall mean that all base atoms in its antecedent are contained in $L(P)$, where P is the consequent of S. A theory is bound by a language conjecture if all its clauses are. A theory is *adequate* for a set of facts if it implies all the true facts and implies no false fact. It is *ground adequate* with language conjecture L if it is adequate and all the true facts bound by L are implied by some ground clause in the theory. It should be noted that a ground adequate theory may imply true facts not bound by L: it may contain substitution instances of terms in the theory.

It is our purpose to build ground adequate theories in finite time from an enumeration. During the process one constructs theories with weaker properties than adequacy. To follow this process we need some further definitions.

Let S_t and S_f be two finite sets of ground clauses with the property that no antecedent of a clause in S_t is a subset of any antecedent of a clause in S_f with the same consequent. In such a case the pair $\langle S_t, S_f \rangle$ will be called a *consistent pair*. The members of S_t will be called *true facts* and the members of S_f, *false facts*.

A theory T will be said to *enclose* a set S of ground clauses if T implies every clause in S. It *ground encloses S with* a language conjecture L if each clause in S bound by L subsumes a ground clause in T.

The ground clauses occurring in an initial segment of an enumeration form a consistent pair since they come from a model of a theory. The theory generated by the algorithm will ground enclose the true facts in this consistent pair with the language conjecture. It should also fail to imply any false facts, but will initially have to have a weaker property described next.

Given a set S of ground clauses and a language conjecture L, a theory T will be said to be *maximal for S with L* if it is bound by L and for each predicate P in S and each $X \subseteq L(P)$ either $X \supseteq A$ for some ground clause $P \leftarrow A$ in T or $X \subseteq B$ for some $P \leftarrow B$ in S. The theory generated by the algorithm will be always maximal for the false clauses with the language conjecture.

The next lemma establishes the fact that if a theory fails to imply a set of true facts with a language conjecture in the course of the algorithm, then the language conjecture is inadequate.

LEMMA 3.1   *Let $\langle S_t, S_f \rangle$ be a consistent pair and T be maximal for S_f with language conjecture L. Let $P \leftarrow A$ in S_t be not implied by T. Then A is not a subset of $L(P)$.*

Proof: If $P \leftarrow A$ is not implied by T then A' is not the subset of A for any clause $P \leftarrow A'$ in T. If $A \subseteq L(P)$ then since T is maximal for S_f with L, $A \subseteq B$ for some $P \leftarrow B$ in S_f. But since $P \leftarrow A$ is in S_t and $\langle S_t, S_f \rangle$ is a consistent pair, this is impossible.   ∎

These lemmata are needed to show that the two procedures ("*Add*" and "*Shrink*" discussed next (which alternately expand and shrink the model) do not cause an infinite loop. *Add* and *Shrink* are needed in the algorithm precisely because we have not restricted the examples to come strictly from the model but to contain redundant predicates. In most of the related work this contingency can be covered by alternative means. These will be commented on when we discuss the procedure "*Dream.*"

2.3.1   *Add*

The procedure *Add* is invoked by the algorithm when it encounters a true fact S which T does not imply. It does two things. First, it unions the base atoms of the antecedent of S to $L(A)$, where A is the consequent of S. If A did not occur as the consequent of any clause in T, then it adds $A \leftarrow true$ to T; else it adds to T the set of clauses $A \leftarrow B$, one for each base atom B in the antecedent of S which was newly added to $L(A)$ by the union process above.

Lemma 3.1 indicates that the enhancement of L is necessary in the circumstance. The next lemma shows that the enhancement of T by *Add* does not destroy the maximality of T.

LEMMA 3.2   *Let $\langle S_t, S_f \rangle$ be a consistent pair. If T is maximal for S_f with L and does not imply $P \leftarrow A$ in S_t, then Add leads to a language conjecture L' and a theory T' such that T' implies $P \leftarrow A$ and is maximal for S_f in L'.*

Proof: Since the base atoms B in the definition of *Add* are elements of A, each of the clauses added to T imply $P \leftarrow A$.

To show that T' is maximal for S_f with L', let $X \subseteq L'(Q)$. If Q is distinct from P then X is also a subset of $L(Q)$ and since every element of T is an element of T', there is nothing to prove. If Q is the same as P, then if $X \subseteq L(P)$ again there is nothing to prove. Else X contains an element B

introduced by *Add* and there is a clause in T' whose antecedent is a subset of X. ∎

It will be noticed that *Add* ground encloses a larger part of S_t at every invocation, by enlarging the language conjecture. We can thus state the following proposition, since S_t is finite.

PROPOSITION 3.1   *A theory encloses S_t after a finite number of invocations of Add.* ∎

In the next section we introduce a procedure which renders a theory ground adequate for a consistent pair.

2.3.2   *Shrink*

The procedure *Shrink* is invoked when the backtrace algorithm finds a clause responsible for the proof of a false fact. If this clause is non-ground, it is merely removed from the theory. Otherwise the clause is replaced by a set of clauses with the same consequent P and the antecedent obtained by adding to the antecedent of this offending clause a literal from $L(P)$ which did not occur in the antecedent previously. Sentences which subsume any clause in the theory are not introduced.

We have seen in lemma 3.1 that in a theory which ground encloses S_t and is maximal for S_f with L, *Add* is only invoked a finite number of times. To show that *Shrink* can, in a finite number of invocations, render a theory ground adequate, we need to indicate that if a theory implies a false fact, then a theory modified with a finite number of invocation of *Shrink* modifies the theory to exclude that false clause from the model.

We need the following lemmata and definitions.

LEMMA 3.3   *Let $\langle S_t, S_f \rangle$ be a consistent pair and L a language conjecture. Let $P \leftarrow A$ be in S_t and bounded by L and let $P \leftarrow B$ be in S_f. Then there is a base atom X in $L(P)$ such that X is in A but not in B.*

Proof: Since $\langle S_t, S_f \rangle$ is a consistent pair, A is not a subset of B. Hence there is an X in A not in B. Since $P \leftarrow A$ is contained in $L(P)$ (being bounded by L), $X \in L(P)$. ∎

Given two theories T and T' we shall say $T' \leq T$ if for each ground clause $P \leftarrow A$ in T there is a ground clause $P \leftarrow B$ in T' with $A \subseteq B$ or the ground clause of T and T' are identical and such that every non-ground clause in T' is in T.

LEMMA 3.4   *Given a consistent pair $\langle S_t, S_f \rangle$ and a language conjecture L. Let theory T ground enclose S_t with L and be maximal for S_f with L. If there is a clause $P \leftarrow B$ in S_f implied by T, then there is a $T' \leq T$ maximal with S_f in L and ground enclosing S_t with L.*

Proof: There may be a subset S of T consisting of non-ground clauses such that $T - S$ does not imply $P \leftarrow B$. Since maximality or ground enclosure do not depend on the non-ground clauses of the theory, $T - S < T$ fulfills the conditions of the lemma. If there is no such subset, there is some ground clause $P \leftarrow A$ in T such that $A \subseteq B$. Let $T' = T - \{P \leftarrow A\} \cup \{P \leftarrow A \cup \{X\} | X \in L(P)\}$. Then $T' \leq T$.

T' is maximal for S_f in L. Let $M \subseteq L(P)$. If $M \subseteq B$ for some $Q \leftarrow B$ in S_f there is nothing to prove. Else $M \supseteq C$ for some $Q \leftarrow C$ in T. If Q is distinct from P or C is not the same as A, there is a $Q \leftarrow C$ in T'. Else if $M \subseteq B$ for some $P \leftarrow B \in S_f$ or $M \supseteq A'$ for some $P \leftarrow A \in T$ with $A \neq A'$ there is nothing to prove. Else there is an $X \in L(P)$ such that $X \in M$ and X is not in A. Then $M \supseteq A \cup \{X\}$.

Since T' is maximal for S_f with L' and $\langle S_t, S_f \rangle$ is a consistent pair, T' ground encloses S_t with L' by lemma 3.1.   ∎

From these the following proposition follows quite readily.

PROPOSITION 3.2   *Given a consistent set of true and false facts, the process of repeated applications of Add and Shrink to an empty theory and language conjecture yields a theory (perhaps consisting entirely of ground clauses) which contains all the true facts in its model and does not have any of the false facts in its model.*

Proof: Proposition 3.1 indicates that *Add* can only be applied a finite number of times, irrespective of other changes in the theory as long as the change leaves the theory ground enclosing S_t and maximal for S_f with the language conjecture. Lemma 3.1 indicates that all true facts bound by a language conjecture are ground enclosed by the enclosing maximal theory. All false facts implied by a theory can be removed by *Shrink* since by lemma 3.4 the existence of such clauses causes the theory to descend down a chain and with a finite language conjecture, such a chain has to be finite. Since the empty theory and language conjecture are trivially a theory maximal for false facts and ground enclosing true facts with the current language conjecture, and both *Shrink* and *Add* preserve maximality, the proposition follows.   ∎

So far there has been no indication of how non-ground clauses enter the theory. We now proceed to introduce them.

2.3.3 Introducing Predicates

In addition to the restrictions we have placed on the class of clauses allowed in the theory, we need to restrict the theories we shall deal with in two ways.

Given any theory in the present language, it is not too difficult to show that any theory has a *useful* subtheory with an identical model. A theory is called useful if all its clauses are *explicit* in the theory and no predicate occurs as a consequent in more than two clauses. A clause is explicit in a theory if all the non-base atoms in its antecedent are the substitution instance of a predicate explicit in the theory. A predicate is explicit in a theory if either it is the consequent of a ground clause in the theory or it is the consequent of a explicit clause in the theory. The concepts involved are analogous to the ideas in language theory (see [5]).

Given a useful theory, one can define *representatives* of the clauses in the theory as follows. The representative of a ground clause is itself. The representatives of all other clauses are obtained by replacing each occurrence $P\sigma$ of a substitution instance of the consequent of a clause S by the substitution instance of the representative of S. We shall state the following without a proof.

PROPOSITION 3.3   *A finite useful theory has a finite set of representatives for its clauses.*   ∎

Let T be a Theoretical Term. Since the theory is useful, there are only two clauses in the theory with T in their consequent. Let R_1 and R_2 be the representatives of these two clauses. Two sentences in the model of the theory, of the forms $A \leftarrow B \cup \{R_1\}$ and $A \leftarrow B \cup \{R_2\}$ (with B non-empty), will be said to constitute an *indicator* for T.

We shall consider only useful theories. However, some further restrictions will be made.

We shall call a theory *learnable* if the two following restrictions are met:

1. If the substitution instances of two predicates appear in the antecedent of the same clause, then the substitution instances of the representatives of the clauses having these predicates as consequents are disjoint from each other as well as from the base atoms in the clause.

2. If every other theory equivalent to it has all the representatives of this theory among its clauses.

3. If there is at least one clause with a Theoretical Term in its antecedent which implies an indicator for that term.

It is our belief that any model having a useful theory satisfying restriction 1 above satisfies restriction 2. But there is not much point to discussing that here.

A sufficient condition for ensuring that a theory obey restriction 3 is that there be at least one clause with a non-Theoretical consequent and with a Theoretical Term and at least one more term in its antecedent. As our example will show later, this condition is not necessary.

In what follows, we shall assume our theories to be learnable. It is to be noted that if a model has a learnable theory, then any theory in which these representatives can be implied by a non-ground clause is false in the model.

2.3.4 *Generalize*

The procedure *Generalize* is invoked only after *Add* and *Shrink* have produced a ground adequate theory for the available facts. If two clauses $A \leftarrow B$ (the *main clause*) and $C \leftarrow D$ (the *secondary clause*) occur in the theory such that $D\sigma$ is a subset of B for some substitution σ, then *Generalize* adds to the theory the clause $A \leftarrow B - D\sigma \cup \{C\sigma\}$. If A is a Theoretical Term, then all occurrences of A in this clause are subsequently replaced by a new predicate. Also a set of new clauses is added to the theory for each sentence in the theory with A as the consequent, replacing each occurrence of A with the new predicate.

The efficacy of *Generalize* as well as the need for condition 2 for learnable theories as well as that for representatives is made clear in the following lemma and proposition.

LEMMA 3.5   *If in a learnable theory $A \leftarrow E \cup \{C\sigma\}$ and $C \leftarrow D$ directly and indirectly imply $A \leftarrow B$ and if no base atom of $D\sigma$ occurs in E, then $A \leftarrow E \cup \{C\sigma\}$ can be obtained from $C \leftarrow D$ and $A \leftarrow B$ by Generalize.*

Proof: From the definition of implication we have $B = E \cup D\sigma$ so that the result of *Generalize* on $A \leftarrow B$ and $C \leftarrow D$ is $A \leftarrow E \cup D\sigma - D\sigma \cup \{C\}$. This is identical to $A \leftarrow E \cup \{C\sigma\}$ if and only if E and $D\sigma$ are disjoint as required in a learnable theory.   ∎

PROPOSITION 3.4 *Let there be a proof tree for the representative for a clause M where each indirect subtree consists of the representatives of clauses whose consequent occurs at the root of the direct subtree. Then the roots of the direct subtrees, including the main clause, can be obtained from the representative and the roots of the indirect subtrees by a series of applications of Generalize.*

Proof: By induction on the number of non-base atoms in the main clause. If the number is 1, then the proposition is identical to lemma 3.5. Else consider the father of the main clause. By condition 1 for a useful theory, the substitution instances of the representatives of all of the non-base atoms in this clause are disjoint from the atoms of this clause. Hence the father can be obtained by a sequence of *Generalize*. From the father and the trivial root of its indirect subtree the main clause can be obtained by *Generalize* according to lemma 3.5.   ∎

Rouveirol's algorithm differs from both our algorithm and Muggleton's in that it makes condition 1 for learnability above unnecessary. For details, see Ling and Narayan [16].

In what has gone above we have been assuming that the representatives of all clauses in the theory would be available to *Generalize*. This would be true if the hypothesis language contained no Theoretical Terms. Representatives of Theoretical Terms in the language have to be obtained from a separate procedure (wich we shall call *Dream*) which has to be invoked before *Generalize*.

2.3.5 *Dream*

The introduction of Theoretical Terms into the theory is brought about by *Dream* acting on the indicators of the Theoretical Terms. *Dream* is brought into action when there are two sentences in the theory with the same head P and whose bodies have a non-empty intersection C. Let A and B be the parts of the two bodies left after removing C. Let T_A be the set of all terms and their subterms that occur in A and let T_B be the similar set corresponding to B. For *Dream* to be invoked T_A and T_B must have the same set of variables (which in general will be a subset of those in P). Thus the set of terms in the intersection of T_A and T_B is non-empty. Let $t_1, \ldots, t_n$ be the set of the deepest subterms in this intersection such that each term in $A \cup B$ has some t_i as its substitution instance. Let σ be the substitution which replaces x_i by t_i ($1 \leq i \leq n$). Then the algorithm adds the following sentences to the theory:

$$P: -C, D(t_1, \ldots, t_n).$$
$$D(x_1, \ldots, x_n): -A'. \tag{1}$$
$$D(x_1, \ldots, x_n): -B'.$$

where A' is such that $A'\sigma$ is A, and similarly for B'. D is a new predicate letter not previously used anywhere in the theory.

The construction of the set $\{t_1 \ldots t_n\}$ is done by a simple depth-first algorithm searching the tree of the subterms. We shall show elsewhere that it yields a unique set having the properties required.

Some properties of *Dream* need to be recorded here.

PROPOSITION 3.5   *Clauses introduced into a theory by Dream do not change the model of the theory. Nor is it changed by an application of Generalize using a Theoretical Clause as the main clause.*   ∎

PROPOSITION 3.6   *The terms $t_1, \ldots, t_n$ introduced by Dream from the indicators of a Theoretical Term will have as subterms the terms occurring in the antecedents of the corresponding Theoretical Clauses.*

From proposition 3.6 one can see that the terms occurring as arguments to a Theoretical Term in the antecedent of a clause in a theory are substitution instances of terms occurring in the terms occurring in the clauses introduced by *Dream* from the indicators of that Theoretical Term. This indicates that the clauses introduced by *Dream* will also be introduced by the Muggleton "W."

It will be noticed that some of the work of *Add* and *Shrink* could be taken over by *Dream* by replacing redundant predicates in the examples by Theoretical Terms representing the disjunction of the redundant predicates. This would require a different set of examples, of course.

We are now in a position to prove the main proposition of the chapter.

PROPOSITION 3.7   *There exists an algorithm which, presented with an enumeration of the model of a learnable theory, can produce a theory for the model in finite time.*

The proof will refer to the following algorithm.

Begin
    $F_+ := \phi; F_- := \phi; L := \phi; T := \phi;$
    Do forever

```
begin
    read a fact ⟨M, v⟩ and place M in F_v;
    FLAG:-false;
    while there is a M ∈ F_+ not implied by T or
        there is a M ∈ F_- implied by T do
      begin
        while there is an M ∈ F_- implied by T do
            begin
                locate Q: − B ∈ T responsible for error;
                if B contains a non-base atom
                    T := T − {Q ← B}
                else begin T := SHRINK(T, L, Q ← B); FLAG = true end
            end
        if there is P ← A ∈ F_+ not implied by T
        then (T, L) := ADD(T, L, P ← A)
      end
    if FLAG
    then
        begin
            for every pair of clauses in T allowing
            Dream, apply it;
            for every pair of clauses in T allowing
            Generalize, apply it, provided no M ∈ F_- is implied by
            the clause added;
        end
    end
end
```

Proof of proposition 3.7:   Our claim is that the algorithm produces a useful theory for the model after it has seen the following facts.

1. The representatives of all the clauses in a learnable useful theory.

2. Subsets of all the clauses in 1 of size one less than the corresponding clause (except the subset containing only the antecedent).

3. An indicator for every Theoretical Term in the learnable useful theory.

4. A representative of every non-Theoretical clause false in the model which could be introduced into the theory by the algorithm at the point when all the facts in sets 1 to 3 above were available.

5. Representatives of all clauses false in the model which are introduced into the theory by the time all the elements of set 4 are seen.

It will be noted that the clauses obtained by *Generalize* have no more terms nor no deeper terms than the representatives, from which they are constructed. Hence they are finite in number and so are their representatives. Thus the facts in 4 and 5 are finite in number.

The "do-forever" loop is reentered after every reading of a fact. In this loop there are the two nested loops calling *Add* and *Shrink*. By the arguments of the previous section, this loop terminates after obtaining a ground adequate theory for the current segment of the enumeration. The lines between the end of this nested loop and the end of the "do-forever" loop do not make the theory ascend the chain of the ordering over theories, since *Generalize* and *Dream* do not activate unless there has been a descent down the lexicographic ordering, as recorded by the Boolean FLAG. Thus the loop always terminates between each reading. Consider the state of the theory after the facts enumerated above have been read. Let the set of facts in the sets 1 to 4 be denoted by F_1. By the time these have been read in, there is no clause in the theory which implies the representatives except the representatives themselves and non-base clauses true in the model. Any non-ground clause implying them is false in the model since the theory is useful and the facts in set 4 will remove them by the invocation of *Shrink*. Thus all the base atoms in the representatives will be in the language conjecture and the theory will contain the representatives. By proposition 3.5, all applications of *Dream* leave the model unchanged. *Generalize* will at this point introduce all the clauses in the theory by proposition 3.4 above. After this, no new clause will be added to the theory, since no true fact will remain unexplained. There will be some false non-ground clauses in the theory, generated by some non-representative ground clauses. These will be removed by the set 5. There will also be clauses obtained by *Generalize* from Theoretical Clauses as well as such clauses obtained by *Dream*. These are not isolated by the backtrace algorithm and hence never removed. However, clauses with non-Theoretical predicates in the consequent which have Theoretical Terms in their antecedent are removed if they are false in the theory. Since *Generalize* applied to Theoretical Terms creates new Theoretical Terms, clauses referring to them which are true in the theory are still true in the theory after the application of *Generalize*. These will therefore not be affected by the removals.   ∎

2.4   An Example

We shall now exemplify the workings of the algorithm on clauses modeling a somewhat complex theory. It will be based on the representation of integers by binary strings. In what follows, the function symbol E is used to denote the least significant digit ("end") of the string, R stands for the "rest" of the string and M stands for the "empty" string. A typical such "numeral" would satisfy the clause

$$n(x): - E(x) = 1, E(R(x)) = 0, E(R(R(x))) = 1, R(R(R(x))) = M. \qquad (2)$$

This ground sentence represents the numeral 5 in binary. Recognizing it as a numeral consists in proving it to be true in the following theory for numerals.

$$n(x): - d(E(x)), R(x) = M. \qquad (3)$$

$$n(x): - d(E(x)), n(R(x)). \qquad (4)$$

$$d(x): - x = 0. \qquad (5)$$

$$d(x): - x = 1. \qquad (6)$$

In a previous paper [4] we illustrated a working of the algorithm on learning this theory. At that time *Dream* was at a rudimentary stage. In what follows we include a few more sentences in the theory describing equality of numerals and the successor relation between them.

$$s(x, y): - E(x) = 0, E(y) = 1, eq(R(x), R(y)). \qquad (7)$$

$$s(x, y): - E(x) = 1, E(y) = 0, s(R(x), R(y)). \qquad (8)$$

$$eq(x, y): - x = M, y = M. \qquad (9)$$

$$eq(x, y): - eqd(E(x), E(y)), eq(R(x), R(y)). \qquad (10)$$

$$eqd(x, y): - x = 0, y = 0. \qquad (11)$$

$$eqd(x, y): - x = 1, y = 1. \qquad (12)$$

It will be noted that in the above set of sentences, the first two describe how the binary strings for two successive integers are related. These descriptions involve the description of *eq*, the equality between binary strings; that in its turn involves the description of *eqd*, the equality between digits. These descriptions occupy the last four statements above.

We shall illustrate our methods in terms of examples motivated by a psychological experiment (described by Bruner [8]) where one needs to develop descriptions of sets of pictures. Imagine that each of the pictures has a number of crosses and a number of borders. Let us try to develop a theory which will describe a set of pictures where the number of borders exceeds the number of crosses by one. Without the use of first order languages, the description of such a concept would have a large number of disjuncts. However, if the relation *s* (for "successor") is defined on numerals, then one could describe the given set of pictures (callled "set" here) as follows:

$$set(x): -s(crosses(x), borders(x)). \tag{13}$$

In what follows we shall consider all predicates except "set" to be Theoretical Terms. Consider starting with the following true facts in the theory (we shall ignore for the time being the way false facts are used in the overall algorithm):

$$set(x): -E(cr(x)) = 0, E(bd(x)) = 1, E(R(cr(x))) = 0,$$
$$E(R(bd(x))) = 0, R(R(cr(x))) = M, R(R(bd(x))) = M. \tag{14}$$

$$set(x): -E(cr(x)) = 0, E(bd(x)) = 1, E(R(cr(x))) = 1,$$
$$E(R(bd(x))) = 1, R(R(cr(x))) = M, R(R(bd(x))) = M. \tag{15}$$

$$set(x): -E(cr(x)) = 0, E(bd(x)) = 1, E(R(cr(x))) = 0,$$
$$E(R(bd(x))) = 0, E(R(R(cr(x)))) = 1, E(R(R(bd(x)))) = 1,$$
$$R(R(R(cr(x)))) = M, R(R(R(bd(x)))) = M. \tag{16}$$

$$set(x): -E(cr(x)) = 1, E(bd(x)) = 0, E(R(cr(x))) = 0,$$
$$E(R(bd(x))) = 1, R(R(cr(x))) = M, R(R(bd(x))) = M. \tag{17}$$

$$set(x): -E(cr(x)) = 1, E(bd(x)) = 0, E(R(cr(x))) = 0,$$
$$E(R(bd(x))) = 1, E(R(R(cr(x)))) = 0, E(R(R(bd(x)))) = 1,$$
$$R(R(R(cr(x)))) = M, R(R(R(bd(x)))) = M. \tag{18}$$

In the above I have used *cr* and *bd* for "crosses" and "borders" respectively in the interest of brevity.

It will be noticed that all these sentences come from the model of the above theory. Inputs to the algorithms of Muggleton and of Ling would have to be of this form. In our case, we would claim that these sentences are introduced into the theory from more redundant examples by *Add* and *Shrink*, using a number of true and false facts in the process. In what follows, only *Generalize* and *Dream* are illustrated. For an illustration of *Add* and *Shrink*, see [4].

One obtains from 14 and 15 by *Dream*

$$set(x): -E(cr(x)) = 0, E(bd(x)) = 1, P(E(R(cr(x))), E(R(bd(x)))),$$
$$R(R(cr(x))) = M, R(R(bd(x))) = M. \qquad (19)$$

$$P(x, y): -x = 0, y = 0. \qquad (20)$$

$$P(x, y): -x = 1, y = 1. \qquad (21)$$

since $E(R(cr(x)))$ and $E(R(bd(x)))$ were the deepest terms common to the terms that occurred in the parts of the antecedent of 14 and 15 that were not common to them.

It will be noticed that 20 and 21 are the same as 11 and 12 above. *P* takes the place of *eqd*.

From 16, one can apply *Generalize* twice, using 20 and 21, to obtain

$$set(x): -E(cr(x)) = 0, E(bd(x)) = 1, P(E(R(cr(x))), E(R(bd(x)))),$$
$$P(E(R(R(cr(x)))), E(R(R(bd(x))))),$$
$$R(R(R(cr(x)))) = M, R(R(R(bd(x)))) = M. \qquad (22)$$

At this point 19 and 22 satisfy the condition for *Dream* and yield the sentences:

$$set(x): -E(cr(x)) = 0, E(bd(x)) = 1, P(E(R(cr(x))), E(R(bd(x)))),$$
$$Q(R(R(cr(x))), R(R(bd(x)))). \qquad (23)$$

$$Q(x, y): -x = M, y = M. \qquad (24)$$

$$Q(x, y): -P(E(x), E(y)), R(x) = M, R(y) = M. \qquad (25)$$

and then one uses *Generalize* on 25, using 24 to obtain

$$S(x, y): -x = M, y = M. \qquad (26)$$

$$S(x, y): -P(E(x), E(y)), R(x) = M, R(y) = M. \tag{27}$$

$$S(x, y): -P(E(x), E(y)), S(R(x), R(y)). \tag{28}$$

It may again be noticed that 26 and 28 are the same as 9 and 10 except for the predicate name. It should also be noted that when *Generalize* is applied to clauses with Theoretical Terms in the consequent, the name of the predicate is changed.

Generalize is again applied twice to 22, using 27 and 28 to yield

$$set(x): -E(cr(x)) = 0, E(bd(x)) = 1, S(R(cr(x)), R(bd(x))). \tag{29}$$

At this point *Generalize* could be applied to 17 using 26 to yield

$$set(x): -E(cr(x)) = 1, E(bd(x)) = 0, E(R(cr(x))) = 0,$$
$$E(R(bd(x))) = 1, S(R(R(cr(x))), R(R(bd(x)))). \tag{30}$$

and *Generalize* applied to 18 using 26 yields

$$set(x): -E(cr(x)) = 1, E(bd(x)) = 0, E(R(cr(x))) = 1,$$
$$E(R(bd(x))) = 0, E(R(R(cr(x)))) = 0, E(R(R(bd(x)))) = 1.$$
$$S(R(R(R(cr(x)))), R(R(R(bd(x))))). \tag{31}$$

which, together with 30 can use *Dream* to yield

$$set(x): -E(cr(x)) = 1, E(bd(x)) = 0,$$
$$T(E(R(cr(x))), E(R(bd(x))), R(R(cr(x))), R(R(bd(x)))). \tag{32}$$

$$T(x, y, u, v): -x = 0, y = 1, S(u, v). \tag{33}$$

$$T(x, y, u, v): -x = 1, y = 0, E(u) = 0, E(v) = 1, S(R(u), R(v)). \tag{34}$$

and then *Generalize* applied to 34 using 33 would yield

$$V(x, y, u, v): -x = 0, y = 1, S(u, v). \tag{35}$$

$$V(x, y, u, v): -x = 1, y = 0, E(u) = 0, E(v) = 1, S(R(u), R(v)). \tag{36}$$

$$V(x, y, u, v): -x = 1, y = 0, V(E(u), E(v), R(u), R(v)). \tag{37}$$

Now *Generalize* could be applied to 29 using 35 or twice to 30 using 36 and 37 to yield

$$set(x): -V(E(cr(x)), E(bd(x)), R(cr(x)), R(bd(x))). \tag{38}$$

This is not the same as 13, nor are 35 and 37 the same as 7 and 8. However, the former are "more general" than the latter in that the latter can be obtained from the former if we define

$$s(x, y) : -V(E(x), E(y), R(x), R(y)). \tag{39}$$

as was indicated in the sequel to proposition 3.6.

2.5   Concluding Remarks

To the extent that the class of learnable theories have any significance, some of the conditions of learnability need further clarification. What is more important, however, is that a major restriction be removed from the class of learnable theories, to wit that variables occur in the consequent if and only if they occur in the antecedent. These are required by *Generalize* and by *Dream*. Muggleton and Buntine [7] have described similar procedures using the techniques of [6] for unification of terms. They still require that all variables in the consequent occur in the antecedent, but it is not clear if the removal of the converse condition gives them any further learning ability—especially since their papers do not clearly specify as to what subset of the hypothesis language can be included in the observation language.

It is our belief that the "refinemement" processes of this algorithm (i.e. the operations inside the "do-forever" loop) will be more efficient than the ones suggested by Shapiro for similar classes of theories, since fewer non-ground clauses are looked at. However, it is still basically exponential in the size of the language conjecture at the end of the reading of F_1. Muggleton and Buntine avoid the use of the *Add* and *Shrink* procedures, relying on reverse unification to remove the inessential base atoms from the theory. However, this procedure is exponential also. One could, of course, include as facts in the observation language only the clauses in the model and clauses using base atoms that occur in the model (as one is prone to do when testing the procedures "experimentally"), but that is not very satisfactory in testing the performance of an algorithm.

As indicated in the introduction, this chapter, except for the rather unusual language used, uses algorithms very similar to those used by a number of authors. Ling and Narayan [16] have made a careful comparison of the techniques. I could do no better than referring the reader to their paper.

It seems to us at this point that we have no precisely described algorithm for learning first order theories which have less than exponential growth rate. Osherson, Stob and Weinstein [9, 10, 11, 12] have shown that this difficulty will remain for many interesting classes of first order theories. However, they have also isolated rather restrictive classes of first order theories which are learnable in the sense of Valiant [14, 13]. The class of theories studied here clearly do not belong to such classes. Attempts at widening the classes discovered by them seem like an exciting challenge.

References

[1] Shapiro, E. *Inductive Inference of Theories from Facts*. Technical Report No. 193, Computer Science Department, Yale University (1981).

[2] Laird, P. *Inductive Inference by Refinement*. Technical Report No. TR-376, Yale University (1986).

[3] Gold, E. M. *Language Identification in the Limit. Information and Control*. 10:447 (1965).

[4] Banerji, R. B. *Learning in the Limit in a Growing Language*. In *Methodologies for Intelligent Systems* (Z. Ras and M. Zemankova, eds.). North Holland, Amsterdam (1987), p. 299.

[5] Hopcroft, J., and Ullman, J. *Introduction to Automata Theory, Languages and Computation*. Addison-Wesley, New York (1979).

[6] Plotkin, G. *A Further Note on Inductive Generalization. Machine Intelligence*, vol. 6. Edinburgh University Press (1971), pp. 101–124.

[7] Muggleton, S., and Buntine, W. *Constructive Induction in First Order Logic*. In *Proceedings of the First International Workshop in Change of Representation and Inductive Bias*. Phillips Laboratories, Briarcliffe Manor (June 1988), p. 279.

[8] Bruner, J., Goodnow T., and Austin, G. *A Study of Thinking*. John Wiley and Sons, New York (1956).

[9] Osherson, D. N., Stob, M., and Weinstein, S. *New Directions in Automated Scientific Discovery. Information Sciences* 57–58:217–230 (1991).

[10] Osherson, D., and Weinstein, S. *Paradigms of Truth Detection. Journal of Philosophical Logic* 18:1 (1989).

[11] Osherson, D., and Weinstein, S. *Identification in the Limit of First Order Structures. Journal of Philosophical Logic* 15:55 (1986).

[12] Osherson, D., Stob, M., and Weinstein, S. *On Approximate Truth*. In *Proceedings of the Second Annual Workshop on Computational Learning Theory*. Morgan Kaufman, San Mateo (1989).

[13] Blumer, A., Ehrenfeucht, A., Haussler, D., and Warmuth, M. Occam's Razor. *Information Processing Letters* 24:377 (1987).

[14] Valiant, L. A Theory of the Learnable. *Communications of the ACM* 27:1134 (1985).

[15] Ling, X. C. Learning and Inventing of Horn Clause Theories—a Constructive Method. In *Methodologies for Intelligent Systems 4* (Z. Ras, ed.). North Holland, Amsterdam (1989), p. 323.

[16] Ling X., and Narayan, M. A. A Critical Comparison of Various Methods based on Inverse Resolution. *Machine Learning* (In press).

[17] Rouveirol, C., and Puget, J. F. Beyond Inversion of Resolution, In *Proceedings of the Seventh International Conference on Machine Learning*. Morgan Kaufman, San Mateo (1990).

[18] Sammut, C., and Banerji, R. B. Learning Concepts by Asking Questions. In *Machine Learning: An Artificial Intelligence Approach*, Vol. 2. (R. Michalski, J. Carbonell, and T. Mitchell, eds.). Morgan Kaufmann, Los Altos (1986), p. 167–191.

3 How Loading Complexity is Affected by Node Function Sets

Stephen Judd

3.1 Introduction

As we pursue implementations and applications of neural networks, one question that we want to answer is what type of node the networks should have. This makes a difference in the capacity of the network, the types of signals it can handle, and its speed, size, complexity, reliability, and cost. We would like some guiding principles with which to select one type of node over another. And we would like to know why Mother Nature has selected the particular ones she has implemented in biological neurons.

Neural networks are often touted as being especially promising tools because of their supposed ability to learn and adapt to unforeseen environments. Part of the black art of using them, though, is knowing what kind of architecture they should have in order to facilitate the learning and generalization. Judd [Jud90] showed that this learning facility is at least under suspicion because the problem of training them (which was formally described as the *loading* problem in that work) is NP-complete. But that result at least has the beneficial possibility of furthering the analysis of neural networks to the point where the black art of network design would become less black, and possibly even a science.

In this chapter I explore the interaction between the type of nodes used in a network and the concomitant complexity of loading it. Is there any hope that studying the loading complexity will guide us in choosing appropriate node designs? Can we glean any arguments that would tell us why brains use nodes that are similar to threshold functions? Answers to these questions are presently unclear. The first section of this chapter discusses work on shallow networks which reveals a resounding equivocality on the issue, but the following section discusses deep networks and reports more complicated interactions. It seems the study of architectures that balance depth and width will be the definitive area.

3.2 The Loading Problem

3.2.1 The Learning Protocol

The type of learning investigated here is known as supervised learning. In this paradigm input patterns (called *stimuli*) are presented to a machine paired with their desired output patterns (called *responses*). The object of the learning machine is to remember all the associations presented during a training phase so that in future tests the machine will be able to emit the associated response for any given stimulus.

In what follows, every stimulus is a fixed-length string of s bits, and every response ρ is a string of r bits with "don't-cares," that is, $\sigma \in \{0, 1\}^s$ and $\rho \in \{0, 1, *\}^r$. The output from a net is an element of $\{0, 1\}^r$. The purpose of a response string is to specify constraints on what a particular output can be: an output string, θ, is said to agree with a response string, ρ, if each bit, θ_i, of the output equals the corresponding bit, ρ_i, of the response whenever $\rho_i \in \{0, 1\}$. (Whenever the ρ_i is a "don't care"—denoted by a *—then any value for θ_i is acceptable.) The notation for such agreement is $\theta \models \rho$. Each stimulus/response pair, (σ, ρ), is called an SR *item*. A *task* is a set of SR items that the machine is required to learn. To be reasonable, each distinct stimulus in a task should be associated with no more than one distinct response. Equivalently, a task T should be extendable to some function $f : \{0, 1\}^s \rightarrow \{0, 1\}^r$. Let us view functions as sets of ordered pairs and use the notation $T \subseteq f$ to mean $T \subseteq \{(\sigma, \rho) : f(\sigma) \models \rho\}$. For the less formally inclined, read "$T \subseteq f$" as "the task is correctly performed."

3.2.2   Network Architecture

The particular style of connectionist machines considered here is that of nonrecurrent, or feed-forward, networks of computing elements. This is a generalized combinational circuit; the connections between nodes form a directed acyclic graph, and the nodes perform some function of their inputs as calculated by previous nodes in the graph.

Define an *architecture* as a 5-tuple $A = (P, V, S, R, E)$ where

P is a set of *posts*,

V is a set of n *nodes*: $V = \{v_1, v_2, \ldots, v_n\} \subseteq P$,

S is a set of s *input posts*: $S = P - V$,

R is a set of r *output posts*: $R \subseteq P$, and

E is a set of directed *edges*: $E \subseteq \{(v_i, v_j) : v_i \in P, v_j \in V, i < j\}$.

The constraints on the edges ensure that no cycles occur in the graph. Denote the *set of input posts* to node v_k as $pre(v_k) = \{v_j : (v_j, v_k) \in E\}$. The size of this set (denoted $|pre(v_k)|$) is called the *fan-in*.

An architecture specifies everything about a circuit except what functions the nodes perform (i.e., what kinds of gates they are).

3.2.3 Node Functions

Each node in a network contributes to the overall retrieval computation by computing an output signal as a function of the signals on its input edges. Although most of our theorems can be extended to apply to important types of node functions that yield real-valued outputs, they will be stated and proved just for the case where the functions are binary-valued:

$$f_i : \{0, 1\}^{|pre(v_i)|} \to \{0, 1\}.$$

The function f_i is a member of a given set, $\mathscr{F}$, of functions, called a *node function set*. Typically, connectionists have used the set of linearly separable functions (LSFns) for $\mathscr{F}$. These functions are characterized by a real-valued threshold and a real-valued weight associated with each input to a node. An activation level is calculated from the weighted sum of the a inputs, and the output is one of two values depending on whether the activation is above or below the threshold.

$$\text{LSFns} = \{ f : \{0, 1\}^a \to \{0, 1\} \,|\, \exists W \in \mathfrak{R}^a, \Theta \in \mathfrak{R}$$

$$\sum_{i=1}^{a} W_i X_i > \Theta \Leftrightarrow f(X) = 1 \}.$$

Without loss of generality, it can be conceptually simpler to ignore this form of LSFns and think of it as merely a set of binary truth tables. A variety of other node function sets are considered:

LUFns	set of all Boolean functions (LU is from Look-Up table)
LSFns	set of linearly separable functions
TSFns	set of threshold symmetric functions (monotonic in the number of active inputs)
MIFns	set of monotonically increasing functions
SAFns	set of functions formed from one AND gate with inverters on inputs and/or output
AOFns	{AND, OR}
LLFns	sigmoid functions on linear (weighted) sums of inputs
QLFns	any functions composed of any bounded, monotonic function applied to a linear combination of the inputs

Note that LLFns and QLFns are real-valued functions. The back-propagation algorithm of [RHW86] is designed to work with LLFns.

A *configuration*, $F = \{f_1, f_2, \ldots, f_n\}$, of a network is a list of n functions corresponding one to one with the set of nodes, V, meaning that f_i is the function that node i computes.

3.2.4   The Computational Problem

In a configured network, every node performs a particular function, and therefore the network as a whole performs a particular function that is a composition of the node functions. An architecture, A, and a configuration, F, together define a mapping from the space of stimuli to the space of responses:

$$\mathcal{M}_F^A : \{0, 1\}^s \to \{0, 1\}^r.$$

The A and F fully define a circuit and thus fully define how the network will behave during retrieval.

A task, as defined above, can be viewed as a collection of constraints on the mapping that a network is allowed to perform. Recall that an SR item in a task is a pair of strings (σ, ρ). When the posts in S are assigned the values of respective elements of σ, the network mapping defines values for each post in R. It is required that these values agree with respective elements of ρ. For stimuli not in the task, any output is acceptable—that is, $\mathcal{M}_F^A$ may be any consistent extension (generalization) of the task.

The process of *loading* can now be defined. In the learning problem being considered, an architecture and a task are given, and loading is the process of assigning an appropriate function to every node in the architecture, $load(A, T) \mapsto F$, so that the derived mapping includes the task. It is a procedure that accepts a pair (A, T) and returns a *solution*, which is a configuration F such that $T \subseteq \mathcal{M}_F^A$. If no such configuration exists, the procedure announces that fact.

The loading problem is a search problem, but it is usual to frame a complexity question in terms of a simple yes/no question usually called a *decision problem*. In the space of all possible (A, T) pairs, some pairs will have solution configurations and some will not; that is, for some pairs the architecture can *perform* the task, and for some it cannot. The *performability* decision problem is simply, "Can the architecture perform the task?" In the style of [GJ79], this is phrased as follows:

Instance: An architecture A and a task T.

Question: Is there a configuration F for A such that $T \subseteq \{(\sigma, \rho) : \mathscr{M}_F^A(\sigma)$ agrees with $\rho\}$?

For purposes of our ensuing complexity questions, this decision problem embodies the crux of the loading problem, and the terms "loading problem" and "performability problem" will be almost interchangeable.

Note that the above statements are technically incomplete because they hold no direct reference to the node function set being used. Our next (and last) rephrasing of the loading problem redresses this oversight and uses classical terminology for expressing decision problems: The performability problem is the problem of recognizing the following (parameterized) language:

$$LOAD_{\mathscr{F}} = \{(A, T) : \exists F \in \mathscr{F}^n \ni T \subseteq \mathscr{M}_F^A\}.$$

The subscripted parameter indicates the node function set, and in what follows questions will be asked about a variety of such sets. Each time the subscript is changed, it will be referring to a slightly different decision problem.

Specifically, the loading problem involves:

1. A given (previously unknown) network,

2. Total, easy, ongoing access to the network structure,

3. A given (previously unknown) task, and

4. Total, easy, ongoing access to all items in the task,

where *total* means freedom from locality constraints, *easy* means linear cost to read the whole data, and *ongoing* means there is no limit to the number of accesses allowed.

3.3 It Doesn't Matter

One central lesson that has been learned is that the nature of the node function set really does not affect the complexity of loading. Witness

THEOREM 1 $LOAD_{LUFns}$ *is NP-complete.*

$LOAD_{LSFns}$ *is NP-complete.*

$LOAD_{MIFns}$ *is NP-complete.*

$LOAD_{SAFns}$ is NP-complete.

$LOAD_{AOFns}$ is NP-complete.

$LOAD_{QLFns}$ is NP-complete.

$LOAD_{LLFns}$ is NP-complete.   ■

These have been proved elsewhere [Jud87, Jud90].

These results seem very uniform and nondiscriminating between the different node function sets, but there is a subtlety here that needs to be addressed. Each of the decision problems represented above is trying to discriminate between two sets of tasks: those that can be computed by a given architecture and those that cannot. The trouble is that for different node function sets these sets are (in general) different. For instance the tasks performable with LSFns are different from (actually a subset of) the tasks that are performable with LUFns. Hence we cannot claim that changing the node function sets has not made any difference because it could be that it is easier to load all the tasks performable with LSFns *if you used LUFns to do it.*

Let $LOAD_{\mathscr{F}}^{\mathscr{G}}$ be the problem of finding a configuration composed of functions from $\mathscr{F}$ for a given architecture under the following more lax criterion: If there is a configuration composed of functions from $\mathscr{G}$ then it must find one composed of functions from $\mathscr{F}$; but if none exists using $\mathscr{G}$ then no particular response is required. As long as $\mathscr{F} \supseteq \mathscr{G}$, this problem is no harder than $LOAD_{\mathscr{G}}$ and might be easier. It allows the extra power in $\mathscr{F}$ to be used without having to load a larger set of tasks—so now the playing field has been leveled out, and we can ask fairer questions about the effect of node function sets here.

By taking $\mathscr{F}$ and $\mathscr{G}$ to extremes, we can maximize the consequences of this question:

THEOREM 2 $LOAD_{LUFns}^{AOFns}$ is NP-complete.   ■

Since we have used a minimal set to define the set of tasks to be loaded, and we have allowed the machine the most unfettered set to do the loading, it seems that all the peculiarities of the node function set have been exorcised from the problem. Nevertheless, the intractability remains. This evidence gives a clear answer that the NP-completeness arises from some other source, and is independent of the node function set.

We now go in search of other ways to ask our question.

3.3.1   Architectural Subcases

The theorems above hold for the set of *all* possible architectures. However, the loading problem can be split up into many different subcases, and one way to do this is to ask about its complexity with respect to some particular family of architectures. When the problem is constrained so that it is not as general a computational problem, it can become easier to compute.

It is not my purpose to explore all the different types of subcases one might imagine; some of that has been done elsewhere [Jud90]. But it is instructive to glance at a summary of some of that work. Figure 3.1 shows a lattice of subfamilies of architectures, where the most general one is represented as the top dot, and dots located further down the chart are subcases of the ones above them. The labels on the edges are constraints; each dot represents a family that is constrained by all the edges above it on the path back to the top. When the loading problem is restricted to deal only with architectures from one of these classes, the lattice also represents special cases of the loading problem.

The subcases are further specified by attaching a node function set to it as well; if there is no discrimination between sets on the general-architecture problem, we would like to see if there is at least some breakup of the classes for some specific classes of architectures.

The complexity of the subcases is shown beside the dot; X's mean it is NP-complete, and checks mean it is polynomial. There are individual marks for each node function set, which appear in this order: LUFns, LSFns, MIFns, SAFns, AOFns. The observation to be made is merely that all the marks are X's or they are all checks: even in all these subcases we have found no interaction between the node function sets and architectures. Hence we are left with an accumulating impression:

The choice of node function set does not affect loading complexity.

3.4   It Does Matter

All the results in the previous section were for families on architectures that had two things in common: they were all shallow (i.e. their depth did not increase as they scaled up), and the fan-in to each node was bounded. In this section, we will examine one class of architectures where the fan-in

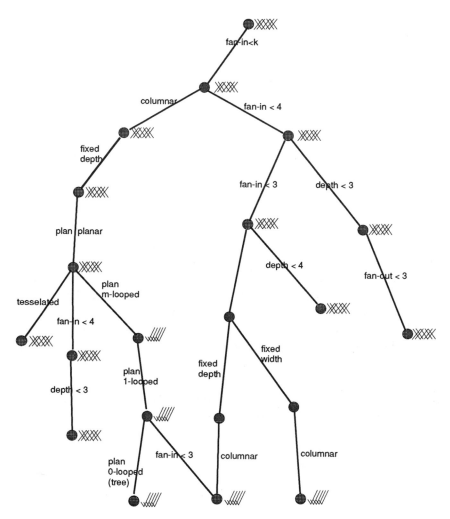

Figure 3.1
A hierarchy of architectural families forming subcases of the loading problem

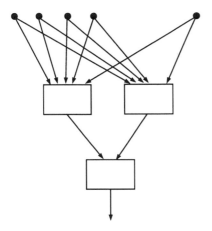

Figure 3.2
The 3-node architecture

is *not* bounded, and one class where the depth is not bounded. In both classes, we will find cases where the node function set makes a difference to the tractability.

3.4.1 Unbounded Fan-in

Blum and Rivest [BR88] looked at the architecture in figure 3.2. It expands only by scaling up the number of inputs.

THEOREM 3 (Blum and Rivest) *Loading the 3-node architecture with LSFns is NP-complete.* ∎

Alas, our hope for a simple uniform world that does not respect node function sets is dashed ...

THEOREM 4 *Loading the 3-node architecture with LUFns is polynomial. Loading the 3-node architecture with TSFns is polynomial. Loading the 3-node architecture with AOFns is polynomial.*

Proof: LUFns scales so fast with inputs that we can get the top left node to remember any task simply by storing it as a lookup table. The other two-node function sets scale so slowly that all possible configurations can be tried. For AOFns there are only eight combinations; for TSFns there are $O(n^2)$. ∎

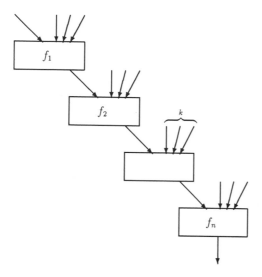

Figure 3.3
Example of 3-injected chain

3.4.2 Unbounded Depth

In order to pry our way into understanding the effect of depth on the complexity of loading, we need to study some network families that are arbitrarily deep, but it is somewhat of an art to decide which families are the most promising ones to explore. The simple family we chose is a single-output architecture where every node has a fixed fan-in and receives no more than one input from another node. We call these *k-injected chains* where *k* is the number of external inputs to each node (one less than the fan-in). See Figure 3.3 for an example.

THEOREM 5   *Loading the k-injected chains using LUFns is NP-complete for any $k \geq 2$.*   ■

To keep matters from being unequivocal, however, we have this disconcerting theorem:

THEOREM 6   *Loading the k-injected chains using TSFns is polynomial.*

Thus we are left to conclude that:

The choice of node function set does affect loading complexity.

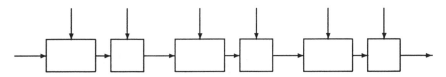

Figure 3.4
Architecture for construction in lemma 7

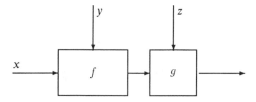

Figure 3.5
The gadget for each variable

We cannot make sweeping statements about its intractability without referring to the set in use.

3.4.3   Proof of Theorem 5

This section contains a proof of one of the results alluded to above:

THEOREM   *Loading the k-injected chains using LUFns is NP-complete for any $k \geq 2$.*

Proof: We begin, of course, by proving something slightly different. Figure 3.4 depicts an architecture where every second node receives a three-valued signal from above, and the alternate nodes receive a two-valued signal from above. All horizontal-moving signals are binary; the nodes perform LUFns.   ∎

LEMMA 7   *Loading these architectures is NP-complete.*

Proof: There are three steps to construct a reduction from SAT.

Step 1:   For each variable, v_i, in the SAT system, we need a gadget as depicted in figure 3.5. It computes a function $h'(x, y, z) = g(f(x, y), z)$ where $f : \{0, 1\} \times \{0, *, 1\} \mapsto \{0, 1\}$ and $g : \{0, 1\}^2 \mapsto \{0, 1\}$. We specify a "tasklet" for this net (thereby implying some constraints on h') in three pieces. Here is piece 1:

$$0 \quad *0 \quad \longmapsto 0$$
$$1 \quad *0 \quad \longmapsto 1.$$

If h' obeys this, then we know $f(0, *) \neq f(1, *)$, and because LUFns is closed under complementation we can, WLOG, assume $f(1, *) = 1$. This implies

$$f(x, *) = x \quad \text{and} \quad g(x, 0) = x. \tag{1}$$

The second piece of the tasklet is

$$1 \quad 0\,0 \quad \longmapsto 1$$
$$1 \quad 1\,0 \quad \longmapsto 1.$$

If h' performs this (as well as the first piece) then $f(1, 0) = f(1, 1) = f(1, *) = 1$, that is,

$$f(1, x) = 1 \quad \text{and} \quad g(f(1, x), 0) = 1. \tag{2}$$

The last piece of the tasklet is

$$0 \quad 0\,1 \quad \longmapsto 0$$
$$0 \quad 1\,1 \quad \longmapsto 1,$$

from which we deduce that

$$f(0, 1) \neq f(0, 0) = 1 - f(0, 1). \tag{3}$$

We use this whole contraption for a single variable, v, of the SAT system, and identify $f(0, 1)$ with $value(v)$. Let $h_v(x, y) = g_v(f_v(x, y), 0)$. Then

$$\text{if } value(v) = 1, \begin{cases} h_v(0, 1) = 1 = value(v) \\ h_v(0, 0) = 0 = \neg value(v) \\ h_v(1, y) = 1 \end{cases}$$

$$\text{if } value(v) = 0, \begin{cases} h_v(0, 1) = 0 = value(v) \\ h_v(0, 0) = 1 = \neg value(v) \\ h_v(1, y) = 1 \end{cases}$$

or more succinctly,

$$h_v(x, y) = \begin{cases} x & \text{if } y = * \\ x \vee (y = value(v)) & \text{otherwise} \end{cases}$$

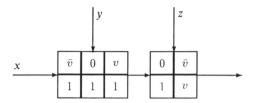

Figure 3.6
The gadget for variable v with Karnaugh maps filled in

All these constraints on h are depicted in figure 3.6.

Step 2: All these pieces can coexist in the composite system whose structure is given in figure 3.4: If there are n variables then piece 1 of the (composite) task is

$$0 \quad (* \, 0)^n \quad \mapsto 0$$
$$1 \quad (* \, 0)^n \quad \mapsto 1,$$

and equation (1) holds for each variable. (The $* \, 0$ are signals to the two upper input lines of each of the n gadgets.) The second piece comes as n pairs of items:

$$1 \quad (* \, 0)^{i-1} \quad 0 \, 0 \quad (* \, 0)^{n-i} \quad \mapsto 1$$
$$1 \quad (* \, 0)^{i-1} \quad 1 \, 0 \quad (* \, 0)^{n-i} \quad \mapsto 1,$$

which preserves equation (2) for each variable v_i separately. The third piece also comes as n pairs of items:

$$1 \quad (* \, 0)^{i-1} \quad 0 \, 1 \quad (* \, 0)^{n-i} \quad \mapsto 1$$
$$1 \quad (* \, 0)^{i-1} \quad 1 \, 1 \quad (* \, 0)^{n-i} \quad \mapsto 1,$$

which preserves equation (3) for each variable v_i separately.

Step 3: Describe the jth clause of the SAT system as a vector

$$(sense_j(v_1), sense_j(v_2), sense_j(v_3), \dots)$$

where $sense_j(v)$ takes one of the values $\{1, 0, *\}$, depending on whether the variable appears respectively as a positive literal, a negative literal, or not at all in clause i. A fourth piece of the task then consists of one item for each clause:

$$0 \quad sense_j(v_1) \quad 0 \quad sense_j(v_2) \quad 0 \quad sense_j(v_3) \quad 0 \quad \dots \quad \mapsto 1.$$

If the network performs this item too, then we know

$$\ldots h_{v_3}(h_{v_2}(h_{v_1}(0, sense_j(v_1)), sense_j(v_2)), sense_j(v_3))\ldots = 1.$$

If the clause involved variables a, b, and c, then after removing all the nonparticipating variables (remember $h_v(x, *) = x$), we have

$$(0 \vee (value(a) = sense(a)) \vee (value(b) = sense(b))$$
$$\vee (value(c) = sense(c))) = 1$$

which is a transparent isomorph of the SAT clause.

The broad strategy is to force the disjuctions of a SAT clause to be complied with during retrieval of one of these final items. The global conjuction arises through requiring *all* items to be performed correctly. ∎

Proof of theorem: The construction for the previous lemma is overtly relevant only to the case where ternary input signals are allowed. We can repair this proof for the case where only binary signals are allowed by simply replacing the ternary inputs by a pair of binary ones (thus giving rise to a fourth column in the Karnaugh map for f), but never using the fourth column. This simple modification proves the theorem for 2-Injected Chains. For larger k, the same proof holds by keeping the extra inputs constant.   ∎

The construction in this proof causes function g to be either $g(x, y) = x$ or $g(x, y) = x \oplus y$, and thus it works fine for LUFns which contains $\oplus$. Neither LSFns nor TSFns has $\oplus$ though, so the proof breaks down for them.

3.4.4 Proof of Theorem 6

This section contains the proof for one of the results alluded to above:

THEOREM (T. X. Brown) *Loading the k-injected chains using TSFns is polynomial.*

Proof: An algorithm is given. First, let the inputs to unit c be called $x_{c,1}, x_{c,2}, \ldots, x_{c,k}$. Node c calculates a function $f_c(y_{c-1}, x_{c,1}, x_{c,2}, \ldots, x_{c,k})$ where y_{c-1} is the output from the previous node except for the first node which has the extra input $y_0 = x_{1,0}$. Since the node function set used is TSFns, an abbreviation of the inputs is used: define $s_c^i = \sum_j x_{c,j}^i$ to be the number of inputs that are active at unit c in stimulus i.

$B(I_0, I_1, c)$:
    if $I_0 = \emptyset$ or $I_1 = \emptyset$
       return true
    if $c = 0$ return false
    calculate $h = \min_{i \in I_1} (s_c^i)$
    calculate $\ell = \max_{i \in I_0} (s_c^i)$
    if $h < \ell$ return false
    if $h > \ell$ return true
    if $h = \ell$
       calculate $I_0' = \{i \in I_0 | s_c^i = \ell\}$
       calculate $I_1^h = \{i \in I_1 | s_c^i = h\}$
       return $B(I_0', I_1^h, c - 1)$.

LEMMA 8 Let $Z_0 = \{i | \rho^i = 0\}$ and $Z_1 = \{i | \rho^i = 1\}$ where ρ^i is the required (single bit) response for item i. $B(Z_0, Z_1, n)$ returns true iff there is a configuration of the k-injected chain that performs the task.

Proof: Clearly, if $h > \ell$ at any point, then the two sets of items indexed by I_0 and I_1 can be separated by setting the threshold for that node function at h. If $h < \ell$ then no solution exists because the input from the node before (which has yet to be tallied in with s_c^i) can only increase the h by one, which would leave no threshold to discriminate between the two sets. Whenever $h = \ell$ the node can discriminate iff the node before it can resolve the items that are currently on the borderline of confusion. ∎

The algorithm recurs at most once for every node in the architecture, and hence it runs in time $O(n|T|)$, linear in the product of the architecture size and task size. This proves the theorem. ∎

3.5 Conclusion

We have sought some guidance as to what type of node function set would be most appropriate for neural networks. The only criterion used was the worst-case complexity of loading various families of architectures. We have found evidence that shows several reasonable node function sets to be equivalent for shallow networks, and we can conclude that all nontrivial sets will follow this rule.

    The complexity of loading a simple net of unbounded fan-in turns out to be dependent on the node function set, and the same goes for a simple family of unbounded depth. These results point to a much more complex world. The job of the researcher trying to make sense of this has thus been shown to be complicated, but it leaves open the possibility of making an argument about the relative merits of node function sets.

References

[GJ79]   Garey, M. R., and Johnson, D. S. *Computers and Intractability: A Guide to the Theory of NP-Completeness.* W. H. Freeman, San Francisco, CA, 1979.

[Jud87]   Judd, J. S. Learning in networks is hard. In *Proceedings of the First International Conference on Neural Networks*, Vol. 2, pp. 685–692. San Diego, CA, IEEE 1987.

[Jud90]   Judd, J. Stephen. *Neural Network Design and the Complexity of Learning.* MIT Press, Cambridge, MA, 1990.

[RHW86]   Rumelhart, David E., Geoffrey E. Hinton, and Ronald J. Williams. Learning internal representations by error propagation. In David E. Rumelhart and Jay L. McClelland, editors, *Parallel Distributed Processing: Explorations in the Microstructure of Cognition*, Vol. 1, *Foundations*, p. 318–362. Bradford Books/ MIT Press, Cambridge, MA, 1986.

4 Defining the Limits of Analogical Planning

Diane J. Cook

4.1 Introduction

Analogy is pervasive in human intelligence. When solving a problem in a relatively new and unfamiliar domain, humans often rely on experience with similar problems to attack the current problem by adapting known techniques, mapping constraints from a solved problem to the new problem, and modifying existing solutions to include new capabilities. Given a novel problem (the *target* case), an analogical planner selects a similar, solved problem (the *base* case), computes a mapping between the base and target problem descriptions, and uses the mapping to adapt the base solution to the current domain. Unfortunately, the process of planning by analogy is nebulous and difficult to capture in a complete implementation. Buchanan goes as far as to say that analogical reasoning is a "pipe dream when matched against the harsh standards of robustness of commercial applications" [1].

One way of strengthening the automation of analogical planning is to develop a formal model of analogical planning that can control the system, predict and measure performance, and compare algorithms. Very little work has been done to formalize analogical reasoning, but Valiant has introduced a complexity-based model of learning concepts from examples that has become widely accepted, known as *probably approximately correctly (PAC)-learning* a concept. As a result of applying this formalism to inductive learning, it is possible to predict how well a given algorithm will classify future examples, based on the size of the concept and the size of the training set.

The purpose of this chapter is to merge the empirical-based work on analogical reasoning with analyses found in computational learning theory. We introduce analogical planning and discuss the application of PAC-learning techniques to analogical planning. The results of the analysis are used to describe formally the analogical planning task and to measure the expected performance of an analogical planner. Section 4.2 defines the analogical planning technique and describes a system that uses graph match to perform analogical planning in a variety of problem domains. Next, the theory of pac-learning is reviewed, and the notion of *probably approximately correctly analogically (PACA)-planning* is introduced. Section 4.4 utilizes the PACA-planning theory to analyze necessary conditions for good analogical planning performance. Finally, we analyze a method of increasing the effectiveness of analogical planning by merging multiple similar base cases.

4.2 Analogical Planning

Analogy can be defined as an inference that if two or more things agree in some respects they will probably agree in others. The strength of the analogically generated inferences depends on the type and strength of the relationship between the known shared properties and the inferred shared properties.

Analogy is a powerful planning tool. Engineers and scientists rarely attack a problem in an unfamiliar domain from scratch. Instead, they rely on their experience with solving problems in similar domains. They adapt known techniques, map constraints from a solved problem to the new problem, and modify existing solutions to fit the current problem specification. When examples are lacking and domain theory is scarce, the intelligent agent draws on past experience in similar situations to attack a new problem.

The three main steps of analogy plan formation are *base selection, map formation*, and *inference generation*. Given the target problem that needs a solution, the analogical planner selects a base problem that has a successful plan and that shares crucial properties of the problem with the target. When the appropriate base case has been found, the system constructs the analogical mapping. Once the mapping is formed, the analogy system uses the information describing the base and the *base → target* mapping to infer the target plan.

For example, a programmer rarely develops his code from scratch. Instead, he pulls ideas and pieces of code from similar programs he has written in the past and modifies them to fit the peculiarities of the current goal. If he wants to implement a program that computes real-number division to a specific accuracy, he may benefit most from analogically deriving the program. First, he finds a program in his database that computes the cube root of a real number to a specific precision (base selection). He senses the underlying similarities between the type of information used and the goal of the programs and pinpoints the correspondences (map formation). Using these correspondences, he maps the existing code to fit the current situation and enters the new analogically implemented program into his database (inference generation).

In recent work we suggest a graph match approach to analogical planning, implemented in a system called ANAGRAM [5, 6, 7]. ANAGRAM has successfully generated analogical plans in the domains of automatic programming and route planning. This approach represents plans as directed acyclic graphs. The nodes in each graph represent objects or object attributes, and the links represent the relations between the nodes. Given a target problem specification represented in graph form, ANAGRAM uses a graph match technique to compare each base case in a database of previously solved problems with the target. ANAGRAM uses the selected base together with the *base → target* mapping output from the graph match to generate a plan which will achieve the target goal. By matching the graph representations of plans, ANAGRAM ensures that the underlying structures of the two problems are the same, which is a fundamental component of analogy.

Figure 4.1 represents a pair of base and target subgraphs which describe the goal state for each problem. The goal of the target problem is to generate a program that will compute q (the quotient of two real numbers c and d) to a given precision e. The selected base is an existing plan to generate a program that computes r (the cube root of a) to a given precision e. ANAGRAM performs a graph match to determine if the two problems are similar and to output the best set of node-to-node mappings. The result of this match is the set of mappings:

$\{$Goal-State $\rightarrow$ Goal-State, $< \rightarrow <$, abs $\rightarrow$ abs, $e \rightarrow e$,
  term0 $\rightarrow$ term1, $- \rightarrow -$, pow $\rightarrow /$, $r \rightarrow q$, $a \rightarrow c$, $1/3 \rightarrow d\}$.

From this mapping the base program segment is transformed to a program that achieves the target goal. The base and target programs are shown below. The program specifications are defined by Dershowitz [8].

Diane J. Cook

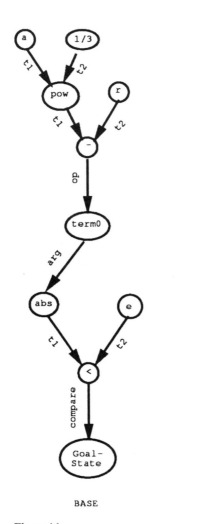
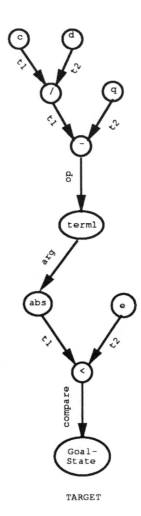

BASE   TARGET

Figure 4.1
Base and target goal state subgraphs

```
/* Compute cube root of a */          /* Compute c/d */
begin cube root                       begin target
    assert a ≥ 0, e > 0                   assert d > c ≥ 0, e > 0
    goal |a^{1/3} − r| < e                goal |c/d − q| < e
    (r, s) := (0, a + 1)                  (q, s) := (0, c + 1)
    loop L₃: until s ≤ e      ⇒          loop L₃: until s ≤ e
        s := s/2                              s := s/2
        if (r + s)³ ≤ a                       if (a + s) × d ≤ c
            then r := r + s                       then q := q + s
        endif                                 endif
        repeat                                repeat
end                                   end
```

Much of the existing analogy research focuses primarily on the creation of the *base → target* mapping. Gentner's theory of *systematicity* [3, 9, 10] shows that humans use analogies between concepts whose underlying *structures* are the same. Other popular methods of map formation include Carbonell's *transformational analogy* approach [2] which uses means-ends analysis to reduce the difference between base and target, and the *explanation-based* approach of Kedar-Cabelli [15], which constructs an *explanation* of the difference between base and target concepts. Other work focuses on the base selection task, such as case-based reasoning research [11, 12, 16] which uses plan keywords to organize the database and select a base case.

Our goal here is to offer a formal analysis of the effectiveness of analogical planning. Very little research focuses on the formal foundations of analogical reasoning. One existing model applied to *metaphors* is presented by Indurkhya [13]. Indurkhya offers a formal model of metaphors that can be applied to analogical reasoning in general. He uses T-MAPS to represent the partial mappings $\langle F, S \rangle$ (F is the *base → target* mapping, and S is the set of sentences in the base that can be transformed using F). Indurkhya uses this formal model to measure the current strength and amount of inference of a metaphor. Unfortunately, this model does not indicate what steps any given analogy system must take to maximize its performance.

4.3   PACA Planning

Until recently analogical reasoning was largely an experimental science. As a result the actual technique used to perform analogical planning is nebulous. Many implementations rely upon a variety of heuristics which are not easily formalized, and no method has been proposed to compare these techniques or combine specialized approaches.

A solution to this problem is to specify a formal analogical reasoning model by which algorithms may be controlled, evaluated, and compared. This section describes a formal analogical planning framework based on the learnability model defined by Valiant. This theory of analogical planning will be used to define algorithms which in a feasible (polynomial) amount of time generate (with high likelihood) analogical plans that are measurably accurate.

Although formalizing the analogical planning task has received little attention, the formal specification of another machine learning task has recently been rigorously investigated: the technique of learning from examples. Computational learning theorists contribute a means of formally defining the inductive learning task and predicting the performance of a given inductive learning algorithm. This contribution is based on Valiant's "learnability framework" [17, 18]. Valiant characterizes inductive learning algorithms according to the properties needed for the algorithm to polynomial-time learn a concept C within an error tolerance ε to a specified probability $1 - \delta$. That is, the resulting concept is predicted to be $1 - \varepsilon$ consistent with future examples with probability $1 - \delta$. An algorithm meeting these requirements is said to be able to probably approximately correctly (pac)-learn the concept C.

Given the size of a concept representation, an error threshold ε, and a probability threshold δ, this model is used to determine how many examples the algorithm must be trained on to learn the concept within these parameters. One algorithm described by Kearns et al. [14] learns the class of monomials over n attributes from positive examples only. The monomial-learning algorithm (algorithm A_1) is given below.

$H \leftarrow x_1 \overline{x_1} x_2 \overline{x_2} \ldots x_n \overline{x_n};$ /* H = all possible variables */
for $i := 1$ to NUM-EXAMPLES do

```
begin
    v ← POS-EXAMPLE;
    for j := 1 to n do                    /* Eliminate inconsistencies */
        if v(j) = 0 then
            delete x_j from H;
        else
            delete x̄_j from H;
end
output H.
```

If some attribute x_j is assigned the value 0 in a positive example, it can never appear in the monomial M being learned, so algorithm A_1 deletes x_j from the hypothesis H. Algorithm A_1 can err only by failing to delete an attribute x_j (or its negation) that does not appear in M and has a good chance (the definition of "good chance" here depends on the value of ε) of being assigned 0 in some positive example.

Because algorithm A_1 is *conservative* (it discards the current hypothesis if and only if the hypothesis incorrectly classifies the next input), *acyclic* (it never conjectures any hypothesis more than once), and *poly-failure-bounded* (it never makes more than a polynomial number of incorrect hypotheses), the number of examples that must be submitted for A_1 to PAC-learn can be computed from the size of the search space. Given that the depth of the search space for this algorithm is $2n$, the upper bound on NUM-EXAMPLES is shown by Kearns et al. to be $\frac{2n}{\varepsilon}\left(ln(2n) + ln\left(\frac{1}{\delta}\right)\right)$.

The monomial-learning algorithm can be used to analyze how much fit is needed between base and target problem descriptions to PACA-plan. Instead of learning the class of monomials, the goal of analogical planning is to learn maximally complete mappings from base to target. The more complete the mapping, the greater chance the inferred target plan has of being accurate.

Instead of being fed examples, the analogical planning algorithm A_2 is fed predicate names that are used in both the base and target plan representation. If the object o_i is an argument of a predicate describing the base, and object o_j is used as an argument of a predicate *of the same name* describing the target, then object o_i has the possibility of being mapped to object o_j. For example, if the predicate (**Maximum** *val*1 *val*2) occurs in the base—**Maximum** is the *predicate name*—and (**Maximum** *valx valy*) occurs in the target, then one possible mapping includes $val1 \rightarrow valx$. If one of the objects is used as an argument in a predicate with name P and the other is not used in any predicate with name P, the objects cannot map to each other. In this way mappings can be deleted from the current hypothesis in the same way that variables were deleted from the hypothesis in the monomial-learning algorithm. The map-learning algorithm A_2 is given below.

$H \leftarrow (b_1, t_1)(b_1, t_2) \ldots (b_1, t_m)$ /* H = all possible object mappings */
$\qquad \vdots$
$\qquad (b_n, t_1)(b_n, t_2) \ldots (b_n, t_m)$
$P_B \leftarrow \{$Set of predicate names describing the base$\}$
$P_T \leftarrow \{$Set of predicate names describing the target$\}$
$P \leftarrow P_B \cap P_T$
for $i := 1$ to NUM-SHARED-PREDICATE-NAMES do
begin
    /* $tuple_{b_i} = (p_i, b_x, \ldots, b_y)$, $tuple_{t_i} = (p_i, t_x, \ldots, t_y)$ */
    tuple$_{b_i} \leftarrow$ PREDICATE $\in B$ described by p_i
    tuple$_{t_i} \leftarrow$ PREDICATE $\in T$ described by p_i
    for $j := 1$ to n do   /* Eliminate all inconsistencies */
      for $k := 1$ to m do
        if $((b_j \in tuple_{b_i}$ AND $t_k \notin tuple_{t_i})$ OR
          $(b_j \in tuple_{b_i}$ AND $t_k \notin tuple_{t_i}))$ then
           delete (b_j, t_k) from H;
end
output H.

In order to find the perfect mapping, each object must be mapped to only one other object. In other words, for any object in the base b_i, there must be only one entry in H of the form (b_i, t_j). Algorithm A_2 is conservative, acyclic, and poly-failure-bounded, so the number of predicates that must describe both base and target in order to PACA-plan (NUM-SHARED-PREDICATE-NAMES) can be calculated in a manner similar to the method we used to calculate NUM-EXAMPLES for algorithm A_1. The number of shared predicate descriptors can also be viewed as the amount of *structural fit* between the base and target plans, because the predicates express relationships between the objects and define the structure of the problem itself. The depth of the search space for this algorithm is *mn*, so NUM-SHARED-

PREDICATE-NAMES must have a lower bound of $\dfrac{mn}{\varepsilon}\left(ln(mn) + ln\left(\dfrac{1}{\delta}\right)\right)$ to PACA-plan, or analogically plan with accuracy $1 - \varepsilon$ and confidence $1 - \delta$.

4.4   Maximizing Performance

The previous section formalizes analogical planning by viewing it as an algorithm that learns a mapping from base to target. This section uses the results of paca-planning to predict the performance of analogical planners. The theory of paca-planning is useful is several ways. First, the result in the previous section calculates the amount of *fit* between base and target needed to generate an analogical plan accurately. Second, we can calculate the number of plans that must reside in the database as potential base cases to paca-plan with probability Ω.

Let p represent the number of shared predicate names required to PACA-plan. The following assumptions are made:

• Let g signify the size of the representation grammar (the number of symbols used to describe the plan's input to the system, including predicate names and predicate arguments), x is the number of symbols used to describe the base plan, and y is the number of symbols used to describe the target plan. The size of g is the same for each base case in the database and for the target,

• The probability of selecting a particular predicate from the grammar is the same for all predicates (it follows a uniform distribution),

• The number of predicates describing each base and target is at least p and at most g, and

• The probability that a particular number of predicates is used to express any given base or target is equal for any number between p and n (it follows a uniform distribution).

The probability ψ that the target will share at least p of the predicates describing the base is calculated by first considering the probability that the base and target share exactly p predicate names.

In probability theory, the value p is said to have a hypergeometric distribution. Using the formula for a hypergeometric distribution, the probability that the base and target share exactly p predicates is

$$\frac{\binom{x}{p}\binom{g-x}{y-p}}{\binom{g}{y}}.$$

However, the number of shared predicate names can range from p to g. Thus, the probability must be summed from p to y, yielding the result

$$\psi = \sum_{z=r}^{min(x,y)} \frac{\binom{x}{y}\binom{g-x}{y-z}}{\binom{g}{y}}.$$

An analogical planner can select the base case from its database that will best fit the target. It is assumed that the probability of any base case sharing p of its predicates with the target is independent of the probabilities for the other base cases. Given n bases in the database, the probability Ω that at least one base has p predicates shared with the target is $1 - (1 - p)^n$. As a result, the number of base cases needed to paca-plan with probability Ω is $log_{(1-p)}(1 - \Omega)$.

Algorithm A_2 assumes that there will be one unique predicate defined for any predicate name from the base plan, and only one unique predicate defined for any predicate name from the target plan. Furthermore, it assumes that the order of predicate arguments is not important; in other words, if the predicate (**Maximum** $val1$ $val2$) exists in the target and the predicate (**Maximum** $valx$ $valy$) exists in the base, then $val1$ can map to either $valx$ or $valy$.

We can remove these constraints from the algorithm without changing the general-case results found in the theoretical analysis. The modifications do not affect the number of shared predicate names needed for the algorithm to pac-learn, because the modified algorithms are still conservative, acyclic, and poly-failure-bounded, and because the depth of the search space is mn in each case. However, the number of (b, t) that can be deleted after processing each input predicate name differs according to the type of constraints imposed on the input data.

Figure 4.2 demonstrates empirically how accuracy is affected by the size of NUM-SHARED-PREDICATE-NAMES with and without each of the constraints mentioned above. For this experiment, 100 base-domain predicates were

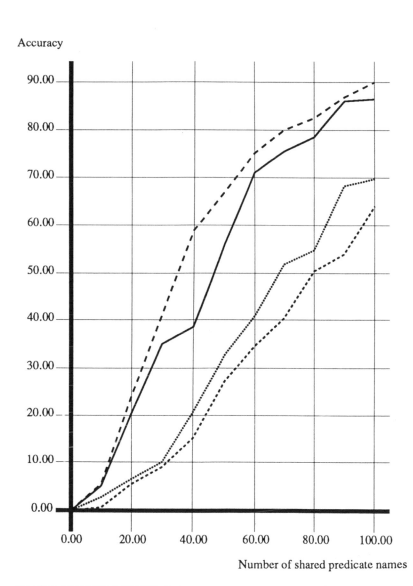

Accuracy

Number of shared predicate names

| No order / Unique predicates |
| Order / Unique predicates |
| No order / Multiple predicates |
| Order / Multiple predicates |

Figure 4.2
Accuracy as a function of the number of shared predicate names

randomly generated from a grammar (collection of predicate names and objects) of size 150. Each predicate has three arguments. The size of NUM-SHARED-PREDICATE-NAMES ranged from 0 to 100, and predicates were randomly generated to describe the target. After the algorithm converged on a mapping, the mapping was applied to the remaining base predicates. The accuracy of the mapping is demonstrated by finding a unique mapping for each symbol in each remaining base tuple. The accuracy is plotted in figure 4.2 against the size of NUM-SHARED-PREDICATE-NAMES.

Four different sets of constraints were imposed on the input data. In the first test, the base and target each had only one predicate for any given predicate name, and the order of the predicate arguments was not enforced. In the second test, single predicates were again used, and a matched ordering of arguments was enforced. In the third and fourth tests, the base and target could use multiple predicates with the same predicate name, and the order of predicate arguments was relaxed in the third test and enforced in the fourth test. When single predicates were used, the number of predicates that described the target corresponded to the number of shared predicate names. When multiple predicates were used, the base and the target both contained two predicates for each shared predicate name.

As is seen from the analysis, the more predicate names that are shared between base and target, the more accurate the resulting analogy will be. Unfortunately, in many cases no base case can be found that shares as many predicate names with the target problem as are required to PACA-plan. As a result we must consider methods of combining several similar base cases.

4.5   Merging Congruent Base Cases

A major limitation of analogical planning is that the strength of an analogical plan depends entirely on the completeness of the match between the base and target cases. Using inductive learning, if the concept is not learned well enough, the algorithm can be fed more training examples. Using analogical learning, the accuracy of the mapping is dependent entirely on the fit between one base case and the target.

A solution to this *single base limitation* is to merge congruent base graphs (base graphs that are structurally similar to each other and the target) into a *virtual base case* that better fits the target. This procedure has

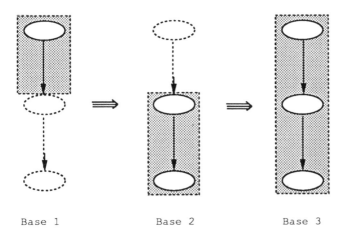

Figure 4.3
Distinct base case merge

the effect of strengthening an analogy by supplying map information where a single base case could not, or of generalizing portions of the base cases to cover the target.

One method of merging bases is to find base cases that match each other and whose differences with the target do not overlap, as shown in figure 4.3. The best of each base case (here represented by graphs) is pulled into the virtual base case. In the PACA-planning theory, each individual base case cannot generate a sufficient analogy, because too few predicates are shared between the base and the target to learn a sufficient number of mappings. Merging cases with distinct *base* → *target* differences allows the "missing pieces" of the mapping to be filled in. Let M represent the desired mapping and assume each base case shares b predicate names with the target. The merged base case must share p predicates with the target to PACA-plan, so the number of distinct base cases that must be merged to PACA-plan is $\frac{p}{b}$, or $\frac{1}{b}\left[\frac{mn}{\varepsilon}\left(ln(mn) + ln\left(\frac{1}{\delta}\right)\right)\right]$.

If the defective/unmatched portions of the base cases *do* overlap, the base cases can be merged by generalizing the overlapping subgraphs. The intent is to generalize portions of the base cases that cannot map to the target enough so the resulting general subplan *does* cover the target specification. There are many methods of generalization that can be used. One such method is the *climbing generalization tree* method. This technique

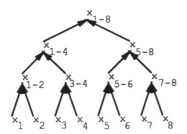

Figure 4.4
Generalization hierarchy for x

replaces each variable in the concept description with the node label that appears one level up in the concept hierarchy. In figure 4.4, x_1 can be generalized to x_{1-2}, and the set of instances $\{x_1, x_2, x_7\}$ can be generalized to the single variable x_{1-8}.

Assume that the branching factor for each generalization tree is a constant b. Also assume that there is a constant height h for each generalization tree, resulting in $l = b^h$ leaves, or distinct symbols, in each generalization tree. Each subplan from the merged cases that does not map to the target is generalized the least possible amount. Let s represent the size of the map which cannot be covered by a single base (the number of individual target symbols that have no corresponding base symbol). In order to PACA-plan, the number of base cases that must be merged using the generalization technique is $\dfrac{s(h+1)}{\varepsilon}\left(ln(h+1) + ln\left(\dfrac{1}{\delta}\right)\right)$.[1]

4.6 Graph Match as a PACA Planner

The PACA-planning model shows that if an algorithm can in polynomial time learn a *base* $\rightarrow$ *target* mapping to $1 - \varepsilon$ accuracy with $1 - \delta$ probability between a base and target with $\dfrac{mn}{\varepsilon}\left(ln(mn) + ln\left(\dfrac{1}{\delta}\right)\right)$ shared predicates, the algorithm is a paca-planner. This section determines if the graph match algorithm can be classified as a paca-planner.

Our graph match algorithm has been proved to operate time polynomial in the number of plans in the database and the size of the plans [4, 5]. The algorithm can be transformed to A_2 described in section 4.4 and thus be proved as a paca-planner. Given information about the initial state and goal states of both the base and target plans, the graph match algorithm matches the graph representations of these descriptions and outputs a set of correspondences between the two cases. To transform the algorithm to algorithm A_2, each link can be represented as the predicate (**link-label**, *from-node, to-node*). In the graph match the link labels must match, so the graph match is performing the same match as algorithm A_2. Each node from the base will only match a node from the target if both are surrounded by similar graph structures with similar link labels. The mapping output by the graph match algorithm represents the hypothesis that algorithm A_2 converged on, and each base symbol not included in the mapping corresponds to each base symbol which has more than one possible mapping in A_2's hypothesis. Thus the graph match algorithm does probably approximately correctly analogically (PACA) plan.

4.7 Conclusions

This chapter has demonstrated the application of computational learning theory to analogical planning. By designing a formal model of analogical planning based on pac-learning theory, we have constructed a method of controlling, evaluating, and comparing analogical planning systems. In this chapter, the idea of probably approximately correctly analogically (PACA)-planning was introduced and used to calculate the amount of fit needed between base and target to accurately analogically plan. These results were also used to compute the number of plans needed in the database to paca-plan, and to compute the number of base cases that can be merged to achieve paca-planning. Once a formal model of analogical reasoning has been adopted for analogical planning, this machine learning method can approach the benefits humans derive from analogically reasoning about everyday problems.

Note

1. The derivation of these formulas is presented by Cook [5]).

References

[1] Buchanan, B. G. Can machine learning offer anything to expert systems? *Machine Learning*, Vol. 4 (3–4): pp. 251–254, 1989.

[2] Carbonell, J. G. Learning by analogy: Formulating and generalizing plans from past experience. In R. S. Michalski, J. G. Carbonell, and T. M. Mitchell, editors, *Machine Learning: An Artificial Intelligence Approach*, Vol. 1, pp. 137–162. Tioga, Palo Alto, CA, 1983.

[3] Clement, C. A., and Gentner, D. Systematicity as a selection constraint in analogical mapping. Technical Report UIUCDCS-R-89-1558, University of Illinois, Urbana-Champaign, IL, 1989.

[4] Cook, D. J. Analogical planning. In *Proceedings of the DARPA Workshop on Innovative Approaches to Planning, Scheduling and Control*, 1990.

[5] Cook, D. J. Base Selection in Analogical Planning. Ph.D. thesis, University of Illinois, Urbana-Champaign, IL, 1990.

[6] Cook, D. J. Application of parallelized analogical planning to engineering design. *International Journal of Applied Intelligence* 1:133–144, 1991.

[7] Cook, D. J. The base selection task in analogical planning. In *Proceedings of the International Joint Conference on Artificial Intelligence*, Vol. 2, pp. 790–795. Morgan Kaufmann, 1991.

[8] Dershowitz, N. Programming by analogy. In R. S. Michalski, J. G. Carbonell, and T. M. Mitchell, editors, *Machine Learning: An Artificial Intelligence Approach*, Vol. 2, pp. 393–421. Morgan Kaufmann, Los Altos, CA, 1986.

[9] Gentner, D. Analogical inference and analogical access. In A. Prieditis, editor, *Analogica*, pp. 63–88. Morgan Kaufmann, Los Altos, CA, 1988.

[10] Gentner, D., and Toupin, C. Systematicity and surface similarity in the development of analogy. *Cognitive Science* 10:277–300, 1986.

[11] Hammond, K. Chef: A model of case-based planning. In *Proceedings of the 1986 National Conference on Artificial Intelligence*, pp. 267–271, 1986.

[12] Hammond, K. J. Case-based Planning: An Integrated Theory of Planning, Learning and Memory. Ph.D. thesis, Yale University, New Haven, CT, 1986.

[13] Indurkhya, B. Constrained semantic transference: A formal theory of metaphors. In A. Prieditis, editor, *Analogica*, pp. 129–157. Morgan Kaufmann, Los Altos, CA, 1988.

[14] Kearns, M., Li, M., Pitt, L., and Valiant, L. G. Recent results on boolean concept learning. In *Proceedings of the Fourth International Workshop on Machine Learning*, pp. 337–352, 1987.

[15] Kedar-Cabelli, S. Toward a computational model of purpose-directed analogy. In A. Prieditis, editor, *Analogica*, pp. 89–108. Morgan Kaufmann, Los Altos, CA, 1988.

[16] Kolodner, J. L., Simpson, R. L., and Sycara, K. A process model of case-based reasoning in problem solving. In *Proceedings of the International Joint Conference on Artificial Intelligence*, pp. 284–290, 1985.

[17] Valiant, L. G. A theory of the learnable. *Communications of the ACM* 27 (11): 1134–1142, 1984.

[18] Valiant, L. G. Learning disjunctions of conjunctions. In *Proceedings of the International Joint Conference on Artificial Intelligence*, pp. 560–566, 1985.

II REPRESENTATION AND BIAS

5 Learning Hard Concepts through Constructive Induction: Framework and Rationale

Larry Rendell and Raj Seshu

5.1 Use and Significance of Constructive Induction

Constructive induction is the formation of new terms during inductive learning (Michalski 1980; Dietterich et al. 1982). Examples of constructions useful in various domains include the maximum element of a set (Michalski 1983), even integers (Muggleton 1987), and transformations that preserve spatial patterns (Rendell 1985). Traditional induction may also be extended without explicit creation of new variables (e.g., Indurkhya and Weiss 1990; Van de Velde 1990), although explicit construction allows concise and modular formation of progressively more abstract concepts (Muggleton and Buntine 1988; Ragavan et al. 1992).

Constructive induction has been the subject of dozens of recent articles found in the proceedings of the Machine Learning Workshop and National and International AI conferences. Slightly older research includes that of Drastal, Czako, and Raatz (1989), Flann and Dietterich (1986), Fu and Buchanan (1985), Pagallo (1989), Schlimmer (1987), and Utgoff (1986). Relevant work includes that by Matheus and Rendell (1989), Mehra, Rendell, and Wah (1989), Ragavan and Rendell (1991b, 1991c), Seshu (1989), Seshu, Rendell, and Tcheng (1989), and Yang, Rendell, and Blix (1991).

Constructive induction is important because many complex applications may be amenable to inductive solutions but cannot be handled with existing inductive or noninductive techniques. In mechanized induction, data are sometimes given as values of attributes (variables) with corresponding values of class membership (dependent variable); the problem is to learn the entire class-membership function, or *concept*. This chapter addresses the induction of "hard" concepts. Early sections focus on these widely used techniques and on the learning problems that elude them. We begin by viewing concept difficulty in terms of a preliminary characterization of inductive difficulty, or *concept dispersion*. This notion allows us to explain why traditional approaches to induction are inadequate when confronted with hard concepts.

Feature construction is the formation of new attributes by applying operators to the original attributes and previously created features (Matheus and Rendell 1989). In this chapter we analyze cases in which feature construction has transformed hard concepts to easy ones. These successes are limited, however, and we also consider open induction problems. In each context, we begin by looking at the inductive difficulty in terms of the notion of concept dispersion. For cases in which the inductive problem has been "solved" by constructing good features, we consider how much easier the inductive problem has been made (in terms of concept dispersion) and consider how these new features were constructed.

Later sections describe variation-reducing utility-invariant-based construction. A *utility invariant* is a transformation that groups together noncontiguous areas of feature space that have the same class-membership values (Banerji 1980; Korf 1980). The notion of variation is a generalization of the simpler measure of difficulty (concept dispersion). An algorithm based on this idea shows how to construct features using a multileveled approach. Each level in this strategy is based on the goal of reducing variation by identifying similarities in the class-membership function. Each level is informed by both domain-dependent and domain-independent sources of knowledge.

5.1.1 The Roles of Selective Induction and Feature Construction

Traditionally, class-membership functions or attribute-based concepts are learned by techniques such as curve fitting (Draper and Smith 1981), neural net training (Hinton 1989; Minsky and Papert 1969), and decision-tree building (Breiman et al. 1984; Quinlan 1983). These methods work in an instance space defined by the attributes, generally using an inductive bias called similarity-based learning or selective induction (SI).

The Fundamental Assumption of SI   SI assumes that sets of contiguous or nearby instances tend to have similar class-membership values (Fig. 1, Rendell 1986). This is the fundamental assumption of selective induction: neighboring points are highly predictive of one another's class-membership values. This assumption may be satisfied to varying degrees. When an instance space fails to satisfy it, the space is "rough" or has high variation; otherwise the space is "smooth." These notions are formally defined in section 5.6.

The fundamental assumption of SI is satisfied in many well-understood problems. Experts are often available who can specify the proper attributes. These representations are appropriate; the attributes relate fairly directly to the concept (see Rendell and Cho 1990; Holte 1991). However, we may need feature construction (FC) if the problem is poorly understood and appropriate features are unknown, but we have features with high intrinsic accuracy. These features may produce poorly behaved class-membership functions, but FC can help by constructing better features as combinations of the primitive attributes.

Intrinsic Accuracy Given a set of attributes, *intrinsic accuracy* is the greatest accuracy attainable in the class-membership function using those attributes and perfect class-membership information. For example, in two-player board games with no chance involved, every position can theoretically be computed as a forced win or not (using minimax) if the attributes express the positions of all the pieces. In contrast, the information about winning is imperfect if the only attribute is piece advantage. In the former case, the intrinsic accuracy is one; in the latter case, it is probably much smaller. Intrinsic accuracy is a quantification of McCarthy's (1977) notion of epistemological adequacy.

Examples of Hard Concepts When the intrinsic accuracy is high and the fundamental assumption of SI is violated by an instance space having extreme roughness or variation, the concept is *hard*. For example, learning how to win checkers or chess from attributes corresponding to piece position is hard even though those attributes have an intrinsic accuracy of one (Quinlan 1983; Rendell 1985). This phenomenon also arises in important applications, such as predicting the structure of protein molecules (Lathrop, Webster, and Smith 1987; Qian and Sejnowski 1988; Seshu, Rendell, and Tcheng 1989).

Comparison of SI and FC Both SI and FC collect instance-space points into sets having similar class membership. SI coalesces points in instance space that are neighbors. This operation works well only if the fundamental assumption of SI is satisfied. If it is not, we can use FC to create new attributes to allow SI to function more effectively. FC constructs new features that implicitly coalesce nonneighboring points in instance space. FC can succeed only if it can learn or be given transformations that preserve class-membership information (i.e., utility invariants). By producing attributes that utilize such transformations, FC reduces the variation by mapping the instance space into one satisfying the fundamental assumption of SI.

Both SI and FC are predictive. When SI estimates a class-membership function, it characterizes instance-space points that were not part of the training set (the set of examples used to build the estimate). This predictive estimation is based on instance space proximity, as SI collects neighboring points into regions, often describing them as disjuncts. Whether the algorithm outputs a decision function in disjunctive normal form (DNF) or in some equivalent representation, SI assumes that the training examples falling into a particular disjunct are typical of the entire subset of instances characterized by the disjunct.

FC is predictive too. FC creates new attributes that correspond to a different notion of proximity. In the instance space defined by the new attributes, two points may become immediate neighbors that were not nearby in the original space (and vice versa). FC learns to construct these new attributes based on the instances in the training set. While SI depends on the "typicality" of attribute values in the training examples to create DNF (or equivalent) decision functions, FC depends on other regularities in the training set to create new attributes. Both the DNF clauses in SI's output and the newly constructed attributes in FC's output characterize the entirety of instance space—even parts of instance space that are unrepresented in the training sample.

Domain Knowledge and Prediction   Concepts are not generally probably approximately correct (PAC) learnable (Ehrenfeucht et al. 1988) if we use only data. PAC learnability means we need a number of examples that are exponential in the number of attributes to guarantee that the estimated class-membership function has classification error no greater than ε for all except proportion δ of the possible training sets for each and every possible concept. Alternatively, one could define learnability to achieve low average error over all possible concepts or to achieve ε and δ for a high proportion of the possible concepts (Buntine 1989). Fortunately, SI also uses knowledge. Since SI's predictive aspects depend on the fundamental assumption that the class-membership variation is relatively smooth and since the attributes themselves are often a product of domain knowledge, SI can learn from experts without appearing to be a knowledge-based approach. Generations of clinicians have cooperated to define, refine, and quantify the measures associated with certain pathologies. Consequently, in some medical problems, SI can produce accurate and concise decision functions without appearing to take advantage of any domain knowledge (Holte and Porter 1989). Without domain knowledge inherent in the attributes, SI can fail to produce accurate and concise decision functions because the fundamental assumption of SI does not hold.

FC also depends on domain knowledge for prediction. Because FC uses transformations applied to existing features, it can exploit domain knowledge to determine when a transformation is likely to preserve class-membership values (Matheus and Rendell, 1989). Both SI and FC experience difficulty if the domain knowledge is incomplete. In SI, the class-membership function becomes less accurate or concise. In FC, the result is often overfitting (Barron and Barron 1988; Draper and Smith 1981; Duda and Hart 1973; Seshu, Rendell, and Tcheng 1989). Since FC is designed to help SI, incomplete or inaccurate domain knowledge possessed by FC raises issues of cooperation between the two systems (Drastal 1991).

Invariant-Based Construction as Merging Later sections define class-membership-preserving transformations as utility invariants and show that they can be induced from the data as well as learned from experts. Feature construction based on utility invariants provides SI with a better set of features by transforming instance space. Over the new instance space, the concept satisfies the fundamental assumption of SI better because variation decreases. In creating these new features, FC smooths the space by merging nonneighboring regions of the original instance space having similar class-membership values.

5.1.2 Outline

This chapter examines the significance and difficulty of variation-reducing invariant-based construction and its associated methods. Section 5.2 formulates the problem of concept learning as the problem of characterizing peaks and valleys—areas of instance space that have particularly high or low class-membership values. Under this view of induction, the problem that SI must overcome is one of concept dispersion, which encompasses three sources of variation: peak multiplicity (how many peaks are there?), peak shape (how difficult are peaks to cover?), and peak arrangement (how many attributes must be considered together?).

In section 5.3, we begin by analyzing a number of existing SI strategies. We present a generic SI splitting scheme and show how it depends on the fundamental assumption of SI. We examine the notion of concept dispersion by presenting empirical studies of its effect on SI. As peak multiplicity, peak shape, and peak arrangement worsen, roughness increases, and concept accuracy and conciseness degrade.

The analysis of SI leads to a view of FC that centers around class-membership-preserving transformations. In particular, we want to construct features that implicitly merge noncontiguous areas of instance space based on utility invariants, which preserve class-membership (truth values). Section 5.4 examines our view in the context of a number of constructive induction problems, focusing on some recent work.

In sections 5.5 through 5.7, we attempt to integrate much of the research on FC and suggest some research directions. Section 5.5 develops our algorithmic framework for performing FC. In section 5.6 we move away from the spatial view of inductive difficulty of concept dispersion and provide a formal definition of variation. Accompanying this definition are several linear FC operations. We show how these operations can reduce the total variation in a transformed instance space. Section 5.6 also introduces our notion of superposition, a particular kind of invariant-based FC. Superposition refines the framework algorithm of section 5.5. Parts of this algorithm have been tested by Rendell (1985) and by Seshu, Rendell, and Tcheng (1989).

Section 5.7 considers the role of knowledge in our FC framework. We show how domain invariants such as superpositions can be inferred from the data or learned from experts, and we detail other ways in which domain-dependent and domain-independent sources of knowledge can be integrated.

5.2   Representing and Learning Concepts as Functions

In machine learning, a concept is usually defined as a rule that describes a class of objects or instances (Mitchell, Keller, and Kedar-Cabelli 1986). In attribute-based learning, each instance of the class is expressed using a set of attributes or features, which are variables taking values in some predefined range. Given a set of attributes, the entire class of objects forms an instance space in which the objects are instances or points. A concept is a dependent variable—a function of the attributes that identifies some subset of instance space (Fig. 1, Haussler 1988; Natarajan 1989; Rendell 1986).

5.2.1   Concepts, Attributes, and Instances

An *attribute* x is a pair (*range, scale*), where *range* X is a set of allowable values, and *scale* includes a partial ordering. A partial ordering is a binary relation (set of pairs) satisfying reflexivity, antisymmetry, and transitivity (Gill 1976). O and possibly a distance measure d defined over X. For a

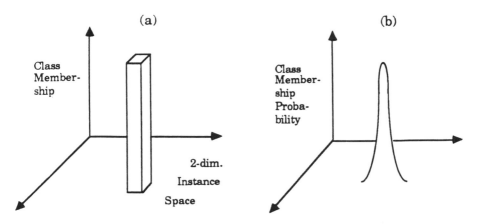

Figure 5.1
Binary-valued versus graded concepts. In (*a*), the concept is binary or all-or-none; in (*b*), it is graded or probabilistic. Here the instance space is two-dimensional and has interval scales. In general a concept is a function over whatever attributes are used to express it

nominal variable, O is the empty set; for a totally ordered variable, O defines relationships for every pair in X. Adding a distance d to a totally ordered variable converts its scale to interval (integer or real).

Suppose $x_1, x_2, \ldots, x_n$ are attributes having ranges $X_1, X_2, \ldots, X_n$ and scales $s_1, s_2, \ldots, s_n$. The *instance space* I defined by $(x_1, x_2, \ldots, x_n)$ is the cross product of $X_1, X_2, \ldots, X_n$, and also the associated scales $(s_1, s_2, \ldots, s_n)$. An instance space is a set of interrelated instances.

Given an n-dimensional instance space I defined by an n-tuple $\mathbf{x}$ of attributes $(x_1, x_2, \ldots, x_n)$, an "all-or-none" concept is a binary-valued function over I (fig. 5.1a). With the uncertainty of many environments, the function becomes probabilistic (fig. 5.1b); then class membership has graded values between 0 (definite exclusion) and 1 (certain membership) (Zadeh 1965). Training examples input to a program are labeled with class-membership values; these values can also be binary or graded. In general a concept is a (binary or graded) *class-membership function u* over instance space, which is a conditional probability:

$$u(\mathbf{x}) = P(\text{class membership}|\mathbf{x}).$$

Concepts are also decision functions, which are often represented as decision trees. A decision tree or a regression tree (Breiman et al. 1984) is basically a DNF estimate of the class-membership function. Another function over instance space is the evaluation function, which has been used for games and puzzles (Doran and Michie 1966; Michie and Ross 1970; Rendell 1983; Samuel 1963). Because concepts are often considered to be binary-valued functions, whereas evaluation functions are usually many valued, some researchers view the two as distinct entities. But evaluation functions can be represented and learned in the same way as decision functions for probabilistic concepts. In fact, evaluation functions *are* probabilistic concepts over the instance space corresponding to a game's state space. In practice, other issues arise in learning evaluation functions, which are not addressed here (e.g., credit assignment to search-tree nodes).

A concept expressed as a function over an instance space depends on the attributes defining that space. The structure of the space and the shape of the concept depend on attribute scales. Figure 5.1 shows familiar interval scales that are ordered and permit a distance measure. If the attributes are real valued, the concept might be a smooth function; if the attributes are integer, the concept might still vary gradually from one point to the next. Partially ordered and nominal scales also determine an instance space, though concepts based on these scales exhibit less structure.

Attributes originally given by the user to describe instances are *ground attributes* or *primitives*. Attributes formed from ground attributes by the system are *constructed features*. Any new representation gives a different class-membership function u over the transformed instance space.

5.2.2   Concept Learning as Function Estimation

Since a concept is a function over its instance space, concept learning is the *discovery of that function*. This learning may take place directly in the space of ground attributes, or it may first transform the space to include constructed attributes. Unless the domain of the function (i.e., the instance space) is small or many data are available, we need interpolation or induction to predict class membership for unseen instances. In other words, we want to estimate the class-membership function u.

Induction is possible only with some assumptions about the form of the function u. When working with real-valued attributes, statisticians call the form a *model* (Draper and Smith 1981); the most common model is a hyperplane (e.g., Samuel's [1963] evaluation function). When working with logic functions, AI researchers refer to the desired functional form as a source of (*inductive*) *bias* (Mitchell 1980); the most common bias is a form having few disjuncts (Utgoff 1986).

In statistics, function learning can be parametric or nonparametric (Barron and Barron 1988). In *parametric* learning, the model is a combination of attributes in which some weights need to be found. This is curve fitting (Draper and Smith 1981). In *nonparametric* learning, the model is a combination of instance-space regions in which their sizes and extents need to be found. This is attribute-based concept learning. What are called nonparametric methods in statistics are given various names in machine learning: decision-tree building, instance-space partitioning, and SI (Michalski 1983; Quinlan 1983; Rendell 1986).

5.2.3 Concept Learning as Peak Estimation

Certain portions of the function u are particularly important to learn. If we want to predict class membership, we are primarily interested in regions of instance space having high and low class-membership values, that is, the peaks and valleys. Since the notion of class membership is just the dual of class exclusion, we simply call these areas *peaks*. Peaks are illustrated in figure 5.2, and we now give a formal definition.

Contiguity   Two distinct elements x and y are *contiguous* in an instance space iff all their corresponding attribute values are equal except the ith ($0 \leq i \leq n$), and the partial ordering O_i of scale s_i contains $[x_i, y_i]$ (or

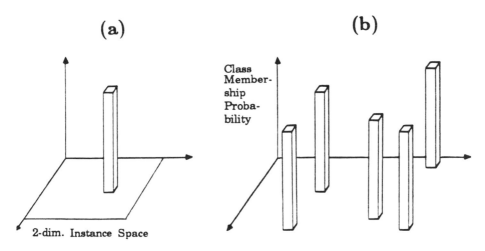

Figure 5.2
Peak multiplicity. In (*a*), the concept is tightly grouped in a single region of instance space. In (*b*), the concept is spread out all over the space

$[y_i, x_i]$) but not both $[x_i, z_i]$ and $[z_i, y_i]$ (or $[y_i, z_i]$ and $[z_i, x_i]$); no other point z can fall between x and y. Binary points having unary Hamming distance are contiguous; two points differing only by the value of a nominal attribute are not contiguous. Nominal scales may be converted to totally ordered scales (Anderberg 1973), which speeds learning and improves accuracy (see proof by Breiman et al. 1984; empirical results of Rendell and Cho 1990). Two points differing by a real-valued attribute are not contiguous by definition; however, real values may be discretized without loss of intrinsic accuracy (Anderberg 1973; Kadie 1988).

Neighborhoods, Regions, and Peaks   The *neighborhood* about a point x is the set of points that are contiguous with x. An *e-region* is a set of overlapping neighborhoods such that the average deviation of u values within their union is e or less. Two neighborhoods *overlap* when they share points. An *e,d-peak* is an *e*-region whose average class membership deviates by d from the average of the entire class-membership function, although we often omit the parameters and simply refer to them as *peaks*.

5.2.4   Problems in Peak Estimation

Although many characteristics of a concept affect its learning (Rendell and Cho 1990), a particularly important characteristic is concept *variation*. We give a formal definition of variation in section 5.6, but for now we characterize the notion spatially by describing its effects on the concept's functional form.

   Define the *concept dispersion* as the union of three measures of inductive difficulty:

• Peak multiplicity. Given a permitted deviation e, what is the smallest number of distinct peaks (collections of overlapping neighborhoods) that describe the concept with some minimal accuracy?

• Shape of the peaks. What is the average number of disjuncts needed to describe each peak (weighted by the number of points in each peak)?

• Arrangement of the peaks. What is the smallest number of features that must be simultaneously considered by an SI strategy in order to achieve a certain accuracy?

These three measures of concept dispersion are not entirely independent; for example, increasing the number of peaks tends to worsen their arrangement. Nevertheless, this characterization will allow some detail.

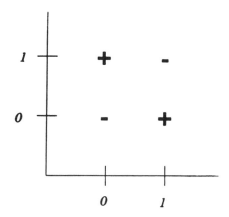

Figure 5.3
Given all the data, *exclusive or* cannot be learned by a selective induction method SI that stops when it detects no difference in class-membership, considering one attribute at a time. To learn such a concept, SI must look ahead in the decision tree; here the projection having smallest dimensionality is the whole space

Figure 5.2 contrasts two extremes of *peak multiplicity* in an integer space. The problem with *peak shape* is that oddly shaped peaks require more disjuncts to cover and may be difficult to learn without axis rotations (Watanabe 1985). As shown in figure 5.3, certain *arrangements* of peaks force induction strategies to consider multiple attributes simultaneously, thereby worsening the computational complexity.

Concept dispersion appears in the literature under a variety of headings. The first two measures of dispersion (peak multiplicity and peak shape) influence the number of disjuncts needed to describe the concept, which is a point of departure for considerable theoretical work on induction (Baum and Haussler 1989; Cover 1965; Ehrenfeucht et al. 1988; Haussler 1988). Surveying experimental results, Holte and Porter (1989) studied several articles and found that the reported concepts tend to have few disjuncts.

Small numbers of peaks is characteristic of concept representations used in many domains, including disease diagnosis (Holte and Porter 1989), games (Samuel 1963), and various pattern-recognition problems (Tou and Gonzalez 1974). For these problems, the class-membership function is often monotonic or singly peaked because good attributes are known. In contrast, some problems are more difficult because they begin with lower-level attributes (Rendell 1983). Extreme examples include learning the letter "A" when the attributes are pixel gray levels or "forced win" when the attributes are contents of squares on a chessboard. Quinlan (1983) reported difficulties with chess end games, a domain characterized by many disjuncts.

The problem of peak arrangement has also been considered under various headings. Breiman et al. (1984) recognized that some functions cannot be learned effectively without constructing features based on attribute weighting. These features are like linear discriminant functions but are used to supplement existing features rather than to replace them. Other systems also enlarge the set of features using weighted combinations of existing features (Utgoff 1990). Pagallo's (1989) algorithm uses symmetry of disjuncts to generate new features. Matheus (1989) compared a number of methods of feature construction that seek to smooth instance space by creating attributes that merge and rearrange peaks. Seshu (1989) investigated the severity of the parity problem, which is the Boolean case of difficult peak arrangement.

The hallmark of peak arrangement is *feature interaction* (Devijver and Kittler 1982; Rendell 1983). Degree-n, tolerance e feature interaction means that for accuracy $1 - e$, n features must be used simultaneously to describe a disjunct or curve. If we demand a high e, n is often greater than one; for example, the degree of feature interaction in *xor* is two. Feature interaction makes it difficult for greedy induction strategies to "divide and conquer" instance space either because it is inefficient to do so or because the design of these algorithms causes them to halt.

This problem also arises in modeling: one cannot parametrically fit a high-order polynomial without overfitting unless the learning sample is large (Draper and Smith 1981). Similar problems occur in pattern recognition (Duda and Hart 1973). If we use a neural network instead, we must provide more hidden units, which drastically increases the required number of training examples (Hinton 1989).

5.3 Selective Induction and Concept Dispersion

This section examines an algorithm SI for selective induction and explains its limitations in terms of concept dispersion. We show how peak multiplicity, peak shape, and peak arrangement can hurt SI because of its algorithmic structure. Later sections give feature construction methods designed to attack the concept dispersion problem by reducing variation.

5.3.1 Traditional Algorithms for Concept Learning

Many methods for inductive learning are based on iterative linear operations that consider only one attribute at a time for efficiency reasons. Although these algorithms have excellent computational complexities (equivalent to a sort; Quinlan 1983; Rendell 1983), their "greediness" prevents them from handling many problems associated with peak multiplicity and peak arrangement. All of these algorithms presume that instance-space proximity is relevant. They require the fundamental assumption of SI (section 5.1).

Splitting Algorithms A number of algorithms developed independently by different researchers have a similar basic design (e.g., CART: Breiman et al. 1984; ID3: Quinlan 1983; PLS1: Rendell 1983). These *partitioning algorithms* use splitting or specialization. Figure 5.4 shows a family SI of such induction algorithms; figure 5.5 gives an example of their use.

These algorithms find and describe hyperrectangular regions in instance space (section 5.2.3). SI estimates the class membership u and its error e, by sampling, to partition I into regions of high and low class membership. Proceeding iteratively, these programs use some criterion μ_B for choosing the best split. A simple choice for μ_B is $\log(u_1/u_2)$, where u_1 is the larger of the two class-membership probability estimates on either side of a split and u_2 is the smaller probability estimate. A more sophisticated measure accounts for uncertainty in the finite sample (Rendell 1983). Quinlan (1983) substitutes a related information criterion; Mingers (1989) studies other choices of μ_B.

Other Approaches Partitioning approaches can be contrasted with a class of generalization strategies (sometimes called agglomeration methods; Anderberg 1973). These methods begin by selecting "seeds" of positive examples and proceed to extend disjuncts against negative examples (Michalski 1983). Some approaches incorporate both specialization and generalization (Lee 1986). Instead of expressing intensional descriptions of the classes themselves, discriminant functions represent their boundaries (Duda and Hart 1973). Nearest-neighbor methods represent concepts extensionally rather than intensionally (Duda and Hart, 1973). Aha and Kibler (1989), Mingers (1989), Rendell, Cho, and Seshu (1989), and Weiss and Kapouleas (1989) compare the behavior of these methods.

Concept Learning Algorithm SI

[This algorithm forms and refines a piecewise-constant estimate of class-membership function.] Given a set of ground attributes *Gnd* to express both the instances and the concept:
Repeat
     gather data *E* from the user or performance task
          [these data are values of *Gnd* annotated with binary or graded class membeship values];
     repeat
          call *Find_best_split*(*E*) to [first] partition or [later] refine the instance space partition
               [this builds the piecewise-constant estimate $\hat{u}$ of the underlying concept *u*];
     until the current data *E* warrant no more splitting;
     perform the task and compute the value of the *SI quality measure* μ_S for this induction
          [in a pure classification task a simple choice of μ_S is the test-sample accuracy];
until all data are exhausted, the task is completed, or the quality μ_S is sufficient.

Procedure *Find_best_split* (set of training examples)

Decide on a set of boundaries to test
     [usually these are orthogonal to the axes, and we use one dimension at a time];
Repeat
     test a boundary using a quality measure μ_B
          [μ_B measures the difference in probability or information induced by the split];
until all the tentative boundaries have been tested;
Return the best boundary and the refined partition $\hat{u}$ as an improved estimate of the function *u*.

Figure 5.4
Algorithm schema for selective induction

(a)

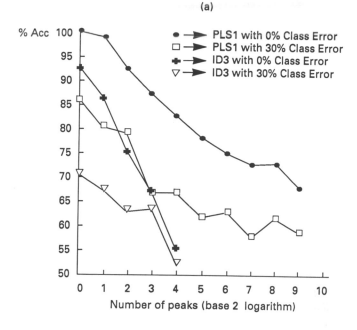

% Acc

PLS1 with 0% Class Error
PLS1 with 30% Class Error
ID3 with 0% Class Error
ID3 with 30% Class Error

Number of peaks (base 2 logarithm)

(b)

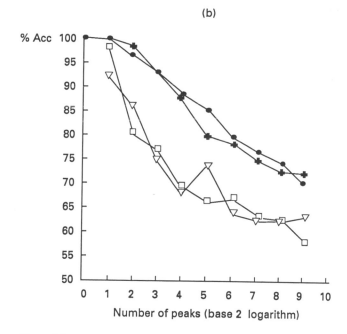

% Acc

Number of peaks (base 2 logarithm)

Figure 5.6
Variation of accuracy with number of peaks. The abscissa is the logarithm of the number of peaks in the underlying concept. Data were generated artificially. In (a) the attribute scales are nominal; in (b) the scales are integer. Data for nominal variables were obtained by scrambling integer data

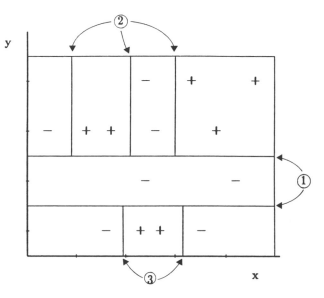

Figure 5.5
Selective induction using splitting. A quality measure μ_B is used to pick the best split; the process is repeated until further refinement is unwarranted by the data. The result is a partition of the instance space, in which each region has annotated class-membership values $\hat{u}$. (Here splitting occurs in the order shown, giving eight regions whose membership values are all binary.)

Commonalities   In all these methods, the instance space and training examples are represented using attributes and class values, although the scales may vary (some strategies cannot handle real variables, others cannot handle nominals). The form of the output class-membership estimator is also similar; decision trees, logic expressions, and discriminant boundaries are more or less interconvertible. Since these algorithms output DNF or equivalent concepts, multiple peaks cause difficulties. Each peak must be learned separately, and oddly shaped peaks require more disjuncts to cover (hence, more training examples). Because the algorithms consider attributes one at a time and are limited to the ground attributes, problems arise with peak arrangement (feature interaction).

5.3.2   Effects of Concept Dispersion

Number of Peaks and Accuracy   Rendell and Cho (1990) studied the effect of peak multiplicity on greedy splitting strategies by observing the decrease in accuracy associated with large numbers of peaks. As shown by the experiment summarized in figure 5.6 accuracy (the number of correct classifications divided by the number of trials, for a separate test sample) degrades as the number of peaks P increases. Here the number of data was fixed at 2000. Figure 5.7 also varies the number of peaks, but here the number of training data was 20 per peak, so a concept having one peak had only 20 data, whereas a concept having 1000 peaks had 20,000 data. The reason for this second experiment was to see if massive data could overcome the detrimental effects of having to spread a fixed number of data over all the peaks. Even if the sample size increases to keep pace with P, the accuracy still decreases (fig. 5.7a).

Number of Peaks and Learning Time   Figure 5.7b shows that the learning time increases as the number of peaks increases because the number of data must also increase to retain the reasonable accuracy of figure 5.7a. This contrasts with figure 5.6, where the required time (not shown) remains about the same while the accuracy drops sharply. In the experiment summarized in figure 5.7, PLS1 took about six hours (using a VAX 780) to learn 1000 peaks. Extrapolating from figure 5.7, Rendell and Cho (1990) estimate that the fastest programs for selective induction would need millions of data and at least one CPU month to learn 100,000 peaks while maintaining reasonable accuracy. If the goal is probably approximately correct (PAC) learning, the minimum size sample set given by Ehrenfeucht et al. (1988) suggests that this extrapolation is optimistic. Since immense numbers of peaks can arise in real-world problems (Rendell 1985), our current algorithms would be completely overwhelmed. As P increases, the accuracy, conciseness, and speed all degrade significantly.

Peak Shape and Accuracy   Because SI is limited to the user-supplied ground attributes and a specific concept form, peaks that are oddly shaped relative to this form require more disjuncts to learn (Breiman et al. 1984; Utgoff 1990; Watanabe 1985). Since each disjunct takes at least two training examples, peak shape can also increase learning time and decrease accuracy.

Peak Arrangement and Accuracy   If we are to retain the excellent complexity bounds of the fastest SI approaches (algorithms such as CART: Breiman et al. 1984; ID3: Quinlan 1983; PLS1: Rendell 1983), we cannot afford to eliminate their one-attribute-at-a-time greedy processing. Even the slower generalization-based (agglomerative) strategies such as AQ15

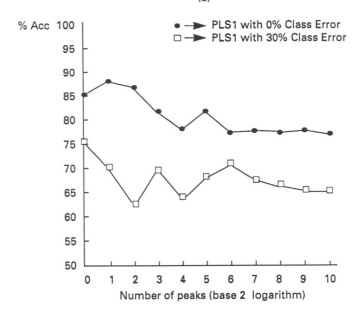

(a)

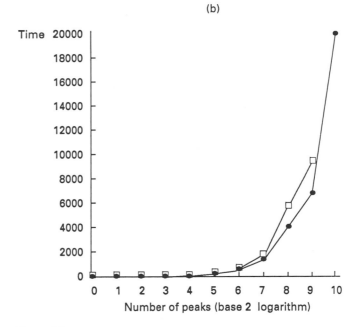

(b)

Figure 5.7
Variation of accuracy (*a*) and speed (*b*) with number of peaks *P* when the sample size increases uniformly with *P* (20 instances per peak)

Table 5.1
Accuracies for maximally liberal iterative splitting

Degree of parity	Degree of lookahead used for learning	Number (and %) missed by lookahead	Avg. errors (and %) per concept
2	1	2 (12.5)	0.25 (6.25)
3	1	72 (28)	0.625 (7.81)
3	2	2 (0.4)	0.004 (0.4)
4	1	38K (58)	1.6 (9.99)
4	2	1414 (2)	0.087 (0.54)
4	3	2 (0.003)	0.002 (0.0015)

(Michalski 1983) extend disjuncts by only one attribute at a time. Alternatives such as lookahead may improve accuracy but at a higher computational cost (but see Ragavan et al. 1992).

Seshu (1989) quantifies the effects of peak arrangement, although a number of other researchers, such as Matheus (1989) and Pagallo (1989), have utilized FC strategies that focus on the problem of peak arrangement to improve SI. Seshu's results are summarized in table 5.1.

This table shows accuracy results for a maximally liberal iterative splitting strategy. A *liberal* splitting algorithm is one that has a weak error component built into the dissimilarity measure μ_B. For example, $\mu_B = \log(u_1/u_2)$ (section 5.3.1) is maximally liberal because it omits error computation entirely. Liberal splitting algorithms are reluctant to cease splitting and define leaves on a decision tree. These algorithms work best in error-free environments because the algorithms have no implicit or explicit pruning (Breiman et al. 1984).

A maximally liberal iterative splitting algorithm was run on all possible Boolean concepts over two, three, and four attributes. For each of the six rows of table 5.1, the algorithm was trained and tested with the entire instance space. All instances were error free.

The *classical parity* concept is the concept corresponding to the N-ary parity function over N-attribute Boolean space. Any N-dimensional space has exactly two classical parity functions, which correspond to *xor* and its complement. A *generalized parity* concept of degree $n \leq N$ is a concept C in an N-dimensional space, where C includes classical parity terms of lower degree, the highest degree being n. For example, if $N = 3$, $C = ([x_1 \; xor \; x_2] \; and \; x_3)$ is a generalized parity concept of degree 2.

Generalized parity is a Boolean form of the peak arrangement problem—a high degree of *feature interaction*. Feature interaction of degree n

means that a maximally liberal SI strategy must use lookahead of degree n in order to achieve 100% accuracy when the example set is exhaustive and error free. Feature interaction is a measure of the difficulty that SI has in fitting the data. In other words, to learn a disjunct having n terms, perfect results demand an instance-space *projection* whose dimension is at least n.

Relationships between generalized parity of degree n and lookahead of degree $k \leq n$ are shown in table 5.1. The first column lists the class of concepts by dimension N. Column 2 gives the degree of lookahead used by SI. Column 3 shows the proportion of hard concepts having parity degree greater than the lookahead used (these are the concepts that cause error). Column 4 is the resulting accuracy for concepts having the given dimension.

The accuracy results are averaged over all Boolean concepts for two, three, and four attributes. The first row shows results for two-dimensional concepts, the next two rows for three-dimensional concepts, and the final three rows for four-dimensional concepts. The number of rows for each number of attributes is one less than N because SI was run for lookaheads of $1, 2, \ldots, N - 1$ (column 2).

These results show that peak arrangement has a significant effect on classification accuracy using standard SI (lookahead = 1). When $N = 2$, column 3 of row 1 shows that 12.5% of all concepts have parity degree 2, although this degrades average SI accuracy per concept by only 6.25% (column 4). When $N = 3$, the number of parity concepts increases to 28%, which degrades average SI accuracy by nearly 8%. When $N = 4$, the number of parity concepts is 58%, which degrades SI accuracy by about 10%. Since many real-world concepts involve several attributes, the generalized-parity effect on standard SI is considerable.

Yet the degradation may be lessened by lookahead (column 2), whose effect is predictable. For example, the second-to-last row shows that a moderate lookahead of 2 decreases the average degradation per concept from 10% error to only .5%. Seshu (unpublished manuscript) proved that degree-k lookahead is equivalent to generating all possible k-ary parity features. In these situations, we can now select lookahead according to the accuracy we desire. In the case of four Boolean attributes, two-ply lookahead will suffice for an accuracy of 0.98. These results suggest that moderate lookahead increases accuracy dramatically.

For PAC learnability (Ehrenfeucht et al. 1988), the general parity problem is NP-hard: the required number of examples is exponential in the number of attributes for a guaranteed classification error no greater than ε for all except proportion δ of the possible training sets for every possible concept. But a weakened notion of learnability is FAC (frequently approximately correct), wherein the goal is to achieve ε and δ for a *high proportion* τ of concepts. This notion is close but not identical to the notions expressed by Buntine (1989), Dietterich (1989), and Pazzani and Sarrett (1990). Buntine (1989) discusses a number of related issues; Dietterich (1989) coins the term *FAC* but assumes a uniform distribution, which we do not. The above experiments are based on FAC splitting.

Summary and Outlook Although traditional systems for SI are good for discovering the sizes and shapes of individual peaks in the class-membership function, each peak must be learned separately. This requires more data and more time. Furthermore, multiple peaks tend to worsen feature interaction. Whereas degree-n feature interaction demands consideration of n attributes simultaneously, greedy SI algorithms consider just one attribute at a time. In other words, standard SI works with one-dimensional projections of the class-membership function over instance space; one-dimensional projections become blurred as n increases, thus degrading accuracy.

In response to this problem, we can use higher-dimensional projections (when deciding how to partition the instance space) or, equivalently, lookahead (in building the decision tree). Deep lookahead is expensive, but empirical results suggest considerable gain with moderate lookahead. Ragavan et al. (1992) investigate a method for dynamically deciding lookahead to minimize the accuracy-speed trade-off.

Another problem with SI methods is that they cannot predict the class-membership function in distant and seemingly unrelated regions of the space. Although traditional learning systems discover rules that describe individual peaks, we need FC for prediction of dispersed peaks. The role of SI is to find and describe individual regions; the role of FC is to find and describe relationships among regions.

5.4   Case Studies in Selective and Constructive Induction

To ground the abstract analysis of the previous sections, we consider various induction contexts having different degrees of concept dispersion. In section 5.3, we defined this as a spatial indicator of inductive difficulty and defined the peak multiplicity (number of peaks in a concept), peak shape (number of disjuncts needed to cover each peak), and peak arrangement (degree of feature interaction).

In this section we also examine some FC methods. In particular, we want to know why they succeed in discovering utility invariants (transformations that preserve class-membership values). If the process of discovering utility invariants involves domain knowledge, we want to find out what kind of knowledge is involved. We also want to see how the problem has been changed in terms of concept dispersion (inductive difficulty). We begin with a short example that sheds some light on the relationship between domain knowledge and the discovery of utility invariants.

5.4.1 Utility Invariants, Domain Knowledge, and the Abduction Problem

Figure 5.8a shows a one-dimensional primitive space x in which even numbers are members of the desired class. In terms of peak multiplicity, the concept is difficult because half the instance are peaks. Figure 5.8b shows that when the concept is expressed using $x \bmod 2$, all peaks of the concept merge into one. This transformation combines concept components from the original instance space. In the new instance space using the constructed feature $x \bmod 2$, SI needs only distinguish two descriptions: even versus odd. $x \bmod 2$ is a utility invariant.

To see how knowledge might be used to discover this invariant, consider four cases. If $x \bmod 2$ is supplied directly by the user (case 1), the FC task is trivial because only one construction is allowed and no search or evaluation is required. The task would be more difficult if the 2 were

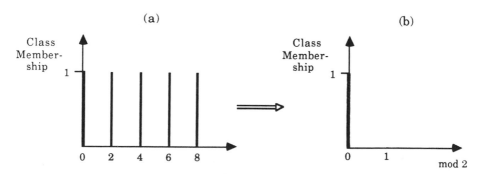

Figure 5.8
The effect of constructing the concept or new attribute "even." Before change of representation (*a*), the concept is dispersed; after introduction of the new attribute $x \bmod 2$ (*b*), the concept has only one peak in its new instance space

replaced by a parameter *a* so the initial expression became *x mod a* (case 2); then an algorithm for FC would need to find a good value for *a*—one that fits the data best. The construction task would be harder still if *x mod a* were given in the context of other, competing rules; then the correct rule would need to be selected and instantiated (case 3). Finally, the induction program might receive no advice whatever from the user (case 4).

One way to characterize these situations is to consider the state of the user's domain theory, a problem that has been faced by workers in explanation-based learning (DeJong and Mooney 1986; Mitchell, Keller, and Kedan-Cabelli 1986). Case 1 is a case of a complete domain theory; the user is simply supplying the inductive system with a closed formula, which is the class-membership function itself. Inductive methods are superfluous.

Case 2 is a simple version of the incomplete-theory problem (Rajamoney and DeJong 1987). The theory *x mod a* predicts a periodic relationship in the variable *x*, but this rule is underspecified. It predicts that peaks in class membership may be superposed in a particular way without loss of information, but more detail (the value of *a*) is required before the knowledge is complete.

Case 3 is roughly analogous to the multiple-explanation problem and the inconsistent theory problem. Multiple rules allow multiple explanations; for example, *x mod a* might be accompanied by another rule x^i, where *i* is an integer. Inconsistencies are resolved using SI with enough data; for example, *x mod a* might predict false positives, while x^i satisfies all the data. Methods for determining the best fit of rules to data are prevalent (Quinlan 1989; Rendell 1985).

In Case 4 the learning system is autonomous. No user is available, and the examples are gathered from data extracted from the surrounding environment. This case raises the difficult problem of *abduction*. Abduction was originally defined by a philosopher of the American pragmatist school, Charles Peirce (Peirce 1931): "The surprising fact C is observed; but if A were true, C would be true as a matter of course, hence there is reason to suspect that A is true." Researchers in explanation-based learning (EBL) and theory formation use abduction when talking about the *plausibility* of an explanation, often one that deals with causality (O'Rorke, Morris, and Schulenburg 1989). In mechanized induction and pattern recognition, researchers have tended to regard the process of model selection as abduction. Watanabe (1969, 1985) notes that no inductive system can form hypotheses if the *extraevidential credibility* of this hypothesis is zero. This may occur if the hypothesis is ignored by the inductive system's *biases* (Mitchell 1980; Utgoff 1986; Rendell, Seshu, and Tcheng, 1987; see also Kuhn 1970).

While these views may seem incompatible, a reconciliation is possible. Consider the similarity among the roles of (1) entailment in the context of propositional logic (e.g., in a blocks world domain), (2) causality in the context of physical or mechanical objects (e.g., chemical distillation; Rajamoney and DeJong 1987), and (3) the family of functions to which a class-membership function belongs in the context of observations (e.g., disease diagnosis; Holte and Porter 1989). In each case, the first member of each pair leads to the second; that is, the first noun or noun phrase in each item plays the role of Peirce's "A" and the second plays the role of Peirce's "C."

The mechanized induction/pattern recognition perspective is also compatible if we see the model A and the data or observations C as the consequents of the model. In other words, the model A entails the data C. Abduction is required when no assumptions can be made about the form of the class-membership function. PAC learning cannot take place in this context (Blumer et al. 1987; but also see Buntine 1989).

Case 4 can help us appreciate what is going on in cases 2 and 3. In both situations, the user has given knowledge to the system, but it is not the same kind of knowledge that the user gives to SI. Instead of telling the system what attributes to consider, the user has told the system what operations on existing attributes may make sense. Whereas the choice of attributes for SI restricts the search for a classification function estimate, the choice of permissible operations over attributes for FC constrains the search for new features. In Watanabe's (1969, 1985) terms, the problem of abduction—the choice of models—has been solved in cases 2 and 3 but not in case 4. The problem was solved by giving FC relevant classes of potential utility invariants.

5.4.2 Specific Constructive and Selective Induction Problems

Table 5.2 summarizes some problems of FC compared with problems of SI. Five examples are arranged roughly in order of their overall difficulty, although difficulty depends on constraints derived from domain knowledge. Column 2 shows the size of the instance space when expressed using the ground attributes selected for the problem. Column 3 estimates the number of peaks in the resulting class-membership function. Column 4

Table 5.2
Problems of selective induction (SI) and feature construction (FC)

Problem or problem type	Ground space size	Number of peaks	SI Acc'y [%]	FC Acc'y [%]	FC space size	Comments
Typical SI problems (e.g., simple diagnosis)	~ 1000	~ 1	100	Not req'd	1	FC not needed since SI accuracy is high.
Natural law discovery (e.g., $pv = c$, etc.)	∞	∞	—	100	~ 100	FC language and procedure uses domain knowledge.
Checkers (abstract attributes)	10^6	$\sim 100?$	$\sim 80?$	Not req'd	$\sim 100?$	Attributes high-level. Accuracy unknown.
Checkers (low-level primitives)	$\sim 10^{18}$	$\sim 10^{16}?$	chance	Never done	$\sim 10^{16}?$	Attributes fine-grained. Intrinsic accuracy 100%
Protein folding (represented as in text)	$> 10^7$	$> \sim 10^6?$	chance	~ 60	$> \sim 10^6?$	Spaces and intrinsic accuracy depend on window size.

shows the best accuracy obtained by any SI method used directly on the original instance space, while column 5 shows the best results found when SI is combined with FC. Column 6 estimates the size of the construction space to be searched.

Typical Selective Induction Problems   The first row in table 5.2 illustrates standard problems in the literature, such as straightforward medical diagnosis. Typically these problems have just a few peaks (often just one); each peak may produce several disjuncts (Holte and Porter 1989). Although the peaks may be oddly shaped, their small number makes them easy to learn by standard SI. The problem of peak arrangement does not arise, and constructive induction is rarely needed.

Discovery of Natural Laws   In BACON (Langley 1977) new attributes are products and quotients of exponentiated ground attributes. Figure 5.9 shows how BACON transforms a set of attributes to simplify a concept drastically. Prior to the transformation, we have a large number of peaks (figure 5.9a), limited only by the degree to which we might discretize the space. Although the peaks are nicely shaped (one disjunct per peak), their arrangement appears to be unfavorable. SI would probably concentrate its efforts on the portions of the curve corresponding to extreme values of p and v, since they have the largest proportion of positive examples (i.e.,

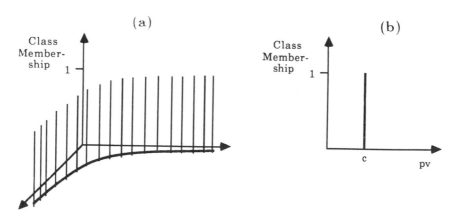

Figure 5.9
The effect of construchng the new term "pv." Before change of representation (*a*), pressure *p* and volume *v* are distinct variables, and a large number of conditions satisfy the concept "allowable states." After introduction of the new term (*b*), there is only one peak, at $pv = c$

more positive examples per unit distance along each axis). Yet the concept is highly dispersed, with numerous peaks.

When the concept is expressed using the transformed pv space, all points in the concept merge into one (figure 5.9b). The transformation superposes concept components from the primitive instance space. This allows prediction of unseen instances, many of which may be distant from each other in the primitive space.

The knowledge given to BACON takes the form of a simple expression $x = \prod e_i^{a_i}$ (where $\prod$ represents iterated products of primitives e_i and the exponents a_i are positive or negative integers). Although the parameters a_i need to be instantiated (case 2), they are assumed to have small values. Since this knowledge is highly constraining, only a few training examples are needed (Muggleton 1987). FC does well in this case, although SI's accuracy is poor. The abduction problem has been solved by the user because the space of possible transformations is small and is explored in an efficient and incremental manner.

Checkers Using High-Level Ground Attributes   Row 3 of table 5.2 shows the game of checkers, which Samuel (1963) studied using high-level features such as piece advantage, mobility, and center control. Such features typically give an instance space size of around 1 million points.

More important than the size is the smoothness of the space: typical features give a gradually varying evaluation function, allowing expression in terms of a linear combination of the ground attributes (Rendell 1983; Samuel 1963). This is because the number of distinct peaks is small or most are weak compared with a global pattern of monotonicity. Constructive induction is not required. Given a feature vector $\mathbf{x}$, the evaluation function (or concept) "win probability" is a graded function $u(\mathbf{x}) = \mathbf{c.x}$, where $\mathbf{c}$ is a vector of weights. Using this simple model, curve-fitting techniques (Draper and Smith 1981) give good estimates using a relatively small sample of board positions. (Training examples could be averaged, for example, with forced wins counting 1, draws 0.5, and losses 0.)

Because the attributes are abstract and the game is complex, the intrinsic accuracy is unknown. As one extreme case, we could use just piece advantage x. Defined over x, the concept "win probability" is a graded function $u_x(x) = cu_x$. This function increases monotonically with x (u_x is an "S" curve with $u(0) = .5$), having one peak where x is maximum. Although u_x is well behaved, it is a poor predictor of winning: many checker positions with a small piece advantage may lose, but some positions are strong for other reasons. In other words, the intrinsic accuracy is poor, although we could estimate u_x using a very small sample. Higher intrinsic accuracy requires additional abstract features or primitive attributes.

Checkers Using Low-Level Attributes Checkers has a board of 64 squares, half of which can be occupied. Suppose the ground attributes are these 32 primitives e_i ($1 \leq i \leq 32$), with values $-2, -1, 0, 1, 2$, representing black king, black man, vacancy, red man, and red king, respectively (where larger values are better for red). The concept "win probability" is a graded function $u_e(\mathbf{e})$, where $\mathbf{e} = (e_1, e_2, \ldots, e_{32})$. We could estimate $u_e(\mathbf{e})$ by taking a very large sample of board positions and averaging as before. The sample would have to be large because u_e is a badly behaved function of $\mathbf{e}$: changing only one primitive e_i can drastically alter the win probability, so $u_e(\mathbf{e})$ may have as many as 10^{16} peaks (Rendell 1983). Furthermore, each peak may require multiple disjuncts to cover, and the peaks are arranged so that feature interaction is severe. The dispersion in this concept effectively incapacitates an SI approach, as table 5.2 claims.

But we can transform the space into one in which the concept dispersion is more manageable by SI. This is precisely what Samuel (1963) did (albeit by hand). Piece advantage x is the sum of the values of all 32 primitives e_i, so this feature may be learned from the primitive representation. Since x comprises contributions from all primitives e_i, a learning program could discover this relationship by hypothesizing that all e_i should be treated equally. Individual attributes can be identified with each other—their projections merged or superposed (figure 5.10). Formally, the hypothesis is $\forall i \neq j \; [u_i(e_i) = u_j(e_j)]$, where $u_i(e_i)$ is the projection of the win function u onto the e_i axis (figure 5.10a).

This hypothesis would be supported by data: the one-dimensional projections $u_i(e_i)$ are roughly equal for all i (figure 5.10b). The projections match because the probability of winning remains roughly invariant if a piece is moved over the board. This utility invariance is hypothesized by a rule that generates all the e_j. The construction is completed by summing the values of e_i over all i, to obtain x. We return to this example in section 5.6.

Protein Folding This domain involves prediction of the secondary structure of a protein molecule. The primary structure of a protein molecule is

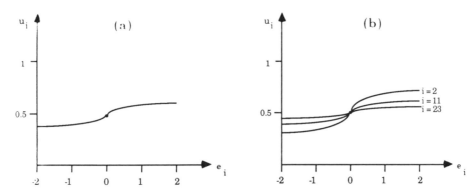

Figure 5.10
A simple construction involving projection. The class membership function u is projected onto subspaces of the primitive instance space (*a*), which are then merged (*b*). If the operation represents some meaningfill relationship, the projections will match. Here the projections are one-dimensional—to find piece advantage in checkers (see text). Structural patterns (features such as forks) require higher-dimensional projections, each dimension corresponding to a piece in the pattern

a chain of amino acids. The secondary structure is determined by the three types of folds or bonds occurring between nonadjacent amino acids. Given any chain of amino acids, one may ask whether a particular fold occurs at a given point. Although chains of amino acids are long, the secondary structure may be determined by a shorter sequence (Lathrop, Webster, and Smith 1987).

In some experiments, data have been represented as sequences of nine amino acids having six types each (row 5 of table 5.2). It is not known whether these nine ground attributes are sufficient to predict all secondary structure, although Qian and Sejnowski (1988) suspect that the intrinsic accuracy of such a representation is limited. The best-known strategies using this representation achieve an accuracy of about 60% (Seshu, Rendell, and Tcheng 1989). A window of amino acids larger than nine would give a higher intrinsic accuracy, but the constructive operations would then be less tractable.

Using a window of only nine gives an instance space size $6^9 \approx 10^7$. While it is difficult to determine the number of peaks or their shape or arrangement, the dispersion of this concept seems unfavorable. Each amino acid position represents a dimension in instance space, many different sequences of amino acids produce the same fold, distant amino acids probably affect the fold, and small changes may alter it. Guessing that folds occupy neighborhoods of 10 instance-space points gives 1 million peaks in the class-membership function for each fold.

Although some aspects of protein folding are understood (King 1977), domain knowledge has not been especially useful so far. Workers who have explored techniques informed by domain knowledge have been no more successful than those who used domain-independent techniques (compare King 1977 with Qian and Sejnowski 1988 and Seshu, Rendell, and Tcheng 1989). Later sections of this chapter argue how knowledge can help.

5.5 Selective Induction with Feature Construction

As long as the ground attributes are intrinsically accurate, SI and FC together can learn any concept. Figure 5.11 shows an algorithm schema CL for concept learning that combines induction with construction. The SI part of CL is SI (figure 5.4) or some other algorithm that describes peaks of class membership. The feature construction part of CL is FC, which constructs utility-invariant descriptions of regions dispersed in instance space. When necessary, CL calls FC to merge peaks and compose new features.

Except for a few novel aspects, CL is a composite of many machine learning systems, including older programs examined by Devijver and Kittler (1982). Some newer aspects of this algorithm have been explored by Rendell (1985) and by Seshu, Rendell, and Tcheng (1989), who implemented and tested a general scheme for feature construction and selection that is the forerunner of CL.

5.5.1 Accommodating Changing Features

The algorithm schema CL has two explicit loops. The outer loop accommodates flexible sampling (Quinlan 1983) and incremental learning (Rendell 1983; Samuel 1963), which is a secondary concern. Here we are more concerned with the inner loop, whose purpose is to choose and improve the set of selected features *Sel* for SI. Replacing *Sel* changes the class-membership function u, because u is defined over the instance space defined by *Sel*.

Besides *Sel*, CL uses two other sets of attributes: the ground set *Gnd* and the active set *Act*. Initially the active set is the ground set, which is

Concept Learning Algorithm *CL*

Let *Gnd* be a set of ground attributes for expressing the concept or function *u*.
Initialize the active set of features *Act* := *Gnd*.
Repeat
    gather data from the user or performance task;
    repeat
        use some measure of *feature quality* μ_x to select from *Act* a subset *Sel*
            (this eliminates subsumed or otherwise useless features);
        if necessary, convert the data from ground form *Gnd* to selected form *Sel*;
        using a standard algorithm for selective induction, attempt to learn or refine
        u(Sel);
        compute the value of the *SI quality measure* μ_S for this induction;
        if μ_S is poor, call *FC* to construct new feature(s) to add to *Act*;
    until μ_S no longer improves;
until the data are exhausted or the quality μ_S is sufficient.

Feature Construction Procedure *FC*

Initialize the new feature set *New* := $\varnothing$.
Repeat
    using *Act* and some technique of peak merging, create a *utility-invariant*
    construction x
        (find and describe a set of neighborhoods hypothesized to have similar
        u-values);
    if the *construction quality* μ_c of *x* is high enough, add this new feature to *New*;
until the desired number of new features is found.
Redefine *Act* := *Act* $\cup$ *New*.

Figure 5.11
Concept learning using feature construction

defined by the user. The reason for using both *Act* and *Sel* is that some
constructed features may be useful for further construction but themselves
perform poorly in SI. During a single call, FC creates one or more new
features *New*. Components for this construction come from *Act*, which
contains the original ground attributes *Gnd* and previously constructed
features. The new features *New* are added to the active set *Act*.

    Some examples of *Gnd*, *Act*, and *Sel* may clarify their use. In Samuel's
(1963) checker player, *Gnd* was a set of 38 ground attributes. *Act* and *Sel*
were equivalent. At any one time, *Act*, whose size was always 16, was some
subset of *Gnd*. There was no constructive induction, only feature selection.
In STAGGER (Schlimmer 1987; Schlimmer and Granger 1986), *Gnd* is a

set of attributes that may be nominal or integer, and *Sel* is a subset of *Act*. *Act* is made Boolean by converting *Gnd* to binary features. Conversion to binary scales also occurs in NTC (Seshu, Rendell, and Tcheng 1989), which builds a large and highly dynamic set *Act* in problems such as protein folding.

CL must constantly reassess perceived quality. As new features are constructed and placed in the active set *Act*, the apparent quality of the old ones may change. New and better features may replace them in the selected subset *Sel*.

5.5.2 Layered Quality Measures

To assess and select features, CL uses two measures of performance. One is the overall SI quality measure μ_S, which evaluates some criterion such as the accuracy, speed, or conciseness of the induction. This measure μ_S provides a stopping criterion for both data presentation during incremental learning and new FC using a given set of data. The other performance measure is the feature quality μ_X. In a sense the SI quality μ_S and the feature quality μ_X both measure the same thing: the effectiveness or discriminatory ability of a set of features. The reason for using both measures is that μ_X provides a fast but useful filter, while μ_S is more accurate but also more expensive. This has been usefully implemented by Gunsch and Rendell (1991). As shown in figure 5.11, CL and FC use three measures to assess components at different stages of feature construction and selection. Each stage should filter less useful components to avoid proliferation of poorer structures. Problems of utility filtering are also studied by Holder (1990) and Markovitch and Scott (1989).

To standardize these measures μ, assume their definitions incorporate a threshold, with acceptance when $\mu > 0$. This allows consistent comparison of various systems in the following discussion of algorithms for feature selection and construction.

Invoking Feature Construction Using Induction Quality   CL assesses its own performance using some quality measure μ_S. One simple definition is: $\mu_S = 1$ unless the concept u becomes inconsistent with the data, in which case $\mu_S = 0$. This corresponds to the criterion in STABB (Utgoff 1986), which looks for new descriptions when current ones fail. In STAGGER, the measure is graded: likelihood ratios are computed to measure correlations between data and Boolean features (Schlimmer 1987). Instead of measuring accuracy, Duce (Muggleton 1987) uses a conciseness criterion. (Duce begins with individual data and repeatedly compresses descriptions using various rules.) In terms of our measure μ_S, Duce might define it as 1—(current number of symbols in the concept description)/(number of symbols after the previous transformation).

Accuracy, conciseness, and speed are related (e.g., see Rissanen 1986). Hence we could base a definition of μ_S on any combination of these qualities. But these performance measures depend on the number of peaks P in the concept. Estimating P can be a by-product of SI, thus providing a ready definition for μ_S. Matheus (1989) discusses this aspect of FC as need detection.

Accepting Features Based on their Quality   Like μ_S, the feature quality μ_X may also be defined in various ways, although they all measure a feature's ability to distinguish class-membership values. Selection of discriminating features occurs in statistical techniques such as stepwise regression, where the feature quality μ_X is essentially the correlation coefficient (Draper and Smith 1981). Such measures for feature selection appear in many learning systems (e.g., Devijver and Kittler 1982; Quinlan 1983; Rendell 1983; Samuel 1963; Schlimmer and Granger 1986; Smith and Medin 1981).

In difficult problems such as protein folding, the differences among competing features tend to be small, because much construction is necessary before low-level ground attributes are converted to useful abstract features. Unless considerable knowledge is available to compress the construction into a few steps, the improvement of any one step is limited. Over many steps, each of which depends on earlier construction, errors in evaluation can easily mask true feature quality differences. Using a technique for multiple objective optimization, Seshu, Rendell, and Tcheng (1989) incorporated several quality measures in an attempt to retain features having any perceptible worth.

Filtering Constructions Using Construction Quality   The procedure FC employs a measure of *construction quality* μ_C to assess a potential feature. The construction quality μ_C may or may not be identical to the feature quality μ_X. In other words, we could assess the value of a new feature before or after CL considers its use.

Individual systems use one or both of these two measures. Muggleton's (1987) quality measure based on conciseness is sufficient for all purposes in Duce. In our context, time is also a factor: the feature quality μ_X involves comparison of a new feature x to other features; in contrast, estimating the construction quality μ_C assesses x in isolation. Hence, FC uses μ_C to evaluate a constructed feature before adding it to *New*. Seshu, Rendell, and Tcheng (1989) found this approach effective.

Basing Construction on Reduced Variation Even more important are decisions made during FC. Because errors proliferate in iterative processing that builds successively more complex structures, it is crucial to restrict constructions to plausible candidates. Constraint may be imposed through data or knowledge. Using data, the procedure FC matches u-values: of all merges, the only useful combinations are those having similar class-membership values. FC is the process of bringing together uniform regions that are dispersed in instance space.

Construction can also be guided by the use of knowledge. Here the role of knowledge is to merge dispersed instance space regions by suggesting merging operations. These operations encode utility invariants—transformations that preserve class membership. The next section details the combined use of data and knowledge to accomplish this merging.

5.6   Details of Feature Construction

Given the goal of reducing variation, improving dispersion, or merging peaks in the class-membership function, several definitions follow naturally. We present several definitions illustrated with examples of their use.

5.6.1   Variation

We begin by refining the spatial view of variation as concept dispersion and examining the utility of the refinement.

Definition Consider an instance space I defined by an n-tuple $\mathbf{x}$ of attributes $(x_1, x_2, \ldots, x_n)$. Assume that each attribute is integer valued between zero and some maximum value. Let $u(\mathbf{x})$ be the class-membership function defined over I. Assume that u is defined for each value of $\mathbf{x}$ and that each such point has an equal chance of appearing in a random sample in I.

Now consider the class-membership variation in small volumes of the space. For each $\mathbf{x}$, average the deviation (absolute value of the difference) in class membership between that point and its immediate neighbors. (Recall that two points are neighbors if they differ in just a single attribute.) This is the *deviation* around a point. If we sum this average over all points **x**, we get a global error estimate for a nearest-neighbor classification algorithm—that is, the total deviation or *variation*. The *variation* is related to the *variance* (Draper and Smith 1981), which uses the square of a difference instead of the absolute value. The resemblance goes further, because the summation of differences in class membership between adjacent points (used in the definition of variation) bears a simple relationship to the summation of differences between class-membership values and the mean of these values. Devroye and Gyorfi (1985) use a metric like the variation (which is continuous rather than discrete) to estimate the number of instances required to learn a real function.

We can interpret this measure in various ways. First, consider the geometrical interpretation. If we transport our integer valued **x** to a Euclidean space of the same dimension and let the class membership u correspond to an additional dimension in an $n + 1$-dimensional space, our notion of variation corresponds roughly to surface area ($n \geq 2$). Next, consider the inductive interpretation. The variation divided by the size of instance space is the expected error for a nearest-neighbor technique using an exhaustive, error-free training set. Even for decision-tree approaches, this estimate may approximate the error in a tree built using a large enough training sample. Finally, our variation measure generalizes number of peaks, which is a source of inductive difficulty for SI algorithms.

The next two sections discuss the limitations of this simplistic definition of variation and its appropriateness compared with two other notions. Readers uninterested in these issues may wish to skip to the discussion of the use of variation in algorithms.

Problems with the Simplified Definition of Variation   Our simplistic definition has omitted some details. First, it can be extended to handle real or nominal attributes. We can discretize real values and impose partial orderings on nominals. For nominals, we modify the definition of variation: *average deviation* is the variation over an instance space under a particular set of choices for attribute partial orderings. *Variation* is the minimum over all average deviations.

More important, our notion of variation is perfect only when we have access to $u(\mathbf{x})$ for all points **x**. Otherwise we are susceptible to consistent underestimates of the true variation. An alternative is to use a distance metric to define "nearest," but metrics are problematic (e.g., they are sensitive to attribute scaling; Duda and Hart 1973; Tou and Gonzalez 1974).

Next, our notion of variation covers only the case of equiprobable instance spaces. In other words, we assume that each x has an equal likelihood of being drawn in a random sample used to measure the overall error of a decision function. If this assumption is violated, our measure will inaccurately estimate the error even in a nearest-neighbor approach, because there may be many values of x that have a high deviation but a low probability mass (or vice versa).

Finally, our definition of variation applies only to a fixed set of attributes, whereas the set can include redundant and interdependent attributes. Our measure could overestimate the true variation in an unknown manner. Fortunately, induction techniques capable of selecting subsets of attributes can tame a space by eliminating redundancies and useless interdependencies.

Variation Versus Other Notions of Inductive Difficulty   There are at least two alternative ideas of concept variation or roughness. First, if each of the x_i has only two values and class membership is binary, we can note the number of disjuncts in an equivalent DNF expression and the maximal size of each minterm (Ehrenfeucht et al. 1988). This definition is superior to ours in that it allows computation of the number of examples needed to guarantee a given inductive accuracy. Unfortunately, there is no notion of averaging. Hence the two measures might disagree if an instance space were locally rocky but globally smooth. Furthermore, the DNF measure of inductive difficulty does not change if irrelevant or redundant attributes are added. We need a measure that is sensitive to the set of features to assess the FC results.

Another approach to the problem of roughness originates in Shannon's rate distortion theory (Berger 1974). The rate-distortion function is a measure of the minimum complexity needed by any estimator of class membership to produce a given average error rate. This function is defined for a *fidelity criterion* (an error measure) and a class of utility estimators (possible decision functions). In particular, the rate-distortion function for a given instance space is a function whose domain is the error rate and whose range is the minimum complexity (measured in units of mutual information between the estimator and the original utility function).

The rate-distortion measure has both advantages and disadvantages. It handles all discrete scales (unlike the DNF model) and allows for feature selection and weighting (like our model). It also handles nonequiprobable instance spaces and many (linear) scale transformations. Unfortunately, rate distortion is very difficult to compute. In general, direct computation is intractable, and no estimator is known. Also, the predicted degree of inductive difficulty does not change when irrelevant or redundant attributes are added.

Variation in Construction Algorithms   A selective induction algorithm SI outputs a set of disjuncts. Hard problems are typically revealed in this output because the number of disjuncts is large (Quinlan 1983; Rendell 1983). Hence, the learning algorithm CL of figure 5.11 has no trouble detecting the need for feature construction. A coarse definition of the SI quality measure μ_S would simply be the inverse of the number of disjuncts.

But for feature selection, such a measure may be too coarse because differences in feature sets are often small until construction is nearly complete (Seshu, Rendell, and Tcheng 1989). To evaluate sets of features, CL uses a quality measure μ_X and selects a subset *Sel*. A suitable choice for μ_X is our variation measure, which can be estimated from the output of SI: given attributes $Sel = \{x_i\}$, SI outputs disjuncts, which are conjunctions of x_i values annotated with their class-membership probabilities; this information derives variation. Although this underestimates the true variation, the results need be accurate only in a comparative sense because we evaluate competing subsets of attributes. Estimated variation is an appropriate choice for μ_X because it is sensitive to the instance-space distribution, which is reflected in the data.

Two Examples of Variation   Consider a simple example based on the target concept of "road-sign visibility." Suppose there are two attributes x_1 and x_2. Let x_1 be the size attribute, having values {small, large}, with a fixed ordering $O_1 = \{(\text{small}, \text{large})\}$. Let x_2 be the color attribute, chosen from the set {red, blue}, with no fixed ordering.

Suppose $u(\text{small, blue}) = .3$, $u(\text{small, red}) = .5$, $u(\text{large, blue}) = .6$, and $u(\text{large, red}) = .8$. These numbers indicate that larger signs in brighter colors are more visible. We can assign a total ordering to the color attribute by choosing either {(red, blue)} or {(blue, red)}. In this case either choice gives the same total deviation $(.6 - .3 + .5 - .3 + .8 - .5 + .5 - .3 + .8 - .5 + .8 - .6 + .8 - .6 + .6 - .3)/2 = 1.0$, which is the variation.

To see that variation is well behaved, suppose we switched the values of the blue instances, defining u' such that $u'(\text{small, blue}) = .3$, $u'(\text{small,}$

red) = .8, u'(large, blue) = .6, and u'(large, red) = .5. This new concept corresponds to the notion of "small xor blue" and has a variation of 1.2. Even in our tiny universe, variation distinguishes more difficult concepts.

Variation plays a part in both SI and FC. In SI the role of variation is coincidental; in FC the role is active. The next section details the constructive operations used by SI and FC.

5.6.2   Inductive Operations

The abstract operations we describe in this section integrate inductive operations found in work by Callan (1989), DeRaedt and Bruynooghe (1989), Devijver and Kittler (1982), Dietterich et al. (1982), Drastal, Czako, and Raatz (1989), Duda and Hart (1973), Flann and Dietterich (1986), Fu and Buchanan (1985), Kokar (1986), Langley (1977), Matheus (1989), Michalski (1983), Muggleton (1987), Muggleton and Buntine (1988), Pagallo (1989), Quinlan (1989), Rendell (1985), Schlimmer (1987), Schlimmer and Granger (1986), Seshu, Rendell, and Tcheng (1989), Utgoff (1990), Wogulis and Langley (1989), and others. We claim that the many operations in such research may be viewed as variations or combinations of our abstract operations. The first two operations are performed by SI. The remainder are used by FC.

Projection (Removal of Attributes or Attribute Selection)   Suppose I is an instance space with attributes x_1, x_2, ..., x_n, ranges X_1, X_2, ..., X_n, and scales s_1, s_2, ..., s_n. If $\{i_1, i_2, ..., i_{n'}\} \subseteq \{1, 2, ..., n\}$ (with $n' \leq n$), then X_{i_1}, X_{i_2}, ..., $X_{i_{n'}}$ and S_{i_1}, S_{i_2}, ..., $S_{i_{n'}}$ produce a *projection I'* of I formed by x_{i_1}, x_{i_2}, ..., x_{i_n}. This is analogous to the corresponding operation in vector spaces.

How does projection affect our measure of variation? The geometrical interpretation seems straightforward: projection leads to summing (integrating) u over an attribute. The effect on a nearest-neighbor algorithm is the same as performing attribute selection. If an attribute is removed, two instances distinguished only by their value in that attribute are merged (their u values are averaged). Moreover, two instances that were not neighbors in the original space can become neighbors in the transformed space. Projection decreases variation as a side effect of SI.

To exemplify projection, suppose instance space I comprises $X_1 = \{$small, large$\}$, with $O_1 = \{$(small, large)$\}$ and $X_2 = \{$red, blue$\}$. One projection I_1 of I is $X_1 = \{$small, large$\}$ and O_1; the other projection is $I_2 =$

$X_2 = \{\text{red, blue}\}$. In our first "sign-visibility" concept, with $u(\text{small, blue}) = .3$, $u(\text{small, red}) = .5$, $u(\text{large, blue}) = .6$, and $u(\text{large, red}) = .8$, u projected onto X_1 becomes u_1, which has values $u_1(\text{small}) = (.5 + .3)/2 = .4$ and $u_1(\text{large}) = (.8 + .6)/2 = .7$.

Puncturing (Removal of Attribute Values)   Suppose I is an instance space with attributes $x_1, x_2, \ldots, x_n$, ranges $X_1, X_2, \ldots, X_n$, and scales $s_1, s_2, \ldots, s_n$. Let $\{i_1, i_2, \ldots, i_{n'}\} \subseteq \{1, 2, \ldots, n\}$, with $n' \leq n$, and consider the subsets of ranges and scales $X'_{i_1}, X'_{i_2}, \ldots, X'_{i_{n'}}$ and $s'_{i_1}, s'_{i_2}, \ldots, s'_{i_{n'}}$, where each X'_j is a restriction of X_j and each S'_j is S_j minus any pairs whose components are missing from X'_j. These restricted ranges X'_{i_j} and scales s'_{i_j} compose a *puncturing* I' of I (a term from coding theory; Blahut 1983). For example, suppose instance space J is $X_J = \{\text{small, medium, large}\}$, $O_J = \{(\text{small, medium}), (\text{medium, large}), (\text{small, large})\}$, and $X_2 = \{\text{red, blue}\}$. One puncture of J is $X_1 = \{\text{small, large}\}$ with $O_1 = \{(\text{small, large})\}$, and X_2 unchanged; this is instance space I of the original example. If there are any medium objects in the space, we distribute their class-membership values by averaging them with those of their neighbors.

   Like projection, puncturing affects both variation and the difficulty of induction. Removing relevant values of relevant attributes can forfeit the attributes' discrimination power. But removal can help induction if it removes attribute values associated with instances that have class-membership values similar to the values of neighboring instances.

Concept Compression   A *compression* is a projection or a puncture or a combination of the two. Given a class-membership function u defined over space I, a *concept compression* maps u' of u onto I', where I' represents a projection of some (not necessarily proper) subset of the original attributes and a puncturing of the ranges of some (not necessarily proper) subset of the remaining attributes. Values of u' are obtained by averaging u over the removed attributes and attribute ranges.

Accurate Concept Compression   Concept compression makes sense only if the subspace I' retains enough class-membership information. To see if it does, we need to compute the error associated with the compression. For every instance $\mathbf{x}$ in the original space, determine its corresponding point in the compressed space and compute the differences in the corresponding u values. An *e-allowable compression* is one whose error is less than some bound e. For example, computing u_1, $(.5 + .3)/2 = .4$ is sensible if the error e is within ± 0.1.

Similarly, an e-allowable compression with confidence bound t is a concept compression whose averaged (possibly weighted) class-membership values match their determining values within tolerance e for at least a fraction t of subspace points. In our example, the projection of size and color onto size is an e-allowable compression with $e = 0.1$ and confidence bound $t = 1$, and therefore is simply e-allowable.

e-Useful Compression   Concept compression is e-useful iff it is allowable and has significant variation. A concept varies significantly over its domain if the value at one point differs from the value at another point by more than the tolerance or error e. Practical SI algorithms such as stepwise regression (Draper and Smith 1981) and decision-tree induction (Breiman et al. 1984) not only find the concept or function but also a useful projection. Attributes selected for a useful projection are *relevant*.

Concept Superpositions: Merging Concept Compressions   A *concept superposition* of two compressions I_1 and I_2 is an averaging of u-values over corresponding attributes. Consider the case in which the compressions are simply projections. In our example, one projection was $I_1 = \{\text{small, large}\}$. Projecting u onto I_1, we obtained $u_1(\text{small}) = .4$ and $u_1(\text{large}) = .7$. The other projection was $I_2 = \{\text{blue, red}\}$. Similarly, projecting u onto I_2, we get $u_2(\text{blue}) = .45$ and $u_2(\text{red}) = .65$. We can superpose projection I_1 on I_2 by imposing the partial order $\{(\text{blue, red})\}$ on its scale, to derive the space I_3. We average class-membership values of the resulting points in this space to get $u_{13}(\text{small} \cup \text{blue}) = .47$ and $u_{13}(\text{large} \cup \text{red}) = .63$.

Accurate Concept Superposition   Concept superposition makes sense only if the merging preserves class-membership information. An e-allowable superposition is a concept superposition whose averaged class-membership values equal their determining values within some tolerance e. Similarly, an e-allowable superposition with confidence bound t is a concept superposition whose averaged class-membership values match their determining values within tolerance e for at least a fraction t of subspace points. Our error values for $u_{13}(\text{small} \cup \text{blue})$ and $u_{13}(\text{large} \cup \text{red})$ average 0.11, so the superposition of size and color is allowable if $e \geq .11$.

Geometrical Interpretation   Intuitively, superposition makes sense because "redness" and "largeness" correspond; they are positively correlated. Since class-membership values in the size projection correspond to those of the color projection, we can merge these two attributes into one without loss of information. Geometrically, this corresponds to taking one hyperrectangle of instance space (and possibly rotating it) before averaging it with another (possibly distant) hyperrectangle. For this reason, superpositions can help with spatial domains, as later examples show.

Useful Concept Superposition (SI-Aiding Construction)   A concept superposition is e-useful iff it is allowable and the concept has significant variation. In our example, the two logic descriptions $x_{13}^{(1)} = $ small $\cup$ blue and $x_{13}^{(2)} = $ large $\cup$ red arose out of allowable projections and superpositions. Such constructions are useful because they compress instances while preserving class-membership values, and the compressed descriptions are more suited to SI. Whereas the original description space had two ground attributes (size and color) and four points, the final description space has one constructed attribute (x_{13}) and two points. The compression identifies small size and blue color, and large size and red color, as two similar groupings, with respect to the concept of road-sign visibility.

Use in Algorithms   In practice, the allowability of the operations is estimated by sampling. For example, the error or tolerance e is often obtained through computation of statistical significance (Rendell 1986). Projection and puncturing are implemented in systems for SI. SI systems perform allowable compression when they collect similar instances into regions and output their descriptions (section 5.2). Programs for FC collect similar regions into allowable superpositions and output their descriptions. Superpositions relate regions at a more abstract level that involves domain knowledge; that is, superpositions code utility invariants (Ragavan and Rendell 1991a).

5.6.3   Construction Examples and Algorithm Refinement

A crucial step in the coarse algorithm schema of figure 5.11 is "using *Act* (the set of features used as operands for construction) and some technique of peak merging, create a *utility-invariant construction x* (find and describe a set of neighborhoods having similar *u*-values)." Procedure *RV* (figure 5.12) shows this instruction expanded into several instructions that use compressions and superpositions. A partial implementation of RV was tested by Rendell (1985). Typical algorithms omit different steps of RV, depending on the problems addressed; essential steps vary from concept to concept, as the following examples show.

Procedure Reduce Variation RV

(1) *Pattern processing.* Find and describe a set of allowable compressions:
    Case A (logic, step-function approach):
        Partition the selected instance space into regions (possibly imposing scale orderings).
        Sort the regions into sets having similar class-membership values.
    Case B (numeric, curve-fitting approach):
        Find useful concept projections, favoring small dimensionality.

(2) *Pattern-class processing.* Sort the compressions by type of peak arrangement:
    Case A (logic representation):
        Divide each set of regions (of uniform class-membership value) into subsets
            based on some factor such as dimensionality of the subspace.
    Case B (numeric representation):
        Sort the allowable projections by dimensionality.

(3) *Pattern group processing.* Merge allowable superpositions:
    For each subset of (A) regions or (B) projections,
        fit its members to superposition rules, which code domain knowledge.

(4) *Feature formation.* Convert the construction to a new feature.

Figure 5.12
Building projections, superpositions, and new features

Basic Processing in Three Simple Cases   Some constructions require little computation. Suppose the ground instance space is Boolean with six dimensions. Consider the concept $C = x_2 x_4$ or $x_1 x_3 x_5$. Since C has only two peaks (regions of high class membership), SI (step 1) would easily locate them. Here superposition (steps 2 and 3) is trivial because C has only two equidimensional sets of terms, and each set has only one member. The only construction is to disjoin the two terms, and this is no help to SI, whose task is finished.

In general, construction for Boolean concepts uses negation, conjunction, and disjunction. Learning systems that use SI for negation and conjunction, and then replace conjunctions with new terms, have been shown to improve accuracy in some cases (Matheus and Rendell 1989; Pagallo 1989).

Consider a second example, a more complex Boolean concept y that exhibits some regularity. Suppose y is the disjunction of two-literal terms in a six-dimensional space such that pairs of adjacent literals agree: $x_i =$

x_{i+1} for odd i. This This parity function has six terms: $x_1 = 0$ *and* $x_2 = 0$ *or* $x_1 = 1$ *and* $x_2 = 1$ *or* $x_3 = 0$ *and* $x_4 = 0$ *or* ... But the higher-order logic description of y expresses it more succinctly.

This concept is a small challenge for RV (figure 5.12). The SI algorithm in step 1 learns individual terms. If SI finds the correct expressions, they will have the form $[x_i = c][x_{i+1} = c]$ for odd $i \in \{1, 3, 5\}$, with $c = 0$ or $c = 1$—the values for i and c would be specific. Step 2 collects these expressions into a set of dimensionality two (the only set in this case). If step 3 has knowledge available, it will narrow the search for superpositions. A highly constraining piece of knowledge is: for all odd $i \le 5$, x_i and x_{i+1} either agree or disagree (parity is known, but evenness or oddness is unknown). Only one example is required to complete this knowledge and predict the other five terms (in this case, the examples are not basic data but, rather, instance-space regions). Knowledge diminishes the data required and predicts missing regions not represented in the data.

Expressions found by SI, such as $[x_i = c][x_{i+1} = c]$ for specific values of i and c, are *patterns*. Patterns become "metadata" for superposition rules. A *superposition rule* is a statement that embodies domain knowledge and constrains candidate superpositions. A superposition rule foresees allowable superposition.

Our third and final example also uses knowledge to reduce search. In BACON (Langley 1977), region formation (step 1) is unnecessary because the regions are the data themselves. As in the parity example, no pattern-class separation (step 2) is required because the regions are (assumed to be) of one type. Given patterns from step 2, step 3 matches them to superposition rules.

BACON fits the data to superposition rules having the form $\{x | x = \prod e_i^{a_i}\}$ (where the e_i are the primitive attributes and the exponents a_i are parameters having small, signed integer values). Since this knowledge is highly constraining, few training examples are needed.

These three examples of FC are relatively simple. They exclude error and incremental learning. They fit only a single superposition rule to the entire set of data or regions. In these examples, RV has no trouble sorting regions by peak arrangement because there is only one kind of arrangement. The next example has none of these advantages.

More Complex Construction in a Harder Case   The low-level ground attributes for checkers in section 5.4.2 were the contents of the 32 legal squares. The values of these primitives e_i ($1 \leq i \leq 32$) were -2, -1, 0, 1, 2, representing black king, black man, vacancy, red man, and red king, respectively. From these primitives we can build any conceivable feature or intermediate concept about checkers. An intermediate concept is any expression built from the primitives to construct the ultimate concept (Fu and Buchanan 1985).

One intermediate concept useful for the goal of winning is piece advantage, which section 5.4.2 described in terms of its construction. Another intermediate concept is *diagonal adjacency*: two friendly pieces next to each other prevent the opponent from jumping. Rendell (1985) converts diagonal adjacency to a useful feature by counting its instances on the board. Like piece advantage, diagonal adjacency employs all the primitives, but unlike piece advantage, this concept interrelates primitives (in pairs).

The order or degree of a concept is the maximum number of primitives in a single term of a disjunction expressing the concept (Ehrenfeucht et al. 1988; Haussler 1988). The order is also the maximum degree of feature interaction in the primitives and the dimensionality of projections in step 2 of RV. Because the relationships in diagonal adjacency are limited to pairs of pieces, the order of this intermediate concept is two.

The individual disjuncts or projections from which an intermediate concept is constructed is a *pattern*. In the parity example (also of order two), each pattern is a pair of Boolean attributes expressed as a Boolean conjunction $x_i x_j$ (for certain i and j); in diagonal adjacency, a pattern is a projection expressed as a function $u_{ij}(e_i, e_j)$ (for certain i and j). In the parity example, the two-dimensional pattern is derived from estimates and projections of the entire function $y(x_1, x_2, \ldots, x_6)$; in diagonal adjacency, the two-dimensional pattern is derived from estimates and projections of the entire function $u(e_1, e_2, \ldots, e_{32})$.

The role of projections becomes clearer if we trace the discovery of diagonal adjacency through figure 5.12. Primitive examples take the form of detailed board positions such as the 32-tuple $(1, -2, \ldots)$, which means that the first square contains a red man and the second square contains a black king... Suppose that two checkerboards differ at squares e_{10} and e_{14} (these squares are diagonally adjacent). Further, suppose that this pair (e_{10}, e_{14}) for these two cases has values (0, 1) and (1, 1), with corresponding win probabilities of .5 and .7. This gives limited evidence that pair adjacency is relevant and that (1, 1) is better than (0, 1).

The two-dimensional subspace defined by (e_{10}, e_{14}) has $5 \times 5 = 25$ points. Given a subset of these 25 points, an SI algorithm (step 1 of figure 5.12) would discover this useful projection (e_{10}, e_{14}). SI would also discover other projections in different two-dimensional subspaces. Since many projections are possible, step 1 would identify many other patterns involving various attributes in different degrees. Hence the number of possible constructions is large. But step 2 simplifies somewhat by extracting a *pattern class*, which can be defined as a set of patterns having the same degree (Rendell 1985).

Suppose step 3 picks the degree-two class. The pair (e_{10}, e_{14}) is one of several pairs that together represent diagonal adjacency. Yet the pairs representing diagonal adjacency constitute only a few of all possible pairs, which number $32 \times 31 \div 2 = 496$, only 49 of which correspond to diagonal adjacency. To construct this intermediate concept, step 3 must select or discover the particular 49 pairs of primitives that constitute the correct set. This is equivalent to compilation (Flann and Dietterich 1986).

The worst situation is when no prior knowledge is available other than the assumptions of step 2 (which assert that equal-degree superpositions are meaningful). (This knowledge-poor situation is case 4 of section 5.4.1.) Nevertheless, step 3 can discover diagonal adjacency by first hypothesizing that arbitrary sets of pairs are equivalent. Pairs are represented as two-dimensional projections, which are tentatively superposed. If the 49 patterns coding adjacency are similar to each other but different from the remaining $496 - 49 = 447$ dispersed patterns, a function-matching technique will extract this information (Rendell 1985). The functions that match are the projections corresponding to the tentative superpositions that represent adjacency.

The discovery of diagonal adjacency may be simplified by using knowledge coded as candidate superpositions (case 2 of section 5.4.1) to produce *pattern groups*. One superposition rule is the family of projections (e_i, e_j) such that $|i - j| = 3$ or $|i - j| = 4$, which roughly represents diagonal adjacency. This rule is one of many possible rules that could be used to constrain candidate superpositions. The strongest constraint includes only the correct (allowable) superpositions (case 1 of section 5.4.1). A more general method is to present numerous choices or biases, one of which works for diagonal adjacency and others of which are useful for different features (case 3 of section 5.4.1). Methods for choosing the best rules have been examined empirically by Bergadano and Giordana (1990) and Quinlan (1987, 1989) using logic descriptions and by Rendell (1985) using group descriptions.

The final step in RV's construction (figure 5.12) is to convert the superposition rules into features for SI to use. This conversion may be accomplished in at least two ways: a rule can be made a Boolean feature that tests for the presence of a structure, or a rule can be made into a counting function that enumerates instances of the structure. For example, the description "any diagonally adjacent pair of pieces" produces a feature that counts instances of diagonal adjacency.

Still More Complex Constructions and Phenomena Humans normally think of checkers in terms of intermediate concepts, including not only piece advantage and diagonal adjacency but many other features (Fu and Buchanan 1985). Checkers without prior knowledge of important intermediate concepts corresponds to hard unsolved problems such as protein folding. Although machine learning systems have had limited success with such problems, this section attempts some extensions based on RV in figure 5.12.

Difficult problems are characterized by primitive class-membership functions having high variation and by incipient knowledge involving considerable uncertainty and incoherence. When the class-membership function is rocky, the dispersed data are hard to coalesce into useful intermediate concepts. When knowledge is uncertain, superposition rules are numerous and conflicting, each representing a different intermediate concept; in extreme cases, a single plausible rule may even confound portions of useful intermediates.

How does this situation appear in term of patterns, pattern classes, and pattern groups? To learn the intermediate concept "diagonal adjacency," first step 1 of RV found useful two-dimensional projections, which step 2 classified as such, and step 3 grouped into adjacent versus nonadjacent patterns. The basis of the grouping of adjacent patterns was matched superpositions.

Viewing this data manipulation from another perspective, we find that regions of the primitive instance space merge because the probability of winning varies roughly independently of the location of the adjacency pattern on the board. This invariance appears as projection similarity across individual patterns. Hence, translation emerges as a utility invariant for adjacency.

The basis for any such intermediate concept is utility invariance, which is discovered by the combination of steps 1, 2, and 3 of RV. But intermediate concepts differ in their degree of primitive interaction; hence, projections vary in dimensionality. Some features involve patterns of several pieces (one for every dimension in the projection), although our knowledge of checkers tells us that many useful features have small order. (Other domains also have low-degree intermediate concepts, paralleling Seshu's results discussed in section 5.3.2.)

Just as translation invariance worked for diagonal adjacency, the application of that same rule will be valid for other cases. Any set of projections that encodes a translation of a pattern over the checkerboard will match when superposed (as in figure 5.10). This occurs whenever the contribution to a win of a pattern is roughly invariant when moved across the board. Thus, a single type of superposition rule applies to many pattern classes.

A superposition rule can be given as a logic expression such as (e_i, e_j) such that $|i - j| = 3$ or $|i - j| = 4$, which we used for diagonal adjacency. But another form of the same knowledge involves groups (Gill 1976). A *pattern group* is a prototypical pattern together with a set of operations to transform the prototype into other patterns. For example, our prototypical pair (e_{10}, e_{14}) generates all pairs composing diagonal adjacency, when translated over the checkerboard and allowed to rotate by 90 degrees. Other kinds of group operations, such as deformations, produce other kinds of structure.

A superposition rule codes a utility-invariant transformation, any function whose domain and ranges are subsets (not necessarily proper) of instance space and which guarantees that the class membership of a point in the domain is identical to the class membership of a point in the range. Hence, a pattern group is a prototypical pattern and a utility-invariant transformation. Two utility-invariant transformations in checkers are translations and 90-degree rotations.

This rosy picture of intermediate construction ignores possible interference among patterns, classes, and groups. The overall task of producing a useful set of features is very difficult because many intermediate features are required before a good win function can be composed. Moreover, different features require different projections. Since many projections are possible, step 1 would identify many patterns involving various primitive attributes in different degrees. The SI algorithm would run repeatedly, for many choices of attributes and degrees of projection. But this complicates pattern-class processing. Which patterns belong to which rules? This is a problem of jumbled information.

The multiplicity of pattern classes is the reason for using step 2 of RV. Sorting patterns by dimensionality is one useful heuristic (Rendell 1985), but much work remains to test the generality of such notions.

5.7   The Role of Knowledge

According to the algorithm schema for concept learning (figure 5.11), abstract features such as piece advantage and diagonal adjacency gradually displace primitives to improve SI performance. SI performance will improve as allowable new features produce class-membership functions having less variation. In sections 4, through 6 we saw that such FC is facilitated by utility invariance to bias region merging. Utility invariance appears in an algorithm for FC (figure 5.11) and a procedure for variation reduction (figure 5.12).

For the overall process of concept learning through change of representation, figures 5.4, 5.11, and 5.12 show various constructions: region boundaries, regions, superpositions of regions, and finally new features. Each component is assessed before participating in further construction. FC itself works in stages, building increasingly structured hypotheses from lower-level components—first patterns, then classes, and finally groups. Testing at an earlier stage (in an inner loop in the algorithm) avoids unpromising structures. Unpromising components can also be eliminated by the use of knowledge in various forms, such as superposition rules. The use of various forms of knowledge to help concept learning is the subject of this section.

5.7.1   Knowledge Application as Test Incorporation

Before we explicitly investigate the sources of domain knowledge, let us consider the underlying purpose of domain knowledge in constructive induction. Domain knowledge reduces the expected effort needed for induction by assessing components of candidate features before constructing those features. This is *test incorporation*, which is the process of "incorporating portions of a test [component utility in our case] into the generator [feature construction in our case]" (Dietterich 1986; Tappel 1980). In our version of test incorporation, the test is an approximation of the original; structures can be assessed incorrectly. But we want to save time without sacrificing too much accuracy.

Test incorporation improves efficiency because it filters components before they proliferate in combinations. For example, if we screen individual primitives before considering them as pairs in hypothetical patterns, we eliminate every case in which the rejected primitives would appear. The elimination of half the primitives reduces the number of pairs by one-quarter, and the advantage increases with the complexity of the structure. The advantage may multiply if constraints are applied in a layered fashion.

5.7.2 Knowledge Inputs to Concept Learning

To help select components preferred for construction, we may use various sources of knowledge, such as user advice (Bratko and Michie 1980; Michie 1977), observation of task performance (Flann and Dietterich 1986; Kadie, 1988; Rendell 1985), and inferences from domain theories (DeJong and Mooney 1986; Mitchell, Keller, and Kedar-Cabelli 1986). In the process of concept learning, especially when feature construction is involved, knowledge appears in various guises. Below are listed some general ways of expressing knowledge at different points during induction and construction in CL (figures 5.11 and 5.12). These rough divisions overlap and do not detail feature construction.

• The classification knowledge in the data. In learning from examples, class-membership values accompany each member of the training set (of k-tuples of ground attributes). From these data, the class-membership function is induced.

• The domain knowledge hidden in the ground attributes. This knowledge can be extensive, contained in appropriate, abstract features. It can also be meager, found in low-level primitives and extractable only after considerable search. In the former case, humans have applied their experience to generate good features; in the latter case, a construction system must form new features.

• The knowledge implicit in the biases of the inductive system SI. Most common is the fundamental assumption of SI—that neighboring points predict one another's class-membership values. If this implicit knowledge matches the ground attributes, the bias is appropriate and constructive induction is unnecessary. Implicit knowledge also involves other aspects of SI, such as the amount of noise in the data. Such knowledge can be used to decide parameter settings for an algorithm. An algorithm may also infer such biases based on previous experience. A static bias can become dynamic and flexible if it is related to previous problems (Rendell, Seshu, and Tcheng 1987) or deduced from the problem at hand (Utgoff 1986).

• General assumptions about the world, such as simplicity. Simplicity extends to FC and favors few elements in any structure, including patterns, classes, and groups.

• Specific knowledge about a domain not coded in the ground attributes and not appropriate for use by SI. Knowledge sources include user advice, observation of task performance, and inference from domain theories. Such knowledge needs to be mapped into preferred components and structures (biases) for FC.

The first three knowledge categories determine the need for FC (Matheus 1989); the fourth and fifth determine its effectiveness and tractability. How can the algorithm schema FC (figure 5.11) accommodate a dynamic interplay among data, domain knowledge, and emerging structures? Given the layered constraints of RV (figure 5.11), the question can be more specific: Which kinds, forms, and sources of knowledge apply at which level? In other words, which knowledge constrains which components?

5.7.3   Meshing the Knowledge with the Structures

Many sources of knowledge may be available to help induction. To organize the application of knowledge to structures, table 5.3 augments the layered scheme of RV to accept knowledge at each stage. This table shows three layers of construction, from primitives (ground attributes), through patterns (conjuncts of primitives), and classes (disjunctions or projections of patterns), to groups (descriptions of classes). At each level, one of these structures (column 1) is built from data (column 2) and knowledge (column 3).

The table assumes that each row builds on the previous one, for a nested hierarchy of candidate structures. The input data are first used directly (row 1) and then in a modified form (other rows): a structure in row k becomes a metadatum for row $k + 1$.

Column 3 lists some kinds and sources of knowledge appropriate at each level. To begin construction at $k = 1$, we might select the ground

Table 5.3
Levels of knowledge application

Level of construction	Data or meta-data	Suitable knowledge to incorporate
1. Patterns (Formation of structures from active primitives)	Raw data expressed using ground attributes	Biases favoring particular ground attributes. Suggested structures or combinations (e.g., pairs of ground attributes).
2. Pattern classes (Selection of pattern classes for superposition)	Patterns (regions or projections)	Simplicity. General knowledge of domain, such as biases favoring continuity, proximity, or adjacency. Domain theory consequences about structures.
3. Pattern groups (Selection of rules for describing superpositions)	Classes (patterns that have begun to be grouped)	Domain knowledge about good transformations. Biases favoring certain kinds of groups (e.g., rotations of 90°). Observations about successful regularities in current and related domains.

attributes that are more relevant. When knowledge is available, it directly constrains the "active" primitives to a subset of all ground attributes. For example, if we wanted the system to learn a feature such as center control in checkers, we would eliminate the peripheral squares. (This would not preclude learning since the system might select a still smaller subset.) When no knowledge is available, heuristics and data produce the active primitives (Rendell 1985). The patterns formed at this level become meta-data for row 2.

Row 2 knowledge aids the formation of pattern classes. The simplest way to constrain pattern classes is to limit their complexity or, at least, to order construction so that simpler classes are attempted first. The simplest class has just one conjunct in each disjunct (the projection degree is one). In checkers, this results in the construction of piece advantage (Rendell 1985), the most important feature (Samuel 1963). After piece advantage and perhaps center control, several two- and three-degree features emerge, such as piece adjacency and double-jumps. (An increasing repertoire of useful features facilitates the discovery of more complex features; Rendell 1985.) These higher-degree features are constructed more quickly and reliably if supporting knowledge is available, such as the notion of proximity used to develop adjacency in section 6.3.

Row 3 knowledge uses superposition rules to create pattern groups. One form of superposition rule is a prototypical pattern and a set of operations to transform the prototype into related patterns. For example, any pattern (e.g., a diagonally adjacent pair) may be translated, rotated, or deformed (Rendell 1985). Hence, general knowledge about the domain helps to identify utility-invariant transformations. For example, rotations and translations in board games preserve the likelihood that one side or the other will win. Although geometrical or spatial invariants are particularly common in these contexts, they can appear in unexpected places (Flann and Dietterich 1986; Seshu, Rendell, and Tcheng 1989). Russell and Grosof (1990) also examine the use of knowledge to determine inductive bias.

Invariants are known or suspected in many domains. In protein folding, for example, knowledge or hunches apply at each of the three levels. Here the sequence of primitives corresponds to (amino acids at) successive positions of the string. At the pattern level (row 1 of table 5.3), knowing that k amino acids take part in a fold translates to patterns made from primitives $i, i + 1, \ldots, i + k$. At the pattern-class level (row 2), knowing the approximate distance $d \pm c$ between two parts of a fold suggests that patterns should be made from primitives whose subscripts differ by $d - c, d - c + 1, \ldots, d + c$. At the group level (row 3), suspecting that a fold is independent of its position on the string leads to superposition rules that code translation: the group of degree-k patterns defined by the prototype i, $i + 1, \ldots, i + k$ and a rule that allows i to vary, may be a good candidate for utility invariance.

Some kinds of knowledge apply at more than one level. For example, the knowledge that patterns can be deformed but not broken (e.g., parts of animals in a visual scene) would apply to the pattern-class and group levels.

5.7.4 Knowledge-In, Knowledge-Out

This chapter began with an examination of selective induction, which is cheap and accurate as long as the attributes are related to the problem at hand. SI can be used not only for ground-level objects of the original problem but also for the other levels of table 5.3. At any level, a component to be selected can be chosen from a space of comparable structures, which are described much like the ground-level objects (Rendell, Seshu, and Tcheng 1987). In other words, the scheme outlined in table 5.3 amounts to *selective induction in higher-order spaces of component descriptions*. These higher spaces can be structured, manually and automatically, into more manageable forms suitable for SI (so that there are few peaks in the function representing probability of usefulness or bias appropriateness). Hence, in reformulating the problem of concept learning, we have simultaneously avoided the drawbacks of SI at the primitive level, facilitated the incorporation of knowledge at several levels, and used SI to surmount the difficulties of it.

5.8 Conclusion

Hard binary concepts are Boolean functions having arbitrary compositions of conjuncts and disjuncts. Hard graded concepts are real-valued functions having any composition of instance-space regions. If examples of concepts are k-tuples of attribute values labeled with (binary or graded) class-membership values, then learning hard concepts from limited samples leads to feature construction, which may incorporate domain knowledge in specific ways. This chapter has characterized the problem and developed an algorithm schema FC, which has been partially tested. The components of FC were analyzed in the light of previous approaches and from the perspective of inherent properties. Layered structures and domain knowledge can be meshed to improve learning performance. Analysis and experiments show:

• Attribute-based concept learning is function estimation, which is straightforward for traditional inductive methods given the fundamental assumption that neighboring points predict class membership.

• In such cases learning can take place over the original instance space of ground attributes, but functions that are difficult to learn because of concept dispersion incapacitate standard selective induction methods because of their algorithmic structure.

• The fundamental assumption of selective induction is satisfied only when problems are well understood, which leads to appropriate ground attributes.

• A useful approach for harder problems is feature construction, which transforms the ground attributes so that a new function over the transformed space has less variation.

• A statistical notion of variation, and variation-reducing transformations motivate feature construction that can incorporate domain knowledge expressed using utility invariance, which predicts class membership for dispersed points in instance space.

• Utility invariance expressed as superposition rules (region merging transformations) can improve the behavior of selective induction and help determine incomplete domain knowledge.

• Since selective induction and feature construction complement each other, they can be combined to improve learning in terms of accuracy, conciseness, and speed for learning hard concepts.

Selective induction combined with constructive induction can outperform selective induction alone because the two processes have different strengths and weaknesses. Selective induction is good for discovering the sizes and shapes of individual peaks in the class-membership function, yet too many peaks incapacitate it. In contrast, feature construction is good for merging peaks, especially when domain knowledge is available, but it is a poor substitute for shaping an individual peak.

Acknowledgments

This research was supported in part by grant IRI 8822031 from the National Science Foundation. Conversations with Ranan Banerji, Andrew Barron, Bruce Buchanan, George Drastal, Pat Langley, Pankaj Mehra, Steve Muggleton, and Derek Sleeman contributed to this chapter. Gunnar Blix, Michael Hall, Rob Holte, Eduardo Perez, Harish Ragavan, Jay Scott, and the anonymous reviewers of *Computational Intelligence* provided helpful criticisms of earlier drafts. Howard Cho ran the experiments of section 5.3.2. We thank Ross Quinlan for a copy of ID3/C4.

References

Aha D. W., and Kibler, D. Noise-tolerant instance-based learning algorithms. *Proc. Eleventh International Joint Conference on Artificial Intelligence*, 1989, 794–799.

Anderberg, M. R. *Cluster Analysis for Applications.* New York: Academic Press, 1973.

Banerji, R. B. *Artificial Intelligence: A Theoretical Approach.* Dordrecht: North-Holland, 1980.

Barron, A. R., and Barron, R. L. Statistical learning networks: A unifying view. In *Computing Science and Statistics: Proceedings of the 20th Symposium on the Interface*, 192–203. Reston, Virginia, 1988.

Baum, E. B., and Haussler, D. What size net gives valid generalization? *Neural Computation 1*, 1989, *1*, 151–160.

Bergadano, F., and Giordana, A. Guiding induction with domain theories. In Kodratoff, Y., and Michalski, R. S. (eds.), *Machine Learning: An Artificial Intelligence Approach III*, 474–492. San Mateo, Calif.: Morgan Kaufman, 1990.

Berger, T. *Rate Distortion Theory: A Mathematical Basis for Data Compression*. Englewood Cliffs, N.J.: Prentice-Hall, 1974.

Blahut, R. E. *Theory and Practice of Error Control Codes*. Menlo Park, Calif.: Addison-Wesley, 1983.

Blumer, A., Ehrenfeucht, A., Haussler, D., and Warmuth, M. Occam's Razor. *Information Processing Letters 24*, 1987, 377–380.

Bratko, I., and Michie, D. An advice program for a complex chess programming task. *Computer Journal*, 1980, *23*, 353–359.

Breiman, L., Friedman, J. H., Olshen, R. A., and Stone, C. J. *Classification and Regression Trees*. Belmont, Calif.: Wadsworth, 1984.

Buntine, W. A critique of the Valient model. *Proc. Eleventh International Joint Conference on Artificial Intelligence*, 1989, 837–842.

Callan, J. P. Knowledge-based feature generation. *Proc. Sixth International Workshop on Machine Learning*, 1989, 441–443.

Cover, T. Geometrical and statistical properties of systems of linear equations with applications to pattern recognition. *IEEE Trans. Elect. Comp.*, 1965, *14*, 326–334.

DeJong, G., and Mooney, R. Explanation-based learning: An alternative view. *Machine Learning*, 1986, *1*, 145–176.

DeRaedt, L., and Bruynooghe, M. Towards friendly concept-learners. *Proc. Eleventh International Joint Conference on Artificial Intelligence*, 1989, 849–854.

Devijver, P. A., and Kittler, J. *Pattern Recognition: A Statistical Approach*. Englewood Cliffs, N.J.: Prentice-Hall, 1982.

Devroye, L., and Gyorfi, L. *Nonparametric Density Estimation: The L1 View*. New York: Wiley, 1985.

Dietterich, T. G. Learning at the knowledge level. *Machine Learning*, 1986, *1*, 287–316.

Dietterich, T. G. Limitations on inductive learning. *Proc. Sixth International Workshop on Machine Learning*, 1989, 124–128.

Dietterich, T. G., London, B., Clarkson, K., and Dromey, G. Learning and inductive inference. In P. R. Cohen and E. A. Feigenbaum (eds.), *The Handbook of Artificial Intelligence*. San Mateo, Calif.: Kaufmann, 1982.

Doran, J., and Michie, D. Experiments with the graph-traverser program. *Proc. Roy. Soc.*, 1966, *A*, 235–259.

Draper, N. R., and Smith, H. *Applied Regression Analysis*. New York: Wiley, 1981.

Drastal, G. Informed pruning in constructive induction. *Proc. Eighth International Workshop on Machine Learning*, 1991, 132–136.

Drastal, G., Czako, G., and Raatz, S. Induction in an abstraction space: A form of constructive induction. *Proc. Eleventh International Joint Conference on Artificial Intelligence*, 1989, 708–712.

Duda, R. O., and Hart, P. E. *Pattern Classification and Scene Analysis*. New York: Wiley, 1973.

Ehrenfeucht, A., Haussler, D., Kearns, M., and Valiant, L. A general lower bound on the number of examples needed for learning. *Proc. Computational Learning Theory*, 1988, 139–154.

Flann, N. S., and Dietterich, T. G. Selecting appropriate representations for learning from examples. *Proc. Fifth National Conference on Artificial Intelligence*, 1986, 460–466.

Fu, L., and Buchanan, B. G. Learning intermediate concepts in constraining a hierarchical knowledge base. *Proc. Ninth International Joint Conference on Artificial Intelligence*, 1985, 659–666.

Gill, A. *Applied Algebra for the Computer Sciences*. Englewood Cliffs, N.J.: Prentice-Hall, 1976.

Gunsch G., and Rendell, L. A. Opportunistic constructive induction: Using fragments of domain knowledge to guide construction. *Proc. Eighth International Workshop on Machine Learning*, 1991, 147–152.

Haussler, D. Quantifying inductive bias: AI learning algorithms and Valiant's learning framework. *Artificial Intelligence*, 1988, *36*, 177–221.

Hinton, G. E. Connectionist learning procedures. *Artificial Intelligence*, 1989, *40*, 185–234.

Holder, L. B. The general utility problem in machine learning. *Proc. Seventh International Conference on Machine Learning*, 1990, 402–410.

Holte, R. C. Very simple classification rules perform well on most datasets. Department of Computer Science, Report No. TR-91-16. Ottawa: University of Ottawa, April 1991.

Holte, R. C., and Porter, B. W. Concept learning and the problem of small disjuncts. *Proc. Eleventh International Joint Conference on Artificial Intelligence*, Detroit, 1989, 813–824.

Indurkhya, N., and Weiss, S. M. *Iterative Rule Induction Procedures*. Laboratory for Computer Science Research Report LCSR-TR-145. New Brunswick, N.J.: Rutgers University, 1990.

Kadie, C. M. Diffy-S: Learning robot operator schemata from examples. *Proc. Fifth International Conference on Machine Learning*, 1988, 430–436.

King, R. D. An inductive learning approach to the problem of predicting a protein's secondary structure from its amino acid sequence. *Proc. Second European Working Session on Learning*. Sigma Press, Wilmslow, 1987, 230–250.

Kokar, M. M. Discovering functional formulas through changing representation base. *Proc. Fifth National Conference on Artificial Intelligence*, 1986, 455–459.

Korf, R. E. Toward a Model of Representation Change. *Artificial Intelligence*, 1980, *14*, 41–78.

Kuhn, T. *The Structure of Scientific Revolution*. Chicago: University of Chicago Press, 1970.

Langley, P. Rediscovering physics with Bacon. *Proc. Fifth International Joint Conference on Artificial Intelligence*, 1977, 505–507.

Lathrop, R., Webster, T., and Smith, T. ADRIADNE: Pattern-directed inference and hierarchical abstraction in protein structure recognition. *Communications ACM*, 1987, *30*, 909–921.

Lee, W. D. *Probabilistic Inference: Theory and Practice*. Department of Computer Science Report UIUCDCS-R-86-1271. Urbana: University of Illinois, 1986.

McCarthy, J. Epistemological problems of artificial intelligence. *Proc. Fifth International Joint Conference on Artificial Intelligence*, 1977, 1038–1044.

Markovitch, S., and Scott, P. D. Utilization filtering: A method for reducing the inherent harmfulness of deductively learned knowledge, *Proc. Eleventh International Joint Conference on Artificial Intelligence*, 1989, 738–743.

Matheus, C. J. *Feature Construction: An Analytic Framework and an Application to Decision Trees*. Department of Computer Science Report UIUCDCS-R-89-1559. Urbana: University of Illinois, 1989.

Matheus, C. J., and Rendell, L. A. Constructive induction on decision trees. *Proc. Eleventh International Joint Conference on Artificial Intelligence*, 1989, 645–650.

Mehra, P., Rendell, L. A., and Wah, B. W. Principled constructive induction. *Proc. Eleventh International Joint Conference on Artificial Intelligence*, 1989, 651–656.

Michalski, R. S. Knowledge acquisition through conceptual clustering: A theoretical framework and an algorithm for partitioning data into conjunctive concepts. *Journal of Policy Analysis and Information Systems*, 1980, *4*, 219–244.

Michalski, R. S. A theory and methodology of inductive learning. *Artificial Intelligence* 20:2, 111–161.

Michie, D. A theory of advice. In E. W. Elcock and D. Michie (eds.), *Machine Intelligence*. American Elsevier, 1977.

Michie, D., and Ross, R. Experiments with the adaptive graph traverser. In B. Meltzer and D. Michie (eds.), *Machine Intelligence*. American Elsevier, 1970.

Mingers, J. An empirical comparison of selection measures for decision-tree induction. *Machine Learning*, 1989, *3*, 319–342.

Minsky, M. L., and Papert, S. *Perceptrons: An Introduction to Computational Geometry*. Cambridge, Mass.: MIT Press, 1969.

Mitchell, T. M. *The need for biases in learning generalizations*. Technical Report CBM-TR-117. May 1980.

Mitchell, T. M., Keller, R. M., and Kedar-Cabelli, S. T. Explanation-based generalization: A unifying view. *Machine Learning*, 1986, *1*, 47–80.

Muggleton, S. Structuring knowledge by asking questions. *Progress in Machine Learning: Proc. Second European Working Session on Learning*, 1987, 218–229.

Muggleton, S., and Buntine, W. Machine invention of first-order predicates by inverting resolution. *Proc. Fifth International Conference on Machine Learning*, 1988, 339–352.

Natarajan, B. K. On learning sets and functions. *Machine Learning*, 1989, *4*, 67–97.

O'Rorke, P., Morris, S., and Schulenburg, D. Abduction and world model revisions. In Ohlson, G., and Smith, E. (eds.), *Proc. Eleventh Annual Conference of the Cognitive Science Society*. Hillsdale, N.J.: Lawrence Erlbaum, 1989.

Pagallo, G. Learning DNF by decision trees. *Proc. Eleventh International Joint Conference on Artificial Intelligence*, 1989, 639–644.

Pazzani, M. J., and Sarrett, W. Average case analysis of conjunctive learning algorithms. *Proc. Seventh International Conference on Machine Learning*, 1990, 339–347.

Peirce, C. S. *Collected Papers. Vol 2*. Cambridge, Mass.: Harvard University Press, 1931.

Qian, N., and Sejnowski, T. J. Predicting the secondary structure of globular proteins using neural network models. *Journal of Molecular Biology*, 1988, *202*, 865–884.

Quinlan, J. R. Learning efficient classification procedures and their application to chess end games. In Ryszard Michalski (ed.), *Machine Learning: An Artificial Intelligence Approach*. Tioga, 1983.

Quinlan, J. R. Simplifying decision trees. *International Journal of Man-Machine Studies 27*, 1987, 221–234.

Quinlan, J. R. *Learning relations: Comparison of a symbolic and a connectionist approach*. Basser Department of Computer Science Technical Report TR-346. Sydney: University of Sydney, 1989.

Ragavan, H., and Rendell, L. A. Relations, knowledge, and empirical learning. *Proc. Eighth International Workshop on Machine Learning*, 1991a, 188–192.

Ragavan, H., and Rendell, L. A. Relieving limitations of feature construction algorithms. *Proc. Change of Representation Workshop, Twelfth International Joint Conference on Artificial Intelligence*, 1991b, 27–36.

Ragavan, H., and Rendell, L. A. Learning disjunctive concepts using domain knowledge, 1991c. This volume.

Ragavan, H., Rendell, L. A., Shaw M., and Canart, A. Improving decision trees through feature construction. Unpublished manuscript, 1992.

Rajamoney, S. A., and DeJong, G. F. The classification, detection and handling of imperfect theory problems. *Proc. Tenth International Joint Conference on Artificial Intelligence*, 1987, 205–207.

Rendell, L. A. Conceptual knowledge acquisition in search. University of Guelph Report CIS-83-15, 1983, Guelph, Canada. Reprinted in L. Bolc (ed.), *Computational Models of Learning*. New York: Springer-Verlag, 1987.

Rendell, L. A. Substantial constructive induction using layered information compression: Tractable feature formation in search. *Proc. Ninth International Joint Conference on Artificial Intelligence*, 1985, 650–658.

Rendell, L. A. A general framework for induction and a study of selective induction. *Machine Learning*, 1986, *1*, 177–226.

Rendell, L. A., and Cho, H. H. Empirical learning as a function of concept character. *Machine Learning*, 1990, *5*, 3, 267–298.

Rendell, L. A., Cho, H. H., and Seshu, R. M. Improving the design of similarity-based rule-learning systems. *International Journal of Expert Systems*, 1989, 2, 1, 97–133.

Rendell, L. A., Seshu, R. M., and Tcheng, D. K. Layered concept learning and dynamically variable bias management. *Proc. Tenth International Joint Conference on Artificial Intelligence*, 1987, 308–314.

Rissanen, J. Stochastic complexity and modelling. *Annals of Statistics*, 1986, *12*, 3, 1080–1100.

Russell, S., and Grosof, B. Declarative bias: An overview. In P. Benjamin (ed.), *Change of Representation and Inductive Bias*. Newton, Mass.: Kluwer Academic Press, 1990. 267–308.

Samuel, A. L. Some studies in machine learning using the game of checkers. *IBM Journal of Research and Development*, 1959, *3*. Reprinted in E. A. Feigenbaum (ed.), *Computers and Thought*. New York: McGraw-Hill, 1963.

Schlimmer, J. C. Learning and representation change. *Proc. Sixth National Joint Conference on Artificial Intelligence*, 1987, 346–389.

Schlimmer, J. C., and Granger, R. H. Incremental learning from noisy data. *Machine Learning Journal*, 1986, 317–354.

Seshu, R. M. Solving the parity problem *Proc. European Working Session on Learning*, 1989, 263–271.

Seshu, R. M., Rendell, L. A., and Tcheng, D. K. Managing constructive induction using subcomponent assessment and multiple-objective optimization. *Proc. Fifth International Conference on Artificial Intelligence Applications*, 1989, 191–197.

Smith, E. E., and Medin, D. L. *Categories and Concepts*. Cambridge, Mass.: Harvard University Press, 1981.

Tappel, S. Some algorithm design methods. *Proc. National Conference on Artificial Intelligence*, 1980, 64–67.

Tou, T. T., and Gonzalez, R. C. *Pattern Recognition Principles*. Reading, Mass.: Addison-Wesley, 1974.

Utgoff, P. E. Shift of bias for inductive concept learning. *Machine Learning: An Artificial Intelligence Approach*, 1986, *2*, 107–148.

Utgoff, P. E. An incremental method for finding multivariate splits for decision trees. *Proc. Seventh International Conference on Machine Learning*, 1990, 58–65.

Van de Velde, W. Incremental induction of topologically minimal trees. *International Machine Learning Conference*, 1990, 66–74.

Watanabe, L., and Rendell, L. A. Learning structural decision trees from examples. *Proc. Twelfth International Joint Conference on Artificial Intelligence*, 1991, 770–776.

Watanabe, S. *Knowing and Guessing: A Formal and Quantitative Study*. New York: Wiley 1969.

Watanabe, S. *Pattern Recognition: Human and Mechanical*. New York: Wiley, 1985.

Weiss, S. M., and Kapouleas, I. An empirical comparison of pattern recognition, neural nets, and machine learning classification methods. *Proc. Eleventh International Joint Conference on Artificial Intelligence*, 1989, 781–787.

Wogulis, J., and Langley, P. Improving efficiency by learning intermediate concepts. *Proc. Eleventh International Joint Conference on Artificial Intelligence*, 1989, 657–662.

Yang, D. S., Rendell, L. A., and Blix, G. A scheme for feature construction and a comparison of empirical methods. *Proc. Twelfth International Joint Conference on Artificial Intelligence*, 1991, 699–704.

Zadeh, L. A. Fuzzy sets. *Information and Control*, 1965, *8*, 338–353.

6 Learning Disjunctive Concepts Using Domain Knowledge

Harish Ragavan and Larry Rendell

6.1 Introduction

To address problems in learning from purely empirical or purely analytical techniques, many approaches apply domain theories to aid learning from multiple examples (e.g., UNIMEM: Lebowitz 1986; MIRO: Drastal, Czako, and Raatz 1989; IOE: Flann and Dietterich 1989; ML-SMART: Bergadano and Giordana 1990). In learning from examples expressed as attribute-value tuples, systems using statistical similarity estimates (Breiman et al. 1984; Quinlan 1983) work well as long as enough training examples are available, their distributions are representative of the unknown population, and instance-space proximity coincides with concept similarity (Rendell and Seshu 1990). For some difficult domains, however, or when data are sparse, classical induction systems break down. In such cases, domain knowledge representing higher-level relationships between the primitive (measurement) attributes is a key to successful learning.

Integrated techniques apply domain knowledge to construct new relations and new representations that help concept learning. Many integrated learning systems combine training examples with domain knowledge to construct new descriptors for representing the examples (constructive induction: Michalski 1983). Some integrated systems use the training examples to drive a domain theory for deducing new descriptors. Such a bias has been found to be at times too strong toward the domain theory unless allowed to vary as search for the concept proceeds (Drastal, Czako, and Raatz 1989; Rendell, Seshu, and Tcheng 1987). In this chapter, we study a flexible method that manipulates concepts, examples, and domain knowledge, all as relations (compare FOIL: Quinlan 1990). The method uses compositions of relations to construct representations that are more effective in classical induction. Specifically, a combination of specialization and generalization (deduction and induction) is used to construct new features, allowing the learning system to strengthen or weaken its bias dynamically.

In section 6.2, we introduce a relational framework. Section 6.3 investigates a process for using domain knowledge to construct new relational features. In section 6.4, we present some set-theoretic results on the interaction between data and knowledge. Section 6.5 gives a learning algorithm that uses relational knowledge and analyzes several empirical results. Section 6.6 discusses related research.

6.2   Concepts and Knowledge

6.2.1   Concepts

We focus on attribute-value data representations, but the approach is extensible to relational domains as well. An n-ary relation over X_1, X_2, ..., X_n is a subset of the Cartesian product $X_1 \times X_2 \times \cdots \times X_n$. A *concept* is a set of objects, each described by an n-tuple of attribute values and all sharing the same class value, that is, a relation expressing the correspondence between objects and their class. The data $E = E^+ \cup E^-$ comprise positive and negative examples, assumed to be free of noise. Each positive example is a member of the concept's extension, and the learning problem is to construct a concise intensional description of the concept (hypothesis).

If R and R' are two relations such that $R \subset R'$, then R' is more general than R. Suppose x_1 and x_2 are attributes over $X = \{0, 1\}$, and C is a class variable over $\{0, 1\}$. Let $R_1 \doteq (x_1 = 1)$ and $R_2 \doteq (x_2 = 1)$ be two relations ($\subset X^2$) in the domain theory. Given R_1 and R_2, to derive the more specific relation $R_3 \doteq R_1 \cap R_2$ corresponds to deducing $(x_1 = 1) \wedge (x_2 = 1)$ from $x_1 = 1$ and $x_2 = 1$. Conversely, given R_3, hypothesizing the more general relation R_1 corresponds to inductively inferring $(x_1 = 1)$ from $(x_1 = 1) \wedge (x_2 = 1)$.

6.2.2   Using Knowledge to Identify Concepts

Many induction methods rely on low-level similarities among the training examples, such as the mean distances between them or instance-space proximity. For difficult concepts, the gap between the primitive attributes used to describe the examples and the concept may be too wide for low-level similarities like instance-space proximity to be meaningful. Domain knowledge becomes a key to bridge this gap by identifying higher-level similarities among training examples, such as relationships between attributes. These new relations are closer to the concept, and the learning problem becomes feasible for classical induction techiques.

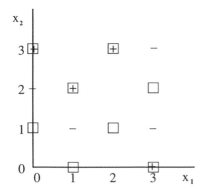

Figure 6.1
The concept $((x1$ is even$) \wedge (x2$ is odd$)) \vee ((x2$ is even$) \wedge (x1$ is odd$))$ has numerous disjuncts, many of which are not caught by the training examples (empty squares)

Figure 6.1 shows the concept $((x_1$ is even$) \wedge (x_2$ is odd$)) \vee ((x_2$ is even$) \wedge (x_1$ is odd$))$, which corresponds to numerous regions in instance space distributed in a checkerboard pattern. Sparse training samples are likely to "miss" several of these regions, indicated by empty boxes in figure 6.1. In general, the more disjunctive the concept is, the greater is the likelihood of missing concept regions. With the knowledge that this concept is symmetric about the two axes, however, the learner needs to search only half the instance space, predicting the other half using symmetry knowledge. This knowledge reduces the number of possible concepts to its square root, by augmenting the training examples.

Even a relatively weak domain theory may contain several knowledge relations, needing efficient indexing mechanisms. In our approach, input examples are used as cues for accessing relevant knowledge relations or stimuli to retrieve stored (generalized) exemplar information for creating a learning context (Smith and Medin 1981). In this manner, relations in the domain theory suggested by the data become useful for constructing new features and for learning the concept.

6.2.3   Two Kinds of Knowledge

We investigate two types of domain relations: relations among primitive attributes (*object-level knowledge*) and properties of relations such as symmetry (*higher-level* knowledge).

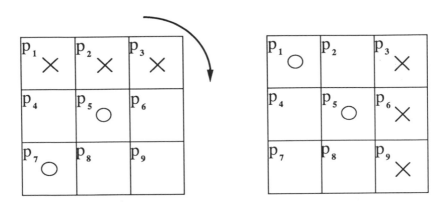

Figure 6.2
Clockwise quarter rotation of tic-tac-toe board values

Object-Level Knowledge   Consider the tic-tac-toe board shown in figure 6.2. p_1 through p_9 are the attributes used for describing the contents of board positions, 'O,' 'X,' or ' .' Let v_x represent the value of the attribute p_x, so training examples are vectors $(v_1, v_2, \ldots, v_9)$. Let $R_1 \doteq (v_1 = X) \wedge (v_2 = X)$ and $R_2 \doteq (v_2 = X) \wedge (v_3 = X)$ be two object-level relations in this domain. $R_3 \doteq R_1 \cup R_2 =$ "2 adjacent X's in the first row" derived from R_1 and R_2, is more general than either R_1 or R_2. Similarly, "3 X's in the first row" is more specific than R_3, formed by $R_1 \cap R_2$. "adjacent X's in any row" is more general than "adjacent X's in the first row." The object-level domain relations form a partially ordered hierarchy.

Higher-Level Knowledge   The second type of knowledge expresses properties of object-level relations, such as symmetry or transitivity for binary relations. Here we investigate only symmetry. A quarter-clockwise rotation of the tic-tac-toe board values in figure 6.2 is expressed by a relation with nine terms:

$$QC\ Rotation = Replace(v_3, v_1) \wedge Replace(v_6, v_2) \wedge \cdots \wedge Replace(v_9, v_7)$$

where $Replace(v_x, v_y)$ denotes replacing attribute value v_x by v_y, all replacements being done simultaneously.

The knowledge that the concept "Win-for-X" (winning, boards for X) is invariant under a quarter-clockwise rotation of the board values is equivalent to a huge number of examples for learning the concept. For instance, if a learner is trying to identify the concept Win-for-X," it could construct the hypothesis term "3-X's-in-a-row" from the training examples and use its knowledge of rotation invariance to identify the symmetric term "3-X's-in-a-column" without searching the instance space explicitly.

6.2.4   Worth of Knowledge

We investigate simple knowledge relations that are more specific than the concept to study their utility for feature construction and for learning the concept. We quantify the amount of knowledge provided by a relation in terms of the number of training examples it represents.

Let C be a concept represented by examples $E = E^+ \cup E^-$. A relation $K \subseteq C$ provides a total of $|K|$ positive examples for learning C, some of which may be present in the training examples. Therefore, K provides $|K - E^+|$ positive examples in addition to the given examples. $|K|$ is the *intrinsic* worth of K for learning C, and $|K - E^+|$ is its *net* worth in number of positive examples. The worth of an arbitrary relation K' is $|K' \cap C - E^+|$ positive examples and $|K' - K' \cap C - E^-|$ negative examples. If $K' \subseteq E$, then its net worth is 0; if K' is completely represented by the training examples, it does not provide additional examples for learning C.

Worth provides a quantitative measure of the value of knowledge relations that are more specific than the concept. The primary difficulty in estimating worth is that C is unknown. Nevertheless, worth is a useful notion for controlled experiments with artificial concepts. We use this notion to investigate relationships between data and knowledge empirically in section 6.5.

6.3   Combining Data with Knowledge

Consider learning the concept "Win-for-X," that is, 3 X's in any row, column or diagonal, in tic-tac-toe. Due to the highly disjunctive nature of this concept, a learning algorithm may not derive the correct concept from sparse training samples, as discussed in section 6.2.2. With prior knowledge about X's in two adjacent board positions and an effective mechanism to determine that this information is relevant to learning "Win-for-X," the learner can derive the correct concept more easily. In this section, we discuss the issue of combining the examples with the domain relations to change learning bias dynamically.

6.3.1 Knowledge Indexing

In the disjunctive relation learner (DRL) algorithm (section 6.5.1), the examples are first intersected with knowledge relations to order the latter based on how well they fit the data based on a probability relevance criterion (section 6.3.1). The ordered relations provide a "semantic bias" (Flann and Dietterich 1989) for hypothesis construction. DRL is similar to MIRO (Drastal, Czako, and Raatz 1989), which also uses data to drive a domain theory to find important relations. In addition, DRL also applies intersection (conjunction) and union (disjunction) to construct new relational descriptors or features. This allows for relationships among the primitive attributes to vary depending upon the domain theory as well as the training examples.

Relevance   Relevance of a knowledge relation for learning a concept is any estimate of the closeness of the relation to the concept, from the training examples. The accuracy of this estimate goes up with more training examples.

We use $p(x)$ to denote the probability estimate of event x. Given data $E = E^+ \cup E^-$, we define the relevance of a knowledge relation $K \subseteq C$ as

$$\rho(K, E) = p(K|E),$$

which denotes the probability of an event of K, given E. This expression may be evaluated by expanding $E = E^+ \cup E^-$, and applying Bayes' rule, noting that E^+ and E^- are disjoint. Alternatively, the information-gain criterion (Quinlan 1986) may also be substituted for this metric. In this chapter, we investigate only relations that are more specific than the concept $K \subseteq C$ to study their utility for induction. We simplify the relevance metric to

$$\rho(K, E) = \frac{|K \cap E^+|}{|E^+|} \times \frac{|\overline{K} \cap E^-|}{|E^-|}.$$

If H is any hypothesis consistent with E, then $p(H, E) = 1$. If $K \subseteq C$, then the second factor reduces to 1.

Relevant Relation   A relevant relation K has $\rho(K, E) > T$, where T is a predefined threshold. We set $T = 0$ in section 6.5.

6.3.2 Predicting Concept Regions

Consider the integers between $\{0, 1, \ldots, 9\}$ and the concept $C \doteq Even(x) = \{x | x \bmod 2 = 0\}$. Consider three knowledge relations:

$$R_1 = \{x | x \bmod 3 = 0\} = \{0, 3, 6, 9\}$$
$$R_2 = \{x | x \bmod 4 = 0\} = \{0, 4, 8\}$$
$$R_3 = \{x | x \bmod 5 = 0\} = \{0, 5\}$$

Given three positive examples of the concept $E = \{4, 6, 8\}$, $\rho(R_1, E) = \frac{1}{3}$, $\rho(R_2, E) = \frac{2}{3}$ and $\rho(R_3, E) = 0$, which gives an ordering $R_2 \succ R_1 \succ R_3$, where $\succ$ denotes "more relevant than." This determines a partial ordering of relational domain knowledge, depending on the particular training examples used to represent a concept. In the example, R_2 is a specialization of C, and the learner would still require additional examples to generalize the hypothesis, but the hypothesis covers the object 0, which need not be given as an example. Knowledge relations can thus help detect concept regions not represented by data.

6.4 Data and Knowledge Interaction

Relationships between data and knowledge relations influence their usefulness for concept learning. In this section, we outline some useful properties of the relevance heuristic of section 6.3.1 and theorems that result from set-theoretic considerations.

THEOREM 1 *If $K \subseteq C$ is a relevant relation for learning a concept C from data $E = E^+ \cup E^-$, then $K \cap C \neq \varnothing$.*

Proof: $\rho(K, E) > 0 \Rightarrow K \cap E^+ \neq \varnothing \Rightarrow K \cap C \neq \varnothing$.

Knowledge indexed using the relevance heuristic thus selects only relations that are "useful" for learning concepts, in the sense that they have non-null intersection with the concept (assuming relations are not used indirectly by finding their complements). Satisfying this condition, however, does not guarantee that K will provide additional information for learning C. Such information could already be fully present in the examples. K will provide additional examples for learning C if E^+ does not contain K—that is, if the worth of $K > 0$.

6.4.1 Properties of Relevance

In this section, we illustrate some useful properties of the relevance heuristic of section 6.3.1.

Subset property: *Any relation is at least as relevant as a less general one for learning any concept.* As relations are used by decreasing relevance, this property biases the learner to specialize more general relations (than the concept) first, before generalizing more specific relations.

Intersection property: *The intersection of two relations is no more relevant than either of them alone.* Applying mathematical induction, we can generalize this result to: *The intersection of relations is no more relevant than any relation alone.* If a given relation is not relevant, it will not help

1. $H := \varnothing$

2. Order the knowledge relations by decreasing ρ in a list, L_R.

3. If L_R is empty THEN $R_c :=$ any positive example.
   ELSE $R_c := R_1$, where R_1 is the first (most relevant) relation in L_R.
   Remove R_1 from L_R.

4. IF (FC is ON) & length(L_R) ≥ 2
   THEN $R_c := R_c \cap R'$.
         where R' is the first relation in L_R.
         R_c is updated only if ρ does not decrease.

5. Maximize $\rho(R_c)$:

   (a) Specialize R_c to exclude negative examples, without excluding any positive examples, giving R'.

   (b) Generalize R' to cover all the neighbouring positive examples, without including negative ones, to give H_t.

6. $H := H \cup H_t$.

7. Remove all the positive examples covered by H_t.

8. Use symmetry knowledge (if any) to construct symmetric terms, H_s.
   $H := H \cup H_s$.

9. IF there are no unclassified positive examples THEN Stop.
   ELSE recursively apply steps 4–9.

Figure 6.3
The DRL algorithm

in deduction for constructing new features and is eliminated. This is important for reducing feature construction search.

Union Property: *The union of two relations is at least as relevant as either relation alone.* We can generalize this to: *The union of relations is at least as relevant any relation alone.*

We can also apply the union property to multiple disjunctive regions in instance space of the same knowledge relation. Although one region of the relation may have null intersection with data, the relation may still be considered relevant because of non-null intersection at other regions. This allows a knowledge relation to "pick up" concept regions not covering even one example, to predict missing concept regions.

THEOREM 2 *The union of two relevant relations is at least as relevant as their intersection.*

Proof: $\rho(R_1 \cup R_2, E) \geq \rho(R_1, E) \geq \rho(R_1 \cap R_2, E)$.

This theorem and the above properties provide a basis for varying bias by constructing new relations from existing ones using $\cap$ and $\cup$, to maximize ρ. Constructing a hypothesis from relevant knowledge relations and data should work toward increasing ρ to 1. A feature construction method using intersection is described in section 6.5.1.

6.5 Effects of Knowledge on Learning

6.5.1 The DRL Algorithm

The DRL algorithm (figure 6.3) extends the AQ algorithm (Michalski 1983) by applying the bias varying methods described in sections 6.2 through 6.4. In addition it uses knowledge relations either as initial seed or to construct new features (seeds).

DRL first orders knowledge relations by relevance in a list L_R. It uses a frequency count of the examples covered by each relation (section 6.3.1) to estimate the degree to which the relation fits the concept. This approach for determining relevance has been found to have human psychological validity (Smith and Medin 1981; Bareiss and Porter 1987). The frequency count determines an initial (partial) ordering on knowledge relations. This is followed by a "lazy specialization" step, which weakens the bias initially and strengthens it later.

DRL applies a specialization and generalization process for finding a consistent (nonminimal) set cover. Knowledge relations are selected in the order of decreasing relevance, either one at a time to provide a "seed" directly for induction or (optionally) two at a time to construct a new feature, which is then used as seed. For this step, DRL uses the feature construction technique: two relevant relations are intersected. If this does not decrease relevance, the resulting feature becomes the seed. If there are no relevant relations left, a positive example is selected. The seed is the initial current relation.

A hypothesis term is constructed by first specializing the current relation to exclude negative examples, without excluding any covered positive examples. DRL then generalizes the specialized relation to cover all the neighboring positive examples, without covering negative examples. Both steps use greedy search, based on the information-gain value of an attribute. Relations are generalized by dropping literals and specialized by conjoining literals. DRL then removes all the positive examples covered by the resulting term and adds the term to the hypothesis. DRL also uses any available symmetry knowledge to predict symmetric concept terms.

DRL recursively applies the previous steps using the next relevant relations in the ordered list, until all the examples are classified correctly or a specified tolerance limit is reached.

DRL represents knowledge relations and data using Prolog (Horn) clauses and features and hypotheses using decision lists. In the next section, we analyze empirical results with DRL on two domains: Boolean functions and tic-tac-toe. Although both domains are simple, learning is exacerbated by sparse training data and highly disjunctive concepts.

6.5.2 Learning Boolean Functions Using Knowledge

In several experiments, DRL's learning behavior was measured by classification accuracy on the entire instance space. The effects of adding measured amounts of relational knowledge incrementally are illustrated for learning Boolean functions in figures 6.4 through 6.6. Artificial Boolean concepts were generated using a data generator that uses a set of propositional rules (or Horn clauses in section 6.5.3) as input. The rules express the concept in terms of intermediate relationships as described in section 6.2.3. In all experiments, domain knowledge comprised intermediate relationships that were more specific than the concept. Knowledge relations were measured by worth. The training data were a uniformly distributed

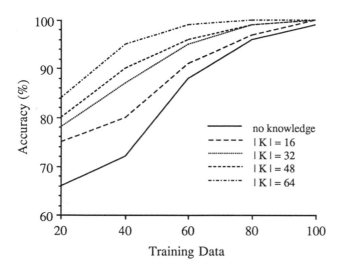

Figure 6.4
DRL learning curve

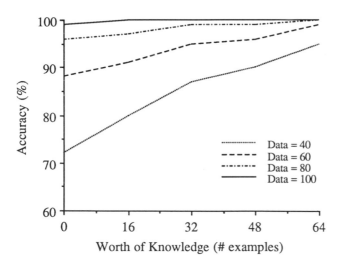

Figure 6.5
Relationship between accuracy and knowledge

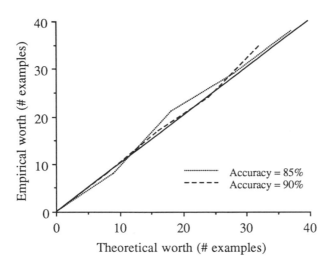

Figure 6.6
Theoretical and empirical worth of knowledge

sample drawn from the instance space. We discuss each of these experiments in detail below.

Variation of Accuracy with Data and Knowledge Figure 6.4 illustrates learning curves for four-term three-DNF boolean functions of seven variables. There is a tendency to reach a given accuracy with fewer training examples as the intrinsic worth of knowledge is increased. With sufficient knowledge, the system achieves 100% accuracy even with few training data. Alternatively, for fixed training sample size, greater accuracy is achieved with more knowledge. The inflexion in the learning curves for little or no knowledge tends to be eliminated with increasing knowledge.

The marginal utility of knowledge goes down with more training examples as more information is already present in the training examples. With sufficient training data, adding more knowledge gives little or no gain. This result delineates the utility of knowledge for improving predictive accuracy.

Figure 6.5 illustrates the relationship between knowledge and accuracy, for fixed training set sizes. The relationship becomes more linear with increasing training set size. With less knowledge, accuracy is lower for a given training size. The average slope decreases with more training data. For training data = 100, the curve is almost a horizontal line, indicating

Table 6.1
Tic-tac-toe results

Adjacency knowledge	Accuracy %	Size literals	Time (secs)
None	59.2	28	112
Row	87.2	16	65
Row and column	97.9	16	52
Row, column, and diagonal	99.3	13	34

the independence of accuracy from knowledge with sufficient training data. At the other end of the spectrum, there is high increase in accuracy with knowledge when the training set sizes are low.

Theoretical and Empirical Worth of Knowledge   Figure 6.6 shows the theoretical (predicted) net worth of the knowledge relations from figure 6.4 on the x-axis and their empirical (actual) value on the y-axis, for a given accuracy.

A fixed original set of training examples was generated. Relational knowledge was added to these examples incrementally, until DRL reached a certain accuracy (e.g., 90%). The theoretical net worth of this knowledge was calculated. The knowledge bias was then removed, and new training examples were added instead to the same original training examples. The number of additional examples was varied until the same accuracy was reached. The number of additional examples gives the empirically observed net worth. The experiment was repeated by varying the original set of training examples, for each of four different accuracy levels. Both curves shown in figure 6.6 lie close to the unit slope line, indicating close correlation between the predicted and observed values.

6.5.3   The Utility of Knowledge in Tic-Tac-Toe

We investigate the utility of domain knowledge for learning tic-tac-toe concepts. Although a relatively simple domain, highly disjunctive concepts occur in tic-tac-toe, and learning them accurately can be exacerbated by lack of sufficient training examples.

Effects of Object-Level Relations   Learning tic-tac-toe concepts with sparse training data covering 10% of instance space gave similar results as Boolean functions. Table 6.1 illustrates the behavior of DRL for learning the concept "Win-for-X" ("3-in-a-row" or "3-in-a-column" or "3-in-a-diagonal"). Domain knowledge ranged from no prior information to complete relational information for two adjacent X's in all rows, columns, and diagonals. As the amount of knowledge is increased, DRL constructs more concise hypotheses, giving greater accuracy. The size of the hypothesis is measured by the number of literals in the decision list. The algorithm also takes less time to converge as the amount of knowledge increases, since all the domain knowledge is relevant for learning this concept. This may not occur in other cases.

Symmetry Knowledge and Feature Construction   Figure 6.7 illustrates the value of symmetry knowledge and relational feature construction for learning the tic-tac-toe concept "Win-for-X" from sparse training data (10% of instance space). The symmetry knowledge is that the concept "Win-for-X" is invariant under a clockwise quarter-rotation of the board values. The *Replace*( ) relations (section 6.2.3) are input to a meta-interpreter, which takes a hypothesis term and substitutes literals.

Figure 6.7 shows considerable increase in accuracy with the addition of symmetry knowledge, compared to using no domain knowledge. DRL searches for a concept term (e.g., "3-X's-in-a-row") using the training examples and uses symmetry knowledge to predict new concept terms (e.g.,

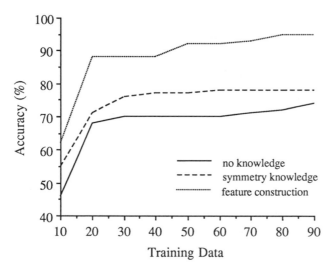

Figure 6.7
DRL accuracy for tic-tac-toe

"3-X's-in-a-column"). Thus, concept search is reduced, as discussed in section 6.2. Properties of relations like symmetries could be powerful for improving learning, exemplified by the large increase in accuracy in figure 6.7 compared to using data alone.

The utility of relational feature construction for tic-tac-toe is also shown in figure 6.7. DRL is given complete adjacency knowledge for X's (X's in two adjacent positions, for all rows, columns, and diagonals). DRL constructs new features like "3-X's-in-a-row," by intersecting relevant relations. Major accuracy improvement is achieved using with feature construction. In figure 6.7, the accuracy with feature construction is higher than even with symmetry knowledge.

Speed Improvements   Figure 6.8 illustrates the utility of knowledge for improving convergence speed. The figure shows that the DRL convergence central processing unit time for the tic-tac-toe function is highest without knowledge, increasing more than linearly with training data. With adjacency knowledge, the time improves considerably, still increasing more than linearly with data. With symmetry knowledge, the time reduces further. With sufficient training data, lowest convergence time is obtained with feature construction, increasing roughly linearly with data. Knowledge that is directly useful for learning the concept can thus help to reduce

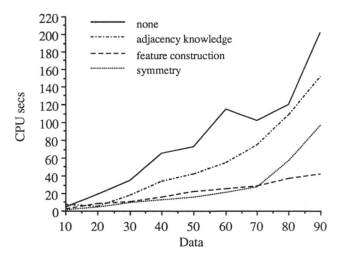

Figure 6.8
CPU convergence times for tic-tac-toe

search. In other cases or as the amount of knowledge is increased, performance could degrade.

6.6   Discussion

In this section, we discuss the relationship of three integrated learning algorithms of other researchers that are related to our approach, before summarizing.

6.6.1   Relationship to Other Methods

Exemplar-Based Learning in PROTOS   The PROTOS learning apprentice system (Bareiss and Porter 1987) is an exemplar-based heuristic classifier. PROTOS learns concepts from natural domains. Such concepts are usually characterized by large variablility and vagueness in their definition. Because matching new cases with generalized concept definitions could involve considerable deductive inference, PROTOS remembers and indexes specific training cases, minimizing deduction. PROTOS assumes "category cohesivesness" uniting all members of the same category, so that it is possible to represent each exemplar of a category by prominent features and explanations of how each feature is relevant to the category.

Exemplars are learned from training examples provided by a teacher, as well as explanations in cases where PROTOS fails to classify. Three indexing mechanisms are discussed for retrieval of exemplars from the knowledge base: reminding cues (Schank 1982), prototypicality of exemplars to their categories (Rosch and Mervis 1975), and differences between neighboring exemplars. Retrieved exemplars are used for problem solving.

DRL's indexing mechanism is similar, based on a directly estimated distance heuristic between knowledge and data. It is less dependent on the quality of the training examples or the teacher, as it also applies domain knowledge to identify similarities in the data. The data are augmented by domain knowledge, and the net composition is used for learning the concept.

Augmenting Explanations with Examples in ML-SMART   The ML-SMART system (Bergadano and Giordana 1988) uses training examples and domain knowledge for learning, integrating deduction with induction. Using a relational framework, ML-SMART uses a deductive mechanism to drive a domain theory, to operationalize tentative concept descriptions for multiple-example explanation-based learning (EBL) (DeJong and Mooney 1986; Mitchell, Keller, and Kedar-Cabelli 1986). The primary difference from pure EBL is that ML-SMART also identifies similarities in the data by obtaining explanations on many examples at the same time, permitting the system to use an incomplete domain theory (Rajamoney 1988). ML-SMART mainly uses two types of heuristics to search for the concept: statistical data-driven strategies and domain-independent heuristics in the form of "metarules," or control knowledge.

DRL does not require that a concept description be provided; it can use data and the domain knowledge to propose promising partial concept descriptions in the domain-knowledge lattice. This technique partly incorporates hypothesis testing into the generation phase itself.

Using Explanations for Constructing Features in MIRO   MIRO (Drastal, Czako, and Raatz 1989) represents a domain theory as an and/or graph denoting relations between primitive attributes. The examples are used to instantiate nodes of the graph, to determine a set of maximally proved descriptors—that is, domain relations that are maximally consistent with the training data. In this manner, MIRO constructs an abstraction language to describe examples. The proofs identify the relevant relations in the domain theory, providing a systematic basis for constructing new features. These abstract descriptors represent the data more effectively for learning.

In our relational framework, MIRO intersects the data and the domain theory, to determine relevant relations through deduction. When this relevance-determination technique provides too strong a bias toward the domain theory, a technique such as the one described in section 6.5.1 may be useful to vary the bias appropriately.

6.6.2   Conclusions

We described a relational framework for characterizing various integrated empirical learning systems combining training examples and domain knowledge. The framework forms the basis for a technique to apply simple relational knowledge in a principled manner to learn highly disjunctive concepts from sparse training samples. The approach links data with domain knowledge through feature construction.

Empirical results with the DRL algorithm illustrate the utility of knowledge for learning such concepts. Knowledge is most useful with few training examples, and its utility falls off with more examples. Symmetry knowledge can be valuable for improving learning. Knowledge-based feature construction can give considerable improvement.

The relational framework provides a perspective for analyzing integrated learning systems using both data and domain knowledge even if they use differing representation languages, by explaining learning behavior at a set-theoretic level using a homogeneous treatment of data and knowledge. Implications of knowledge quantification on results from computational theory such as sample complexity bounds (Blumer et al. 1986) or the strength of bias (Haussler 1988) remain to be investigated.

Acknowledgments

This research was supported in part by National Science Foundation grant IRI-88-22031 and an Artificial Intelligence/Cognitive Science Fellowship at the Beckman Institute. We thank the Inductive Learning Group at the Beckman Institute for useful comments on an earlier version.

References

Bareiss, E. R., and B. W. Porter. 1987. Protos: An Exemplar-Based Learning Apprentice. *Proceedings of the Fourth International Machine Learning Workshop*, 12–23.

Bergadano, F., and A. Giordana. 1990. Guiding Induction with Domain Theories. In Machine Learning: An Artificial Intelligence Approach. Vol. 3. San Mateo, Calif.: Morgan Kaufmann.

Blumer, A., A. Ehrenfeucht, D. Haussler, and M. Warmuth. 1986. Classifying Learnable Geometric Concepts with the Vapnik-Chervonenkis Dimension. *18th ACM Symposium on Theoretical Computing*, Berkeley, California, 346–389.

Breiman, L., J. Friedman, R. Olshen, and C. Stone. 1984. Classification and Regression Trees. Belmont, Calif.: Wadsworth.

DeJong, G. F., and, R. Mooney. 1986. Explanation-Based Learning: An Alternative View. Machine Learning 1:2, 145–176.

Drastal, G., G. Czako, and S. Raatz. 1989. Induction in an Abstraction Space: A Form of Constructive Induction. *Proceedings of the International Joint Conference on Artificial Intelligence*, 707–712.

Flann, N. S., and T. G. Dietterich. 1989. A Study of Explanation-Based Methods for Inductive Learning. Machine Learning 4:2.

Haussler, D. 1988. Quantifying Inductive Bias: AI Learning Algorithms and Valiant's Learning Framework. Artificial Intelligence 36:177–221.

Lebowitz, M. 1986. UNIMEM, a General Learning System: An Overview. *Proceedings of the European Conference on Artificial Intelligence*.

Michalski, R. S. 1983. A Theory and Methodology of Inductive Learning. Artificial Intelligence 20:2, 111–161.

Mitchell, T. M., R. M. Keller, and S. T. Kedar-Cabelli. 1986. Explanation-Based Generalization: A Unifying View. Machine Learning 1:1, 47–80.

Quinlan, J. R. 1986. Induction of Decision Trees. Machine Learning 1:1, 81–106.

Quinlan, J. R. 1990. Learning Logical Definitions from Relations. Machine Learning 5:3, 239–266.

Rajamoney, S. A. 1988. Explanation-based Theory Revision: An Approach to the Problems of Incomplete and Incorrect Theories. Ph.D. dissertation, University of Illinois.

Rendell, L., and R. Seshu. 1990. Learning Hard Concepts: Framework and Rationale. Computational Intelligence 6:4, 247–270.

Rendell, L., R. Seshu, and D. Tcheng. 1987. Layered Concept Learning and Dynamically-Variable Bias Management. *Proceedings of the International Joint Conference on Artificial Intelligence*. 308–314.

Rosch, E., and C. B. Mervis. 1975. Family resemblance studies in the internal structure of categories. Cognitive Psychology 7:573–605.

Schank, R. 1982. Dynamic Memory: A Theory of Reminding and Learning. Cambridge: Cambridge University Press.

Smith, E., and D. Medin. 1981. Categories and Concepts. Cambridge: Harvard University Press.

7 Learning in an Abstraction Space

George Drastal

7.1 Introduction

The concept of abstraction has played an important and well-known role in artificial intelligence since the mid-1960s. The difficulty in making use of abstraction has always been the construction of an *explicit* mapping between the problem definition in the initial space and its definition in an abstraction space. As Amarel (1968) noted, "The main difficulty in finding an appropriate abstraction ... lies in the discovery of the topology ... of its connections to the problem space." In this chapter, I report on the learning system MIRO, which performs supervised concept formation in an abstraction space constructed by the process of deduction. The mapping is exactly the set of proof structures used in this construction. I describe the method in detail for domain theories represented by rules composed of attribute-value pairs and discuss issues involved in the extension to domain theories in first-order Horn clause logic. Extensive empirical results are given that illustrate the basic ideas.

In essence, the algorithm is a two-stage process: first, construct an abstraction space, and then apply an induction method over this space. Given a domain theory, the method first builds all possible proof structures, including partial proof structures, from deduction on a set of positive and negative training instances. It then performs induction over a language defined by these *proof structures* rather than the language defined by the instances, to yield a new characteristic concept description. The set of descriptors (or predicates) that are consequences of this deduction is viewed as the abstraction space, the set of descriptors used to describe the instances is viewed as the initial space, and the set of proof structures is viewed as the mapping between the two spaces. While the concept description formed is not justifiable in the sense of explanation-based generalization (Mitchell, Keller, and Kedar-Cabelli 1986), the descriptors from which it is composed are justifiable. The method is able to extend an incomplete domain theory with a set of rules that represent a disjunctive concept derived from a batch of training instances. These inductively derived rules may be used in the same way as the original domain theory, when a new batch of instances is presented and can support incremental refinement of the concept. It is also possible to regard this method as a form of constructive induction (Michalski 1983) in which "probably useful" relations are encoded in the domain theory. However, I propose a strong form of deductive bias as a means of limiting the number of constructed descriptors.

The motivation for this work is to address the known weaknesses associated with both induction and explanation-based learning methods. In the case of conventional induction methods, it may take an exponential number of training instances to form a concept description (Haussler 1987); coincidental patterns may be "noticed" and incorporated erroneously into the concept description, and attribute noise—the presence of random errors in the training data—is difficult for many methods to handle (Laird 1988). The explanation-based methods incorporate the weaknesses associated with knowledge-based systems: intractable, incomplete, brittle, or difficult-to-construct domain theories. I consider a knowledge-based approach coupled with induction that allows for a meaningful trade-off between the added cost of deduction and solving the above problems.

I present empirical studies that yield evidence for the following conjectures about learning in an abstraction space (as opposed to learning in the initial space). First, such learning can be more efficient because the abstraction space is by construction more compact than is the initial space. Second, forming a concept description in an abstraction space can reduce the number of misclassifications, because the deduction process biases the induction process in favor of constructed features that are more relevant in the task domain. I show evidence that a significant improvement in generalization can be expected. Third, this approach can offer an effective method of handling the problem of attribute noise. I show that even with injection of 30% of attribute noise into the training set, the method presented here is able to construct a "corrected" characteristic concept description. The empirical studies are based not on single runs or even a few trials but on controlled, randomized, and exhaustive testing of many hundreds of trials.

In the next section I present the basic idea of constructing an abstraction space via deduction and set the terminology for the chapter. I also relate this construction to the learning model due to Valiant (1984). In section 7.3, I give an overview of the method, which is implemented as the program MIRO. In section 7.4, I describe a heuristic technique related to postpruning that detects and *corrects* for feature noise in training

instances. Section 7.5 presents the empirical results of applying this induction method in the abstraction space. I point out in section 7.6 the
connections to related work, including attempts to combine empirical and
explanation-based learning and constructive induction. Finally, I draw
some conclusions and discuss open problems. This chapter is an expanded
version of Drastal and Raatz (1988), Drastal, Raatz, and Czako (1989),
and Drastal (1991).

7.2   Abstraction Spaces

This section presents the central ideas related to the use of an abstraction space in induction.

7.2.1   Abstraction and Learnability

I start by giving a detailed geometric example that introduces the relationship between the ideas of abstraction, induction, and domain theory. Consider an instance or *initial* space $\mathscr{I} = \{0, 1\}^n$ in which an instance may be
viewed as a vector $(x_1, \ldots, x_n)$ of n binary descriptors. Thus, in the case of
$n = 3$, the triple $(1, 0, 1)$ denotes the instance in which descriptor x_1 is
present, x_2 is absent, and x_3 is present. Such a vector can be viewed
geometrically as a vertex of an n-dimensional cube on the axes of the
descriptors $x_1, \ldots, x_n$. A concept can be viewed in terms of an n-dimen-
sional region, so that points inside the region are positive instances of the
concept and points outside are negative instances. Given a sample S of
positive and negative instances of an unknown target concept R_T, where
$S \subseteq \mathscr{I}$, the problem of selective induction is to find a concept description
$u(\mathbf{x})$ such that for any instance $\mathbf{x} \in \mathscr{I}$, $u(\mathbf{x}) = 1$ if $\mathbf{x}$ is a positive instance
and $u(\mathbf{x}) = 0$ if $\mathbf{x}$ is a negative instance.[1]
  Consider the following example in which $n = 3$.

EXAMPLE 2.1   *Let Pos* $= \{(0, 0, 0), (1, 1, 1)\}$, *and Neg* $= \{(0, 1, 0), (1, 1, 0)\}$, *as
depicted in figure* 7.1.

  The concept description

$$R = x_3 \vee \neg x_2$$

correctly labels every vertex in the cube as either positive or negative.
Notice that this concept description is not specific in that it classifies four

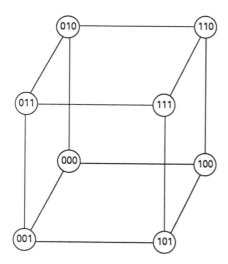

Figure 7.1
Instance space

instances (001), (011), (101), (100) as positive in addition to the positive instances (000), (111) given in the problem statement. In fact, there are other concept descriptions consistent with the above observed instances, and a particular induction method with a particular bias will prefer one over others. I will argue that induction in an abstraction space constructed by deduction can be more effective if the domain theory encodes a preference for certain concept descriptions.

Since there are 2^{2^n} possible labelings in an n-dimensional cube, one well-known problem in selective induction is to find a computationally efficient method to form the concept description. A second problem for selective induction is that it works well only when the target concept encloses a small number of contiguous regions of instance space (Rendell 1988). In general, a concept R is arbitrarily disjunctive, and the complexity of selective induction is NP-hard (Rivest 1989). We would like a method that can predict disjuncts that are "distant" from positive training instances in the sense that they define regions that are not contiguous with regions containing only observed positive instances. This can be accomplished only by applying some kind of prior knowledge that supports an *expectation* of class membership in a region A based on evidence for class membership in region B (figure 7.2). However, arbitrary application of

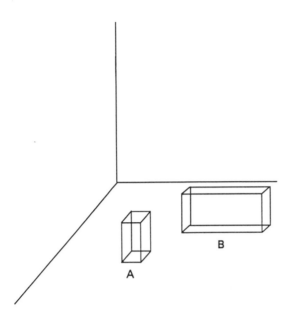

Figure 7.2
Noncontiguous concept

such a strategy can result in the proliferation of descriptors constructed to describe class membership in distant regions. Thus, the problem becomes how to pick the useful constructed descriptors.

Amarel (1968) has shown that the choice of representation can have a crucial effect on computational complexity of problem solving and that, in particular, a shift in representation from the initial problem definition to a more abstract problem definition is a potentially powerful technique. Selective induction depends fundamentally upon the premise that implicit disjunction is a valid representational shorthand, which in the case of binary descriptors means that the values of some descriptors are uncorrelated with $u(\mathbf{x})$. This is indeed a valid premise if "typical" or "useful" classes are representable by contiguous regions of space built up from primitive regions, by applying few union and intersection operations.[2] That is, $u(\mathbf{x})$ is well behaved over the domain of $\mathbf{x}$. If the initial space $\mathscr{I}$ does not have this property, we can attempt to create the property by applying a transformation to $\mathscr{I}$ that preserves the correct assignment of labels to positive and negative instances, giving a descriptor space where concept descriptions are well behaved. We call the result of such a transformation an *abstraction* space $\mathscr{A}$ and the descriptors of which it is composed *abstract* descriptors. We think of the domain theory D as a lens that focuses the information of the initial space into a more compact representation in the abstract space.

In terms of our geometric view of induction, such a transformation maps a vertex $\mathbf{x}$ in an n-dimensional cube representing the initial space onto a vertex $\mathbf{x}'$ of an m-dimensional cube representing the space of abstract descriptors, such that a topologically complex region surrounding some positive instances $\{\mathbf{x}_1, \ldots, \mathbf{x}_k\}$ in the initial space corresponds to a simple region around their image $\{\mathbf{x}'_1, \ldots, \mathbf{x}'_l\}$ in the abstract space.

The previous example illustrates this principle for a simple problem in discriminant concept formation. In the initial space, no purely conjunctive concept is consistent, although several disjunctive ones exist. One consistent disjunction is the union of two overlapping regions that cover other vertices outside the training set. Without prior knowledge about the interpretation of this domain, there is no basis (other than the Occam's razor bias that favors short conjunctions) for believing that instances (001), (011), (101), (100) should necessarily be classified positive. However, if we introduce the following rules for shifting the representation to an abstract space $\mathscr{A}$,

$$x_4 = equal(x_1, x_3)$$
$$x_5 = notequal(x_1, x_2),$$

and then redescribe the problem in terms of descriptors x_4, x_5 *alone*, a simple conjunctive solution can be found (figure 7.3).

Now the concept description

$$R_{\mathscr{A}} = x_4 \wedge \neg x_5$$

correctly classfies all instances in the abstract space $\mathscr{A}$. I argue in the next section that a typical learning method will find this solution in the abstraction space with less computation than would be possible in the initial space. But the crucial point is that the result is also more likely to generalize beyond the training set since it incorporates the bias that was deliberately engineered into the transformation rules and expresses exactly the concept that x_1, x_2, and x_3 have the same value.

Returning to the example, we assume that an induction method can form a concept description using only regions parallel to the faces of the

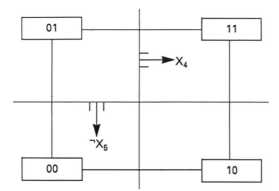

Figure 7.3
Abstract space

cube. Thus, the concept description in the initial space is the union of the front face for x_3 and the bottom face for $\neg x_2$. But this is not the most specific description since it covers six instances rather than two. We cannot expect a general induction method with a fixed bias to prefer our intended concept that x_1, x_2, and x_3 have the same value. However, if prior knowledge is available in the form of a domain theory (of transformation rules), an abstraction space can be constructed that encodes this bias. To operationalize the domain theory in the sense of explanation-based learning, the descriptor x_4 corresponds to all instances such that $x_1 = x_2$, for instance. In our example, it is as if an induction method can use a plane at any pitch to form its concept description. Thus, the node $(0, 1)$ in figure 7.3 corresponds to the intersection of the regions shown in figure 7.4, resulting in an exact description of the target concept.

We investigate the use of domain theory to construct an abstraction space and its effect on concept learning for classification tasks. Sections 7.2.3 and 7.3 describe a general method based on the intuitions presented here. The example illustrates two of the three central points that I will focus on throughout this chapter. First, careful use of domain theory can reduce the computational cost of induction. Second, induction can exploit the a priori information contained in a domain theory to select a concept that more closely approximates the target concept with a fixed number of training instances. I also show in section 7.4 that the approach offers a method of successfully dealing with attribute noise. First I give a relation-

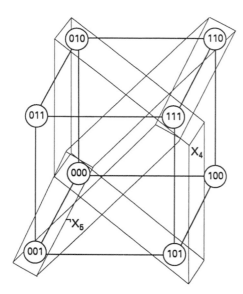

Figure 7.4
R_A in the initial space

ship between the initial space and the abstraction space in terms of the Vapnik-Chervonenkis dimension.

7.2.2 Abstraction and the Vapnik-Chervonenkis Dimension

The task of finding a perfect concept description from examples is generally intractable if it is well defined at all (Valiant 1984). A more useful expression of the computational complexity of learning is given in Blumer et al. (1986) by the relationship between a problem's Vapnik-Chervonenkis (VC) dimension and the number of training instances required to attain a probably approximately correct (PAC) concept. If a shift in representation from an initial space to an abstract space improves complexity within this framework, this improvement will manifest itself by reducing the problem's VC dimension. I give a brief review the relevant terminology and refer the reader to Blumer et al. (1986) for details.

As before, assume that training instances are given in the space $\mathscr{I} = \{0,1\}^n$ and a specific instance $\mathbf{x}$ is given by a set

$$\mathbf{x} = \{x_1, \ldots, x_k, \bar{x}_{k+1}, \ldots, \bar{x}_l\},$$

where for each $x_j \in \mathbf{x}$ $(1 \leq j \leq l)$, x_j is intepreted as descriptor x_j is present in instance $\mathbf{x}$ and $\bar{x}_j$ is interpreted as descriptor x_j is absent from instance $\mathbf{x}$. For a set $S = Pos \cup Neg$ of training instances, we say

$$L = \{x | x \in \mathbf{x}, \mathbf{x} \in S\}$$

is the *initial concept description language*. Let R_T be the target concept, and let the rule space $\mathscr{R}$ in which it is represented be all k-term-disjunctive normal form (DNF) formulas over L. In this model we assume that there is a fixed but arbitrary probability density function P defined on $\mathscr{I}$ such that for any instance $\mathbf{x} \in \mathscr{I}$, the probability that the next sample drawn is $P(\mathbf{x})$. Each sample consists of an instance and its classification as either positive, $\mathbf{x} \in R_T$, or negative, $\mathbf{x} \notin R_T$. We refer to the learning problem in the *initial space* $\mathscr{I}$ as the problem of forming a characteristic concept description for R_T using the descriptors in L.

In the next section I will give a detailed method for construction of an abstraction space through the process of deduction. For now, we assume $\mathscr{L}_{\mathscr{A}}$ to be the *abstract concept description language* constructed through deduction from a domain theory and refer to the learning problem in an *abstraction space* $\mathscr{A}$ as the problem of forming a characteristic concept description for R_T using the descriptors in $L_{\mathscr{A}}$.

A learning method (in either an initial or abstraction space) accepts an accuracy parameter ε and a confidence parameter δ (Valiant 1984). After drawing a number of samples, the induction method produces a concept description R, which may or may not be different from the target concept R_T. The concept R is *approximately correct* if the probability that R and R_T will classify an instance drawn according to P differently is at most ε. If for any rule space $\mathscr{R}$, probability distribution P, parameters ε and δ, the probability that the output is approximately correct is at least $1 - \delta$, the induction method is said to be probably approximately correct, and the space $\mathscr{R}$ is said to be PAC-learnable.

In order for the induction method to learn any R_T representable in $\mathscr{R}$, the measured error rate of each concept $R \in \mathscr{R}$ must be a good estimate of the true error rate. In 1971, Vapnik and Chervonenkis gave a characterization of classes of concepts for which the measured error rate converges uniformly to the true error rate.

DEFINITION 7.1   *The Vapnik-Chervonenkis dimension of a rule space $\mathscr{R}$ is the largest d such that there exists a set S of d instances, such that for every* subset $U \subset S$ there exists a concept $R \in \mathcal{R}$ such that $U = S \cap R$ (Vapnik and Chervonenkis 1971).

Blumer et al. (1986) subsequently gave an upper bound on the number $m(\varepsilon, \delta)$ of examples needed by an induction method to learn in a rule space $\mathcal{R}$ in terms of its VC dimension d:

$$m(\varepsilon, \delta) = max\left(\frac{4}{\varepsilon} ln \frac{2}{\delta}, \frac{8d}{\varepsilon} ln \frac{13}{\varepsilon}\right).$$

What improvement should we expect as a result of a shift in representation from an initial space to an abstract space? If we assume that a hard induction task is one that exhibits high dimensionality and disjunctiveness, the effects of $\mathcal{R}$ should dominate this bound on sample complexity. Since the number of samples needed to learn a concept depends on d, we measure the complexity of the rule space $\mathcal{R}$ in which the target concept R_T is representable. For a finite $\mathcal{R}$, the VC dimension of the rule space $\mathcal{R}$ is given by the formula $d = log|\mathcal{R}|$ as developed in Rivest (1989).

Our representation is k-term-DNF over n descriptors. Since a descriptor can be true, false, or unknown, there are 3^n possible 1-term-DNF rules and

$$|\mathcal{R}| = \binom{3^n}{k}$$

possible k-term-DNF formulas. Thus the VC dimension is just

$$d = log|\mathcal{R}| = log\binom{3^n}{k}.$$

Using Stirling's approximation for $n!$ and the assumption that 3^n is much greater than k, we can simplify this to $d = k(n \, log \, 3 - log \, e)$. When d is sufficiently large, sample complexity will be proportional to d, and we can measure the expected improvement simply in terms of the dimensionality n and disjunctiveness k. Let $m_{\mathcal{I}}(\varepsilon, \delta)$ and $m_{\mathcal{A}}(\varepsilon, \delta)$ represent sample complexity in the initial and abstract space, respectively. Let $k_{\mathcal{A}}$ stand for the value of k in the k-term-DNF representation of the abstraction space, $k_{\mathcal{I}}$ for the value of k in the initial space, $n_{\mathcal{A}}$ for the number of descriptors in the abstract language $L_{\mathcal{A}}$, and $n_{\mathcal{I}}$ for the number of descriptors in the initial language L. If $k_{\mathcal{A}} < k_{\mathcal{I}}$ and $n_{\mathcal{A}} < n_{\mathcal{I}}$, the expected improvement is a ratio

$$\frac{m_{\mathscr{I}}(\varepsilon, \delta)}{m_{\mathscr{A}}(\varepsilon, \delta)} = O\left(\frac{k_{\mathscr{I}} n_{\mathscr{I}}}{k_{\mathscr{A}} n_{\mathscr{A}}}\right).$$

If $R \in \mathscr{R}_{\mathscr{I}}$ implies that $R \in \mathscr{R}_{\mathscr{A}}$, then ε will either be smaller in the abstraction space, or for fixed ε, $m_{\mathscr{A}}(\varepsilon, \delta)$ can be smaller than $m_{\mathscr{I}}(\varepsilon, \delta)$.

It is important to remember that the number $m(\varepsilon, \delta)$ of examples needed by an induction method to learn in a rule space $\mathscr{R}$ is an asymptotic worst-case number. It remains to be seen if learning problems exist that exhibit the behavior that $m_{\mathscr{A}}(\varepsilon, \delta)$ is substantively smaller than $m_{\mathscr{I}}(\varepsilon, \delta)$. In section 7.5, I will present empirical results suggesting that this is the case. In fact, I will argue that this can be expected in the presence of a "well-engineered" or "appropriate" domain theory. In order to make the concept of a well-engineered domain theory more precise, I introduce the following terminology. If whenever R_T is a member of the initial hypothesis space, R_T is also contained in the abstract hypothesis space, the mapping is *appropriate*. Assuming the mapping is *appropriate*, we call it *effective* if $k_{\mathscr{A}} < k_{\mathscr{I}}$, and *compact* if $n_{\mathscr{A}} < n_{\mathscr{I}}$.

Why should the mapping be compact? In naturally occurring problems, the members of a class are grouped together because of a common function, a shared intent of an intelligent agent that constructed them, or a common causal antecedent (i.e., a set of defining preconditions). This set of essential properties can be realized in many ways. Although instances may exhibit such great diversity in their initial space representation that it is difficult to find patterns empirically, each instance is a manifestation of a class that has an underlying intent or functionality. Mapping each instance into relevant abstract descriptors will reveal intraclass similarities and interclass differences. Deduction from this diversity of observable features has the purpose in concept formation of highlighting the invariants in the class. Once deduction has recovered the essential properties of each instance, represented by a smaller set of abstract descriptors, characterization of the class by its members' common properties is simplified.

Why should the mapping be effective? We argue from the nature of the classification task, which must identify an instance's essential properties despite superficially variable patterns and from engineering the domain theory. The efficacy of the method depends on how well, for typical or useful problems, the domain theory can map a complex and irregularly shaped region of initial space onto a simple region of abstract space. Its efficiency depends on quickly finding an appropriate set of abstract descriptors, and thus of simple regions, so that $L_{\mathscr{A}}$ is small. This, in turn, requires that despite the absence of a prior characterization for the class to be learned, the domain theory contains appropriate descriptors at or near its most abstract level. In other words, an effective mapping is one that constructs a small number of descriptors that are subsequently used in a compact encoding of R_T. Conversely, the method is inefficient if the only way of discriminating training instances is by examining patterns of initial descriptors. Stated in terms of Rendell's (1986) framework, the *inductive gain* attributable to restriction of the language increases as L contains more abstract descriptors, because they typically permit a greater *inductive compression*. Since the total inductive gain in $u(\mathbf{x})$ is fixed by the number of classes (two) and the number of possible initial descriptors, the inductive load on the algorithm decreases with more abstract descriptors in L.

7.2.3   Discussion: The Role of Knowledge Engineering

We consider the role of knowledge engineering in the method and the question of the relevancy of abstract descriptors in a domain theory for solving a given problem, that is, of acquiring an unknown concept. In order for a domain theory to provide a large inductive gain when solving a "typical" problem, it should be engineered with care to separate its abstract deductive consequences as much as possible from the details of how that abstract concept is realized or manifested in initial descriptors. This is best done by keeping in mind that a class is cohesive by virtue of its members' common purpose, function, or intent of an intelligent agent that created or gathered them together. Indeed, this pushes part of the learning problem back into the realm of knowledge engineering.

It is reasonable to assume that a characteristic concept description constructed out of partial proofs is useful, since the domain theory is engineered so that most rules encode causal relations between possible states that are shared across the whole domain, or they encode definitions of functional properties that are believed to be potentially relevant for explaining behavior in the domain. An abstract descriptor infrequently will be used to denote a class name, in contrast to explanation-based learning, where a goal concept is exactly the name of the concept to be learned. Abstract descriptors that do represent a class should not be defined directly in terms of operational descriptors, since such rules are specific to that class and are unlikely to match training instances of a new class.

Deduction is used to recover the essential properties of an instance. But why deduction, and why use a domain theory for mapping? Why is this shift of representation different from deriving descriptors in constructive induction? Watanabe (1985) has argued that preference in forming a class is an artificial consequence of the choice of a formal language in which to characterize the class. In constructive induction, care must be taken to ensure that derived descriptors do not multiply uncontrolled. Deduction exploits the focus on essential properties that can be engineered into the domain theory. This approach provides a deductive justification for the selection of a concept description language, while utilizing the empirical evidence found in a set of training data.

Even with a perfectly correct domain theory and noise-free instances, a concept representable in $R_{\mathcal{I}}$ might not be representable in $R_{\mathcal{A}}$. For example, any domain theory (which is an acyclic forest) can be augmented by a rule from every root of a tree to the abstract descriptor *thing*. Then the most abstract description of every instance is truly *thing*, but they are no longer distinguishable in this space. Because deduction has an explicit sequence of derivations, when the deductive bias is too strong (as in this example), it is possible to relax the bias systematically, while preserving it as much as possible consistent with finding a solution. It is important to be able to do that since we require that R_T be representable in $R_{\mathcal{A}}$.

If we assume the deductive theory is free of error (though it may be incomplete) and if $R_T \in R_{\mathcal{I}}$ implies $R_T \in R_{\mathcal{A}}$, then an unbiased inductor can in principle find an assignment of labels to vertices in $\mathcal{A}$ that corresponds to a correct assignment of labels to vertices in the initial descriptor space. However, the problem remains of finding a sufficient set of abstract descriptors that will form the language $L_{\mathcal{A}}$. Thus, we have the search through a space of languages that terminates when an L is found such that a discriminant can be constructed in L. We will see that evaluating the appropriateness of L can be costly, so we want to ensure that the cost of this search does not eliminate the savings that accrue from the fact that $n_{\mathcal{A}} < n_{\mathcal{I}}$.

7.3 Constructing the Concept Description

The method outlined in this section has been implemented as the program MIRO and is the basis for the experimental results presented in section 7.5.

7.3.1 Overview of the Method

The analytic stage that constructs the language $L_{\mathscr{A}}$ is directly applicable only to domain theories of rules composed of descriptor-value pairs but illustrates topics that are applicable in other types of domain theories. In section 7.5, I will offer strong empirical evidence to back up the three claims mentioned in the introduction for domain theories constructed of rules composed of descriptor-value pairs. However, the construction is general and can be applied to any domain theory representable as an and/or graph. The inductive stage is based on the one-sided variant (Haussler 1987) of the candidate elimination (or version space) algorithm (Mitchell 1978). The algorithm is applied to a seed $x_s \in Pos$ and to all negative instances to yield a set G of discriminant concept descriptions. Each element of G is a conjunction of descriptors drawn from a concept description language, and an element of G covers a subset of Pos, including the seed. I will call it a *partial concept description* if it covers only a subset of Pos and a *complete concept description* if it is a disjunction of partial descriptions that covers all of Pos. Since we require a complete description, candidate elimination is applied repeatedly in order to construct a disjunction of terms. A new seed is used and one partial concept description is selected from the G set on each cycle. Selection from the G set depends on a measure of credibility described shortly. This method resembles the AQ11 algorithm (Michalski 1973) and shares with it a degree of tolerance to errors in the instances.

In order to obtain a characteristic partial description, each discriminant partial description is specialized by adding descriptors from an augmented language into the conjunction. This entails a search guided by the same heuristic measure used to select an element from the G set. The instances covered by each partial characteristic description are then removed from the set Pos. The algorithm terminates when a complete description is found or some positive instances remain that have been tried as seeds and cannot be discriminated from the set Neg. In addition, there is a facility for detecting and correcting instances with attribute noise. I summarize the method in pseudo-code as follows.

Construct abstract language $L_{\mathscr{A}}$.
set characteristic concept description $R \leftarrow \varnothing$;
set initialize concept description language L to a subset of $L_{\mathscr{A}}$;

do while *Pos* ≠ ∅
    Choose a seed $\mathbf{x}_s \in Pos$;
    set $G \leftarrow \varnothing$;
    Invoke Candidate Elimination on $\mathbf{x}_s \cup Neg$,
           returning general version space G;
    do while $G = \varnothing$
      if All initial descriptors are already in L
        then Fail due to indistinguishable training instances
        else Select a descriptor and add to L;
      Restart Candidate Elimination with augmented L;
    end;
    Perform search from G, returning conjunction C;
    set $R \leftarrow R \vee C$;
    set $Pos \leftarrow Pos - \{\mathbf{x} | \mathbf{x} \in Pos, \mathbf{x} \text{ covered by } C\}$;
end;
Perform heuristic error correction on R;

7.3.2 Construction of the Abstraction Space

Let D be a set of rules forming a domain theory. These rules may be first-order Horn clauses, rules in an expert system, or rules composed of descriptors as in

$$x \leftarrow x_1, \ldots, x_k, \overline{x}_{k+1}, \ldots, \overline{x}_n.$$

The key restriction is that D must be representable as a finite acyclic and/or graph (Nilsson 1980) (so that arbitrary first-order theories, for instance, are not allowed). However, D may contain rules composed of descriptors that are not in the set L, and thus it is possible for the domain theory to introduce descriptors that are not in the initial language L. It is useful to note that a rule of the form $x \leftarrow x_1, \ldots, x_k, \overline{x}_{k+1}, \ldots, \overline{x}_n$ is equivalent to a first-order Horn clause with monadic descriptors, as in,

$$\forall v [x(v) \leftarrow x_1(v), \ldots, x_k(v), \overline{x}_{k+1}(v), \ldots, \overline{x}_n(v)],$$

so that we can speak of substitutions, negation, proofs and other terms related to deductive logic. We will use such a domain theory to construct an alternate concept description language.

    Let $G_D = (V, E)$ be the *and/or* graph induced by a set D of rules in which V is a set of nodes labeled with pairs $(A, bool)$, where A is a descriptor in

D, and *bool* a syntactic variable over the values **t** for truth and **f** for falsehood. The set E of edges is defined as usual so that an *and*-edge is represented by a set of edges with the same index label and an *or*-edge by a singleton edge. A deduction from a training instance on this representation is performed by a *bottom-up propagation of truth* according to the following rules. Truth is propagated from node n_1 to node n_2 along an *or*-edge if n_1 is true. Truth is propagated from nodes $n_1, \ldots, n_k$ to node m along an *and*-edge if the nodes $n_1, \ldots, n_k$ are all true. A graph is initialized with all truth values *bool* set to **f**. The deduction mechanism is uniform for both positive and negative training instances. Finally, for domain theory D and training instance **x**, the graph G_D with the "truth" of **x** fully propagated is denoted G_D^x.

Given a set of instances that includes both positive and negative examples, the proof of some positive instances may overlap the proof of some negative instances; that is, some node in G_D may be marked **t** in the explanation of both a positive and negative instance. In this case, an induction method may form a characteristic concept description containing the negation of descriptors in order to cover positive instances without covering negative instances. We represent negation by marking the edge from a negative literal as a *negative edge* and invoking a kind of negation as failure (Clark 1978) rule: if a node labeled x cannot be marked **t**, then a node labeled $\bar{x}$ may be marked **t**, and if a node labeled x can be marked **t**, then a node $\bar{x}$ cannot be marked **t**. Rules with negative consequents are not permitted in the domain theory. It is possible to have a combinatorial number of deductions depending on the order of the instances. Although this has not been a problem in practice, it is straightforward to impose a linear ordering on the predicates and automatically rearrange a training instance to obey this ordering. With this refinement, it can be shown that the number of proofs for any training instance is linear in the number of edges and nodes of a graph.

We will say a descriptor is a *root descriptor* if it is the label of a node in a graph G_D that has outdegree 0 (a root) and a *minimal* or *initial descriptor* if it is a node with indegree 0 (a leaf). We say **x** *proves* x, denoted $\mathbf{x} \vdash x$, if for instance **x**, truth can be propagated to a node labeled x. If $\mathbf{x} \vdash x$ and the node labeled with x has no successor proved in the graph G_D^x, we say x is a *maximally proved descriptor*, denoted $\mathbf{x} \vdash x$ *maximal*. We also write $\mathbf{x} \vdash x$ *initial* for a node that is a leaf and has no successor proved. Note

that a maximally proved descriptor is *not* necessarily maximal in that it
need not be a root.

The set of maximally proved descriptors plays a central role in the work
to follow. Let

$$L_{\mathscr{A}} = \{(x, \alpha) | \exists \mathbf{x} \in \{Pos \cup Neg\}, \mathbf{x} \vdash x \ maximal,$$
$$\alpha \ a \ pointer \ to \ the \ node \ in \ G_D^{\mathbf{x}} \ labeled \ x\}.$$

The set $L_{\mathscr{A}}$ is *explicitly constructed* as a set of pairs consisting of a descriptor x and the *proof* that established x. Each instance $\mathbf{x}$ potentially generates a set

$$\{(x_1, \alpha_1), (x_2, \alpha_2), (x_3, \alpha_3)\}$$

of pairs of maximally proved descriptors and pointers to $G_D^{\mathbf{x}}$. In a sense,
Amarel's (1968) term *connections* is appropriate, since we will need to
perform a tree traversal of these proof structures in order to define an
induction method that makes use of the abstraction space. We do not pass
proof structures to induction but keep these structures, so that if induction
using maximal descriptors fails, we have information as to how to recon-
struct (augment) the language. This will be explained in detail in the next
section.

As before, we let $L_{\mathscr{A}}$ be the *abstract concept description language* and
refer to the learning problem in an *abstraction space* $\mathscr{A}$ as the problem of
forming a concept description for R_T using the descriptors in $L_{\mathscr{A}}$. The set
of proofs or proof structures is the mapping from the initial to the abstraction space. The set $L_{\mathscr{A}}$ does not necessarily have to be more compact than
L (since the domain theory can introduce new descriptors). However, this
will almost always be the case for reasonable examples. Note that the
concept description language used in the induction component is initialized to a subset of the abstraction space $L_{\mathscr{A}}$.

7.3.3 The Role of the Candidate Elimination Algorithm

The deductive stage provides a means of constructing a concept description language that is deductively biased in the sense that the abstract
descriptors are deductive consequents of the set of initial descriptors. This
bias is exploited to its fullest if only maximal abstract descriptors are
admitted into the language, which has the additional advantage of controlling the size of the concept description language L. However, a maxi-

mally biased language may not be adequate for inducing a discriminant concept description, because even a noise-free positive instance that is distinguishable from *Neg* in the instance language may be indistinguishable in *L*. Since we do not know how to adjust the amount of deductive bias in advance but prefer to use the strongest possible bias, it is important that the induction algorithm be able to tell when the bias is too strong. The candidate elimination algorithm is an efficient method that meets this requirement. It is an *unbiased inductor* that generates all expressions in *L* consistent with its training sets. If the training sets input to candidate elimination are indistinguishable by any expression in *L*, the algorithm returns an empty version space and terminates. This signals that *L* is insufficiently expressive to distinguish the classes. Although we will not define it formally, by analogy we can think in terms of searching a space of concept description languages in the direction of strong to weak bias, where candidate elimination has the role of testing for a goal state. Of course, candidate elimination also returns a version space when it "finds" a goal state.

The most straightforward use of candidate elimination is to construct a disjunctive version space that is consistent with *Pos* and *Neg*, using the standard two-sided strategy, resulting in a set *S* of maximally specific concept descriptions. However, this strategy could expend extensive computational resources only to determine that *L* is inadequate. Instead, we construct a conjunctive version space using a one-sided strategy, resulting in a set *G* of maximally general partial concept descriptions. This permits the introduction of a controllable bias in choosing each seed, without defeating the unbiased inductor property that is required to search the space of languages. The cost of discovering that *L* is inadequate with respect to the seed and *Neg* is also much smaller.

The concept description language *L* is defined as the set

$$L = \{x | \exists \mathbf{x} \in \{Pos \cup Neg\}, \mathbf{x} \vdash x \text{ maximal}\}$$
$$- \{x | \exists \mathbf{x} \in \{Pos \cup Neg\}, \mathbf{x} \vdash x \text{ initial}\}$$
$$- \{x | \forall \mathbf{p} \in Pos, \mathbf{p} \vdash x \text{ and } \forall \mathbf{n} \in Neg, \mathbf{n} \vdash x\}$$

Since the set of descriptors

$$\{x | \exists \mathbf{x} \in \{Pos \cup Neg\}, \mathbf{x} \vdash x \text{ maximal}\}$$

is the definition of the abstract language $L_{\mathscr{A}}$, the concept description language L is a subset of $L_{\mathscr{A}}$. The language L is strongly biased toward constructing a concept description out of the most abstract descriptors proved in any instances. Descriptors whose value is invariant over all training instances clearly do not occur in the G set. Therefore they can be removed from the concept description language without loss of generality. Descriptors that are true in all instances are readmitted later when searching for a characteristic description.

Suppose that the seed cannot be discriminated from *Neg* in the language L (i.e., the G set collapses in the candidate elimination algorithm), but there exists a discriminant description in the instance language. Then at least one abstract descriptor $x \in L$ must have antecedent descriptors in different proof structures that are needed for a discriminant description in *some* adequate language. Since we wish to find an adequate language having the strongest possible deductive bias, we define the candidates to augment L as the set

$Cand = \{x \mid x \notin L$ and x has different values in the seed and
                 the negative instance causing the G set to collapse$\}$

We throw out all nonmaximal candiates. If more than one candidate is left, the choice of candidate x attempts to maximize the potential discriminant value of its proof subtrees by a heuristic related to heuristics used in optimal decision-tree methods (Quinlan 1986). In the event that a seed is indistinguishable from *Neg* in the instance language, no descriptor can be added, and the seed is set aside as a special case for the error-correction module. Note that the choice of x is not guaranteed to result in an adequate language L', and successive additions may be needed. In principle, the entire set of initial descriptors could be added one at a time this way. This would amount to retracting gradually and completely the deductive bias encoded in a (presumably inappropriate) domain theory. In practice, the addition of more than two descriptors was a rare event in our series of experiments.

If all version space candidates generated prior to the collapse have been retained (including marking those instances covered by each candidate conjunction), then it is possible to generate all the new candidate conjunctions that contain new descriptors without regenerating old candidates. This may be an important consideration for efficiency, but in fact we simply restart the candidate elimination algorithm with a new language L'. Once a nonempty G set is returned, it becomes the basis for constructing a characteristic partial description. However, it is first necessary to establish what is desired in a characteristic description.

7.3.4   A Heuristic Measure over Concept Descriptions

We define a measure of credibility $\Gamma(C)$ for a partial concept description C, which attempts to measure the "correctness" of C ($\mu(C)$ in Rendell's (1986) terminology). The quantity $\Gamma(C)$ is designed to balance the empirical support propagated through a proof structure, with the extraevidential support that is intrinsic to the proof structure itself. Intuitively, the extraevidential component measures how much prior domain knowledge is used in explaining the data. It influences three steps in the process of building an inductive hypothesis: choosing a seed, searching for an adequate language, and specializing a partial discriminant description.

Let the *structural value* of a descriptor x proved in instance $\mathbf{x}_k$, denoted $\gamma_k(x)$, be defined as

$$\gamma_k(x) = \begin{cases} 1, & \text{if } x \text{ is an initial descriptor in } \mathbf{x}_k; \\ 1 + \sum_i \gamma_k(x_i), & \text{otherwise} \end{cases}$$

where x_i, $1 \le i \le n$, is a descriptor in the antecedent of a rule

$$x \leftarrow x_1, \ldots, x_j, \bar{x}_{j+1}, \ldots, \bar{x}_n$$

used to prove x in instance $\mathbf{x}_k$. Thus $\gamma_k(x)$ is a simple measure of the syntactic complexity of the proof of x that instance $\mathbf{x}_k$ induces. When several proof trees exist, $\gamma_k(x)$ is computed over the largest tree, and for a negated descriptor the method uses the smallest tree that could have proved x.[3] The total structural value of a descriptor over all instances is given by

$$\gamma_{sum}(x) = \sum_{\mathbf{x}_p \in Pos} \gamma_p(x).$$

Many formulas for the structural value are possible. The one I have given weights the extraevidential support of each inference in the domain theory equally with the empirical support of an initial descriptor.

Let C be the conjunction, that is, a partial concept description,

$$C = x_1 \wedge \cdots \wedge x_i \wedge \bar{x}_{i+1} \wedge \cdots \wedge \bar{x}_n.$$

The *credibility* of conjunction C with respect to instance $\mathbf{x}_p$ that proves C is defined as

$$\Gamma_p(C) = \sum_{j=1}^{n} f(x_j),$$

where f is the contribution of a single descriptor:

$$f(x_j) = \begin{cases} \gamma_p(x_j), & \text{if } 1 \leq j \leq i; \\ \gamma_p(x_j), & \text{if } i < j \leq n \text{ and } negZero = nil; \\ 0, & \text{if } i < j \leq n \text{ and } negZero = true; \\ -\gamma_p(x_j), & \text{if } 1 \leq j \leq i \text{ and } x_j \text{ is in the proof of descriptor } x_m \neq x_j; \\ -\gamma_p(x_j), & \text{if } i < j \leq n \text{ and } \bar{x}_j \text{ is in the proof of descriptor } x_m \neq x_j. \end{cases}$$

The flag $negZero$ determines whether negated descriptors are given the same structural value as positive descriptors. Our experiments indicate that giving zero structural value to negated descriptors in C results in more reasonable concept descriptions. Although a characteristic concept description containing negated descriptors is often logically consistent and may even be the shortest one, people tend to characterize a class in terms of absent properties only when absolutely necessary (Medin, Wattenmaker, and Michalski 1986). There are also obvious computational advantages to minimizing the number of negated terms. The value Γ_p is defined to discourage specialization of a conjunction with redundant information by penalizing reuse of the same proof subtree. Finally, the credibility of a conjunction C with respect to the set of positive instances is given by the summation

$$\Gamma(C) = \sum_{\mathbf{x}_p \in Pos, \, \mathbf{x}_p \vdash C} \Gamma_p(C).$$

Note that since C is assumed to be an element of a G set or its specialization, $\Gamma(C)$ does not account for the possibility of covering negative instances.

7.3.5   Selecting a Seed

In selective induction based on the implicit disjunction of sets of descriptors, a concept description can be viewed as a region built out of overlapping primitive regions in the descriptor space. A given region can be expressed in many different ways as the union of primitive regions, which is equivalent to saying that the concept description can be expressed by many logically equivalent disjunctive formulas. Several advantages accrue from sequencing the discovery of regions so that the largest ones are found first. Since a larger region is likely to cover a larger number of positive training instances, the number that remain to be covered decreases quickly. This in turn may reduce the number of disjunctions required to cover the entire training set *Pos*.

The error tolerance of an AQ algorithm is enhanced when the shortest possible conjunction is generated in each cycle, if training errors are uniformly distributed across the initial descriptors. Suppose a conjunction $C = x_1 \wedge \cdots \wedge x_j$ is in the G set returned by candidate elimination. The likelihood that this conjunction's empirical coverage of *Pos* will be distorted by training-set error increases with its length j, since any of the x_i may be incorrect in some instance. Conversely, a conjunction containing no descriptor x_i that is incorrect in an instance **e** may still cover **e** because it matches descriptors in **e** with correct values, regardless of the incorrect value recorded for x_i. Once **e** is covered, it is removed from *Pos*, and its erroneous value can no longer potentially complicate the search for successive partial concepts. More important, when an erroneous positive instance is fortuitously covered by a conjunction that was induced by a different seed, that instance will never be responsible for producing an erroneous conjunction that is subsequently saved as an extension to the domain theory.

When each cycle of the induction algorithm attempts to cover only a single positive instance, how can we control the sequencing of induction so that the first conjunction found also covers the greatest number of instances? The answer, in part, is by selecting a seed that represents a point in descriptor space that lies within the largest possible region. How can such a seed be selected? Our approach is to choose an instance that is most *similar* to the positive instances that remain uncovered by any prior cycle of candidate elimination. Similarity is measured inexpensively by the number of maximal abstract descriptors that two instances have in common, weighting a match by the descriptor's structural value. We attempt to choose a seed that will induce a desirable conjunction by estimating an upper bound on the heuristic value of the (as-yet-undiscovered) conjunction C. This is computed for a potential seed **s** as:

$$\Gamma_{est}(\mathbf{s}) = \sum_{x_n} \gamma_{sum}(x_n),$$

where the summation is over all maximal descriptors x_n proved in candidate seed **s**.

7.3.6 Specializing a Conjunction

The outcome of candidate elimination is a set of conjunctions, each of
which covers the seed and possibly other positive instances as well and
excludes all negative instances. Each conjunction is also maximally general. Any member of this set is a consistent discriminant description of a
class with respect to the instances. However, we intend that as a result of
concept acquisition, we have new domain theory rules that are valid for
proving a new instance of the learned class but exclude new instances
drawn from the universe of classes within the domain. That is, we want a
characteristic concept description, not a discriminant one. This is obtained
by specializing a conjunction C to include more information about the
instances that it covers, without specializing it so far that it covers many
fewer positive instances. In this general-to-specific search of conjunctions
formed by descriptors in the language L, we augment L by the set

$$L = L \cup \{x | \forall \mathbf{p} \in Pos, \mathbf{p} \vdash x \text{ and } \forall \mathbf{n} \in Neg, \mathbf{n} \not\vdash x\}.$$

This readmits to the language descriptors that were excluded from consideration by the candidate elimination algorithm on grounds of efficiency. A
descriptor that is proved in every positive and negative instance has no
discriminant value in the version space but nevertheless is ubiquitous to
the positive class.

Candidates are generated by a modified beam search, guided by $\Gamma(C)$.
Each successive level is generated by adding one descriptor to each of the
k_1 conjunctions with highest $\Gamma(C)$ in the previous level, where only the k_2
descriptors with highest values of $\gamma_{sum}(x)$ are considered. The integers k_1
and k_2 are adjustable parameters, typically set to 3 in our experiments.
The beam search may be cut off by remembering the highest value of $\Gamma(C)$
computed in each value and stopping when the highest value for the current level is lower than the highest level in the general version space set.
This strategy is reasonable because $\Gamma(C)$ increases with the size of the
proof structure supporting each additional descriptor, provided it is not
redundant. However, as a conjunction becomes more specific it is likely to
cover fewer instances, which has the effect of quickly forcing down its
credibility, as shown in figure 7.5.

This search terminates either when no descriptors remain with which to
specialize any of the conjunctions or upon cutoff. At termination, the
conjunction with the highest value of $\Gamma(C)$ is selected as a partial charac-

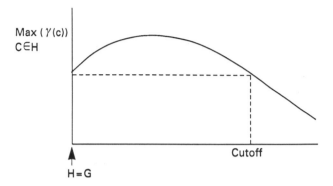

Figure 7.5
Typical $\Gamma(C)$ vs. specificity of C

teristic concept description, and all instances that it covers are removed from the positive training set.

7.4 Correction of Training Noise

Much attention has been given to pruning or postpruning techniques that simplify a concept description based on evidence extracted from the training set or from a separate test set, for example, Fisher and Schlimmer (1988) and Quinlan (1987). The reader may wish to consult Mingers (1989) for a comparative study of decision-tree pruning algorithms. This section explores the use of explicit, prior bias in a domain theory as an additional source of evidence and presents a pruning method for the restricted case of Boolean features subject to noise in the positive training instances. Noise of this kind occurs in situations such as entering a patient's medical record, whenever interpretive judgment or an imperfect measuring device intervenes between observation and recording of an event.

In geometric terms, a noisy positive instance is a vertex **v** originally contained within the region R_T that has been translated to a vertex **v'** outside R_T. Assuming that enough uncorrupted instances remain in the training set, a partial region approximating R_T can be found, though it may not contain **v'**. Since we assume that induction must account for all training instances, **v'** may spawn a region that covers only itself or a few other noisy instances. This results in an overgeneralized concept, exhibiting a higher false-positive rate in testing.

We show a correspondence between this method and the nearest-neighbor algorithm for decoding error-correcting block codes, used in a binary symmetric communications channel. The correspondence becomes clearer if we view a domain theory as a natural, linguistic representation of two distinct types of bias: *disjunctions* encode prior belief about how multiple peaks in the concept membership function may be merged, and *conjunctions* encode redundancy in the instance features with respect to the target concept. The redundancy that exists in an appropriate domain theory can be exploited to identify and correct the effect of noise much as the deliberate addition of redundancy to an encoded message makes it tolerant of errors in transmission. The method offers a decision mechanism that augments rather than replaces statistical or information-based criteria. We call this combination of evidential and a priori criteria *informed pruning*.

7.4.1   Informed Pruning

Supervised induction, with the added complications of a domain theory and errors in the training instance features, can be understood in terms of a standard model of communication. The teacher holds a copy of domain theory D and the target concept R_T represented as a DNF over abstract features in D. The teacher generates correctly labeled positive training instances represented in the initial language $\{x_1, \ldots, x_n\}$ by sampling from the deductive closure of $\{R_T \cup D\}$. Since both R_T and D may be disjunctive, there is variability in the expression of R_T, but an instance can be viewed as a redundant encoding of one term in the message R_T. Each positive instance is sent on a channel subject to noise, and negative instances are sent undisturbed. The learner accumulates a batch of examples with no classification noise but with feature noise in its positive instances.

Clearly, if R_T were known to the receiver, negative instances would have no purpose. The receiver's only task would be to use $\{R_T \cup D\}$ as a block code and decode each message to the proper term, giving a frequency estimate for each term in R_T. Nearest-neighbor decoding could be used to correct feature noise (within bounds determined by the minimum distance of the domain theory) since the Hamming distance between "legal" messages can be computed.[4] The nearest-neighbor strategy does not guarantee to decode an instance to the correct term, but it is optimal when the probability of error in a feature is less than 0.5 (Gallager 1968). Bounds on the performance of the class of random codes can be derived when the noise distribution is known (Peterson and Weldon 1972), but these are not directly applicable since (at best) the decoder $\{R_T \cup D\}$ that defines legal instances can be said to be probably approximately known to the learner.

The communication metaphor is complicated by the fact that the learner has a copy of D but does not know R_T. What can be done when the receiver has an incomplete decoder? The first step is to find an approximation to R_T. MIRO finds an approximation R as described in section 7.2 by induction over the classified instances that have been partially decoded using D. Since the approximation R covers all positive training instances, it typically overfits the noise. The next step is to hypothesize a dichotomization of the instances covered by R into legal and illegal messages. We call this error detection. The final step, error correction, applies a simplified nearest-neighbor decoding. The information returned by error correction can be used in various ways to adjust R; I present only one strategy, which is to delete terms.

7.4.2   Detecting Errors

Labeling each instance $\mathbf{x} \in Pos$ as legal or illegal by considering all $2^{|Pos|}$ dichotomizations is infeasible. Instead, the algorithm assigns tentative labels to terms in $R = C_1 \vee \cdots \vee C_k$ by evaluating the strength of support for each term C_j. The method is similar to conventional postpruning, except that no terms are discarded at this stage. Indeed, many methods have been reported that could be adapted for use here. The decision function I use is not proposed as a replacement for information-theoretic or statistical criteria. It only provides a simple baseline for measuring the effect of error correction.

The same Γ weight used before to select covering terms is used again to evaluate each term, and the instances it covers, for labeling. Recall that $\Gamma(C)$ increases with the complexity of the proof subgraph in D supporting the features in C, summed over all instances covered by C. Two assumptions are implicit in the use of Γ to identify possibly noisy instances. First, a large group of instances that are compactly represented by C are probably legal; conversely, a noisy outlier tends to force the induction algorithm to cover it with a term that accounts for few other instances. Second, abstract features behave like noise filters that fail to propagate truth when a noisy instance is missing some expected pattern of redundancy in its initial representation. Our experiments confirm that the addition of noise induces extra terms containing relatively less abstract features, an effect roughly proportional to the probability of noise.[5] Let

$$\rho = \varepsilon \sum_{i=1}^{k} \Gamma(C_i)$$

for some arbitrary threshold $0 < \varepsilon < 1$. The decision function labels C and the instances covered by C possibly illegal if $\Gamma(C) < \rho$. Using ρ instead of a simple ratio test on coverage, it is possible for C to cover fewer than $\varepsilon * 100\%$ of the instances and still be labeled legal. The advantage is that if C represents a rare subclass of the true concept R_T and there are relatively few samples from C that would otherwise be submerged in noise, the strength of domain theory support for them can cause $\Gamma(C)$ to peak above the ρ threshold.

7.4.3 Correcting Errors

After the possibly illegal instances have been marked, error correction can find for each illegal instance $\mathbf{x}_{bad}$ some legal instance $\mathbf{x}_{good}$ that minimizes the Hamming distance $d(\mathbf{x}_{bad}, \mathbf{x}_{good})$ between them. Note that $\mathbf{x}_{good}$ need not have been in *Pos*, as long as it would have been covered by a legal term C_i in R. If $\mathbf{x}_{bad}$ is replaced by its correction $\mathbf{x}_{good}$, we say that $\mathbf{x}_{bad}$ is *coerced* into C_i. The decision whether to coerce $\mathbf{x}_{bad}$ depends in principle on knowing the probability distribution of noise over the instance features. Assuming a uniform probability P gives a hyperspherical probability distribution on the length of error transitions centered about $\mathbf{x}_{good}$. Then a reasonable decision might be to coerce $\mathbf{x}_{bad}$ if $d(\mathbf{x}_{bad}, \mathbf{x}_{good}) <$ expected value of number of errors in $\mathbf{x}_{good}$.

Let C_i be a legal term, and let C_i^* denote the subset of initial features that could be used in some proof of C_i. For some illegal instance $\mathbf{x}_{bad}$ and Hamming distance α, we call $\mathbf{x}_{bad}^*$ the α-*perturbations* of $\mathbf{x}_{bad}$, which is the set of all instances that differ from $\mathbf{x}_{bad}$ by at most α features in C_i^*. From a geometric point of view, $\mathbf{x}_{bad}^*$ does not include all points in the hypersphere of radius α about $\mathbf{x}_{bad}$, since some of them cannot prove C_i.

The implementation of error correction was simplified by assuming uniform noise of unknown probability P and fixing $\alpha = 1$. There are $|C_i^*|$ 1-perturbations of $\mathbf{x}_{bad}$, and they are easily generated by adding or removing one feature at a time. Feature x can be marked an error and corrected if $\mathbf{x}_{bad} \not\vdash C_i$ and $\exists x \in C_i^*$ such that $\mathbf{x}_{bad} - \{x\} \vdash C_i$, or $\mathbf{x}_{bad} \not\vdash C_i$ and $\exists x \in C_i^*$ such that $\mathbf{x}_{bad} \cup \{x\} \vdash C_i$.

When more than one correction to $\mathbf{x}_{bad}$ is possible, the domain theory may be used to express a preference by choosing the one that would most increase $\Gamma(C_i)$. A correction is not guaranteed valid, but the choice is informed by domain-theory bias in both the detection and the correction steps. Alternatively, knowledge of the noise distribution can be used to break ties by choosing the feature with the highest prior probability of error. For these experiments, a random correction was chosen when more than one was possible.

Error correction attempts to coerce each illegal instance into a legal term beginning with the term ranked first in order of decreasing Γ. If that fails, it tries the second legal term, and so on. An illegal instance is coerced at most once, and error correction stops when all illegal instances have been tried. If, and only if, a possibly illegal term C_j no longer covers any instances, C_j is removed from R.

7.5   Experimental Validation

This section presents the results of the empirical studies supporting the claims made in section 7.2. Recall that I asserted that learning in an abstraction space can (1) be more efficient because the abstraction space is by construction more compact than is the initial space, (2) reduce the number of false-negative and false-positive classifications, and (3) successfully handle training instances with significant amounts of feature noise.

The results from section 7.2 indicate how upper bounds on the sample complexity for PAC learnability may change due to shifting representation to an abstraction space. However, this alone does not argue convincingly for an average case improvement in either error rates or computational complexity. My approach to validating MIRO for classification domains has been an empirical one that depends on repeating randomized learning trials to obtain averaged error curves.[6] The relative effect of initial and abstract concept description languages on the computational cost of finding a consistent set of classification rules is easily observed. Similarly, their accuracy or predictive quality in the limit can be compared.

7.5.1   The Effect of Abstraction

A synthetic problem domain was invented that would exhibit sufficiently high dimensionality and disjunctiveness to represent difficult problems for a selective induction algorithm. The domain represents household cooking implements (e.g., soup bowls, forks) with an instance language of 28 observable, structural features. Many of the interesting classes that are representable in this language share functional properties (e.g., insulated against heat) that are not included in the instance language. I invented a domain theory of 36 rules that represents such a functional property as the consequent of a rule, or chain of rules, grounded in the instance language. These included four rules that could be interpreted as defining a class (glass, cup, plate, cooking vessel) but did not include any rules defining the target class for the learning experiments.

Training instances were created by pseudorandom mechanical generation of structure and features in order to preclude the introduction of unconscious bias by the investigators. Several thousand rather bizarre objects resulted, and these were screened and mechanically sorted into training classes by using a classification rule base that was unknown to the learning program. A total of 78 usable instances resulted, of which 30 "spoons" were chosen for a pool of positive training instances. All remaining instances were used in the negative pool. An average instance of "spoon" has 14 features, and an average instance of any type has 15 features. The target concept is exactly represented by an eight-term-DNF expression in instance space.

A single learning trial consists of choosing k positive and k negative training instances from each pool, running MIRO to give a set of classification rules (i.e., a characteristic concept description), and then testing that concept against 10 positive and 10 negative instances chosen randomly from each pool, excluding training instances used in that trial. By varying k from 2 through 20 by 2 we obtain a series. Each point in an error rate curve reported here is an average of 20 series. Thus, each graph in this section (except figures 7.6 through 7.9, where $k \leq 16$) summarizes performance over 200 concept learning runs and 4000 tests of instance coverage.

Figure 7.6 presents the false-negative (solid line) and false-positive (dotted line) error rates obtained in the initial feature space, using no domain theory. Here the false-negative rate has not stabilized after 16 positive and negative instances, beyond which these trials often could not be completed due to exhausting LISP virtual memory. This explosion of memory use is clearly visible from figure 7.7, which plots growth of the version space G set during candidate elimination. The independent axes are the number of training instances (horizontal) and the number of negative instances eliminated (projection of axis perpendicular to the page). The dependent verti-

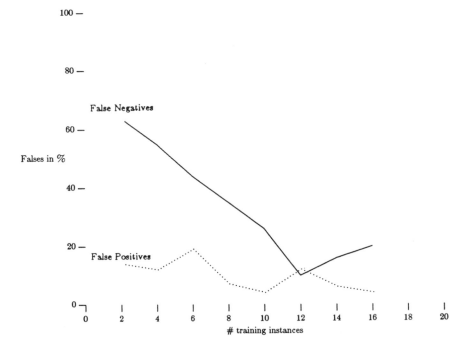

Initial descriptor space / zero training noise

Figure 7.6
Initial space error rate

cal axis shows the average size of G. We see clearly that induction is very underconstrained, owing to the highly disjunctive nature of the target concept when represented in the initial feature space.

Examining the concept descriptions that result from training on 10 positive and 10 negative instances, near the midpoint of the error curve, we find that they contain an average of 2.7 conjunctions with an average of 4.6 features in each conjunction (or 2.7-term 4.6-DNF). The computation time used in the induction step is approximately proportional to $T * X^2$, where T is the number of terms in the concept and X is the maximum size of G over the trial.

In the next series of experiments, the domain theory was used to introduce maximal proved descriptors. However, as in naive constructive induction, all the initial descriptors from the instance language were re-

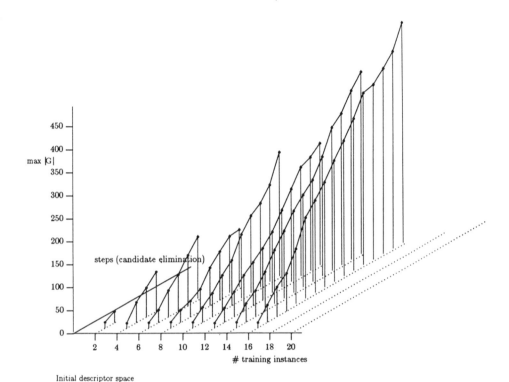

max |G|

steps (candidate elimination)

training instances

Initial descriptor space

Figure 7.7
Initial space *G* set growth

tained. We can see from figure 7.8 that error rates reached low plateaus far more rapidly. This is intuitively plausible since the domain theory has introduced "appropriate" descriptors, making it possible for selective induction to find a geometrically contiguous region enclosing the positive instances. As this transformation is deductively justified, the resulting concept description is more accurately predictive of unseen members of the target class. An average concept description size stabilizes at one-term three-DNF around six training instances.

Computation cost is still excessive, as shown in figure 7.9. Although the deductive bias has dramatically reduced error, it has not been fully exploited to filter out irrelevant features. The algorithm is clogged with consistent yet undesirable conjunctions on each pass, which are discarded only when the Γ heuristic is used to select one having the highest combination of coverage and domain theory support.

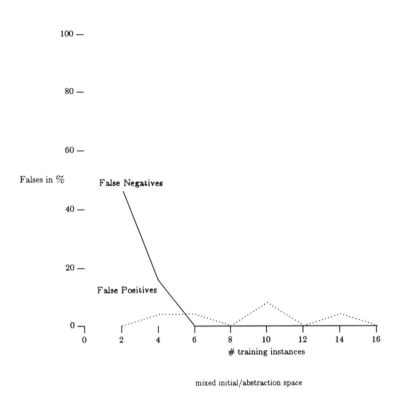

Figure 7.8
Mixed space error rate

The following experimental series defines the performance baseline for MIRO in our synthetic domain. In this and all succeeding experiments, the concept description language was constructed as described in section 7.3.3 to exclude any initial descriptors from the instance language. The resulting error curve in figure 7.10, which is now extended through 20 training instances, shows performance comparable to that in figure 7.8, except for a slight and stable tendency toward overgeneralization made visible in the false-positive curve. An average concept was observed to converge at one-term three-DNF around four training instances. Essentially no cases of version space collapse were observed. As I will show later, feature noise is more likely to cause version space collapse.

The effect of fully exploiting deductive bias is more visible in figure 7.11, which shows a slow growth in the G set as more training instances are

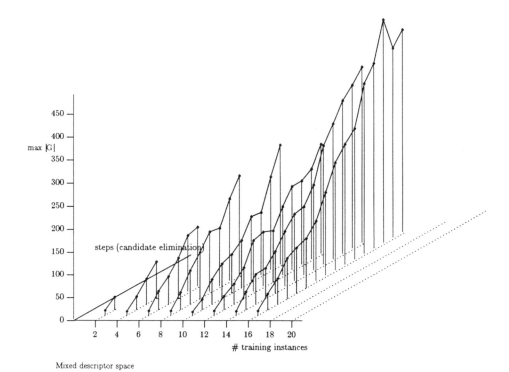

Mixed descriptor space

Figure 7.9
Mixed space *G* set growth

used. This suggests that an appropriate domain theory can reduce both the dimensionality and disjunctiveness of a learning problem, although very little effort was made to engineer a "correct" or "complete" domain theory.

By simply adding one rule that defines the target concept into the domain theory, we obtain the error curve shown in figure 7.12. Although one expects to observe a zero error rate in the case that the concept is known, there appears a 24% false-negative error when training on two instances. This is due to the system's using the correct rule but overspecializing it to account for coincidental patterns that it can readily find in a small training set. Although this does not increase coverage, it does appear to the system to strengthen the learned concept by bringing in more support from the domain theory. This tendency vanished with more than two training instances in this experiment, because the instances were consistent with an

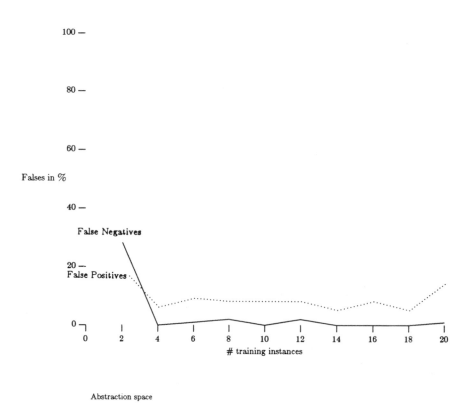

Figure 7.10
Abstraction space error rate

existing rule. In the presence of concept drift, MIRO is in principle able to specialize or replace a concept that was previously believed correct but that is inconsistent with a more current batch of training instances.

7.5.2 Handling Feature Noise

An important dimension for evaluating any method is resistance to training noise. We have thus far studied only one variety of noise, a uniform distribution of error in recording the features of positive training instances. In this situation, the teacher correctly assigns class membership (+ or −) to each instance, and that information is correctly communicated to the learning program. However, features of positive instances are transmitted to the learning program over a communication channel that inverts each feature value with probability P.

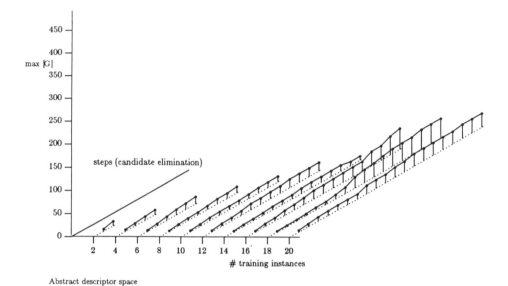

Figure 7.11
Abstraction space G set growth

For the following experiments, sets of positive training instances were generated for $P = 0.05, 0.1, 0.15, 0.2, 0.25, 0.3, 0.35,$ and 0.4 by perturbing the original pool of zero-noise instances. Trials were conducted as shown in figures 7.10 and 7.11, except that test instances were chosen from the zero-noise pool and no test instance would be used in a given trial if its perturbed "descendant" were already used as a training instance in the same trial.

Noise can make a positive instance look identical to a negative instance when viewed in the abstraction space. This induces a version space collapse, which triggers MIRO to add a new descriptor to the language. Collapse has been observed to occur an average of 1.6 times per trial when training on 10 negative and 10 positive instances at the 25% noise level. Since each pass through candidate elimination creates a much smaller G set in the abstraction space compared with the initial or mixed space, the computational advantages of using the abstraction space are considerable, although each collapse entails recomputing the G set from scratch. Figure 7.13 shows the growth of an average G set, which is only slightly faster than its growth at the zero training noise level.

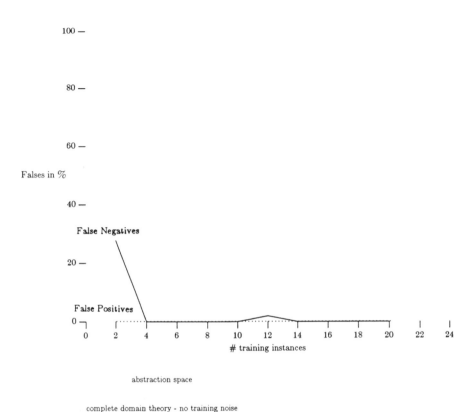

abstraction space

complete domain theory - no training noise

Figure 7.12
Complete domain theory error rate

Figure 7.14 shows a typical error curve as a function of k instances containing 30% noise. Without any pruning, false negatives fall to near zero by $k = 14$, but false positives have leveled off near 20% due to the spurious terms in R. Using informed pruning with a detection threshold set (empirically) to $\varepsilon = 0.1$, the false-positive rate is 4% at $k = 20$ and still falling gradually. This 16% drop is traded against a 2% increase in false negatives.[7] At the $P = 0.3$ noise level, an average concept output by MIRO is three-term 3.6-DNF, and a version space collapse causes a new feature to be added to the language 1.8 times. After informed pruning, an average concept is two-term 2.9-DNF, indicating that longer terms are more likely to be removed. The resulting description is improved in conciseness as well as generalization when tested against noise-free instances.

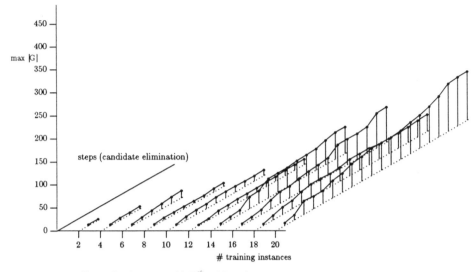

Abstract descriptor space with 25% training noise

Figure 7.13
25% Noise *G* set growth

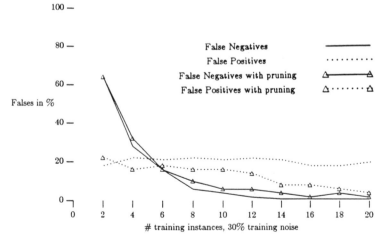

Figure 7.14
Effect of informed pruning on test error

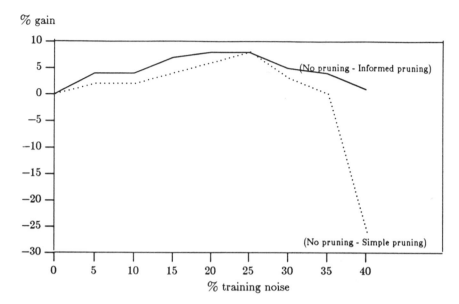

Figure 7.15
Improvement in test error rate

Since the algorithm is a hybrid of conventional pruning and knowledge-intensive error correction, how much of the improvement in error rate can be attributed to error correction? All experiments were repeated, unconditionally removing terms that were marked illegal in the error-detection step, without using the correction step. This "simple pruning" method is compared with informed pruning in figure 7.15. Each point represents an average, over 100 trials, of the difference (total error with no pruning) − (total error with simple or informed pruning), taken over $k = 12, 14, 16, 18, 20$. Both give comparable results (within 3% of each other) from $P = 0.1$ through $P = 0.3$, but simple pruning is much worse than none at all at $P > 0.3$ due to a high false-negative rate.

This suggests that as P increases and R becomes more fragmented, a fixed ρ threshold becomes less effective at discriminating bad terms. Although the error-correction step uses the same labeling of terms given by ρ, it is more conservative about discarding them. An exact analysis of this effect is difficult, but a crude approximation follows from considering the redundant information in a term. For the simple domain theory D used here, an average term with 3.6 abstract features is a decoding of 7 initial

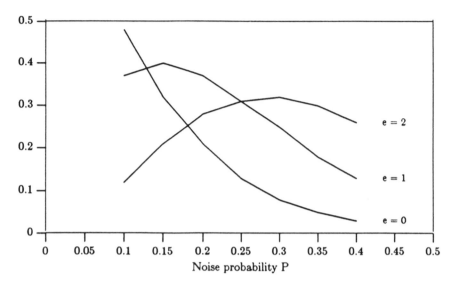

Figure 7.16
Probability of exactly *e* errors in 7 features

features. If *D* represented a perfect (7,4) block code, it would have a minimum distance 3, sufficient to correct all single errors but insufficient to justify setting $\alpha > 1$. Figure 7.16 shows how the probability of exactly *e* errors in 7 features varies with *P* for $e = 0, 1, 2$. At high noise rates, $\Pr[e = 2]$ dominates, and we would expect that most instances have been translated away from their original legal positions by distance 2. Fewer instances are marked legal in the error-detection step at high noise rates, and the general dispersion of all instances leaves fewer within range of error correction. This reduces the chance of coercing all instances covered by a term. Conversely, at low *P*, where $\Pr[e = 0]$ dominates, few instances are marked illegal by error detection. Figure 7.15 shows that informed pruning gave the greatest improvement in generalization for $0.15 \leq P \leq 0.25$, where $\Pr[e = 1]$ dominates and a correction over distance $\alpha = 1$ is likely to be successful.

7.6   Relationship to Other Work

An intelligent agent presented with a learning task has two sources of information available: the training instances drawn from the sample space and the prior knowledge about the task that has been accumulated from previous experience. These two sources of information are compatible and complementary. Prior knowledge guides and organizes the process of learning from new instances, and new instances are the basis for incremental additions to knowledge. This intuition about the interplay between the role of prior knowledge and the role of induction in a learning task has motivated many researchers recently to develop learning systems that combine aspects of both explanation-based learning and inductive learning. In the continuum of learning methods ordered by how they make use of the two sources of information available to a learning agent, explanation-based learning (Mitchell, Keller, and Kedar-Cabelli 1986; DeJong and Mooney 1986) is an end point representing total dependence on prior knowledge. The second end point is the class of conventional induction methods, which represents total dependence on the set of training instances.

Explanation-based learning is based on "explaining," by application of domain knowledge, how a single training instance is an example of a concept and then generalizing this explanation to a characteristic concept description. The properties of this approach are that a characterization can be obtained from a single training instance and that this characterization relies on domain theory rather than an inductive bias. However, it does not work in the presence of domain theories that are intractable or incomplete, it is intolerant of error, and finally, it cannot make use multiple training instances. In fact, the method requires *complete* prior knowledge because it uses only a single training instance.

The MIRO system can be viewed as intermediate between explanation-based and inductive learning. It uses prior knowledge of the task domain to re-represent a sample of training instances in a simplified abstraction space that facilitates the empirical induction of a target concept. The method does not go the extreme of total dependence on prior knowledge, since we wanted a system that is robust in the presence of noisy or incomplete domain theory. The method also does not go the extreme of conventional induction methods that are totally dependent on training instances. Prior knowledge is, after all, available in many learning problems.

A central concern for any method of concept formation from examples is identification of those features that are relevant, when the class to be learned may manifest itself in a vast variety of measurable forms. In explanation-based learning, the domain theory unambiguously identifies indirectly relevant initial descriptors in the instance language, because they are necessary in the proof of a directly relevant descriptor, which is given as the goal concept. Since the domain theory is assumed to be complete with respect to the goal, any descriptors not used in the proof may be regarded as irrelevant. It is this strong "deductive bias" that makes standard explanation-based learning rigid in the presence of noise. Conventional empirical methods exploit multiple instances and assumptions about the well behavedness of underlying probability densities to reveal the recurring patterns of relevant descriptors. In constructive induction (Michalski 1983), patterns of descriptors that are believed a priori to be relevant may be rewritten as more abstract descriptors in order to simplify the resulting concept description. Thus, an induction task that is difficult in the initial descriptor space would be simple in an abstract space, if only it were possible to identify the relevant descriptors from among many derived, abstract descriptors. In effect, constructive induction demands that we know which are the useful initial patterns, whereas explanation-based learning requires that we know how to define the goal concept abstractly. Both approaches share the idea that deductive knowledge should support the task of characterizing a class from limited examples drawn from the class.

In the MIRO system, the relevant descriptors are identified by the prior domain theory, and the deduction process is used to focus on essential properties of a particular learning domain that have been encoded into this domain theory. In MIRO, the selection of concept description language for induction is deductively justified, whereas in constructive induction, the concept description language is defined by arbitrarily derived descriptors, with only guidance from the data on which of these descriptors is really useful. MIRO can be considered a variant of constructive induction in which a strong bias is applied to the construction of the concept description language but which includes a systematic means for relaxing that bias when it has been found to be inappropriate for the concept formation task at hand.

Flann and Dietterich (1986) describe a system Wyl that also constructs a new concept description language. We will carefully compare the Wyl and MIRO systems in order to highlight their similarities and differences. Wyl is based on a very general multiple-representation strategy that translates training instances given in one representation into a second that is compatible with induction. After induction in this second representation, the resulting concept is "compiled" into a third representation that is suitable for performance. An example is given in which the system learns the checkers end-game concept of "trap" from two training examples of a "loss." What Wyl and MIRO have in common is the framework of a multiple-representation strategy, not the methods, motivation, or details. Wyl attempts to be very general, admitting highly dissimilar representations for training instances, induction, and concept description (up to and including the full first-order logic). A set-theoretic or algorithmic definition of the relationships and/or restrictions between these representations is not given in their paper. It is important to emphasize that Wyl admits unrelated languages between different stages of the method—at one point, the language is structural and at another functional. In MIRO both the instance language and the language used to construct a concept are forms of monadic predicate calculus.

Utgoff (1984, 1986) introduces and analyzes the concept of a shift of bias for an inductive concept learning method. He shows that programs that learn inductive generalizations from examples are guided not only by the training instances but by a bias encoded in the concept-description language that determines how generalizations are to be formed. He describes a system, STABB, that is able to shift its bias dynamically during execution automatically. Our method of induction in an abstraction space can be viewed in this context as using domain theory to implement a shift in bias from the concept-description language of the initial space to that of the abstraction space.

Lebowitz (1986a) develops a system UNIMEM, which searches a database of voting records for empirical generalizations and verifies these generalizations via a domain theory. In later work, Lebowitz (1986b) proposes that empirical techniques can be used to formulate a hypothesis that provides focus for the deduction mechanism of explanation-based learning. In essence, an inductive method is used to control the search space for a version of a deductive method. This work can be considered the dual of the work reported in this chapter, in the sense that I use a deductive technique to construct descriptors for induction. Lebowitz presents his work by example and explanation and includes neither an algorithm nor empirical studies. In later work (Lebowitz 1986c), he has given some philosophical arguments why "robust machine learning must involve the integration of similarity-based [inductive] and explanation-based methods."

Pazzani, Dyer, and Flowers (1986) describe a system OCCAM that builds generalization rules used to suggest causal and intentional relationships. In domains for which a prior causal theory is available, these relationships are confirmed or denied by the theory by differentiating between relevant and irrelevant features. In domains without a causal theory, the relationships serve as a basis for the construction of a causal theory. In a later paper, Pazzani (1988) argues that OCCAM can be viewed as an integration of explanation-based and empirical learning and, like Lebowitz, gives a convincing argument that such an integration can be more than the sum of the parts. The work has the same top-level goals as the work reported in this chapter but differs in the specifics of approach, validation, analysis, and error correction. The OCCAM system is also presented by explanation of examples represented by either conceptual dependencies or situation-action rules.

An area of work indirectly related to integrating inductive and explanation-based learning is work on learning based on analogy or function. Concepts are analogous when they have certain attributes in common, and this commonality is often expressed functionally. Kedar-Cabelli (1985) proposes an approach called *purpose-directed analogy*, which constructs multiple explanations by analogy with known examples and then combines these explanations to produce a more general concept description. Winston et al. (1983) describe a system that learns concept descriptions from functional definitions. Mitchell (1979) uses the results of explanation-based generalizations of training instances to refine a version space set, which finds a concept description more efficiently because of the smaller version space.

7.7   Conclusions and Open Problems

I have presented a method for supervised concept formation that I call induction in an abstraction space and described its implementation as the system MIRO. The MIRO system demonstrates three properties about learning in an abstraction space. First, there exist instances of the concept formation problem for which a substantial reduction in computational resources can be expected by shifting the problem from an initial space to an abstraction space. In fact, I believe that this reduction is typical for problems that admit a well-engineered domain theory. Second the MIRO system demonstrates that learning in an abstraction space can reduce the

number of false-negative and false-positive classifications. Since coincidental patterns are filtered by the deduction process, the MIRO system does
not incorporate these patterns into the concept description. Third, the
MIRO system is able to construct a "corrected" concept description even
in the presence of substantial attribute noise in the training set.

The work reported in this chapter is a first step in an attempt to develop
a general framework or architecture that takes a form of knowledge and
couples this knowledge with an induction algorithm to realize an instance
of the paradigm of induction in an abstraction space. To be more precise,
the MIRO system uses a descriptor-valued domain theory to construct the
abstraction space

$$L_{\mathscr{A}} = \{(x, \alpha) | \exists \mathbf{x} \in \{Pos \cup Neg\}, \mathbf{x} \vdash x \ maximal,$$

$$\alpha \ \text{a pointer to the node in} \ G_D^{\mathbf{x}} \ \text{labeled} \ x\},$$

where the set $L_{\mathscr{A}}$ is explicitly constructed as a set of pairs consisting of
a descriptor x and the proof that established x. And the MIRO system
then uses the candidate elimination algorithm as the basis of its induction.
We want to define the issues associated with an architecture where other
forms of domain theory, such as MYCIN-like rule-based classification
rules, Horn clause logic, or even simulation or a qualitative model can be
used to construct the set $L_{\mathscr{A}}$, and other induction algorithms can be used
in tandem with it.

It is clear that every pair $\langle D, A \rangle$, where D is a type of domain theory
with its associated conventions of deduction and A is an induction algorithm, will generate open problems. Consider, for instance, the extension
to MIRO of accepting first-order Horn clause domain theories. The extension of the bottom-up deduction method to Horn clause theories is
straightforward, but adapting the induction algorithm to accept an abstraction space composed of terms instead of descriptors presents problems. Vere (1975) has shown by reduction from the subgraph isomorphism
problem that it is NP-complete to determine whether a single instance is a
generalization or specialization of another instance. There is a consensus
(Haussler 1987) that induction methods incorporating this step will not
be computationally effective. It is possible to give an "ad hoc" induction
method by restricting classes of substitution instances of descriptors in the
domain theory. Multiple-place descriptors then describe only relationships between individual objects, not relationships between objects and

classes of objects. For example, the term *parent*(X, Y) is compatible with this assumption because it gives the relationship between objects X and Y. The term *color*$(X, blue)$ is not, since it describes the membership of object X in the class of blue objects. But this restriction is not automatically verifiable, as it induces a merging of the syntax and semantics of descriptor symbols.

It is reasonable to expect that domain theories even more unlike those used here will lead to further open areas. For example, one can imagine replacing a logical domain theory by a qualitative model to construct the set

$$L_{\mathscr{A}} = \{(x, \alpha) | \exists \mathbf{x} \in \{Pos \cup Neg\}, \mathbf{x} \vdash x \text{ } maximal,$$

$$\alpha \text{ a pointer to the reasoning in the qualitative model for } x\}.$$

The deductive bias encoded in a qualitative model is far removed from that of a domain theory composed of descriptor-value rules, and yet it is there. How can the notion of abstraction be defined here and used in the context of induction?

I believe that it will be important to find a principled way of combining the evidential support from a sample with the extraevidential support encoded in a domain theory. MIRO combines these two forms of support in the heuristic function Γ. This function is used at three crucial points: to choose from among competing abstract descriptors, to choose a seed for the candidate elimination algorithm, and to identify and correct noisy instances within a sample. This function encodes belief in the relative value of different proof structures, and I have argued why this encoding is reasonable. However, a principled and mathematically rigorous combination of evidential and extraevidential support for a hypothesis requires a framework based on other than heuristics chosen from obervation or argument. I am exploring an information-theoretic approach in which the evidential support of examples is interpreted as the source of information and the extraevidential support of a prior domain theory is interpreted as part of the encoding/decoding function of the system. The hope is to measure by some common metric the contribution of each type of support.

Another open problem is to understand the relationship between the problem domain and more complex control strategies that interleave deduction and induction, such as the blackboard architecture of Rule Writer (Drastal 1984; Drastal and Kulikowski 1982). The inductive and deductive components in the MIRO system have been kept cleanly separated, which permits us to experiment with benchmarks, varying such parameters as the domain theory or the induction algorithm, and observe trade-offs between the computational load in the deductive and inductive stages. But is such a clean separation in fact necessary or wanted in combining deduction with induction?

Hirsh (1989) describes an application of incremental version space merging (IVSM) to learning from noisy data. The method assumes that every noisy instance x is a perturbation of some good instance that lies within a "nearby" hypersphere about x. Informed pruning uses the bias in D to constrain the α-perturbations of x, which is equivalent to imposing a size and complex shape on the region of instance space about x. This suggests that an analogous use of domain theory (for real-valued features) may be a principled way of bounding regions in IVSM to account for prior knowledge of correlations between features.

The algorithm I have described is based on an assumption of noise-free negative instances. I have implemented an extension that corrects negative-instance feature noise before induction, in one pass over the training set. It requires that D contain a complete classification rule for every category of instance represented in the negative training set. Since instances are correctly labeled by assumption, this preprocessing simply corrects any negative instance that fails to match its classification rule by coercing it to the nearest matching point in instance space. The preliminary experiments are encouraging. It is an open question whether the approach be extended to cope with feature noise in the negative instances, without introducing a separate domain theory for them.

The detection step relies on a threshold ε that is fixed in advance, and no doubt better empirical pruning methods could be used to label instances. The complexity of R decreases as terms are discarded but at the risk of removing a good term. Adapting the minimum description length principle (Rissanen 1978) to account for the complexity of an abstract feature may lead to an algorithm that finds a principled compromise on the number of terms in R without using ε. In such a case, a separate step to identify noisy instances would become unnecessary; the correction step would repeatedly attempt to remove the weakest term until the overall complexity of R becomes justified by the data. This requires more knowledge or assumptions about the noise distribution.

Acknowledgments

I thank the following people for their valuable contributions: Pat Langley, Larry Rendell, Raj Seshu, and Stan Raatz for insightful advice and criticism; Gabe Czako for implementing most of MIRO and the thoughtful discussions that were a part of that; Regine Meunier for implementing and carefully verifying postpruning; and Uwe Clausen for assistance preparing graphs.

Notes

1. We are assuming that descriptors take only binary values here. More generally, induction hypothesizes a utility function $u(\mathbf{x})$ that probabilistically assigns a degree of membership of instance $\mathbf{x}$ to the positive class (Rendell 1986).

2. What we call a primitive region depends on the convention chosen for labeling vertices of the instance space. For a suitably labeled n-dimensional cube, it is the rectangular region on one side of an $(n-1)$-dimensional plane that bisects axis x_i. Then all vertices in the rectangle have the same value for descriptor x_i.

3. Since the negation of x is always proved by failure, the structural value of the smallest proof tree is a kind of least upper bound on $\gamma_k(x)$. Recall that rules with negated consequents are not permitted in the domain theory, and the method does not introduce such rules.

4. Such a random code has none of the algebraic structure of a practical code that permits efficient computation of the nearest term in R_T. The required table lookup can be realized by matching terms against the proof completed by an instance, however. This immediately suggests a method for error correction in certain explanation-based learning systems.

5. The seed selection heuristic has an important role in finding a compact, abstract term early in the cycle of covering and removing positive instances. If it chooses poorly, the noisy seed may introduce new features into L too soon, and the number of terms in R tends to rise.

6. These are related but not identical to learning curves seen in the psychology literature.

7. Training ID3 at $k = 20$ without a domain theory or pruning gave decision rules that tested at a 20 percent false-negative and 16 percent false-positive rate, using the $P = 0.3$ training set and the noise-free test set.

References

Amarel, S. (1968). On representations of problems of reasoning about actions. In *Machine Intelligence* 3. D. Michie, ed. Edinburgh: Edinburgh University Press, 131–171. Also, in *Readings in Artificial Intelligence*. Palo Alto, Calif.: Tioga Press, 1981.

Blumer, A., Ehrenfeucht, A., Haussler, D., and Warmuth, M. (1986). Classifying learnable geometric concepts with the Vapnik-Chervonenkis dimension. In *Proceedings of the Eighteenth Annual ACM Symposium on Theory of Computing*, Berkeley, Calif., 273–282.

Clark, K. (1978). Negation as failure. In H. Gallaire and J. Minker (eds.), *Logic and Databases*. New York: Plenum Press, 293–322.

DeJong, G, and Mooney, R. (1986). Explanation-based learning: An alternate view. *Machine Learning* 1:2, 145–176.

Dietterich, T., and Michalski, R. (1981). Inductive learning of structural descriptors: Evaluation criteria and comparative review of selective methods. *Artificial Intelligence* 16, 257–294.

Drastal, G. (1984). Experiments with Rule Writer, a tool for building expert systems. *Proceedings 17th Hawaii International Conference on System Sciences*, Honolulu.

Drastal, G. (1991). Informed pruning in constructive induction. *Proceedings 8th International Workshop on Machine Learning*, Evanston, Ill.

Drastal, G., and Kulikowski, C. (1982). Knowledge-based acquisition of rules for medical diagnosis. *Journal of Medical Systems* 6:433–445.

Drastal, G., and Raatz, S. (1988). Empirical Results on Induction in an Abstraction Space. Department of Computer Science DCS-TR-248, Rutgers University.

Drastal, G., Raatz, S., and Czako, G. (1989). Induction in an abstraction space: A form of constructive induction. *Proceedings 11th International Joint Conference on Artificial Intelligence*, Detroit.

Duda, R., and Hart, P. (1973). *Pattern Classification and Scene Analysis*. New York: Wiley.

Fisher, D., and Schlimmer, J. (1988). Concept simplification and prediction accuracy. *Proceedings 5th International Conference on Machine Learning*, Ann Arbor Mich.

Flann, N., and Dietterich, T. (1986). Selecting appropriate representations for learning from examples. *AAAI-86*, Philadelphia, 460–466.

Gallager, R. (1968). *Information Theory and Reliable Communications*. New York: Wiley.

Haussler, D. (1987). Bias, version spaces and Valiant's learning framework. 4th *International Workshop on Machine Learning*, 324–336, Irvine, Calif.

Hirsh, H. (1989). Incremental Version-Space Merging: A General Framework for Concept Learning. Ph.D. thesis, Stanford University.

Kedar-Cabelli, S. (1985). Purpose-directed analogy. *Cognitive Science Society Conference*, Irvine, Calif.

Laird, P. (1988) *Learning from Good and Bad Data*. Norell, Mass.: Kluwer.

Lebowitz, M. (1986a). Integrated learning: Controlling explanation. *Cogitive Science* 10, 219–240.

Lebowitz, M. (1986b). Concept learning in a rich input domain: Generalization based memory. In *Machine Learning: An Artificial Intelligence Approach*, R. Michalski, J. Carbonell, and T. Mitchell (eds.), Los Altos, Calif.: Morgan Kaufmann, 193–214.

Lebowitz, M. (1986c). Not the path to perdition: The utility of similarity-based learning. *AAAI-86*, Philadelphia, 533–537.

Medin, D., Wattenmaker, W., and Michalski, R. (1986). Constraints and Preferences in Inductive Learning. Report ISG86-1. Department of Computer Science, University of Illinois at Urbana-Champaign.

Mingers, J. (1989). An empirical comparison of pruning methods for decision tree induction. *Machine Learning* 4, 227–243.

Michalski, R. (1973). AQVAL-1: Computer implementation of a variable-valued logic system VL1 and examples of its application to pattern recognition. In *Proceedings 1st International Joint Conference on Pattern Recognition*, Washington D.C., 3–17.

Michalski, R. (1983). A theory and methodology of inductive learning. In *Machine Learning: An Artificial Intelligence Approach*. Los Altos, Calif.: Morgan Kaufmann.

Michalski, R., Carbonell, J., and Mitchell, T. (eds.) (1986). *Machine Learning: An Artificial Intelligence Approach. Volume 2*. Los Altos, Calif.: Morgan Kaufmann.

Mitchell, T. (1978). Version Spaces: An Approach to Concept Learning. Ph.D. dissertation, Stanford University.

Mitchell, T. (1984). Toward combining empirical and analytic methods for inferring heuristics. In *Artificial and Human Intelligence*, A. Elithorn and R. Banerji (eds.), Amsterdam: North-Holland Publishing Co.

Mitchell, T., Keller, R., and Kedar-Cabelli, S. (1986). Explanation-based generalization: A unifying view. *Machine Learning* 1:1, 47–80.

Nilsson, N. J. (1980). *Principles of Artificial Intelligence*. Polo Alto, Calif.: Tioga Press.

Pazzani, M. (1988). Integrating explanation-based and empirical learning methods in *OCCAM*. 3rd *European Working Session on Learning*, Glasgow, 147–166.

Pazzani, M., Dyer, I., and Flowers, M. (1986). The role of prior theories in generalization. *AAAI-86*, Philadelphia, 545–550.

Peterson, W., and Weldon, E. (1972). *Error-Correcting Codes*. Cambridge, Mass.: MIT Press.

Plaisted, D. (1981). Theorem proving with abstraction. *Artificial Intelligence* 16, 47–108.

Quinlan, J. (1986). Induction of decision trees. *Machine Learning* 1:1, 81–106.

Quinlan, J. (1987). Simplifying decision trees. *International Journal of Man-Machine Studies* 27, 221–234.

Rendell, L. (1986). A general framework for induction and a study of selective induction. *Machine Learning* 1, 177–226.

Rendell, R. (1988). Learning hard concepts. 3rd *European Working Session on Learning*, Glasgow, 177–200.

Rissanen, J. (1978). Modeling by shortest data description. *Automatica* 14 465–471.

Rivest, R. (1989). Notes on machine learning. Unpublished draft.

Russell, S. (1985). The Compleat Guide to MRS. Report KSL-85-12. Knowledge Systems Laboratory, Department of Computer Science, Stanford University.

Tenenberg, J. (1986). Planning with abstraction. *AAAI-86*, Philadelphia.

Utgoff, P. (1986). Shift of bias for inductive concept learning. In *Machine Learning: An Artificial Intelligence Approach. 2*. Michalski, Carbonell, J., and T. Mitchell (eds.). Los Altos, Calif.: Morgan Kaufmann, 2:107–148.

Utgoff, P. (1984). Shift of Bias for Inductive Concept Learning. Ph.D. dissertation. Rutgers University.

Valiant, L. (1984). A Theory of the learnable. CACM 27:11, 1134–1142.

Vapnik, V., and Chervonenkis, A. (1971). On the uniform convergence of relative frequencies of events to their probabilities. *Theory of Probability and its Applications* 16:2, 264–280.

Vere, S. (1975). Induction of concepts in the predicate calculus. *IJCAI-4*, Tbilisi, USSR, 281–287.

Watanabe, S. (1985). *Pattern Recognition: Human and Mechanical*. New Tork: Wiley Interscience.

Winston, P., Binford, T., Katz, B., and Lowry, M. (1983). Learning physical descriptions from functional definitions, examples and precedents. *AAAI-83*, Washington, D.C.

8 Binary Decision Trees and an "Average-Case" Model for Concept Learning: Implications for Feature Construction and the Study of Bias

Raj Seshu

8.1 Introduction

This chapter has two parts. The first section describes an "average-case" model of learning and presents some experimental results. Under this model, we assume that all learning examples have uniform probability weight and that all possible target concepts are equally likely (also see Kadie 1991 and Pazzani and Sarrett 1990). Even if we assume a uniform distribution on the examples, this model is clearly no stronger than the Valiant model (Valiant 1984) since satisfying the latter's ε-δ rule guarantees average error less than $\delta + \varepsilon(1 - \delta)$. Furthermore, the method of measuring performance has two important limitations. First, it can be used only in learning problems with hypotheses spaces that can be explicitly generated. Second, the example spaces must be discrete (unlike the Valiant model; see appendix A in Blumer et al. 1986).

However, in the context of binary decision trees (BDTs), this method allows accurate measurement of the sample sizes needed to achieve certain error bounds for small-concept classes. I apply this method to a number of such concept classes, and the results suggest that there is an *intimate connection between the base-2 logarithm of the class size and the sample size*. In particular, the experiments are consistent with the proposition that sample sizes that are much smaller than half of the hypothesis space logarithm cannot achieve high accuracies, whereas those that are at least twice this size can produce error rates significantly less than 10 percent. The reported error rates are considerably more optimistic than those predicted by the Valiant-model bounds (also see Kadie 1991).

Mitchell (1980) defines *bias* as any tendency of a learning procedure to prefer one hypothesis over another other than consistency with the training data. *If use assume that BDT algorithms can do no better than to choose at random between a set of consistent hypotheses, then the average-case model can be used to analyze biases associated with BDT algorithms.* Given a particular sample set, some biases allow BDT strategies to construct more complex trees. These biases are essentially increasing the size of the algorithm's *effective hypothesis space* (EHS) (Haussler 1988). Since the average-error model's results imply that the base-2 logarithm of the EHS should not be much larger than the number of examples used for learning, we may be able to reject certain biases as inappropriate for the induction task at hand.

In the second half of the chapter, I analyze three sources of bias. One source appears when the learner attempts to use BDTs in learning problems with nonbinary attributes. I refer to these biases as *feature-conversion* biases. Feature-conversion biases necessarily crop up in BDT algorithms when attributes have more than two values. Even in the case of ID3 (Quinlan 1983), which creates offspring nodes for *each value* of a multivalued attribute, these issues arise when attributes are real valued.

A second source of bias arises from methods used to prevent decision trees from "overfitting" the data (e.g., see Brieman et al. 1984). I refer to these as *pruning* biases. Finally, a third source of bias inheres in *constructive induction* (CI) approaches. CI methods allow the BDT algorithm to grow smaller trees that have more discriminating power (Utgoff 1988; Pagallo 1989; Seshu 1989; Tcheng, Lambert, and Lu 1990).[1]

Each of these sources of bias may be independently manipulated by the user of BDT algorithms, but normally the pruning biases appear in the form of some user-specified parameters. Since these parameters are often real valued, it is reasonable to ask whether an algorithm may be able to set them automatically through optimization performed over subsamples. In particular, it is possible that the learner can undo some of the damage done to it when the user erroneously sets some of the other biases, for example, by using CI methods that are more powerful than the sample size will tolerate.

The experiments in the second half of the chapter test the hypothesis that all three kinds of biases can work independently to change the size of the algorithm's effective hypothesis space and, hence, to slow or speed learning. The results are consistent with the following propositions:

• *It is difficult to study any of the commonly analyzed kinds of biases in isolation since they all interact.* For example, a pruning or feature conversion bias that may be useful in the absence of feature construction may be damaging when feature construction is used.

• An algorithm that can *dynamically* adjust its biases (Tcheng et al. 1989; Holder 1990) may be able to manipulate pruning biases in order to overcome the ill effects of excessively powerful feature-construction methods. However, this same kind of correction seems more difficult when the user is using undesirable feature conversion methods.

• *In situations where the learner has insufficient data, domain knowledge may become misleading. This happens when a bias that appears to be reasonable for a problem places the learner into an effective hypothesis space that is too large for the number of examples.* For example, a BDT having the power to distinguish all subsets of a nominal attribute may perform less well than if we restrict it to choosing each nominal value individually.

8.2 Average-Case Learning for Binary Decision Trees

This section begins by briefly reviewing the Vapnik-Blumer bound for Valiant-model concept learning.

8.2.1 The Vapnik-Blumer Bound

Let ε $(0 > \varepsilon \leq 1/2)$ be the maximum error we are willing to tolerate. Suppose our sample consists of m examples and the class of H's that we are trying to learn is finite. If δ is the probability of failure, then:

$$|H|(1 - \varepsilon)^m \leq \delta. \tag{8.1}$$

This is because there can be at most $|H|$ hypotheses that have error ε and the probability that a sample of size m is consistent with any of the $\varepsilon - bad$ hypotheses is no more than $(1 - \varepsilon)^m$. The probability of picking any one of them is no more than the sum of the probabilities of picking one, so the result follows by statistical independence.

If we know that $-Ln(1 - \varepsilon) \geq \varepsilon$, we can produce the familiar result:

$$m \geq \frac{Ln(1/\delta) + Ln(|H|)}{\varepsilon}. \tag{8.2}$$

This bound has been improved and extended by the replacement of $Ln(|H|)$ by the Vapnik-Chervonenkis (VC) dimension (Blumer et al. 1989) and by other workers (e.g., Schapire 1990; Littlestone, 1988).[2]

8.2.2 Average-Error Bounds as an Alternative

Critics of the Valiant model have pressed the case for average-error results. Many workers, such as Buntine (1989a), Dieterich (1989), and Rendell and Seshu (1990), have focused on the "worst-case" nature of the derivation. In particular, the bound is "worst case" in at least two senses. First, the learner makes no assumptions about the example distribution;

this fact is relied upon in both Blumer et al. (1989) and Schapire (1990). Second, the resulting $\varepsilon - \delta$ rule may be overly conservative because it applies to *all* possible choices of a target concept (Dietterich 1989). Haussler (1990) and Kadie (1991) have also argued that the VC dimension fails to take into account other aspects of the learning problem, such as background knowledge and noise.

For the data analyst who wishes to select biases or the programmer who wants the learning algorithm to do so automatically, we might restate some of these criticisms in a more succinct manner: The Vapnik-Blumer bounds give no indication of how much error to expect with a given learning bias and sample size that is too small to support reasonable values of ε and δ.

8.2.3 Analytical and Empirical Average-Error Bounds

Unfortunately, just one analytical approach to average-error bounds has been pioneered, that of Pazzani and Sarrett (1990), and it may be difficult to apply to decision trees. Seshu (1989) has used an average-error model to show that a particular feature construction technique can overcome errors due to certain unfavorable configurations of examples labeled as "generalized parity problems," but the method has nothing to offer us in the context of error resulting from insufficient samples (indeed, it could not, since it applies to the unrestricted class of concepts).

Kadie (1991) has used an empirical approach to estimate what he calls the *effective VC dimension*. His results suggest that this strategy is very useful when we are trying to analyze the future performance of a particular bias in a specific learning problem. Because Kadie's approach can account for the effect of errors in the training sample and arbitrary biases of the learning algorithm, it seems to be more generally applicable when the issue is to estimate the rate of accuracy improvement for a particular algorithm-problem combination.

8.2.4 Estimating Average-Error Lower Bounds for Small Classes of Decision Trees

An alternative empirical approach to average-error bounds might be obtained simply by computing them directly. One could generate random concepts from a class of decision trees and use statistical techniques to estimate the average error. Random concepts drawn from classes of decision trees have been used frequently (e.g., Matheus 1990; Kadie 1990). Unfortunately, one must use a large number of such concepts to get a result that may be reliable, and one is faced with bounding the variance resulting from different choices of training samples and the error resulting from different choices of concepts.

The strategy I present here revolves around the use of what I will call a *concept tree* and superficially resembles a technique used in Kushilevitz and Mansour (1990). It can be used only for small classes of decision trees since its complexity is governed by the product of $|H|$ (the hypothesis space size) and the number of events. Nevertheless, this method provides a result that appears to be extremely accurate, and the space requirements can be limited to almost exactly $\dfrac{2^N |H|}{8}$ bytes via bit-vector operations.

Procedure *Calc_Lower_Avg* produces an estimated lower bound for the average error. First, no **BDT** algorithm can do better than randomly selecting a concept that is consistent with all the examples. Second, in my experiments, I have designed my version of this procedure to refrain from choosing an event e in step 2 that has already been chosen in the path to the root. This assumption is not especially optimistic when the parameter E (the number of training examples) is small compared to the total number of possible examples in the space.

Procedure *Calc_Lower_Aug* (H_{node}: **Concept_List**;
   E: **#_Events_Left_To_Choose**)

1. If E is 0, call *Calc_Leaf_Error*(H_{node}) and return.
2. Randomly select an event, e.
3. Let $H1$ be the members of H_node which classify the event as a positive.
4. Call *Calc_Lower_Avg*($H1, E\text{-}1$).
5. Let $H2$ be the members of H_{node} which classify the event as a negative.
6. Call *Calc_Lower_Avg*($H2, E\text{-}1$).

Procedure *Calc_Error* (H_{leaf}: **Concept_List**)

1. For each member of H_{leaf}, h, calculate h_d, the average distance between h and all members of H_{leaf}.
2. Average all of the h_d's and multiply by the proportion of concepts in H_{leaf}. (This is the contribution to the total average error.)

Table 8.1
Decision-tree concept classes

No. of features	No. of nodes	Maximum tree depth	No. of concepts
7	5	2	184
7	7	2	1066
4	11	3	3078
5	9	4	9232
5	11	3	16992
7	9	4	58466

The starting hypotheses spaces, H, were generated with several parameters: the number of features, the number of nodes in the decision tree, and the tree's maximum depth (starting from 0 for the root). Table 8.1 summarizes the six surveyed spaces.

Figure 8.1 shows the results of the experiments. Only three runs were used for each concept class, because the variation between runs with this method tends to be quite small—no more than 2 percent for the smallest class and in the tenths and hundredths of a percentage point for the others. *The fact that the runs are this close together indicates that considerable averaging is already present in each run.* Note that figure 8.1 shows the number of examples used for learning in units of $\lceil Log_2 |H| \rceil$.

8.2.5 Analysis of Results

Because I have surveyed a relatively small number of decision-tree concept classes and because the method does not lend itself easily to classes that are many orders of magnitude larger than the largest one shown (with 58,466 concepts), it would be rather difficult to make detailed conclusions involving expected accuracies. The one hypothesis that may be suspected from figure 8.1 is that the $\lceil Log_2 |H| \rceil$ is an important breakpoint for average-case error with these classes of decision trees. This suggests that the "pessimism" inherent in the worst-case analysis of the Vapnik-Blumer bound is mainly associated with the ε divisor for these concept classes.

Assuming, then, that the shapes of corresponding curves for decision-tree concept classes tend toward the same form as in figure 8.1, we may tentatively conclude that the $\lceil Log_2 |H| \rceil$ is a good average-error heuristic. That is, one cannot expect to do very well (above, say, 90%) if the learner does not have at least $\lceil Log_2 |H| \rceil$ examples.

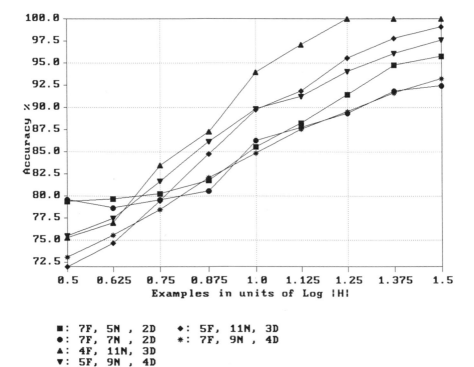

Figure 8.1
Experiment 1: Average D-tree class accuracy (uniform). (Described by number of features, number of nodes, and maximum depth.)

8.2.6 Feature Construction and $\lceil Log_2|H| \rceil$

Consider a learner that is given n examples, and suppose that we are willing to generate 2^n features at random; that is, each such "constructed" feature is generated by flipping a coin n times, once for each training example. Even if we do not know how many of the learning events are positive examples, we can still observe that the expected number of "perfect splits" available in our randomly generated set of features is 2; that is, on the average, there will be two features available from that set that completely separate the positive events in the training sample from the negative events. This means that no learner that relies on the data alone to select features for node tests can save itself from selecting one of our randomly generated attributes.[3]

But if the learner chooses one of these attributes, the learner is effectively guessing the class values of the examples that are not in the training set. In other words, no "learning" has occurred; the mutual information between the decision function and the target concept will be zero, and there will be no compression (Blumer et al. 1989). The learner will build a three-node tree (provided that there are some positive and some negative examples), and the tree will predict the class value of unseen events no more accurately than guessing.

This example is not as pathological as it appears at first blush. The same phenomenon can occur, albeit in a less striking manner, when the learner is presented with a smaller number of additional attributes constructed in this manner. Since the algorithm may now build a more detailed tree, whole subtrees of this tree may end up consisting of our "garbage" features.

8.2.7 Simplicity Criteria and Difficulty Measures

Define a *simplicity criterion* as a limitation on the complexity of the model class that may be instantiated when estimating a particular function. For example, when one is performing a polynomial fit, it seems fairly apparent that the degree of the polynomial must be less than the number of data points. Simplicity criteria have been studied by statisticians for a number of years; one of the most important early efforts was the *Akaike information criterion* (AIC) (Akaike 1977).

The essential idea here is to figure out how many parameters, k, to include in a model. Minimizing AIC means minimizing k minus the log-likelihood function for the model, based on some assumed variance, $\hat{\sigma}$. In particular, if k is allowed to get too large, it does not matter that the likelihood of the data given a k-parameter model is very great; one will not achieve a minimal AIC. Unfortunately, the log-likelihood function cannot be calculated without an assumed family of distributions and a reasonable estimate of $\hat{\sigma}$. Nevertheless, the AIC had an important *structural* feature, and that is the existence of a *penalty term* for model complexity.

Within the statistical community, there is considerable debate about both the proper viewpoint (communications theory or statistics; compare Barron 1984 and Rissanen 1983) and the nature of the penalty term (compare Barron 1984 and Rissanen 1983 with Friedman 1990 and Schwartz 1977).

In the machine-learning community, this controversy often appears in the search for pruning techniques, though some work is not easily classifiable as belonging solely to machine learning or solely to statistics (e.g. Brieman et al. 1984; Quinlan and Rivest 1988). But one trend that seems to be established is that any algorithm that selects models must do so based on some kind of trade-off between model complexity and model fit—normally implemented as a "penalty" for model complexity. Traditional pruning strategies (Brieman et al. 1984) and more modern approaches (Cestnik and Bratko 1991) reflect this basic notion.

On the other hand, much work has been done in trying to establish *difficulty measures*. Measures of difficulty often apply to classes of concepts (models), such as their VC dimension, or may apply to comparisons between classes of concepts (e.g., Pagallo's notion of the strength of representations; see Pagallo 1990, ch. 2). Alternatively, these difficulty measures may apply to individual concepts (e.g., dispersion in Rendell and Seshu 1990 or Shannon's rate distortion theory, or the use of the L_1 norm in Kushilevitz and Mansour 1990).

In this chapter I am proposing that average-case error analysis can serve to bridge the gap between these two perspectives. If the data are insufficient to guarantee satisfactory average-error results in a particular model class, then we should not choose models from that class. In particular, for finite hypothesis spaces, I am proposing $\lceil Log_2 |H| \rceil$ as an approximate lower bound on the number of examples that we will be willing to use when attempting to produce hypotheses from $|H|$. If we do not have enough examples, I am advocating that we either attempt to find a smaller H or abandon the search for an estimate of the class function, *regardless* of how successful we are in fitting the training data.

8.3   Experiments with Feature Conversion and Pruning Biases

This set of experiments involves just two of the three kinds of biases mentioned earlier: *feature conversion* biases and *pruning biases*. Recall that feature conversion biases center around how a particular feature is "Booleanized", given that an attribute of a learning problem may have m values, how many of the $2^{m-1} - 1$ reasonable partitions can the BDT method use in a *single* node test? I defined pruning biases as those biases used to prevent the tree from having "too many" leaf nodes.

Table 8.2
Test domain characteristics

Domain	No. of classes	No. of features	No. of examples	Class populations	Best (%) in Holte (1991)	Best (%) here
Lymphography	4	18	148	81, 61, 4, 2	85.1	84.8
Breast cancer	2	9	286	201, 85	78.5	76.4

8.3.1   The Domains

Two domains were used, both from standard "test-bed" problems. One is the lymphography problem and the other is the breast cancer domain. Both data sets were first used in Michalski et al. (AQ15, 1986), Cestnik, Konenenko, and Bratko (ASSISTANT-86, 1987), and Clark and Niblett (CN2, 1987).[4] Both domains have been widely used since then; Holte (1991) has collected the citations. Table 8.2 summarizes the results.

Although my primary purpose in this chapter is not to compare my accuracy results with those of other systems, the best result reported here for lymphography is (insignificantly) below the best result reported in Holte (1991).[5] The best result reported here for breast cancer is significantly below the best result reported in Holte.[6]

8.3.2   The Learner

All the experiments in this and the following section were done with the New Term Constructor/2 (NTC/2), a descendant of the older NTC algorithm (Seshu, Rendell, and Tcheng, 1989).[7] NTC/2 uses the PLS1 clusterer as a subroutine (Rendell 1981) but is capable of applying a large number of additional techniques to the induction process. For purposes of this chapter, the portions of NTC/2 that are relevant are the PLS1 clusterer and the feature construction operations (described in the next section). (See Seshu 1991 for a more complete description.)

8.3.3   Feature Conversion Biases

I examined four basic methods of feature conversion. None of the methods differs for 2-valued (binary) attributes, but there can be great variation in the number of possible binary distinctions for multivalued attributes.

Unary conversion is the simplest. Just assign one binary attribute to each value of a multiple-valued attribute. *Range-based* conversion is more

Table 8.3
Feature conversion biases

Conversion bias	No. binary features for $V > 2$ values	Actual features generated for a 4-valued attribute	No. features gen'd in lymphog.	No. features gen'd in br. canc.
Unary	V	$\{1\}, \{2\}, \{3\}, \{4\}$	50	47
E-Range	$V - 1$	$\{1\}, \{1,2\}, \{1,2,3\}$	82	65
Ranges	$\binom{V}{2} + V$	union of above 2 entries & $\{2,3\}$	139	134
Full binary	$2^{(V-1)} - 1$	All proper subsets minus mirror images	300	629
"Fiddling"	N/A	N/A	57	46

complex and can be used on attributes whose values have an ordering.[8] Range-based conversion picks out each attribute value range (up to mirror images).

Extreme-range (or *e-range*) conversion is like range-based conversion, except that a binary feature corresponding to a particular range is not generated if one of the original attribute's extreme values is not present in the range. *Full binary* conversion can be used with interval-, integer-, or nominal-valued features alike. We simply generate new Boolean features for every subset of the original attribute values (except that mirror images are not used). Table 8.3 summarizes the number of (Boolean) features generated under each conversion bias for attributes with 4 and V values.

One additional conversion bias shown in table 8.3 is labeled "fiddling." This bias was obtained in the obvious manner: I tried to handpick the best possible combination of feature conversion biases for the problem, based primarily on average-error and best-error results. I will describe this process and its result in more detail subsequently.

8.3.4   Pruning Biases

Nearly every BDT strategy has either been introduced with a built-in pruning mechanism or has had some sort of companion pruning operation proposed for it: Brieman et al. (1984)—CART with cost-complexity pruning; Rendell (1981)—the PLS1 clusterer; Quinlan (1987)—ID3 with various methods; Quinlan and Rivest (1988)—ID3 with the minimum description length principle;[9] and Cestnik and Bratko (1991)—ASSIS-

TANT-86 with Laplace method. Mingers (1989) collects the citations (also see Quinlan 1987). Pruning operations are essential to BDT methods because accuracy tends to degrade as the tree becomes "too large" (Holder 1990; Schaffer 1991).

Because the experiments were done with NTC/2, I used the pruning biases that come with the PLS1 clusterer (Rendell 1981). These biases take the form of *prepruning* rather than *post-pruning*; they control the PLS1 cluster's willingness to *stop splitting* rather than some additional algorithm's willingness to *chop leaves off an already-built tree*. While prepruning may be preferable to postpruning for conceptual economy or because it might run faster, neither advantage seems particularly significant.

Since one of the major issues here is whether biases can be learned based on experience with the current learning problem (Tcheng et al. 1989), I wanted to select a number of pruning biases in a "grid" pattern that would cover a portion of the bias space for these parameters (by "bias space," I simply mean the set of choices for these parameters).

All of the PLS1 clusterer's biases are pruning biases, and there are three: the minimum number of training events per leaf, minimum dissimilarity, and t_α, a confidence parameter. The original PLS1 cluster splitting metric used by Rendell (1981) involved taking the average-class value on each side of the candidate split (μ_1 and μ_2, where $\mu1 \geq \mu2$) and treating them as normally distributed (using the normal approximation to the binomial) with variance σ^2. The standard error of $\mu1$ is $\dfrac{\sigma}{\sqrt{n_1}}$ (similarly for $\mu2$). Rendell used the logarithm of the ratio of the means and a confidence parameter, t_α, which measures the degree of certainty wanted by the user to define the *dissimilarity*:[10]

$$d = \log\left(\frac{\mu_1}{\mu_2}\right) - t_\alpha \log(\sqrt{n_1}\sqrt{n_2}) + 2t_\alpha \log(\sigma). \tag{8.3}$$

Table 8.4
Pruning biases for domains

Domain	Minimum events at a leaf	Minimum dissimilarity	t_α (as used in NTC/2)
Lymphography	$\{1, 2, 3\}$	$(0.15, 0.20, 0.25\}$	$\{0.10, 0.20, 0.30\}$
Breast cancer	$\{8, 12\}$	$\{0.10, 0.15\}$	$\{0.10\}$

Since NTC/2 was coded to run on DOS machines (lacking a numeric coprocessor), I allowed the user to use an alternative but equivalent splitting metric that involves the difference of the means and reinterpreted t_α as a "preference for equality," since all candidate splits deal with the same node population ($n_1 + n_2$ are always the same). (See Seshu 1991 for more detail.) For our purposes, what is important is that each bias retards the growth of large trees when set to high values.

8.3.5 Experimental Design and Error Analysis: Lymphography

Each of the pruning biases was run with each of the feature-conversion methods on each domain for 20 runs with each fraction of the entire sample. Because the pruning biases interacted heavily with the sample size and with the conversion biases, I show the average (over all pruning biases) and the best and the worst biases for each sample fraction for

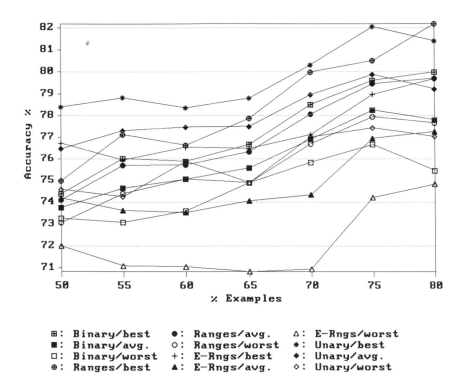

Figure 8.2a
Experiment 2a: Feature conversion, lymphography—best, average, and worst P-biases

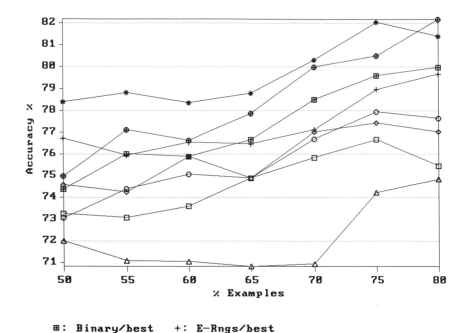

☐: **Binary/best**   +: **E-Rngs/best**
☐: **Binary/worst**   △: **E-Rngs/worst**
⊕: **Ranges/best**   *: **Unary/best**
○: **Ranges/worst**   ◇: **Unary/worst**

Figure 8.2b
Experiment 2a: Feature conversion, lymphography—best and worst P-biases

lymphography in figure 8.2a. Since there are 27 pruning biases and 4 conversion biases run 20 times each on 7 sample percentages, figure 8.2a summarizes 15,120 runs.

There are only 148 examples in the data set, and the variance is roughly estimable from the two larger classes that contain all but 6 of the examples. Essentially, we have a Bernoulli distribution with parameter $p = \dfrac{81}{148}$, so the variance is about 0.23. The most highly inaccurate points are those in which 80% of the sample was used for learning—about 590 examples in all. So one standard deviation is approximately $\sqrt{\dfrac{0.23}{590}}$, or about 2%. For the points calculated with 65% for learning, this number drops to just over 1%.

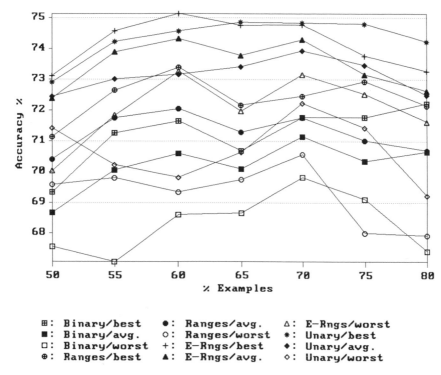

Figure 8.3a
Experiment 2a: Feature conversion, breast cancer—best, average and worst *P*-biases

For the average biases, we have much more accurate results, since there are 15,930 examples averaged over the 20 runs for each of the 27 biases even when 80% of the examples were used for learning. Each of the averages hence has a standard error of about one-third of a percentage point (0.37%). When 65% of the examples were used for learning, this drops to about 0.2%. Figure 8.2b is just like figure 8.2a except that I have only shown the best and the worst pruning biases.

8.3.6   Experimental Design and Error Analysis: Breast Cancer

Each of the pruning biases was run with each of the feature-conversion methods on each domain for 20 runs with each fraction of the entire sample. Again, the pruning biases interacted heavily with the sample size and with the conversion biases, so I show the average (over all pruning biases) and the best and the worst biases for each sample fraction for

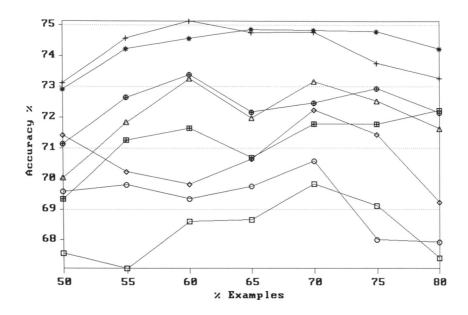

⊞ : **Binary/best**   + : **E-Rngs/best**
□ : **Binary/worst**   △ : **E-Rngs/worst**
⊕ : **Ranges/best**   * : **Unary/best**
○ : **Ranges/worst**   ◇ : **Unary/worst**

Figure 8.3b
Experiment 2a: Feature conversion, breast cancer—best and worst *P*-biases

breast cancer in figure 8.3a. Since there are 4 pruning biases and 4 conversion biases run 20 times each on 7 sample percentages, figure 8.3a summarizes 2240 runs.

There are 286 examples in the data set, and we treat the distribution as
Bernoulli, with parameter $p = \dfrac{205}{286}$, so the variance is about 0.20. The
most inaccurate points are those in which 80% of the sample was used for
learning—about 57 points per run, or 1140 points in all. One standard
deviation is approximately $\sqrt{\dfrac{0.20}{1140}}$, or about 1.3%. For the points calculated with 65% of the examples used for learning, this drops to just below
1%.

For the average biases, the inaccuracy is roughly two-thirds of a percentage point when 80% of the examples were used for learning and about

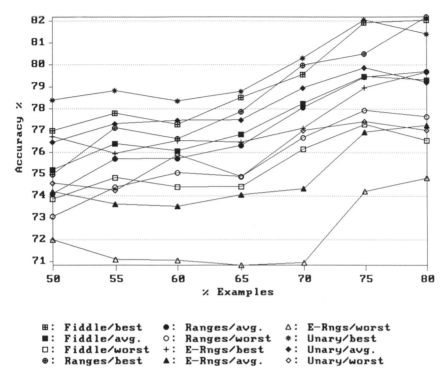

⊞: Fiddle/best	●: Ranges/avg.	△: E-Rngs/worst
■: Fiddle/avg.	○: Ranges/worst	✳: Unary/best
□: Fiddle/worst	+: E-Rngs/best	◆: Unary/avg.
⊕: Ranges/best	▲: E-Rngs/avg.	◇: Unary/worst

Figure 8.4a
Experiment 2a: Feature conversion, lymphography—best, average, and worst *P*-biases

one-half of a percentage point where 65% of the examples were used. Figure 8.3b is just like figure 8.3a except that I have only shown the best and the worst pruning biases.

8.3.7 "Fiddling" to Improve Feature-Conversion Biases

Arguably, the preceding experiment is somewhat unnatural. Although the range of results shown here is certainly within the established norms for these domains (Holte 1991), one might reasonably ask whether it seems reasonable to perform full binary feature conversion on an attribute such as the number of infected lymph nodes. From the view of common sense, it certainly does not make sense to generate all subsets of the legal lymph node counts (see Leng and Buchanan, 1991), so I tried to change the feature-conversion bias so that it would more accurately reflect the tiny amount of domain knowledge inhering in our interpretation (as lay-

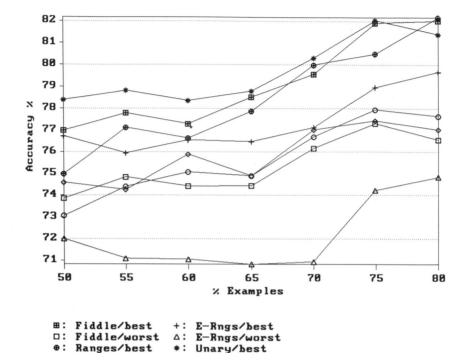

Figure 8.4b
Experiment 2a: Feature conversion, lymphography—best and worst *P*-biases

persons) of the attributes used in both data sets. I also experimented with
omitting attributes that I thought were confusing. Figures 8.4a, and 8.4b
summarizes these results for lymphography, with my "best fiddle" replacing binary conversion (the least successful method). Figure 8.4b is the same
as figure 8.4a except that I have only shown the best and worst pruning
biases. Figure 8.5a and 8.5b summarizes results analogous to figures 8.4a
and 8.4b but for breast cancer.

To my surprise, "fiddling" did not work well with lymphography. I was
unable to find any combination of feature conversion biases that worked
as well as unary conversion, even on attributes that did not appear to
merit it. Tables 8.5 and 8.6 summarize attributes, their values, and the best
conversion bias that I was able to produce (other than the four standard
ones previously discussed).[11]

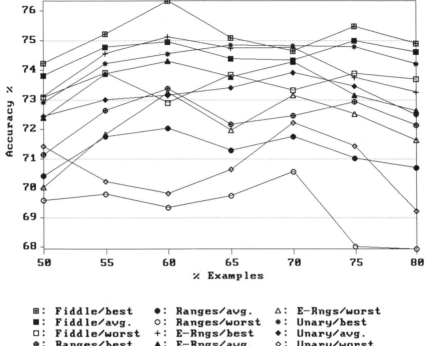

⊞: Fiddle/best	●: Ranges/avg.	△: E-Rngs/worst
■: Fiddle/avg.	○: Ranges/worst	*: Unary/best
□: Fiddle/worst	+: E-Rngs/best	◆: Unary/avg.
⊕: Ranges/best	▲: E-Rngs/avg.	◇: Unary/worst

Figure 8.5a
Experiment 2a: Feature conversion, breast cancer—best, average, and worst *P*-biases

8.3.8   Analysis of Results

Accuracy and Size of Effective Hypothesis Space   Given the analysis in section 8.2.1 about the log of the H-space, one might believe that the feature-conversion biases should make a good deal more difference, especially considering the much larger number of features generated during binary conversion. In lymphography, this trend seems to be weakly supported by figure 8.2. The 50 features generated under unary conversion seem to do substantially better than the higher number of features used for other methods (82 for extreme ranges, 139 for ranges, and 300 for full binary conversion; see table 8.3). However, the difference does not seem to be especially substantial between the three groups, implying that some saturation point is reached when we add interdependent features. Interestingly, e-ranges seem to do worst of all, which suggests that some attributes

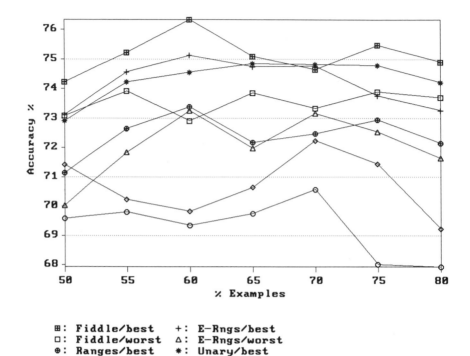

**: Fiddle/best   +: E-Rngs/best
□: Fiddle/worst   △: E-Rngs/worst
⊕: Ranges/best   *: Unary/best
○: Ranges/worst   ◇: Unary/worst

Figure 8.5b
Experiment 2a: Feature conversion, breast cancer—best and worst *P*-biases

may not be linearly correlated with the class value. This would help to explain the closing gap between range features and unary features as the number of examples increases (although this trend is just barely statistically significant).

In breast cancer (figure 8.3), there seems to be a slightly better relationship between the number of features and the accuracy; unary and e-range features tend to do quite a bit better. But there is no evidence that feature-conversion methods that generate more features do relatively better with more data, although the average performance of range-based and full binary conversion is significantly below the performance of the two more frugal feature-conversion methods. Finally, there appears to be no correlation between the number of examples used for learning and the relative accuracy of different conversion methods.

Table 8.5
Attributes and "best fiddle" for lymphography

Attribute Name	No. of values	Type of values	Best conversion by "fiddling"
Lymphatics	4	Nominal	Unary
Block of affere	2	Nominal	Unary
Block of lymph c	2	Nominal	Unary
Block of lymph s	2	Nominal	Unary
By-pass	2	Nominal	Unary
Extravasates	2	Nominal	Unary
Regeneration of	2	Nominal	Unary
Early uptake in	2	Nominal	Unary
No. nodes diminished	3	Interval	Unary
No. nodes enlarged	4	Interval	Unary
Changes in lymphatics	3	Interval	Unary
Defect in node	4	Nominal	Unary
Changes in node	4	Nominal	Unary
Changes in structure	8	Nominal	Unary
Special forms	3	Nominal	Unary
Dislocation of	2	Nominal	Unary
Exclusion of	2	Nominal	Unary
No. of nodes in	8	Interval	E-Range

Table 8.6
Attributes and "best fiddle" for breast cancer

Attribute Name	No. of values	Type of values	Best conversion by "fiddling"
Age†	6	Interval	Unary
Menopause	3	Interval	Unary
Tumor size†	10	Interval	E-Range
Inv-nodes†	7	Interval	E-Range
Node-caps	2	Nominal	Removed
Degree of malignancy	3	Interval	E-Range
Breast (left/right)	2	Nominal	Removed
Breast-quad location	4	Nominal	Removed
Irradiation	2	Nominal	Removed

Relative Importance of Pruning and Conversion Biases For lymphography (figure 8.2), the *best* pruning biases for e-range and full binary conversion do not seem to be much above the average pruning biases for the best two conversion methods (unary and ranges), suggesting that feature conversion has a more serious impact than the choice of pruning parameters (for the options in table 8.4).

For breast cancer, the *worst* pruning biases of the two *best* feature-conversion methods are not substantially below the *best* pruning biases of the two *worst* pruning methods (figure 8.3b), so feature conversion seems to be a more important bias in this case than pruning. Still, these results are tentative, because there is no way of knowing whether more "conservative" pruning biases (those that retarted the growth of trees even more) might have helped the weaker feature-conversion methods.

Use of Common Sense in Converting Features My attempt to "fiddle" with the feature-conversion bias and optimize it failed for lymphography (figure 8.4) and was not especially successful for breast cancer (figure 8.5). It is interesting to note that I started out in each case using the "natural" feature conversions (end-point ranges for most interval-valued features, binary for nominals) but soon replaced binary conversions with unary ones for both data sets. Oddly, in lymphography the unary conversions seem to do even better than the two forms of range-based conversions, even on variables that should be interval (such as the number of enlarged or diminished nodes). This suggests that domain knowledge may be misleading. In some data sets the "natural" way to convert features may fail because there just are not enough data. Lymphography, with a mere 150 examples, may be such a case. However, I ran out of patience with the large number of possibilities when "fiddling," so is not clear that this has much significance. Also, I am not a clinician and have no formal basis for interpreting the meaning of the attribute labels in order to make conclusions about their data types (see Breiman et al. 1984; Leng and Buchanan 1991).

Optimal Training Sample Sizes in Breast Cancer For all biases in breast cancer, there appears to be a sampling proportion that produces optimal results. This may be because the best breast cancer runs involve very simple trees. If the attributes in breast cancer have high intrinsic accuracy, that is, the potential to predict the class well (Rendell and Seshu 1990), then perhaps there are many very small disjuncts (Holte, Acker, and Porter 1989) causing the problem. With smaller samples, NTC/2 does not try to learn these disjuncts and therefore does better. On the other hand, it may be that the attributes for breast cancer are very poor, in which case larger training samples simply encourage induction strategies to "fit the noise." This question cannot be resolved with the small test data set (although Michalski et al. 1986 do not suggest that the experts do better than the best results in Holte 1991). However, it does suggest that feature-conversion methods that produce fewer features may do better in such situations.

8.4   Feature Construction Experiments

In the final set of experiments, my focus was on feature-construction methods. I used three methods: no construction, a reduced form of look-ahead, and FRINGE-class strategies. The feature-conversion biases were those that performed the best in the previous experiment: unary conversions for breast cancer and the "fiddled" conversions for lymphography. Other than that, the domains, number of runs, and pruning biases were all identical to the previous experiment (hence, the error analysis in the previous section also applies).

8.4.1   Lookahead Feature Construction

Exhaustive lookahead greatly increases the complexity of BDT algorithms since it involves squaring the number of features or some higher power (Rendell, Cho, and Seshu 1989). NTC/2 instead offers the user the option of picking the most promising features whenever a decision tree node is split and using those for lookahead. These most promising features are those with the best dissimilarity ratings, except that NTC/2 knows about feature conversion and makes sure that there is as little duplication as possible.[12] The user can select two-feature lookahead to generate these features from each pair of the most promising features:

- A AND B
- $\overline{A}$ AND B
- A AND $\overline{B}$
- $\overline{A}$ AND $\overline{B}$
- A XOR B

Under three-feature lookahead, we again choose the set of the most promising features and generate the above features for every pair in that set, but we also generate these additional features for each trio:

- $\overline{A}B$ OR AC
- $\overline{A}\overline{B}$ OR AC
- AB OR $\overline{A}C$
- $A\overline{B}$ OR $\overline{A}C$

I have shown (Seshu 1991) that three-feature lookahead essentially allows the D-tree to "jump" two levels at once. A tree with four leaves can have at most three features used in the internal nodes, and the feature-construction operations above cover all possible distinctions. In the experiments, I used three-feature lookahead over the set of the four most promising features; 40 features were generated for every split. This is the equivalent of using 90 features in lymphography (40 plus the 50 generated by unary conversion) and 86 in breast cancer (40 plus the 46 used in the "fiddled" conversion). I used a set size of four promising features based strictly on my experience with running NTC/2 over the data sets.

8.4.2   FRINGE* Feature Construction

NTC/2 does not use the complete FRINGE/symFRINGE algorithm as implemented by Pagallo (1989, 1990) or the extensions to FRINGE implemented by Yang's DCFringe (Yang 1990; Yang, Blix, and Rendell 1991). NTC/2 uses all the feature-construction methods, but it only applies these methods once. In other words, we grow the tree to purity (what Brieman et al. 1984 refer to as T_{max}) and construct features just once before rerunning the algorithm. During the first run, the pruning biases are set so that the tree can easily be grown to purity (NTC/2 uses zero minimum dissimilarity and allows leaf nodes to contain only a single example). On the second run, NTC/2 reverts to the user-requested bias. Only the second run's accuracy measurement is recorded. This scenario is quite different from what has been envisioned by Pagallo (1989) and Yang (1990). Under their schemes, the algorithm keeps on trying to construct new features by splitting to purity until some stopping criterion is reached. As this process continues, constructed features that have not been used in the last few runs are removed.

The reason that FRINGE/symFRINGE and/or DCFringe are not implemented in their entirety is that I wanted to see how the feature-construction operations themselves affected learning. Moreover, my experience with allowing multiple rounds of feature construction on both data sets is that overfitting begins to occur very rapidly. The feature-construction operations used are the union of those used in FRINGE, symFRINGE, and DCFringe.

The pseudocode used to implement these operations is shown in figure 8.6. In the figure, the term Current's parity of parent-feature means:

- If the current node is a right-child, use the parent's feature.
- If the current node is a left-child, use the negation of the parent's feature.

The term Parent's parity of grandparent-feature means:

- If the parent node is a right-child, use the grandparent's feature.
- If the parent node is a left-child, use the negation of the grandparent's feature.

8.4.3 Analysis of Results

Accuracy and Size of Effective Hypothesis Space   For lymphography, figures 8.7a and b show no apparent correlation between the number of features generated by feature construction and the accuracy, except as the training sample size approaches 80%. Only at that point does any form of feature construction (lookahead) appear to do much better.[13] In figures 8.8a and b (breast cancer), there seems to be little correlation between increasing sample size and an increasing likelihood that feature-construction methods can do well. Indeed, feature construction seems to hurt the learner all along the sample-size (x) axis, although it has less impact in the areas where accuracy is highest.

Relative Importance of Pruning Biases and Feature Construction   In lymphography, the separation between the best, average, and worst pruning biases is relatively consistent, suggesting that pruning biases are indeed much more important. This separation is blurred a little bit toward the right side of the graph, as the average pruning bias for lookahead seems to be doing as well as the best pruning bias for no feature construction.

For breast cancer (figure 8.8), the two feature-construction methods seem to do substantially worse than no construction at all, but this gap

For all leaves of depth 2 or more:
   {if (the sibling isn't a leaf)
/* – – – – – – – – – Case 1: Sibling isn't a leaf – – – – – – – – – – – – – – – */
     {if ((the current node is positive ‖ /* Originally from FRINGE   */
       (running as DCFringe+)   ) /* The DCFringe + extension */
       {Build & add the feature:
           [Parent's parity of grandparent-feature] AND
           [Current's parity of parent-feature   ]
       }
     else /* do absolutely nothing */;
     }
   else
/*– – – – Case 2: Sibling is leaf, but parent's sibling not leaf – – – – – – – – */
/* – – – –   and the current node is positive – – – – – – – – – – – – – – */
     {if ((the parent's sibling isn't a leaf) && /* originally from   */
      (the current node is positive)   ) /* FRINGE.   */
      {Build & add the feature:
          [Parent's parity of grandparent-feature] AND
          [Current's parity of parent-feature   ]
      }
     else
/* – – – – – – Case 3: both sibling & parent's sibling are leaves – – – – – – */
/* – – – – – –   and the parent's sibling is negative – – – – – – – – – – */
      {if ((the parent's sibling is a leaf   ) &&   /* originally   */
       (the current node is positive   ) &&   /* from   */
       (the parent's sibling is negative)   )   /* FRINGE   */
       {Build & add the feature:
           [Parent's parity of grandparent-feature] AND
           [Current's parity of parent-feature   ]
       }
      else
/* – – – – – – Case 4: both sibling & parent's sibling are leaves – – – – – – */
/* – – – – – –   and the parent's sibling is positive – – – – – – – – – – */
       {if ((the parent's sibling is a leaf   ) && /* the   */
        (the current node is positive   ) && /* DCFringe   */
        (the parent's sibling is positive)   ) /* extension   */
        {Build & add the feature:
          [Current's parity of parent-feature] OR
          [Reverse-of-Parent-parity of grandparent-feature]
        }   /* case 4 satisfied   */
       }   /* case 1–3 not satisfied   */
      }   /* Cases 1–2 not satisfied   */
    }   /* Cases 1 not satisfied   */
  }   /* for all leaves of depth 2 or more */

Figure 8.6
Pseudocode for FRINGE* methods

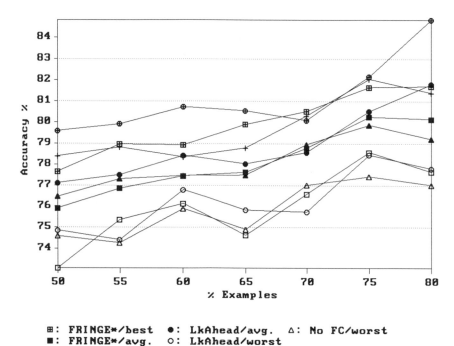

Figure 8.7a
Experiment 3: Feature construction, lymphography—best, average, and worst P-biases

does seem to narrow significantly as the number of examples increases. Figure 8.8a seems to indicate that a small number of pruning biases are especially inappropriate for the problem, since the average and best pruning biases for all methods seem particularly close as the number of training examples approach 80%. At the percentage of examples for learning with the highest accuracies (60%), all three methods appear to do about equally well, with the best, worst, and average pruning bias performances clearly separated.

Also as before, it is unclear whether more sophisticated methods for constructing features based on lookahead or whether the original FRINGE* algorithms might do better or worse than the methods implemented for these experiments.

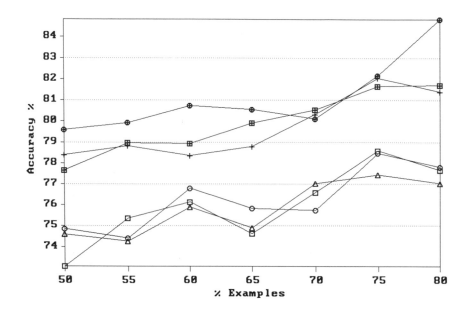

Figure 8.7b
Experiment 3: Feature construction, lymphography—best and worst *P*-biases

8.5   Conclusion

I have advocated the following propositions in this chapter:

• Average-case lower-bound estimates for BDT concepts/algorithms can be obtained via an accurate sampling method and are considerably more optimistic than the Valiant-model worst-case bounds.

However, the method has severe limitations and may not be sufficiently predictive for some problems.

• Feature-conversion biases may be more important than pruning or feature-construction biases.

In particular, it may not be possible for an algorithm dynamically manages its pruning biases to recover from a poor choice of feature-conversion

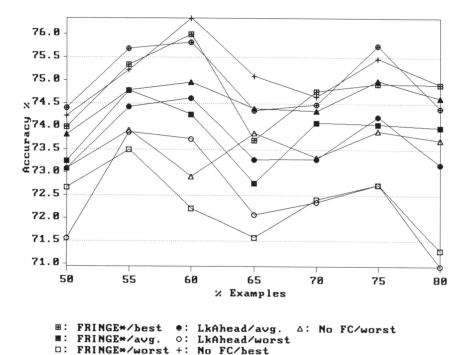

Figure 8.8a
Experiment 3: Feature construction, breast cancer—best, average, and worst P-biases

methods by the user. The optimal feature-conversion biases may depend on the size of the training sample, as well as the nature of the domain. Where data are sparse, a conservative approach to feature conversion may do better, even if the domain knowledge suggests otherwise.

• Pruning biases may be more important than feature-construction biases.

Powerful feature-construction biases such as lookahead and FRINGE* methods allow the learner to compress several levels of a tree into one level. If a learner has an ability to subsample and to evaluate its success, it may be able to moderate the effects of excessively powerful feature-construction methods by pruning more aggressively.

• The interaction between feature construction, feature conversion, and pruning biases may be substantial—perhaps so significant that it is diffi-

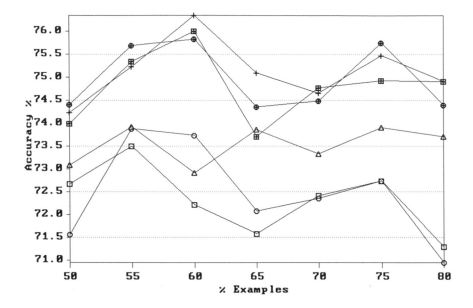

⊞: FRINGE*/best   +: No FC/best
□: FRINGE*/worst △: No FC/worst
⊕: LkAhead/best
○: LkAhead/worst

Figure 8.8b
Experiment 3: Feature construction, breast cancer—best and worst P-biases

cult to draw conclusions from studying any one of these forms of bias
in isolation.

Many studies, particularly those involving artificial data or randomly
generated concepts (Kadie 1991; Rendell and Cho 1990), use only Boolean
features, so the question of feature conversion does not arise. But some
analyses of feature-construction algorithms may be flawed because no
effort was made to allow the learner to compensate by changing its pruning biases. The same argument can be made about comparative studies of
BDT algorithms, such as Rendell, Cho, and Seshu (1989).

The conclusions, however, are tentative, and further research is needed
in a large number of areas, among them:

• How much does the size of the effective hypothesis space increase with
powerful feature-construction and/or -conversion methods?

Evidently we cannot get an idea of how much larger the effective hypothesis space is just by counting the number of features generated or the number of dichotomies induced (Haussler 1988) by a feature-construction method or created by a feature-conversion strategy. To the extent that both approaches create a large number of poor features, it may be that the increase in the number of samples required for average-case learning is quite moderate and, therefore, that the risk of "overfitting" is minimal. In particular, when the extra features do little to distinguish the events in the "true" concept, these strategies may have no impact whatsoever.

• To the extent that pruning biases matter, can they be effectively optimized?

Some evidence on this subject already exists (Seshu, Rendell, and Tcheng 1989; Tcheng, Lambert, and Lu 1990), but the number of surveyed problems is small. The results presented here are not especially persuasive because they involved a small number of pruning biases in a limited area of NTC/2's bias space.

• What is the impact of small disjuncts and attribute or class error on methods that generate a large number of features?

One would expect that a very conservative approach to feature conversion and feature construction would do best in a situation in which the target concept had a great number of small disjuncts or the training sample was infected with a large amount of error in the feature or class values, but this is still an open question.

• Can domain knowledge actually hurt the feature-construction or feature-conversion process?

Surely this is not the case in domains where certain transformations are *rational* in nature (Ragavan 1991); for example, rotating a tic-tac-toe board can never be harmful. But are there other kinds of domain knowledge that can have the effect of increasing the number of examples needed to produce good average-error results?

Acknowledgments

This research was partially supported by National Science Foundation grant IRI-88-22031 and partially done while the author was in the Inductive Learning Group at the University of Illinois at Urbana-Champaign.

Notes

This paper presents results from an *average-case* model of learning in the context of *binary decision tree* (BDT) algorithms. Under this model, all concepts in some specific class have an equal chance of being the target concept for a particular example, and all examples in the space are equally weighted. I first present results using a sampling.

1. Among many others. See citations in Matheus (1990) or Rendell and Seshu (1990). The analysis given here concerning feature construction biases is inapplicable to systems that use domain knowledge (e.g., Drastal, Czako, and Raatz 1989; Ragavan 1991).

2. More precisely, by replacing $Ln(|H|)$ by a factor proportional to the VC dimension over $\log(\varepsilon)$.

3. This analysis was first suggested to me by Dave Tcheng (personal communication). A similar argument appears in Ehrenfeucht et al. (1988) and Blumer et al. (1989).

4. Thanks go to M. Zwitter and M. Soklic of the University Medical Centre, Institute of Oncology, Liubljana, Yugoslavia, for providing the data. I am also grateful to David Aha and the administrators of the University of California—Irvine machine-learning database.

5. The best result on lymphography so far is from Buntine (1989b), who used a modified Bayesian classifier. The result reported here is significantly above the second-best accuracy of 83 percent reported in Holte (obtained by Clark and Niblett 1987, 1989 with CN2).

6. In fact, of the 66 results reported, 16 of them are at least 75.4 percent; about one in four of these accuracy ratings are equal or significantly higher than what I obtained.

7. NTC/2 is supported for users at the University of Illinois at Urbana-Champaign on several machines, including a VAX, some Suns, and an HP. NTC/2 also runs on IBM-compatible PCs. Send e-mail to rseshu@du.edu if you would like a copy of the code that may be installed on Unix- or DOS-based machines.

8. Note that the algorithm can impose an ordering on nominal-attribute values based on the conditional probability of a given class given the attribute value's cue validity; this is the method used in Brieman et al. (1984) and Rendell and Cho (1990). See also Quinlan (1985).

9. See Rissanen (1978, 1983).

10. The last term is constant and gets absorbed into the user's minimum dissimilarity value.

11. Breast cancer features marked with a dagger were preprocessed to add missing values with the most common value for the class of the event. This was done for just 9 events of 286.

12. For example, if a particular feature with many values is very important and feature conversion generates many resulting features, there is a chance that only those features will be selected as the most promising. NTC/2 tries to prevent this by making sure that no pair of features descended from an original, user-specified feature is included in this set of most promising features. Of course, this computationally inexpensive technique does not stop NTC/2 from being deceived when the user-specified features are insufficiently independent. No algorithm that runs in time linear in the number of features can solve this problem.

13. The FRINGE* operations were executed only once. In FRINGE and SymFRINGE (Pagallo 1989) and in DCFringe (Yang 1991), the feature-construction operations are performed repeatedly, and unpromising features are dropped. The point of this research is not to compare algorithms per se but rather to compare the effects of different biases. Interestingly, the highest accuracy reached by lookahead is insignificantly below the highest accuracy reported by Holte (1991).

References

Akaike, H. (1977). On the entropy maximization principle. In *Applications of Statistics*, P. R. Krishnaiah, ed. North-Holland.

Barron, A. R. (1984). Predicted squared error: A criterion for automatic model selection. In *Self-organizing Methods in Modelling*, S. J. Farlow, ed. Marcel Dekker, New York.

Barron, A. R., and Barron, R. L. (1988). Statistical learning networks: A unifying view. *Computing Science and Statistics: Proc. 20th Symposium on the Interface*, E. Wegman, ed. American Statistical Association, Alexandria, Va.

Blumer, A., Ehrenfeucht, A., Haussler, D., and Warmuth, M. (1986). Learnability and the Vapnik-Chervonenkis dimension. JACM 36 no. (4) October 1989, 929–965.

Brieman, L., Friedman, J., Olshen R. A., and Stone, C. J. (1984). *Classification and Regression Trees*. Wadsworth, Belmont, Calif.

Buntine, W. (1989a). A critique of the Valiant model. *Proc. Eleventh International Joint Conference on Artificial Intelligence*, 837–842.

Buntine, W. (1989b). Learning classification rules using Bayes. *Proc. Sixth International Workshop on Machine Learning*, A. Segre, ed. Morgan Kaufmann. 94–98.

Cestnik, G., and Bratko, I. (1991). On estimating probabilities in tree pruning. *Proc. European Working Session on Learning*.

Cestnik, G., Konenenko, I., and Bratko, I. (1987). Assistant-86: A knowledge-elicitation tool for sophisticated users. In I. Bratko and N. Lavrac (eds.), *Progress in Machine Learning*, 31–45. Sigma Press, Wilmslow.

Clark, P., and Niblett, T. (1987). Induction in noisy domains. In *Progress in Machine Learning*. I. Bratko and N. Lavrac (eds.), 11–30. Sigma Press, Wilmslow.

Clark, P., and Niblett, T. (1989). The CN2 induction algorithm. *Machine Learning* 3(4): 261–283.

Dietterich, T. G. (1989). Limitations on inductive learning. *Proc. Sixth International Workshop on Machine Learning*, 124–128.

Drastal, G., Czako G., and Raatz, S. (1989). Induction in an abstraction space: A form of constructive induction. *Proc. Eleventh International Joint Conference on Artificial Intelligence*, 708–712.

Ehrenfeucht, A., Haussler, D., Kearns, M., and Valiant, L. G. (1988). A general lower bound on the number of examples needed for learning. *Proc. 1988 Workshop on Computational Learning Theory*, 139–154.

Friedman, J. H. (1990). Multivariate adaptive regression splines. *Annals of Statistics* 2:1–67.

Haussler, D. (1988). Quantifying inductive bias: AI learning algorithms and Valiant's learning framework. *Artificial Intelligence* 36:177–221.

Haussler, D. (1990). Probably approximately correct learning. *Proc. AAAI*, 1101–1108.

Holder, L. (1990). The general utility problem in machine learning. *Proc. Seventh International Conference on Machine Learning*.

Holte, R. C. (1991). *Very Simple Classification Rules Perform Well on Most Datasets*. Report No. TR-91-16. University of Ottawa Department of Computer Science, April.

Holte, R. C., Acker, L., and Porter, B. W. (1989). Concept learning and the problem of small disjuncts. *Proc. of the Eleventh International Joint Conference on Artificial Intelligence*, 813–818.

Kadie, K. M. (1990). Quantifying the effects of representation, noise, and method on inductive learning. Workshop on Computational Theory and Natural Learning Systems, September, Princeton, N.J.

Kadie, K. M. (1991). Quantifying the value of constructive induction, knowledge, and noise filtering on inductive learning. *Proc. Eighth International Workshop on Machine Learning*, 153–158.

Kushilevitz, E., and Mansour, Y. (1990). Learning decision trees using the Fourier spectrum. *Proc. Conference on Learning Theory*.

Leng, B., and Buchanan, B. (1991). Constructive induction on symbolic features: Introducing new comparative terms. *Proc. Eighth International Workshop on Machine Learning*, 163–168.

Littlestone, N. (1988). Learning quickly when irrelevant attributes abound: A new linear-threshold algorithm. *Machine Learning*, 2 (2): 285–318.

Matheus, C. J. (1989). *Feature Construction: An Analytic Framework and an Application to Decision Trees* (Ph.D thesis), Report no. UIUCDCS-R-89-1559a. University of Illinois, Department of Computer Science, December.

Mitchell, T. M. (1980). *The need for biases in inductive learning*. Technical Report CBM-TR-117. Department of Computer Science, Rutgers University, May.

Michalski, R., Mozetic, I., Hong, J., and Lavrac, N. (1986). The multi-purpose incremental learning system AQ15 and its testing applications to three medical domains. *Proc. Fifth National Conference on Artificial Intelligence*, 1041–1045.

Mingers, J. (1989). An empirical comparison of selection measures for decision tree induction. *Machine Learning* 3 (4): 319–342.

Pagallo, G. M. (1989). Learning DNF by decision trees. *Proc. Eleventh International Joint Conference on Artificial Intelligence*.

Pagallo, G. M. (1990). *Adaptive Decision Tree Algorithms for Learning from Decision Trees* (Ph.D thesis). Report No. UCSC-CRL-90-27. University of California at Santa Cruz, June.

Pazzani, M., and Sarrett, W. (1990). Average Case Analysis of Conjunctive Learning Algorithms. *Proc. Seventh International Conference on Machine Learning*, 339–347.

Quinlan, J. R. (1983). Learning efficient classification procedures and their application to chess endgames. In *Machine Learning: An Artificial Intelligence Approach*, R. Michalski, J. Carbonell, and T. Mitchell, eds. Tioga, Palo Alto, Calif.

Quinlan, J. R. (1985). Decision trees and multi-valued attributes. In *Machine Intelligence 11*, J. E. Hayes and D. Michie, eds. Oxford University Press.

Quinlan, J. R. (1987). Simplifying decision tree. *International Journal of Man-Machine Studies* 27:221–234.

Quinlan, J. R., and Rivest, R. (1989). Inferring decision trees using the minimum description length principle. *Information and Computation* 80 (3): 227–248.

Ragavan, H. (1991). Relations, knowledge, and empirical learning. *Proc. Eighth International Workshop on Machine Learning*, 188–192.

Rendell, L. A. (1987). *An Adaptive Plan for State-Space Problems*. Ph.D thesis, University of Waterloo.

Rendell, L. A., and Cho, H. K. (1990). Empirical concept learning as a function of concept character. *Machine Learning* 5 (3): 267–298.

Rendell, L. A., Cho, H. H., and Seshu, R. M. (1989). Improving the design of similarity-based learning systems. *International Journal of Expert Systems* 2 (1): 97–133.

Rendell, L. A., and Seshu, R. M. (1990). Learning hard concepts through constructive induction: Framework and rationale. *Computational Intelligence* 6 (4): 247–270.

Rissanen, J. (1978). Modeling by shortest data description. *Automatica* 14:465–471.

Rissanen, J. (1983). A universal prior for integers and estimation by minimum description length. *Annals of Statistics* 11 (2): 416–431.

Schaffer, C. (1991). *Overfitting Avoidance as Bias.* Unpublished manuscript.

Schapire, R. (1990). The strength of weak learnability. *Machine Learning* 5:197–227.

Schlimmer, J. (1989). Incremental adjustment of representations for learning. *Proc. Sixth International Workshop on Machine Learning*, 79–90.

Schwartz, G. (1977). Estimating the dimension of a model. *Annals of Statistics* 6 (2): 461–464.

Seshu, R. M. (1989). Solving the parity problem. In *Proc. European Working Session on Learning*, pp. 191–197.

Seshu, R. M. (1991). *The NTC/2 User's Guide.* Unpublished manuscript.

Seshu, R. M., Rendell L. A., and Tcheng, D. (1989). Managing constructive induction with subcomponent assessment and multiple-objective optimization. *Proc. Fifth International Conference on Artificial Intelligence Applications*, 191–197.

Tcheng, D., Lambert, B., Lu, S. C-Y., and Rendell, L. (1989). Building robust learning systems by combining induction and optimization. *Proc. Eleventh International Joint Conference on Artificial Intelligence.*

Tcheng, D. K., Lambert, B., and Lu, S. C-Y. (1990). Generalized recursive splitting algos for learning hybrid concepts. In *Proc. AAAI*, 601–606.

Utgoff, P. E. (1988). Perceptron trees: A case study in hybrid concept representation. *Proc. Sixth Annual Workshop on Machine Learning.*

Valiant, L. G. (1984). A theory of the learnable. *CACM* 27 (11): 1134–42.

Yang, D. S. (1991). Feature Discovery in Decision Tree Representation. Master's thesis, University of Illinois.

Yang, D. S., Blix, G., and Rendell, L. A. (1991). The replication problem: A constructive induction approach. In Y. Kodratoff (ed.), *Proc. European Working Session on Learning*, 44–61.

9 Refining Algorithms with Knowledge-Based Neural Networks: Improving the Chou-Fasman Algorithm for Protein Folding

Richard Maclin and Jude W. Shavlik

9.1 Introduction

When addressing an unsolved problem, a normal approach is to start by researching the problem and seeing which approaches have been taken. The direction one takes often builds on earlier work. This strategy is generally ignored by most computerized empirical learning systems— systems that try to learn new concepts. Empirical learning systems often try to acquire a concept from scratch, ignoring knowledge that already exists about a problem. Ignoring this existing knowledge is dangerous, since the resulting learned concept may not contain important factors already identified in earlier work. The learning system may even be unable to solve the problem without the head start prior knowledge would give it. The approach we present allows an empirical learning system to take advantage of prior knowledge about a problem in a systematic way. Our learning system takes the initial knowledge and, rather than attempting to learn the whole concept from scratch, refines the initial knowledge to address the problem better.

Our work extends the KBANN system (for Knowledge-Based Artificial Neural Networks) [Towell90]. We use the extended system to refine the Chou-Fasman algorithm [Chou78] for predicting the folded structure of globular proteins, a particularly difficult problem in molecular biology. KBANN uses knowledge represented as simple, propositional-calculus rules (referred to as a *domain theory*) to create an initial neural network that represents the knowledge contained in the rules. This network will, it is hoped, be a better starting point for learning than a randomly configured initial network. This technique has proved effective for complex problems such as gene recognition [Noordewier91, Towell90], even when the original domain theory is not particularly good at solving the problem. The main limitation of the KBANN technique is that it can only translate rules that are propositional (have no variables) and are nonrecursive. This chapter describes an addition to KBANN that extends it for a simple type of recursion.

We extend KBANN to include a simple form of recursion by representing state information in the neural network. State in the network represents the context of the problem. For example, if the problem is how to cross a room, the state variables may represent (among other things) whether the light is on in the room. The rules introduced to solve this problem can therefore take into account the state of the problem. Rules to turn on the light would be considered only when the state of the problem indicated that the light is off. In this style of problem solving, the problem is solved not in one step but instead as a series of actions, each leading to a new state that, it is hoped, leads to the goal state (turning on the light, navigating to the couch, moving Cindy's toy fire engine out of the way, etc.). The network similarly attempts to determine the resulting next state given the current state and input. This approach is recursive because the state calculated is used in the next step as the previous state for the network. The extended KBANN system, called Finite-State KBANN (FSKBANN), translates domain theories that use state information, usually represented as generalized finite-state automata [Hopcroft79]. As in KBANN, FSKBANN first translates the domain theory into a neural network and then refines the network using backpropagation [Rumelhart86] with a set of examples.

The choice of neural networks as the empirical learning system on which to build was made for a couple of reasons. One basic reason is that networks provide a very general mechanism for representing concepts. A neural network, given the proper number of hidden units and hidden layers, can learn almost any type of concept [Hornik89]. A second reason for using neural networks is that they generally deal very well with noisy and incorrect data [Shavlik91]. As for limitations of neural networks, one basic problem is how to go about selecting the topology of the network. Determining the best topology for a neural network is problem dependent and is often done by experimentation [Weiss89], which can be a long and costly process. Another problem is deciding what to input to the network. This choice can greatly affect a neural network, since if not enough features are provided, the network may be unable to learn the concept, but if too many are provided, the network may be unable to determine which features are critical. Both of these problems are handled to some extent by the KBANN approach. The rules in the domain theory not only determine the initial topology for the network but are also used to tell the network which variables to focus on initially.

We chose the problem of protein secondary-structure prediction (defined in section 9.3) for a number of reasons. The secondary-structure prediction problem is an open problem that will become increasingly critical as the Human Genome Project [Watson90] continues to pro-

Table 9.1
An overview of our approach to the protein-folding problem

Given:	An algorithm for predicting secondary structure (e.g., the Chou-Fasman algorithm [Chou78]).
	and
	Sample proteins with known secondary structure from the Brookhaven X-ray Crystallography Database [Berstein77].
Do:	Refine the initial algorithm using sample proteins.
Predict:	The secondary structure of new proteins.

duce more data. The problem is attractive because there exist a number of algorithms, proposed by biological researchers, that attempt to solve this problem, but with only limited success. The Chou-Fasman algorithm [Chou78] is the focus of our work because it is one of the best-known and widely used algorithms in the field. This algorithm cannot be represented using the original KBANN system but can be represented for FSKBANN. The secondary-structure problem is also of interest because a number of researchers have applied standard neural networks to it [Holley89, Qian88]. Our work combines these two approaches to achieve a more accurate result than either neural networks or the Chou-Fasman algorithm does alone; table 9.1 illustrates a broad overview of our task.

This chapter presents and empirically analyzes the FSKBANN algorithm for problem solving in domains where prior knowledge exists. The next section presents the basic KBANN algorithm and discusses how we extended the algorithm to handle state information. Section 9.3 contains a description of the protein-folding problem, including a discussion of a number of approaches that have been taken. Following that are a number of experiments we performed to test the utility of the FSKBANN approach for this problem. The fourth section describes some enhancements to our approach that we are currently exploring. We conclude with a review of work in related fields, specifically other work that attempts to solve the protein-structure problem, network methods that use state information, and other algorithms that refine domain theories.

9.2   The KBANN Algorithm

The KBANN algorithm [Towell90] translates a domain theory represented as simple rules into a promising initial neural network; it uses the rules to define a network topology and also to initialize the weights of the network. This section outlines standard KBANN and gives a simple example of

Table 9.2
Overview of the KBANN algorithm

1.	Translate the domain theory into a neural network.
2.	Add extra links and input units to the network.
3.	Train the network using backpropagation.

how the algorithm works. This is followed by a description of an extension to the standard algorithm for domain theories represented as finite-state automata (FSAs).

9.2.1   Standard KBANN

KBANN translates domain theories represented as propositional, nonrecursive rules. An overview of the algorithm appears in table 9.2. The algorithm takes as input a set of rules along with a specification of which propositions are to be used as input and output units. KBANN produces a network where each proposition has a corresponding unit that is highly active when the proposition is true and inactive when the proposition is false. The process of assigning propositions to units is described below in step 1. After it creates the initial network, KBANN adds extra links with low weights to the network, as described in step 2. In step 3, KBANN trains the network using backpropagation, thereby refining the original domain theory.

Step 1: Setting the Initial Topology and Weights   The rules in the domain theory determine the topology of the network. KBANN represents each rule by a separate unit. For each antecedent of a rule, KBANN adds a connection in the network from the unit representing the antecedent to the unit representing the rule's consequent. The weight of the connection is equal to a constant, ω (generally 4.0), for positive antecedents and $-\omega$ for negated antecedents. The bias of the new unit is $(n - \frac{1}{2})\omega$ where n is the number of positive antecedents in the rule being translated. The resulting unit is active only when all of the positive antecedents are on and all of the negative antecedents are off.

As an example, consider translating rule 3 in figure 9.1a. KBANN creates the unit marked 3 in figure 9.1b, which has connections from the input units V and W with weights of ω. The bias of this unit is set to $\frac{3}{2}\omega$. Each of the units corresponding to one of figure 9.1a's rules is marked with the rule number in figure 9.1b. Links with weight ω appear as solid lines, and links with weight $-\omega$ are dashed.

$$
\begin{array}{llll}
(1) & A & \leftarrow & U \wedge \neg V \\
(2) & B & \leftarrow & W \wedge \neg Y \\
(3) & C & \leftarrow & V \wedge W \\
(4) & C & \leftarrow & X \wedge Y
\end{array}
$$

(a)

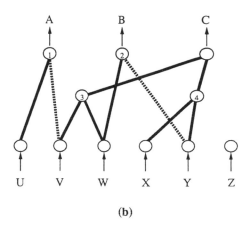

(b)

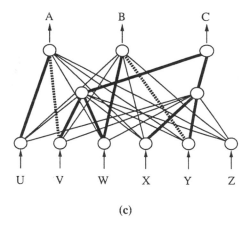

(c)

Figure 9.1
Example of the KBANN process: (a) a set of sample rules, (b) the neural network representing
the rules, and (c) the network after adding extra links

The units in figure 9.1b representing rules 1 and 2 from figure 9.1a represent the propositions A and B, respectively. However, C is represented by a unit that does not correspond to a rule. When a proposition is the consequent of only one rule (as A and B are), then the unit representing that rule directly corresponds to that proposition, but when more than one rule implies a proposition (as with C), that proposition must be handled slightly differently. In this latter case (an implicit disjunction), KBANN generates a unit for each rule. It then generates a new unit to represent their disjunction. Each of the units representing rules is connected to the unit representing the consequent with connections of weight ω. The bias of the unit representing the consequent is set to $\frac{1}{2}\omega$. Thus, in the example in figure 9.1, the unit representing C is active when *either* of the units representing rules 3 and 4 is active.

Step 2: Adding Connections   Once the initial topology and initial weights are set, KBANN adds lowly weighted connections to the network. These connections allow the network to add antecedents to rules during the learning phase. The basic algorithm for connecting units is to connect every unit at level n to every unit at level $n - 1$ (unless there is a connection already). KBANN determines the level of a unit recursively: a unit's level is one higher than the level of the highest unit connected to it. In figure 9.1b, assuming the input units are all at level zero, the units labeled 1–4 are at level 1, and the unit corresponding to proposition C is at level 2. KBANN then connects each of the level 1 units to the level 0 units, and the level 2 units to the level 1 units (an exception is made for output units; output units are never connected to other output units). The resulting network appears in figure 9.1c, with the low-weight connections shown as thin, solid lines.

Step 3: Refining the Domain Theory   After setting up the network, KBANN trains the network on a set of examples using backpropagation [Rumelhart86], though any neural-network learning algorithm could be used. The domain theory serves as a bias giving the network a (hopefully) good starting point for backpropagation search through weight space.

Evaluation of KBANN   KBANN has proved to be very effective in the *promoter* problem [Towell90] and the *splice-junction* problem [Noordewier91], two tasks from molecular biology. KBANN achieves for the promoter problem an error rate of only 3.8% as compared to an error rate of 7.6% for neural networks alone and 11.3% for a nonlearning solution. For the splice-junction problem, KBANN and standard neural networks have about the same error rate for large numbers of examples, but for small numbers of training examples, KBANN makes fewer than half the number of errors standard neural networks do.

9.2.2 Finite-State KBANN

One limitation of KBANN is that its domain theories must be expressed as propositional, nonrecursive rules. This makes it impossible easily to represent domain theories such as the Chou-Fasman algorithm, which predicts protein secondary structure. We address this limitation by extending KBANN to represent finite-state automata. The difficulties in representing an FSA in a neural network are representing the state of the automaton and capturing the notion of "scanning" an input string. FSKBANN addresses both of these issues.

Maintaining Past State FSKBANN uses a neural network structure similar to the networks introduced in both [Elman90, Jordan86] to represent state. The network takes as input the previous state and the input values and determines the next state. It uses this new state as the previous-state input in the next step. This "copying-back" process acts as if there were recurrent links, with fixed weights, from the output units representing the current state to the input units representing the previous state. We chose this representation over a fully recurrent neural network implementation because of its simplicity. The major difference between our networks and fully recurrent networks is that no weight adjustment occurs in our network for the links from the output units to the inputs.

Scanning the Input FSKBANN captures the notion of scanning a series of input values and successively determining the current state by activating the network once for each input value, as in [Sejnowski87]. Each input value is combined with the previously determined state as input to the network, and the network determines the resulting state. The concept of input value is generalized for our networks. An FSA generally examines a single input value at a time. Instead of requiring a single input value, FSKBANN takes a vector of values representing the current input (an input value may be represented by many input propositions; for example, the input could contain an amino acid and its twelve neighbors in a protein).

Mapping FSAs to Neural Networks The final addition needed to the standard KBANN algorithm to handle FSAs is a step that transforms an

FSA into a set of rules involving state. FSKBANN translates each of the transition arcs in the FSA into a rule where the antecedents of the rule are the original state plus the predicate with which the arc is labeled, and the consequent of the rule is the resulting state. As an example, consider the arc labeled $U \wedge \neg V$ from state C to state A in the FSA in figure 9.2a. FSKBANN translates this arc into rule 1 in figure 9.2b. Figure 9.2b displays the rules derived from the FSA in figure 9.2a.

FSKBANN maps these rules into a network where the input units are the input propositions and the previous state; the output of the network represents the resulting state. The network resulting from figure 9.2b's rules is shown in figure 9.2c. FSKBANN concludes by adding extra links to the network and then training the network.

Algorithmic Details   An important consideration in training neural networks with state information is which output to use as the previous state. There are two possibilities: the teacher's (correct) output or the actual output produced by the network. Each approach has its advantages and drawbacks. If the network's output is used and that output is incorrect, then in the next training step the network will be trying to learn the wrong transition. Using the teacher's output avoids this problem, but it is possible that the network will become dependent on receiving the correct last output as input. This can be a problem in domains where the trained network will not achieve very high accuracy. In this case, using the actual output is an advantage because the network can still learn to use the state information but will not place too much faith in the correctness of the information. Our experiments for the protein-folding problem (see section 9.4) used the approach of training with the actual output value because we did not expect to achieve perfect accuracy for our predictions. In preliminary testing, using the teacher' s output led to substantially worse results.

Our additions to KBANN extend it to a larger class of problems by enriching the vocabulary with which the user can express domain theories. In the next section, we describe how FSKBANN can represent and refine the Chou-Fasman algorithm for predicting protein secondary structure.

9.3   The Protein-Folding Problem

Globular proteins are long strings of amino acids, several hundred elements long on average. There are twenty amino acids in all (represented

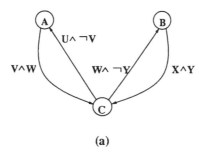

(a)

(1) A_i ← $C_{i-1} \wedge U \wedge \neg V$

(2) B_i ← $C_{i-1} \wedge W \wedge \neg Y$

(3) C_i ← $A_{i-1} \wedge V \wedge W$

(4) C_i ← $B_{i-1} \wedge X \wedge Y$

(b)

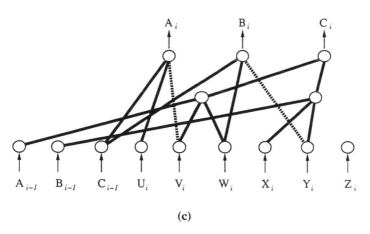

(c)

Figure 9 2
Example of the FSKBANN process: (a) a sample finite-state automaton, (b) the rules derived from the FSA, and (c) the initial FSKBANN translation of the FSA

by different capital letters). The string of amino acids making up a given protein constitutes the *primary* structure of the protein. Once a protein forms, it folds into a three-dimensional shape; the spatial location of each of the amino acids in this structure is known as the *tertiary* structure of the protein. Tertiary structure is important because the form of the protein strongly influences its function.

9.3.1   Predicting Protein Secondary Structure

Few means exist to determine the tertiary structure of a protein. These include X-ray crystallography and magnetic resonance processes, both of which are costly and time-consuming. An alternative solution is to predict the *secondary* structure of a protein as an approximation to the tertiary

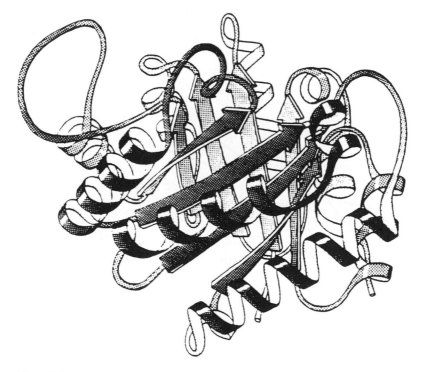

Figure 9.3
Ribbon drawing of the three-dimensional structure of a protein (from [Richardson89, pg. 35]). The areas resembling springs are α-helix structures, the flat arrows represent β-sheets, and the remaining regions are random coils.

structure. The secondary structure of a protein is a description of the local structure for each amino acid. One prevalent system of determining secondary structure divides a protein into three different types of structures: (1) α-helix regions, (2) β-sheet regions, and (3) random coils (all other regions). Figure 9.3 is a diagram of the tertiary structure of a protein and how the shape is divided into regions of secondary structure.

Table 9.3 shows a sample mapping between a protein's primary and secondary structures. The basic task is usually defined as follows: given the primary structure of the protein, produce a secondary-structure assignment for each of the amino acids in the protein. In section 9.4's experiments, we focus on learning how to perform this task.

Predicting the secondary structure from the primary structure is only one part of the protein-folding problem. Other methods attempt to predict *super-secondary* structures, which are descriptions of combinations of secondary structures [Chothia84]. Another problem is how to combine the information about secondary structure and primary structure (and possibly super-secondary structure) to determine the tertiary structure [Cohen89]. For a more complete review of the protein-folding problem, see [Fasman89].

9.3.2 Approaches to Predicting Secondary Structure Based on Biological Information

A number of different algorithms have been proposed in the biological literature for predicting protein secondary structure. Generally these algorithms focus on predicting the secondary structure for an amino acid using only local information (information about the string of amino acids immediately before and after it in the protein). The algorithm we focus on is that of Chou and Fasman [Chou78]. Their algorithm is similar for both α-helix and β-sheet prediction, so we will discuss only α-helix prediction. Figure 9.4 provides an overview of the algorithm. The first step of the

Table 9.3
Primary and secondary structures of a sample protein

Primary (20 possible amino acids)	P	S	V	F	L	F	P	P	K	P	...
Secondary (three possible local structures)	c	c	β	β	β	β	c	c	c	α	...

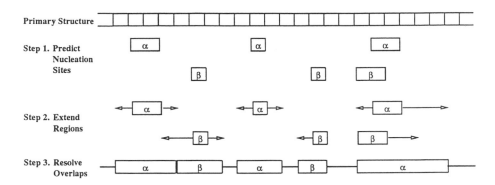

Figure 9.4
Steps of the Chou-Fasman algorithm

Table 9.4
Accuracies of various (nonlearning) structure-prediction algorithms

Method	Accuracy %	Comments
Chou-Fasman [Chou78]	48	original algorithm, data from [Qian88]
Chou-Fasman [Chou78]	58	reworked version, from [Nishikawa83]
Chou-Fasman [Chou78]	58	reworked version, data from [Qian88]
Lim [Lim74]	50	from [Nishikawa83]
Robson et al. [Robson76]	50	from [Nishikawa83]
Garnier and Robson [Garnier89]	58	data from [Qian88]

process is to find α-helix nucleation sites. Nucleation sites are amino acids that are very likely to be part of α-helix structures, according to the conformation probabilities and rules reported by Chou and Fasman. From these sites, their algorithm extends the structure both forward and backward along the protein, as long as the probability of being part of a α-helix structure remains high enough. After both α-helix and β-sheet regions have been predicted, the Chou-Fasman algorithm compares the relative probabilities of regions to resolve predictions that overlap.

Table 9.4 contains results from the Chou-Fasman and some related nonlearning algorithms. Note that in the data sets used to test the algorithms, 54 to 55% of the amino acids in the proteins are part of coil structures, so 54% accuracy can be achieved trivially by always predicting coil. Another important point is that many biological researchers believe that algorithms that take into account only local information can achieve only limited accuracy [Wilson85] (generally believed to be at most 80% accuracy). Accuracy is limited because the structure can be affected by a portion of the protein that is far away along the protein but has come back into proximity due to three-dimensional folding. The relatively limited success of these results has led other researchers to try different means of creating prediction algorithms, including neural network approaches.

9.3.3   Neural-Network Approaches

Several researchers have attempted to use neural networks to solve the protein-folding problem [Holley89, Qian88]. The neural networks in these efforts have as input a window of amino acids consisting of the central amino acid being predicted, plus some number of the amino acids before and after it in the sequence. The amino acid for each window position is represented by twenty-one input units (one for each of the amino acids, plus one for "off the end"). The network output, which predicts the structure of the central amino acid, includes a unit for each type of secondary structure, though Holley and Karplus use only two output units for α-helix and β-sheet, predicting coil if neither of these is active. The networks also include some number of hidden units in a single layer between the input and output units (the number was varied in both studies); figure 9.5 is a diagram of this type of network. The networks are trained on a set of proteins with known secondary structure and then tested on a separate set of proteins. Table 9.5 presents results from two studies using this approach. One reason for the differences in the results is that these studies use different sets of proteins for testing. Since the results are still somewhat disappointing, a possible strategy is to combine the neural network approach with the knowledge from the Chou-Fasman algorithm to produce a better network solution. This is our approach.

9.3.4   Representing the Chou-Fasman Algorithm as a Finite-State Automaton

The primary problem in representing the Chou-Fasman algorithm as a set of rules is capturing the notion of extending a region. In a neural network without state information, to know if an α-helix region can be extended to

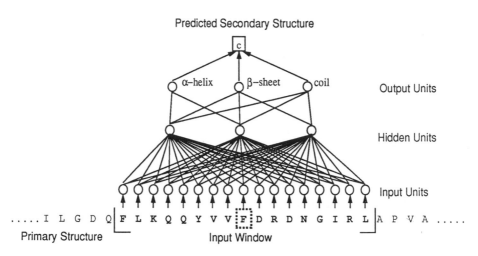

Figure 9.5
General neural network architecture used by Holley and Karplus and Qian and Sejnowski

Table 9.5
Neural network results for the secondary-structure prediction task

Method	Accuracy %	Number of hidden units	Window size
Holley and Karplus [Holley89]	63.2	2	17
Qian and Sejnowski [Qian88]	62.7	40	13

the current window position, the network would have to determine if a nucleation site is predicted just to the left of the window, two steps to the left of the window, three steps to the left of the window, and so forth. Not only does this require a lot of replication of rules (since the rules to recognize a nucleation site would have to be copied for each window position), but the nucleation site might actually be outside the window. We solved this problem by representing the Chou-Fasman algorithm as an FSA (see figure 9.6); once the algorithm goes into state `helix`, it will remain there until `break-helix` is true.

The notion of transition in figure 9.6's automata is complex. Each transition is actually a set of rules dependent on the input window and the current state. Table 9.6 displays some samples of different types of rules

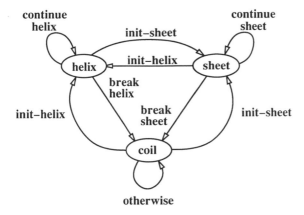

Figure 9.6
The finite-state automaton used to represent the Chou-Fasman algorithm

Table 9.6
Sample rules from the Chou-Fasman finite-state automaton

(1)	break-helix ← helix-break@0 ∧ helix-break@1
(2)	$helix_i$ ← init-helix
(3)	$coil_i$ ← $helix_{i-1}$ ∧ break-helix

derived from the FSA (the full set of rules appear in the chapter appendix). Not all of the rules involve state information; some of the rules are used to prove propositions that are used in other rules. Rule 1 is an example that does not involve state. It is used to prove the proposition break-helix, which is used in rule 3. Break-helix is defined in terms of the propositions helix-break@0[1] and helix-break@1; these propositions are then defined by other propositions (see the appendix). Rule 2 is an example that results in a new state but does not refer to the previous state. This type of rule occurs when a transition to a state should occur no matter what the previous state. Rule 2 says that no matter what the previous state is, if init-helix is true, the resulting state should be helix. Rule 3 is an example of a transition made from one state to another. It says that the automaton should transition from state helix to state coil if break-helix is true.

Figure 9.7 is a diagram of the type of network we used to represent the Chou-Fasman domain theory. One important aspect to consider about

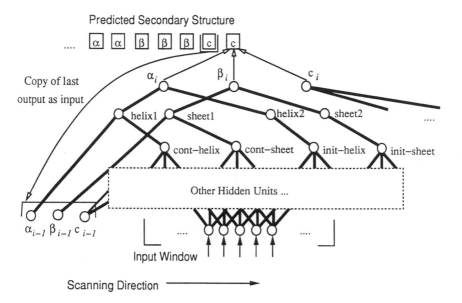

Figure 9.7
General neural network architecture used to represent the Chou-Fasman algorithm

our approach is that the FSA extends the structure only in a single direction as it scans the primary structure. To extend the structure in both directions, our network actually scans the primary structure in both directions and averages the predictions.

9.4   Experimental Study

We performed a number of experiments on the protein structure-prediction problem to evaluate FSKBANN. Our study demonstrates that FSKBANN has a small but statistically significant gain in accuracy over both standard artificial neural networks (ANNs) and over a nonlearning version of the Chou-Fasman algorithm.

This section describes the data used in our experiments and our training method. Following that, we present and analyze a number of experiments. The experiments evaluate (1) the effectiveness of the FSKBANN approach versus standard ANNs and the Chou-Fasman algorithm, (2) the value of using state information in ANNs, and (3) performance on test-set proteins as a function of the number of training examples. We conclude with an in-depth empirical analysis of the strengths and weaknesses of the three different methods.

9.4.1 Experimental Details

We performed our experiments using the data set from Qian and Sejnowski [Qian88]. Their data set consists of 128 proteins with 21,623 amino acids, for an average length of 169 amino acids per protein. Of these amino acids, 54.5% are part of coil structures, 25.2% part of α-helix structures, and 20.3% part of β-sheet structures. We divided the proteins randomly into training and test sets containing two-thirds (85 proteins) and one-third (43 proteins) of the original proteins, respectively.

We used backpropagation [Rumelhart86] to train the neural networks in the two network approaches (FSKBANN and standard ANNs). *Patience* [Fahlman90] was our criterion for stopping learning on the training set. The patience criterion states that training should continue until the error rate has not decreased for some number of training cycles. For this study, we set the number of epochs to be four. We use patience rather than some minimum accuracy on the training set because the noisiness of the data set prevents anything close to perfect learning on the training set.

During training, we divided the training proteins into two portions: a training set and a tuning set [Lang90, 41–42]. We employ the training set to train the network and the tuning set to estimate the generalization of the network. For each epoch, the system trains the network on each of the amino acids in the training set; it then assesses accuracy on the tuning set. We retain the set of weights achieving the highest accuracy for the tuning set and use this set of weights to measure test-set accuracy. The system randomly chooses a "representative" tuning set; it considers a tuning set representative if the percentages of each type of structure in the tuning set roughly approximate the percentages of all the training proteins (the percentages of α-helix, β-sheet, and random coil structures in the tuning set should be close to the percentages present in the training proteins). The system does not consider the testing set when comparing the percentages. It chooses the tuning set by randomly picking a set of proteins and then evaluating their "representativeness" and repeating the process until a tuning set is chosen that meets the criterion. Through empirical testing (not reported here), we found that a tuning set size of five proteins achieved the best results for both FSKBANN and ANNs. It is important to consider that this style of training is different from that reported by Qian and Sejnowski. They tested their network periodically and retained the network that achieved the highest accuracy for the test set.

Our experiment-running system trains the FSKBANN networks twice for each protein—scanning forward and then in reverse over the protein. It then averages the two predictions for each amino acid. This simulates extending secondary structure in both directions. The system trained the ANNs both ways—scanning both directions and scanning only one direction (as in [Qian88]). We report results for ANNs of scanning only one direction, because these results are slightly superior to the results for scanning both directions. Our ANNs use the same number of hidden units that we used in the FSKBANN networks (28) to represent the domain theory. We use 28 hidden units rather than the 40 suggested by Qian and Sejnowski, for two reasons: (1) we wished to hold the network size constant when comparing FSKBANN and standard ANNs, and (2) Qian and Sejnowski found only minor differences in accuracy when the number of hidden units ranged from 0 to 40.

A final item to note is that for ANNs and FSKBANN we do some postprocessing of the network output (as suggested in [Holley89]). For each amino acid the system predicts the secondary structure by choosing the output unit with the highest activation. The system then eliminates any "short" sequences. Short sequences are sequences of α-helix or β-sheet predictions that are fewer than four or two amino acids in length, respectively. Since such short sequences do not in general occur in real proteins [Kabsch83], the prediction for these sequences is replaced with coil.

9.4.2 Results and Analysis

Table 9.7 contains results averaged over the 10 test sets. The statistics reported are the percentage accuracy overall, the percentage accuracy by secondary structure, and the correlation coefficients for each secondary

Table 9.7
Comparison of FSKBANN, ANN, and the nonlearning Chou-Fasman algorithm

Method	Accuracy %				Correlation coefficients		
	Total	Helix	Sheet	Coil	Helix	Sheet	Coil
Chou-Fasman	57.3	31.7	36.9	76.1	0.24	0.23	0.26
ANN	61.8	43.6	18.6	86.3	0.35	0.25	0.31
FSKBANN	63.4	45.9	35.1	81.9	0.37	0.33	0.35

structure. The correlation coefficient [Mathews75] is defined by the formula:

$$C_s = \frac{TP_s TN_s - FP_s FN_s}{\sqrt{(TP_s + FP_s)(TP_s + FN_s)(TN_s + FP_s)(TN_s + FN_s)}}.$$

In this formula, s is the secondary structure whose coefficient is being calculated, and TP_s, TN_s, FP_s, and FN_s are the number of true positives. true negatives, false positives, and false negatives for that structure, respectively. The correlation coefficient is good for evaluating the effectiveness of the prediction for each of the classes of secondary structure separately. The resulting gain in overall accuracy for FSKBANN over both ANNs and the nonlearning Chou-Fasman method is statistically significant at the 0.5% level (with 99.5% confidence) using a t-test.

The apparent gain in accuracy for FSKBANN over ANN networks appears fairly small (only 1.6 percentage points), but this number is somewhat misleading. The correlation coefficients give a more accurate picture. They show that the FSKBANN does better on both α-helix and coil prediction and much better on β-sheet prediction. The reason that the ANN solution still does fairly well in overall accuracy is that it predicts a large number of coil structures (the largest class) and does very well on these predictions.

The gain in accuracy for FSKBANN over the Chou-Fasman algorithm is fairly large and exhibits a corresponding gain in all three correlation coefficients. It is interesting to note that the FSKBANN and Chou-Fasman solutions produce approximately the same accuracy for β-sheets, but the correlation coefficient demonstrates that the Chou-Fasman algorithm achieves this accuracy by predicting a much larger number of β-sheets.

To evaluate the usefulness of the domain theory as the number of training instances decreases and also to estimate the value of collecting more proteins, we performed a second series of tests. We divided each of the training sets into four subsets: the first contained the first 10 of the 85 proteins, the second contained the first 25, the third contained the first 50, and the fourth had all 85 training proteins. This process produced 40 training sets. Each of these training sets was then used to train both the FSKBANN and ANN networks. Figure 9.8 contains the results of these tests. FSKBANN shows a gain in accuracy for each training-set size (statistically significant at the 5% level—95% confidence).

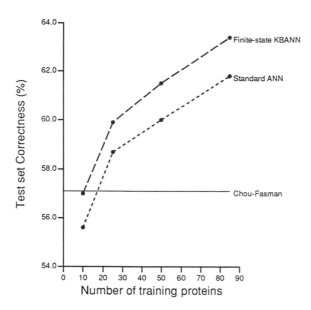

Figure 9.8
Percent correctness on test proteins as a function of training-set size

The results in figure 9.8 demonstrate a couple of interesting trends: the FSKBANN networks do better no matter how large the training set, and the shape of the curve indicates that accuracy might continue to increase if more proteins were used for training. The one anomaly for this curve is that the gain in accuracy for the 10 training proteins is not very large. One would expect that when the number of training instances is very small, the domain knowledge would be a big advantage. The problem here is that for a small training set, it is possible to obtain random sets of proteins that are not very indicative of the overall population. Individual proteins generally do not reflect the overall distribution of secondary structures for the whole population; many proteins have large numbers of α-helix regions and almost no β-sheets, and others have large numbers of β-sheet regions and almost no α-helices. Thus, in trying to learn to predict a very skewed population, the network may produce a poor solution. This is mitigated as more proteins are introduced, causing the training population to match the overall population more closely.

FSKBANN networks are different from standard ANNs in two ways: (1) their topology is determined by the domain theory, and (2) they copy the

Table 9.8
Effect of state variables on the standard neural network approach

Method	Accuracy %				Correlation coefficients		
	Total	Helix	Sheet	Coil	Helix	Sheet	Coil
ANN	61.8	43.6	18.6	86.3	0.35	0.25	0.31
ANN (with state)	61.7	39.2	24.2	86.0	0.32	0.28	0.31

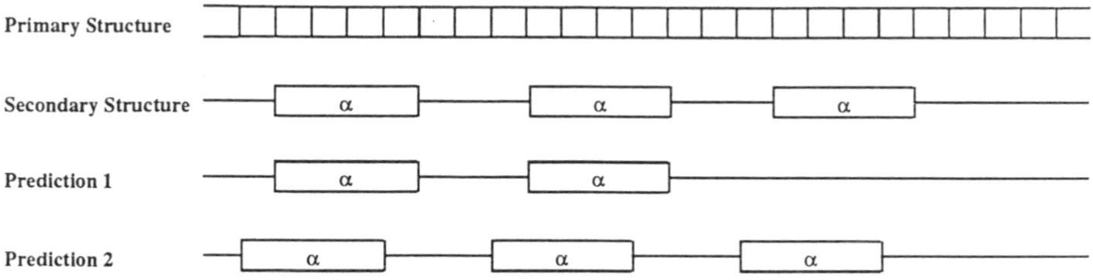

Figure 9.9
Two possible predictions for secondary structure

output of the network back as the state of the network in the next step. To evaluate the utility of the second feature alone, we trained ANNs similar to those in Qian and Sejnowski's work but added to these networks state information (i.e., the output was copied back as part of the input for each step). Table 9.8 compares results from these tests with results from using standard ANNs alone. These results show that state information alone is not enough to increase the accuracy of the network prediction.

Finally, to analyze the detailed performance of the various approaches, we gathered a number of additional statistics concerning the FSKBANN, ANN, and Chou-Fasman solutions. These statistics analyze the results in terms of regions. A *region* is a consecutive sequence of amino acids with the same secondary structure. We consider regions because the measure of accuracy obtained by comparing the prediction for each amino acid does not adequately capture the notion of secondary structure as biologists view it [Cohen91]. For biologists, knowing the number of regions and the approximate order of the regions is nearly as important as knowing exactly the structure within which each amino acid lies. Consider the two predictions in figure 9.9. The first prediction misses completely the third α-helix region, so it has four errors. The second prediction is slightly skewed for each α-helix region and ends up having six errors, although it

Table 9.9
Region-oriented statistics for α-helix prediction

Occurrence		Description	FKKBANN	ANN	Chou-Fasman
Actual	α-helix	Average length of an actual helix region (number of regions).	10.17 (1825)	10.17 (1825)	10.17 (1825)
Predicted	α-helix	Average length of a predicted helix region (number of regions).	8.52 (1774)	7.79 (2067)	8.00 (1491)
Actual	α-helix	Percentage of time an actual helix region is overlapped by a predicted helix region (length of overlap).	67% (6.99)	70% (6.34)	56% (5.76)
Predicted	α-helix				
Actual	other	Percentage of time a predicted helix region does not overlap an actual helix region.	34%	39%	36%
Predicted	α-helix				

appears to be a better answer. The statistics we have gathered try to assess how well each solution does on predicting α-helix regions (table 9.9) and β-sheet regions (table 9.10).

The results of tables 9.9 and 9.10 give a picture of the strengths and weakness of each approach. Table 9.9 shows that the FSKBANN solution overlaps slightly fewer actual α-helix regions than the ANNs but that these overlaps tend to be somewhat longer. On the other hand, the FSKBANN networks *overpredict* fewer regions than ANNs (i.e., predict fewer α-helix regions that do not correspond to an actual α-helix region). Table 9.9 also indicates that the FSKBANN and ANN networks more accurately predict the occurrence of regions than the Chou-Fasman algorithm does.

Table 9.10 demonstrates that FSKBANN's predictions overlap a much higher percentage of actual β-sheet regions than either the Chou-Fasman algorithm or ANNs alone. The overall accuracy for β-sheet predictions is approximately the same for FSKBANN and the Chou-Fasman method, because the length of overlap for the Chou-Fasman method is much longer than for FSKBANN (at the cost of predicting much longer regions). The ANN networks do extremely poorly at predicting overlapping actual β-sheet regions. The FSKBANN networks do as well as the ANNs at not overpredicting β-sheets, and both do better than the Chou-Fasman method. Taken together, these results indicate that the FSKBANN solution does

Table 9.10
Region-oriented statistics for β-sheet prediction

Occurrence		Description	FKKBANN	ANN	Chou-Fasman
Actual	β-sheet	Average length of an actual sheet region (number of regions).	5.00 (3015)	5.00 (3015)	5.00 (3015)
Actual Predicted	β-sheet β-sheet	Average length of a predicted sheet region (number of regions).	3.80 (2545)	2.83 (1673)	6.02 (2339)
Actual Predicted	β-sheet other	Percentage of time an actual sheet region is overlapped by a predicted sheet region (length of overlap).	54% (3.23)	35% (2.65)	46% (4.01)
Actual Predicted	other β-sheet	Percentage of time a predicted sheet region does not overlap an actual sheet region.	37%	37%	44%

significantly better than the ANN solution on predicting β-sheet regions without having to sacrifice much accuracy in predicting α-helix regions.

Finally, the results indicate that the FSKBANN solution does a much better job of avoiding the problem of overpredicting coil regions than the ANN solution. The results also suggest that more work needs to be done on developing methods of evaluating solution quality, so that solutions that accurately predict all three classes are favored over solutions that only do well at predicting the largest class.

9.5 Future Work

We are considering a number of extensions to FSKBANN in the hope of increasing the gain in predictive accuracy. The extensions for the structure-prediction problem can be broken down into two classes: changes to the architecture and training style of the neural network and additions to the domain theory. Beyond producing a better structure-prediction network, we are also studying the problem of translating the trained network back into a human-readable form. Finally, we are interested in applying FSKBANN to biological (e.g., recognizing splice-junctions, finding reading frames) and other problems (such as natural language understanding).

Table 9.11
Predictive accuracy and coverage as a function of output-unit activation

Threshold	Accuracy	% Predicted
0.6	69%	70
0.7	75	49
0.8	80	32
0.9	86	16

9.5.1 Different Neural-Network Architectures

Our studies and other work in the field [Holley89, Qian88] suggest a number of changes to the method of training the networks. One such observation noted by Holley and Karplus [Holley89] is that the activity of the units corresponding to helix and sheet prediction seems to correlate with how likely the prediction is correct. Table 9.11 indicates that this trend is even more apparent in our networks. This table reports the accuracy of those predictions when only one of the three output units (helix, sheet, coil) is above the *threshold* and the others are below (1 − threshold). So, for example, 32% of the time one of the unit's activation was above 0.8, the others below 0.2, and the accuracy of these predictions was 80%.

This observation suggests a possible change to the prediction method: instead of predicting all of the protein's structure in one scan, predict only the strongest activated areas first and then feed these predictions back into the network for the next scan. This might be an advantage since helix and sheet regions consist of multiple amino acids, so predicting one indicates others might be adjacent. Figure 9.10 outlines how this process of structure prediction might work. The question then becomes, How should the information be fed back into the network, and which predictions should be chosen? Figure 9.11 illustrates the general structure of the type of net-. work we plan to use to feed the information back in. There is only one difference between this and the networks in previous figures. The input for each window position not only represents the amino acid in the primary sequence but also the current estimate of the probability of each of the three types of secondary structure (initially these values would be the a priori probabilities for each category). The network then predicts a set of probabilities for each of the positions on the protein. The algorithm would next evaluate this vector of probabilities for the best predictions and threshold the best predictions before the next scan. This type of network would

Primary Structure	P	S	V	F	L	F	P	P	K	P	...
Initial Prediction	·	·	·	·	·	·	·	·	·	·	...
Step 1	·	·	·	·	β	·	·	c	·	·	...
Step 2	c	·	·	·	β	β	·	c	·	·	...
Step 3	c	c	·	β	β	β	·	c	α	α	...
		·									
		·									
		·									
Final Prediction	c	c	β	β	β	β	c	c	α	α	...

Figure 9.10
Predicting structure by filling in the most likely structures and using that information for subsequent predictions

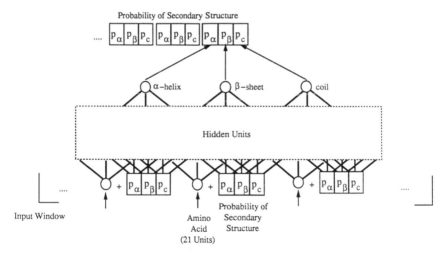

Figure 9.11
Network that includes current prediction probabilities as part of the input

allow the system to take advantage of information about predictions that have already been made. The network would be trained similarly to FSKBANN networks—scanning a protein and making a prediction for each amino acid, or it would be trained using a recurrent technique.

A second idea, originally suggested in Qian and Sejnowski's work [Qian88], is to use two neural networks instead of one (which they call *cascaded networks*). This idea is appropriate for translating the Chou-Fasman algorithm, since this algorithm has two largely separate parts: finding nucleation sites and extending sequences. Figure 9.12 sketches a scheme for using two networks. For FSKBANN, the first network would be constructed using a domain theory about nucleation sites and would try to predict just the probability for each position's being part of a particular structure. The second neural network would use these probabilities, along with primary-structure information and knowledge about extending structures. It would incorporate knowledge about the past predictions as it was scanning along the protein (since this information is needed for the rules to extend structures). This second network might exhibit the effects discussed by Qian and Sejnowski of connecting areas of secondary structure separated by one anomalous prediction.

A final idea is to redefine the task of learning an FSA somewhat. Instead of focusing on predicting the state at each step, one can view the problem as predicting locations where state transitions occur. That is, rather than predicting the structure for a particular amino acid, the goal would be to find places between amino acids where the structure changes from one type to another. Figure 9.13 contains a sample network for this approach. The transition that the network predicts is between the middle two amino acids. The network has output units representing transitions from one type of structure to a different type of structure. In the cases where the structure does not change between amino acids, the network would predict no transition. An open problem with this approach is deciding how to combine the predicted transitions into a consistent secondary structure.

9.5.2 Additions to the Structure-Prediction Domain Theory

Besides altering the network architecture, we are considering a number of changes to the domain theory and problem representation. KBANN uses a domain theory to give the network a "good" set of initial weights, since

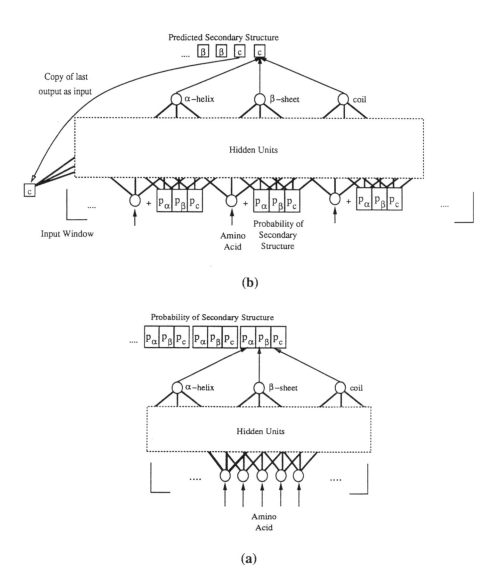

Figure 9.12
Networks for cascaded prediction: (*a*) first network that calculates the probability for each structure for each amino acid, and (*b*) second network that combines predictions from first network with primary structure to predict secondary structure

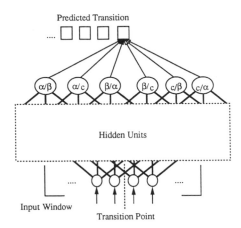

Figure 9.13
Network to predict finite-state transitions

search starts from that location in weight space. Therefore, augmenting the Chou-Fasman domain theory with other information might increase the accuracy of the solution, since training will start from a "better" location.

A basic way of augmenting the domain theory is to include information from other domain theories, such as the GorII and GorIII algorithms [Garnier89] and Lim's method [Lim74]. The advantage of adding these other approaches is that they may have strengths in prediction where Chou-Fasman is weak. Another advantage is that we can add these domain theories without having to consider how they interact with the others, since backpropagation training can incorporate the different pieces of information together [Jacobs91].

Hunter [Hunter91] suggests using an input representation of the amino acids that is more meaningful. As with other neural network approaches to this problem, our input encoding uses one bit for each of the possible amino acids (so for each amino acid, one bit is on and the others are off). Hunter instead suggests a 37-bit representation where the bits encode properties of the amino acid that are meaningful to biologists and are shared with other amino acids. The encoding is still unique for each of the amino acids, so no information is lost, but the network might be able to find a better solution since it can focus not only on different amino acids but on different properties of the amino acids.

9.5.3   Translation of Trained Networks into Symbolic Terms

A basic problem of the KBANN approach is extracting information in a human-readable form from the trained network. Towell and Shavlik have approached this problem in the KBANN system [Towell92], and the problem has also been examined by other researchers [Fu91]. We need to address rule extraction for the augmented networks of FSKBANN that include state information, so as to extract learned FSAs.

9.5.4   Other Problems

Finally, there is the question of using FSKBANN in other domains. A couple of biological problems that seem natural for this type of approach are the splice-junction problem [Noordewier91], where the states are *intron* and *exon*, and the reading-frame problem [Staden90] where the states are *reading frames 1, 2, and 3*. Also of interest is evaluating this approach for problems in other fields such as natural language (as in [Elman90]). The task could involve learning to recognize simple sentences involving a simple (regular) grammar where some information about the grammar is known, but some is missing or incorrect.

9.6   Related Research

Our work shares similarities with research in three areas: algorithms for predicting protein structure, neural networks that use state information, and systems that refine domain theories.

9.6.1   Methods of Predicting Protein Secondary Structure

There have been a number of different algorithms proposed for predicting protein secondary structure. These can loosely be divided into ones that use biological knowledge (and are nonlearning methods) and those that use a learning mechanism.

Nonlearning Methods   The three most widely used approaches in the biological literature [Fasman89] for predicting protein secondary structure are the Chou-Fasman [Chou78, Prevelige89], Robson [Garnier89, Robson76], and Lim [Lim74] algorithms. Chou-Fasman relies on information concerning the likelihood for each type of amino acid to be part of a particular secondary structure. This information is summed over local areas of the protein to determine the likelihood for that area to be part of a particular structure. The Robson et al. [Robson76] and the later GorII and GorIII [Garnier89] solutions are based on information theory. These approaches, like neural networks, base prediction on a window of information around a central amino acid (from position -8 to $+8$ around the central amino acid). For every window position, the Robson algorithm determines the relevance of the amino acid for predicting each type of secondary structure. Computerized versions of the Chou-Fasman and Robson techniques that we implemented and tested on the Qian and Sejnowski test data exhibit 58% accuracy (see table 9.4). The Lim method [Lim74] is the only one that tries to account for long-range interactions; it uses a stereochemical theory of globular proteins' secondary structure. Later solutions [Garnier89, Prevelige89] include theories of a fourth type of secondary structure, β-turns, which usually are classified as coils. The main advantage of FSKBANN over these algorithms is that while FSKBANN contains some of the biological information, it also has a mechanism for learning.

Learning Methods   A number of investigators use learning algorithms and sample folded proteins to try to predict secondary structure of new proteins. Holley and Karplus [Holley89] and Qian and Sejnowski [Qian88] use simple one-hidden-layer neural networks to try to predict secondary structure. Both studies focus on varying the hidden unit size and window size, achieving very different results (as shown in table 9.5) for these parameters, though both report test-set accuracies around 63%. Qian and Sejnowski also use a cascaded architecture, which produces a 1.6 percentage point improvement in accuracy over their single network results. Stolorz et al. [Stolorz92] use a perceptron architecture to evaluate a different error function, *mutual information*, which produces a one percentage point gain in accuracy over a standard perceptron. The Stolorz measure improves helix and sheet prediction at the expense of coil prediction, a desirable effect since coil (making up 54% of the training data) tends to be overpredicted in many other neural-network techniques.

Zhang et al. also use machine learning [Zhang92]. Their method combines information from a statistical technique, a memory-based reasoning algorithm, and a neural network. They divide the training set into halves, with each of the three components trained on one-half of the training set. Further training is done using the other half of the training set to learn to combine results from the three different components, using a second neural network. The best results they report are 66.4% for a training set size of 96 proteins.

The major difference between these learning approaches and FSKBANN is that only FSKBANN incorporates domain knowledge. FSKBANN also differs in that the neural networks in our studies use state information, unlike the other approaches.

9.6.2   Methods of Representing State Information in Neural Networks

Several researchers have proposed neural network architectures for incorporating information about state. The idea of retaining a state or context across training patterns occurs in work aimed at solving natural language problems [Cleeremans89, Elman90, Mozer91, Porat91, Servan-Schreiber91, St. John90]. Each of these approaches provides a mechanism for preserving one or more of the past activations of some units for the next input sequence.

Jordan [Jordan86] and Elman [Elman90] introduced the particular recurrent network topology we use in FSKBANN. Their networks have a set of hidden units, called *context units*, which preserve the state of the network. At each time step, the previous value of the context units is copied back as input to the system. These networks allow for the possibility of keeping multiple past contexts as input to the system. One difference between our networks and those of Elman and Jordan is that our context units are output units instead of hidden units, since the output of our network is the state.

The idea of using the type of network introduced by Jordan to represent a finite-state automaton was first discussed by Cleeremans et al. [Cleeremans89]. They state that this type of network can perfectly learn to recognize a grammar derived from a finite-state automaton. The major difference between our research and that of Cleeremans et al. is we focus on using an initial domain theory expressed as a finite-state automaton rather than attempting to learn it from scratch.

9.6.3   Methods of Refining Domain Theories

There have been a number of efforts aimed at refining approximate domain theories. Ourston and Mooney's EITHER system [Ourston90] uses a domain theory to focus the corrections that an inductive learning system performs. This system constructs an explanation (a proof), possibly incomplete, of instances of a concept. The inductive learner examines the missing portions or errors in the concept's explanation to suggest changes to the domain theory that would make the explanations correct.

Flann and Dietterich [Flann89] examine a method that could fix a domain theory that is too general. Their system takes several examples of the concept being refined and produces explanations for each using the domain theory. These explanations are passed to an inductive learning system, which finds the maximally specific shared explanation structure. Our research differs with these efforts in that FSKBANN refines domain theories with recursive rules and does not assume the domain theory is overly general.

VanLehn's SIERRA system [VanLehn87] extends a domain theory expressed as a grammar. This system constructs the maximal partial parse of a set of training examples to determine where there are gaps (or "holes") in the parse for the examples. SIERRA uses an inductive learning algorithm to fill the gap in the grammar so that these examples can be correctly parsed. SIERRA depends on receiving a good sequence of training examples because it assumes that each set of training examples presented shares the same gaps and will not have too many gaps. Since FSKBANN uses a neural network methodology to refine the domain theory, it is less vulnerable to poor sequences of data.

9.7 Conclusions

We present and evaluate FSKBANN, a system that broadens the KBANN approach to a richer, more expressive vocabulary. FSKBANN provides a mechanism for translating domain theories represented as generalized finite-state automata into neural networks. These networks can be further trained, using techniques such as backpropagation, to refine the initial domain knowledge. The extension of KBANN to domain theories that include knowledge about state significantly enhances the power of KBANN; rules expressed in the domain theory can take into account the current problem-solving context (the state of the solution).

We tested FSKBANN by refining the Chou-Fasman algorithm for predicting protein secondary structure. The FSKBANN-refined algorithm proved to be more accurate than both standard neural network approaches to the problem and a nonlearning version of the Chou-Fasman algorithm. The FSKBANN solution proved even more effective when considered in terms of how well it does for each class of secondary structure; FSKBANN shows gains in predictive power for all three classes over both ANNs and the nonlearning Chou-Fasman algorithm.

Finally, our work demonstrates the need for better criteria for evaluating solutions to the protein-structure problem, since a direct, straightforward measure of how predicted structures match the actual structures is often misleading. A better definition of solution quality, possibly based on edit distance [Cohen91], might favor solutions that do well at predicting all three classes of secondary structure.

The success of FSKBANN for the secondary-structure problem indicates that it may prove to be a useful tool for addressing other problems that include state information. However, more work must be done both in improving the neural network refinement process and the extraction of symbolic knowledge from the trained network.

Appendix: The Chou-Fasman Domain Theory

The Chou-Fasman algorithm [Chou78] involves three activities: (1) recognizing nucleation sites, (2) extending sites, and (3) resolving overlapping predictions. In this appendix, we provide more details of these three steps and describe our representation of their algorithm as a collection of rules.

To recognize nucleation sites, Chou and Fasman assign two *conformation* values to each of the 20 amino acids. The conformation values represent how likely an amino acid is to be part of either a helix or sheet structure, with higher values being more likely. They also group the amino acids into classes of similar conformation value. The classes for helix are *formers, high-indifferent, indifferent,* and *breakers.* Those for sheet are *formers, indifferent,* and *breakers.* Table 9.12 defines the values for the various types of breakers and formers.

Table 9.13 contains the rules we use to represent the Chou-Fasman algorithm; $x@N$ is true if x is the amino acid N positions from the one whose secondary structure the algorithm is predicting. It predicts an α-helix nucleation site if for some consecutive set of six amino acids, at least four are helix formers and fewer than two are helix breakers. (Two helix high-indifferent amino acids count as a helix former.) A rule to determine if a location is a nucleation site simply adds the helix-former and helix-breaker values for a window of amino acids six wide, and if the totals are greater than four and fewer than two respectively, predicts a helix nuclea-

Table 9.12
Former and breaker values for the amino acids

helix-former(E)	= 1.37	helix-former(A)	= 1.29	helix-former(L)	= 1.20
helix-former(H)	= 1.11	helix-former(M)	= 1.07	helix-former(Q)	= 1.04
helix-former(W)	= 1.02	helix-former(V)	= 1.02	helix-former(F)	= 1.00
helix-former(K)	= 0.54	helix-former(I)	= 0.50		
helix-former(*others*)	= 0.00				
helix-breaker(N)	= 1.00	helix-breaker(Y)	= 1.20	helix-breaker(P)	= 1.24
helix-breaker(G)	= 1.38				
helix-breaker(*others*)	= 0.00				
sheet-former(M)	= 1.40	sheet-former(V)	= 1.39	sheet-former(I)	= 1.34
sheet-former(C)	= 1.09	sheet-former(Y)	= 1.08	sheet-former(F)	= 1.07
sheet-former(Q)	= 1.03	sheet-former(L)	= 1.02	sheet-former(T)	= 1.01
sheet-former(W)	= 1.00				
sheet-former(*others*)	= 0.00				
sheet-breaker(K)	= 1.00	sheet-breaker(S)	= 1.03	sheet-breaker(H)	= 1.04
sheet-breaker(N)	= 1.14	sheet-breaker(P)	= 1.19	sheet-breaker(E)	= 2.00
sheet-breaker(*others*)	= 0.00				

Note: We produced these values using the tables reported by Chou and Fasman [Chou78, pg. 51]. We normalized the values for formers by dividing the conformation value of the given former by the conformation value of the weakest former. So for example, the helix former value of alanine (A) is 1.29 since the helix conformation value of alanine is 1.45 and the conformation value of the weakest helix former phenylalanine (F) is 1.12. Breaker values work similarly except that the value used to calculate the breaker value is the multiplicative inverse of the conformation value.

We did not directly use the values of Chou and Fasman for two reasons. One, we wanted smaller values, to decrease the number of times three very strong helix-formers would add up to more than 4 (and similarly for sheets). Two, breaker conformation values tend to be numbers between 0 and 1 with the stronger breakers being close to 0. We wanted the breaker value to be larger the stronger the breaker, so we used the inverse of the breaker's conformation value (restricting the result to not exceed 2).

tion site (proposition `init-helix` in our rules). Nucleation of β-sheets is similar to α-helix nucleation, except that the window is only five amino acids wide and a sheet nucleation site is predicted if there at least three sheet formers and fewer than two sheet breakers.

The third step of the algorithm—resolving overlaps—is the reason we use the numbers in table 9.12 rather than making the formers and breakers Boolean properties. Chou and Fasman suggest that the conformation values of regions be compared to resolve overlaps. This is done in our networks by weighting the links from various amino acids according to the numbers in table 9.12. For example, a combination of four alanines (A's) will produce a higher activation of the `init-helix` unit than a combination of four phenylalanines (F's).

Table 9.13
The Chou-Fasman algorithm expressed as inference rules

Rules for recognizing nucleation sites.

$$init\text{-}helix \quad \leftarrow \left(\sum_{position=0}^{5} helix\text{-}former(amino\text{-}acid @ position) \right) > 4$$

$$\wedge \left(\sum_{position=0}^{5} helix\text{-}breaker(amino\text{-}acid @ position) \right) < 2$$

$$init\text{-}sheet \quad \leftarrow \left(\sum_{position=0}^{4} sheet\text{-}former(amino\text{-}acid @ position) \right) > 3$$

$$\wedge \left(\sum_{position=0}^{4} sheet\text{-}breaker(amino\text{-}acid @ position) \right) < 2$$

Rules for pairs of amino acids that terminate helix structures.
$helix\text{-}break @ 0 \leftarrow N @ 0 \vee Y @ 0 \vee P @ 0 \vee G @ 0$
$helix\text{-}break @ 1 \leftarrow N @ 1 \vee Y @ 1 \vee P @ 1 \vee G @ 1$
$helix\text{-}indiff @ 1 \leftarrow K @ 1 \vee I @ 1 \vee D @ 1 \vee T @ 1 \vee S @ 1 \vee R @ 1 \vee C @ 1$
$break\text{-}helix \quad \leftarrow helix\text{-}break @ 0 \wedge helix\text{-}break @ 1$
$break\text{-}helix \quad \leftarrow helix\text{-}break @ 0 \wedge helix\text{-}indiff @ 1$

Rules for pairs of amino acids that terminate sheet structures.
$sheet\text{-}break @ 0 \leftarrow K @ 0 \vee S @ 0 \vee H @ 0 \vee N @ 0 \vee P @ 0 \vee E @ 0$
$sheet\text{-}break @ 1 \leftarrow K @ 1 \vee S @ 1 \vee H @ 1 \vee N @ 1 \vee P @ 1 \vee E @ 1$
$sheet\text{-}indiff @ 1 \leftarrow A @ 1 \vee R @ 1 \vee G @ 1 \vee D @ 1$
$break\text{-}sheet \quad \leftarrow sheet\text{-}break @ 0 \wedge sheet\text{-}break @ 1$
$break\text{-}sheet \quad \leftarrow sheet\text{-}break @ 0 \wedge sheet\text{-}indiff @ 1$

Rules for continuing structures.
$cont\text{-}helix \quad \leftarrow \neg P @ 0 \wedge \neg break\text{-}helix$
$cont\text{-}sheet \quad \leftarrow \neg P @ 0 \wedge \neg E @ 0 \wedge \neg break\text{-}sheet$

Rules for predicting helix: either by nucleation or propagating from the last state.
$helix_i \quad \leftarrow init\text{-}helix$
$helix_i \quad \leftarrow helix_{i-1} \wedge cont\text{-}helix$

Rules for predicting sheet: either by nucleation or propagating from the last state.
$sheet_i \quad \leftarrow init\text{-}sheet$
$sheet_i \quad \leftarrow sheet_{i-1} \wedge cont\text{-}sheet$

Rules for predicting coil (the default).
$coil_i \quad \leftarrow helix_{i-1} \wedge break\text{-}helix$
$coil_i \quad \leftarrow sheet_{i-1} \wedge break\text{-}sheet$
$coil_i \quad \leftarrow coil_{i-1}$

The Chou-Fasman algorithm continues to predict α-helix as long as the predicate `cont-helix` is true. The rules define `cont-helix` mostly in terms of helix-brealcing rules—a helix continues as long as a break region is not encountered. An α-helix break region occurs when a helix-breaker amino acid is immediately followed by either another helix breaker or a helix-indifferent amino acid. A helix is also broken when encountering the amino acid proline (P). The process of extending β-sheet structures works similarly. The algorithm predicts coil as the default.

Acknowledgments

This research was partially supported by National Science Foundation Grant IRI-9002413 and Office of Naval Research Grant N00014-90-J-1941. The authors thank Terrence Sejnowski for providing the data used in testing. We also thank Geoffrey Towell, Mark Craven, Lorien Pratt, Charles Squires, and Gary Lewandowski for their valuable discussion.

Note

1. The "@" in these propositions refers to a window position. For example, `Helix-break@0` means that the proposition `helix-break` is true about the amino acid at window position 0 (the central amino acid).

References

[Bernstein77]   Bernstein, R., T. Koeyzle, G. Williams, J. Meyer, M. Brice, J. Rodgers, O. Kennard, T. Shimanouchi, and M. Tatsumi. "The protein data bank: A computer-based archival file for macromolecular structures." *Journal of Molecular Biology 112* (1977), pp. 525–542.

[Chothia84]   Chothia, C. "Principles that determine the structure of proteins." *Annual Review of Biochemistry 53*(1984), pp. 537–572.

[Chou78]   Chou, P., and G. Fasman. "Prediction of the secondary structure of proteins from their amino acid sequence." *Advances in Enzymology 47*(1978), pp. 45–148.

[Cleeremans89]   Cleeremans, A., D. Servan-Schreiber, and J. McClelland. "Finite state automata and simple recurrent networks." *Neural Computation 1*, 3 (1989), pp. 372–381.

[Cohen89]   Cohen F., and I. Kuntz. "Tertiary structure prediction." In *Prediction of Protein Structure and the Principles of Protein Conformation*, pp. 647–705. G. Fasman (ed.). Plenum Press, New York, 1989.

[Cohen91]   Cohen, B., S. Presnell, F. Cohen, and R. Langridge. "A proposal for feature-based scoring of protein secondary structure predictions." *Proceedings of the AAAI-91 Workshop on Artificial Intelligence Approaches to Classification and Pattern Recognition in Molecular Biology*, pp. 5–20, Anaheim, CA, July 1991.

[Elman90]   Elman, J. "Finding structure in time." *Cognitive Science 14*, 2 (1990), pp. 179–211.

[Fahlman90]   Fahlman, S., and C. Lebiere. "The cascade-correlation learning architecture." In *Neural Information Processing Systems 2*, pp. 524–532. D. Touretzky (ed.), 1990.

[Fasman89]   Fasman, G. "The development of the prediction of protein structure." In *Prediction of Protein Structure and the Principles of Protein Conformation*, pp. 193–316. G. Fasman (ed.). Plenum Press, New York, 1989.

[Flann89]   Flann, N., and T. Dietterich. "A study of explanation-based methods for inductive learning." *Machine Learning 4*, 2 (1989), pp. 187–226.

[Fu91]   Fu, L. "Rule learning by searching on adapted nets." *Proceedings of the Ninth National Conference on Artificial Intelligence*, pp. 590–595. Anaheim, CA, July 1991.

[Garnier89]   Garnier, J., and B. Robson. "The GOR method for predicting secondary structures in proteins." In *Prediction of Protein Structure and the Principles of Protein Conformation*, pp. 417–465. G. Fasman (ed.). Plenum Press, New York, 1989.

[Holley89]   Holley, L., and M. Karplus. "Protein structure prediction with a neural network." *Proceedings of the National Academy of Sciences (USA) 86* (1989), pp. 152–156.

[Hopcroft79]   Hopcroft, J., and J. Ullman. *Introduction to Automata Theory, Languages, and Computation*. Addison-Wesley, Reading, MA, 1979.

[Hornik89]   Hornik, K., M. Stinchcombe, and H. White. "Multilayer feedforward networks are universal approximators." *Neural Networks 2* (1989), pp. 359–366.

[Hunter91]   Hunter, L. "Representing amino acids with bitstrings." *Proceedings of the AAAI-91 Workshop on Artificial Intelligence Approaches to Classification and Pattern Recognition in Molecular Biology*, pp. 110–117. Anaheim, CA, July 1991.

[Jacobs91]   Jacobs, R., M. Jordan, S. Nowlan, and G. Hinton. "Adaptive mixtures of local experts." *Neural Computation 3*, 1 (1991), pp. 79–87.

[Jordan86]   Jordan, M. "Serial order: A parallel distributed processing approach." Technical Report 8604. University of California, Institute for Cognitive Science, San Diego, 1986.

[Kabsch83]   Kabsch, W., and C. Sander. "Dictionary of protein secondary structure: Pattern recognition of hydrogen-bonded and geometric features." *Biopolymers 22* (1983), pp. 2577–2637.

[Lang90]   Lang, K., A. Waibel, and G. Hinton. "A time-delay neural network architecture for isolated word recognition." *Neural Networks 3* (1990), pp. 23–43.

[Lim74]   Lim, V. "Algorithms for prediction of α-helical and β-structural regions in globular proteins." *Journal of Molecular Biology 88* (1974), pp. 873–894.

[Mathews75]   Mathews, B. "Comparison of the predicted and observed secondary structure of T4 Phage Lysozyme." *Biochimica et Biophysica Acta 405* (1975), pp. 442–451.

[Mozer91]   Mozer, M., and J. Bachrach. "SLUG: A connectionist architecture for inferring the structure of finite-state environments." *Machine Learning 7*, 2/3 (1991).

[Nishikawa83]   Nishikawa, K. "Assessment of secondary-structure prediction of proteins: Comparison of computerized Chou-Fasman method with others." *Biochimica et Biophysica Acta 748* (1983), pp. 285–299.

[Noordewier91]   Noordewier, M., G. Towell, and J. Shavlik. "Training knowledge-based neural networks to recognize genes in DNA sequences." In *Advances in Neural Information Processing Systems*, Vol. 3. Morgan Kaufmann, Denver, 1991.

[Ourston90]   Ourston, D., and R. Mooney. "Changing the rules: A comprehensive approach to theory refinement." *Proceedings of the Eighth National Conference on Artificial Intelligence*, pp. 815–820. Boston, July 1990.

[Porat91]   Porat, S., and J. Feldman. "Learning automata from ordered examples." *Machine Learning 7*, 2/3 (1991).

[Prevelige89] Prevelige, P. J., and G. Fasman. "Chou-Fasman prediction of the secondary structure of proteins: The Chou-Fasman-Prevelige algorithm." In *Prediction of Protein Structure and the Principles of Protein Conformation*, pp. 391–416. G. Fasman (ed.). Plenum Press, New York, 1989.

[Qian88] Qian, N., and T. Sejnowski. "Predicting the secondary structure of globular proteins using neural network models." *Journal of Molecular Biology 202* (1988), pp. 865–884.

[Richardson89] Richardson, J., and D. Richardson. "Principles and patterns of protein conformation." In *Prediction of Protein Structure and the Principles of Protein Conformation*, pp. 1–98. Fasman (ed.). Plenum Press, New York, 1989.

[Robson76] Robson, B., and E. Suzuki. "Conformational properties of amino acid residues in globular proteins." *Journal of Molecular Biology 107* (1976), pp. 327–356.

[Rumelhart86] Rumelhart, D., G. Hinton, and R. Williams. "Learning internal representations by error propagation." In *Parallel Distributed Processing: Explorations in the Microstructure of Cognition.* Vol. 1: *Foundations*, pp. 318–363. D. Rumelhart and J. McClelland (eds.). MIT Press, Cambridge, MA, 1986.

[Sejnowski87] Sejnowski, T. J., and C. R. Rosenberg. "Parallel networks that learn to pronounce English text." *Complex Systems 1* (1987), pp. 145–168.

[Servan-Schreiber91] Servan-Schreiber, D., A. Cleeremans, and J. McClelland. "Graded state machines: The representation of temporal contingencies in simple recurrent networks." *Machine Learning 7*, 2/3 (1991).

[Shavlik91] Shavlik, J., R. Mooney, and G. Towell. "Symbolic and neural learning algorithms: An experimental comparison." *Machine Learning 6* (1991), pp. 111–143.

[St. John90] St. John, M., and J. McClelland. "Learning and applying contextual constraints in sentence comprehension." *Artificial Intelligence 46*, 1–2 (1990), pp. 217–257.

[Staden90] Staden, R. "Finding protein coding sequences in genomic sequences." *Methods in Enzymology 183* (1990), pp. 163–180.

[Stolorz92] Stolorz, P., A. Lapedes, and Y. Xia. "Predicting protein secondary structure using neural net and statistical methods." *Journal of Molecular Biology 225* (1992), pp. 363–377.

[Towell90] Towell, G., J. Shavlik, and M. Noordewier. "Refinement of approximate domain theories by knowledge-base neural networks." *Proceedings of the Eighth National Conference on Artificial Intelligence*, pp. 861–866. Boston, July 1990.

[Towell92] Towell, G., and J. Shavlik. "Interpretation of artificial neural networks: Mapping knowledge-based neural networks into rules." In Advances in Neural Information Processing Systems, Vol. 4. Morgan Kaufmann, Denver, 1992.

[VanLehn87] VanLehn, K. "Learning one subprocedure per lesson." *Artificial Intelligence 31* (1987), pp. 1–40.

[Watson90] Watson, J. "The human genome project: Past, present, and future." *Science 248* (1990), pp. 44–48.

[Weiss89] Weiss, S., and I. Kapouleas. "An empirical comparison of pattern recognition, neural nets, and machine learning classification methods." *Proceedings of the Eleventh International Joint Conference on Artificial Intelligence*, pp. 781–787. Detroit, August 1989.

[Wilson85] Wilson, I., D. Haft, E. Getzoff, J. Tainer, R. Lerner, and S. Brenner. "Identical short peptide sequences in unrelated proteins can have different conformations: A testing ground for theories of immune recognition." *Proceeding of the National Academy of Sciences (USA) 82* (1985), pp. 5255–5259.

[Zhang92] Zhang, X., J. Mesirov, and D. Waltz. "Hybrid system for protein secondary structure prediction." *Journal of Molecular Biology 225* (1992), pp. 1049–1063.

III SAMPLING PROBLEMS

10 Efficient Distribution-free Learning of Probabilistic Concepts

Michael J. Kearns and Robert E. Schapire

10.1 Introduction

Consider the following scenarios:

A meteorologist is attempting to predict tomorrow's weather as accurately as possible. He measures a small number of presumably relevant parameters, such as the current temperature, barometric pressure, and wind speed and direction. He then makes a forecast of the form "chances for rain tomorrow are 70 percent." The next day it either rains or it does not rain.

A statistician wishes to compile an approximate rule for predicting when students will be admitted to a particular college. There are some students whose records are so strong they will be accepted regardless of which admissions officer reviews their files; similarly, there are others who are categorically rejected. For many students, however, their admission may be highly dependent on the particular admissions officer that evaluates their applications; thus the best model for the chances of these borderline students involves a probability of acceptance. However, every student is either accepted or rejected.

A physicist is attempting to determine the orientation of spin for particles in a certain magnetic field. Presumably, the orientation of spin is at least partially determined by a genuinely random process of Nature. The spin of any particle is always oriented either up or down.

We wish to produce a good model for the recognition of common objects such as chairs. For most objects in the world, there is nearly universal agreement as to whether that object is a chair or a nonchair. A few objects that may provoke disagreement do exist, however, such as stools and benches. This is due to the fact that the concept of "chair" is not absolute, and semantic boundaries of this concept may be exposed by both naturally occurring and artificially constructed objects. Most young children, however, are not explicitly told about such definitional shortcomings; they are simply told whether or not something is a chair.

There are some obvious common themes in each of the above situations. First, in each there is *uncertain* or probabilistic behavior. This uncertainty may arise for rather different reasons. For example, in the case of the meteorologist, it could be that while the weather is in principle a deterministic process, the parameters measured by the meteorologist and the limited accuracy of these measurements are insufficient to determine this process. In the case of the physicist, the electron spin is believed to be governed to some degree by an ideal random process. In the case of the statistician, the uncertainty arises from the diversity of human behavior, and in the case of chair recognition, a probability may model the difficulties of providing a perfectly precise definition to an inherently uncertain or "fuzzy" concept.

A second theme that is common to each of these settings is the fact that even though the best model may be a conditional probability $c(x)$ that the event (rain, acceptance to the college, etc.) occurs given x (where x represents the measured weather variables or a student's application), the observer only witnesses whether or not the event occurs. Thus, examples are of the form $(x, 0)$ or $(x, 1)$—not $(x, c(x))$—and the $\{0, 1\}$ label provided with x is distributed according to the conditional probability $c(x)$. Furthermore, we should not expect to be able to compute even an *estimate* of $c(x)$ from the given $\{0, 1\}$-labeled examples, since in general we are unlikely to ever see the same x twice (each day's weather is at least slightly different, as is each student's application).

Finally, although there is uncertainty in each of these settings, there is also some *structure* to this uncertainty. For instance, days with nearly identical atmospheric conditions and students with very similar high school records can be expected to have nearly equal probabilities of rain and acceptance to the college, respectively. We also expect some inputs to be assigned conditional probabilities that are very near 0 or 1; for example, days on which the sky is cloudless, or students with straight A's. This structured behavior strongly distinguishes these learning scenarios from a "noisy" setting, such as the one considered by Angluin and Laird [3], Kearns and Li [17], and Sloan [27]. In a model of learning with noise, the noise is typically "white" (that is, all inputs have either an equal probability of corruption or a probability determined by an adversary), and the noise is regarded as something an algorithm wishes to "filter out" in an attempt to uncover some underlying *deterministic* concept. In the examples given above, the probabilistic behavior is both *structured* (possibly in a manner that can be exploited by a learning algorithm) and *inherently part of the underlying phenomenon*. Thus, whenever possible we do not wish to filter this probabilistic behavior out of the hypothesis, but rather to *model* it.

In this chapter we wish to study a model of learning in such uncertain environments. We formalize these settings by introducing the notion of a *probabilistic concept* (or *p-concept*). A p-concept c over a domain set X is simply a mapping $c: X \to [0, 1]$. For each $x \in X$, we interpret $c(x)$ as the probability that x is a positive example of the p-concept c. Following the discussion above, a learning algorithm in this framework is attempting to infer something about the underlying target p-concept c solely on the basis of labeled examples (x, b), where $b \in \{0, 1\}$ is a bit generated randomly according to the conditional probability $c(x)$, that is, $b = 1$ with probability $c(x)$.

The value $c(x)$ may be viewed as a measure of the degree to which x exemplifies some concept c. In this sense, p-concepts are quite similar to the related notion of a *fuzzy set*, a kind of "set" whose boundaries are fuzzy or unclear, and whose formal definition is nearly identical to that of a p-concept. An axiomatic theory of fuzzy sets was introduced by Zadeh [33], and they have since received much treatment by researchers in the field of pattern recognition. (See Kandel's book [15] for a good introduction.)

We distinguish two possible goals for a learning algorithm in the p-concept model. The first and easier goal is that of *label prediction*: the algorithm wishes to output a hypothesis that maximizes the probability of correctly predicting the $\{0, 1\}$ label generated by c on an input x. We call this kind of learning *decision-rule learning*, since we are not primarily concerned with actually modeling the underlying uncertainty but instead wish to predict accurately the observable $\{0, 1\}$ outcome of this uncertainty. We will see that the more difficult and more interesting goal is that of finding a good *model of probability*. Here the algorithm wishes to output a hypothesis p-concept $h: X \to [0, 1]$ that is a good real-valued approximation to the target c; thus, we want $|c(x) - h(x)|$ to be small for most inputs x. Following the motivation given above, we are mainly concerned with this latter notion of learning.

As mentioned above, the quantity $c(x)$ is simply the conditional probability of the label 1 being assigned to a given instance x. Equivalently, in this setting, $c(x)$ is the conditional expectation of the label b assigned to the given instance x. Thus, the problem of learning a model of probability can be described in statistical terms as that of modeling the conditional distribution of some random variable b (the label) given the value of some other random variable x (the instance). This problem, commonly known to statisticians as *regression*, has received much attention in the statistics literature. (See, for instance, Dobson's book [8].) The problem of learning a model of probability is also equivalent (with slight restrictions) to that of learning a *stochastic rule* as defined in the parallel work of Yamanishi [32].

As noted above, we will typically assume that the probabilistic behavior exhibited by the target p-concept is, to some degree, structured. To model this structure, we study the learnability of classes of p-concepts that obey natural mathematical properties intended to model some realistic environments. As a simple example, in constructing a p-concept model of the subjective notion of "tall," it is reasonable to assume that $x \geq y$ implies $c(x) \geq c(y)$ (where x represents height)—the taller a person actually is, the higher the percentage of people who will agree he is tall (or the greater the "degree of tallness" we wish to assign). This motivates us to consider learning the class $\mathscr{C}$ of all nondecreasing p-concepts over the positive real line. In general, we wish to study the learnability of p-concept classes that are restricted in such a way as to capture plausibly some realistic situation, but are not so restricted as to make the learning problem trivial or uninteresting.

We adopt from the Valiant model for learning deterministic concepts [28] the emphasis on learning algorithms that are both efficient (in the sense of polynomial time) and general (in the sense of working for the largest possible p-concept classes and against any probability distribution over the domain). After formalizing the learning model and the two possible goals for a learning algorithm (decision-rule learning and model-of-probability learning), we embark on a systematic study of techniques for designing efficient algorithms for learning p-concepts and the underlying theory of the p-concept model.

We begin by giving examples of efficient algorithms producing a good model of probability that employ what we call the *direct approach*; the analyses of these algorithms give first-principles arguments that the output hypothesis is good. These include algorithms for arbitrary nondecreasing functions motivated above, a probabilistic analogue of Rivest's decision lists [25], and a class of "hidden-variable" p-concepts, motivated by settings such as weather prediction where the apparently probabilistic behavior may in part be due to the fact that some relevant quantities remain undiscovered.

We then consider the problem of *hypothesis testing* in the p-concept model. Working in the same framework as Haussler [11, 12], we define a *loss function* that assigns a measure of goodness to any hypothesis p-concept on a $\{0, 1\}$-labeled sample. After observing that the *quadratic loss* measure has some well-studied mathematical properties that make it a convenient and appropriate choice for our setting, we next give an example of an efficient algorithm for finding a model of probability that first does some direct computation to narrow the search and then uses quadratic loss to choose the best hypothesis among a small remaining pool. This algorithm learns a class of p-concepts in which only a small number of variables are relevant, but the dependence on these variables may be arbitrary.

Next we consider the related but more difficult issue of *uniform convergence* of a p-concept class. More precisely, how many $\{0, 1\}$-labeled examples must be taken before we have high confidence that every p-concept in the class has an empirical quadratic loss that accurately reflects its true performance as a model of probability? In a more general formulation, this question has received extensive consideration in the statistical pattern recognition literature, and its importance to learning has been demonstrated by many recent papers. We show that the sufficient sample size for uniform convergence is bounded above by the *pseudo dimension* of the p-concept class, a combinatorial measure discussed by Pollard [24], Haussler [12], and other authors.

We then give efficient algorithms that apply the uniform convergence method (that is, take a large enough sample as dictated by the pseudo dimension, and find the hypothesis minimizing the empirical loss over the sample) in order to find a good model of probability. In particular, we prove the effectiveness of an algorithm for learning p-concepts represented by linear combinations of d given basis functions. We then show that the pseudo dimension, when finite, is also a lower bound on the required sample size for learning any p-concept class with a model of probability; thus the pseudo dimension, when finite, characterizes the sample complexity of p-concept learning with a model of probability in the same way that the Vapnik-Chervonenkis (VC) dimension characterizes sample complexity in Valiant's model. (See Blumer et al.'s paper [6] for a full discussion of the VC-dimension.) However, we show that p-concept classes of *infinite* pseudo dimension may sometimes be learned efficiently, in contrast to classes of infinite VC-dimension in the Valiant model, which are not learnable in *any* amount of time. (Technically, this is not always true if "dynamic" sampling is allowed; see Linial, Mansour, and Rivest's paper [20] for further details.)

We conclude with an investigation of Occam's Razor in the p-concept model. In the Valiant model, Blumer et al. [5] show that it suffices for learning to find a consistent hypothesis that is slightly shorter than the sample data. We look for analogies in our setting: namely, when does "data compression" imply a good model of probability? We formalize this question and argue briefly that several of our algorithms can be interpreted as implementing a form of data compression.

The primary contribution of this research is that of providing initial positive results for efficient learnability in a natural and important extension to Valiant's model. This may be significant because the Valiant model has been criticized for its strong hardness results and drought of powerful positive results, as well as for the unrealistic deterministic and noise-free view it takes of the concepts to be learned.

At first, it may seem paradoxical that we are able to generalize the model and obtain several positive results simultaneously; perhaps this can be intuitively explained by the fact that since we generalize the form of the representations being learned, there are more ways that concepts capturing some natural and realistic setting may be simply expressed. In contrast, since the Valiant model tends to emphasize concept classes based on standard circuit complexity, one is quickly led to study very powerful and apparently difficult classes such as disjunctive normal form Boolean expressions.

Another contribution of this research is in demonstrating the feasibility and practicality of the approach suggested by Haussler [11]. His work addressed the issue of sample complexity upper bounds in great generality, even encompassing the case where the input-output relation to be learned has no prescribed functional form. This generality prevents Haussler from obtaining either good sample size lower bounds or efficient learning algorithms; indeed, he cites both of these as important areas for further research. Our results may be regarded as a first demonstration of applying some of Haussler's general principles to a specific and realistic model in which computation time is of foremost significance.

10.2   The Learning Model

Let X be a set called the *domain* (or *instance space*). A *probabilistic concept* (or *p-concept*) is a real-valued function $c: X \rightarrow [0, 1]$. When learning the p-concept c, the value $c(x)$ is interpreted as the *probability* that x exemplifies the concept being learned (i.e., the probability that x is a positive example). A *p-concept class* $\mathscr{C}$ is a family of p-concepts. On any execution, a learning algorithm for $\mathscr{C}$ is attempting to learn a distinguished *target* p-concept $c \in \mathscr{C}$ with respect to a fixed but unknown and arbitrary *target distribution D* over X. We think of D as modeling the natural distribution of objects in the domain, and c represents the probabilistic concept to be learned in this domain. (More formally, D is a probability measure on a σ-algebra of measurable subsets of X. We assume implicitly that all of the p-concepts considered are measurable functions with respect to this σ-algebra on X, and the Borel σ-algebra on $[0, 1]$.)

The learning algorithm is given access to an oracle EX (short for "examples") that behaves as follows: EX first draws a point $x \in X$ randomly according to the distribution D. Then with probability $c(x)$, EX returns the labeled example $(x, 1)$, and with probability $1 - c(x)$ it returns $(x, 0)$. Thus, $c(x)$ is the conditional probability that example x is labeled 1. Further note that the learning algorithm never has direct access to these conditional probabilities $c(x)$, but only to random examples whose labels are distributed according to these unknown probabilities.

Let h be a function mapping X into $\{0, 1\}$; we call such a function a *decision rule*. We define the *predictive error* of h on c with respect to D, denoted $R_D(c, h)$, as the probability that h will misclassify a randomly drawn point from EX. If h minimizes $R_D(c, \cdot)$, then we say that h is a *best decision rule*, or a *Bayes optimal decision rule*, for c. We say that h is an ε-*good* decision rule for c if $R_D(c, h) \leq R_D(c, \tilde{h}) + \varepsilon$, where $\tilde{h}$ is a best decision rule. Thus we ask that h be nearly as good as the best decision rule for c.

The *projection* of the p-concept c is the function $\pi_c: X \to \{0, 1\}$ that is 1 if $c(x) \geq 1/2$ and 0 if $c(x) < 1/2$. It is well known and easy to show that for any target p-concept c, its projection π_c is a Bayes optimal decision rule.

In this chapter we are primarily interested not in the problem of finding a good decision rule, but in that of producing an accurate real-valued approximation to the target p-concept itself. Thus, we wish to infer a good *model of probability* with respect to the target distribution. We say that a p-concept h is an (ε, γ)-*good model of probability* of c with respect to D if we have $\mathbf{Pr}_{x \in D}[|h(x) - c(x)| > \gamma] \leq \varepsilon$. Thus, the value of h must be near that of c on most points x.

We are now ready to describe our model for learning p-concepts. Let $\mathscr{C}$ be a p-concept class over domain X. We say that $\mathscr{C}$ is *learnable with a model of probability* (respectively, *learnable with a decision rule*) if there is an algorithm A such that for any target p-concept $c \in \mathscr{C}$, for any target distribution D over X, for any inputs $\varepsilon > 0$, $\delta > 0$, and $\gamma > 0$, algorithm A, given access to EX, halts and with probability at least $1 - \delta$ outputs a p-concept h that is an (ε, γ)-good model of probability (respectively, an ε-good decision rule) for c with respect to D. Note that this model of learning p-concepts generalizes Valiant's model for learning deterministic concepts.

We say that $\mathscr{C}$ is *polynomially learnable* (with either a model of probability or a decision rule) if there is a learning algorithm A that runs in time polynomial in $1/\varepsilon$, $1/\delta$ and, where appropriate, $1/\gamma$. (In fact, an equivalent formulation is obtained by requiring the running time to be polynomial in $\log(1/\delta)$, rather than $1/\delta$. See section 10.4.) Often the p-concept class $\mathscr{C}$ will be parameterized by a complexity parameter n, that is, $\mathscr{C} = \bigcup_{n \geq 1} \mathscr{C}_n$, and all p-concepts in $\mathscr{C}_n$ share a common subdomain X_n, and $X = \bigcup_{n \geq 1} X_n$. In such cases we also allow a polynomial dependence on n.

Our first lemma shows that a good model of probability can always be efficiently used as a good decision rule; thus, learning with a model of probability is at least as hard as decision-rule learning.

LEMMA 2.1 *Let $\mathscr{C}$ be a class of p-concepts. If $\mathscr{C}$ is (polynomially) learnable with a model of probability, then $\mathscr{C}$ is (polynomially) learnable with a decision rule.*

Proof: To prove the lemma, we show that the projection of a good model of probability can be used as a good decision rule. In particular, we show that if h is an (ε, γ)-good model of probability, then π_h is an $(\varepsilon + 2\gamma)$-good decision rule. Thus, by choosing ε and γ appropriately, an arbitrarily good decision rule can be found by the assumed algorithm for learning with a model of probability.

Let $x \in X$, and suppose $|h(x) - c(x)| \leq \gamma$. If $|c(x) - 1/2| > \gamma$, then clearly $\pi_h(x) = \pi_c(x)$. On the other hand, if $|c(x) - 1/2| \leq \gamma$, then it may be that $\pi_h(x) \neq \pi_c(x)$. However, the chance that $\pi_c(x)$ agrees with a random label for x (chosen according to c) is at most $1/2 + \gamma$, while the chance that $\pi_h(x)$ agrees with the random label is at least $1/2 - \gamma$.

Thus, the difference in predictive error between π_c and π_h (taken over a random choice of an instance and its label) is at most $\varepsilon + (1 - \varepsilon) \cdot 2\gamma \leq \varepsilon + 2\gamma$.   ∎

10.2.1 Alternative Formulations

In addition to the formulation given above, there are various other natural ways of expressing the fact that some hypothesis p-concept h is "close" to the target c. For example, we might say that h is a good model of probability for c if the average difference between the two functions is small, that is, if the *variational distance* $\mathbf{E}_{x \in D}[|h(x) - c(x)|]$ is small. Alternatively, our goal might be to make small the *quadratic distance* (i.e., the expected square of the difference between the functions).

As we will see in the following sections, these alternative definitions are sometimes easier to work with than the "official" definition given above. The next lemma and theorem show that the three formulations are equivalent modulo polynomial-time computations.

LEMMA 2.2 *Let h and c be p-concepts, and let $\mathscr{D}$ be a target distribution on domain X. Let $e_1 = \mathbf{E}_{x \in D}[|h(x) - c(x)|]$ and let $e_2 = \mathbf{E}_{x \in D}[(h(x) - c(x))^2]$. Then*

- *$e_2 \leq e_1 \leq \sqrt{e_2}$;*
- *for any $\gamma > 0$, h is both an $(e_1/\gamma, \gamma)$- and an $(e_2/\gamma^2, \gamma)$-good model of probability for c;*
- *if h is an (ε, γ)-good model of probability, then $e_1 \leq \varepsilon + \gamma$, and $e_2 \leq \varepsilon + \gamma^2$.*

Proof: Since $|h(x) - c(x)| \leq 1$ for all x, it is clear that $e_2 \leq e_1$. Also, it is well known that $(\mathbf{E}[Y])^2 \leq \mathbf{E}[Y^2]$ for any random variable Y. Thus, $e_1 \leq \sqrt{e_2}$.

Let $\gamma > 0$. Then by Markov's inequality,

$$\mathbf{Pr}_{x \in D}[|h(x) - c(x)| > \gamma] \leq e_1/\gamma.$$

Similarly,

$$\mathbf{Pr}_{x \in D}[|h(x) - c(x)| > \gamma] = \mathbf{Pr}_{x \in D}[(h(x) - c(x))^2 > \gamma^2] \leq e_2/\gamma^2.$$

These imply the second part of the lemma.

Finally, suppose h is an (ε, γ)-good model of probability. Then

$$e_1 \leq \mathbf{Pr}_{x \in D}[|h(x) - c(x)| > \gamma] \cdot 1 + \mathbf{Pr}_{x \in D}[|h(x) - c(x)| \leq \gamma] \cdot \gamma$$
$$\leq \varepsilon + (1 - \varepsilon)\gamma \leq \varepsilon + \gamma.$$

Similarly, $e_2 \leq \varepsilon + \gamma^2$. ∎

THEOREM 2.3   *Let $\mathscr{C}$ be a class of p-concepts, let c be the target p-concept, and let D be a target distribution on domain X. Then, assuming access to oracle EX, the following computational problems are equivalent (i.e., if one is solvable, then so are the others):*

1. *Finding, with probability at least $1 - \delta$, an (ε, γ)-good model of probability in time polynomial in $1/\varepsilon$, $1/\delta$, and $1/\gamma$;*

2. *Finding, with probability at least $1 - \delta$, a hypothesis h such that $\mathbf{E}_{x \in D} [|h(x) - c(x)|] \le \varepsilon$ in time polynomial in $1/\varepsilon$ and $1/\delta$;*

3. *Finding, with probability at least $1 - \delta$, a hypothesis h such that $\mathbf{E}_{x \in D} [(h(x) - c(x))^2] \le \varepsilon$ in time polynomial in $1/\varepsilon$ and $1/\delta$.*

Proof: Lemma 2.2 implies the following:

• Given an algorithm A_1 for solving problem 1, problem 2 can be solved by running A_1 with ε and γ each set to $\varepsilon/2$.

• Given an algorithm A_2 for solving problem 2, problem 3 can be solved by running A_2 directly.

• Given an algorithm A_3 for solving problem 3, problem 1 can be solved by running A_3 with ε set to $\varepsilon\gamma^2$.   ∎

In addition to the formulations given by Theorem 2.3, Yamanishi [32] shows that an equivalent problem is to find, in polynomial time with high probability and for given ε, a hypothesis h such that $\mathbf{E}_{x \in D} [(\sqrt{h(x)} - \sqrt{c(x)})^2] \le \varepsilon$. (This quantity is known as the *Hellinger distance.*) Finally, Abe, Takeuchi, and Warmuth [1] have shown that all of these problems are equivalent (modulo polynomial-time computation) to the problem of finding, with high probability and for given ε, a hypothesis with *Kullback-Liebler divergence,* that is, a hypothesis h for which

$$\mathbf{E}_{x \in D}\left[c(x) \lg \left(\frac{c(x)}{h(x)} \right) + (1 - c(x)) \lg \left(\frac{1 - c(x)}{1 - h(x)} \right) \right] \le \varepsilon.$$

10.2.2   Chernoff Bounds

Several times, in later sections of this chapter, we will make use of the following bounds on the tails of a binomial distribution [4, 14].

LEMMA 2.4 (Chernoff Bounds)   *Let $X_1, \ldots, X_m$ be a sequence of m independent Bernoulli trials, each succeeding with probability p so that $\mathbf{E}[X_i] = p$.*

Let $S = X_1 + \cdots + X_m$ be the random variable describing the total number of successes. Then for $0 \leq \gamma \leq 1$, the following hold:

- *(additive form)* $\mathbf{Pr}[S > (p + \gamma)m] \leq e^{-2m\gamma^2}$, *and* $\mathbf{Pr}[S < (p - \gamma)m] \leq e^{-2m\gamma^2}$;
- *(multiplicative form)* $\mathbf{Pr}[S > (1 + \gamma)pm] \leq e^{-\gamma^2 mp/3}$, *and* $\mathbf{Pr}[S < (1 - \gamma)pm] \leq e^{-\gamma^2 mp/2}$.

The additive form (also known as Hoeffding's inequality) holds also if X_1, ..., X_m are independent identically distributed random variables with range in $[0, 1]$.

10.3   Efficient Algorithms: The Direct Approach

In this section we describe efficient algorithms for learning good models of probability based on first principles and proved correct by direct arguments. Later arguments will rely on an underlying theory of p-concept learning that is developed in subsequent sections. We begin with a p-concept class motivated by the problem of modeling "tallness" discussion in the Introduction.

10.3.1   Increasing Functions

THEOREM 3.1   *The p-concept class of all nondecreasing function $c: \mathbf{R} \rightarrow [0, 1]$ is polynomially learnable with a model of probability.*

Proof: We prove the result in slightly greater generality for any domain X linearly ordered by some ordering "$\leq$." Given positive ε, δ, and γ, let $t = \lceil 4/\varepsilon\gamma \rceil$, and let

$$s = \left\lceil \max \left\{ \frac{64 \ln(2^{21}/(\varepsilon\gamma)^2\delta)}{\varepsilon\gamma}, \frac{2\ln(4t/\delta)}{\gamma^2} \right\} \right\rceil.$$

Our algorithm begins by drawing a labeled sample of $m = st$ examples (x_i, b_i). The examples are sorted and reindexed so that $x_1 \leq \cdots \leq x_m$. In fact, we assume initially that no instance occurs twice in the sample so that $x_1 < \cdots < x_m$. Later, we show how this assumption can be removed.

The set X can naturally be partitioned into t disjoint intervals I_j, each containing exactly s instances of the sample; specifically, we let $I_1 = (-\infty, x_s]$; $I_j = (x_{(j-1)s}, x_{js}]$ for $j = 2, 3, \ldots, t - 1$; and $I_t = (x_{(t-1)s}, \infty)$. For $1 \leq j \leq t$, let $\hat{p}_j = (1/s) \cdot \sum_{x_i \in I_j} b_i$. Thus, $\hat{p}_j$ is an estimate of the probability

p_j that a random instance in I_j is labeled 1. Our algorithm outputs a step function h defined in a natural manner: for $x \in I_j$, we define $h(x) = \hat{p}_j$.

This algorithm clearly runs in polynomial time. We argue next that the output hypothesis h is an (ε, γ)-good model of probability (with high probability). Here are the high-level ideas: first, we show that (with high probability) each interval has weight approximately $\varepsilon\gamma$ under the target distribution. Next we show that if c increases by roughly γ or less on the interval I_j, then h is close to c on all points in the interval. On the other hand, since c is nondecreasing and bounded between 0 and 1, c can increase by more than γ in at most $1/\gamma$ intervals; since these "bad" intervals have total weight at most ε, h is a good model of probability.

Specifically, we can apply the uniform convergence results of Vapnik and Chervonenkis [30] to show that, with high probability, each interval I_j has probability at most $\varepsilon\gamma/2$. Let S be the set of all intervals on X. Then Theorem 2 of their paper shows that, with probability at least $1 - \delta/2$, for the sample size m chosen by our algorithm, the relative fraction of points of the sample occurring in *any* interval of S is within $\varepsilon\gamma/4$ of the true weight of the interval under the target distribution. In particular, since each interval I_j contains $1/t \leq \varepsilon\gamma/4$ of the instances in the sample, the weight of I_j under the target distribution is at most $\varepsilon\gamma/2$. (Technically, their results rely on certain measurability assumptions which may depend on the choice of X. However, these assumptions are satisfied when $X = \mathbf{R}$.)

Let $q_j = c(x_{j_s})$ for $1 \leq j < t$, and let $q_0 = 0$ and $q_t = 1$. Then for $x \in I_j$, it is clear that $q_{j-1} \leq c(x) \leq q_j$ since c is nondecreasing. In particular, this is true for each $x_i \in I_j$. Thus, each point $x_i \in I_j$ is labeled 1 with probability $c(x_i) \geq q_{j-1}$, and so, for each j, $\hat{p}_j \geq q_{j-1} - \gamma/2$ with probability at least $1 - \delta/4t$; this follows from the fact that $s \geq (2/\gamma^2) \cdot \ln(4t/\delta)$, and by applying the additive form of Chernoff bounds given in Lemma 2.4. Similarly, $\hat{p}_j \leq q_j + \gamma/2$ with probability at least $1 - \delta/4t$. Thus, it follows that $q_{j-1} - \gamma/2 \leq \hat{p}_j \leq q_j + \gamma/2$ for all j with probability at least $1 - \delta/2$. Hence, if $q_j - q_{j-1} \leq \gamma/2$, then $|h(x) - c(x)| \leq \gamma$ for $x \in I_j$.

On the other hand, $q_j - q_{j-1}$ can exceed $\gamma/2$ for at most $2/\gamma$ values of j since c is nondecreasing and bounded between 0 and 1. Since each of these "bad" intervals has probability weight at most $\varepsilon\gamma/2$, the sum total probability of these intervals under D is at most ε. Thus, h is an (ε, γ)-good model of probability.

Finally, we show how to ensure that the sample does not contain the same instance more than once. Such a situation could be problematic for our algorithm since it might cause some of the intervals defined above to be empty, or to contain too many sample points.

The idea is to replace the given domain X and target distribution D with a new domain X' and distribution D' under which the same instance is very unlikely to occur twice. In particular, we let $X' = X \times T$ and $D' = D \times U$ where U is the uniform distribution on the set $T = \{0, \ldots, 2^k - 1\}$, and $k = \lceil 2 \lg m + \lg(1/\delta) \rceil$. Then X' is linearly ordered under the lexicographic ordering (i.e., $(x, r) \leq (y, s)$ if and only if $x < y$, or $x = y$ and $r \leq s$). Also, the chance that any pair of instances are the same in a sample of size m drawn according to D' is at most $\binom{m}{2} \cdot 2^{-k} \leq m^2 \cdot 2^{-k-1} \leq \delta/2$.

In addition, given a random source of instances from X drawn according to D, we can easily simulate the random choice of instances from X' according to D': given $x \in X$, we simply draw a random number r uniformly from T, yielding an instance (x, r) with distribution D' (x's label is not altered). Thus, the previously described algorithm can be simulated (with δ replaced by $\delta/2$) on domain X'. If the same instance occurs twice in the sample, the algorithm simply fails—as argued above, this will happen with probability at most $\delta/2$. Thus, with probability at least $1 - \delta$, the algorithm returns an (ε, γ)-good hypothesis h (with respect to X'). This hypothesis can be used to estimate $c(x)$ for a given point $x \in X$ by randomly choosing $r \in T$ and evaluating $h((x, r))$. Although this yields a randomized hypothesis h', it remains true that the probability (over choices of $x \in X$ and the randomization of h') that h' differs by more than γ from c is at most ε. Thus, h' is an (ε, γ)-good model of probability if h is. ∎

This algorithm can be modified to learn with a model of probability any function over the real line with at most d extremal points; the running time is then polynomial in d, $1/\varepsilon$, $\log(1/\delta)$, and $1/\gamma$.

In principle, the algorithm of Theorem 3.1 could be used to learn the p-concept class of nondecreasing functions with a decision rule (by applying Lemma 2.1). However, a much simpler and more efficient algorithm exists that we give in section 10.5.

10.3.2 Probabilistic Decision Lists

We turn next to the problem of learning a probabilistic analogue of Rivest's decision lists [25]. We define such lists with respect to a basis $\mathscr{F}_n$ of Boolean-valued functions on the domain $\{0, 1\}^n$. We assume always that

$\mathscr{F}_n$ contains the constant function 1. Then a *probabilistic decision list c over basis* $\mathscr{F}_n$ is given by a list $(f_1, r_1), \ldots, (f_s, r_s)$, where each $f_i \in \mathscr{F}_n$, and each $r_i \in [0, 1]$. We also assume that f_s is the constant function 1. For any assignment x in the domain, $c(x)$ is defined to be r_j, where j is the least index for which $f_j(x) = 1$. In other words, the functions in $\mathscr{F}_n$ are tested one by one in the order specified by the list, until a function which evaluates to 1 on x is encountered; the corresponding real number r_j is then the probability that x is labeled 1.

Rivest does not define decision lists with respect to a general basis as is done here. Rather, in his definition, a decision list only tests the values of monomials. That is, he defines decision lists specifically with respect to the basis consisting of all conjunctions of literals. He goes on to define the class k-DL of decision lists in which each monomial occurring in the list is a conjunction of k or fewer literals. Thus, this class is over the basis of all monomials of size at most k. Rivest describes an efficient algorithm for learning the class k-DL, when k is any fixed constant.

Below, we describe an efficient algorithm for learning a special class of probabilistic decision lists over any basis $\mathscr{F}_n$. The running time of this algorithm is polynomial in all of the usual parameters, in addition to $|\mathscr{F}_n|$, and the maximum time needed to evaluate any function f in $\mathscr{F}_n$. Thus, in particular, this implies a polynomial-time algorithm for the same basis considered by Rivest, namely, the set of all conjunctions of k or fewer literals, for k a fixed constant.

Let c be a probabilistic decision list over basis $\mathscr{F}_n$, given by the list $(f_1, r_1), \ldots, (f_s, r_s)$. For $\omega \in [0, 1]$, we say that c is a probabilistic decision list *with ω-converging probabilities* if $|r_i - \omega| \geq |r_{i+1} - \omega|$ for $1 \leq i < s$. Below we describe an algorithm for inferring such lists when ω is known. As a special case, when $\omega = 0$, this algorithm can be used to learn probabilistic decision lists *with decreasing probabilities*, that is, lists in which $r_i \geq r_j$ for $i \leq j$.

Perhaps the most natural case occurs when $\omega = 1/2$. In this case, we say that c is a probabilistic decision list *with decreasing certainty* since instances with the most certain outcomes (labels) are handled at the beginning of the list. For instance, a college's admissions process (see section 10.1) might be naturally modeled in this manner as a list of criteria for determining admission, ordered by importance: for example, if the student has straight A's, then he should be admitted with 90% probability; otherwise, if he did poorly on his SAT's, then he should be rejected with 85%

probability; otherwise, if he was class president, then he should be accepted with 75% probability; and so on. Note that the class of probabilistic decision lists with decreasing certainty includes the class of ordinary (deterministic) decision lists over the same basis.

We also note that the algorithm given below in Theorem 3.2 can be applied to learn ordinary decision lists when the supplied examples are "noisy." Specifically, consider the problem of learning a deterministic decision list c given by the list $(f_1, b_1), \ldots, (f_s, b_s)$ where each f_i is in the basis $\mathcal{F}_n$, and, since the list is deterministic, each $b_i \in \{0, 1\}$. Suppose further that the label of each example is flipped (i.e., reversed) randomly with probability $\eta < 1/2$. This random misclassification noise model is considered, for instance, by Angluin and Laird [3]. Note that the observed behavior in such a situation can be modeled naturally by the probabilistic decision list c' given by $(f_1, |b_1 - \eta|), \ldots, (f_s, |b_s - \eta|)$. That is, $c'(x)$ is the probability that x is labeled 1 by a noisy oracle for c. Clearly, c' is a probabilistic decision list with 1/2-converging probabilities. Thus, we can apply the efficient learning algorithm for this class (described below) to obtain a good model of probability h for c'. If we choose $\gamma < 1/2 - \eta$, then it can be seen that the projection of h is a good approximation of c; that is, with probability at least $1 - \delta$, a hypothesis h is obtained for which $\mathbf{Pr}_{x \in D} [\pi_h(x) \neq c(x)] \leq \varepsilon$. (Technically, this algorithm assumes that η, or an upper bound on η, is known. However, if no such bound is known, Angluin and Laird [3] give a technique for finding a good bound using a kind of "binary search.")

Thus, a corollary of Theorem 3.2 is a proof that deterministic decision lists are efficiently learnable even when the supplied examples are randomly misclassified with probability η. The running time is then polynomial in $1/(1 - 2\eta)$, in addition to the usual other parameters. This specifically answers an open question proposed by Rivest [25] concerning the learnability of decision lists in such a noisy setting. (This problem of learning noisy decision lists was solved independently by Sakakibara [26].)

THEOREM 3.2   Let $\omega \in [0, 1]$ be fixed, and let $\mathcal{F}_n$ be a basis of functions. Then the p-concept class of probabilistic decision lists over basis $\mathcal{F}_n$ with ω-converging probabilities is learnable with a model of probability (assuming both ω and $\mathcal{F}_n$ are known). Specifically, this class can be learned in time polynomial in $1/\varepsilon$, $1/\gamma$, $\log(1/\delta)$, n, $|\mathcal{F}_n|$, and the maximum time needed to evaluate any function in $\mathcal{F}_n$.

Input: $\omega \in [0, 1]$
             basis $\mathscr{F}_n = \{f_1, \ldots, f_s\}$
             $\varepsilon, \delta, \gamma > 0$
             access to random examples of a probabilistic decision list over basis $\mathscr{F}_n$
                with ω-converging probabilities

Output: with probability at least $1 - \delta$, an (ε, γ)-good model of probability

Procedure:
1 $L \leftarrow$ empty list
2 $J \leftarrow \{1, \ldots, s\}$
3 obtain a sample S of $m = \lceil (32s/\varepsilon^3 \gamma^2) \cdot \ln(2^{s+2}s/\delta) \rceil$ random examples
4 **repeat**
5   **if** $|\{(x, b) \in S : f_j(x) = 1\}| \leq m\varepsilon/4s$ for some $j \in J$ **then**
6      $t \leftarrow j$
7      $\hat{p}_t \leftarrow 0$
8   **else**
9   **for** $j \in J : \hat{p}_j \leftarrow |\{(x, b) \in S : f_j(x) = 1 \wedge b = 1\}| \div |\{(x, b) \in S : f_j(x) = 1\}|$
10   choose t that maximizes $|\hat{p}_j - \omega|$
11    $L \leftarrow L, (f_t, \hat{p}_t)$
12    $S \leftarrow \{(x, b) \in S : f_t(x) = 0\}$
13    $J \leftarrow J - \{t\}$
14 **until** $J = \varnothing$
15 **output** L

Figure 10.1
An algorithm for learning probabilistic decision lists with ω-converging probabilities

Proof: Our learning algorithm for this p-concept class is shown in Figure 10.1. As usual, the algorithm begins by drawing a large sample S of size m which will be used to construct a hypothesis probabilistic decision list L. (Note that S and all subsets derived from S are *multisets*—they are "sets" which may contain multiple copies of the same example.)

Assume for convenience that the functions in $\mathscr{F}_n$ are indexed so that the target p-concept c is given by the list $(f_1, r_1), \ldots, (f_s, r_s)$. (Of course, the learning algorithm is not aware of this.) We also assume without loss of generality that every function in the basis $\mathscr{F}_n$ occurs in the target list so that $s = |\mathscr{F}_n|$.

Here is the intuition behind our algorithm: using the sample, we might estimate the probability p_i that a positive random example $(x, 1)$ is drawn, given that $f_i(x) = 1$. It can be shown to follow from the definition of ω-converging decision lists that $|p_1 - \omega| \geq |p_i - \omega|$ for all i. This suggests a technique for identifying the first variable in the list: if our estimates $\hat{p}_i$ are sufficiently accurate, we would expect $|\hat{p}_i - \omega|$ to be maximized when $i = 1$. This is the approach taken by our algorithm: the function f_i for which $|\hat{p}_i - \omega|$ is greatest is placed at the head of the hypothesis list. The remainder of the list is constructed iteratively using the part of the sample on which $f_i(x) = 0$.

For $I \subset \{1, \ldots, s\}$ and $j \in \{1, \ldots, s\}$, let $A(I, j)$ be the set of all instances x for which $f_j(x) = 1$ and $f_i(x) = 0$ for all $i \in I$. Let

$$u(I, j) = \mathbf{Pr}_{x \in D} [x \in A(I, j)]$$

and

$$v(I, j) = \mathbf{Pr}_{(x,b) \in EX} [b = 1 | x \in A(I, j)].$$

Also, let $\hat{u}(I, j)$ and $\hat{v}(I, j)$ be empirical estimates of these quantities derivable from the sample S in the obvious manner.

Let $I \subset \{1, \ldots, s\}$ and $j \in \{1, \ldots, s\}$ be fixed. Then, using the multiplicative form of Chernoff bounds given by Lemma 2.4, it follows that if $u(I, j) > \varepsilon/2s$ then, since $m \geq (16s/\varepsilon) \cdot \ln(2^{s+1}s/\delta)$,

$$\hat{u}(I, j) \geq \tfrac{1}{2} \cdot u(I, j)$$

with probability at least $1 - \delta/(s \cdot 2^{s+1})$. Furthermore, if $\hat{u}(I, j) > \varepsilon/4s$, then the number of instances $x \in A(I, j)$ included in S is at least $m\varepsilon/4s \geq (8/\varepsilon^2\gamma^2) \cdot \ln(2^{s+2}s/\delta)$. Thus, applying the additive form of Chernoff bounds, we see that

$$|v(I, j) - \hat{v}(I, j)| \leq \varepsilon\gamma/4$$

with probability at least $1 - \delta/2^{s+1}s$, assuming $\hat{u}(I, j) > \varepsilon/4s$.

Thus, with probability at least $1 - \delta$, a sample S is chosen such that for all $I \subset \{1, \ldots, s\}$ and for all $j \in \{1, \ldots, s\}$, we have that

$$u(I, j) \leq \max\left(\frac{\varepsilon}{2s}, 2\hat{u}(I, j)\right), \tag{1}$$

and, whenever $\hat{u}(I, j) > \varepsilon/4s$, we also have that

$$|v(I, j) - \hat{v}(I, j)| \leq \frac{\varepsilon\gamma}{4}. \tag{2}$$

We assume henceforth that all of the empirical estimates $\hat{u}(I, j)$ and $\hat{v}(I, j)$ satisfy the conditions described above. As just argued, this will be the case with probability at least $1 - \delta$. To complete the proof, we show that this assumption implies that the algorithm's output hypothesis h is an (ε, γ)-good model of probability.

Suppose h is given by the list $(f_{t_1}, r'_1), \ldots, (f_{t_s}, r'_s)$. Let $T_i = \{t_1, \ldots, t_i\}$. To prove that h is an (ε, γ)-good model of probability, we show that, for $1 \leq i \leq s$, either

$$\mathbf{Pr}_{x \in D} [x \in A(T_{i-1}, t_i)] \leq \varepsilon/2s \tag{3}$$

or

$$\mathbf{Pr}_{x \in D} [|h(x) - c(x)| > \gamma | x \in A(T_{i-1}, t_i)] \leq \varepsilon/2. \tag{4}$$

Note that the sets $A(T_{i-1}, t_i)$ are disjoint. Thus, this implies

$$\mathbf{Pr}_{x \in D} [|h(x) - c(x)| > \gamma]$$

$$= \sum_{i=1}^{s} \mathbf{Pr}_{x \in D} [|h(x) - c(x)| > \gamma | x \in A(T_{i-1}, t_i)] \cdot \mathbf{Pr}_{x \in D} [x \in A(T_{i-1}, t_i)]$$

$$\leq \varepsilon$$

as can be seen by breaking the sum into two parts based on whether $\mathbf{Pr}_{x \in D}$ $[x \in A(T_{i-1}, t_i)]$ exceeds or does not exceed $\varepsilon/2s$.

Fix i and consider the ith iteration of our algorithm. Prior to the extension of L at line 11, the hypothesis list is $(f_{t_1}, r'_1), \ldots, (f_{t_{i-1}}, r'_{i-1})$. Let $C_j = A(T_{i-1}, j)$. Also, let $p_j = v(T_{i-1}, j)$, and observe that, as defined in the figure $\hat{p}_j = \hat{v}(T_{i-1}, j)$. This follows from the fact that, at this point in the execution of the algorithm, all examples (x, b) in S are such that $f_k(x) = 0$ for $k \in T_{i-1}$.

Let t be as in the figure (i.e., $t = t_i$). If t was chosen at line 6, then $\hat{u}(T_{i-1}, t) \leq \varepsilon/4s$, and so $u(T_{i-1}, t) \leq \varepsilon/2s$ by Equation (1). Thus, in the case, Equation (3) holds by definition of $u(I, j)$.

Otherwise, for all $j \in J$, $\hat{u}(T_{i-1}, j) > \varepsilon/4s$, and thus, $|p_j - \hat{p}_j| \leq \varepsilon\gamma/4$ by Equation (2). We wish to prove that Equation (4) holds in this case, that is, that

$$\mathbf{Pr}_{x \in D} [|\hat{p}_t - c(x)| > \gamma | x \in C_t] \leq \varepsilon/2.$$

Let u be the smallest member of J. Then $p_u = r_u$ by definition of decision lists. Also, since c is given by a list with ω-converging probabilities, $|r_u - \omega| \geq |r_j - \omega|$ for $j \geq u$. Thus, by our choice of t, for $j \in J$,

$$|r_j - \omega| \leq |r_u - \omega| = |p_u - \omega| \leq |\hat{p}_u - \omega| + \varepsilon\gamma/4 \leq |\hat{p}_t - \omega| + \varepsilon\gamma/4.$$

Suppose $\hat{p}_t \geq \omega$. Then clearly $r_j \leq \hat{p}_t + \varepsilon\gamma/4$ for $j \in J$, and thus $c(x) \leq \hat{p}_t + \varepsilon\gamma/4 \leq \hat{p}_t + \gamma$ whenever $x \in C_t$. Let z be the probability that an x is chosen for which $c(x) < \hat{p}_t - \gamma$, given that x is in C_t:

$$z = \mathbf{Pr}_{x \in D}[c(x) < \hat{p}_t - \gamma | x \in C_t].$$

Then

$$p_t = \mathbf{E}_{x \in D}[c(x) | x \in C_t]$$
$$\leq z(\hat{p}_t - \gamma) + (1 - z)(\hat{p}_t + \varepsilon\gamma/4)$$
$$\leq z(p_t + \varepsilon\gamma/4 - \gamma) + (1 - z)(p_t + \varepsilon\gamma/2)$$
$$\leq p_t + \varepsilon\gamma/2 - \gamma z.$$

This implies $z \leq \varepsilon/2$, and so Equation (4) holds in this case. The proof of Equation (4) is symmetric when $\hat{p}_t \leq \omega$.

The algorithm of Figure 10.1 clearly runs in polynomial time. ∎

It is an open question whether this class is learnable when ω is unknown.

The class of probabilistic decision lists has also been considered by Yamanishi [32]. He describes an algorithm, based on the principle of minimum description length, for learning a model of probability for p-concepts in this class; however, his algorithm is *not* computationally efficient. Also, Aiello and Mihail [2] have recently described an efficient algorithm for learning arbitrary probabilistic decision lists over the basis consisting of all literals in the special case that D is the uniform distribution.

10.3.3 Hidden-variable Problems

We next consider p-concept classes motivated by *hidden-variable* problems, in which there is an underlying deterministic concept, but the settings of some of the relevant variables are invisible to the learning algorithm, resulting in apparent probabilistic behavior. A *visible monomial* p-concept is defined over $\{0, 1\}^n$ by a pair (M, α), where M is a monomial over the *visible* Boolean variables $x_1, \ldots, x_n$ and $\alpha \in [0, 1]$. The associated p-concept c is defined for $x \in \{0, 1\}^n$ to be $c(x) = \alpha \cdot M(x)$. We conceptually regard the true deterministic concept as having the form $M \wedge I$, where I is a deterministic concept over the *hidden variables*. We interpret α as the probability that the settings of the invisible variables satisfy I. Note that we assume independence between the settings for the variables of M and those for I.

For instance, I might itself be a monomial, in which case the underlying target concept is a conjunction of literals, some which are visible and some which are hidden.

Visible monomials model well situations in which certain observable conditions are requisite to some outcome, but in which these conditions are not in themselves enough to determine the outcome with certainty. Thus, the conditions are necessary, but not sufficient, and, when the conditions are met, the final outcome may be uncertain. For instance, if you are handed a drink that is brown and fizzes and tastes sweet, then the drink might be Coke; on the other hand, it might not be Coke (it could be Pepsi). In any case, if the drink lacks any one of these qualities, then it certainly cannot be "the real thing."

We note that the algorithm described in the proof below can be easily extended to learn any p-concept c of the form $c = \alpha c_0$ where α is an unknown constant in $[0, 1]$ and c_0 is a deterministic concept from some known concept class for which there exists an efficient algorithm that, like the algorithm V described in the proof, requires positive examples only, and outputs hypotheses with one-sided error on the positive-examples distribution only. For instance, Valiant [28] describes such an algorithm for learning k-CNF (the class of Boolean formulas consisting of a conjunction of clauses, each a disjunction of at most k literals).

THEOREM 3.3   *The class of visible monomial p-concepts is polynomially learnable with a model of probability.*

Proof: Let the target p-concept c be defined by the pair (M, α), and let the target distribution over $\{0, 1\}^n$ be D. We describe an algorithm that, given ε, $\delta > 0$, outputs with probability at least $1 - \delta$ a hypothesis h for which $\mathbf{E}_{x \in D} [|h(x) - c(x)|] \leq \varepsilon$; Theorem 2.3 implies that such an algorithm can be converted into one that learns a good model of probability.

The first step of the learning algorithm is to obtain an estimate $\hat{p}$ of $p = \mathbf{Pr}_{(x,b) \in EX} [b = 1]$ that, with probability at least $1 - \delta/3$, is such that $|p - \hat{p}| \leq \varepsilon/3$. If $\hat{p} \leq 2\varepsilon/3$, then the algorithm outputs the hypothesis $h(x) \equiv 0$. Assuming $\hat{p}$ has the desired accuracy, we have $\mathbf{E}_{x \in D} [|c(x) - h(x)|] \leq \varepsilon$ in this case as desired, since $p = \mathbf{E}_{x \in D} [c(x)] \leq \varepsilon$. Otherwise, $\hat{p} > 2\varepsilon/3$, and we can assume henceforth that $p \geq \varepsilon/3$ (as is the case with probability at least $1 - \delta/3$).

Next our algorithm attempts to learn a good approximation of M. This is done using Valiant's algorithm [28], here denoted V, for learning monomials from positive examples only in the distribution-free deterministic model. Algorithm V, which we here use as a "black-box" subroutine, has the following properties: the algorithm takes as input positive ε and δ, and a source of positive examples of some monomial M, each chosen randomly according to some fixed, arbitrary distribution D^+ on the set of all positive examples. After running for time polynomial in $1/\varepsilon$, $\log(1/\delta)$, and n, V outputs a monomial $\hat{M}$ that, with high probability, has error at most ε for the positive examples of M, and has zero error for the negative examples. That is, with probability at least $1 - \delta$, $\hat{M}$ is such that:

$$\mathbf{Pr}_{x \in D^+} [\hat{M}(x) = 0] \leq \varepsilon,$$

and also

$$M(x) = 0 \quad \Rightarrow \quad \hat{M}(x) = 0.$$

Our algorithm simulates V with V's parameter ε set to $\varepsilon/4$, and δ set to $\delta/3$. We provide V with a simulated oracle EX' that supplies V with only positively labeled examples. Specifically, when V requests an example, EX' draws examples from EX until an example $(x, 1)$ is received; this instance x is then provided to V.

Note that if x is labeled positively by EX, then $c(x) > 0$ and so $M(x) = 1$. Thus, V is only supplied with positive examples. Note also that the probability of drawing a positively labeled example from EX equals p. Since $p \geq \varepsilon/3$, it follows that the expected running time of EX' is at most $O(1/\varepsilon)$.

The probability that EX' outputs some instance x is just

$$D^+(x) = \mathbf{Pr}_{(y,b) \in EX} [y = x | b = 1]$$

$$= \frac{\mathbf{Pr}_{(y,b) \in EX} [y = x \wedge b = 1]}{\mathbf{Pr}_{(y,b) \in EX} [b = 1]}$$

$$= \frac{\alpha M(x) \cdot D(x)}{\alpha \cdot \mathbf{Pr}_{y \in D} [M(y) = 1]}$$

$$= \frac{M(x)D(x)}{\mathbf{Pr}_{y \in D} [M(y) = 1]}$$

$$= \mathbf{Pr}_{y \in D} [y = x | M(y) = 1].$$

With probability at least $1 - \delta/3$, V outputs a hypothesis $\hat{M}$ which is such that $\hat{M}(x) = 0$ whenever $M(x) = 0$, and

$$\mathbf{Pr}_{x \in D^+} [\hat{M}(x) = 0] \le \varepsilon/4.$$

Our algorithm next obtains an estimate $\hat{\alpha}$ of $\alpha' = \mathbf{Pr}_{(x,b) \in EX}$ $[b = 1 | \hat{M}(x) = 1]$ that, with probability at least $1 - \delta/3$, is such that $|\alpha' - \hat{\alpha}| \le \varepsilon/2$. Such an estimate can be derived from a polynomial-size sample since

$$\mathbf{Pr}_{x \in D} [\hat{M}(x) = 1] \ge (1 - \varepsilon/4) \cdot \mathbf{Pr}_{x \in D} [M(x) = 1] \ge (1 - \varepsilon/4)p$$
$$\ge (1 - \varepsilon/4)(\varepsilon/3).$$

The algorithm outputs the hypothesis h defined by $(\hat{M}, \hat{\alpha})$; we argue next that h is, with probability at least $1 - \delta$, within ε of c on average.

As noted above, $\hat{M}$ has the property that

$$\mathbf{Pr}_{x \in D} [\hat{M}(x) = 0 | M(x) = 1] = \mathbf{Pr}_{x \in D^+} (\hat{M}(x) = 0) \le \varepsilon/4.$$

Also, $\hat{M}$ logically implies M. Since

$$\alpha = \mathbf{Pr}_{(x,b) \in EX} [b = 1 | M(x) = 1]$$
$$= \mathbf{Pr}_{(x,b) \in EX} [b = 1 | \hat{M}(x) = 1] \cdot \mathbf{Pr}_{x \in D} [\hat{M}(x) = 1 | M(x) = 1],$$

it follows that $\alpha \ge \alpha' \ge \alpha(1 - \varepsilon/4) \ge \alpha - \varepsilon/4$, and so $|\alpha - \hat{\alpha}| \le 3\varepsilon/4$. Thus, again making use of the fact that $\hat{M}$ has one-sided error, it can be seen that

$$\mathbf{E}_{x \in D} [|h(x) - c(x)|] \le \mathbf{Pr}_{x \in D} [\hat{M}(x) = 0 \wedge M(x) = 1]$$
$$+ |\alpha - \hat{\alpha}| \cdot \mathbf{Pr}_{x \in D} [\hat{M}(x) = 1]$$
$$\le \mathbf{Pr}_{x \in D} [\hat{M}(x) = 0 | M(x) = 1] + |\alpha - \hat{\alpha}|$$
$$\le \varepsilon. \qquad \blacksquare$$

Finally, we remark that Kearns, Schapire, and Sellie [18] have recently extended this result beyond the class of partially visible monomials to the class of partially visible k-term DNF formulas. Specifically, if f is a k-term DNF formula over a set of hidden and visible variables, then Kearns, Schapire, and Sellie give an efficient algorithm for learning with a model of probability the p-concept induced by regarding f as a probabilistic function over only the visible variables. (This assumes that the random assignment to the hidden variables is chosen independently of the assignment to the visible variables.) Their procedure uses as a subroutine the algorithm of section 10.3.2 for learning probabilistic decision lists with increasing probabilities.

10.4 Hypothesis Testing and Expected Loss

In this section we address the problem of *hypothesis testing* in the p-concept model. More precisely, given a labeled sample, and a hypothesis p-concept, how do we decide how good h is with respect to the sample? As will be seen, the answer to this question depends on what our goal is (a decision rule or a model of probability).

We begin with a description of the learning framework that was proposed by Haussler [12], and that extends the work of Pollard [24], Dudley [10], Vapnik [29], and others. In this framework the learner observes pairs (x, y) drawn randomly from some product space $X \times Y_0$ according to some fixed distribution. For instance, in the p-concept model, X is the domain, and $Y_0 = \{0, 1\}$; the target distribution on X and the target p-concept together induce a distribution on the space $X \times Y_0$.

Roughly speaking, in Haussler's model, the learner tries to find a hypothesis that accurately predicts the y-value of a random pair (x, y), given only the observed x-value. Thus, the hypothesis h should be such that $h(x)$ is "near" y for most random pairs (x, y).

It is often convenient not to restrict the range of h to the set Y_0; for instance, if $Y_0 = \{0, 1\}$, then we may want to allow h to map into $[0, 1]$. In general, then, we assume that h is a function which maps X into some set $Y \supset Y_0$.

In Haussler's model the learner must choose a hypothesis from some given hypothesis space $\mathscr{H}$ of functions (each mapping X into Y). The goal of the learner is to find the hypothesis from $\mathscr{H}$ that minimizes the "discrepancy" on random pairs (x, y) between the observed value y, and the predicted value $h(x)$. This discrepancy between y and $h(x)$ is measured by a real-valued "loss" function. Formally, a *loss function* L is a function mapping $Y \times Y_0$ into $[0, 1]$. (The extension of such results to general bounded functions is straightforward.) Thus, the formal goal of the learner in this framework is to find a function $h \in \mathscr{H}$ that minimizes the average loss $\mathbf{E}[L(h(x), y)]$, where the expectation is over points (x, y) drawn randomly from $X \times Y_0$ according to the distribution on this product space.

Following Haussler [12], we adopt the notation $L_h(x, y) = L(h(x), y)$ for loss function L and hypothesis h. Moreover, we will write $\mathbf{E}[L_h]$ to denote the expected loss of h (with respect to L) under the unknown distribution on $X \times Y_0$. For a given sample $S = ((x_1, y_1), \ldots, (x_m, y_m))$ of m labeled examples, we will also be interested in the *empirical loss* of h:

$$\hat{\mathbf{E}}_S[L_h] = \frac{1}{m} \sum_{i=1}^{m} L_h(x_i, y_i).$$

Note that the empirical loss does not depend on the underlying distribution. Also, when the sample is clear from context, the subscript S is usually dropped.

We can cast the problems of learning decision rules and models of probability into this general framework. As mentioned above, in our setting $Y_0 = \{0, 1\}$ since an algorithm only sees $\{0, 1\}$-labels. For decision-rule learning, the algorithm outputs $\{0, 1\}$-valued hypotheses, and thus $Y = Y_0 = \{0, 1\}$ in this case. Similarly, for model-of-probability learning, we assume that hypotheses have range $[0, 1]$, and so $Y = [0, 1]$. The distribution on $X \times Y_0$ is naturally determined by the joint behavior of the target distribution D on X and the conditional probabilities $c(x)$ given by the target p-concept.

For finding the best decision rule, the *discrete* loss function is most appropriate, that is, the loss function Z given by the rule

$$Z(y, y') = \begin{cases} 0 & \text{if } y = y' \\ 1 & \text{if } y \neq y'. \end{cases}$$

Then $\mathbf{E}[Z_h]$ is just the probability that h will misclassify a randomly drawn point, so minimizing $\mathbf{E}[Z_h]$ is equivalent to minimizing the predictive error.

For finding a model of probability, the *quadratic loss function* $Q(y, y') = (y - y')^2$ has some nice properties that make it the appropriate choice. These properties, which follow from the following theorem, are well known to statisticians. (See, for instance, White's review article [31].) Also, note that the empirical loss $\hat{\mathbf{E}}[Q_h]$ is the *average squared-error* statistic commonly used by researchers in pattern recognition and statistical decision theory.

THEOREM 4.1   *For any target p-concept c, target distribution D, and p-concept h,*

$$\mathbf{E}[Q_h] - \mathbf{E}[Q_c] = \mathbf{E}_{x \in D} [(h(x) - c(x))^2].$$

Proof: For fixed $x \in X$, the probability that x is labeled 1 is $c(x)$, and in this case, h has loss

$$Q_h(x, 1) = Q(h(x), 1) = (1 - h(x))^2.$$

Likewise, x is labeled 0 with probability $1 - c(x)$, and in this case, h has loss $(h(x))^2$. Thus,

$$E[Q_h] = \int_X [c(x)(1 - h(x))^2 + (1 - c(x))h(x)^2]\, dD(x).$$

Similarly,

$$E[Q_c] = \int_X [c(x)(1 - c(x))^2 + (1 - c(x))c(x)^2]\, dD(x).$$

Applying straightforward algebra and linearity of integrals, it follows that

$$E[Q_h] - E[Q_c] = \int_X [h(x) - c(x)]^2\, dD(x)$$

$$= E_{x \in D}[(h(x) - c(x))^2]$$

as desired.

(All these integrals are defined, assuming as usual that c and h are measurable.) ■

Combined with Theorem 2.3, this theorem immediately suggests a computationally efficient method of choosing a good model of probability from a small (polynomial-size) class of candidate hypotheses. Suppose that a learning algorithm A has done some initial sampling and computation and has produced a class $\mathscr{H}$ of hypotheses, one of which is a good model of probability. Then A may simply use the empirical loss $E[Q_h]$ on a large enough labeled sample (a second sample) as an accurate estimate of the true loss $E[Q_h]$ for each $h \in \mathscr{H}$, and then output the hypothesis with the smallest empirical loss. This hypothesis h must have near-minimal true loss, and so, by the preceding theorem and our assumption that $\mathscr{H}$ contains a good model of probability, h must itself be a good model of probability.

For instance, we can use this method to prove that any efficient algorithm in the p-concept model (whose running time may be polynomial in $1/\delta$) can be converted into one whose running time is only polynomial in

$\log(1/\delta)$. More precisely, suppose that A is an algorithm that, with probability at least $1/2$, succeeds in finding a "good" decision rule or model of probability h. Then we can convert A into an algorithm that successfully finds a good hypothesis with probability at least $1 - \delta$ in time polynomial in $\log(1/\delta)$. The idea is to simply run A repeatedly, say $t = O(\log(1/\delta))$ times, producing hypotheses $h_1, \ldots, h_t$. With high probability, one of these hypotheses is "good," and we can find the best one by hypothesis testing each h_i and outputting the one with the lowest discrete or quadratic loss. (This technique is due to Haussler et al. [13] who prove the analogous result for the deterministic PAC model.)

The remainder of this section describes another example of an efficient learning algorithm that employs the approach outlined above.

10.4.1 Probabilistic Concepts of k Relevant Variables

For a p-concept c on n Boolean variables, we say that variable x_i is *relevant* if $c(x) \neq c(y)$ for two vectors x and y which differ only in their ith bit. We say that c is a *p-concept of k relevant variables* if c has only k relevant variables. Such p-concepts are good models of situations in which there are a small number of variables whose settings determine the probabilistic behavior in a possibly very complicated manner, but most variables have no influence on this behavior.

THEOREM 4.2   *Let $k \geq 1$ be fixed. Then the class of all p-concepts of k relevant variables is polynomially learnable with a model of probability.*

Proof: For any set $I \subset \{1, \ldots, n\}$, we say that two assignments x and y in $\{0, 1\}^n$ are *equivalent with respect to I* if $x_i = y_i$ for all $i \in I$. Then this equivalence relation partitions $\{0, 1\}^n$ into $2^{|I|}$ equivalence classes, called *I-blocks.*

Let c be the target p-concept, and let I_* be the set of indices of the k relevant variables of c.

Our algorithm begins by drawing a sample S_1 of size $m_1 = O((2^k/\varepsilon^3) \cdot \log(2^k/\delta))$. For each of the $\binom{n}{k}$ sets I of k indices, and for each I-block B, our algorithm obtains from S_1 an estimate $\hat{p}_B$ of $p_B = \mathbf{Pr}_{(x,b) \in EX} [b = 1 | x \in B]$. A hypothesis h_I is then defined by the rule $h_I(x) = \hat{p}_B$ for $x \in B$.

By our choice of m_1, it follows from Chernoff bounds (Lemma 2.4) that, with probability at least $1 - \delta/2$, a sample S_1 is chosen for which

$|\hat{p}_B - p_B| \le \varepsilon/4$ for every I_*-block B which satisfies $\mathbf{Pr}_{x \in D}\,[x \in B] > \varepsilon/2^{k+2}$. This implies that, with high probability,

$$\mathbf{E}_{x \in D}[|h_{I_*}(x) - c(x)|] = \sum_B \mathbf{Pr}_{x \in D}[x \in B] \cdot |\hat{p}_B - c(x)| \le \varepsilon/2$$

where the sum is taken over all I_*-blocks B. This bound follows from the fact that $c(x) = p_B$ for $x \in B$, and by breaking the sum into two parts according to whether $\mathbf{Pr}_{x \in D}\,[x \in B]$ exceeds or does not exceed $\varepsilon/2^{k+2}$.

Next, our algorithm tests each hypothesis h_I; that is, an estimate $\hat{\mathbf{E}}[Q_{h_I}]$ is found from a sufficiently large sample S_2 that, with high probability, is within $\varepsilon/4$ of $\mathbf{E}[Q_{h_I}]$. Specifically, this will be the case with probability at least $1 - \delta/2$ for all hypotheses h_I if we choose a sample S_2 of size $O((1/\varepsilon^2) \cdot \log(n^k/\delta))$. The algorithm outputs the hypothesis $h = h_I$ with the minimum empirical loss. Then, applying Theorem 4.1, we have

$$\begin{aligned}
\mathbf{E}_{x \in D}\,[(h(x) - c(x))^2] &= \mathbf{E}[Q_h] - \mathbf{E}[Q_c] \\
&\le \hat{\mathbf{E}}[Q_h] - \mathbf{E}[Q_c] + \varepsilon/4 \\
&\le \hat{\mathbf{E}}[Q_{h_{I_*}}] - \mathbf{E}[Q_c] + \varepsilon/4 \\
&\le \mathbf{E}[Q_{h_{I_*}}] - \mathbf{E}[Q_c] + \varepsilon/2 \\
&= \mathbf{E}_{x \in D}\,[(h_{I_*}(x) - c(x))^2] + \varepsilon/2 \le \varepsilon.
\end{aligned}$$

Applying Theorem 2.3, it follows that this efficient algorithm can be used to learn a good model of probability.   ∎

10.5   Uniform Convergence Methods

When is minimization of the empirical loss over a hypothesis class $\mathscr{H}$ sufficient to ensure good learning of a decision rule or a model of probability? Note that even with computational issues set aside, the hypothesis-testing methods of the preceding section fall apart in the case of an infinite class $\mathscr{H}$: directly estimating the empirical loss of each $h \in \mathscr{H}$ separately would take an infinite number of examples and an infinite amount of time. What is required is a characterization of the number of examples required for uniform convergence of empirical losses to expected losses analogous to that provided by the VC-dimension in the case of deterministic concepts. This is particularly pressing in our model of p-concepts, where even when the domain is finite (e.g., $\{0, 1\}^n$), the target p-concept class is usually infinite due to the different values allowed for the probabilities. We now turn to a discussion of such uniform convergence techniques applicable to p-concept classes.

Haussler [12], Pollard [24], and others have described the *pseudo dimension* of a class of real-valued functions $\mathscr{F}$ on domain X and have shown that the pseudo dimension is a powerful tool for obtaining uniform convergence results.

Specifically, the pseudo dimension of $\mathscr{F}$ is defined as follows: Let $T = \{(x_1, r_1), \ldots, (x_d, r_d)\}$ be a set of d pairs, where each $x_i \in X$ and each $r_i \in \mathbf{R}$. We say that $\mathscr{F}$ *shatters* T if for every string $v \in \{0, 1\}^d$ there is a function $f \in \mathscr{F}$ such that for $1 \le i \le d$, if $v_i = 0$ then $f(x_i) \le r_i$ and if $v_i = 1$ then $f(x_i) > r_i$. Thus on the points $x_1, \ldots, x_d$ the class $\mathscr{F}$ exhibits all 2^d possible "above-below" behaviors with respect to the r_i. A geometric interpretation of this definition is to regard $(r_1, \ldots, r_d)$ as the origin of a coordinate system in d-dimensional Euclidean space; then $\mathscr{F}$ shatters T if the set $\{(f(x_1), \ldots, f(x_d)) : f \in \mathscr{F}\}$ intersects all 2^d orthants of the coordinate system. For this reason we will sometimes refer to $(r_1, \ldots, r_d)$ as the *origin of shattering*. The *pseudo dimension* of $\mathscr{F}$, denoted $PD(\mathscr{F})$, is defined as the largest value of d for which there exists some set T of d pairs that is shattered by $\mathscr{F}$; if no such d exists, then $PD(\mathscr{F})$ is infinite.

For us, the most important property of the pseudo dimension is that it allows us to upper bound the size of a sample sufficient to guarantee uniform convergence of empirical estimates for an entire class of functions. We state this formally in the following theorem which is adapted directly from Haussler's Corollary 2 [12].

For a hypothesis space $\mathscr{H}$ and loss function L, we define $L_{\mathscr{H}} = \{L_h : h \in \mathscr{H}\}$.

THEOREM 5.1   *Let $\mathscr{H}$ be a hypothesis space of functions mapping X into Y which satisfies certain "permissibility" assumptions (see Haussler's paper). Let D be a probability distribution on $X \times Y_0$, let $L: Y \times Y_0 \to [0, 1]$ be a loss function, let $d < \infty$ be the pseudo dimension of $L_{\mathscr{H}}$, and let S be a sample of m points from $X \times Y_0$ chosen randomly according to D. Assume*

$$m \ge m(d, \varepsilon, \delta) = \frac{64}{\varepsilon^2}\left(2d \ln\left(\frac{16e}{\varepsilon}\right) + \ln\left(\frac{8}{\delta}\right)\right).$$

Then

$$\mathbf{Pr}[\exists h \in \mathscr{H} : |\hat{\mathbf{E}}[L_h] - \mathbf{E}[L_h]| > \varepsilon] \le \delta,$$

where the probability is taken over the random generation of S according to D.

Theorem 5.1 suggests the following canonical algorithm for finding a hypothesis from $\mathcal{H}$ with near-minimum loss, when the pseudo dimension d is finite: take a sample S of at least $m(d, \varepsilon/2, \delta)$ labeled examples from the oracle EX, and output any $h \in \mathcal{H}$ that minimizes the empirical loss $\hat{\mathbf{E}}[L_h]$ with respect to S. Then the theorem guarantees that the output hypothesis has true loss within ε of the best possible with probability at least $1 - \delta$. This of course ignores the computational problem of actually finding such a hypothesis.

We can apply Theorem 5.1 to our learning problems by determining what the pseudo dimension is for each of the loss functions Z and Q. For the loss function Z, Haussler points out that the pseudo dimension is just the VC-dimension of the hypothesis class. That is, if $\mathcal{H}$ is a hypothesis space of functions with range $\{0, 1\}$, then the pseudo dimension of the set of functions $Z_{\mathcal{H}}$ is just the VC-dimension of $\mathcal{H}$. Thus, the number of examples needed for decision-rule learning is bounded by the VC-dimension of the space of hypotheses used by the learning algorithm. (That the VC-dimension can be used in this manner was also observed by Blumer et al. [6].)

For example, consider the problem of learning a decision rule for an increasing function over **R**. Note that the best decision rule for such a p-concept is always of the form $h_a(x) = 1$ for $x > a$, and 0 otherwise, for some a. Thus, a natural and efficient decision-rule learning algorithm for this problem is the following: draw a "large" sample from EX. Then, for each x_i in the sample, determine the empirical predictive error of hypothesis h_{x_i}, that is, the fraction of points in the sample whose labels disagree with h_{x_i}. Finally, output that h_{x_i} with the minimum empirical predictive error. Since the VC-dimension of this class of decision rules is 1, it follows from Theorem 5.1 that a polynomial-size sample suffices to ensure the correctness of this algorithm.

For the problem of learning a model of probability, we will be interested in characterizing the pseudo dimension of $\mathcal{L}_{\mathcal{H}}$ when L is the quadratic loss function Q, and $\mathcal{H}$ is a class of p-concepts over domain X. In fact, the following theorem shows that, in the p-concept model, the pseudo dimension of $Q_{\mathcal{H}}$ is equal to the pseudo dimension of $\mathcal{H}$.

THEOREM 5.2 *For any p-concept class $\mathcal{H}$, the pseudo dimension of $Q_{\mathcal{H}}$ is equal to the pseudo dimension of $\mathcal{H}$.*

Proof: Let $\{(x_i, r_i)\}_{i=1}^d$ shatter $\mathcal{H}$. For all $v \in \{0,1\}^d$, there exists $h \in \mathcal{H}$ such that

$$sign(r_i - h(x_i)) = v_i,$$

where $sign(y) = 1$ if $y \geq 0$ and $sign(y) = 0$ if $y < 0$. Since all quantities are nonnegative, $h(x_i) \leq r_i$ if and only if $Q_h(x_i, 0) = (h(x_i))^2 \leq r_i^2$. Thus,

$$v_i = sign(r_i^2 - Q_h(x_i, 0)),$$

and so $\{((x_i, 0), r_i)\}_{i=1}^d$ shatters $Q_{\mathcal{H}}$. Thus, the pseudo dimension of $Q_{\mathcal{H}}$ is at least $PD(\mathcal{H})$.

Conversely, let $\{((x_i, b_i), r_i)\}_{i=1}^d$ shatter $Q_{\mathcal{H}}$. Since d is finite, we can assume without loss of generality that the r_i's are chosen so that strict inequality holds in the definition of pseudo dimension, that is, for all $v \in \{0,1\}^d$ there exists $h \in \mathcal{H}$ such that $Q_h(x_i, b_i) < r_i$ if $v_i = 1$ and $Q_h(x_i, b_i) > r_i$ if $v_i = 0$. Then

$$sign(r_i - Q_h(x_i, b_i)) = sign(r_i - (h(x_i) - b_i)^2) = sign(\sqrt{r_i} - |h(x_i) - b_i|)$$

which equals $sign(\sqrt{r_i} - h(x_i))$ if $b_i = 0$, and equals $sign(h(x_i) - (1 - \sqrt{r_i}))$ $= 1 - sign((1 - \sqrt{r_i}) - h(x_i))$ if $b_i = 1$. It follows that $\{(x_i, |b_i - \sqrt{r_i}|)\}_{i=1}^d$ shatters $\mathcal{H}$, and thus the pseudo dimension of $Q_{\mathcal{H}}$ is at most $PD(\mathcal{H})$.   ∎

Note that the second part of the proof of this theorem relies critically on the fact that, in the p-concept model, instances are only $\{0,1\}$-labeled.

10.5.1   Linear Function Spaces

Armed with the definition of pseudo dimension and the sample size upper bounds provided by Theorem 5.1, we can now seek efficient algorithms that work by directly minimizing the quadratic loss over an infinite class of functions. This is the approach taken in our next theorem. For any domain X, let $f_i: X \to \mathbf{R}$, $1 \leq i \leq d$ be any d functions, and let $\mathscr{C}(f_1, \ldots, f_d)$ denote the class of all p-concepts of the form $c(x) = \sum_{i=1}^d a_i f_i(x)$ for $a_i \in \mathbf{R}$, where we assume that the f_i and a_i are such that $c(x) \in [0, 1]$ for all $x \in X$. We describe below an algorithm that learns a model of probability for p-concepts in the class $\mathscr{C}(f_1, \ldots, f_d)$. The running time of this algorithm is polynomial in the usual parameters, d, and the time needed to evaluate the functions f_i.

This result can be applied to prove the polynomial learnability of several natural p-concept classes. For instance, consider the generalization of deterministic disjunctions in which the target p-concept has the form $c(x) = (x_{i_1} + \cdots + x_{i_t})/t$, where the x_{i_j} are Boolean variables chosen from $x_1, \ldots, x_n$, and $+$ denotes ordinary addition. Thus, such a p-concept is "more positive" on vectors $x \in \{0, 1\}^n$ that have many of the relevant variables set to 1. Such a p-concept class is clearly of the form required by Theorem 5.3 and so is polynomially learnable with a model of probability.

As a more subtle application, consider a class of p-concepts over $\{0, 1\}^n$ that are partially specified by a canonical positive example $z \in \{0, 1\}^n$. We wish to model a setting in which z is the prototypical positive instance, and those examples "most like" z are more likely to be labeled positively. Thus, the target p-concept might have the form $c(x) = a - b \cdot d(x, z)$ where $d(x, z)$ denotes the Hamming distance and a and b are positive real-valued coefficients such that c is maximized at z and is always in the range $[0, 1]$. Here the p-concept class $\mathscr{C}$ is obtained by ranging over the choices of the prototype z and the coefficients a and b, and the "decay function," which specifies the rate at which vectors farther away from the prototype fail to exemplify the concept, is linear. It is not difficult to show that each function in $\mathscr{C}$ can in fact be written as a weighted linear sum of the variables $x_1, \ldots, x_n$, so $\mathscr{C}$ is polynomially learnable with a model of probability.

Finally, we remark that Theorem 5.3 can be applied to learn so-called "t-transform functions" considered by Mansour [22].

THEOREM 5.3   *For any set of d known computable functions $f_i : X \to \mathbf{R}$, $1 \leq i \leq d$, the class $\mathscr{C}(f_1, \ldots, f_d)$ is learnable with a model of probability. Specifically, there exists a learning algorithm for this class whose running time is polynomial in $1/\varepsilon$, $\log(1/\delta)$, $1/\gamma$, d, and the maximum time needed to evaluate any of the functions f_i.*

Proof: Given ε, $\delta > 0$, our algorithm draws a sample of size $m = \lceil m(d, \varepsilon/2, \delta) \rceil$ as given by Theorem 5.1 and attempts to find the choice of coefficients $a_1, \ldots, a_d$ that minimizes the quadratic loss over the sample. This can be done using a standard least-squares approximation. For instance, this can be done directly by differentiating with respect to each unknown coefficient a_i the expression $\sum_{j=1}^{m} [(\sum_{i=1}^{d} a_i f_i(x_j)) - b_j]^2$ (where $\{(x_j, b_j)\}_{j=1}^{m}$ is the labeled sample), and setting the resulting partial derivative to 0. This yields a system of d linear equations in the d variables a_i that is of a special form and that can be solved using standard techniques.

Cormen, Leiserson, and Rivest [7, chap. 31] describe in detail how this can be done efficiently; see also Duda and Hart [9].

Let $\hat{a}_1, \ldots, \hat{a}_d$ be the resulting solution, and let $h_0 = \sum_{i=1}^d \hat{a}_i f_i$. Note that h_0 may not be bounded between 0 and 1, and so may not be in $\mathscr{C} = \mathscr{C}(f_1, \ldots, f_d)$. We show below how to handle this difficulty.

For any real-valued function f, let $clamp(f)$ denote the function obtained by "clamping" f between 0 and 1; that is, $clamp(f) = g \circ f$ where $g : \mathbf{R} \to \mathbf{R}$ is defined as

$$g(x) = \begin{cases} 0 & \text{if } x \leq 0 \\ x & \text{if } 0 \leq x \leq 1 \\ 1 & \text{if } x \geq 1. \end{cases}$$

Let $\mathscr{H} = \{clamp(\sum_{i=1}^d a_i f_i) : a_i \in \mathbf{R}\}$. Our algorithm outputs the hypothesis $h = clamp(h_0)$. Clearly h is in $\mathscr{H}$, as is the target c.

Dudley [10] shows that a d-dimensional linear function space has pseudo dimension d. (This is reproved by Haussler [12], Theorem 4.) Combined with Haussler's Theorem 5 (which concerns the pseudo dimension of families of functions constructed in the same way as $\mathscr{H}$), this immediately implies $PD(\mathscr{H}) \leq d$. Thus, by Theorem 5.1 and our choice of m, with probability at least $1 - \delta$, $|\mathbf{E}[Q_{h'}] - \hat{\mathbf{E}}[Q_{h'}]| \leq \varepsilon/2$ for every $h' \in \mathscr{H}$. Also, note that $\hat{\mathbf{E}}[Q_h] \leq \hat{\mathbf{E}}[Q_{h_0}]$ since all instances in the sample are $\{0, 1\}$-labeled, so clamping the hypothesis only improves its performance. Thus, with probability at least $1 - \delta$, we have:

$$\begin{aligned} \mathbf{E}_{x \in D}[(h(x) - c(x))^2] &= \mathbf{E}[Q_h] - \mathbf{E}[Q_c] \\ &\leq \hat{\mathbf{E}}[Q_h] - \mathbf{E}[Q_c] + \varepsilon/2 \\ &\leq \hat{\mathbf{E}}[Q_{h_0}] - \mathbf{E}[Q_c] + \varepsilon/2 \\ &\leq \hat{\mathbf{E}}[Q_c] - \mathbf{E}[Q_c] + \varepsilon/2 \leq \varepsilon. \end{aligned}$$

As usual, Theorem 2.3 can be applied to convert this algorithm into one that learns a good model of probability for this class. ∎

10.6. A Lower Bound on Sample Size

Theorem 5.1 provides a kind of general upper bound on the sample size required for learning a model of probability. We turn now to the problem of lower bounds on sample complexity in this framework. For this, we need to introduce a refined notion of shattering.

Let $\mathscr{H}$ be a class of p-concepts over domain X. Let $T = \{(x_1, r_1), \ldots, (x_d, r_d)\}$ be a set of d pairs, where each $x_i \in X$ and each $r_i \in [0, 1]$. For $w > 0$, we say that $\mathscr{H}$ *w-shatters* T if for every string $v \in \{0, 1\}^d$ there is a p-concept $h \in \mathscr{H}$ (a *witness*) such that for $1 \leq i \leq d$, if $v_i = 0$ then $h(x_i) < r_i - w$ and if $v_i = 1$ then $h(x_i) > r_i + w$. Thus, in addition to T being shattered by $\mathscr{H}$ we require that there be a *separation* of width w between r_i and $h(x_i)$ for each witness h; we call w the *width of shattering*. Note that if $\mathscr{H}$ has pseudo dimension at least d then there always exists some $w > 0$ such that some set of d pairs over $X \times [0, 1]$ is w-shattered.

Based on this stronger notion of shattering, we can now prove the following lower bound on sample complexity in our model. This lower bound, combined with Theorems 5.1 and 5.2, shows that when the pseudo dimension is finite it characterizes the sample size required for learning with a model of probability (that is, the bound obtained by applying Theorem 5.1 is tight within a polynomial factor of $1/\varepsilon$ and $1/\delta$). This lower bound may also be of theoretical interest, since in Haussler's general learning framework [12] the pseudo dimension is used only to upper bound approximately the so-called *covering number*, which is directly used to obtain sample-size bounds.

THEOREM 6.1 *Let $\mathscr{C}$ be a p-concept class that w-shatters a set of cardinality d. Then for $\gamma \leq w$ and $\varepsilon + \delta \leq 1/8$, any algorithm for learning $\mathscr{C}$ with a model of probability requires at least $\lfloor d(\lg e)/8 \rfloor = \Omega(d)$ examples.*

Proof: Our proof is based on the analogous lower bound proof given by Blumer et al. [6] for learning deterministic concepts. However, the analysis is considerably more involved in the probabilistic case.

Let $T = \{(x_1, r_1), \ldots, (x_d, r_d)\}$ be w-shattered by the p-concept class $\mathscr{C}$. Let $\mathscr{C}_0 \subseteq \mathscr{C}$ be any fixed subclass of $\mathscr{C}$ such that $\mathscr{C}_0$ w-shatters T and $|\mathscr{C}_0| = 2^d$. Let A be a learning algorithm for $\mathscr{C}$ taking m examples for the given choices of ε, δ, and γ, and let h_S denote the hypothesis output by A, with input a labeled sample S of size m. (We assume for simplicity that A is deterministic—the proof is easily modified to handle randomized algorithms.)

Let the target distribution D be uniform over the points $x_1, \ldots, x_d$. We define a weak error measure $e(c, S)$ for target $c \in \mathscr{C}_0$ and input sample S as follows: the error $e_i(c, S)$ at x_i is defined to be 0 if $c(x_i)$ and $h_S(x_i)$ are either both less than r_i, or both greater than r_i; otherwise, $e_i(c, S) = 1$. Then e is just the average of the e_i's:

$$e(c, S) = \frac{1}{d} \sum_{i=1}^{d} e_i(c, S).$$

Note that if $e(c, S) > \varepsilon$, then h_S cannot be an (ε, w)-good model of probability for c since if $c(x_i)$ and $h_S(x_i)$ are not "on the same side" of r_i, then they differ by more than w.

This definition allows us to examine the expectation

$$\mathbf{E}_S[e(c, S)] = \sum_S \mathbf{Pr}[S|c] \cdot e(c, S)$$

which is taken over S drawn randomly according to D and labeled randomly according to c, and $\mathbf{Pr}[S|c]$ is the conditional probability that S is generated by D and c.

We will also be interested in the expectation of $e(c, S)$ when both $c \in \mathscr{C}_0$ is generated uniformly at random and S is generated according to the randomly chosen c and the target distribution D:

$$\mathbf{E}_{c,S}[e(c, S)] = \frac{1}{2^d} \sum_S \sum_{c \in \mathscr{C}_0} \mathbf{Pr}[S|c] \cdot e(c, S).$$

We wish to lower bound $e(c, S)$ for most of the p-concepts in $\mathscr{C}_0$. For any sample S, let $\mathscr{C}_S = \{c \in \mathscr{C}_0 : e(c, S) < 1/4\}$. Then for $c \in \mathscr{C}_0 - \mathscr{C}_S$, $e(c, S) \geq 1/4$, and so we obtain the lower bound

$$\mathbf{E}_{c,S}[e(c, S)] \geq \frac{1}{2^{d+2}} \sum_S \sum_{c \in \mathscr{C}_0 - \mathscr{C}_S} \mathbf{Pr}[S|c]$$

$$= \frac{1}{2^{d+2}} \left(\sum_S \sum_{c \in \mathscr{C}_0} \mathbf{Pr}[S|c] - \sum_S \sum_{c \in \mathscr{C}_S} \mathbf{Pr}[S|c] \right).$$

Now

$$\sum_S \sum_{c \in \mathscr{C}_0} \mathbf{Pr}[S|c] = \sum_{c \in \mathscr{C}_0} \sum_S \mathbf{Pr}[S|c] = |\mathscr{C}_0| = 2^d$$

since for any c, $\sum_S \mathbf{Pr}[S|c] = 1$. To upper bound $\sum_{c \in \mathscr{C}_0} \sum_S \mathbf{Pr}[S|c]$, we will first derive upper bounds on the total number of possible samples S, the cardinality of $\mathscr{C}_S$, and the value of $\mathbf{Pr}[S|c]$. First, the number of possible samples S is at most $(2d)^m$, since each of the d points may appear with either label and the number of examples in S is m. To bound $|\mathscr{C}_S|$, consider drawing a p-concept c uniformly at random from the class $\mathscr{C}_0$. By choice of $\mathscr{C}_0$, the probability that $e(c, S) < 1/4$ is bounded by the probability of fewer than $d/4$ heads occurring in d flips of a fair coin. Thus, applying Chernoff bounds (Lemma 2.4), we conclude

$$|\mathscr{C}_S| \leq |\mathscr{C}_0| \cdot e^{-d/8} = 2^{(1-a_0)d}$$

where $a_0 = (\lg e)/8$. Finally, $\Pr[S|c] \leq 1/d^m$ since if we ignore the labels on the points in S, the probability of any particular set of m points being generated by the target distribution D is at most $1/d^m$.

Piecing together these bounds, we may now write

$$\mathbf{E}_{c,S}[e(c,S)] \geq \frac{1}{2^{d+2}}(2^d - (2d)^m \cdot 2^{(1-a_0)d} \cdot d^{-m}) = \frac{1}{4}(1 - 2^{m-a_0 d}).$$

Thus, if $m \leq a_0 d - 1$ then $\mathbf{E}_{c,S}[e(c,S)] \geq 1/8$. From this it follows that for some fixed $c_0 \in \mathscr{C}_0$, $\mathbf{E}_S[e(c_0,S)] \geq 1/8$ where the expectation is taken over S drawn according to D and labeled according to c_0. By assumption A learns with a model of probability. Thus, with probability at least $1 - \delta$, a sample S is chosen such that h_S is an (ε, w)-good model of probability. As noted above, in such a case, $e(c,S) \leq \varepsilon$. Thus, $\mathbf{E}_S[e(c_0,S)] \leq (1-\delta)\varepsilon + \delta < \varepsilon + \delta$. Therefore, if $\varepsilon + \delta \leq 1/8$ then m is at least $\lfloor a_0 d \rfloor$, proving the theorem. ∎

Any theorem giving a sample-size lower bound must incorporate the width of shattering; for instance, ours holds only for $\gamma \leq w$. To see that this is necessary, note that the p-concept class of all functions mapping X into $\{1/2 - w, 1/2 + w\}$ shatters all of X, but for $\gamma \geq w$ this class can be learned with *no* examples with the hypothesis $h(x) \equiv 1/2$. A more natural example is provided by the nondecreasing functions of section 10.3.1. Here the pseudo dimension is infinite, but we have an efficient learning algorithm. An interesting open problem is to give improved general upper bounds on sample size that incorporate the width of shattering.

10.7 Occam's Razor for General Loss Functions

In this section we present a generalized form of Occam's razor [5] applicable to the minimization of bounded loss functions, and in particular to learning p-concepts with a model of probability or a decision rule. Here we have several motivations: first, it is of philosophical interest to investigate the most general conditions under which learning is equivalent to some form of data compression; second, as in the Valiant model, we hope that Occam's razor will help isolate and simplify the probabilistic analysis of learning algorithms; third, Occam's razor may be easier to apply than uniform-convergence methods in the case that the pseudo dimension is unknown or difficult to compute; and fourth, Occam's razor may give better sample-size bounds than direct analyses.

An *Occam algorithm* for hypothesis class $\mathcal{H}$ over parameterized domain X, with respect to a loss function $L: Y \times Y_0 \to [0, 1]$, is a polynomial-time algorithm A that takes as input a labeled sample $S \in (X_n \times Y_0)^m$, and outputs a hypothesis h with the properties that:

1. $\hat{\mathbf{E}}[L_h] - \inf_{h' \in \mathcal{H}} \hat{\mathbf{E}}[L_{h'}] \leq \tau = \tau(n, m) = n^a m^{-\alpha}$ for some constants $a \geq 0$, and $\alpha > 0$; and

2. h can be represented by a string over the finite alphabet $\{0, 1\}$ of encoded length $\ell = \ell(n, m) = n^b m^\beta$ for some constants $b \geq 0$ and $\beta < 1$.

Thus, as in the nonprobabilistic setting, we require an Occam algorithm to perform some kind of data compression, that is, to output a hypothesis significantly smaller than the given sample. Furthermore, the output hypothesis must come close to minimizing the empirical loss on the sample over the entire hypothesis space $\mathcal{H}$.

THEOREM 7.1 *Let A be an Occam algorithm as described above. Let S be a labeled sample of size m generated according to some target p-concept c. Let h be the result of running A on S. Assume m is so large that $\tau \leq \varepsilon/4$ and $2(2^\ell + 1)e^{-\varepsilon^2 m/8} \leq \delta$. Then*

$$\mathbf{Pr}[\mathbf{E}[L_h] - \inf_{h' \in \mathcal{H}} \mathbf{E}[L_{h'}] > \varepsilon] \leq \delta.$$

In particular, this will be the case if

$$m \geq \max \left\{ \left(\frac{4n^a}{\varepsilon} \right)^{1/\alpha}, \left(\frac{16(\ln 2)n^b}{\varepsilon^2} \right)^{1/(1-\beta)}, \frac{16 \ln(4/\delta)}{\varepsilon^2} \right\}.$$

Proof: The proof is analogous to that of Blumer et al. [5].

Let $\mathcal{H}_A$ be the set of (at most) 2^ℓ hypotheses which might potentially be output by A. Let $h_* \in \mathcal{H}$ be such that $\mathbf{E}[L_{h_*}] \leq \inf_{h' \in \mathcal{H}} \mathbf{E}[L_{h'}] + \varepsilon/4$. Then, by Chernoff bounds (Lemma 2.4), the probability that either $\mathbf{E}[L_{h'}] > \hat{\mathbf{E}}[L_{h'}] + \varepsilon/4$ for any $h' \in \mathcal{H}_A$, or that $\hat{\mathbf{E}}[L_{h_*}] > \mathbf{E}[L_{h_*}] + \varepsilon/4$ is at most $2(2^\ell + 1)e^{-\varepsilon^2 m/8} \leq \delta$. So, with probability at least $1 - \delta$,

$$\mathbf{E}[L_h] \le \hat{\mathbf{E}}[L_h] + \varepsilon/4$$
$$\le \inf_{h' \in \mathcal{H}} \hat{\mathbf{E}}[L_{h'}] + \varepsilon/2$$
$$\le \hat{\mathbf{E}}[L_{h_*}] + \varepsilon/2$$
$$\le \mathbf{E}[L_{h_*}] + 3\varepsilon/4$$
$$\le \inf_{h' \in \mathcal{H}} \mathbf{E}[L_{h'}] + \varepsilon.$$

We show next that the stated bound on m is sufficient. Clearly, from the first bound on m, $\tau \le \varepsilon/4$. Further, from the second bound, we have that $\ell = n^b m^\beta \le (\lg e)\varepsilon^2 m/16$. Thus, $2(2^\ell + 1)e^{-\varepsilon^2 m/8} \le 4 \cdot 2^\ell e^{-\varepsilon^2 m/8} \le 4 \cdot e^{-\varepsilon^2 m/16} \le \delta$ by the last bound on m. ∎

As an example, Theorem 7.1 can be applied to the problem of learning p-concepts with k relevant variables. Essentially, the algorithm given in Theorem 4.2 can be modified so that a single initial sample of size m can be used for all of the estimates made by that algorithm. Note that a hypothesis output by this algorithm can be represented by the names of k of the variables, plus the probabilities for the 2^k equivalence classes. Each name requires $\lg n$ bits, and, moreover, each probability is a rational number (being an empirical probability estimate) that requires only $O(\log m)$ bits; thus, the hypothesis has size $O(k \log n + 2^k \log m)$. Finally, it can be shown that the hypothesis has the minimum empirical loss over the *entire* class of p-concepts with k relevant variables. Thus, Theorem 7.1 can be used to determine easily an appropriate sample size for this algorithm.

Note that Theorem 7.1 is only applicable to algorithms which output hypotheses over a finite alphabet. However, the theorem can be extended to apply to other algorithms in a manner similar to the approach taken by Littlestone and Warmuth [21] in the Valiant model. The basic idea is to allow the learning algorithm to output hypotheses that can be represented over the alphabet $S \cup \{0, 1\}$, where S is the given sample. That is, the representation of the hypothesis may include individual examples from the sample itself. For example, the hypothesis output by the algorithm for learning increasing functions with a decision rule (section 10.5) can be represented by a single example from the sample, despite the fact that this hypothesis would require an infinite number of bits to represent over a fixed finite alphabet. Thus, this alternate form of Occam's razor can be used to provide a good sample-size bound. Similarly, the algorithm given in Theorem 3.1 (slightly modified) for learning increasing functions with a model of probability can be cast in this light as an Occam algorithm.

10.8   Conclusions and Open Problems

In this chapter we have explored an extension of Valiant's model that incorporates the uncertainty inherent in many real-world learning problems. We have focused primarily on techniques for the design of efficient algorithms in this model.

Naturally we would like to find efficient algorithms for much broader classes of p-concepts than the simple classes considered here. For example, can the algorithm of section 10.3.2 be extended to learn arbitrary (not necessarily ω-converging) probabilistic decision lists? As is often the case in the deterministic Valiant model, sample size is not the problem: from Theorem 7.1, one can fairly easily derive a polynomial sample-size bound for learning this class using a computationally inefficient Occam algorithm that, given a sample, finds the decision list with the minimum quadratic loss by trying all permutations of the list order. The problem here is computational: how can we learn this class efficiently? The development of further techniques for learning p-concepts is a vitally important direction for further research.

Although the p-concept model captures realistic aspects of many learning problems, it might still be criticized for its assumption that the target p-concept belongs to an a priori known class of p-concepts. More realistic is a so-called *agnostic* learning model in which the target p-concept is *any* function from X into [0, 1], and the learner's goal is to find the best hypothesis from some fixed space of hypotheses. This is actually the framework assumed by Haussler [12] in deriving his sample-size bounds, and some further progress in this direction has been made recently by Kearns, Schapire, and Sellie [18]. A few of the algorithms described in this chapter are effective agnostic learners, such as the algorithm of Theorem 4.2 for p-concepts with k relevant variables. An important open problem is the extension of other algorithms to agnostic learning. For instance, do there exist efficient agnostic algorithms for probabilistic decision lists with ω-converging probabilities (section 10.3.2), or for linear function spaces (section 10.5.1)?

It is also important to continue to develop a theoretical foundation for p-concept learning. For instance, are there other loss functions that might be appropriate, such as the log loss function? (See Abe, Takeuchi, and Warmuth [1] in this regard.) Also, can the lower bound proof of Theorem 6.1 be significantly improved?

Finally, consistent with our quest for efficient algorithms is the need to be able to recognize that a learning problem is computationally intractable. Various techniques in this regard have been developed in the Valiant model, such as those of Pitt and Valiant [23], and Kearns and Valiant [19, 16]. Can such techniques be extended to the p-concept model? Both of these results seem to depend crucially on the deterministic nature of the Valiant model. What then would a negative, computational result look like in the p-concept model?

Acknowledgments

We are deeply indebted to David Haussler and Ron Rivest for their considerable help and guidance in preparing this chapter. We also wish to thank Avrim Blum, Yoav Freund, Umesh Vazirani, and two anonymous referees for their comments and suggestions.

Financial support for this chapter was provided through ARO grant DAAL03-86-K-0171, DARPA contract N00014-89-J-1988, NSF grant CCR-8914428, and a grant from the Siemens Corporation.

References

[1] Abe, Naoki, Jun-ichi Takeuchi, and Manfred K. Warmuth. Polynomial learnability of probabilistic concepts with respect to the Kullback-Liebler divergence. In *Proceedings of the Fourth Annual Workshop on Computational Learning Theory*, pp. 277–289, 1991.

[2] Aiello, William, and Milena Mihail. Learning the Fourier spectrum of probabilistic lists and trees. In *Proceedings of the Second Annual ACM-SIAM Symposium on Discrete Algorithms*, pp. 291–299, 1991.

[3] Angluin, Dana, and Philip Laird. Learning from noisy examples. *Machine Learning* 2 (4): 343–370, 1988.

[4] Angluin, Dana, and Leslie G. Valiant. Fast probabilistic algorithms for Hamiltonian circuits and matchings. *Journal of Computer and System Sciences* 18 (2): 155–193, 1979.

[5] Blumer, Anselm, Andrzej Ehrenfeucht, David Haussler, and Manfred K. Warmuth. Occam's razor. *Information Processing Letters* 24 (6): 377–380, 1987.

[6] Blumer, Anselm, Andrzej Ehrenfeucht, David Haussler, and Manfred K. Warmuth. Learnability and the Vapnik-Chervonenkis dimension. *Journal of the Association for Computing Machinery* 36 (4): 929–965, 1989.

[7] Cormen, Thomas, H. Charles E. Leiserson, and Ronald L. Rivest. *Introduction to Algorithms*. MIT Press, Cambridge, MA, 1990.

[8] Dobson, Annette, *J. An Introduction to Generalized Linear Models*. Chapman and Hall, New York, 1990.

[9] Duda, Richard, O., and Peter E. Hart. *Pattern Classification and Scene Analysis*. John Wiley and Sons, New York, 1973.

[10] Dudley, R. M. Central limit theorems for empirical measures. *Annals of Probability* 6 (6): 899–929, 1978.

[11] Haussler, David. Generalizing the PAC model: Sample size bounds from metric dimension-based uniform convergence results. In *30th Annual Symposium on Foundations of Computer Science*, pp. 40–45, 1989.

[12] Haussler, David. Decision theoretic generalizations of the PAC model for neural net and other learning applications. *Information and Computation* 100 (1): 78–180, 1992.

[13] Haussler, David, Michael Kearns, Nick Littlestone, and Manfred K. Warmuth. Equivalence of models for polynomial learnability. *Information and Computation* 95 (2): 129–161, 1991.

[14] Hoeffding, Wassily. Probability inequalities for sums of bounded random variables. *Journal of the American Statistical Association* 58 (301): 13–30, 1963.

[15] Kandel, Abraham. *Fuzzy Techniques in Pattern Recognition*. John Wiley and Sons, New York, 1982.

[16] Kearns, Michael. *The Computational Complexity of Machine Learning*. MIT Press, Cambridge, MA, 1990.

[17] Kearns, Michael, and Ming Li. Learning in the presence of malicious errors. In *Proceedings of the Twentieth Annual ACM Symposium on Theory of Computing*, 267–280, 1988. *SIAM Journal on Computing*, to appear.

[18] Kearns, Michael, J., Robert E. Schapire, and Linda M. Sellie. Toward efficient agnostic learning. In *Proceedings of the Fifth Annual Workshop on Computational Learning Theory*, pp. 341–352, 1992.

[19] Kearns, Michael, and Leslie G. Valiant. Cryptographic limitations on learning Boolean formulae and finite automata. In *Proceedings of the Twenty First Annual ACM symposium on Theory of Computing*, pp. 433–444, 1989.

[20] Linial, Nathan, Yishay Mansour, and Ronald L. Rivest. Results on learnability and the Vapnik-Chervonenkis dimension. In *29th Annual Symposium on Foundations of Computer Science*, pp. 120–129, 1988.

[21] Littlestone, Nick, and Manfred Warmuth. Relating data compression and learnability. Unpublished manuscript, November 1987.

[22] Mansour, Yishay. Learning via Fourier transform. Unpublished manuscript, April 1990.

[23] Pitt, Leonard, and Leslie G. Valiant. Computational limitations on learning from examples. *Journal of the Association for Computing Machinery* 35 (4): 965–984, 1988.

[24] Pollard, David. *Convergence of Stochastic Processes*. Springer-Verlag, New York, 1984.

[25] Rivest, Ronald L. Learning decision lists. *Machine Learning* 2 (3): 229–246, 1987.

[26] Sakakibara, Yasubumi. *Algorithmic Learning of Formal Languages and Decision Trees*. Ph.D. thesis, Tokyo Institute of Technology, 1991. Research Report IIAS-RR-91-22E, Inter-

national Institute for Advanced Study of Social Information Science, Fujitsu Laboratories, Ltd.

[27] Sloan, Robert H. Types of noise in data for concept learning. In *Proceedings of the 1988 Workshop on Computational Learning Theory*, pp. 91–96, August 1988.

[28] Valiant, L. G. A theory of the learnable. *Communications of the ACM* 27 (11): 1134–1142, 1984.

[29] Vapnik, V. N. *Estimation of Dependences Based on Empirical Data*. Springer-Verlag, New York, 1982.

[30] Vapnik, V. N., and A. Ya. Chervonenkis. On the uniform convergence of relative frequencies of events to their probabilities. *Theory of Probability and Its Applications* 16 (2): 264–280, 1971.

[31] White, Halbert. Learning in artificial neural networks: A statistical perspective. *Neural Computation* 1 (4): 425–464, 1989.

[32] Yamanishi, Kenji. A learning criterion for stochastic rules. In *Proceedings of the Third Annual Workshop on Computational Learning Theory*, pp. 67–81, 1990. *Machine Learning* 9 (2–3): 165–203.

[33] Zadeh, L. A. Fuzzy sets. *Information and Control* 8 (3): 338–353, 1965.

11　VC Dimension and Sampling Complexity of Learning Sparse Polynomials and Rational Functions

Marek Karpinski and Thorsten Werther

11.1　Introduction

This chapter presents the recent results (see [KW 89, We 91]) on the Vapnik-Chervonenkis (VC) dimension and the learnability of sparse univariate polynomials over the real numbers. The framework is the model of Probably Approximately Correct (PAC) learning concepts from examples introduced by Valiant ([Val 84]). The results presented here crucially depend on the connection between pac learnability and the VC dimension.

We derive linear upper $(4t - 1)$ and lower $(3t)$ bounds on the VC dimension of the class of t-sparse polynomials over the real numbers implying uniform pac learnability of this function class. We transfer these results to sparse rational functions and sparse, degree-bounded polynomials. The results generalize to uniform distribution-free learnability of sparse polynomials even in the extended metric model of Haussler ([Ha 89]). Applying this result, we solve Vapnik's open problem on uniform estimation of the polynomial regression function ([Vap 82]).

The interest in the computational complexity in learning sparse polynomials and rational functions has several motivations. The first motivation is the growing interest in sparse polynomials from the complexity theoretic point of view. The complexity analysis of algorithms manipulating polynomials usually measures the input length in terms of the degree of polynomials. For polynomials with a small number of terms, this model is not reasonable since sparse polynomials are usually represented by a list of nonzero coefficients and the corresponding exponents. Hence, the natural measure of the size of a polynomial is given in terms of its sparsity when applying the uniform cost model of computation (see [AHU 74]). Recent results also indicate that sparse polynomials play a key role in the harmonic analysis of Boolean circuits ([Br 90, BS 90]) and, surprisingly, in the area of learnability of Boolean functions as well ([KM 91]).

The issues of sparse polynomial interpolation are the second motivation. In the black box model, a learning algorithm for sparse polynomials has access to an oracle which gives the value of the polynomial for an arbitrary evaluation point Karpinski ([Kar 89]). Grigoriev and Karpinski ([GK 87]), Ben-Or and Tiwari ([BeTi 88]), and Grigoriev et al. ([GKS 90]) show that in this oracle model there are efficient algorithms for exact learning (interpolation) of sparse determinants ([GK 87]) and sparse polynomials over fields of characteristic zero ([BeTi 88]) and over finite fields ([GKS 90]).

It is known (see [WD 81, Fl 89]) that elements of vector spaces of real-valued functions are pac learnable. Therefore, the third motivation of this chapter is to explore the learnability of sparse polynomials as a function class which is not embedded in some vector space.

11.2 Previous Work

Throughout this chapter, we employ the model of machine learning introduced by Valiant ([Val 84]), usually referred to as the PAC model. Valiant used this new model of distribution-free learning from examples to exhibit and analyze several learning algorithms for Boolean functions.

In this section we review the definition of Valiant's distribution-free model of learning. This model was extended by Blumer et al. ([BEHW 86, BEHW 89]) to classes of concepts defined by regions in Euclidean space E^n. Blumer et al. applied results of the pioneering work of Vapnik and Chervonenkis ([VC 71]) on the uniform convergence of empirical dependences to provide the necessary and sufficient conditions for feasible learnability.

The reader is referred for the basic notations of set theory, probability theory, and stochastic processes to [Coh 82, Po 84, Vap 82]. For a set X, 2^X will denote the set of all subsets of X. Whenever we talk of an unknown probability distribution P on X, P is assumed to be arbitrary but fixed. For a collection $C \subseteq 2^X$ of subsets of X, we assume each member of C to form a Borel set, such that unions, intersections, sequences, and limits of events result also in events, that is, probabilities are assigned to them by any probability distribution P on X. This assumption is of crucial importance for the connection of learnability and convergence of stochastic processes.

11.2.1 The PAC Model and the Vapnik-Chervonenkis Dimension

There are many approaches proposed in the literature, especially from the area of artificial intelligence, to formalize the notation of *learning* and to give it a precise meaning. This chapter explores the learnability of sparse polynomials in the framework of Valiant's model of *distribution-free learning from examples*.

In Valiant's probabilistic model of learning (concepts) from examples, each concept c from a nonempty class $\mathscr{C} \subseteq 2^X$ is a subset of a given instance space X (for example, X might be $\{0, 1\}^n$ ([Val 84]) or n-dimensional Euclidean space E^n ([BEHW 86])). The unknown target concept t to be learned is assumed to be a member of the class $\mathscr{C}$.

In this model of learning we assume a fixed but arbitrary (and unknown) probability distribution P defined on X. It is assumed that a learning algorithm has access to a finite set of *examples* of the unknown target concept t. Each example (x, c) consists of an instance $x \in X$, which is drawn independently according to P, and its classification $c \in \{0, 1\}$ as either a positive instance ($x \in t$) or a negative instance ($x \notin t$). This set is called a *sample* of the target concept.

In the PAC (Probably Approximately Correct) model, a *learning function* for $\mathscr{C}$ is a function that, given a large enough randomly drawn sample, returns a *hypothesis* which is, with high probability, a good approximation (with respect to P) to the target concept, no matter which concept from $\mathscr{C}$ we are trying to learn. The error of the hypothesis is the probability that the hypothesis disagrees with the target on a (with respect to P) randomly drawn example.

We formalize this using the notation from [BEHW 89].

Let $\mathscr{C} \subseteq 2^X$ be a nonempty class of concepts, and $c \in \mathscr{C}$ is a Borel set. For $x = (x_1, \ldots, x_m) \in X^m$, $m \geq 1$, the m-sample of $c \in \mathscr{C}$ generated by x is given by

$$\text{sam}_c(x) = (\langle x_1, I_c(x_1) \rangle, \ldots, \langle x_m, I_c(x_m) \rangle),$$

where I_c is the $\{0, 1\}$-valued indicator function for c, that is, $I_c(x_i) = 1$ iff $x_i \in c$. The sample space of $\mathscr{C}$, denoted $S_\mathscr{C}$, is the set of all m-samples over all $c \in \mathscr{C}$ and all $x \in X^m$, for all $m \geq 1$.

The learning algorithm takes an m-sample as an input and produces a hypothesis from some hypothesis space H. Usually the hypothesis space is $\mathscr{C}$ itself, but in some cases it is preferable to approximate concepts from $\mathscr{C}$ in a different class H.

Let $H \subseteq 2^X$ now be a set of Borel sets, called the hypothesis space. Let $A_{\mathscr{C}, H}$ denote the set of all functions that map the sample space $S_\mathscr{C}$ to the hypothesis space H. $A \in A_{\mathscr{C}, H}$ is called consistent if, for each sample $s = (\langle x_1, a_1 \rangle, \ldots, \langle x_m, a_m \rangle)$, the hypothesis produced by A, $h = A(s)$, agrees with s, that is, $a_i = I_h(x_i)$ for all $1 \leq i \leq m$.

In the PAC model the sample is generated according to an unknown, but fixed probability distribution P on X. The error rate of a hypothesis $h \in H$ (with respect to the target concept $t \in \mathscr{C}$ and P) is the probability that h and t classify a randomly drawn example differently, which is $P(h \oplus t)$, the probability of the symmetric difference of h and t.

Let $\mathscr{C} \subseteq 2^X$ be a nonempty class of concepts and let $H \subseteq 2^X$ be a hypothesis space. For $0 < \varepsilon, \delta < 1$, let $m(\varepsilon, \delta)$ be an integer-valued function of ε and δ. Let P be a probability distribution on X.

We say $\mathscr{C}$ is *uniformly learnable by H under the distribution P* if there is (a learning function) $A \in A_{\mathscr{C}, H}$ such that for a randomly drawn sample of size $m(\varepsilon, \delta)$ of any target concept in $\mathscr{C}$, A produces, with probability at least $1 - \delta$, a hypothesis in H with error rate no more than ε.

If there exists $A \in A_{\mathscr{C}, H}$ such that A is a learning function for $\mathscr{C}$ with sample size $m(\varepsilon, \delta)$ for all probability distributions P on X, $\mathscr{C}$ *is uniformly learnable by H*. The smallest sample size $m(\varepsilon, \delta)$ is called the *sample complexity* of A.

Note that this general definition of uniform learnability imposes no restrictions of feasibility or even computability of the learning function.

For finite concept classes $\mathscr{C} \subseteq 2^X$, Vapnik ([Vap 82]) gave an upper bound on the sample complexity for any uniform learning algorithm. For infinite classes, such as geometric concept classes on E^n, there was no general characterization of uniform learnability known until Blumer et al. ([BEHW 86]) employed ideas from Vapnik and Chervonenkis ([VC 71]) to show that the essential condition for distribution-free learnability is finiteness of a combinatorial parameter of the concept class C, called the Vapnik-Chervonenkis dimension.

Let $\mathscr{C} \subseteq 2^X$ be a concept class on X. For any finite set $F \subseteq X$, let $\Pi_\mathscr{C}(F) = \{c \cap F \mid c \in \mathscr{C}\}$ denote the restriction of $\mathscr{C}$ to the set F. If $\Pi_\mathscr{C}(F) = 2^F$, then the set F is *shattered* by $\mathscr{C}$. In other words, each subset of F is of the form $c \cap F$ for some $c \in \mathscr{C}$. The *Vapnik-Chervonenkis dimension* (VC dimension) of the class $\mathscr{C}$ is the largest integer d such that some $S \subseteq X$ of size d is shattered by the class $\mathscr{C}$. If arbitrary large subsets of X are shattered by the class $\mathscr{C}$, then the VC dimension of $\mathscr{C}$ is infinite. The class consisting of one concept is of VC dimension 0, and, by convention, the empty class is of VC dimension -1. Let $VCdim(\mathscr{C})$ denote the VC dimension of $\mathscr{C}$.

Vapnik and Chervonenkis ([VC 71]) give necessary and sufficient conditions for the uniform convergence of the empirical risk functional to the expected risk functional in terms of the VC dimension. Their work has been extended to handle much more general situations ([Po 84]). Blumer et al. ([BEHW 86]) were the first to draw the connection between distribution-free learning and the VC dimension.

To avoid measurability difficulties in Theorem 1, Blumer et al. assume that the concept class is *well-behaved*, which is a relatively benign measure-theoretic condition. It is not likely to exclude any concept class considered in the context of machine learning applications. For common use it is sufficient to show that a concept class is *universally separable* (see [Du 78]). The well-behavedness of the concept class follows from this.

THEOREM 1 [BEHW 86]   *Let $\mathscr{C}$ be a nontrivial, well-behaved concept class. $\mathscr{C}$ is uniformly learnable iff the VC dimension of $\mathscr{C}$ is finite.*

Blumer et al. and Ehrenfeucht et al. give upper and lower bounds on the sample complexity $m(\varepsilon, \delta)$ for distribution-free learning of a concept class $\mathscr{C}$ of finite VC dimension $d < \infty$.

THEOREM 2 [BEHW 86]   *Let $\mathscr{C}$ be a nontrivial, well-behaved concept class of VC dimension $d < \infty$. Then, for $0 < \varepsilon, \delta < 1$ and sample size at least*

$$\max\left(\frac{4}{\varepsilon}\log\frac{2}{\delta}, \frac{8d}{\varepsilon}\log\frac{13}{\varepsilon}\right),$$

any consistent function $A : S_{\mathscr{C}} \to \mathscr{C}$ is an (ε, δ)-learning function for $\mathscr{C}$.

Blumer et al. also give a lower bound on the sample size. This bound was improved by Ehrenfeucht et al.

THEOREM 3 [EHKL 89]   *Let $\mathscr{C}$ be a concept class of VC dimension $d > 1$. Then, for $0 < \varepsilon \le \frac{1}{8}, 0 < \delta \le \frac{1}{100}$, any (ε, δ)-learning function A for $\mathscr{C}$ must use sample size*

$$m(\varepsilon, \delta) \ge \max\left(\frac{1-\varepsilon}{\varepsilon}\log\frac{1}{\delta}, \frac{d-1}{32\varepsilon}\right).$$

11.2.2   The Extended PAC Model

One of the shortcomings of the standard PAC model is that it is only defined for $\{0, 1\}$-valued functions. Haussler ([Ha 89]) proposes a generalization of the PAC model for distribution-free learning of functions that take values in an arbitrary metric space. This is of particular interest when learning real-valued functions. Haussler generalizes the notation of VC dimension and shows that, similar to the standard model, small VC dimension implies fast uniform distribution-independent convergence. We recall some of his results briefly.

Let $\mathscr{F}$ (the hypothesis space) be a family of functions from a domain X to a set Y with metric d_Y. Let $\mathscr{D}$ be a family of probability distributions on $S = (X \times Y)$. A pair $(x, y) \in S$ is called an example, a sequence of examples is called a sample. A learning problem P is stated as follows: Given a sample chosen independently at random with respect to some unknown distribution $D \in \mathscr{D}$, find a hypothesis h from $\mathscr{F}$ that is close to the target t from $\mathscr{F}$, where the target is the element from $\mathscr{F}$ which is closest to the sample.

More formally: Let $\mathrm{er}_D(f)$ be the expectation (with respect to D) of $d_Y(f(x), y)$ when (x, y) is drawn at random from S (with respect to D). Let $\mathrm{opt}(D, \mathscr{F})$ be the infimum of $\mathrm{er}_D(f)$ over all $f \in \mathscr{F}$. Let $d_v(r, s) = \dfrac{|r - s|}{v + r + s}$, for $r, s, v \in \mathbb{R}^+$, be a metric on $\mathbb{R}^+$.

The set $\mathscr{F}$ is called *uniformly learnable* ([Ha 89]) iff there exists a function L from the set of all samples into $\mathscr{F}$ such that for all $v > 0, 0 < \alpha < 1$, $0 < \delta < 1$ there exists a finite sample size $m = m(v, \alpha, \delta)$ such that for all $D \in \mathscr{D}$ and samples s of size m the (learning) function L produces with probability at least $1 - \delta$ a hypothesis that is acceptably close to the optimal hypothesis in $\mathscr{F}$, that is

$$d_v(\mathrm{er}_D(L(s)), \mathrm{opt}(D, \mathscr{F}))) \leq \alpha.$$

Similar to the results of Blumer et al. ([BEHW 86]), Haussler shows that the essential condition for distribution-free uniform learnability of $\mathscr{F}$ is the finiteness of the "VC dimension of the graphs of functions in $\mathscr{F}$," which is an extension of the standard VC dimension.

For each $f \in \mathscr{F}$, we denote by $I(f)$ the function from $X \times Y \times \mathbb{R}^+$ into $\{0, 1\}$ defined by

$$I(f)(x, y, \varepsilon) = \begin{cases} 1 & \text{if } d_Y(f(x), y) \leq \varepsilon \\ 0 & \text{otherwise} \end{cases}.$$

Let $I(\mathscr{F}) = \{I(f) \mid f \in \mathscr{F}\}$. We define the *metric VC dimension* of $\mathscr{F}$ as the (standard) VC dimension of $I(\mathscr{F})$. Let $m\text{-VCdim}(\mathscr{F})$ denote the metric VC dimension of $\mathscr{F}$.

In section 11.3 we investigate learnability of sparse real polynomials in this generalized model. In this case, $Y = \mathsf{R}$ and $d_Y(x, y) = |x - y|$, and the notation of metric VC dimension is similar to the notation of VC dimension of real-valued functions given in [Po 84] and [Vap 89].

Haussler gives bounds on the sample size required for uniform learnability in this generalized model depending on the metric VC dimension of $\mathscr{F}$ and on the metric dimension of the metric space (Y, d_Y). These bounds reduce to the bounds given in Theorem 2 for the standard PAC model.

11.3 Learnability of Sparse Polynomials

In this section we prove uniform learnability of sparse univariate polynomials over the real numbers in the standard PAC model as well as in the generalized model defined by Haussler (see section 11.2.2).

We prove upper and lower bounds on the VC dimension of sparse polynomials and apply results of Blumer et al. to derive bounds on the sample size required for uniform learning.

Combining these bounds with the results for degree-bounded polynomials (see section 11.3.2), we derive bounds on the VC dimension of the class of sparse and degree-bounded polynomials.

11.3.1 Notation

Let $\mathscr{C} \subseteq 2^X$ be a concept class on X. For a sample $s = (\langle x_1, a_1 \rangle, \ldots, \langle x_m, a_m \rangle) \in S_{\mathscr{C}}$, we call the vector $a = (a_1, \ldots, a_m) \in \{0, 1\}^m$ the *labeling* of s. A concept $c \in \mathscr{C}$ is said to satisfy the labeling a on $(x_1, \ldots, x_m)$ if c is consistent with the sample s.

Let $\mathscr{F}$ be a collection of real-valued functions on a set X. We investigate learnability of the concept class $\mathrm{pos}(f_0 - \mathscr{F})$ defined as the collection of all concepts

$$\mathrm{pos}(f_0 - f) = \{x \in X \mid f_0(x) - f(x) > 0\},$$

for $f \in \mathscr{F}$ and $f_0 \notin \mathscr{F}$ an arbitrary real function on X.

For each $t \in \mathsf{N}$, let $\mathscr{P}_t \subset \mathsf{R}[x]$ denote the set of t-sparse univariate polynomials over the real numbers, that is, for each $p \in \mathscr{P}_t$, the number of nonzero coefficients in the expansion of p is bounded by t. Let $\mathscr{P}_t^+ \subset \mathsf{R}[x]$ denote the set of t-sparse polynomials where the domain is restricted to R^+. We identify the VC dimension of $\mathscr{P}_t(\mathscr{P}_t^+)$ with the VC dimension of the concept class $\mathrm{pos}(y - \mathscr{P}_t) \subset \mathsf{R}^2$ $(\mathrm{pos}(y - \mathscr{P}_t^+) \subset \mathsf{R}^+ \times \mathsf{R})$.

11.3.2 Learnability of Degree-bounded Polynomials

In this section we briefly survey results on the learnability of regions defined by elements of vector spaces of real-valued functions. Real polynomials of bounded degree fit in this setting as a special case.

Let $X = R^2$, and consider the set $\mathscr{P}_n \subset R[x]$ of univariate polynomials of degree less than n. Let $f_0(x, y) = y$. For $p \in \mathscr{P}_n$, the concept $\text{pos}(f_0 - p) = \{(x, y) \in R^2 | y > p(x)\}$ consists of all points in the plane that lie "above" the graph of p. It is simple to see that the VC dimension of $\mathscr{C} = \text{pos}(f_0 - \mathscr{P}_n)$ equals n. First, any subset $S \subset X$ of size n is shattered by $\mathscr{C}$ since a satisfying polynomial from $\mathscr{P}_n$ can be retrieved via interpolation for each labeling in $\{0, 1\}^n$. Assume that a set $R \subset X$ of size $n + 1$ is shattered by $\mathscr{C}_n$. Then there are polynomials $p_1, p_2 \in \mathscr{P}_n, p_1 \not\equiv p_2$ satisfying the two alternating labelings $\sigma_1 = (1, 0, 1, 0, \ldots)$ and $\sigma_2 = (0, 1, 0, 1, \ldots)$ of size $n + 1$. Hence, there are at least n points with $p_1(x) = p_2(x)$. This implies $p_1 \equiv p_2(x)$. From Theorem 1, the class of polynomials of degree less than n is uniformly learnable for each fixed $n > 0$.

This result holds in the much more general case of vector spaces of real-valued functions. Wenocur and Dudley ([WD 81]) extended a result of Cover ([Cov 65]) and proved that the VC dimension equals the dimension of the vector space.

THEOREM 4 [WD 81] *Let $\mathscr{F}$ be an m-dimensional vector space of real functions on a set X. Let $f_0 \notin \mathscr{F}$ be a real function on X. Then the VC dimension of $\text{pos}(f_0 - \mathscr{F})$ equals m.*

11.3.3 Bounds on the VC Dimension of $\mathscr{P}_t$

We show that the VC dimension of $\mathscr{P}_t$ is linear in t. For $\mathscr{P}_t^+$, we determine its VC dimension exactly.

11.3.3.1 Lower bounds   We start with a lower bound on the VC dimension of $\mathscr{P}_1$.

LEMMA 5 *The VC dimension of $\mathscr{P}_1$ is bounded from below by 3.*

Proof: We show that for each labeling $\sigma \in \{0, 1\}^3$ there is a 1-sparse polynomial f_σ satisfy σ on the set $S = \{(-3, 4), (1, 2), (7, 6)\}$ of size 3. Choose, for example, $f_{000} = 7$, $f_{001} = 5$, $f_{010} = x^2$, $f_{011} = -2x$, $f_{100} = 3x$, $f_{101} = 3$, $f_{110} = x$, and $f_{111} = 1$ (see figure 11.1). Note that the VC dimension of $\mathscr{P}_t^+$ is at least 2. ∎

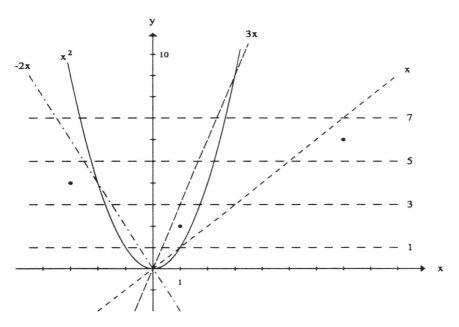

Figure 11.1
Monomials shattering the set S of size 3

In the following proofs it will be convenient to assume that no element of a set S, which is shattered by some set of sparse polynomials, lies on the graph of these polynomials.

REMARK 6   *Let a set S of size d be shattered by the class of t-sparse polynomials. Then there are a set $Z = \{(x_i, y_i)\}_{i=1,\ldots,d}$ and constants $\varepsilon_i > 0$, $i = 1, \ldots, d$ such that every set $S' = \{(\bar{x}_i, \bar{y}_i)\}_{i=1,\ldots,d}$ with $|(\bar{x}_i, \bar{y}_i) - (x_i, y_i)| \le \varepsilon_i$ is shattered by t-sparse polynomials.*

Proof: For each $\sigma \in \{0, 1\}^d$, there is a t-sparse polynomial f_σ satisfying σ on S. For $i = 1, \ldots, d$, we define the regions

$$M_i = \left\{ (x, y) \,|\, \forall \sigma \in \{0, 1\}^d : \begin{cases} y > f_\sigma & \text{if } \sigma(i) = 1 \\ y < f_\sigma & \text{if } \sigma(i) = 0 \end{cases} \right\}.$$

Since S is shattered by $\{f_\sigma\}_{\sigma \in \{0, 1\}^d}$, there exists a point (x_i, y_i) and a constant $\varepsilon_i > 0$ such that the ball

$$B_{\varepsilon_i}(x_i, y_i) = \{(x, y) \,|\, |(x, y) - (x_i, y_i)| \le \varepsilon_i\}$$

is a proper subset of M_i. Hence, each set S' defined as above is shattered by the t-sparse polynomials $\{f_\sigma\}_{\sigma \in \{0,1\}^d}$. ∎

Lemma 7 states that the VC dimension of sparse polynomials is sub-additive. We use this lemma to derive a lower bound.

Given a set shattered by t_1-sparse polynomials and a set shattered by t_2-sparse polynomials, we construct a set shattered by $(t_1 + t_2)$-sparse polynomials.

LEMMA 7 *For $t_1, t_2 \in \mathbb{N}$, let d_1, d_2 denote the VC dimension of $\mathcal{P}_{t_1}, \mathcal{P}_{t_2}$ respectively. Then the VC dimension of $\mathcal{P}_{t_1+t_2}$ is at least $d_1 + d_2$.*

Proof: Let S_1 and S_2 denote some sets of points of size d_1, d_2 respectively, shattered by t_1-sparse polynomials, t_2-sparse polynomials respectively.

Let $S_1 = \{(x_i^{(1)}, y_i^{(1)})\}_{i=1,\ldots,d_1}$ and $S_2 = \{(x_j^{(2)}, y_j^{(2)})\}_{j=1,\ldots,d_2}$. For a labeling $\sigma^{(1)} \in \{0,1\}^{d_1}$ let $f_{\sigma^{(1)}}$ satisfy $\sigma^{(1)}$ on S_1, and for a labeling $\sigma^{(2)} \in \{0,1\}^{d_2}$ let $g_{\sigma^{(2)}}$ satisfy $\sigma^{(2)}$ on S_2.

In order to show that VC dimension of $\mathcal{P}_{t_1+t_2} \geq d_1 + d_2$, we modify the sets S_1 and S_2 (and the corresponding polynomials shattering S_1 and S_2) such that the union of these modified sets is shattered by polynomials derived by adding some of the modified polynomials.

First, we pull the sets S_1 and S_2 apart such that the absolute values of the x-coordinates of points in S_1 are at most $\frac{1}{2}$ and the absolute values of the x-coordinates of points in S_2 are at least 2.

Let

$$c_1 > 2 \cdot \max_{(x_i, y_i) \in S_1} \{|x_i|\} \quad \text{and} \quad c_2 < \frac{1}{2} \cdot \min_{(x_j, y_j) \in S_2} \{|x_j|\}.$$

By Remark 6, we may assume that $c_2 > 0$.

Then, the set

$$\bar{S}_1 = \{(\bar{x}_i, \bar{y}_i)\}_{i=1,\ldots,d_1} \quad \text{with} \quad (\bar{x}_i, \bar{y}_i) = \left(\frac{x_i}{c_1}, y_i\right), (x_i, y_i) \in S_1$$

is of size d_1 and is shattered by the set of t_1-sparse polynomials $\{\bar{f}_{\sigma^{(1)}}\}_{\sigma^{(1)} \in \{0,1\}^{d_1}}$, where $\bar{f}_{\sigma^{(1)}}(x) = f_{\sigma^{(1)}}(c_1 x)$.

Similarly, the set

$$\bar{S}_2 = \{(\bar{x}_j, \bar{y}_j)\}_{j=1,\ldots,d_2} \quad \text{with} \quad (\bar{x}_j, \bar{y}_j) = \left(\frac{x_j}{c_2}, y_j\right), (x_j, y_j) \in S_2$$

is of size d_2 and is shattered by the set of t_2-sparse polynomials $\{\bar{g}_{\sigma^{(2)}}\}_{\sigma^{(2)} \in \{0,1\}^{d_2}}$, where $\bar{g}_{\sigma^{(2)}}(x) = g_{\sigma^{(2)}}(c_2 x)$.

$\bar{S}_1$ and $\bar{S}_2$ satisfy the conditions claimed above, that is, $\forall (x, y) \in \bar{S}_1 : |x| < \frac{1}{2}$ and $\forall (x, y) \in \bar{S}_2 : |x| > 2$.

Let ε_i be the minimal distance of the point $(x_i, y_i) \in \bar{S}_1$ to some shattering polynomial in $\{f_{\sigma^{(1)}}\}$, that is,

$$\varepsilon_i = \min_{f \in \{\bar{f}_{\sigma^{(1)}}\}} |f(x_i) - y_i|.$$

Similarly, for each point $(x_j, y_j) \in \bar{S}_2$, define δ_j by

$$\delta_j = \min_{g \in \{\bar{g}_{\sigma^{(2)}}\}} |g(x_j) - y_j|.$$

Again, by Remark 6, we assume that $\varepsilon_i, \delta_j > 0$.

Our goal is to modify the polynomials from $\{f_{\sigma^{(1)}}\}$ and $\{g_{\sigma^{(2)}}\}$ such that the polynomials from $\{\bar{f}_{\sigma^{(1)}}\}$ do not interfere the shattering of the set $\bar{S}_2$ and vice versa.

We define a polynomial $F(x)$ to be an upper bound on the polynomials shattering S_1 in the region according to $\bar{S}_2$, that is,

$$F(x) > \max_{f \in \{\bar{f}_{\sigma^{(1)}}\}} |f(x)| \quad \text{for all} \quad |x| \geq 2.$$

$F(x)$ is an upper bound on the influence of the polynomials shattering $\bar{S}_1$ on the shattering of the set $\bar{S}_2$.

For some even integer N, we transform the set $\bar{S}_2$ into the set $\bar{S}_2^N$ by

$$(x_j, y_j) \in \bar{S}_2 \quad \Rightarrow \quad (x_j, x_j^N \cdot y_j) \in \bar{S}_2^N.$$

Since N is even, x^N is positive, and the set $\bar{S}_2^N$ is shattered by the set of t_2-sparse polynomials $\{x^N \cdot \bar{g}_{\sigma^{(2)}}\}$. The minimal distance of the point $(x_j, y_j) \in \bar{S}_2^N$ to some shattering polynomial in $\{x^N \bar{g}_{\sigma^{(2)}}\}$ is $x_j^N \cdot \delta_j$.

We choose the parameter N to be large enough such that the following two conditions are fulfilled:

• The polynomials $\{x^N \cdot \bar{g}_{\sigma^{(2)}}\}$ may not interfere with the shattering of $\bar{S}_1$, that is,

$$x_i^N \cdot \bar{g}_{\sigma^{(2)}}(x_i) < \varepsilon_i \quad \text{for all} \quad (x_i, y_i) \in \bar{S}_1 \quad \text{and for all} \quad \sigma^{(2)} \in \{0,1\}^{d_2}.$$

Let G be the maximum of the absolute values of the polynomials $\{\bar{g}_{\sigma^{(2)}}(x)\}$ for $|x| \leq 1/2$ (all $|x_i| < \frac{1}{2}$), and ε the maximum over all ε_i. Then we choose N according to

$$G \cdot \left(\frac{1}{2}\right)^N < \varepsilon, \quad \text{that is,} \quad N > \log_2\left(\frac{G}{\varepsilon}\right).$$

- The polynomials $\{\bar{f}_{\sigma(1)}\}$ may not interfere with the shattering of $\bar{S}_2^N$, that is,

$$F(x_j) < x_j^N \cdot \delta_j \quad \text{for all} \quad (x_j, y_j) \in \bar{S}_2.$$

There exists such an N since the absolute value of the x_j's is at least 2 and N is even.

Let $\bar{S}_1 = \{(x_i', y_i')\}_{i=1,\ldots,d_1}$ with $x_1' < \cdots < x_{d_1}'$, and let $\bar{S}_2^N = \{(x_j'', y_j'')\}_{j=1,\ldots,d_2}$ with $x_1'' < \cdots < x_{d_2}''$.

Let $S = \bar{S}_1 \cup \bar{S}_2^N$. $S = \{(x_k, y_k)\}_{k=1,\ldots,d_1+d_2}$ and $x_1 < \cdots < x_{d_1+d_2}$. For $\sigma \in \{0, 1\}^{d_1+d_2}$, we define $\sigma_1 \in \{0, 1\}^{d_1}$ and $\sigma_2 \in \{0, 1\}^{d_2}$ by

$$\sigma_1(i) = \sigma(k) \quad \text{iff} \quad x_k = x_i' \quad \text{and} \quad \sigma_2(j) = \sigma(k) \quad \text{iff} \quad x_k = x_j''.$$

S is of size $d_1 + d_2$ and is shattered by the set of $(t_1 + t_2)$-sparse polynomials $\{h_\sigma\}_{\sigma \in \{0,1\}^{d_1+d_2}}$, where $h_\sigma = \bar{f}_{\sigma_1} + x^N \bar{g}_{\sigma_2}$. Hence, the VC dimension of the class of $(t_1 + t_2)$-sparse polynomials is at least $d_1 + d_2$. ∎

We are now able to state our lower bound on the VC dimension of t-sparse polynomials.

LEMMA 8   *The VC dimension of t-sparse polynomials is at least $3t$.*

Proof: Combine Lemmas 7 and 5. ∎

Note that Lemma 7 is also valid for $\mathscr{P}_t^+$. Hence $2t$ is a lower bound for the VC dimension of $\mathscr{P}_t^+$.

11.3.3.2   Upper bounds   In section 11.3.2 we have derived an upper bound on the VC dimension of degree-bounded univariate polynomials from the maximal number of roots.

The main tool in this section is *Descartes's Rule of Signs* used to derive an upper bound on the number of roots of t-sparse polynomials. This leads to a first upper bound on the VC dimension of t-sparse polynomials. Considering the structure of sparse polynomials with the maximal number of roots, we derive a (slight) improvement of the upper bound.

We begin with the well-known Descartes's Rule (see [Coh 82]).

Let $f_t = \sum_{i=1}^t c_i x^{e_i} \in \mathsf{R}[x]$, $f \not\equiv 0$ be a t-sparse polynomial for $e_i < e_{i+1}$, $i = 1, \ldots, t-1$. The sequence $c = (c_1, c_2, \ldots, c_t)$ is said to have a sign alternation at position i if $c_i c_{i+1} < 0$ (zero coefficients are deleted from the sequence). Denote by $s(f_t)$ the number of sign alternations in c. Let $n^+(f_t)$ denote the number of positive real roots of f_t counted with multiplicity.

THEOREM 9 [Descartes's Rule]   *Let $f \in \mathsf{R}[x]$, $f \not\equiv 0$ be a t-sparse polynomial. Then $s(f) - n^+(f)$ is a nonnegative even integer.*

Hence, the number of positive real roots of a t-sparse real polynomial $f \not\equiv 0$ is strictly less than its sparsity t. The (total) number of real roots of f is bounded by $2t - 1$ (where the root at the origin is counted without multiplicity).

Let $f \in \mathsf{R}[x]$. f is said to be *even* iff $f_t(x) = f_t(-x)$ (i.e., $\forall i = 1, \ldots, t : e_i$ is even), and f is said to be *odd* iff $f_t(x) = -f_t(-x)$ (i.e., $\forall i = 1, \ldots, t : e_i$ is odd). We call f *symmetric* iff f is odd or even.

LEMMA 10   *Let $f_t \in \mathsf{R}[x]$, $f_t \not\equiv 0$ be a t-sparse polynomial. If f_t has the maximal number of $2t - 2$ nonzero real roots, then f is symmetric.*

Proof: Let $f_t = \sum_{i=1}^{t} c_i x^{e_i} \in \mathsf{R}[x]$, for $e_i < e_{i+1}$, $i = 1, \ldots, t - 1$. Assume f_t has $2t - 2$ nonzero real roots. Then, f_t has $t - 1$ positive roots. Hence, the sequence of coefficients c of f has $t - 1$ sign alternations. Furthermore the $t - 1$ negative roots are positive roots for $f_t(-x)$. Let $c' = ((-1)^{e_1} c_1, \ldots, (-1)^{e_t} c_t)$ denote the sequence of coefficients of $f_t(-x)$. Suppose f_t is not symmetric. Then there is an index i such that e_i and e_{i+1} are not both even or odd. Therefore, $(-1)^{e_i} c_i \cdot (-1)^{e_{i+1}} c_{i+1} = (-1) \cdot c_i c_{i+1} > 0$, since $c_i c_{i+1} < 0$. Hence, c' has at most $t - 2$ sign alternations, contradicting the assumption that f_t has $t - 1$ negative real roots. ∎

Using Descartes's estimate on the number of positive real roots of a sparse polynomial, we deduce the (exact) VC dimension of $\mathscr{P}_t^+$.

LEMMA 11   *The VC dimension of the concept class $pos(y - \mathscr{P}_t^+)$ equals $2t$.*

Proof: Let d denote the VC dimension of $\mathscr{P}_t^+$. In section 11.3.3.1 we proved $d \geq 2t$. Hence, we have to show $d \leq 2t$.

Let $S = \{(x_i, y_i)\}_{i=1,\ldots,d}$, where $0 < x_1 < x_2 < \cdots < x_d$, be a set of points shattered by t-sparse polynomials. Let f_1 and f_2 be t-sparse polynomials satisfying the two alternating labelings $\sigma_1 = (1, 0, 1, 0, \ldots, 1, 0)$ and $\sigma_2 = (0, 1, 0, 1, \ldots, 0, 1)$. Let $F = (f_1 - f_2)$. Note that F is $2t$-sparse and $s(F) \leq 2t - 1$. Furthermore, $F(x_i) \cdot F(x_{i+1}) < 0$ for $i = 1, \ldots, d - 1$, forcing

F to have at least $d - 1$ positive real roots. By Descartes's Rule $d - 1 < 2t$, proving the statement. ∎

By Lemma 11 the VC dimension of $\mathscr{P}_t$ is bounded by $4t$. With Lemma 8 the VC dimension of $\mathscr{P}_t$ is linear in t.

Lemma 12 gives an improvement of the upper bound on the VC dimension of $\mathscr{P}_t$. As a consequence, the VC dimension of 1-sparse polynomials is exactly 3.

LEMMA 12   *The VC dimension of $\mathscr{P}_t$ is at most $4t - 1$.*

Proof: Assume, for purpose of contradiction, that the set $S = \{(x_i, y_i)\}_{i=1,\dots,4t}$, for $x_1 < x_2 < \cdots < x_{2t} < 0 < x_{2t+1} < \cdots < x_{4t}$ is shattered by t-sparse polynomials.

Consider the following four labelings on the set S:

$$\sigma_1 = (\underbrace{1,0,1,0,\dots,1,0}_{2t}, \underbrace{1,0,1,0,\dots,1,0}_{2t}),$$

$$\sigma_2 = (\underbrace{0,1,0,1,\dots,0,1}_{2t}, \underbrace{0,1,0,1,\dots,0,1}_{2t}),$$

and

$$\gamma_1 = (\underbrace{0,1,0,1,\dots,0,1}_{2t}, \underbrace{1,0,1,0,\dots,1,0}_{2t}),$$

$$\gamma_2 = (\underbrace{1,0,1,0,\dots,1,0}_{2t}, \underbrace{0,1,0,1,\dots,0,1}_{2t}).$$

Let the t-sparse polynomials f_1, f_2 and g_1, g_2 satisfy the labelings σ_1, σ_2 and γ_1, γ_2.

Define $F = f_1 - f_2$ and $G = g_1 - g_2$. Note that both F and G are $2t$-sparse. By the alternating structure of the labelings, both F and G have at least $4t - 2$ nonzero real roots. From Lemma 10, F and G are symmetric.

We show that F is odd and G is even. Assume F is even and let $|x_{2t}| < x_{2t+1}$. Then, $F(-x_{2t}) = F(x_{2t}) > 0$ and $F(x_{2t+1}) < 0$, that is, F has an "extra" positive root in the interval $(-x_{2t}, x_{2t+1})$, contradicting the upper bound on the number of positive real roots. For $|x_{2t}| > x_{2t+1} F$ has an "extra" negative root in the interval $(x_{2t}, -x_{2t+1})$. The proof that G is even is similar.

Note that F is odd implies that both f_1 and f_2 are odd (if some monomial occurs in f_1 and in f_2 as well, F would be at most $2t - 1$-sparse). Similarly, both g_1 and g_2 are even. Then, wlog, we may assume (for sake of simplicity of notation) that the x-values of the points from S are symmetric as well, that is, $x_i = -x_{4t+1-i}$, $i = 1, \ldots, 2t$.

We define $2t - 1$ intervals J_i on the negative real line by $J_i = (x_i, x_{i+1})$, $i = 1, \ldots, 2t - 1$. We prove that for each $i = 1, \ldots, 2t - 1$ at least two polynomials from $\{f_1, f_2, g_1, g_2\}$ have a (negative) root in the interval J_i. We distinguish two cases:

1. Let y_i and y_{i+1} have different signs. Assume $y_i < 0$, $y_{i+1} > 0$ and i odd. Then, by definition of the labelings, $f_1(x_i)$, $g_2(x_i) < y_i < 0$ and $f_1(x_{i+1})$, $g_2(x_{i+1}) > y_{i+1} > 0$. Hence, f_1 and g_2 have a root in J_i. If i is even, f_2 and g_1 have a root in J_i. The case $y_i > 0$, $y_{i+1} < 0$ is symmetric.

2. Let y_i and y_{i+1} have equal signs. We show that f_1 or g_2 and f_2 or g_1 have a root in J_i. Assume y_i, $y_{i+1} > 0$ and i odd. Then $f_1(x_{i+1})$, $g_2(x_{i+1}) > y_{i+1} > 0$. Assume f_1 has no root in J_i (f_1 is strictly positive in J_i). Then, f_1 is strictly negative in the interval (x_{4t-i}, x_{4t-i+1}) (f_1 is odd). Since g_2 is even, $g_2(x_{4t-i+1}) > 0$ and $g_2(x_{4t-i}) < f_1(x_{4t-i}) < 0$. Hence, g_2 has a root in the interval (x_{4t-i}, x_{4t-i+1}), and (g_2 is symmetric) g_2 has a root in J_i. Similarly, we can show that either f_2 or g_1 has a root in J_i. The remaining cases are symmetric.

Hence, the total number of negative roots of the polynomials from $\{f_1, f_2, g_1, g_2\}$ is at least $2 \cdot (2t - 1) = 4t - 2$ contradicting the assumption that each polynomial from $\{f_1, f_2, g_1, g_2\}$ is t-sparse (each polynomial has at most $t - 1$ negative roots summing up to at most $4t - 4$ negative roots). This proves the claimed upper bound of $4t - 1$ on the VC dimension of t-sparse polynomials. ∎

We state the main result of this section:

THEOREM 13   For fixed $t \in \mathbf{N}$, the class of t-sparse polynomials is uniformly and distribution-free learnable. The sample size required for (ε, δ)-learning is at most

$$\frac{4}{\varepsilon} \cdot \max\left(\log\frac{2}{\delta}, (8t - 2)\log\frac{13}{\varepsilon}\right).$$

Proof: Apply the results of Blumer et al. (Theorems 1 and 2). Note that the concept class $\mathrm{pos}(y - \mathcal{P}_t)$ is universally separable since any real polynomial can be written as the pointwise limit of some polynomial over the rational numbers.   ∎

Note that the bounds derived in this subsection remain valid when restricted to t-sparse polynomials over the rational numbers and t-sparse polynomials over the integers.

Let $\mathcal{R}_t$ denote the set of real rational functions with t-sparse numerator and t-sparse denominator. Following the proof of Lemma 11, we derive the upper bound of $4t^2$ on the VC dimension of $\mathrm{pos}(y - \mathcal{R}_t)$ proving uniform learnability of t-sparse rational functions for any fixed t.

THEOREM 14   *The VC dimension of $\mathcal{R}_t$ is at most $4t^2$.*

Proof: Let d denote the VC dimension of $\mathrm{pos}(y - \mathcal{R}_t)$. Consider the two rational functions $f_1 = \dfrac{g_1}{h_1}, f_2 = \dfrac{g_2}{h_2}$ from $\mathcal{R}_t$ satisfying the alternating labelings. Then $f_1(x) = f_2(x)$ for at least $d - 1$ points, that is, the $2t^2$-sparse polynomial $g_1 h_2 - g_2 h_1$ has to have at least $d - 1$ real roots. From Theorem 9 we have $d - 1 \leq 4t^2 - 1$.   ∎

REMARK 15   It is interesting to compare our results on the learnability of polynomials with the learnability of trigonometric polynomials. Since degree-bounded trigonometric polynomials form a vector space of finite dimension, this concept class is of finite VC dimension (see Theorem 4) and, hence, uniformly learnable (see Theorem 1). On the other hand, sparse trigonometric polynomials may oscillate arbitrarily often. It is easily verified that the VC dimension of the class of sparse trigonometric polynomials is infinite and, hence, not learnable.   ∎

11.3.4   Related Results

11.3.4.1   VC dimension of degree-bounded sparse polynomials   We give now sharp bounds on the VC dimension of sparse and degree-bounded univariate real polynomials. For practical applications this is the most important case.

For each $t, n \in \mathbb{N}$, $t \leq n$, let $\mathcal{P}_{t,n} \subset \mathbb{R}[x]$ denote the set of t-sparse univariate polynomials of degree less than n, that is, $\mathcal{P}_{t,n} = \{p \in \mathcal{P}_t | \deg(p) < n\}$. Let $\mathcal{P}_{t,n}^+ = \{p \in \mathcal{P}_t^+ | \deg(p) < n\}$.

From sections 11.3.2 and 11.3.3.2 we derive an upper bound of $\min\{n, 4t - 1\}$ on the VC dimension of $\mathcal{P}_{t,n}$ and $\min\{n, 2t\}$ on the VC dimension of $\mathscr{P}_{t,n}^+$. In this section we investigate the corresponding lower bounds.

LEMMA 16

1. $\text{VCdim}(\mathscr{P}_{t,n}) \geq \text{VCdim}(\mathscr{P}_{t-1,n-3}) + 3.$
2. $\text{VCdim}(\mathscr{P}_{t,n}^+) \geq \text{VCdim}(\mathscr{P}_{t-1,n-2}^+) + 2.$

Proof: Let $d = \text{VCdim}(\mathscr{P}_{t-1,n-3})$. Then there exists a set $S = \{(x_i, y_i)\}_{i=1,\dots,d}$ that is shattered by the set $\{f_\sigma\}_{\sigma \in \{0,1\}^d}$ of $(t-1)$-sparse polynomials of degree less than $n-3$.

As shown in the proof of Lemma 7, we may assume $\max_i |x_i| < 1$. Let

$$0 < \varepsilon < \min_{i,\sigma} |f_\sigma(x_i) - y_i|$$

be the minimal distance of some point from S to some shattering polynomial in $\{f_\sigma\}_{\sigma \in \{0,1\}^d}$. Since $\deg(f_\sigma) < n - 3$, there exists $a > \max\left\{\dfrac{\varepsilon}{27}, \dfrac{\varepsilon^2}{243}\right\}$ such that

$$\forall \sigma \in \{0,1\}^d \forall x \geq 1 : |f_\sigma(x)| < a \cdot |x|^{n-4} =: M(x).$$

We show that three additional points are shattered by adding monomials of degree at most $n-1$ to the polynomials in $\{f_\sigma\}_{\sigma \in \{0,1\}^d}$, that is, by increasing the sparsity by 1 and the degree by 3.

Consider, for instance, the points $(x_0, y_0) = \left(-81\dfrac{a}{\varepsilon}, (-1)^n 30 \cdot M\left(-81\dfrac{a}{\varepsilon}\right)\right)$, $(x_{d+1}, y_{d+1}) = \left(9\dfrac{a}{\varepsilon}, 2 \cdot M\left(9\dfrac{a}{\varepsilon}\right)\right)$ and $(x_{d+2}, y_{d+2}) = \left(81\dfrac{a}{\varepsilon}, 60 \cdot M\left(-81\dfrac{a}{\varepsilon}\right)\right)$.

In Figure 11.2 we give monomials $\{g_j\}_{j=1,\dots,8}$ of degree less than n shattering these three points.

Note that the minimal distance of the g_i's to (x_0, y_0), (x_{d+1}, y_{d+1}), and (x_{d+2}, y_{d+2}) is at least $M(x_0)$, $M(x_{d+1})$, and $M(x_{d+2})$ respectively, hence greater than the absolute values of each $f \in \{f_\sigma\}_{\sigma \in \{0,1\}^d}$ at these points. On the other hand, $g_j(x) < \varepsilon$ for $x < 1$, $j = 1, \dots, 8$.

Hence, the set $S' = \{(x_i, y_i)\}_{i=0,\dots,d+2}$ is shattered by the set $\{f_\sigma + g_j | \sigma \in \{0,1\}^d, j = 1,\dots,8\}$ of t-sparse polynomials of degree less than n. This proves the first statement.

	$\dfrac{g_i(x_0)}{M(x_0)}$	$\dfrac{g_i(x_{d+1})}{M(x_{d+1})}$	$\dfrac{g_i(x_{d+2})}{M(x_{d+2})}$	n even	n odd
$g_1 =$ $\quad 0$	0	0	0	0 1 1	1 1 1
$g_2 = \quad \frac{\epsilon}{3} \cdot x^{n-3}$	$-27(-1)^n$	3	27	0 0 1	1 0 1
$g_3 = \quad \frac{\epsilon^2}{81a} \cdot x^{n-2}$	$81(-1)^n$	1	81	0 1 0	1 1 0
$g_4 = \quad \epsilon \cdot x^{n-3}$	$-81(-1)^n$	9	81	1 0 0	0 0 0
$g_5 = \quad \frac{\epsilon^2}{27a} \cdot x^{n-2}$	$243(-1)^n$	3	243	0 0 0	1 0 0
$g_6 = \quad \frac{2\epsilon}{3} \cdot x^{n-3}$	$-54(-1)^n$	6	54	1 0 1	0 0 1
$g_7 = -\frac{\epsilon^2}{27a} \cdot x^{n-2}$	$-243(-1)^n$	-3	-243	1 1 1	0 1 1
$g_8 = \frac{\epsilon^3}{243a^2} \cdot x^{n-1}$	$-2187(-1)^n$	1	2187	1 1 0	0 1 0

Figure 11.2
Monomials $\{g_i\}$ shattering the three additional points

Note that the monomials $\{g_j\}_{j=1,\ldots,4}$ of degree at most $n-2$ shatter the two points (x_{d+1}, y_{d+1}) and (x_{d+2}, y_{d+2}). Hence the second statement follows.   ∎

LEMMA 17

1. $\mathrm{VCdim}(\mathscr{P}_{1,n}) = \min\{n, 3\}$.
2. $\mathrm{VCdim}(\mathscr{P}_{1,n}^+) = \min\{n, 2\}$.

Proof: The statement is clear for $n = 1, 2$. Note that $\mathrm{VCdim}(\mathscr{P}_1^+) = 2$ and $\mathrm{VCdim}(\mathscr{P}_1) = 3$. For the first statement, we proved in Lemma 5 that for each labeling $\sigma \in \{0,1\}^3$ there is a monomial f_σ of degree less than 3 satisfying σ on the set $S = \{(-3, 4), (1, 2), (7.6)\}$ of size 3.   ∎

COROLLARY 18

1. $\min\{n, 4t - 1\} \geq \mathrm{VCdim}(\mathscr{P}_{t,n}) \geq \min\{n, 3t\}$.
2. $\mathrm{VCdim}(\mathscr{P}_{t,n}^+) = \min\{n, 2t\}$.

Proof: Note that $\mathrm{VCdim}(\mathscr{P}_{t,n}) \leq \min\{n, 4t - 1\}$, since $\mathrm{VCdim}(\mathscr{P}_n) = n$, $\mathrm{VCdim}(\mathscr{P}_t) \leq 4t - 1$, and $\mathrm{VCdim}(\mathscr{P}_{t,n}^+) \leq \min\{n, 2t\}$, since $\mathrm{VCdim}(\mathscr{P}_n^+) = n$, $\mathrm{VCdim}(\mathscr{P}_t^+) = 2t$.

The statement follows by induction with Lemma 16 and Proposition 17. Then

$$\min\{n, 4t - 1\} \geq \text{VCdim}(\mathcal{P}_{t,n})$$
$$\geq \text{VCdim}(\mathcal{P}_{t-1,n-3}) + 3$$
$$= \min\{n - 3, 3(t - 1)\} + 3 = \min\{n, 3t\}$$

and

$$\min\{n, 2t\} \geq \text{VCdim}(\mathcal{P}_{t,n}^+)$$
$$\geq \text{VCdim}(\mathcal{P}_{t-1,n-2}^+) + 2$$
$$= \min\{n, 2t\}. \qquad \blacksquare$$

11.3.4.2 Learnability of sparse polynomials in the metric PAC model In this subsection we investigate the learnability of sparse polynomials in the generalized PAC model of Haussler (see section 11.2.2). The essential condition for distribution-free uniform learnability (in this model) of the class of sparse polynomials is the finiteness of the metric VC dimension of $\mathcal{P}_t$. We prove linear bounds for $m\text{-VCdim}(\mathcal{P}_t)$.

First, we construct a lower bound on the metric VC dimension of the class $\mathcal{P}_t$.

LEMMA 19 $m\text{-VCdim}(\mathcal{P}_t) \geq \text{VCdim}(\mathcal{P}_t)$.

Proof: Let $d = \text{VCdim}(\mathcal{P}_t)$, and let $S = \{(x_i, y_i)\}_{i=1,\ldots,d}$ be a set of points shattered (in the standard sense) by the set of t-sparse polynomials $\{f_\sigma\}_{\sigma \in \{0,1\}^d} \subset \mathcal{P}_t$, that is,

$$\forall i = 1, \ldots, d \ \forall \sigma \in \{0,1\}^d : f_\sigma(x_i) - y_i \begin{cases} \leq 0 & \text{if } \sigma(i) = 1 \\ > 0 & \text{if } \sigma(i) = 0 \end{cases}.$$

Let ε be defined by

$$\varepsilon = \max_{i=1,\ldots,d} \max_{\sigma, \sigma(i)=1} y_i - f_\sigma(x_i).$$

Then

$$\forall i = 1, \ldots, d \ \forall \sigma \in \{0,1\}^d : |f_\sigma(x_i) - (y_i - \varepsilon)| \begin{cases} \leq \varepsilon & \text{if } \sigma(i) = 1 \\ > \varepsilon & \text{if } \sigma(i) = 0 \end{cases},$$

that is, the set $S_\varepsilon = \{(x, y - \varepsilon, \varepsilon) | (x, y) \in S\}$ of size d is shattered (in the metric sense) by the set of t-sparse polynomials $\{f_\sigma\}_{\sigma \in \{0,1\}^d} \subset \mathcal{P}_t$. Hence, $m\text{-VCdim}(\mathcal{P}_t) \geq \text{VCdim}(\mathcal{P}_t)$. $\qquad \blacksquare$

We introduce the following lemma to derive an upper bound on m-VCdim$(\mathscr{P}_t)$.

LEMMA 20   *Let* $S = \{(x_i, y_i, \varepsilon_i)\}_{i=1,\ldots,4}$ *where* $x_1 < x_2 < x_3 < x_4$. *Let* $\sigma_1 = (1,0,0,1)$, $\sigma_2 = (0,1,1,0)$, $\sigma_3 = (1,0,1,0)$, $\sigma_4 = (0,1,0,1)$ *be labelings on* S. *Let* $\{f_i\}_{i=1,\ldots,4}$ *be continuous functions satisfying* σ_i *on* S *(in the metric sense). Then at least one of the pairs of functions* (f_1, f_2), (f_1, f_3), (f_1, f_4), (f_3, f_4) *have an intersection point in the interval* (x_1, x_4).

Proof: Consider the 2^8 cases for $f_i(x_j) > y_j + \varepsilon_j$ or $f_i(x_j) < y_j - \varepsilon_j$ if $\sigma_i(j) = 0$.   ∎

THEOREM 21   *The metric VC dimension of the class of t-sparse polynomials is at most* $48t - 9$.

Proof: Let $d = $ m-VCdim$(\mathscr{P}_t)$ and $S = \{(x_i, y_i, \varepsilon_i)\}_{i=1,\ldots,d}$, where $x_1 < x_2 < \cdots < x_d$. Assume S is shattered by t-sparse polynomials. Consider the labelings $\sigma_1 = (1,0,0,1,0,0,1,0,0,\ldots)$, $\sigma_2 = (0,1,1,0,1,1,0,1,1,\ldots)$, $\sigma_3 = (1,0,1,0,1,0,\ldots)$, and $\sigma_4 = (0,1,0,1,0,1,\ldots)$. Let $f_1, \ldots, f_4$ be t-sparse polynomials satisfying $\sigma_1, \ldots, \sigma_4$. Then, by Lemma 20, there are two polynomials with at least $d/12$ intersections, and, with Lemma 10, we conclude that $d \le 12(4t - 1) + 2 = 48t - 10$ (there may exist two additional points, where we cannot apply Lemma 20).   ∎

COROLLARY 22   *For any fixed* $t \in \mathbf{N}$, *the class of t-sparse polynomials is uniformly and distribution-free learnable in the metric PAC model.*

11.3.4.3 Approximating the polynomial regression   As an application of the results derived in the previous section, we consider the open problem stated by Vapnik ([Vap 82]) on computational approximation of the general regression functions used in the theory of empirical data dependences.

One of the central problems in computational regression theory is the problem of determining the number of terms in an arranged system of functions. The most important case of this problem is the approximation of polynomial regression (cf. [Vap 82], pp. 254–258).

The classical scheme of approximating polynomial regression, which involves the determination of the true degree n of regression and the expansion in a system of n orthogonal polynomials of degree $1, 2, \ldots, n$, can be successfully implemented only when large samples are used. The reason for this is the (possibly) large degree of regression and therefore the large metric VC dimension (capacity) of the class of polynomials of degree n. The problem for small samples remained open.

We prove linear bounds (Theorem 21) on the metric VC dimension of t-sparse polynomials (independent of the degree) implying Corollary 23.

COROLLARY 23   *The polynomial regression can be estimated for small samples (depending only on the number of required terms).*

11.4   Open Problems and Further Research

In section 11.3 we have proved uniform and distribution-free learnability of sparse univariate polynomials, but several related problems remain open. In this section we list some of the open problems in the area of learnability of sparse polynomials.

11.4.1   Learnability of Multivariate Polynomials

From Theorem 4, degree-bounded multivariate polynomials are of finite VC dimension for any fixed number of variables. There is no corresponding result for sparse multivariate polynomials. As described in section 11.3, the main tool for proving the finiteness of the VC dimension in the sparse univariate case is the upper bound on the number of roots of sparse polynomials derived from Descartes's Rule. A promising approach for the multivariate case might be the work of Khovanskii ([Kh 83]). Khovanskii generalizes Descartes's estimate to the sparse multivariate case and proves that the number of nondegenerate roots of sparse polynomials as well as the number of connected components of a singular real algebraic variety can be estimated in terms of the sparsity and the number of variables. In spite of these results, it is not clear in the multidimensional case how to relate the VC dimension to the upper bounds on the roots of multivariate polynomials.

11.4.2   Efficient Learning Algorithms

It is an open problem if there exists a hypothesis finder for the class of t-sparse polynomials such that the time complexity of the algorithm is bounded only in terms of the sparsity and the sample size.

A related problem is the problem of whether the class of sparse polynomials is learnable with respect to target complexity. The results of Linial et al. ([LMR 88]) imply that this is equivalent to the question of whether or not the class of sparse polynomials is polynomially uniformly decomposable. This reduces to the problem of the existence of a polynomial-time algorithm for sparse linear programming. Note that the existence of such an algorithm would not imply polynomial learnability of the class of t-sparse polynomials for fixed t since the appropriate degree is unknown.

11.4.3 Exact VC Dimension of Sparse Polynomials

From Lemma 11, the VC dimension of sparse univariate polynomials on the right half space equals $2t$. Lemmas 8 and 12 give a lower bound of $3t$ and an upper bound of $4t - 1$ on the VC dimension in the unrestricted case. The exact VC dimension remains unknown. For the metric VC dimension the tradeoff between lower bound ($3t$) and upper bound ($48t - 10$) is even larger.

11.4.4 Data Compression Schemes

Given a finite set of examples, labeled consistently with some concept from a concept class, a data compression scheme of size d saves at most d of those examples. From the d saved examples, the data compression scheme reconstructs a hypothesis that is consistent with the original sample. Data compression schemes are of crucial importance in the context of on-line and space-bounded learning algorithms. It is an open problem whether or not there exists a data compression scheme of small size for the class of sparse univariate polynomials. For the case of univariate real polynomials of degree less than n, Floyd ([Fl 89]) shows that there is a data compression scheme of size n and gives an on-line learning algorithm saving at most n examples at a time. The techniques used by Floyd depend mainly on the vector space structure, induced by degree-bounded polynomials, implying that any interpolation problem is solvable. For sparse polynomials, these techniques are not applicable.

Acknowledgments

We thank Manuel Blum, Allan Borodin, Sally Floyd, Dima Grigoriev, Les Valiant, and Manfred Warmuth for a number of interesting conversations. The discussion with Vladimir Vapnik has led us to the solution of the general regression problem.

Notes

Supported in part by Leibniz Center for Research in Computer Science, by the DFG grant KA 673/2-1, and by the SERC grant GR-E 68297.

References

[AHU 74] Aho, A., Hopcroft, J., and Ullman, J. *The Design and Analysis of Computer Algorithms*. Addison-Wesley, London, 1974.

[BEHW 86] Blumer, A., Ehrenfeucht, A., Haussler, D., and Warmuth, M. K. Classifying Learnable Geometric Concepts with the Vapnik-Chervonenkis Dimension. In *Proc. 18th ACM STOC*, pp. 273–282, 1986.

[BEHW 89] Blumer, A., Ehrenfeucht, A., Haussler, D., and Warmuth, M. K. Learnability and the Vapnik-Chervonenkis Dimension. *Journal ACM* 36 (4): 929–965, 1989.

[BeTi 88] Ben-Or, M., and Tiwari, P. A. A Deterministic Algorithm for Sparse Multivariate Polynomial Interpolation. In *Proc. 20th ACM STOC*, pp. 301–309, 1988.

[Br 90] Bruck, J. Harmonic Analysis of Polynomial Threshold Functions. *SIAM J. Discrete Math.* 3 (2): 282–287, 1990.

[BS 90] Bruck, J., and Smolensky, R. Polynomial Threshold Functions, AC^0 Functions, and Spectral Norms. In *Proc. 31th IEEE FOCS*, pp. 632–641, 1990.

[Coh 82] Cohn, P. M. *Algebra*, Vol. 1. 2nd ed. John Wiley and Sons, New York, 1982.

[Cov 65] Cover, T. M. Geometrical and Statistical Properties of Systems of Linear Inequalities with Applications in Pattern Recognition. *IEEE Trans. Electron. Comput.* 14: 326–334, 1965.

[Du 78] Dudley, R. M. Central Limit Theorems for Empirical Measures. *Annals of Probability* 6 (6): 899–929, 1978.

[EHKL 89] Ehrenfeucht, A., Haussler, D., Kearns, M., and Valiant, L. A General Lower Bond on the Number of Examples Needed for Learning. *Information and Computation* 82 (3): 247–261, 1989.

[Fl 89] Floyd, S. On Space-bounded Learning and the Vapnik-Chervonenkis Dimension. Technical Report TR-89-061, Ph.D. diss. International Computer Science Institute, Berkeley, 1989.

[GK 87] Grigoriev, D. Yu., and Karpinski, M. The Matching Problem for Bipartite Graphs with Polynomially Bounded Permanent is in NC. In *Proc. 28th IEEE FOCS*, pp. 166–172, 1987.

[GKS 90] Grigoriev, D. Yu., Karpinski, M., and Singer, M. Fast Parallel Algorithms for Sparse Multivariate Polynomial Interpolation over Finite Fields. *SIAM J. Comp.* 19 (6): 1059–1063, 1990.

[Ha 89] Haussler, D. Generalizing the PAC Model: Sample Size Bounds from Metric Dimension-based Uniform Convergence Results. In *Proc. 30th IEEE FOCS*, pp. 40–45, 1989.

[Kar 89] Karpinski, M. Boolean Circuit Complexity of Algebraic Interpolation Problems. In *Proc. CSL '88, LNCS 385*, pp. 138–147, 1989.

[KW 89] Karpinski, M., and Werther, T. VC Dimension and Learnability of Sparse Polynomials and Rational Functions. Technical Report TR-89-060, International Computer Science Institute, Berkeley, 1989; to appear in *SIAM J. Comput.* 22 (6), 1993.

[Kh 83]   Khovanskii, A. G. Fewnomials and Pfaff Manifolds. In *Proc. Intern. Congress of Math.*, Warsaw, 1983.

[KM 91]   Kushilevitz, E., and Mansour, Y. Learning Decision Trees Using the Fourier Spectrum. In *Proc. 23th ACM STOC*, pp. 455–464, 1991.

[LMR 88]   Linial, N., Mansour, Y., and Rivest, R. L. Results on Learnability and the Vapnik-Chervonenkis Dimension. In *Proc. 29th IEEE FOCS*, pp. 120–129, 1988.

[Po 84]   Pollard, D. *Convergence of Stochastic Processes.* Springer-Verlag, New York, 1984.

[Val 84]   Valiant, L. G. A Theory on the Learnable. *Comm. ACM* 27 (11): 1134–1142, 1984.

[Vap 82]   Vapnik, V. N. *Estimation of Dependences Based on Empirical Data.* Springer-Verlag, New York, 1982.

[Vap 89]   Vapnik, V. N. Inductive Principles of the Search for Empirical Dependences (Methods Based on Weak Convergence of Probability Measures). In *Proc. 2nd Workshop on Computational Learning Theory*, pp. 3–21, 1989.

[VC 71]   Vapnik, V. N., and Chervonenkis, A. Y. On the Uniform Convergence of Relative Frequencies of Events and their Probabilities. *Th. Prob. and its Appl.* 16 (2): 264–280, 1971.

[WD 81]   Wenocur, R. S. and Dudley, R. M. Some Special Vapnik-Chervonenkis Classes. *Discrete Mathematics* 33: 313–318, 1981.

[We 91]   Werther, T. VC Dimension and Learnability of Sparse Polynomials. Ph.D. thesis, University of Bonn, 1991.

12 Learning from Data with Bounded Inconsistency: Theoretical and Experimental Results

Haym Hirsh and William W. Cohen

12.1 Introduction

The problem of inductive concept learning—forming general rules from specific cases—has been well studied in machine learning and artificial intelligence. In the simplified case that is often studied, the concept learning problem is to find some general description in a concept description language that covers all given positive examples of an unknown concept and covers no negative examples of the concept. However, in real-world applications data are often subject to error, and there may be no concept that correctly classifies all the data. When data are inconsistent, the learner will be unable to find a description classifying all instances correctly. General-purpose learning systems must generate reasonable results even when there is no concept definition consistent with all the data.

Much of the past work on learning from inconsistent data forms concept definitions that perform well but not perfectly on the data, viewing those instances not covered as anomalous (e.g., [Michalski and Larson 1978; Quinlan 1986]). Instances are effectively thrown away, even if they are merely slightly errant. The approach taken here to learning from inconsistent data is to forego a solution to the full problem, and instead to solve a subcase of the problem for one particular class of inconsistency that can be exploited in learning. The underlying assumption for this class of inconsistency, called *bounded inconsistency*, is that some small perturbation to the description of any bad instance will result in a good instance (such as when all errors are the result of small perturbations to the training instances). When this is true, a learning system can search through the space of concept definitions that correctly classify either the original data, or small perturbations of the data. The definition that does best can be taken as the result of learning.

This is the approach taken in this chapter. The approach is implemented using a generalization of Mitchell's [1978] version-space approach to concept learning. Mitchell defines a version space to be the set of all concept definitions in a prespecified language that correctly classify

Portions of this chapter were previously published in a dissertation titled *Incremental Version-Space Merging: A General Framework for Concept Learning*, Kluwer Academic Publishers, 1990.

training data—the positive and negative examples of the unknown concept. The generalized approach [Hirsh 1990a; Hirsh 1990b], called *incremental version-space merging*, removes the assumption that there is always some concept definition that correctly classifies all the given data.

The chapter begins with a description of bounded inconsistency, the form of inconsistency considered here. It continues with the general solution to this problem, followed by its implementation with incremental version-space merging. Experimental results are then presented, followed by an overview of related work and a general discussion. A formal analysis of how the quality of results is influenced by the amount of data used in learning concludes the chapter. Further details are presented elsewhere [Hirsh 1990a; Hirsh 1990c].

12.2   Bounded Inconsistency

This chapter addresses the problem of learning from inconsistent data by solving a subcase of the problem called bounded inconsistency. The underlying assumption for this class of inconsistency is that some small perturbation to the description of any bad instance will result in a good instance. Whenever an instance is misclassified with respect to the desired final concept definition, some nearby instance description has the original instance's classification.

Figure 12.1 shows a simple way to view this. Concepts (such as C) divide the set of instances (I) into positive and negative examples. I_1^+ is an example of a representative positive example. It is correctly classified with

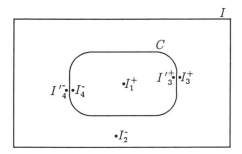

Figure 12.1
Pictorial representation of bounded inconsistency

respect to the desired concept C. Similarly, I_2^- is a correctly classified representative negative example. I_3^+, however, is incorrectly classified as positive even though the desired concept would label it negative. However, I_3^+ is a small perturbation of the neighboring instance $I_3'^+$ which is correctly classified, and similarly for the incorrectly classified negative instance I_4^- and its neighbor $I_4'^-$. Roughly speaking, if misclassifications only occur near the desired concept's boundary, the data have bounded inconsistency.

As an example of a situation in which bounded inconsistency is likely to occur, consider a learning problem in which instances are described by features whose values are determined by measuring devices of limited tolerance. Suppose a positive instance has a feature whose value was measured as 5.0. If the tolerance on the measurement of the feature's value is 0.1, the true feature value of the instance could have been 4.9. If the "true" positive instance were 4.9, and the instance that really has value 5.0 would have been negative, a misclassification error has occurred. However, if the tolerance information is correct, for every incorrect instance there is a neighboring correct instance description, all of whose feature values are no more than the tolerance away from the original instance's value for that feature. This is an example of bounded inconsistency.

12.3 Approach

The approach taken to solve this problem of learning from data with bounded inconsistency is most easily described through the classic view of concept learning as search [Simon and Lea 1974; Mitchell 1978; Mitchell 1982], namely, that the goal of learning is to determine some concept definition out of a space of possible definitions as the desired result of learning. For consistent data this problem is simply one of finding a description that correctly classifies all the data. When data are inconsistent, however, there is no such definition. The approach taken here is to select concept definitions such that for each training instance I, either the concept definition correctly classifies I, or it correctly classifies some perturbation of I. Each instance is effectively "blurred," and the concept definitions to be considered are those that generate a correct classification for at least one instance in each "blur."

Note, however, that in general there will be many possible definitions that correctly classify some instance in each blur. Not all of the remaining concept definitions are equal, though. Fortunately, the original, unperturbed training data can be used to define metrics over the space of possible results, which can be used to select a final result for learning.[1] Two such metrics are discussed in section 12.4.

12.4 Implementation

The method used to implement this approach is based on version spaces [Mitchell 1978]. However, version spaces assume the data to be noise-free, and therefore some modification of the method is necessary.[2] The approach taken here is to use *incremental version-space merging* (*IVSM*) [Hirsh 1990a; Hirsh 1990b], a generalization of version spaces [Mitchell 1978] that removes its assumption of strict consistency with data. A version space is generalized to be any set of concept definitions in a concept description language representable by boundary sets.[3] The key observation is that concept learning can be viewed as the two-step process of specifying sets of relevant concept definitions and intersecting these sets. For each piece of information obtained—typically an instance and its classification—incremental version-space merging forms the version space containing all concept definitions that are potentially relevant given the information (determined as appropriate for the given learning task). The resulting version space is then intersected with the version space based on all past data. This intersection takes place in boundary-set form (using the *version-space merging algorithm* [Hirsh 1990a; Hirsh 1990b]) and yields the boundary-set representation for a new version space that reflects all the past data plus the new information.

The general algorithm proceeds as follows:

1. Form the version space for the new piece of information.

2. Intersect this version space with the version space generated from past information.

3. Return to step 1 for the next piece of information.

The initial version space contains all concept descriptions in the language and is bounded by the S-set that contains the empty concept that says nothing is an example, and by the G-set that contains the universal concept that says everything is an example.

Use of incremental version-space merging requires a specification of how the individual version spaces should be formed in step 1 for each iteration. For example, using simple consistency with instances (i.e., forming the version space of all concept definitions that correctly classify the current instance) results in an emulation of Mitchell's [1978] candidate-elimination algorithm. This and other examples are presented elsewhere [Hirsh 1989; Hirsh 1990a; Hirsh 1990b], as are further details of the generalized version-space approach (including a discussion of the computational complexity of the method). The key idea in this work is to include in individual version spaces all of the concept definitions that are consistent with either the instance or some other term in the instance language near the given instance (where proximity is defined as appropriate for the given learning task). The version space of concept definitions to be considered for each instance will then be those concept definitions consistent with the instance or one of its neighbors within the region. The net effect is that all instances are "blurred," and version spaces reflect all instances within the blur.

The general technique can be viewed as follows:

Given:

• *Training Data*: Positive and negative examples of the concept to be identified.

• *Definition of Nearby*: A method that determines all instances near a given instance.

• *Concept Description Language*: A language in which the final concept definition must be expressed.

Determine:

• A set of concept definitions in the concept description language consistent with the data or nearby neighbors of the data.

The method proceeds as follows:

1. (a) Determine the set of instances near a given instance.
   (b) Form the version space of all concept definitions consistent with some instance in this set.
2. Intersect this version space with the version space generated from all past data.

3. Return to the first step for the next instance.

If an instance is positive, the version space of all concept definitions consistent with some instance in the set of neighboring instances has as an S-set the set of most specific concept definitions that cover at least one of the instances, and as a G-set the universal concept that includes everything. If the single-representation trick holds (i.e., for each instance there is a concept definition whose extension only contains that instance) [Dietterich et al. 1982], the S-set contains only the instance and its neighboring instances. If an instance is negative, the S-set contains the empty concept that includes nothing, and the G-set contains all minimal specializations of the universal concept that excludes the instance or one of its neighbors.

Ideally the result of this learning process would be a singleton version space containing the desired concept definition. However, if not enough data are given, the final version space will have more than one concept definition. This also may happen if the definition of nearby is too "generous"—that is, if every instance has many nearby instances. In this case there will be many consistent concept definitions in each instance version space; in some cases no set of instances will permit convergence to a single concept definition. The definition of nearby should be generous enough to guarantee that the desired concept definition is never thrown out by any instance, but not too generous to include too many things (or in the worst case, everything).

In fact, it is often impractical to wait for enough instances to converge to a single concept definition. As each instance throws away candidate concept definitions, the version space gets smaller and smaller. As the version space decreases in size, the probability that a randomly chosen instance will make a difference—will be able to remove candidate concept definitions—becomes smaller and smaller. The more data processed, the longer the wait for another useful instance. Therefore it will sometimes be desirable due to time considerations to use the small but nonsingleton version space (before converging to a single concept) to determine a usable result for learning.

Thus a situation can arise in which the final version space after processing data has multiple concept definitions. As mentioned earlier, however, not all of the remaining concept definitions are equal, and the original, unperturbed training data can be used to define metrics over the space of possible results that can be used to select a final result for learning. For example, one such metric uses the observation that each concept definition is consistent with only some of the original, unperturbed data; some of the original data must be "blurred" to be consistent with the definition. This suggests computing the portion of the original, unperturbed data that is covered by the given concept definition. The concept definition with best coverage is then selected as the final generalization. A second possible metric uses the observation that for each concept definition the classification of some of the original data is unchanged even if perturbed by the maximum amount allowed by the definition of nearby. This suggests computing the number of instances whose classifications remain unchanged even if maliciously perturbed. Whichever definition maintains the classification of the largest number of correctly classified instances should be selected as the result of learning.

Using such metrics to find a "best" concept definition is computationally feasible only if the version space is reasonably small in size. Section 12.6 gives some formal results on the consequences of omitting this step and instead returning an arbitrary element of the version space.

12.5   Experimental Results

To demonstrate this technique Fisher's [1936] iris data is used. In addition to providing a test of the quality of the technique, it has been in use for fifty years and thus permits a comparison to the results of several other techniques.

12.5.1   Problem

The particular problem is that of classifying examples of different kinds of iris flowers into one of three species of irises: setosa, versicolor, and viginica. The goal is to learn three nonoverlapping concept definitions that cover the space of all irises; this requires a slight extension to the version-space approach, which is described in the next subsection. There are 150 instances, 50 for each class; instances are described using four features: sepal width, sepal length, petal width, and petal length. The units for all four are centimeters, measured to the nearest millimeter. For example, one example of setosa had sepal length 4.6 cm, sepal width 3.6 cm, petal length 1.0 cm, and petal width 0.2 cm.

The concept description language was chosen to be conjunctions of ranges of the form a $a \leq x < b$ for each feature, where a and b are limited to multiples of 8 mm. An example of a legal concept description is "[0.8 cm $\leq$ petal length < 2.4 cm] and [petal width < 1.6 cm]." The range for defining neighboring instances was taken to be 3 mm for each feature— that is, as much as 3 mm can be added to or subtracted from each feature value for each instance (defining a range of size 6 mm centered on each feature value). There is no restriction on the number of features that may be blurred—anywhere from all to none may require blurring.

Note that although this means that each instance could be blurred to be any of an infinite number of instances within the range specified by the nearness metric (or if values are limited to the nearest millimeter, feature values can be blurred to any of a large number of nearby values), many of the instances are equivalent with respect to the concept description language. Two feature values, although different, can still fall in the same range imposed by the concept description language. Thus only a much smaller set of nearby instances need be considered and enumerated, one from each grouping of values imposed by the concept description language.

Also note that this language does not use the single-representation trick, and its features do not form a tree-structured hierarchy, two properties that are commonly used to guarantee computational tractability.

12.5.2 Method

The general approach of section 12.4 was used to find rules. All neighboring instances for each example are generated, by perturbing the instance in all ways possible—0.3 is added to and subtracted from each feature value, and the concept definitions consistent with each combination of potential feature values were formed. The union of all these concept definitions forms the version space for individual instances. For example, the positive instance of setosa given earlier (with sepal length 4.6 cm, sepal width 3.6 cm, petal length 1.0 cm, and petal width 0.2 cm) has four elements in its S-set. All have [3.2 cm $\leq$ sepal width < 4.0 cm] and [0.0 cm $\leq$ petal width < 0.8 cm]. They differ, however, on their restrictions on sepal length and petal length: the different concept definitions correspond to the four different combinations obtainable by choosing one of [4.0 cm $\leq$ sepal length < 4.8 cm] and [4.8 cm $\leq$ sepal length < 5.6 cm], and one of [0.0

cm ≤ petal length < 0.8 cm] and [0.8 cm ≤ petal length < 1.6 cm]. The *G*-set for the instance contains the universal concept that includes everything as positive. The same instance, if viewed as a negative instance of one of the other two classes, would have the empty set as its *S*-set, and its *G*-set would have seven concept definitions: [sepal length < 4.8 cm], [sepal length ≥ 4.8 cm], [sepal width < 3.2 cm], [sepal width ≥ 4.0 cm], [petal length < 0.8 cm], [petal length ≥ 0.8 cm], and [petal width ≥ 0.8 cm].

The goal of learning is to form three disjoint concept definitions that cover the space of instances, and this requires two extensions to the technique described above. The first exploits the fact that the learned concept definitions must not overlap. The simple approach would be to take the 100 examples of two of the classes as negative examples for the third class. However, not only must the concept definitions for the third class exclude these instances, they must exclude all instances included by the final concept definition for each of the other two classes. It is not known what the final definitions will be, but it is known that they must be more general than some element of the *S*-set for its class. That is, whatever the concept definition, it must at least include all instances covered by some most specific concept definition generated from the positive data for that class. In the iris domain the *S*-set for each class after processing the positive data for that class was always singleton, so the final concept definition for each class must include all examples included by the final *S*-set element. Therefore, rather than taking the fifty examples of each class as negative data for the other two classes, initially only positive data are processed for each class; the generalization in the *S*-set that results from this initial stage is taken as a generalized negative instance for the other two classes, replacing the use of the 100 negative instances with two generalizations that include the negative instances plus additional instances that must also be excluded. Thus, for example, all positive data are processed for the setosa class, and the result in the *S*-set is taken as a single generalized negative instance for versicolor and viginica. It summarizes the setosa data, as well as additional instances that will also be included by the final definition for setosa.

The second extension is that, since the three concept definitions that are formed must cover the space, many of the more specific definitions for each class can be removed, since no combination of definitions in the version spaces for the other two classes will cover the space of irises. This fact is used in the final stage of learning, in which the version space is searched for a "best" concept description (section 12.4). In this step, instead of searching the entire version space to find the best definition, only the subset of the version space that could lead to class definitions that cover the entire space of irises is considered. The search then takes place in the cross products of the three much smaller version spaces. One additional heuristic is used to prune this search: selection of a hypothesis in one space allows using it as a generalized negative instance for the other version spaces, and thus not all triples of concept definitions from the three version spaces need be considered.

12.5.3   Results

Since there is only a fixed amount of data, the learning technique was evaluated by leave-one-out cross-validation [Weiss and Kulikowski 1991]. This simply involves learning on each subset of size 149 and testing on the single instance that was left out, and then averaging the results of the 150 single-instance test runs.

All 150 runs on the different 149-instance training sets yielded the same results: when only those nonoverlapping rules that cover the space of irises are considered, just five concept descriptions remained in the version space for setosa, and only three remained for each of versicolor and viginica. Furthermore, for each of the five definitions for setosa only one definition for versicolor and one for viginica were legal. Thus training effectively yielded five candidate results (each with three rules, one for each of the classes), and these were the same for all 149-instance training sets.

The final step of learning is to select a best result from these five using the metrics of section 12.4. Using the first metric, in 149 of the 150 training-set runs two results were ruled out; in the remaining training-set run none was ruled out since all five had the same metric value.

However, in all 150 runs the second metric pruned three results, and only two apparently equivalent results remained.[4] The two results were as follows. Both required the definition for versicolor to have [petal length ≥ 2.4 cm] and [petal width < 1.6 cm]. The first result defined setosas to have [petal length < 2.4 cm] and viginica to have [petal length ≥ 2.4 cm] and [petal width ≥ 1.6 cm]. The second result defined setosas to have [petal length < 2.4 cm] and [petal width < 1.6 cm] and defined viginica to have [petal width ≥ 1.6 cm].

Table 12.1
Overall error rates

Method	Err_{App}	Err_{CV}
Linear	.020	.020
Optimal rule size 2	.020	.020
Neural net (ODE)	.007	.027
Quadratic	.020	.027
Neural net (BP)	.017	.033
Nearest neighbor	.000	.040
PVM rule	.027	.040
CART tree	.040	.047
IVSM	**.053**	**.053**
Bayes independence	.047	.067
Bayes 2nd order	.040	.160

Ideally at this point either some other way to discriminate further between the results should be used, or one of the two should arbitrarily be picked as the result of learning. The second path was followed since no further ideas for discriminating between the two came to mind; however, the leave-one-out cross-validation results for these two results are exactly the same, and thus it did not even matter which of the two was selected.

The overall leave-one-out error rate on all three classes was 5.3%. For setosa alone the rate was 0.0%, as the class is separable from the other two. For versicolor alone the rate was 10.0%, and for viginica 6.0%. For comparison this error rate (labeled "IVSM") is compared to the error rates for other learning algorithms (also estimated using leave-one-out cross-validation) presented in Weiss and Kulikowski's [1991] book and shown in Table 12.1. Err_{App} is the apparent error rate, namely the error rate when training and testing on the complete set of data. Err_{CV} is the leave-one-out cross-validated error rate, which is generally a better estimate of the true error rate. The resulting error rates demonstrate that the approach described here performs well, although other methods do outperform it. We conjecture that these error rates are as good as is possible if learning is constrained to form a single conjunctive rule specifying some axis-parallel rectangle with multiple of 8 mm sides, as it was for this work.

12.5.4 Comparison to Related Work

This chapter describes one approach to learning from inconsistent data by only addressing the subcase of data with bounded inconsistency. Drastal,

Meunier, and Raatz [1989] have proposed a related method that works in cases where only positive data have bounded inconsistency. Their approach is to overfit the inconsistent data, using a learning technique capable of forming multiple disjuncts, some of which only exist to cover anomalous instances. After learning, they remove disjuncts that only cover instances that can be perturbed to fit under one of the other disjuncts, in effect removing the disjunctions that only exist to cover the anomalous data. One benefit of their technique is that it is applied after learning, focusing on only those instances covered by small disjuncts, whereas here all instances must be viewed as potentially anomalous. However, they make the stronger assumption that all such inconsistent data fall into small disjuncts. They furthermore only handle positive data.

As mentioned earlier, Mitchell [1978] presented an alternative approach to learning from inconsistent data with version spaces. The key idea was to maintain in parallel version spaces for various subsets of the data. When no concept definition is consistent with all data, Mitchell's approach considers those concept definitions consistent with all but one instance. As more inconsistency is detected, the system uses version spaces based on smaller and smaller subsets of the data, which the system has been maintaining during learning. The number of boundary sets that need be maintained by this process is linear in the total number of instances to be processed (in the worst case). This is still unacceptably costly. In the iris domain, assuming that at most 10% of the data should be discounted, this would have required updating thirty boundary sets for each instance. Even using the less reasonable assumption that only 4% of the data need be ignored will result in an order of magnitude slowdown. Furthermore, Mitchell's approach requires knowing the absolute maximum number of incorrectly classified instances, in contrast to allowing an unlimited number of errors as done here (replacing it with a bound on the distance any instance may be from a correct instance). Finally, the boundary sets for Mitchell's approach are much larger than for the noise-free case, since Mitchell modifies the candidate-elimination algorithm S-set updating method to ignore negative data, and similarly positive data are ignored by the modified G-set updating method (this allows the use of a linear number of boundary sets by keeping the boundary sets for multiple version spaces in a single boundary set).

A significant distinction can be made between this work and Mitchell's approach, as well as much other work in learning from inconsistent data (e.g., [Michalski and Larson 1978; Quinlan 1986]). These approaches form concept definitions that perform well but not perfectly on the data, viewing those instances not covered as anomalous. Instances are effectively thrown away, whereas here every instance is viewed as providing useful information, and the final concept definition must be consistent with the instance or one of its neighbors. The approach presented here works on data with bounded inconsistency. Other approaches handle a wider range of inconsistency, but cannot utilize any instances that are just a small ways off from correct; they instead throw out such instances as nonhelpful. Furthermore, unlike other approaches that degenerate as more inconsistency is imposed on the data, the incremental version-space merging approach described here still succeeds even when all of the data are subject to bounded inconsistency.

To further demonstrate this point a series of runs of the learning method were done on a simple, artificial domain. There are three attributes that take on real values in the range of 0 to 9. The concept description language partitions attributes into three regions: greater than or equal to 0 and less than 3, greater than or equal to 3 and less than 6, and greater than or equal 6 and less than or equal to 9. A concept definition is a conjunction of such ranges over the various attributes. A single preselected concept definition serves as the target of learning.

Data were created by randomly generating some value for each attribute in its legal range (0 to 9). This instance was then classified according to the preselected target concept definition for learning. The identity of each instance is then perturbed by up to one unit—a random number between −1 and 1 is added to the given value of each attribute. This new instance is given the classification of the instance on which it is based. Training data generated in this manner have bounded inconsistency, since any incorrect instance is never more than 1 away from a correct instance on any attribute.

The test runs perturb different percentages of the data to test the sensitivity of the approach to this factor. The definition of "nearby" used by the learning method defines one instance to be near another if the value of each attribute of the first is within one unit of the corresponding value for the second (i.e., the appropriate definition of nearby was selected). All attribute values for a single instance may be perturbed. Eighty randomly generated instances were used.

Table 12.2 summarizes the results of the test. The arnount of data that was perturbed was allowed to vary from 0% (no data perturbed—data are

Table 12.2
Correct concept identification for different amounts of inconsistency

%	Correct?
0	Yes
20	Yes
40	Yes
60	Yes
80	Yes
100	Yes

consistent) to 100% (all data perturbed). In all cases learning used a definition of "nearby" that added 1 to and subtracted 1 from the value of each attribute. The result of the experiment was that, in all cases, incremental version-space merging (with the additional step of selecting the best classifier from the version space) converged to the target concept definition that was used to generate the data. Unlike most other learning algorithms that degenerate as more noise is introduced to the data, the technique was able to learn correctly the desired concept definition even when all data are perturbed within known bounds. One way to interpret these results is that the approach described here provides a way to use the knowledge that bounded inconsistency exists, which permits successful learning even when all the data are incorrect (within the known bounds).

12.5.5   Discussion

The general approach described here is to consider concept definitions consistent with the instance or some neighbor of the instance. The technique requires a method for generating all instances near a given instance, but it does not constrain a priori the particular definition of "nearby." For example, in tree-structured description languages one such definition would be that two feature values are in the same subtree: rhombus and square might be close, whereas rhombus and oval might not.

However, the approach described here is extremely sensitive to both the concept description language and the definition of "nearby." For a fixed language, if the notion of nearby is too small, the version space will collapse with no consistent concept; if it is too large, each instance will have many neighbors, and instance boundary sets will be quite large, which makes the approach computationally infeasible. Furthermore, the final version space will likely be too big to search for a best concept after processing the data. Similarly, for a fixed definition of nearby, if the concept description language is too coarse, instances will have no neighbors, whereas if the language is too fine, then instances will have too many neighbors. The choice of language and definition of nearby affects the size of version spaces and the convergence rate for learning (how many instances are required to converge, if it is even possible).

The ideal situation for this approach would be when the definition of nearby is given or otherwise known for the particular domain, as well as when the desired language for concepts is provided. However, it is often the case that one or both are not known, as was the case for the iris domain of the previous section, which required three iterations before a successful concept description language and definition of nearby were found. The first description language chosen used intervals of size 4 mm, rather than 8 mm as was finally selected. The first definition of nearby considered instances with feature values within 2 mm of given feature values as "nearby," but the version space collapsed—no concept definition remained after processing the data—for the versicolor and viginica classes. However, a definition of nearby of 3 mm resulted in too many neighbors for each instance, making the process too computationally expensive (the program ran out of memory). Since measurements were only given to the nearest millimeter, there was no intermediate definition of nearby to try. Since adjusting the definition of nearby failed to work, the next step was to adjust the language, and 8 mm intervals were chosen. Fortunately the first attempt using the new language with a definition of nearby of 3 mm yielded nonempty version spaces of reasonable size. Criteria for selecting appropriate description languages and definitions of nearby are an area for future work.

To further demonstrate this issue, a number of runs were made on the artificial learning task of the previous section. In these experiments the concept description language was fixed (using the same language as in the previous section), and the definition of nearby (the amount of inconsistency assumed present by the learning method) was varied. This set of experiments explores how the definition of nearby affects the size of the final version space and the number of neighbors each instance will have.[5]

The results of these experiments are summarized in Table 12.3. There are three attributes, and altogether there are 216 concept definitions in the language. The different rows correspond to different definitions of near-

Table 12.3
Version space size and number of neighbors for different definitions of "nearby"

Nearby	Average $|VS|$	Average no. neighbors
0	0	1
1	1	3
2	4	6.48
3	38	12.91

by—how much is added to or subtracted from each instance. This was varied from 0 to 3—the maximum distance apart the feature values of two instances can be so that the instances are still considered neighbors (column 1 in the table). 100% of the attribute values were perturbed by up to one unit. Note that the real amount of variance imposed on values when generating data was at most 1—no more than 1 was added to or subtracted from the randomly generated value for the feature. The second column of Table 12.3 summarizes the size of the final version space after all eighty instances have been processed. Note that, while learning is impossible here if the data are assumed consistent, and convergence is possible using the eighty instances if the definition of nearby adds or subtracts only 1 to each value (the actual value used in generating the inconsistent data), as the value for nearby increases to 2 and 3, the final version-space size increases.

The third column presents the average number of neighbors for each instance. As would be expected, these numbers increase as the amount by which values may be perturbed increases and are close to their expected values of 1.0, 3.0 ($=(13/9)^3$), 6.7 ($=(17/9)^3$), and 12.7 ($=(21/9)^3$). In general, if there are k features, each with m ranges of size w (here k, m, and w are all 3), and the amount of noise is $d \leq w$ (here d ranged from 0 to 3), the expected number of neighbors (assuming a uniform distribution of values for each feature and independence of features) is $\left(1 + \dfrac{2d}{w}\left(1 - \dfrac{1}{m}\right)\right)^k$.

These results emphasize the need for a sufficiently generous, but not overly generous, definition of nearby. They furthermore suggest a method for automating the selection of an appropriate definition of nearby given a fixed concept description language. The method would begin by assuming consistency, then slowly increase the amount of inconsistency

assumed to be present in the data (i.e., increase the generosity of the definition of nearby) until either a nonempty version space is generated
or enough time has passed to believe that the approach is not computationally feasible on the given data with the given concept description
language.

12.6   Theoretical Results

Recent theoretical work on concept learning (e.g., [Valiant 1984; Haussler
1988; Laird 1988]) has developed techniques for analyzing how the
quality of results is influenced by the amount of data used in learning.
This section gives two such results for learning from data with bounded
inconsistency.

In section 12.6.2 we analyze the sample complexity of the algorithm
presented in this chapter under the assumptions usual in Valiant-style
learnability analysis: in particular, we assume that that examples are
stochastically chosen (with replacement) by an oracle according to some
fixed probability distribution D, and that the goal is to find a concept that
predicts, as well as possible, the classifications given by the true concept on
later examples.

In section 12.6.3 we analyze the sample complexity of a variant of the
algorithm presented in this chapter, in which, after all examples are processed, an *arbitrary* element of the final version space (rather than the best
concept definition in the final version space) is returned. There are two
motivations for this analysis. First, it can be that while the boundary sets
of the final version space are small, the version space itself is large; in this
case the final step of selecting the best element of the version space may be
computationally expensive. Thus it is useful to know what sort of performance guarantees can be made for *any* element of the final version space.
Second, it helps indicate what aspects of the algorithm's behavior result
from the version-space processing of the data, and what aspects of the
algorithm's behavior result from the final step of selecting the best concept
definition in the final version space.

In the analysis we do not consider the computational complexity of the
learning algorithm. It is known to require exponential time in the worst
case; however, experimental evidence shows that the average case performance is acceptable, on at least some learning problems. Further details
are presented in [Hirsh 1990a].

12.6.1   Notation

It is first necessary to present some terminology and notation. X is used to denote the set of all instances; t denotes the target concept; $class(x)$ denotes the classification of an instance x with respect to a target concept t and is 1 if x is a member of t and 0 if it is not; N denotes the number of possible concept definitions in the concept description language.

Bounded inconsistency is viewed as a random process that takes an instance and generates a new instance not too far from it, that is, that there is a random process

$$P : X \rightarrow X$$

that generates the description of observed instances. Thus, an *example* is a pair of the form $\langle P(x), class(x) \rangle$. Examples are generated by an *oracle* randomly according to a probability distribution function D. To keep things simple, we will assume that X is finite, D is a point probability function

$$D : X \rightarrow [0, 1],$$

and that an example x' of class b, $\langle x', b \rangle$, is generated by the oracle with probability

$$\sum_{x \in X : class(x) = b} D(x) \cdot \mathrm{Prob}[P(x) = x'].$$

The function $Neighbors(x)$ gives the set of examples in the instance description language that are near x (for the learning-task specific definition of nearby), namely

$$Neighbors(x) = \{ y \mid y \text{ is near } x \}.$$

The symmetric difference of two concepts h_1 and h_2 is denoted $h_1 \triangle h_2$. The *error* of a hypothesis h is defined to be the probability of the region that is the symmetric difference of h and the target concept t, that is,

$$error(h) \equiv \sum_{x \in h \triangle t} D(x).$$

A hypothesis h is ε-*bad* if and only if $error(h) > \varepsilon$.

In the following analysis it will be assumed that the target concept t is in the final version space. This implies that, first, t must be expressible in the given concept description language, and also that the definition of nearby is generous enough to account for all the noise actually present in the data.

12.6.2   Accuracy of the Best Concept Definition from a Version Space

This first result will give the sample complexity to guarantee traditional consistency with data. Some additional terminology and notation are necessary, however. First, we will introduce a second notion of error with the following definition. For a hypothesis h, define

$o\text{-}error(h) \equiv \text{Prob}[h \text{ disagrees with oracle}].$

The *o-error* of a hypothesis h is the expected rate of disagreement with a noisy sample; the *error* of a hypothesis h measures its expected disagreement with a noise-free sample.

Also, we define

$$\eta \equiv \sum_{x \in X} D(x) \cdot \text{Prob}[class(P(x)) \neq class(x)].$$

The parameter η represents the probability that a randomly selected example x will be moved across the concept boundary by the random noise process P.

Also, the following well-known lemma will be used:

LEMMA 1 (Hoeffding)   *Consider a Bernoulli random variable with probability p of having the value "success" and probability $1 - p$ of having the value "failure". If $0 \leq p \leq 1, 0 \leq s \leq 1$, and m is any positive integer, then*

$Prob[at\ most\ \lfloor (p - s)m \rfloor\ successes\ in\ m\ trials] \leq e^{-2s^2 m}$

$Prob[at\ least\ \lceil (p + s)m \rceil\ successes\ in\ m\ trials] \leq e^{-2s^2 m}.$

Our analysis of sample complexity closely parallels Theorem 5.3 of Laird's thesis [Laird 1988]. Two propositions are required.

PROPOSITION 1 $o\text{-}error(t) = \eta$.

Proof: By definition, t always agrees with an example of the form $\langle x, class(x) \rangle$. So t will agree with the oracle's example $\langle P(x), class(x) \rangle$ if and only if $class(P(x)) = class(x)$, and disagree if and only if $class(P(x)) \neq class(x)$. Thus a disagreement occurs only when, first, x is chosen (according to D) by the oracle, and second, x is mapped to an $P(x)$ so that $class(P(x)) \neq class(x)$; the probability of this sequence of events is given by

$$\sum_{x \in X} D(x) \cdot \text{Prob}[class(P(x)) \neq class(x)]$$

which is precisely the definition of η.   ∎

PROPOSITION 2   *If $error(h) > \varepsilon$, that is, h is ε-bad, then*

o-error(h) $\geq \eta + \varepsilon(1 - 2\eta_b)$,

where η_b is some number so that $\eta < \eta_b < \frac{1}{2}$.

Proof: There are two disjoint ways that h can disagree with the oracle.

1. h agrees with t and disagrees with the oracle. By Proposition 1, this occurs with probability $(1 - \varepsilon)\eta$.

2. h disagrees with t and disagrees with the oracle. By Proposition 1, this occurs with probability $\varepsilon(1 - \eta)$.

Thus

$$\begin{aligned}
o\text{-}error(h) &= (1 - \varepsilon)\eta + \varepsilon(1 - \eta) \\
&= \eta - \varepsilon\eta + \varepsilon - \varepsilon\eta \\
&= \eta + \varepsilon(1 - 2\eta) \\
&\geq \eta + \varepsilon(1 - 2\eta_b).
\end{aligned}$$

The last step follows because $\eta_b > \eta$.   ∎

THEOREM 1   *Let $\eta = o\text{-}error(t)$, where t denotes the target concept, let ε and δ be numbers so that $0 < \varepsilon < 1, 0 < \delta < 1$, and let η_b be some bound on η so that $\eta < \eta_b < \frac{1}{2}$. Finally, let h be the best concept definition (i.e., the concept definition with the lowest observed error rate) in a version space generated from at least m examples, where*

$$m \geq \frac{2}{\varepsilon^2(1 - 2\eta_b)^2} \ln \frac{2N}{\delta}.$$

Then the probability that $error(h) > \varepsilon$ is less than δ.

Proof: By the propositions, on a random example,

Prob[a good hypothesis fails] $= \eta$

Prob[an ε-bad hypothesis fails] $= \eta + \varepsilon(1 - 2\eta)$,

where "fails" means "disagrees with an example provided by the oracle" and a "good hypothesis" is a hypothesis that is equivalent to the target t. The difference between these probabilities is at least

$$\varepsilon(1 - 2\eta) \geq \varepsilon(1 - 2\eta_b) = s.$$

The proof now follows the proof of Theorem 5.3 of Laird's thesis [Laird 1988]. Let F_i be the number of successes for some ε-bad hypothesis h_i on the m examples and let F_t be the number of successes for t on the sample (where a "success" refers to an occasion on which the concept agreed with the oracle.) If h_i is returned, then either

$$\frac{F_i}{m} \leq \eta + \frac{s}{2}$$

or

$$\frac{F_t}{m} \geq \eta + \frac{s}{2}$$

or both. Notice, however, that the expected value of $\frac{F_i}{m}$ is $\eta + s$ and the expected value of $\frac{F_t}{m}$ is η; thus the above only happens if either $\frac{F_i}{m}$ or $\frac{F_t}{m}$ is different from its expected value by at least $\frac{s}{2}$. By applying Hoeffding's inequalities and simplifying, we see that the probability of both of these is bounded by $\frac{\delta}{2N}$. Thus the probability of the learning algorithm picking any ε-bad hypothesis h_i is bounded by $\frac{\delta}{N}$; since there are fewer than N such hypotheses, the total probability that an ε-bad hypothesis is chosen by the learning algorithm is less than δ.   ∎

One surprising point about the result is that, given the assumption that $\eta < \frac{1}{2}$, we are able to bound the probability that h is ε-bad without assuming that $\varepsilon > \eta$. In other words, we are able to obtain hypotheses that agree with t arbitrarily closely, in spite of the fact that the noise process is such that (perhaps) every instance is corrupted to some degree.

Notice that this is slightly different from the Laird result (as stated). Laird's oracle draws an example x according to D, and then with probability η returns $\langle x, \neg class(x) \rangle$ and with probability $(1 - \eta)$ returns $\langle x, class(x) \rangle$. One might think that it is possible to define D' to be a new probability distribution function so that D' is the distribution of $P(x)$'s, and let η be as defined above; so we return $\langle P(x), class \rangle$ and with probability η, $class$ is different from $class(P(x))$. However, Laird's statement of the theorem requires the probability of noise on the example x to be independent of x; for us, the probability of noise is *not* independent of x, since instances closer to the concept boundary are more likely to have their classifications changed.

A tighter sample complexity bound of

$$m \geq \frac{2}{\varepsilon(1 - 2\eta_b)^2} \ln \frac{2N}{\delta}$$

can be shown, by analogy to the proof of the tighter bound found in an appendix to Laird's thesis [Laird 1988]. Laird also gives a technique for estimating η_b from the data, which can be applied to our problem as well.

Finally, it should be noted that this result applies to any algorithm that returns a hypothesis h that has the lowest observed error rate in a space of concept definitions of size N.

12.6.3   Accuracy of Any Concept Definition from a Version Space

If the final version space is large, it may be computationally expensive to search for the best element of the version space. For this reason we also consider the performance of the algorithm if an arbitrary element of the final version space is returned as a hypothesis, rather than the element which agrees best with the data.

This second result will give the sample complexity necessary to guarantee a weaker notion of consistency, called *b-consistency*, for learning from a set of examples. A concept is *b-consistent* with an example if it correctly classifies the example or one of its neighbors: more precisely, h is b-consistent with x if and only if

$x \in h$ and $\exists y \in Neighbors(x) : y \in t$

or $x \notin h$ and $\exists y \in Neighbors(x) : y \notin t$.

(Notice that the target concept t is an implicit parameter of this definition.) We then define the *b-error* of h to be the probability of selecting an x such that h is not b-consistent with x:

$$b\text{-}error(h) \equiv \sum_{x : h \text{ not b-consistent with } x} D(x).$$

With these definitions it is possible to map over Lemma 2.2 from Haussler's [1988] *Artificial Intelligence Journal* paper, as follows:

THEOREM 2   *Let t denote the target concept, let ε and δ be numbers so that $0 < ε < 1, 0 < δ < 1$, and let h be any concept definition in a version space generated from at least m examples, where*

$$m \geq \frac{ln(N) + ln\left(\frac{1}{δ}\right)}{ε}.$$

Then the probability that b-error(h) $\geq ε$ is less than δ.

Proof: We begin by showing that the probability that some element of the version space generated from m examples of t has b-error greater than ε is less than $Ne^{-εm}$. Assume that some set of hypotheses $h_1, \ldots, h_k$ in the concept description language H have b-error greater than ε. This means that the probability that an example is b-consistent with a particular h_i is less than $(1 - ε)$. The probability that h_i is b-consistent with m independent examples is therefore less than $(1 - ε)^m$. Finally, the probability that *some* $h_i \in h_1, \ldots, h_k$ is b-consistent with m instances is bounded by the sum of their individual probabilities; thus the probability that some h_i with b-error greater than ε is b-consistent with m examples of t is less than $k(1 - ε)^m$. Since $k \leq N$, and $(1 - ε)^m \leq e^{-εm}$, the probability of getting some hypothesis with b-error greater than ε b-consistent with m independent examples of t is less than $Ne^{-εm}$.

Solving $δ < Ne^{-εm}$ for m now gives the desired result.   ∎

At first these results may appear somewhat surprising since they give the same guarantees as Haussler, yet address learning from inconsistent data. The reason for this is that these results use a weaker definition of consistency, and hence use a weaker notion of error, than the traditional definition used by Haussler. The definition of b-error can perhaps be clarified by noticing that $b\text{-}error(h) \leq ε$ implies that all but a fraction h of the errors made by h occur near the concept boundary of the target t; in other words, for all but a fraction ε of the instances x that are misclassified by h, there is some neighbor of x that is classified differently by t. The number of errors that occur away from the concept boundary is thus bounded by ε; however, the number of errors that occur *near* a concept boundary, and hence the absolute error rate of h as compared to t, is not bounded.

Finally, notice that these results do not only apply to the version space approach presented here. Any learning method that generates concept descriptions b-consistent with m examples of some concept t will have these guarantees.

12.7   Concluding Remarks

This chapter has described an approach to learning from inconsistent data that focuses on a subcase of the problem, when data have bounded inconsistency. The key idea to learning from such data is to find concept definitions that miss some of the data, but only by a small amount. This approach was implemented using a generalization of Mitchell's version-space approach to concept learning called incremental version-space merging. The central idea is to allow version spaces to contain concept definitions not consistent with the data, but instead consistent with neighboring data. This results in considering more concept definitions than the original version-space approach would ordinarily consider, decreasing the chance that the desired concept definition is removed due to an anomalous instance.

The learning algorithm developed in this chapter has been validated in two ways. First, we have investigated its behavior experimentally on Fisher's iris data [Fisher 1936] and on synthetic data; second, we have investigated its behavior theoretically by bounding its sample complexity under a formal model of learnability. Experimentally the algorithm obtains hypotheses on the iris problem of roughly comparable accuracy to those obtained by other learning methods. The major formal result is that the sample complexity under the Valiant model can be bounded by a polynomial in the logarithm of version-space size, the inverse of the absolute error rate, and a confidence parameter.

The results of this chapter use an algorithm based on version spaces. However, the notion of bounded inconsistency applies to data, not to learning algorithms. It is therefore interesting to consider how knowledge of the presence of bounded inconsistency can be exploited in other learning algonthms. For example, straightforward extensions to ID3 [Quinlan 1986] and Rivest's decision-list learning algorithm [Rivest 1987] should enable them to learn when given data with bounded inconsistency. Future work will explore such modifications of these and other algorithms, such as neural network learning, to see if they yield comparable experimental results.

Notes

1. This, of course, requires retaining *all* data for this later check of coverage. An alternative suategy would be to retain only some subset of the data to lessen space requirements.

2. However, Mitchell [1978] describes one possible way to extend his technique to learn from inconsistent data. This is discussed in section 12.5.4.

3. The boundary sets S and G contain the most specific and general concept definitions in the set. These bound the set of all concept definitions in the version space—the version space contains all concept definitions as or more general than some element in S and as or more specific than some element in G.

4. The second metric pruned the same two results as the first metric, plus one additional result.

5. The size of the final version space is a useful measure of performance since it affects the time required to search for the best concept definition; the number of neighbors determines the size of boundary sets, which is in turn closely correlated to the computational complexity of incremental version-space merging [Hirsh 1990a].

References

[Dietterich el al. 1982]   Dietterich, T. G., London, B., Clarkson, K., and Dromey, G. Learning and inductive inference. In P. Cohen and E. A. Feigenbaum, editors, *The Handbook of Artificial Intelligence*, Vol. 3, pp. 325–334. William Kaufmann, Los Altos, CA, 1982.

[Drastal et al. 1989]   Drastal, G., Meunier, R., and Raatz, S. Error correction in constructive induction. In *Proceedings of the Sixth International Workshop on Machine Learning*, pp. 81–83. Ithaca, NY, 1989.

[Fisher 1936]   Fisher, R. A. The use of multiple measurements in taxonomic problems. *Annual Eugenics* 7:179–188, 1936. Also in *Contributions to Mathematical Statistics*, John Wiley and Sons, New York, 1950.

[Haussler 1988]   Haussler, D. Quantifying inductive bias: AI learning algorithms and Valiant's learning framework. *Artificial Intelligence* 26 (2): 177–221, 1988.

[Hirsh 1989]   Hirsh, H. Combining empirical and analytical learning with version spaces. In *Proceedings of the Sixth International Workshop on Machine Learning*, pp. 29–33. Ithaca, NY, 1989.

[Hirsh 1990a]   Hirsh, H. *Incremental Version-Space Merging: A General Framework for Concept Learning*. Kluwer, Boston, MA, 1990.

[Hirsh 1990b]   Hirsh, H. Incremental version-space merging. In *Proceedings of the Seventh International Conference on Machine Learning*, pp. 330–338. Austin, TX, 1990.

[Hirsh 1990c]   Hirsh, H. Learning from data with bounded inconsistency. In *Proceedings of the Seventh International Conference on Machine Learning*, pp. 32–39. Austin, TX, 1990.

[Laird 1988]   Laird, P. *Learning from Good and Bad Data*. Kluwer, Boston, MA, 1988.

[Michalski and Larson 1978]   Michalski, R. S., and Larson, J. B. Selection of most representative training examples and incremental generation of v11 hypotheses: The underlying methodology and description of programs ESEL and AQ11. Report 867, University of Illinois, 1978.

[Mitchell 1978]   Mitchell, T. M. Version Spaces: An Approach to Concept Learning. Ph.D. thesis, Stanford University, 1978.

[Mitchell 1982]   Mitchell, T. M. Generalization as search. *Artificial Intelligence* 18 (2): 203–226, 1982.

[Quinlan 1986]   Quinlan, J. R. The effect of noise on concept learning. In R. S. Michalski, J. G. Carbonell, and T. M. Mitchell, editors, *Machine Learning. An Artificial Intelligence Approach*, Vol. 2, pp. 149–166. Morgan Kaufmann, Los Altos, CA, 1986.

[Rivest 1987]   Rivest, R. L. Learning decision lists. *Machine Learning* 2 (3): 229–246, 1987.

[Simon and Lea 1974]   Simon, H., and Lea, G. Problem solving and rule induction. In H. Simon, editor, *Models of Thought*, pp. 329–346. Yale University Press, New Haven, CT, 1974.

[Valiant 1984]   Valiant, L. G. A theory of the learnable. *Communications of the ACM* 27 (11): 1134–1142, 1984.

[Weiss and Kulikowski 1991]   Weiss, S. M., and Kulikowski, C. A. *Computer Systems That Learn*. Morgan Kaufmann, Los Altos, CA, 1991.

13 How Fast Can a Threshold Gate Learn?

Wolfgang Maass and György Turán

13.1 Introduction

A *threshold gate* G with weights $w_1, \ldots, w_d \in \mathbf{R}$ and threshold $t \in \mathbf{R}$ computes the following function from $\{0,1\}^d$ to $\{0,1\}$: for inputs $x_1, \ldots, x_d \in \{0,1\}$ it outputs 1 if $\sum_{i=1}^d w_i x_i \geq t$, else it outputs 0. Any function that can be computed by such a gate G is called a *threshold function*. For any $\mathbf{w} = (w_1, \ldots, w_d) \in \mathbf{R}^d$ and $t \in \mathbf{R}$ one also refers to

$$H_{\mathbf{w},t} := \left\{ (x_1, \ldots, x_d) \in \{0,1\}^d \,\middle|\, \sum_{i=1}^d w_i x_i \geq t \right\}$$

as a *halfspace over* $\{0,1\}^d$. This is motivated by the fact that $H_{\mathbf{w},t} = F_{\mathbf{w},t} \cap \{0,1\}^d$, where

$$F_{\mathbf{w},t} = \left\{ (x_1, \ldots, x_d) \in \mathbf{R}^d \,\middle|\, \sum_{i=1}^d w_i x_i \geq t \right\}$$

is a halfspace over $\mathbf{R}^d$. Thus the notions of a threshold gate, a threshold function, and a halfspace over $\{0,1\}^d$ are equivalent and will be used interchangeably. The class of all halfspaces over $\{0,1\}^d$ is denoted by HALFSPACE$_2^d$.

A threshold gate may be viewed as a simple mathematical model of the computational abilities of a neuron (McCulloch and Pitts 1943, Rosenblatt 1962, Minsky and Papert 1988, Hopfield 1982), and it forms the basic building block of neural networks (Rumelhart and McClelland 1986). Particular attention has been given to the question whether it is necessary to "program" a threshold gate by explicitly providing the parameters $\mathbf{w}$ and t, or whether the threshold gate can automatically *learn* these parameters from its own *errors* in a feasible number of steps.

This question can be made more precise by introducing some standard notions from computational learning theory (Angluin 1988).

The learning task is to identify an unknown *target* halfspace H_T from HALFSPACE$_2^d$. A *learning algorithm* (or *learner*) A proposes *hypotheses* H from HALFSPACE$_2^d$. If the current hypothesis H is incorrect, that is, $H \neq H_T$, then the learner receives a *counterexample* $\mathbf{x}$ from $(H_T \setminus H) \cup (H \setminus H_T)$. In other words, $\mathbf{x}$ is an input which is processed incorrectly by the threshold gate with the current weights and the current threshold. After such an *error* the values of the parameters are changed according to the learning algorithm A, to obtain a new hypothesis. The new hypothesis may also depend on the previous counterexamples, that is, on the "history" of the learning process.

The learning complexity $LC(A)$ of the learning algorithm A is the largest number of errors that may occur before A identifies the target halfspace, for any target halfspace and any choice of the counterexamples. $LC(A)$ is also called the *mistake bound* of A (Littlestone 1988). The *learning complexity* LC (HALFSPACE$_2^d$) of HALFSPACE$_2^d$ is

$LC(\text{HALFSPACE}_2^d) := \min\{LC(A) | A$ is a learning algorithm for HALFSPACE$_2^d\}$.

One can now rephrase the question whether a threshold gate can learn within a feasible number of steps as the question whether $LC(\text{HALFSPACE}_2^d)$ is bounded by a polynomial in d.

This learning problem has been studied in particular in the context of *perceptrons* (Rosenblatt 1962, Minsky and Papert 1988, Nilsson 1965). These are circuits consisting of several gates where only the last gate is a threshold gate with variable weights and threshold.

Rosenblatt has shown that the learning complexity of the so-called perceptron algorithm (or Hebb's rule) for learning a halfspace over $\{0, 1\}^d$ is finite (Rosenblatt 1962, Minsky and Papert 1988). However, the learning complexity of this algorithm is clearly not polynomial in d (see section 13.6). Littlestone (1988) proposed other learning algorithms for threshold gates (Winnow 1, Winnow 2), but it has remained open whether these can learn all monotone target halfspaces in HALFSPACE$_2^d$ with a polynomial number of mistakes (as the Winnow algorithms only produce nonnegative weights they cannot learn nonmonotone target halfspaces).

In this chapter we show that $LC(\text{HALFSPACE}_2^d)$ is polynomial in d.

More generally, we consider threshold gates with d inputs from $\{0, \ldots, n - 1\}$. This gives a somewhat more realistic model (see the discussion in Hampson and Volper 1990) and leads to interesting learning problems even in the case when $d = 2$. A threshold gate with d inputs from $\{0, \ldots, n - 1\}$ accepts the set

$$H_{\mathbf{w},t} := \left\{ (x_1, \ldots, x_d) \in \{0, \ldots, n - 1\}^d \, \middle| \, \sum_{i=1}^{d} w_i x_i \geq t \right\} = F_{\mathbf{w},t} \cap \{0, \ldots, n - 1\}^d,$$

called a *halfspace over* $\{0, \ldots, n - 1\}^d$. The class of all halfspaces over

$\{0, \ldots, n-1\}^d$ is denoted by HALFSPACE$_n^d$. The learning complexity $LC(\text{HALFSPACE}_n^d)$ is defined analogously to $LC(\text{HALFSPACE}_2^d)$ above. In section 13.3 we show that

$$LC(\text{HALFSPACE}_n^d) = O(d^2(\log d + \log n)),$$

that is, there is an algorithm for learning a halfspace over $\{0, \ldots, n-1\}^d$ which makes at most $O(d^2(\log d + \log n))$ errors. Furthermore, the number of computation steps executed by the algorithm is polynomial in d and $\log n$.

The new learning algorithms presented in this chapter are based on the existence of efficient algorithms in *convex optimization* for finding a point in a convex body given by a *separation oracle*. The latter algorithms can be used in particular to find a point in a polytope; thus as a special case one gets those linear programming algorithms which, instead of using an explicit representation of the input in the form of a list of the faces, access their input through a separation oracle. Both the *ellipsoid method* (Khachian 1979; see Grötschel, Lovász, and Schrijver 1988) and *Vaidya's algorithm* (Vaidya 1989) fit into this framework. Grötschel, Lovász, and Schrijver (1988) give a general theory, presenting several applications of this class of algorithms.

We observe that in fact *every* algorithm for finding a point in a convex body (given by a separation oracle) gives rise to a halfspace learning algorithm. The $O(d^2(\log d + \log n))$ learning algorithm is obtained by using the algorithm of Vaidya (1989).

It is substantially easier to design an efficient learning algorithm for halfspaces in Valiant's PAC-model (Valiant 1984) for batch learning. In this model one assumes the examples are drawn according to an arbitrary time-invariant distribution over the underlying domain, and it is sufficient to output an approximation to the target concept. It turns out that for a learning algorithm in the PAC-learning model it is sufficient to output any hypothesis that is consistent with the given set of examples (Blumer et al. 1989). Hence one can design a polynomial time computable learning algorithm for halfspaces in the PAC-learning model in the following way: one uses a computationally feasible algorithm for linear programming for the given set of positive and negative examples in order to compute some halfspace that is consistent with these examples. It is easy to see that this method is too weak to yield a learning algorithm with polynomial error bound in the model considered here for on-line learning. An on-line learning algorithm for halfspaces that always outputs hypotheses that are consistent with all previously seen counterexamples may make up to 2^d errors in the LC-model considered here. Hence a different approach is needed.

We also exhibit in this chapter an efficient learning algorithm for threshold gates that have more than two output values. A *multithreshold gate* G with weights $w_1, \ldots, w_d \in \mathbf{R}$ and s different thresholds $t_1 \leq \cdots \leq t_s$ $(t_1, \ldots, t_s \in \mathbf{R}, s \in \mathbf{N})$ is assumed to compute the following function $f_G : \{0, \ldots, n-1\}^d \to \{0, \ldots, s\}$:

$$f_G(x_1, \ldots, x_d) = \begin{cases} \max\left\{ j \,\middle|\, \sum_{i=1}^{d} w_i x_i \geq t_j \right\}, & \text{if this set is not empty,} \\ 0 & , \quad \text{otherwise.} \end{cases}$$

We write MULTITHRESHOLD$_n^{d,s}$ for the class of all functions computable by such multithreshold gates, for arbitrary weights and thresholds from $\mathbf{R}$. Note that MULTITHRESHOLD$_n^{d,s}$ contains various discrete approximations to the frequently considered *sigmoid* continuous threshold functions (Rumelhart and McClelland 1986). Another motivation for the investigation of multithreshold gates is the desire to explore simple models for the (very complicated) information processing capabilities of a neuron in a natural neural system. In a first approximation one may view the current firing rate of a neuron as its current output (see Rumelhart and McClelland 1986, Schwartz 1990). The firing rates of neurons are known to change between a few and several hundred firings per second. Hence a multithreshold gate provides a somewhat better computational model for a neuron than a gate that has only two different output signals. Muroga (1971), and Olafsson and Abu-Mostafa (1988) have previously investigated nonmonotone multilevel threshold functions. Multithreshold automata have been studied by Goles and Martinez (1981).

After defining a suitable extension of the learning model to the case of learning functions, we give in Theorem 4.1 an algorithm for learning multithreshold gates, for which the number of hypotheses required and the total amount of computation time of this learning algorithm are both bounded by a polynomial of d, s, and $\log n$.

We also consider in section 13.4 the problem of learning a halfspace over an *arbitrary* finite set $X \subseteq \mathbf{R}^d$, that is, learning a concept from the class

HALFSPACE$_X^d := \{ C \subseteq X \,|\, \text{for some } \mathbf{w} \in \mathbf{R}^d, t \in \mathbf{R} \text{ it holds that} \\ C = X \cap F_{\mathbf{w},t} \},$

where $F_{w,t}$ is a halfspace in $\mathbf{R}^d$ as defined above. Using a similar approach as in the previous learning algorithms and the existence of a centerpoint for every finite set in $\mathbf{R}^d$ (Yaglom and Boltyanskii 1961; see Edelsbrunner 1987), we present in Theorem 4.3 a learning algorithm that makes at most polynomial in d and $\log|X|$ many errors. This algorithm does not appear to have a computationally efficient implementation.

We also discuss in this chapter various lower bounds for the error bounds that can be achieved by arbitrary on-line learning algorithms for threshold gates. It is shown that the learning complexity of *every* algorithm learning a halfspace over $\{0,\ldots,n-1\}^d$ is $\Omega(d^2\log n)$ (without any assumption on the computational feasibility of the algorithm). Thus the upper bound mentioned above is optimal up to a factor of $\log d$. The lower bound in fact applies to a larger class of learning algorithms, where a hypothesis may be *any* subset of $\{0,\ldots,n-1\}^d$, and not just a halfspace. Recent results of Littlestone (see Maass 1991) imply that this lower bound remains valid even if the learner is allowed to use randomization, and the environment is assumed to be oblivious in presenting the examples.

One of the simplest threshold circuits consisting of more than one gate is the conjunction of two threshold gates, with two inputs from $\{0,\ldots,n-1\}$. Sets accepted by such circuits correspond to intersections of two halfplanes in $\{0,\ldots,n-1\}^2$. It is shown in Theorem 5.6 that *every* learning algorithm for this class requires $\Omega(n)$ hypotheses in the worst case. This complements the negative results of Blum and Rivest (1988) for the case of threshold gates with n Boolean input variables.

The perceptron learning algorithm (Hebb's rule) differs from our new learning algorithm for threshold gates insofar as it is a *distributed* algorithm: each weight can be thought of being controlled by a separate processor. We show that *every* distributed halfspace learning algorithm which satisfies a condition called *boundedness* (see section 13.6) is inherently slow. This condition is satisfied by all known distributed learning algorithms for threshold gates. In particular, it follows that the learning complexity of the Winnow algorithms of Littlestone (1988) is exponential in d.

This chapter is organized as follows. In section 13.2 we give a formal definition of the learning model considered. Section 13.3 contains the new learning algorithms for threshold gates. In section 13.4 we discuss learning a threshold gate with several outputs, and learning a halfspace over an arbitrary set. Section 13.5 contains the lower bound results. Distributed learning algorithms are considered in section 13.6. Open problems are discussed in section 13.7. The Appendix contains some technical details and the description of the convex optimization algorithms used in section 13.3.

This chapter provides complete proofs for a number of results that were announced in Maass and Turán (1989, 1990a). Complete proofs of other results from these papers are given in Maass and Turán (1990b, 1992).

13.2   Definitions

In this section we describe the general on-line learning model of Angluin (1988), which generalizes the classical learning models for perceptrons and neural networks. Littlestone (1988) introduced an equivalent version of this model.

A learning problem is specified by a *domain X* and a *concept class* $\mathscr{C} \subseteq 2^X$. The sets $C \in \mathscr{C}$ are called *concepts*. In this chapter X will always be a finite subset of $\mathbf{R}^d$.

The goal of the *learner* (or *learning algorithm*) is to identify an unknown *target concept* $C_T \in \mathscr{C}$, fixed in the beginning of the learning process by the *environment*. The learner proposes *hypotheses* $H \in \mathscr{C}$. If $H = C_T$ then the environment responds "yes." Otherwise, it responds with a *counterexample* x from the symmetric difference $H \triangle C_T := (C_T \setminus H) \cup (H \setminus C_T)$. If $x \in C_T \setminus H$ then it is called a *positive* counterexample; if $x \in H \setminus C_T$ then it is called a *negative* counterexample.

A learning algorithm for $\mathscr{C}$ is any mapping A which produces hypotheses

$$H_{i+1}^A := A(H_1^A, \ldots, H_i^A, x_1, \ldots, x_i)$$

from $\mathscr{C}$ which may depend on the previous hypotheses H_j^A and the counterexamples $x_j \in H_j^A \triangle C_T$ received. As in this chapter we only consider deterministic learning algorithms, the previous hypotheses may be suppressed as arguments of A.

The *learning complexity* of a learning algorithm A is defined by

$$LC(A) := \max\{i \in \mathbf{N} \mid \text{there is some } C_T \in \mathscr{C} \text{ and some choice of}$$
$$\text{counterexamples } x_j \in H_j^A \triangle C_T \text{ for}$$
$$j = 1, \ldots, i - 1 \text{ such that } H_i^A \neq C_T\}.$$

Note that in the definition of $LC(A)$ the amount of computation performed by A to determine the next hypothesis is not taken into consideration. The attention is focused on the amount of interaction between the learner and the environment. As will be noted later on, the learning algorithms presented in this chapter (with one exception) have the additional property that they are *computationally feasible* as well, in the sense that the required number of computation steps is bounded by a polynomial function of the input parameters.

The *learning complexity* $LC(\mathscr{C})$ of the concept class $\mathscr{C}$ is defined by

$$LC(\mathscr{C}) := \min\{LC(A)|A \text{ is a learning algorithm for } \mathscr{C}\}.$$

In sections 13.3 and 13.4 we consider the domain $\{0,\ldots,n-1\}^d$ and the concept class

$$\text{HALFSPACE}_n^d := \{C \subseteq \{0,\ldots,n-1\}^d | \text{for some } \mathbf{w} \in \mathbf{R}^d, t \in \mathbf{R} \text{ it holds}$$
$$\text{that } C = H_{\mathbf{w},t}\},$$

where for $\mathbf{w} = (w_1,\ldots,w_d) \in \mathbf{R}^d$, $t \in \mathbf{R}$,

$$H_{\mathbf{w},t} := \left\{(x_1,\ldots,x_d) \in \{0,\ldots,n-1\}^d \left| \sum_{i=1}^d w_i x_i \geq t\right.\right\}.$$

The definition of the other learning problems discussed will be given in the corresponding sections.

13.3 A Polynomial Time On-line Learning Algorithm for Threshold Gates

In this section we present learning algorithms for threshold gates with d inputs from $\{0,\ldots,n-1\}$, or equivalently, algorithms for learning halfspaces over $\{0,\ldots,n-1\}^d$.

There are several learning algorithms in artificial intelligence which proceed by updating the *version space*, that is, the set of concepts not ruled out by previous counterexamples (Mitchell 1977, Cohen and Feigenbaum 1982). The learning algorithms to be presented proceed similarly by maintaining an *approximation* of the version space. Typically the "real" version space is slightly enlarged to obtain a more tractable representation. The goal of a fast learning algorithm is to find a new hypothesis with the property that *every* counterexample to this hypothesis eliminates a *large* part of the version space. This guarantees that the version space shrinks fast, and the target concept is identified in few learning steps.

In the case of learning halfspaces we represent the considered concepts $C \in \text{HALFSPACE}_n^d$ by suitable points in $\mathbf{R}^d$. More precisely, we represent C by a point $\mathbf{w} \in \mathbf{R}^d$ such that $C = F_{\mathbf{w},1} \cap \{0, \ldots, n-1\}^d$, where $F_{\mathbf{w},1} = \left\{ \mathbf{x} \in \mathbf{R}^d \,\middle|\, \sum_{i=1}^{d} x_i w_i \geq 1 \right\}$. Hence we may view the version space as a subset of $\mathbf{R}^d$, and we can exploit its *geometrical structure*. The key property of the chosen representation of the version space is the following: any counterexample to some hypothesis $C \in \text{HALFSPACE}_n^d$ (represented by some point $\mathbf{w} \in \mathbf{R}^d$) does not just eliminate the point $\mathbf{w}$, but a whole halfspace in $\mathbf{R}^d$ that contains the point $\mathbf{w}$. Hence in order to guarantee fast learning, it is sufficient to choose as next hypothesis some $C \in \text{HALFSPACE}_n^d$ such that its representation $\mathbf{w}$ lies in the *center* of the remaining version space in $\mathbf{R}^d$. Different algorithms are obtained by using different notions of a center. In each case the essential property of the center $\mathbf{w} \in \mathbf{R}^d$ of the version space is that *every* halfspace that contains $\mathbf{w}$ contains a large portion of the version space.

This strategy is closely related to the *ellipsoid method for linear programming*, or more generally, for *convex optimization* (Khachian 1979; see Grötschel, Lovász, and Schrijver 1988, Schrijver 1986). It may be viewed as an extension of the paradigm of binary search to higher dimensions. The learning algorithm for halfspaces that is induced by the ellipsoid method maintains a d-dimensional ellipsoid which contains the current version space. In a learning step the algorithm poses that halfspace which is represented by the center of the ellipsoid as the next hypothesis. It turns out that a counterexample to this hypothesis eliminates a whole half-ellipsoid from the version space. The remaining half-ellipsoid is included in a new ellipsoid (having smaller volume than the previous one), and the algorithm proceeds to the next learning step. In order to show that this process identifies the target concept $C_T \in \text{HALFSPACE}_n^d$ after polynomially many iterations, one shows that the version space contains a small ball $B_T \subseteq \mathbf{R}^d$ such that *every* point in B_T is a representation for C_T. Obviously the described algorithm will identify C_T at the latest when the volume of the current ellipsoid is as small as the volume of B_T.

More generally, it holds that every convex optimization algorithm which can be formulated in a certain *oracle* model (to be defined below) can be used directly as a halfspace learning algorithm. Therefore we first formulate the convex feasibility problem in the oracle model and describe the reduction of halfspace learning to this problem. Having this reduction, one can simply "plug in" any convex feasibility algorithm which uses the oracle model to obtain a learning algorithm for halfspaces. In particular, the convex feasibility algorithm of Vaidya (1989) leads to the halfspace learning algorithm which is optimal up to a factor of log d.

The goal of the convex feasibility problem is to find a point in an unknown convex body $P \subseteq \mathbf{R}^d$ which has a *guarantee* r and is given by a *separation oracle*.

A guarantee $r \in \mathbf{N}$ for the convex body P is a number such that the *volume* of P within the ball of radius r around $\mathbf{0}$ is at least r^{-d}. Having a guarantee means that it is known in advance that the unknown convex body is "not too small."

Information about P can be obtained through the separation oracle. The oracle can answer queries of the form "$\mathbf{y} \in P$?," where $\mathbf{y} \in \mathbf{R}^d$. If $\mathbf{y} \in P$ then the response to the query is "yes," and the problem is solved. Otherwise the response is a halfspace $F = \{\mathbf{x} : \mathbf{c}^T\mathbf{x} \geq b\}$ such that $P \subseteq F$ but $\mathbf{c}^T\mathbf{y} \leq b$ (such a halfspace separates $\mathbf{y}$ from P, hence the name of the oracle). Furthermore, it is assumed that there is a polynomial p such that if $\mathbf{y}$ is m bits long then the response $(\mathbf{c}, b)$ of the oracle is not longer than $p(m, \log r, d)$ bits. In the case of separation oracles that arise in the learning problem considered here one has $p(m, \log r, d) = m + \log r + d$.

We will reduce the learning of halfspaces to the following problem in combinatorial optimization.

Convex feasibility problem: given a separation oracle and a guarantee r for an unknown convex body P, find a point in P.

We consider algorithms for the convex feasibility problem for which the number of oracle queries and the total number of computation steps performed are both bounded by functions of d and $\log r$. The *query complexity* $q(d, \log r)$ of such an algorithm is the number of queries required in the worst case. The *time complexity* $t(d, \log r)$ is the number of computation steps performed in the worst case.

THEOREM 3.1 *Assume that there is an algorithm A^* solving the convex feasibility problem with query complexity $q(d, \log r)$ and time complexity $t(d, \log r)$. Then there is a learning algorithm A for $HALFSPACE_n^d$ such that $LC(A) \leq q(d, 4d(\log d + \log n + 3)) + 1$, and the total amount of computation performed by A is at most $t(d, 4d(\log d + \log n + 3)) + q(d, 4d(\log d + \log n + 3)) \cdot p(d, \log n)$ for some polynomial p.*

Proof: Let the first hypothesis of A be $\{0,\ldots,n-1\}^d$. If a counterexample is received then this must be a negative counterexample $\mathbf{x}^* = (x_1^*,\ldots,x_d^*)$. This point will be considered the origin by transforming the domain to $U = \underset{i=1}{\overset{d}{\times}}\ \{-x_i^*,\ldots,n-1-x_i^*\}$. The subsequent steps of the learning algorithm will be described as learning a halfspace over this domain. It is straightforward to translate the hypotheses and the counterexamples between the two domains, contributing the overhead $q(d, 4d(\log d + \log n + 3)) \cdot p(d, \log n)$ to the total number of computation steps.

Let $C_T = \left\{\mathbf{x} \in \{0,\ldots,n-1\}^d \middle| \sum_{i=1}^{d} w_i x_i \geq t\right\}$ be the target concept. Because of the preceding first step of the learning algorithm and the subsequent transformation of the coordinate system we have $\mathbf{0} \notin C_T$. This implies that $t > 0$. Hence by multiplying with a positive constant it may be assumed that $t = 1$, that is, $C_T = F_{\mathbf{w},1} \cap U$. Define

$$\text{SOL}_{C_T} := \{\mathbf{u} \in \mathbf{R}^d | C_T = F_{\mathbf{u},1} \cap U\}.$$

If $\mathbf{x} \in C_T$ (resp. $\mathbf{x} \notin C_T$) then every $\mathbf{u} \in \text{SOL}_{C_T}$ must satisfy $\mathbf{u}^T\mathbf{x} = \sum_{i=1}^{d} u_i x_i \geq 1$ (resp. $\mathbf{u}^T\mathbf{x} < 1$). Conversely, if $\mathbf{u}$ satisfies these conditions for every $\mathbf{x} \in U$ then it belongs to SOL_{C_T}. Hence

$$\text{SOL}_{C_T} = \bigcap_{\mathbf{x} \in C_T} F_{\mathbf{x},1} \cap \bigcap_{\mathbf{x} \in U \backslash C_T} \overline{F_{\mathbf{x},1}}.$$

Thus SOL_{C_T} is the intersection of n^d halfspaces (the halfspaces corresponding to $U \backslash C_T$ are open). In particular, SOL_{C_T} is convex. Hence A^* can be used to find a point in SOL_{C_T}.

We need some standard bounds for linear inequalities to get a guarantee for SOL_{C_T}. The proof of the following lemma is given in the Appendix for completeness.

LEMMA 3.2 $2^{4d(\log d + \log n + 3)}$ *is a guarantee for* SOL_{C_T}.

Proof: See Lemma A2 in the Appendix.

The learning algorithm A proceeds as follows. It simulates A^* by presenting the hypothesis $F_{\mathbf{y},1} \cap U$ whenever A^* asks a query "$\mathbf{y} \in \text{SOL}_{C_T}$?". Hence to prove the theorem it is sufficient to show that a response to a query "$\mathbf{y} \in \text{SOL}_{C_r}$?" of algorithm A^* can be obtained from the counter-example $\mathbf{z}$ received after presenting the hypothesis $F_{\mathbf{y},1} \cap U$. Of course, if this hypothesis is correct, the learning process terminates.

Case 1: $\mathbf{z}$ is a positive counterexample.

This means that $\mathbf{y}^T\mathbf{z} < 1$ but $\mathbf{z} \in C_T$. Hence for every $\mathbf{u} \in \text{SOL}_{C_r}$ it holds that $\mathbf{u}^T\mathbf{z} \geq 1$. Thus $F_{\mathbf{z},1}$ is a separating halfspace for $\mathbf{y}$.

Case 2: $\mathbf{z}$ is a negative counterexample.

In this case $\mathbf{y}^T\mathbf{z} \geq 1$ but $\mathbf{z} \notin C_T$. Hence for every $\mathbf{u} \in \text{SOL}_{C_r}$ it holds that $\mathbf{u}^T\mathbf{z} < 1$. Thus $F_{-\mathbf{z},-1}$ is a separating halfspace for $\mathbf{y}$.

Therefore A can indeed simulate A^*, and the bounds for the complexity of A^* directly imply the claimed bounds for the complexity of A, taking also into account the overhead mentioned at the beginning of the proof.

Now we turn to the informal description of algorithms for the convex feasibility problem.

ALGORITHM 1   *the ellipsoid method (Khachian 1979, Grötschel, Lovász, and Schrijver 1988).*

The algorithm maintains a d-dimensional ellipsoid containing the unknown convex body. Initially the ellipsoid is the ball of radius r around the origin. The next query to the separation oracle is the center of the ellipsoid. The response to the query determines a halfspace. The intersection of this halfspace and the ellipsoid forms a half-ellipsoid containing the convex body. This half-ellipsoid is then included in an ellipsoid. As calculations are performed with finite precision, it is necessary to slightly enlarge this ellipsoid to compensate for rounding errors. This slightly enlarged ellipsoid is used in the next iteration. The volume of the new ellipsoid is smaller by a factor $e^{-1/5d}$ than the volume of the original ellipsoid. Hence as the volume of the initial ball is at most $(2r)^d$ and the volume of the unknown convex body within this ball is at least r^{-d}, the number of iterations necessary is at most $10d^2 \ln 2r$. In one iteration one has to perform $O(d^3)$ arithmetic operations assuming that the standard algorithm is used for multiplying matrices. It is sufficient to do the calculations with a precision of $O(d^2 \log r)$ bits. Hence, again assuming that the standard algorithms are used for the multiplication and division of numbers, the time complexity of the algorithm is $O(d^9 (\log r)^3)$.

Applying Theorem 3.1 with the ellipsoid method one obtains a half-space learning algorithm with learning complexity $O(d^3(\log d + \log n))$ and with time complexity polynomial in d and $\log n$.

We refer to the Appendix for further details.

ALGORITHM 2   *Vaidya's algorithm* (*Vaidya* 1989).

The algorithm maintains a full-dimensional polytope P defined by some of the halfspaces obtained as responses to previous queries. Thus P always contains the unknown convex body. The next query to the separation oracle is an *approximation* to the so-called *volumetric center* of P. Also, in order to prevent P from becoming too complicated, some of the inequalities defining P may be dropped.

The volume of P decreases by a constant factor on the average, where the constant is independent of d. Therefore the query complexity of the algorithm is $O(d \log r)$, and so one obtains a speedup d in query complexity compared to the ellipsoid method. The time complexity of the algorithm is given in Vaidya (1989) in the unit cost model, that is, each arithmetic operation is counted as one step. The number of arithmetic operations needed in one iteration is $O(d^3)$, again assuming that we use standard matrix multiplication. The precision required is polynomial in d and $\log r$ (Vaidya (1990)). Hence the time complexity of the algorithm is also polynomial in d and $\log r$.

We again refer to the Appendix for further details.

Thus we obtain the following upper bound for the complexity of learning a threshold gate.

THEOREM   3.3 $LC(\text{HALFSPACE}_n^d) = O(d^2(\log d + \log n))$. *The upper bound is achieved by a learning algorithm for which the total number of computation steps is polynomial in d and* $\log n$.

Proof: Apply Theorem 3.1 with the convex feasibility algorithm of Vaidya (1989).

13.4   Adaptive Threshold Gates with Graded Response and Real Valued Inputs

First we consider learning a function computed by a multithreshold gate, that is, identifying a *target function* from the class MULTITHRES-

HOLD$_n^{d,s}$ defined in the Introduction. We recall that a function f: $\{0,\ldots,n-1\}^d \to \{0,\ldots,s\}$ is in this class if there are $\mathbf{w} = (w_1,\ldots,w_d) \in \mathbf{R}^d$ and $\mathbf{t} = (t_1,\ldots,t_s) \in \mathbf{R}^s$ with $t_1 \leq \cdots \leq t_s$ such that for every $\mathbf{x} \in \{0,\ldots,n-1\}^d$ it holds that

$$f(\mathbf{x}) = \begin{cases} \max\left\{ j \,\middle|\, \sum_{i=1}^{d} w_i x_i \geq t_j \right\}, & \text{if this set is not empty,} \\ 0 & , \quad \text{otherwise.} \end{cases}$$

As the original learning model is defined for learning sets, one has to specify an extension of this model to the case of learning functions. We distinguish three different extensions M_1, M_2, and M_3, which differ in the type of feedback information that the learner receives when he makes an error. Analogously as before, the learner makes an *error* when for a hypothesis f he encounters an input $\mathbf{x}$, for which $f(\mathbf{x}) \neq f_T(\mathbf{x})$, where f is the current *hypothesis*, that is, the function computed by the gate with the current values of the parameters $\mathbf{w}$ and $\mathbf{t}$, and f_T is the target function.

In the weakest model M_1 the learner only receives the point $\mathbf{x}$ and the information that $f(\mathbf{x}) \neq f_T(\mathbf{x})$.

In the intermediate model M_2 the learner receives a pair $(\mathbf{x}, a)$, where $a \in \{0, 1\}$. If $a = 0$ then $f(\mathbf{x}) > f_T(\mathbf{x})$, that is, $f(\mathbf{x})$ is *too high*. If $a = 1$ then $f(\mathbf{x}) < f_T(\mathbf{x})$, that is, $f(\mathbf{x})$ is *too low*.

In the strongest model M_3 the learner receives the pair $(\mathbf{x}, f(\mathbf{x}))$, that is, he is told the correct output for $\mathbf{x}$.

The other aspects of these models are the same as before. In particular, a learning algorithm is a function which produces a new hypothesis, that is, new parameter values $\mathbf{w}'$ and $\mathbf{t}'$, in dependence of the total information received from the previous errors. The learning complexity of an algorithm is the number of errors it can make in the worst case, before identifying the target function f_T. The learning complexity $LC(\text{MULTITHRESHOLD}_n^{d,s})$ of the class of multithreshold functions is the minimum of the learning complexities of learning algorithms for this class.

Note that in the case $s = 1$ each model coincides with the original one.

The question we consider is whether there is a learning algorithm for MULTITHRESHOLD$_n^{d,s}$ which has learning complexity polynomial in d, s, and $\log n$.

It turns out that the first model M_1 is too weak for the existence of such an algorithm, even if both d and s are assumed to be constants ($d = s = 2$).

A lower bound demonstrating this will be presented in section 13.5 (Theorem 5.7). On the other hand, it is possible to give such algorithm in the *intermediate* model M_2 (which appears to be more realistic than the strongest model M_3). This follows from the observation that every half-space learning algorithm can be used to learn multithreshold functions and the results of the previous section. A reduction from multithreshold symmetric automata to binary threshold symmetric automata was previously given by Goles and Martinez (1981).

THEOREM 4.1 $LC(\text{MULTITHRESHOLD}_n^{d,s}) \leq LC(\text{HALFSPACE}_n^{d+s})$.

Proof: First we define a representation for multithreshold functions which is slightly more general than the one given above. For $\mathbf{u} :=
(w_1, \ldots, w_d, t_1, \ldots, t_s, b) \in \mathbf{R}^{d+s+1}$ we also write $\mathbf{u} = (\mathbf{w}, \mathbf{t}, b)$. Define $f_{\mathbf{u}}:
\{0, \ldots, n-1\}^d \to \{0, \ldots, s\}$ by

$$f_{\mathbf{u}}(\mathbf{x}) = \begin{cases} \max\left\{ j \,\middle|\, \sum_{i=1}^{d} w_i x_i \geq t_j + b \right\}, & \text{if this set is not empty,} \\ 0 & , \quad \text{otherwise.} \end{cases}$$

Clearly $f_{\mathbf{u}}$ is a multithreshold function with thresholds $t_1' \leq \cdots \leq t_s'$ defined by $t_j' := \min\{t_k + b \,|\, j \leq k \leq s\}$ for $j = 1, \ldots, s$. For each $\mathbf{u} = (\mathbf{w}, \mathbf{t}, b)$ we associate with $f_{\mathbf{u}}$ the halfspace $C = H_{(\mathbf{w}, -\mathbf{t}), b}$ from HALFSPACE_n^{d+s}, that is,

$$C = \left\{ (\mathbf{x}, \mathbf{y}) \in \{0, \ldots, n-1\}^{d+s} \,\middle|\, \sum_{i=1}^{d} w_i x_i - \sum_{j=1}^{s} t_j y_j \geq b \right\}.$$

In order to prove the theorem it is sufficient to show that for every learning algorithm A^* for HALFSPACE_n^{d+s} there is a learning algorithm A for $\text{MULTITHRESHOLD}_n^{d,s}$ simulating A^*, with $LC(A) \leq LC(A^*)$. Assume that a target function $f_T \in \text{MULTITHRESHOLD}_n^{d,s}$ has been fixed. Let $\tilde{\mathbf{w}} = (\tilde{w}_1, \ldots, \tilde{w}_d)$ and $\tilde{\mathbf{t}} = (\tilde{t}_1, \ldots, \tilde{t}_s)$ be parameters with $\tilde{t}_1 \leq \cdots \leq \tilde{t}_s$ such that

$$f_T(\mathbf{x}) = \begin{cases} \max\left\{ j \,\middle|\, \sum_{i=1}^{d} \tilde{w}_i x_i \geq \tilde{t}_j + b \right\}, & \text{if this set is not empty,} \\ 0 & , \quad \text{otherwise.} \end{cases}$$

We construct a learning algorithm A for $\text{MULTITHRESHOLD}_n^{d,s}$ that simulates the given learning algorithm A^* for HALFSPACE_n^{d+s} in a learning process for a corresponding target concept $C_T = H_{(\mathbf{w}, -\mathfrak{t}), 0} \in$ HALFSPACE$_n^{d+s}$. If A^* presents a hypothesis $H_{(\mathbf{w}, -\mathfrak{t}), b}$, then A presents the hypothesis $f_\mathbf{u}$, for $\mathbf{u} = (\mathbf{w}, \mathbf{t}, b)$. (To be precise, A outputs the standard representation $(\mathbf{w}, \mathbf{t}')$ for $f_\mathbf{u}$ with $t'_j := \min\{t_k + b | j \le k \le s\}$. But this is not relevant for the following.)

Now assume that A receives a pair $(\mathbf{x}, 0)$, that is, it gets a vector $\mathbf{x}$ such that $j := f_\mathbf{u}(\mathbf{x})$ is too high. Since $f_\mathbf{u}(\mathbf{x}) = j$ one has $\sum\limits_{i=1}^{d} w_i x_i \ge t_j + b$. This implies that $(\mathbf{x}, \mathbf{e}_j) \in H_{(\mathbf{w}, -\mathfrak{t}), b}$, where $\mathbf{e}_j := (0, \ldots, 0, 1, 0, \ldots, 0)$ is the jth unit vector in $\mathbf{R}^s$. Since $f_T(\mathbf{x}) < j$ it holds that $\sum\limits_{i=1}^{d} \tilde{w}_i x_i < \tilde{t}_j$, hence $(\mathbf{x}, \mathbf{e}_j) \notin C_T$. Thus $(\mathbf{x}, \mathbf{e}_j)$ is a negative counterexample for the hypothesis $H_{(\mathbf{w}, -\mathfrak{t}), b}$ of A^*.

If A receives as response a pair $(\mathbf{x}, 1)$, then $j := f_\mathbf{u}(\mathbf{x})$ is too low. This implies that $\sum\limits_{i=1}^{d} w_i x_i < t_{j+1} + b$, thus $(\mathbf{x}, \mathbf{e}_{j+1}) \notin H_{(\mathbf{w}, -\mathfrak{t}), b}$. On the other hand, $f_T(\mathbf{x}) > j$ implies that $(\mathbf{x}, \mathbf{e}_{j+1}) \in C_T$ (since $\tilde{t}_1 \le \cdots \le \tilde{t}_s$). Hence in this case $(\mathbf{x}, \mathbf{e}_{j+1})$ is a positive counterexample for $H_{(\mathbf{w}, -\mathfrak{t}), b}$.

Thus every hypothesis of A^* is translated to a hypothesis of A, and every counterexample for the hypothesis of A is translated to a counterexample for the hypothesis of A^*. Hence A can receive at most $LC(A^*)$ counterexamples, and thus $LC(A) \le LC(A^*)$, proving the theorem.

COROLLARY 4.2 $LC(\text{MULTITHRESHOLD}_n^{d,s}) = O((d+s)^2(\log(d+s) + \log n))$. The upper bound is achieved by a learning algorithm for which the total number of computation steps is polynomial in d, s, and $\log n$.

Proof: This follows directly from Theorems 3.3 and 4.1. Note that in the proof of Theorem 4.1 the computational overhead needed by A compared to A^* is clearly polynomial in d, s and $\log n$.

Now we turn to another extension of halfspace learning. Instead of the domain $\{0, \ldots, n-1\}^d$ we now consider as domain an arbitrary finite subset $X \subseteq \mathbf{R}^d$ and the concept class

HALFSPACE$_X^d := \{C \subseteq X | \text{for some } \mathbf{w} \in \mathbf{R}^d, t \in \mathbf{R} \text{ it holds that } C = X \cap F_{\mathbf{w}, t}\}$

of halfspaces over X. Learning a concept from this class corresponds to learning a threshold gate with d real valued input variables with inputs ranging over X.

How many hypotheses are needed to learn a halfspace over X? If we neither know anything about the number of digits needed to represent the elements of X, nor have any other information ensuring that X is not "too degenerate," then the approach of the previous section cannot be used. Without the guarantee r there is no upper bound on the number of iterations required before finding a point in the solution set. Nevertheless we show that by a different combinatorial argument one can give a learning algorithm of learning complexity $O(d^2 \log|X|)$ for every $X \subseteq \mathbf{R}^d$. For $X = \{0, \ldots, n - 1\}^d$ the learning complexity of this algorithm is comparable to the previous algorithms (the upper bound is slightly better than that of the ellipsoid method). On the other hand the algorithm seems to be inefficient computationally.

THEOREM 4.3   For every $X \subseteq \mathbf{R}^d$ it holds that

$LC(\text{HALFSPACE}_X^d) = O(d^2 \log|X|)$.

Proof: The proof is based on the notion of a centerpoint. A point $\mathbf{w} \in \mathbf{R}^d$ is called a centerpoint of a finite set $Y \subseteq \mathbf{R}^d$ if every open halfspace not containing $\mathbf{w}$ contains at most $\dfrac{d}{d+1}|Y|$ points from Y.

LEMMA 4.4   (Yaglom and Boltyanskii 1961; see Edelsbrunner 1987). Every finite set has a centerpoint.

Now let $X = \{\mathbf{x}_1, \ldots, \mathbf{x}_m\}$. The first hypothesis of the learning algorithm is again X. If a counterexample is received then this must be a negative counterexample, which will considered to be the origin. Thus we may assume that the target concept is of the form $C_T = X \cap F_{\mathbf{w},1}$ with $\tilde{\mathbf{w}} \in \mathbf{R}^d$. The second hypothesis is $\varnothing$. If a counterexample is received then this must be a positive counterexample $\mathbf{x}^*$.

Consider the hyperplanes E_i defined by $\mathbf{x}_i^T \mathbf{y} = 1$ in $\mathbf{R}^d$ for $i = 1, \ldots, m$. These hyperplanes partition $\mathbf{R}^d$ into convex regions such that $\mathbf{w}_1, \mathbf{w}_2 \in \mathbf{R}^d$ belong to the same region iff $\mathbf{x}_i^T \mathbf{w}_1 - 1$ and $\mathbf{x}_i^T \mathbf{w}_2 - 1$ have the same sign $(+, -, \text{ or } 0)$ for every $i = 1, \ldots, m$. One can easily show that for every target concept C_T the points $\mathbf{w}$ such that $C_T = X \cap F_{\mathbf{w},1}$ form one of these regions having a nonempty interior and some of the lower dimensional regions on its boundary.

Now select points $\mathbf{w}_1, \ldots, \mathbf{w}_s$, one from each full dimensional region contained in the halfspace $\{\mathbf{y}|(\mathbf{x}^*)^T\mathbf{y} \geq 1\}$. We shall use the fact that $s = O(m^d)$ (see Edelsbrunner 1987). The learning algorithm will identify that one of these points determines the target concept.

During the course of the algorithm we maintain a set $CAND$ of points which are not eliminated by previous counterexamples. Initially $CAND = \{\mathbf{w}_1, \ldots, \mathbf{w}_s\}$. If $|CAND| = 1$ then the learning process is completed.

If $|CAND| > 1$ then the next hypothesis is $X \cap F_{\mathbf{w},1}$ where $\mathbf{w}$ is a center-point of $CAND$. We have $\mathbf{w} \neq 0$ since $CAND \subseteq \{\mathbf{y}|(\mathbf{x}^*)^T\mathbf{y} \geq 1\}$ and $\mathbf{w}$ belongs to the convex hull of $CAND$.

If $\mathbf{x}$ is a positive counterexample to this hypothesis then $CAND$ can be updated to $CAND \cap \{\mathbf{y}|\mathbf{x}^T\mathbf{y} \geq 1\} \subseteq CAND \cap \{\mathbf{y}|\mathbf{x}^T\mathbf{y} > \mathbf{x}^T\mathbf{w}\}$, using $\mathbf{x}^T\mathbf{w} < 1$.

If $\mathbf{x}$ is a negative counterexample then $CAND$ can be updated to $CAND \cap \{\mathbf{y}|\mathbf{x}^T\mathbf{y} < 1\} \subseteq CAND \cap \{\mathbf{y}|\mathbf{x}^T\mathbf{y} < \mathbf{x}^T\mathbf{w}\}$, using $\mathbf{x}^T\mathbf{w} \geq 1$.

Thus in both cases one can apply Lemma 4.4 to conclude that $|CAND|$ decreases by a factor of at least $\dfrac{d}{d+1}$. Hence, using that $s = O(m^d)$ as noted above, the number of iterations needed to achieve $|CAND| \leq 1$ is $O(\log_{(d+1)/d}(m^d)) = O(d^2 \log m)$. This gives the claimed upper bound for the learning complexity of the algorithm.

13.5 Lower Bounds to the Complexity of Learning Algorithms for Threshold Gates

In this section we show that the learning algorithms of the previous sections are not too far from being optimal. Furthermore we show that there does not exist a fast learning algorithm for learning the intersection of two halfspaces.

First we consider the problem of learning a threshold gate with d inputs from $\{0, \ldots, n-1\}^d$, that is, learning a concept from HALFSPACE$_n^d$. In section 13.3 a computationally feasible learning algorithm was given for this problem, which identifies the target concept after at most $O(d^2(\log d + \log n))$ counterexamples.

The next theorem shows that *every* halfspace learning algorithm (even if it is not computationally feasible) requires in the worst case $\Omega(d^2 \log n)$ counterexamples.

THEOREM 5.1   If $d \geq 2$ then $LC(\text{HALFSPACE}_n^d) \geq \binom{d}{2}\log n$. If $d = 1$ then $LC(\text{HALFSPACE}_n^d) \geq \lfloor \log(n+1) \rfloor$.

Proof: In order to describe the argument it is useful to introduce the concept of a *decision tree*. A decision tree T for HALFSPACE$_n^d$ is a rooted binary tree with the following properties:

• Each inner node is labeled by an element **x** of $\{0,\ldots,n-1\}^d$ (representing a *query* "$\mathbf{x} \in C_T$?").

• There are two edges leaving each inner node, labeled "yes," resp. "no" (corresponding to possible answers to the query asked at the node).

• Each leaf is labeled by a concept from HALFSPACE$_n^d$ in such a way that each concept occurs as the label of exactly one leaf, and the label of every leaf is consistent with all labels along the path leading from the root to the leaf (the number of inner nodes along this path is the depth of the leaf).

Thus a decision tree can be thought of as describing an algorithm to learn a concept from HALFSPACE$_n^d$ in a learning model different from the one used in this chapter. In that model the learner can ask queries (called *membership queries*) to determine the membership of elements in the target concept.

The following lemma is a special case of a result of Littlestone (1988).

LEMMA 5.2   (*Littlestone* 1988). *Assume that there is a decision tree T for $HALFSPACE_n^d$ such that the depth of every leaf of T is at least t. Then $LC(HALFSPACE_n^d) \geq t$.*

Proof: Let A be an arbitrary learning algorithm for HALFSPACE$_n^d$. It has to be shown that for some target concept and for some choice of the counterexamples to the hypotheses of A, A needs at least t hypotheses before it can identify the target concept. It is convenient to imagine that the target concept is not decided in advance, but that there is an *adversary* providing the counterexamples to the hypotheses of A. The adversary uses T to determine his responses. The first counterexample is the element at the root. In general, the adversary moves down the tree, always giving the element **x** labeling the current node as a counterexample. If **x** was a positive (resp. negative) counterexample then he moves along the edge labeled "yes" (resp. "no"). As all concepts occurring as labels of leaves in the subtree below the current node are still candidates for being the target concept, the learning process has to continue until a leaf is reached. Thus by the assumption on T, the adversary forces A to ask at least t hypotheses.

This lemma is useful as it reduces the problem of proving a lower bound for every learning algorithm to the problem of constructing a single decision tree with the required property. Such a tree can be constructed using the standard proof for the lower bound to the number of threshold functions (see Muroga 1971, generalized to non-Boolean inputs in Hampson and Volper 1990).

LEMMA 5.3 *There is a decision tree T_n^d for $HALFSPACE_n^d$ with all its leaves having depth at least $\sum_{i=1}^{d} \lfloor \log((n-1)n^{i-1} + 1) \rfloor$.*

Proof: We argue by induction on d. For $d = 1$ the claim follows by considering the decision tree corresponding to binary search over the domain $\{0,\ldots,n-1\}$. For the induction step one relates $HALFSPACE_n^d$ to $HALFSPACE_n^{d-1}$ in a way that is easy to visualize for the case $d = 3$. Each concept in $HALFSPACE_n^2$ corresponds to a line L through the plane $\{0,\ldots,n-1\}^2 \times \{0\}$. Consider a hyperplane $H \subseteq \mathbf{R}^3$ that contains L. By rotating H around the axis L one can realize $|\{0,\ldots,n-1\}^2 \times \{1,\ldots,n-1\}| + 1 = (n-1) \cdot n^2 + 1$ different halfspaces from $HALFSPACE_n^3$ (provided that the angle of L is chosen in such a way that no hyperplane H with $L \subseteq H$ contains more than one point from $\{0,\ldots,n-1\}^2 \times \{1,\ldots,n-1\}$). For a precise proof of the induction step fix for any $d \geq 2$ a decision tree T_n^{d-1} for $HALFSPACE_n^{d-1}$ that exists by the induction hypothesis. Let T be a variation of T_n^{d-1} where every query $(x_1,\ldots,x_{d-1}) \in \{0,\ldots,n-1\}^{d-1}$ is replaced by the query $\{x_1,\ldots,x_{d-1},0\} \in \{0,\ldots,n-1\}^d$.

Now consider an arbitrary leaf ℓ of T_n^{d-1}. If $C_\ell \in HALFSPACE_n^{d-1}$ denotes the concept arriving at ℓ, and ℓ' denotes the leaf corresponding to ℓ in T, then it holds that

$$\mathscr{C}_\ell := \{C \in HALFSPACE_n^d \,|\, C \cap \{0,\ldots,n-1\}^{d-1} \times \{0\} = C_\ell\}$$

is the class of concepts arriving at ℓ'.

We fix weights $w_1, \ldots, w_{d-1} \in \mathbf{R}$ and a threshold $t \in \mathbf{Q}$ such that $C_\ell = \left\{ x \in \mathbf{R}^{d-1} \,\middle|\, \sum_{i=1}^{d-1} w_i x_i \geq t \right\}$ and $1, w_1, \ldots, w_{d-1}$ are linearly independent over $\mathbf{Q}$. The linear independence can be achieved since for a suitable fixed threshold $t \in \mathbf{Q}$ one can choose the representation $(w_1,\ldots,w_{d-1})$ of C_ℓ arbitrarily from some small ball in $\mathbf{R}^{d-1}$ (see Lemma 3.2).

Now add a dth weight $w_d \in \mathbf{R}$ and let $\mathbf{w} := (w_1, \ldots, w_d)$. Then

$$
H_{\mathbf{w},t} = \left\{ (x_1, \ldots, x_d) \in \{0, \ldots, n-1\}^d \,\middle|\, \sum_{i=1}^{d-1} w_i x_i + w_d x_d \geq t \right\}
$$

$$
= C_l \times \{0\} \cup \left\{ (x_1, \ldots, x_d) \in \{0, \ldots, n-1\}^{d-1} \right.
$$

$$
\left. \times \{1, \ldots, n-1\} \,\middle|\, \sum_{i=1}^{d-1} w_i x_i + w_d x_d \geq t \right\}.
$$

As w_d increases from $-\infty$ to $+\infty$, $H_{\mathbf{w},t}$ increases from $C_l \times \{0\}$ to $C_l \times \{0\} \cup (\{0, \ldots, n-1\}^{d-1} \times \{1, \ldots, n-1\})$. An element $(x_1, \ldots, x_d) \in \{0, \ldots, n-1\}^{d-1} \times \{1, \ldots, n-1\}$ enters $H_{\mathbf{w},t}$ for

$$
w_d = \frac{t - \sum_{i=1}^{d-1} w_i x_i}{x_d}.
$$

Thus by the assumption on the w_i's we get $(n-1)n^{d-1} + 1$ different concepts, ordered under inclusion corresponding to the linear ordering $\prec$ of $\{0, \ldots, n-1\}^{d-1} \times \{1, \ldots, n-1\}$ according to the value of $\dfrac{t - \sum_{i=1}^{d-1} w_i x_i}{x_d}$.

Hence one can perform a binary search on $\prec$ to identify one of these concepts. As there may be other extensions of $C_l \times \{0\}$ which are not in this sequence of concepts, it may be necessary to add further queries after completing the binary search to identify a concept.

Let T_n^d be the decision tree for HALFSPACE$_n^d$ obtained from T by appending to each leaf of T the subtree that implements the queries described above. As the depth of each subtree is at least $\lfloor \log((n-1)n^{d-1} + 1) \rfloor$, Lemma 5.3 follows from the induction hypothesis.

To complete the proof of Theorem 5.1 note that the bound for $d = 1$ follows directly from considering binary search. If $d \geq 2$, $n \geq 3$ then

$$
\sum_{i=1}^{d} \lfloor \log((n-1)n^{i-1} + 1) \rfloor \geq d \log(n-1) + \binom{d}{2} \log n - d \geq \binom{d}{2} \log n,
$$

and if $d \geq 2$, $n = 2$ then

$$
\sum_{i=1}^{d} \lfloor \log(2^{i-1} + 1) \rfloor = \binom{d}{2}.
$$

With the same induction argument as in the proof of Lemma 5.3 one can derive the following lower bound for the number of concepts in $HALFSPACE_n^d$. This lower bound is a slight improvement of the lower bound of $n^{(d/2)}$ in Hampson and Volper (1990). We will use this lower bound in the proof of Theorem 6.1.

PROPOSITION 5.4 $|HALFSPACE_n^d| \geq n^{(d/2)} \cdot (n-1)^d$.

We note that the lower bound of Theorem 5.1 holds for a larger class of learning algorithms, where the learner may propose *arbitrary* subsets of the domain $\{0, \ldots, n-1\}^d$ as hypotheses. It is easy to see that Lemma 5.2 remains valid with the same proof. (Littlestone 1988 also proved a converse of the lemma for this class of algorithms; see also Maass and Turán 1990b.) Hence one obtains the following lower bound result.

THEOREM 5.5 *Let A be a learning algorithm for $HALFSPACE_n^d$ which is allowed to use arbitrary subsets of $\{0, \ldots, n-1\}^d$ as hypotheses. Then for some target concept C_T and some choice of the counterexamples, the number of hypotheses used by A to learn C_T is at least $\binom{d}{2} \log n$ if $d \geq 2$, and at least* $\lfloor \log(n+1) \rfloor$ *if $d = 1$.*

Comparing the lower bound with the $O(d^2(\log d + \log n))$ upper bound of Theorem 3.4, one can conclude that allowing arbitrary hypotheses does not increase significantly the speed of on-line learning for halfspaces. There are classes for which this is not the case (see Angluin 1988 and Maass and Turán 1990b for surveys of the power of different formal models of on-line learning).

We note that recent results of Maass (1991) and Littlestone imply that the lower bound (multiplied by $\frac{1}{2}$) remains valid even if the learner can use randomization and the environment is assumed to present the examples in an oblivious manner.

In the remainder of this section we will present lower bounds for on-line learning of threshold circuits and multithreshold gates.

First we consider on-line learning for a simple type of *threshold circuit*, which is the conjunction of two threshold gates having fan-in 2, where the inputs of these threshold gates are from $\{0, \ldots, n-1\}$. The subsets accepted by the circuit with different choices of the weights and thresholds form the concept class

$2 - \text{HALFSPACE}_n^2 := \{C \cap C' | C \in \text{HALFSPACE}_n^2\}.$

As $LC(\text{HALFSPACE}_n^2) = O(\log n)$, it would be interesting to have a similarly efficient learning algorithm for $2 - \text{HALFSPACE}_n^2$ as well. It turns out that this is not possible.

THEOREM 5.6 $LC(2 - HALFSPACE_n^2) = \Omega(n)$.

Proof: We describe an adversary strategy which forces every learning algorithm to use $\Omega(n)$ hypotheses before it can identify the target concept.

Let $Q := \{(i,j) \in \{0,\ldots,n-1\}^2 | i \in \{0, n-1\} \text{ or } j = \{0, n-1\}\}$ be the perimeter of the domain $\{0,\ldots,n-1\}^2$ and $U := \left\{ \left(\left\lfloor \dfrac{n}{2} \right\rfloor + k, \left\lfloor \dfrac{n}{2} \right\rfloor + \ell \right) \right|$ $k = 0, 1, \ell = 0, 1 \right\}$ be the four corners of the unit square in the middle of the domain.

We observe that if H is a concept from $2 - \text{HALFSPACE}_n^2$ such that $U \subseteq H$ then it holds that $H \cap Q \neq \emptyset$. Indeed, consider a representation of H as $F_{w_1,t_1} \cap F_{w_2,t_2} \cap \{0,\ldots,n-1\}^2$, where F_{w_1,t_1} and F_{w_2,t_2} are halfplanes in $\mathbf{R}^2$. As the convex hull of U contains a circle of diameter 1, $F_{w_1,t_1} \cap F_{w_2,t_2}$ either contains one of the four cornerpoints $\{0,0\}, \ldots, \{n-1, n-1\}$ from Q, or it contains a segment of length at least 1 on one of the sides of the square determined by the cornerpoints. The latter implies that it contains a point from Q.

The adversary uses the following strategy. If the hypothesis $H \in 2 - \text{HALFSPACE}_n^2$ is such that $U \setminus H \neq \emptyset$ then he responds with an element of $U \setminus H$ as a positive counterexample. Otherwise the observation above implies that $H \cap Q \neq \emptyset$, and the response of the adversary is any element from $H \cap Q$ given as a negative counterexample.

Let us call a concept from $2 - \text{HALFSPACE}_n^2$ a *strip* if it is of the form $S \cap \{0,\ldots,n-1\}^2$, where S is bounded by two parallel lines touching the circumscribed circle of U. Clearly there are $\Theta(n)$ strips, and each element of Q is contained in only constantly many strips.

Now a positive counterexample of the adversary does not eliminate any strip as a candidate for being the target concept. A negative counterexample x from Q rules out only those concepts which contain x; hence it eliminates only constantly many strips. Thus every learning algorithm is forced to use the $\Omega(n)$ hypothesis before being able to identify the target concept.

Finally we show that the same argument implies a negative result for learning multithreshold gates, as mentioned in section 13.4.

We consider learning a target function f_T from MULTITHRES-HOLD$_n^{2,2}$, that is, a multithreshold function with inputs from $\{0,\ldots,n-1\}^2$, having two thresholds, assuming the weak model M_1. Here the response to each hypothesis f is counterexample $\mathbf{x}$ such $f(\mathbf{x}) \neq f_T(\mathbf{x})$. Thus the learner is not told whether $f(\mathbf{x}) > f_T(\mathbf{x})$ or $f(\mathbf{x}) < f_T(\mathbf{x})$.

THEOREM 5.7 *Every algorithm for learning a function from MULTI-THRESHOLD$_n^{2,2}$ in the model M_1 requires $\Omega(n)$ hypotheses for some target function and some choice of the counterexamples.*

Proof: A strip considered in the proof of Theorem 5.6 corresponds to two multithreshold functions with two thresholds, each assigning value 1 to points between the parallel lines, and 0, resp. 2 to the other two parts of the domain.

The adversary strategy is the following. If for the hypothesis function f there is some $\mathbf{x} \in U$ such that $f(\mathbf{x}) \neq 1$, then $\mathbf{x}$ is given as a counterexample. Otherwise, as outlined above, there must be a $\mathbf{y} \in Q$ such that $f(\mathbf{y}) = 1$, and this element is given as a counterexample.

As there are $\Theta(n)$ multithreshold functions corresponding to strips and each counterexample eliminates only constantly many from being a candidate for the target function, every learning algorithm is forced to present $\Omega(n)$ hypotheses.

13.6 Distributed Learning Algorithms

In this section we consider algorithms for learning a threshold gate which are *distributed* in the sense that the weights $w_1, \ldots, w_d$ and the threshold t are controlled by separate processors, with some limited amount of communication. Such learning algorithms are of particular interest in the context of computational brain models, where emphasis is on learning without a global control.

There are several important examples of distributed learning algorithms for threshold gates such as the perceptron algorithm (also called Hebb's rule; see Rosenblatt 1962, Minsky and Papert 1988, Rumelhart and McClelland 1986) and the Winnow algorithms (Winnow 1 and Winnow 2) of Littlestone (1988). All these learning algorithms have in common that w_i remains unchanged if for the current counterexample $\mathbf{x} = (x_1, \ldots, x_d)$ it holds that $x_i = 0$. Otherwise, if **x** is a positive counterexample then the perceptron algorithm replaces w_i by $w_i + 1$, and the Winnow algorithms replace w_i by αw_i (for some fixed constant $\alpha > 1$); if **x** is a negative counterexample then the perceptron algorithm replaces w_i by $w_i - 1$, Winnow 1 replaces w_i by 0, and Winnow 2 replaces w_i by $\dfrac{w_i}{\alpha}$. These algorithms have in common that there is a bounded number of different updating operations and that these operations commute. Hence they are *k-bounded* according to the following definition. We will show in Theorem 6.1 that all *k*-bounded learning algorithms are inherently slow.

DEFINITION *A learning algorithm A for $HALFSPACE_n^d$ is k-bounded (for some $k \in \mathbf{N}$) if the following conditions are satisfied.*

(a) There are $d + 1$ sets $S_1, \ldots, S_{d+1}$, where each S_i consists of at most k functions $h : \mathbf{R} \to \mathbf{R}$, such that $h \circ h' = h' \circ h$ for all $h, h' \in S_i$ $(i = 1, \ldots, d + 1)$.

(b) The hypotheses of A are updated in the following manner: assume that the sth hypothesis of A is $H_{\mathbf{w}(s), t(s)}$, where $\mathbf{w}(s) = (w_1(s), \ldots, w_d(s))$, and **x** is a counterexample to $H_{\mathbf{w}(s), t(s)}$. Then the next hypothesis $H_{\mathbf{w}(s+1), t(s+1)}$ is obtained by setting $w_i(s + 1) = h_i(w_i(s))$ for $i = 1, \ldots, d$, $t(s + 1) = h_{d+1}(t(s))$, where $h_i \in S_i$ for $i = 1, \ldots, d + 1$ (there is no limitation on the way in which the operations $h_i \in S_i$ are selected in each learning step).

We note that the definition of a k-bounded learning algorithm does not attempt to capture the intuitive notion of a distributed learning algorithm. However, a distributed learning algorithm where each processor can receive at any step only one of k possible signals from its environment (i.e., from the part of the input to which it has access, from other processors, and from the feedback device) is likely to be k-bounded (provided that the weight-change operations of each processor are commutative). In particular, the perceptron algorithm and the Winnow algorithms are k-bounded for $k = 3$. An example for a distributed learning algorithm for threshold gates that is not k-bounded can be found in Duda and Hart (1973). They discuss in Table 5.1 a variation of Hebb's rule where the increment depends also on the time step at which it occurs. Note that this algorithm requires more global control than Hebb's rule or the Winnow rule, since each processor must have access to a global clock. The following result gives a lower bound for the complexity of all k-bounded learning algorithms.

THEOREM 6.1 *Let A be a k-bounded learning algorithm for HALF-SPACE$_n^d$. Then A requires $n^{\Omega(d/k)}$ hypotheses for some target concept and some choice of the counterexamples.*

Proof: As the weight-change operations of A are commutative, the hypothesis of A depends only on *how often* each operation has been applied to the weights and the threshold. Thus within t steps A can produce at most $(t + 1)^{k(d+1)}$ different hypotheses. Hence if A can learn any target concept from HALFSPACE$_n^d$ within t steps it must be the case that

$$(t + 1)^{k(d+1)} \geq |\text{HALFSPACE}_n^d|.$$

From Proposition 5.4 one gets then

$$t + 1 \geq |\text{HALFSPACE}_n^d|^{1/k(d+1)} \geq (n^{(d/2)}(n - 1)^d)^{1/(k(d+1))} = n^{\Omega(d/k)}$$

if $d \geq 2$. If $d = 1$ then the bound follows as well, as $|\text{HALFSPACE}_n^1| \geq n$.

In several cases it is also of interest to study the efficiency of a halfspace learning algorithm for the case where all target concepts belong to a subclass of HALFSPACE$_n^d$ (e.g., monomials, in the case $n = 2$). Therefore we formulate a generalization of Theorem 6.1 which is proved by the same argument.

THEOREM 6.2 *Let A be a k-bounded learning algorithm which can learn with at most t hypotheses any concept from some concept class $\mathcal{C} \subseteq$ HALFSPACE$_n^d$. A is allowed to produce hypotheses from HALFSPACE$_n^d$ not belonging to $\mathcal{C}$. Then $t \geq |\mathcal{C}|^{1/(k(d+1))} - 1$.*

It is easy to see that the perceptron algorithm requires $n^{\Omega(d)}$ hypotheses to learn some target concepts as it increases each weight by at most 1, and there are concepts requiring weights of size $n^{\Omega(d)}$. This follows by a counting argument from Proposition 5.4; one can also construct concrete examples with this property (Hampson and Volper 1990). Thus Theorem 6.1 does not imply a new lower bound for this algorithm.

The Winnow algorithms modify the weights by multiplication, and thus they can produce exponential size weights in polynomially many steps. Hence the above counting argument cannot be used to prove a lower bound. On the other hand it follows from Theorem 6.2 that the Winnow algorithms need $2^{\Omega(d)}$ steps to learn some monotone Boolean threshold function, using the fact that there are at least $2^{(d/2)-d}$ such functions. This argument provides the first lower bound for the Winnow algorithms that is superpolynomial in d.

We close this section with a remark showing that in a sense the perceptron algorithm is an optimal k-bounded distributed halfspace learning algorithm.

Theorem 6.2 implies that if any k-bounded distributed learning algorithm can learn a class $\mathscr{C} \subseteq \text{HALFSPACE}_2^d$ with the number of hypotheses bounded by a polynomial in d, then $|\mathscr{C}| \leq 2^{O(d \log d)}$. The following proposition implies that this upper bound on the size of $\mathscr{C}$ is in fact optimal up to a constant factor in the exponent.

Let p be a polynomial and consider the concept class

$$\mathscr{C}_p := \{C \in \text{HALFSPACE}_2^d | C = H_{\mathbf{w},t} \text{ for some } \mathbf{w} = (w_1, \ldots, w_d) \in \mathbf{Z}^d, t \in \mathbf{Z}$$
$$\text{such that } |w_i| \leq p(d), i = 1, \ldots, d\}.$$

PROPOSITION 6.3   If $p(d) \geq d$ for every d, then $|\mathscr{C}_p| = 2^{\Theta(d \log d)}$, and the perceptron algorithm can learn any target concept from $\mathscr{C}_p$ with at most $O(d^2 p^2(d))$ hypotheses.

Proof: Consider $H_{\mathbf{w},t} \in \text{HALFSPACE}_2^d$ such that $\mathbf{w} = (w_1, \ldots, w_d)$, $(w_1, \ldots, w_{\lfloor d/2 \rfloor})$ is a permutation of $(1, 2, \ldots, \lfloor d/2 \rfloor)$, $w_{\lfloor d/2 \rfloor+1} = \cdots = w_d := -1$, and $t := 0$. Then it is easy to see that different permutations correspond to different concepts; thus $|\mathscr{C}_p| = 2^{\Omega(d \log d)}$. The upper bound for $|\mathscr{C}_p|$ is obvious. The upper bound for the learning complexity of the perceptron algorithm on concepts from $\mathscr{C}_p$ follows from the familiar upper bound on the complexity of this algorithm (see Minsky and Papert 1988).

13.7   Some Open Problems

Let $\mathscr{C}_{k,d}$ be the class of all monotone threshold functions for which only k of the d input variables are "relevant," that is,

$$\mathscr{C}_{k,d} := \Big\{ C \subseteq \{0,1\}^d | \exists \alpha_1, \ldots, \alpha_d, t \in \mathbf{R} \text{ such that } \alpha_1, \ldots, \alpha_d \geq 0,$$

$$\alpha_i > 0 \text{ for at most } k \text{ indices } i \in \{1, \ldots, d\},$$

$$\text{and } \forall x_1, \ldots, x_d \in \{0,1\} \Big((x_1, \ldots, x_d) \in$$

$$C \Leftrightarrow \sum_{i=1}^{d} \alpha_i x_i \geq t \Big) \Big\}.$$

Littlestone (1988) has shown that with the Winnow learning algorithm one can learn any target concept C_T from $\mathscr{C}_{k,d}$ with $O\left(\dfrac{k \log d}{\delta^2}\right)$ hypotheses from HALFSPACE$_2^d$, where δ is a separability parameter of C_T that may be exponentially small in k. It remains an open problem whether $LC^{\text{HALFSPACE}_2^d}(\mathscr{C}_{k,d})$ can be bounded from above by a polynomial in k and $\log d$ (the superscript HALFSPACE$_2^d$ indicates that the learning algorithm for $\mathscr{C}_{k,d}$ is allowed to use hypotheses from the larger concept class HALFSPACE$_2^d$).

It is shown in Theorem 5.6 that $LC(2 - \text{HALFSPACE}_n^2) = \Omega(n)$. However, it remains an open problem whether $LC(2 - \text{HALFSPACE}_2^d) = O(d^{O(1)})$. Note that the results of Blum and Rivest (1988) only imply that this polynomial error bound cannot be realized by a polynomial time computable algorithm (provided that $P \neq NP$).

Another important open problem is whether one can achieve polynomial upper bounds in the LC-model for these and other concept classes that correspond to feedforward neural nets of small depth, if one allows a larger hypothesis space (e.g., corresponding to neural nets of larger depth and size).

Finally some interesting problems related to *distributed* learning algorithms for threshold gates are left open by the results of section 13.6. In particular it remains open whether the lower bound of Theorem 6.1 remains valid without the condition of commutativity for the weight-change operation (see (a) of the definition of k-boundedness at the beginning of section 13.6).

Appendix

Lemma A1 is a standard upper bound for the size of a solution of a system of linear inequalities. In Lemma A2 we restate and prove Lemma 3.2.

LEMMA A1   *Let C be a halfspace over* $\{-n, \ldots, n\}^d$. *Then there are integers* $w_1, \ldots, w_d$, t *having absolute value at most* $2^{3d(\log d + \log n + 3)}$, *such that* $C = F_{\mathbf{w},t} \cap \{-n, \ldots, n\}^d$, *where* $F_{\mathbf{w},t} = \left\{(x_1, \ldots, x_d) \in \mathbf{R}^d \,\middle|\, \sum_{i=1}^{d} w_i x_i \geq t\right\}$.

Proof: Let $\tilde{\mathbf{w}} = (\tilde{w}_1, \ldots, \tilde{w}_d) \in \mathbf{R}^d$, $\tilde{t} \in \mathbf{R}$ such that $C = F_{\mathbf{w},t} \cap \{-n, \ldots, n\}^d$. Thus

$$\sum_{i=1}^{d} \tilde{w}_i x_i \geq \tilde{t} \quad \text{for every } (x_1, \ldots, x_d) \in C,$$

$$\sum_{i=1}^{d} \tilde{w}_i x_i < \tilde{t} \quad \text{for every } (x_1, \ldots, x_d) \in \{-n, \ldots, n\}^d \setminus C.$$

It may also be assumed w.l.o.g. that for every $(x_1, \ldots, x_d) \in \{-n, \ldots, n\}^d \setminus C$,

$$\sum_{i=1}^{d} \tilde{w}_i x_i \leq \tilde{t} - 1.$$

Indeed, as

$$\min \left\{ \tilde{t} - \sum_{i=1}^{d} \tilde{w}_i x_i | (x_1, \ldots, x_d) \in \{-n, \ldots, n\}^d \setminus C \right\} > 0$$

this can be achieved by multiplying with a sufficiently large positive constant. Hence $\tilde{w}_1, \ldots, \tilde{w}_d, \tilde{t}$ is a solution to the following system of $(2n + 1)^d$ linear inequalities in the variables $y_1, \ldots, y_{d+1}$:

$$\sum_{i=1}^{d} x_i y_i \geq y_{d+1} \quad \text{for every } (x_1, \ldots, x_d) \in C, \tag{1}$$

$$\sum_{i=1}^{d} x_i y_i \leq y_{d+1} - 1 \quad \text{for every } (x_1, \ldots, x_d) \in \{-n, \ldots, n\}^d \setminus C.$$

By setting

$$y_i = y_i^+ - y_i^- \quad \text{for } i = 1, \ldots, d + 1 \tag{2}$$

and adding $(2n + 1)^d$ slack variables δ_x we obtain the system

$$-\sum_{i=1}^{d} x_i(y_i^+ - y_i^-) + (y_{d+1}^+ - y_{d+1}^-) + \delta_x = 0 \quad \text{for every } \mathbf{x} = (x_1, \ldots, x_d) \in C,$$

$$\sum_{i=1}^{d} x_i(y_i^+ - y_i^-) - (y_{d+1}^+ - y_{d+1}^-) + \delta_x = -1 \quad \text{for every } \mathbf{x} = (x_1, \ldots, x_d)$$

$$\in \{-n, \ldots, n\}^d \setminus C, \tag{3}$$

$$y_i^+ \geq 0, \, y_i^- \geq 0 \quad \text{for every } i = 1, \ldots, d + 1,$$

$$\delta_x \geq 0 \quad \text{for every } \mathbf{x} \in \{-n, \ldots, n\}^d.$$

Clearly (3) has a solution which can be obtained from $\tilde{w}_1, \ldots, \tilde{w}_d, \tilde{t}$. The rows of the matrix A describing the first $(2n + 1)^d$ inequalities of (3) are linearly independent, as the coefficients of the δ's form an identity matrix.

Hence (3) has a basic feasible solution z (i.e., a solution for which the columns of A corresponding to positive components are linearly independent; this statement is Theorem 2.1 on p. 31 in Papadimitriou-Steiglitz 1982). The submatrix B formed by these columns has the following form (after rearranging some rows and columns):

C	0
D	I

where the elements of C and D are $0, \pm 1, \ldots, \pm n$, and C is a square matrix of size at most $2(d + 1)$. Hence $|\det B|$, and the absolute value of all sub-determinants of B is at most $(2(d + 1))! n^{2(d+1)}$. The right-hand sides of (3) are $0, -1$, and in each column of B there are at most $2d + 3$ elements for which the determinant of the matrix obtained by deleting the row and the column containing the given element is nonzero. Thus from Cramer's rule each component z_j of the basic feasible solution z can be written as $z_j = \dfrac{u_j}{\det B}$, where $u_j \in \mathbf{Z}$ and $|u_j| \leq (2(d + 1))! n^{2(d+1)}(2d + 3)$. Now an integer solution to (1) can be obtained from z using (2) and finally multiplying everything with the common denominator $|\det B|$. The absolute values of $w_1, \ldots, w_d, t$ obtained in this way are at most

$$2(2(d + 1))! n^{2(d+1)}(2d + 3) < 2^{1 + 2(d+1) \log(2(d+1)) + 2(d+1) \log n + \log(2d+3)}$$
$$< 2^{1 + 3d \log 3d + 3d \log n + \log 4d} = 2^{3d(\log d + \log n) + (1 + (3 \log 3)d + \log(4d))}$$
$$< 2^{3d(\log d + \log n + 3)},$$

where we use that $\log 3 < \tfrac{8}{5}$ and $d \geq 2$ (if $d = 1$, the claim is trivial).

LEMMA A2 $2^{4d(\log d + \log n + 3)}$ is a quarantee for SOL_{C_T}.

Proof: We have to show that the volume of $\mathrm{SOL}_{C_T} \cap B$ is at least r^{-d}, where $r = 2^{4d(\log d + \log n + 3)}$ and B is the ball of radius r around the origin. Let $\tilde{w} \in \mathbf{R}^d, \tilde{t} \in \mathbf{R}$ be values such that $C_T = F_{w,t} \cap U$, where $U = \underset{i=1}{\overset{d}{\times}} \{-x_i^*, \ldots, n - 1 - x_i^*\}$. Consider $C := F_{\tilde{w},\tilde{t}} \cap \{-n, \ldots, n\}^d$. By Lemma A1 there exist integers $w_1, \ldots, w_d, t$ of absolute value $\leq 2^{3d(\log d + \log n + 3)}$ such that $C = F_{\tilde{w},\tilde{t}} \cap \{-n, \ldots, n\}^d$. Then clearly $C_T = F_{\tilde{w},\tilde{t}} \cap U$ and as $0 \notin C_T$ it holds that $t > 0$.

Now let $\mathbf{w}^* := (w_1^*, \ldots, w_d^*)$, where $w_i^* = \dfrac{2w_i}{2t-1}$ for $i = 1, \ldots, d$. It is obvious that $C_T = F_{\mathbf{w}^*,1} \cap U$.

We will show that

$$\overset{d}{\underset{i=1}{\text{X}}} \left[w_i^* - \frac{1}{2tn\,d}, w_i^* + \frac{1}{2tn\,d} \right] \subseteq \text{SOL}_{C_T} \cap B.$$

Consider any $\mathbf{u} = (u_1, \ldots, u_d) \in \mathbf{R}^d$ with $u_i = w_i^* + \varepsilon_i$ for some arbitrary $\varepsilon_i \in \left[-\dfrac{1}{2tn\,d}, \dfrac{1}{2tn\,d} \right]$. We show that $C_T = F_{\mathbf{u},1} \cap U$. Consider any $(x_1, \ldots, x_d) \in U$.

(a) Assume $\mathbf{x} = (x_1, \ldots, x_d) \in C_T$. Then as $\mathbf{w}^T\mathbf{x} \geq t$, we get

$$\sum_{i=1}^{d} u_i x_i = \sum_{i=1}^{d} w_i^* x_i + \sum_{i=1}^{d} \varepsilon_i x_i = \sum_{i=1}^{d} \frac{2w_i}{2t-1} x_i + \sum_{i=1}^{d} \varepsilon_i x_i$$

$$\geq \frac{2t}{2t-1} - \frac{1}{2tn\,d} n\,d = 1 + \frac{1}{2t-1} - \frac{1}{2t} > 1.$$

Hence $(x_1, \ldots, x_d) \in F_{\mathbf{u},1}$.

(b) Assume $\mathbf{x} = (x_1, \ldots, x_d) \in U \setminus C_T$. Then as $\mathbf{w}^T\mathbf{x} \leq t - 1$, we get

$$\sum_{i=1}^{d} u_i x_i = \sum_{i=1}^{d} \frac{2w_i}{2t-1} x_i + \sum_{i=1}^{d} \varepsilon_i x_i \leq \frac{2(t-1)}{2t-1} + \frac{1}{2tn\,d} n\,d$$

$$= 1 - \frac{1}{2t-1} + \frac{1}{2t} < 1.$$

Hence $(x_1, \ldots, x_d) \notin F_{\mathbf{u},1}$.

Clearly $\mathbf{u} \in B$, thus $\overset{d}{\underset{i=1}{\text{X}}} \left[w_i^* - \dfrac{1}{2tn\,d}, w_i^* + \dfrac{1}{2tn\,d} \right] \subseteq \text{SOL}_{C_T} \cap B$. The volume of this box is $(tn\,d)^{-d} \geq (2^{3d(\log d + \log n + 3)} n\,d)^{-d} \geq r^{-d}$, proving the lemma.

Finally we give some details of the ellipsoid method and Vaidya's algorithm.

ALGORITHM 1   *The ellipsoid method.*

The bounds and the formulas are from Grötschel, Lovász, and Schrijver (1988). An ellipsoid $E(A, \mathbf{a})$ is given by its matrix A and its center $\mathbf{a}$ such that $E(A, \mathbf{a}) := \{\mathbf{x} \in \mathbf{R}^d | (\mathbf{x} - \mathbf{a})^T A^{-1}(\mathbf{x} - \mathbf{a}) \leq 1\}$.

The algorithm computes a sequence of ellipsoids $E(A_k, \mathbf{a}_k)$. The next query presented to the oracle is the center $\mathbf{a}_k$.

Initially $A_0 = r^2 I$, $\mathbf{a}_0 = \mathbf{0}$ (where r is the guarantee for the unknown convex body).

If the oracle returns the separating halfspace $F = \{\mathbf{x} | \mathbf{c}^T \mathbf{x} \geq b\}$ for the query $\mathbf{a}_k$, then the next ellipsoid $E(A_k, \mathbf{a}_k)$ is given by

$$\mathbf{a}_{k+1} :\approx \mathbf{a}_k + \frac{1}{d+1} \frac{A_k \mathbf{c}}{\sqrt{\mathbf{c}^T A_k \mathbf{c}}},$$

$$A_{k+1} :\approx \frac{2d^2 + 3}{2d^2} \left(A_k - \frac{2}{d+1} \frac{A_k \mathbf{c} \mathbf{c}^T A_k}{\mathbf{c}^T A_k \mathbf{c}} \right).$$

Here "$\approx$" means that all computations have to be done with a precision of $80d^2 \log 2r$ bits. The upper bound for the number of iterations necessary is $10d^2 \log 2r$.

ALGORITHM 2   *Vaidya's algorithm.*

The bounds and the formulas are from Vaidya (1989).

The algorithm maintains a pair $(Q, \mathbf{z})$, where $Q = \{\mathbf{x} \in \mathbf{R}^d | \mathbf{a}_i^T \mathbf{x} \geq b_i,\ i = 1, \ldots, m\}$ is a full-dimensional polytope and $\mathbf{z} \in Q$. The point $\mathbf{z}$ is an approximation to the *volumetric center* of Q, which is defined as follows.

The *logarithmic barrier* for Q is the function $-\sum_{i=1}^{m} \ln(\mathbf{a}_i^T \mathbf{x} - b_i)$. The Hessian of this function is given by

$$H(\mathbf{x}) = \sum_{i=1}^{m} \frac{\mathbf{a}_i \mathbf{a}_i^T}{(\mathbf{a}_i^T \mathbf{x} - b_i)^2}.$$

The volumetric center ω of Q is the minimum of

$$F(\mathbf{x}) := \frac{1}{2} \ln(\det(H(\mathbf{x}))).$$

The heuristic for considering ω given in Vaidya (1989) is that this is the point where the ellipsoid $\{\mathbf{y} \in \mathbf{R}^d | (\mathbf{y} - \mathbf{x})^T H(\mathbf{x})(\mathbf{y} - \mathbf{x}) \leq 1\} \subseteq Q$ (providing a local quadratic approximation to Q) has the largest volume. Hence using this point as the next query can be expected to eliminate a large portion of Q from consideration.

Let ε and δ be fixed constants such that $\delta \leq 10^{-4}$ and $\varepsilon \leq 10^{-3}\delta$.

The sequence of pairs generated by the algorithm is $(P_k, \mathbf{z}_k)$. Initially
$$P_0 := \left\{ \mathbf{x} \in \mathbf{R}^d \,\middle|\, x_i \geq -r \text{ for } i = 1, \ldots, d, \text{ and } \sum_{i=1}^{d} x_i \leq dr \right\} \text{ is a simplex, and } \mathbf{z}_o$$
is the explicitly computable volumetric center of P_0.

For a given pair $(P_k, \mathbf{z}_k)$ the algorithm performs the following computation. (In order to avoid additional indices, assume that $P_k = \{ \mathbf{x} \in \mathbf{R}^d \,|\, \mathbf{a}_i^T \mathbf{x} \geq b_i, \ i = 1, \ldots, m \}$.)

Compute $H(\mathbf{x})$, the quantities

$$\sigma_i(\mathbf{x}) := \frac{\mathbf{a}_i^T H(\mathbf{x})^{-1} \mathbf{a}_i}{(\mathbf{a}_i^T \mathbf{x} - b_i)^2} \quad \text{for } i = 1, \ldots, m,$$

$$\nabla F(\mathbf{x}) := -\sum_{i=1}^{m} \sigma_i(\mathbf{x}) \frac{\mathbf{a}_i}{\mathbf{a}_i^T \mathbf{x} - b_i}$$

and

$$Q(\mathbf{x}) := \sum_{i=1}^{m} \sigma_i(\mathbf{x}) \frac{\mathbf{a}_i \mathbf{a}_i^T}{(\mathbf{a}_i^T \mathbf{x} - b_i)^2}.$$

There are two cases.

Case 1: (Querying the oracle)

If $\sigma_i(\mathbf{z}_k) \geq \varepsilon$ for $i = 1, \ldots, m$ then present the query $\mathbf{z}_k$ to the oracle. Assume that the oracle provides a separating halfspace $F = \{ \mathbf{x} \in \mathbf{R}^d \,|\, \mathbf{c}^T \mathbf{x} \geq b \}$. Choose a β such that $\mathbf{c}^T \mathbf{z}_k \geq \beta$ and

$$\frac{\mathbf{c}^T H(\mathbf{z}_k)^{-1} \mathbf{c}}{(\mathbf{c}^T \mathbf{z}_k - \beta)^2} = \frac{\sqrt{\delta \varepsilon}}{2}.$$

Let P_{k+1} be obtained from P_k by adding the inequality $\mathbf{c}^T \mathbf{x} \geq \beta$. The point $\mathbf{z}_{k+1}$ is obtained by executing the following iteration $\lceil 30 \ln(2\varepsilon^{-4.5}) \rceil$ times:

$$\mathbf{z} \leftarrow \mathbf{z} - 0.18 Q(\mathbf{z})^{-1} \nabla F(\mathbf{z}).$$

Case 2: (Simplifying the polytope)

If the condition of case 1 does not hold then let i be a value for which $\sigma_i(\mathbf{z}_k)$ is as small as possible ($1 \leq i \leq m$). Let P_{k+1} be obtained from P_k by deleting the defining inequality $\mathbf{a}_i^T \mathbf{x} \geq b_i$. The point $\mathbf{z}_{k+1}$ is determined by executing the iteration

$$\mathbf{z} \leftarrow \mathbf{z} - 0.18Q(\mathbf{z})^{-1}\nabla F(\mathbf{z})$$

$\lceil 30 \ln(4\varepsilon^{-3}) \rceil$ times.

Now Vaidya (1989) showed that the volume of P_k is at most

$$d\left(\log r + \ln\left(\frac{2d}{\varepsilon}\right) + 1\right) + \ln(d + 1) - \frac{(k + 1)\varepsilon}{2}.$$

Hence the guarantee implies that the number of iterations needed is $O(d \log r)$.

Acknowledgment

We would like to thank David Haussler and Carsten Lund for their valuable remarks.

Note

Written under partial support by NSF grant CCR 890 3398 to W. Maass. G. Turán was partially supported by OTKA-501.

References

Angluin, D. (1988). Queries and concept learning. *Machine Learning* 2:319–342.

Blum, A., and Rivest, R. L. (1988). Training a 3-node neural network is NP-complete. In *Proceedings of the 1988 Workshop on Computational Learning Theory*, pp. 9–18. San Mateo, CA: Morgan Kaufmann.

Blumer, A., Ehrenfeucht, A., Haussler, D., and Warmuth, M. K. (1989). Learnability and the Vapnik-Chervonenkis dimension. *Journal of the ACM* 36:929–965.

Cohen, P. R., and Feigenbaum, E. T. (1982). *The Handbook of Artificial Intelligence.* Vol. 3. Los Altos, CA: William Kaufmann.

Duda, R. O., and Hart, P. E. (1973). *Pattern Classification and Scene Analysis.* New York: John Wiley and Sons.

Edelsbrunner, H. (1987). *Algorithms in Combinatorial Geometry.* (EATCS monographs on theoretical computer science. Vol. 10). Berlin, New York: Springer-Verlag.

Goles, E., and Martinez, S. (1981). A short proof on the cyclic behaviour of multithreshold symmetric automata. *Information and Control* 51:91–97.

Grötschel, M., Lovász, L., and Schrijver, A. (1988). *Geometric Algorithms and Combinatorial Optimization.* (*Algorithms and Combinatorics.* Vol. 2). Berlin, Heidelberg: Springer-Verlag.

Hampson, S. E., and Volper, D. J. (1990). Representing and learning Boolean functions of multivalued features. *IEEE Transactions on Systems, Man, and Cybernetics* 20:67–80.

Hebb, D. O. (1949). *Organization of Behavior.* New York: John Wiley and Sons.

Hopfield, J. J. (1982). Neural networks and physical systems with emergent collective computational abilities. *Proceedings of the National Academy of Sciences of the U.S.A.* 79:2554–2558.

Khachian, L. G. (1979). A polynomial algorithm in linear programming. *Doklady Akademii Nauk SSSR* 244, 1093–1096. English translation: *Soviet Mathematics Doklady* 20:191–194.

Littlestone, N. (1988). Learning quickly when irrelevant attributes abound: a new linear-threshold algorithm. *Machine Learning* 2:285–318.

Maass, W. (1991). On-line learning with an oblivious environment and the power of randomization. In *Proceedings of the 1991 Workshop on Computational Learning Theory*, pp. 167–175. San Mateo, CA: Morgan Kaufmann.

Maass, W., and Turán, Gy. (1989). On the complexity of learning from counterexamples. In *Proceedings of the Thirtieth Annual Symposium on Foundations of Computer Science*, pp. 262–267. Washington, DC: IEEE Computer Society Press.

Maass, W., and Turán, Gy. (1990a). On the complexity of learning from counterexamples and membership queries. In *Proceedings of the Thirty-First Annual Symposium on Foundations of Computer Science*, pp. 203–210. Washington, DC: IEEE Computer Society Press.

Maass, W., and Turán, Gy. (1990b). Algorithms and lower bounds for on-line learning of geometrical concepts. To appear in *Machine Learning*.

Maass, W., and Turán, Gy. (1992). Lower bound methods and separation results for on-line learning models. *Machine Learning* 9:107–145.

McCulloch, W. S., and Pitts, W. (1943). A logical calculus of ideas imminent in neural nets. *Bulletin of Mathematical Biophysics* 5:115–137.

Minsky, M., and Papert, S. (1988). *Perceptrons: an Introduction to Computational Geometry*, Expanded edition. Cambridge, MA: MIT Press.

Mitchell, J. M. (1977). Version spaces: a candidate elimination approach to rule learning. In *Fifth International Joint Conference on Artificial Intelligence*, Morgan Kaufmann, Los Altos. pp. 305–310.

Muroga, S. (1971). *Threshold Logic and Its Applications*. New York: John Wiley and Sons.

Nilsson, N. J. (1965). *Learning Machines*. New York: McGraw-Hill.

Olafsson, S., and Abu-Mostafa, Y. S. (1988). The capacity of a multilevel threshold function. *IEEE Transactions on Pattern Analysis and Machine Intelligence* 10:277–281.

Papadimitriou, C. H., and Steiglitz, K. (1982). *Combinatorial Optimization: Algorithms and Complexity*. Englewood Cliffs, NJ: Prentice-Hall.

Rosenblatt, F. (1962). *Principles of Neurodynamics*. New York: Spartan Books.

Rumelhart, D. E., and McClelland, J. L. (1986). *Parallel Distributed Processing: Explorations in the Microstructure of Cognition*. Cambridge, MA: MIT Press.

Schrijver, A. (1986). *Theory of Linear and Integer Programming*. New York: John Wiley and Sons.

Schwartz, E. L. (1990). *Computational Neuroscience*. Cambridge, MA: MIT Press.

Vaidya, P. M. (1989). A new algorithm for minimizing convex functions over convex sets. In *Proceedings of the Thirtieth Annual Symposium on Foundations of Computer Science*, pp. 338–343. Washington, DC: IEEE Computer Society Press.

Vaidya, P. M. (1990). Personal communication.

Valiant, L. G. (1984). A theory of the learnable. *Communications of the ACM* 27:1134–1142.

Yaglom, M., and Boltyanskii, V. G. (1961). *Convex Figures*. Translated by P. Kelly and L. Walton. New York: Holt, Rinehart and Winston.

14 When Are k-Nearest Neighbor and Backpropagation Accurate for Feasible-Sized Sets of Examples?

Eric B. Baum

14.1 Introduction

When we learn in a natural environment, we are confronted with a rich and varied world. There is a nearly endless number of features we might observe. Almost all of these, however, will be irrelevant to any specific learning goal. Any particular concept we wish to learn may depend only on some simple, low-parameter function of some subset of the possible features. For example, one would like a learning algorithm that, shown images of hand-drawn numerals, could learn to read them correctly. Is it possible just to feed into our learning algorithm the images, containing as many features as there are pixels, or must we preprocess and extract relevant features such as line ends? A key question, then, is whether it is possible to learn simple concepts in a high-dimensional feature space using resources—time and information—bounded by some (hopefully low order) polynomial in n, the number of features.

The observation that various simple statistical pattern-recognition algorithms seem to require a number of examples exponential in the dimension of the feature space has been dubbed the curse of dimensionality (Duda and Hart 1973, 95). Recently it has been possible in a quite general context to analyze how many examples are necessary for training a neural net, provided they can be successfully loaded. The answer does not seem catastrophic and in fact bodes well for learning. Theorems have been proved that give upper and lower bounds that differ only by constant and log factors, on the number of examples necessary to achieve generalization. Very roughly speaking, these results indicate that if M random examples can be loaded onto a feedforward neural net with W weights and one output, one expects generalization so that about a fraction W/M of future test examples will be missclassified. In section 14.2, I will briefly review these results and give some intuitive arguments as to why they hold. In section 14.3, I discuss some simple experiments that clarify the practical consequences of these results. The experiments indicate that the large constant factors appearing in the theorems are close to one in actual practice but also seem to indicate that the degree of generalization actually achieved depends in some measure on the complexity of the target function. The key assumption in these theorems, of course, is that we are able to load the examples. Thus, while we have achieved some handle on how much information is necessary for learning, we have almost no understanding of when we can learn in a feasible amount of time.

The PAC learning model proposed by Valiant (1984) provides a reasonable theoretical model in which to consider this question. We assume we are given examples drawn from some probability distribution D over some feature space, $\Re^n$ or $\{1, -1\}^n$, say, and classified according to some Boolean target function f. Thus, examples consist of pairs $\vec{x}, f(\vec{x}))$, where $\vec{x}$ is a feature vector drawn acording to some natural distribution D of examples and $f(\vec{x})$ is a classification that $\vec{x}$ is either a positive or negative example of the target concept. We are told that $f \in F$, where F is some simple class of Boolean functions. We ask when there is some learning algorithm A that can look at examples and produce, in time polynomial in n, ε^{-1}, and δ^{-1} a hypothesis g that will with probability $1 - \delta$ correctly classify at least a fraction $1 - \varepsilon$ of future examples drawn from D. The acronym PAC stands for "probably almost correct"—probably (with confidence $1 - \delta$) the learning algorithm generates a classifier that is almost correct (makes a fraction smaller than ε of classification errors).

Thus, for example, the class F might consist of the class of half-spaces: $F = \{f(x): f(x) = \theta(w \cdot x - t), w \in \Re^n, t \in \Re\}$ where $\theta(x)$ is the Heaviside function, $\theta(y) = 1, y \geq 0; \theta(y) = 0, y < 0$. F therefore consists of the class of functions computable by a single linear threshold unit. Notice here that there is one simple feature that sums up the relevant information: $w \cdot x$. Other components of $\vec{x}$ are irrelevant. For this simple case, one can in fact give fast-learning algorithms. Under reasonable assumptions about the distribution D, the perceptron algorithm can be proved to learn very rapidly (Baum 1989b). With no assumptions on D at all, learning algorithms based on Karmarkar's algorithm can be proved to work rapidly (Blumer et al. 1987). However, already when the class F consists of a union of two half-spaces, $F = \{f: f(x) = 1 \text{ if } w_1 \cdot x - t_1 > 0 \text{ or } w_2 \cdot x - t_2 > 0, \text{ else } f(x) = 0 \text{ for some } w_1, w_2 \in \Re^n, t_1, t_2 \in \Re\}$, it is far from clear that an algorithm can be given that will learn in polynomial time. In this case there are two simple features that would suffice to render the problem trivial, but it is unclear whether there is any learning algorithm that can rapidly uncover them.[1]

If we could prove that it is not possible to learn rapidly the class F of unions of two halfspaces, that would be evidence that automatic learning is impossible. My personal philosophy in answering this would be that humans are capable of learning in the natural world. Therefore, a proof within some model of learning that learning is not feasible is an indictment of the model. We should examine the model to see what constraints can be relaxed and made more realistic. One area in which the PAC learning model is generally too restrictive is in making no assumptions regarding the distribution D of examples. In Valiant's definition, and in most of the work of the computational learning theory community, no assumption is made regarding D, and a class F of functions is called learnable only if a learning algorithm exists that works for every distribution D. Some elegant results are possible in this context, but this requirement is much too restrictive for natural learning and available evidence indicates that natural distributions are frequently trivial, much more tractable even than uniform distributions. We will mostly work in this chapter with simple uniform distributions.

On the other hand, if we gave an algorithm that was able to learn a union of two halfspaces from examples but made detailed use of the assumption that the function to be learned was a union of two halfspaces, it is problematic whether that would be helpful in a real-world context. In practical situations, we desire to learn functions that may be simple but are not drawn from any particular, explicitly parametrized class of functions. Many workers from the computational learning theory community hope to deal with this problem by giving algorithms for a specific class of functions that are robust against noise or distortion of the functions. Known positive results in this direction are, however, extremely limited.[2]

In this chapter, we will study the performance of an algorithm that intuitively might be expected to be effective in natural environments, learning relatively smooth functions, but that makes no evident explicit assumptions about the class F of functions to be learned.[3] We will study the k-nearest neighbor algorithm in the PAC learning model, for simple uniform distributions. This algorithm is the following: one has a database of M classified examples. One hypothesizes the following classification for new examples: find the k-nearest examples in the database, and guess that x is positive if more than half of these are positive examples, else guess x is a negative example. This algorithm has the following nice property: it can be proved that as M goes to infinity, k-nearest neighbor yields a classifier having error rate no worse than twice the Bayes risk. This result is independent of both the choice of D and of F (except for reasonable regularity conditions) (Cover and Hart 1967).

Unfortunately, it is easy to see that even if $n = 1$, that is, we consider the case of only one feature, the rate of convergence of this algorithm can be arbitrarily slow (Cover 1968). Our interest here will be in making reasonable simplifying assumptions about D and F, and asking whether k-nearest neighbor will converge to give error rate less than ε in time bounded by a polynomial in n and ε^{-1}.

Our results are as follows. We take D to be the uniform distribution on S^n, the unit n-sphere. For F the class of half-spaces, for k appropriately chosen ($k \sim n\varepsilon^{-2}\ln(\varepsilon^{-1})$), k-nearest neighbor converges to ε accuracy using $M = O(n\varepsilon^{-2}\ln(\varepsilon^{-1}))$ examples. When F is the class of unions of two halfspaces, however, the k-nearest neighbor algorithm will require a number of examples, which is $\Omega(\varepsilon^{-n})$ to converge to ε accuracy. This is traced to a certain breaking of symmetry. In a certain sense, which will be detailed, the k-nearest neighbor algorithm is locally but not globally able to solve this problem. It is unclear whether some variant might be devised that will work, or whether one indeed must use the global information that the target function is a union of halfspaces, or even if this global knowledge will suffice. More generally, it appears that k-nearest neighbor will not be able to learn any function (with polynomially many examples) unless a strong and unrealistic symmetry is respected.

Section 14.2 briefly reviews some results regarding the sample complexity of learning. Section 14.3 discusses some recent experimental results indicating some natural and optimistic extensions of previous theorems to uniform distributions and multilayer nets. Sections 14.4 and 14.5 can be read independently of sections 14.2 and 14.3. Section 14.3 presents positive results on convergence of k-nearest neighbor for a single halfspace. Section 14.5 discusses convergence for a union of halfspaces and presents my negative conclusion that nearest neighbor will require an exponential number of examples except in trivial circumstances such as described in section 15.4. Section 14.6 is a brief discussion.

14.2 Sample Complexity of Learning

In Baum and Haussler (1989), the following result is demonstrated. Assume random examples are chosen from some probability distribution D on $\mathfrak{R}^n \times \{1, -1\}$.[4] Say one attempts to load[5] these on a feedforward net of linear threshold units[6] with W weights and N units. If one can find a choice of weights such that at least a fraction $1 - \varepsilon/2$ of a set of m random training examples are correctly loaded, for m sufficiently large, then one has high confidence that the net will correctly classify all but a fraction ε of future examples. In fact, for $m \geq \dfrac{32W}{\varepsilon} \ln \dfrac{32N}{\varepsilon}$ one has confidence at least $1 - 8e^{-1.5W}$; and for $m \geq \dfrac{64W}{\varepsilon} \ln \dfrac{64N}{\varepsilon}$, one has confidence at least $1 - 8e^{-\varepsilon m/32}$. Thus, assuming only that one's training set and testing set are drawn from the same distribution, one has assurance that is exponential in the size of the training set that, if we are able to load the training set successfully, we expect to achieve good generalization.

The intuition behind these results is straightforward. The point is that it is highly unlikely that a choice of the W weight values would exist that loads the training set unless the net also agreed with the underlying distribution. For any particular choice of weights, we have some hypothesis net. Say hypothesis net A had probability greater than ε of misclassifying a random example. Then the probability that A would correctly classify m examples is less than $(1 - \varepsilon)^m$, which is exponentially small as m grows.[7] Now although, since we use real valued weights, there are an uncountable number of possible choices of weights, it turns out that the number of functions implementable on any m examples by W weight, N node nets is bounded by $(Nem/W)^W$. This is a generalization of Cover's (1965) well-known capacity result for simple perceptrons to nets with hidden layers (Baum 1988). Thus, for fixed W, the effective number of nets is bounded by a polynomial in m. Since the probability that any given net would load the training examples but not generalize well is exponentially small and the effective number of nets is only polynomially large, it is clear that for sufficiently large sample size, the probability that any net would exist that loads the training sample but does not generalize is exponentially small.[8] This is the intuition behind the theorem.

We were also able to analyze in the same way learning procedures that start with W' weights but in learning kill off many synapses, arriving at a hypothesis net with W weights and N nodes. My previous conclusion that good generalization could be expected for large-enough sample size holds again, for only slightly larger sample size: $m \geq \dfrac{32W}{\varepsilon} \ln \dfrac{32NW'}{\varepsilon}$. This bound differs from the previous bound only in the logarithmic factor, so that very few extra examples are necessary. This follows as the number of ways of choosing W weights remaining from the W' initially present is bounded crudely by $(W')^W$, so that the total number of functions implementable on m points by such nets is bounded by $(W')^W(Nem/W)^W$. Because only W and not W' appears in the exponent, $W \ln W'$ appears in the bound.

Notice that these results do not say anything about when it will be possible to load the examples or how to load them. The result is that if the examples can be loaded, then good generalization is ensured.

We have also given the following lower bound on the number of examples needed to ensure generalization (Baum and Haussler 1989). Consider training a net that has n inputs completely connected to a hidden layer of k units, which are then connected to the output unit. Any learning algorithm that uses fewer than (roughly) $m_L \sim W/\varepsilon$ training examples[9] will be fooled by some distributions. That is, one can construct a distribution D such that there exists a choice of weights such that the net exactly agrees with the target classification; the error rate is zero. On the other hand, there will be a finite probability that the learning algorithm will find some other choice of weights and will in fact output a hypothesis net that makes a fraction greater than ε of errors. Thus, one cannot achieve high confidence of valid generalization.

The intuition behind this result is also clear. Using a net with W weights, thus roughly W parameters, to fit fewer than $O(W/\varepsilon)$ examples, is overfitting and one can not guarantee generalization. More precisely, one can find a set S of kn input vectors (in fact any kn points in general position will do [Baum 1988]) such that for any Boolean function on S, there is a choice of weights that implements it. Thus, knowledge of the value of the target function on a subset of these kn points gives no knowledge whatever about its value on the other points, since all possible extensions can be realized by some choice of weights. Now one can specify a distribution D on the set S having the property that with some fixed probability a random set of m_L examples will not include any examples from some subset S_1 that has probability measure greater than 2ε (Ehrenfeucht et al. 1988). Thus, the set of examples one sees simply does not contain sufficient information to specify an extension to the unseen input vectors, which will achieve less than ε error rate.

Notice that both the upper and lower bounds on number of examples necessary for learning depend on the size of the net trained. (We call this the trainee net.) The complexity of the target function does not enter these bounds. Of course, if the target function is very complex, we will not be able to load the examples, in which case the theorems will not apply.

For practical applications, there are several problems with these results. One problem is that although the upper and lower bounds are reasonably tight in their scaling behavior, differing only by a logarithmic factor, the constant coefficients differ by a factor of a thousand. No serious effort has been made to address this, and no doubt with some work this could be substantially improved. Still, it appears that it would be difficult to prove results rigorously with tight constants (i.e., with the upper bound constant close to the lower bound constant) even if such results are true. Another problem is that the lower bound on the number of examples needed has the property that if you have fewer examples, there are distributions that fool you. One might ask whether fewer examples might suffice for typical, reasonable, or practical distributions. A third problem is that we have not been able to give tight lower bounds on the number of examples needed for training nets with more than one hidden layer of threshold units.

In fact one finds in the literature many examples of applications of backpropagation to practical problems where high rates of generalization are obtained using sample sizes comparable to or in fact smaller than the number of weights in the net (see, e.g., Denker et al. 1988). A reasonable explanation for this is that the natural distributions in these cases are in fact trivial. Consider an input distribution consisting of probability 1/2 the input is x_0, probability 1/2 the input is x_1, and probability 0 that any other point occurs. Independent of the target function or the size of the net we train, we can learn with only two examples, provided we have one of each and the target function is deterministic. This is not an unnatural situation. For example, in optical recognition of handwritten characters, a reasonable approximation to such a case might be expected. The character "1" and the character "2" are specifically designed to be distinct, and people, when writing them, are attempting to reproduce the template. Thus, we might expect that the distribution is roughly two delta functions, with some scatter, and we might expect to achieve high rates with very few training examples—in fact, a number of training examples independent of the size of the net we train. Of course (as has been emphasized to me by G. Hinton) there might be a small number of exceptions that are hard to learn. To get these right, we presumably need a large training set. If one can succeed in getting 95% accuracy when loading 5000 examples on a 10,000-weight net, then perhaps such exceptions account for less than 5% of the measure.

In Valiant's (1984) protocol for learning (which has been extensively studied; see, e.g., Rivest, Haussler, and Warmuth 1989) a class of functions is called learnable only if there is a learning algorithm that works for all possible distributions. I have criticized this restriction elsewhere as being too strong for practical interest (Baum 1989b). I have many reasons for my opinion. One is that it appears very difficult to give algorithms that can be proved to work in polynomial time for interesting classes of functions (Baum 1989a). Perhaps with less restrictive assumptions, one might fare better. Another reason is that one has lower bounds on the number of examples needed, which imply great restrictions on the classes that can be learned. These imply that one must have considerable knowledge about the function to be learned (that it come from a particular class of finite Vapnik-Chervonenkis [VC] dimension), and this is unrealistic in practice. One is making a trade-off between assuming enormous knowledge about the target function to achieve no assumption about the distribution. In practice, I would argue the distributions are well controlled, whereas the function class is largely unknown. For this reason, I will work in the remainder of this chapter with uniform distributions. One can show, for example, that some classes of infinite VC dimension are learnable for the uniform distribution. Thus, it is interesting to ask whether, for the uniform distribution, we can learn without making very restrictive assumptions on the function to be learned.

14.3   Experimental Results

The following type of simple experiment can address the various practical shortcomings in our rigorous results by measuring generalization directly. Choose a target net. Choose a distribution on the input space. Generate examples by calling input vectors from the distribution and classifying them according to the target net. Load a set of M examples onto a W weight net, for example, by backpropagation. Then see how that trainee net generalizes to a test set of examples drawn from the same distribution and classified according to the target net. By varying the size of the net being trained and the number of training examples used, one can directly see how training-set size affects generalization for particular distributions.

In the experiments reported on here, I generated input vectors that have each component chosen independently, with probability one-third of being -1, one-third of being 0, and one-third of being 1. I have used randomly chosen multilayer perceptrons as target functions. Here each input is connected to every node in the hidden layer, and every node in the hidden layer is connected to the output node. Each node implements a randomly chosen threshold function. That is, I choose a vector w_i randomly and uniformly on the unit sphere, and node i has value 1 for inputs x such that $x \cdot w_i > 0$, else node i has value -1. Thus, I have been testing a uniform distribution on the input space and random feedforward networks as target functions.[10]

The results are displayed in table 14.1. Notice that the example of row 2, where the trainee net has 441 weights, achieved 5% generalization for 8800 training examples, or almost exactly 20 times as many examples as weights; that the net of the third row, with 881 weights, achieved 6.2% generalization, for 17,600 examples (again roughly 20 times as many examples as weights); and the net of row 4 achieved 5.1% generalization

Table 14.1
Percentage error on testing set/Percentage error on training set

| | Weights | Number of examples in training set | | | | |
		2200	4400	8800	17600	35200
$T: 20 \rightarrow 10 \rightarrow 1$	221		10.8/4.1			
$L: 20 \rightarrow 10 \rightarrow 1$	221		$\sigma = 3.2$			
$T: 20 \rightarrow 10 \rightarrow 1$	221	17.7/1.4	12.2/1.2	5.0/1.8		
$L: 20 \rightarrow 20 \rightarrow 1$	441	$\sigma = 3.0$	$\sigma = 1.7$	$\sigma = 1.2$		
$T: 20 \rightarrow 10 \rightarrow 1$	221		13.0/1.1	9.6/.9	6.2/1.1	
$L: 20 \rightarrow 40 \rightarrow 1$	881		$\sigma = 3.6$	$\sigma = 1.0$	$\sigma = .36$	
$T: 20 \rightarrow 10 \rightarrow 1$	221		14.3/0.9	12.3/.8	7.1/.8	5.1/1.
$L: 20 \rightarrow 80 \rightarrow 1$	1761		$\sigma = 3.25$	$\sigma = 1.0$	$\sigma = .59$	$\sigma = 0.2$
$T: 20 \rightarrow 20 \rightarrow 1$	441		17.6/3.6			
$L: 20 \rightarrow 20 \rightarrow 1$	441		$\sigma = 2.7$			
$T: 20 \rightarrow 20 \rightarrow 1$	441		17.5/1.0		8.4/2.2	
$L: 20 \rightarrow 40 \rightarrow 1$	881		$\sigma = 2.7$		$\sigma = .3$	
$T: 20 \rightarrow 40 \rightarrow 1$	881		22.2/2.0			
$L: 20 \rightarrow 60 \rightarrow 1$	1321		$\sigma = 2.4$			

Note: Left column gives size of target net (labeled T:) and size of net trained (labeled L: for learner) as: input units $\rightarrow$ hidden units $\rightarrow$ output unit. Next column gives number of weights in nets (counting thresholds). First row gives number of examples in training set. Percentages are an average over five runs. Each of these five runs used a different (randomly chosen) target net, a different (random) training set, and different (random) initial conditions. Standard deviation (σ) is given for the percentage error on testing set.

for 35,200 examples. These all seem roughly consistent with the rule $\varepsilon = W/M$ where ε is the error rate, W is the number of weights in the trainee net, and M is the number of examples. The 7.1% generalization achieved by the net of row 4 for 17,600 examples is somewhat anomalous, as the heuristic rule would predict 10%.[11]

Also somewhat anomalous is the 8.4% generalization achieved by the net of column 6, for 17,600 examples. The heuristic would have predicted 5%, the same as for the net of row 3, since the trainee nets of rows 3 and 6 are the same (only the target nets are different). There are at least two possible explanations. The first is that the heuristic is wrong, and the degree of generalization depends on the size of the target net as well as the size of the trainee net. The second is that the lower degree of generalization for the net of row 6, with the larger target net, was caused by my inability to load the training set completely.

The results obtained in the 4400-example column clearly seem to indicate that for low generalization, $\varepsilon > 10\%$, $M \leq 10W$, generalization depends more on the complexity of the target net than on the complexity of the trainee net. The sixth row, for example, has much worse generalization than the third. These two had the same size trainee net but different target nets. Similarly one may compare the fourth row and the seventh.

It was evident in performing these runs that it is far easier to load examples from a small target net into a substantially larger trainee net than into a net of the same size. Not only was a substantially higher fraction of the training set loaded in each instance where the trainee net was much larger than the target net than in those instances where they were comparable, but also the training process was much faster, requiring many fewer epochs.

This phenomenon may account in part for the success of backpropagation. A key question is, Why does backpropagation, which finds only local optima, work so well? This question has been emphasized by results (Judd 1988) showing that the loading problem for a fixed net is NP-complete. The answer may lie in that one does not address the NP-complete loading problem for a fixed net. Instead, in practice, one picks a large enough net to train for backpropagation to load one's data successfully. Say the data are generated by some net with 20 weights. In order to achieve error rate ε, we do not need to solve the loading problem for a net of 20 weights; rather, it suffices to load W/ε examples onto a net with W weights. If we choose $W = 200$, say, we need only find a very poor locally optimal solution to the problem: given these examples, find the smallest net that loads them.

It is worth remarking that the experiments performed here are rather larger than most practical circumstances. It is a rare real-world database that contains 35,000 examples. I have here been interested in scaling properties. It would be interesting to perform similar experiments for smaller nets.

I have also studied nets with two hidden layers. My results so far are indicated in tables 14.2 and 14.3. Table 14.2 compares a one-hidden-layer net to a two-hidden-layer net. The one-hidden-layer target net has 121 weights (counting thresholds), and the two-hidden-layer target net has 231. The one-hidden-layer trainee net has 241 weights, and the two-

Table 14.2
Percentage error on testing set/Percentage error on training set

		Number of examples in training set	
	Weights	1200	4800
T: 10 → 10 → 1	121	14.7/.8	7.2/2.0
L: 10 → 20 → 1	241	σ = 3.5	σ = 0.2
T: 10 → 10 → 10 → 1	231	22.4/2.2	15.4/5.0
L: 10 → 20 → 10 → 1	441	σ = 7.1	σ = 2.3

Note: Left column gives size of target net (labeled *T*:) and size of net trained (labeled *L*: for learner) as: input units → first layer hidden units → second layer hidden units → output unit. Next column gives number of weights in net. First row gives number of examples in training set. Percentages are an average over at least five runs. Each of these runs used a different (randomly chosen) target net, a different (random) training set, and different (random) initial conditions. Standard deviation (σ) is given for the percentage error on testing set.

Table 14.3
Percentage error on testing set/Percentage error on training set

		Number of examples in training set	
	Weights	8610	17220
T: 20 → 10 → 5 → 1	271	10.5/.8	4.6/2.
L: 20 → 20 → 20 → 1	861	σ = 2.2	σ = 0.4

Note: Left column gives size of target net (labeled *T*:) and size of net trained (labeled *L*: for learner) as: input units → first layer hidden units → second layer hidden units → output unit. Next column gives number of weights in net. First row gives number of examples in training set. Percentages with 17220 examples is an average over six runs; percentage with 8610 examples is an average over two runs. Each of these runs used a different (randomly chosen) target net, a different (random) training set, and different (random) initial conditions. Standard deviation (σ) is given for the percentage error on testing set.

hidden-layer trainee net has 441 weights. The two-hidden-layer nets thus have roughly twice as many weights as their one-hidden-layer counterparts. Generalization is substantially worse for the two-hidden-layer nets, very roughly by a factor of two. The formula $\varepsilon \sim W/M$ seems roughly valid, for W the total number of weights in the net.

A major problem with table 14.2 was my inability to load the training set successfully for the two-hidden-layer net. For this reason, in table 14.3, I studied a net with 20 input units and a smaller target net. (It has been my experience that more input units and output units make it easier to load, whereas more hidden units makes it harder to load. This is intuitively reasonable since more external units means more information guiding convergence.) Results in table 14.3 are consistent with $\varepsilon = W/M$, for W the total number of weights in the net.

These simulations might lead one to conjecture that the VC dimension of a multilayer net is equal to its total number of weights. Recently, however, Maas has shown that the VC dimension of layered depth three nets may grow more rapidly than quadratic in the number of nodes (Maas 1993). There are at least two plausible explanations of the discrepancy. It may be that our experiments are not on large enough nets to detect this asymptotic rate of growth. Alternatively it may be that in some sense the effective dimension of nets trained by backpropagation is substantially lower than the true VC dimension of the class of such nets with arbitrary weights.

It is evident that further simulations are warranted. In particular, the comparisons I have made are somewhat suspect because I was unable to load the training set in table 14.2 on the two-hidden-layer net as completely as for the case of the one-hidden-layer net. I do not believe this was a major problem because in the few runs when I was able to load the training set completely, the generalization percentage was similar to the averages quoted. It would also be desirable to try bigger and smaller nets, nets with many hidden layers, and to load more examples, and thus achieve lower error rates on test data.

14.4   *k*-Nearest Neighbor Learns a Single Halfspace Fast

k-nearest neighbor is an algorithm that, given a set S of classified examples, produces a hypothesis function predicting the classification of future examples by the following method. Given an example, x, of which one wishes to guess the classification, one finds the k examples in S closest in Euclidean distance[12] and hypothesizes that x is positive if more than half of these are positive; else one guesses that x is a negative example. We will assume that the examples are drawn from the uniform distribution on S^n, the unit sphere embedded in n dimensions,[13] and classified as positive according to whether they lie in a certain halfspace. (In the next section we will consider more complicated target functions.) We will study the size M of database necessary to achieve accuracy ε, as n gets large.

Previous results (Cover and Hart 1967) have shown that for any (suitably continuous) deterministic target function and any distribution of examples, the k-nearest neighbor algorithm (for any k) provably converges to yield a classifier with error rate 0 as M, the size of the data set, goes to infinity. Intuitively this is clear; if we have a large enough database, we will have k examples so close to the example we are trying to classify that they will all have the same classification as it. It is also evident, however, that if the distribution is very dense near a separating region, we may need a very large database indeed for this to occur (Cover 1968).

The question we are studying here is, what happens when the distribution is uniform but the dimension is large? Now for large n, if we pick any point on S^n and then ask how many more points we must call before we are likely to get another one within a distance $1/2$, say, this number will be exponential in n, as the volume of the sphere of radius r goes like r^n. Thus, for any point near a separating plane, say, there will be a probability only slightly less than $1/2$ that its nearest neighbor will be on the other side of the separating plane, if our database contains only polynomially many examples. For this reason, 1-nearest neighbor will be hopeless in high dimensions. Nonetheless, we will see that, for large k, k-nearest neighbor can be an effective algorithm for learning a single halfspace, since we will take a vote of many examples, each of which is slightly more likely than not to vote correctly. On the other hand, this method does not appear to work for more complicated target functions, so the conclusion is essentially negative. We do not know how to use k-nearest neighbor or any related algorithm to learn more complicated target functions, even for uniform distributions.

THEOREM 14.1 *For any $\vec{w} \in S^n$, $0 < \varepsilon < 1$, $n \geq 2$, let $k = 36\ln\left(\dfrac{\varepsilon}{4}\right)\dfrac{n}{\varepsilon^2}$ and $M = \max\left(7k, 600\ln\left(\dfrac{\varepsilon}{4}\right)\right)$. Call M examples from the uniform distribu-*

tion on S^n; classify these as positive if $\vec{w} \cdot x > 0$ and as negative otherwise. Use these examples as a database for k-nearest neighbor. With probability at least $1 - \varepsilon$, the classifier produced will correctly classify the next random example chosen uniformly from S^n.

Proof: Assume for simplicity, without loss of generality, that w points along the x_1 axis, so that points are classified as positive if their first component is positive, and otherwise are classified as negative. Consider a point p on the unit sphere with first component p_1. We assume for definiteness that $p_1 > 0$, so we are considering a positive example. We will lower bound the probability that the nearest-neighbor algorithm correctly classifies point p. By symmetry, this probability depends only on the first component, and (as is intuitively evident) it will turn out the probability of correctly classifying p monotonically increases with $|p_1|$ (the distance from the separating hyperplane). We will be particularly interested in the case where $p_1 = \varepsilon/\sqrt{n}$. As we will see, it will be possible to show that it is highly likely that k-nearest neighbor will classify this point correctly, for appropriate k. This will show high likelihood of classifying correctly any particular point with larger first component. This set includes a fraction $1 - \varepsilon$ of the total measure.

We proceed as follows. Define $P(r, p_1)$ to be the conditional probability, given that there is an example a distance r from p, that the example is positive. Observe that if $r < p_1$, then $P(r, p_1) = 1$, and also that P is monotonic nonincreasing with increasing r. We will then find a distance r_0, such that with high confidence we will find k examples within distance r_0. Then the probability of misclassifying p can be bounded by the probability, given k examples each with probability at least $P(r_0, p_1)$ of being positive, that at most $k/2$ are positive.

Let S_r be the sphere of radius r centered at p. The intersection of S_r and S^n (the unit sphere on which the probability distribution lies) is an $n - 1$ dimensional sphere with radius $R = r\sqrt{1 - r^2/4}$ (figure 14.1). Indeed the intersection is defined by the locus of $\vec{x}$ such that $\vec{x} \cdot \vec{x} = 1$ and $(\vec{x} - \vec{p})^2 = r^2$. Recall $\vec{p}^2 = 1$. Solving we find $\vec{x} \cdot \vec{p} = 1 - r^2/2$. Let $\vec{x}_\parallel$ be the vector $(\vec{x} \cdot \vec{p})\vec{p}$ and $\vec{x}_\perp$ be $\vec{x} - \vec{x}_\parallel$. Then the intersection is defined by $|x_\parallel| = (1 - r^2/2)$ and $x_\perp^2 = R^2$, which is an $n - 1$ sphere of radius R lying in the hyperplane defined by $\vec{x} \cdot \vec{p} = 1 - r^2/2$. Call this sphere $S'(r)$.

Now $P(r, p_1)$ is equal to the fraction of $S'(r)$ above the plane $x_1 = 0$. Simple trigonometry (figure 14.2) shows that this plane passes a distance

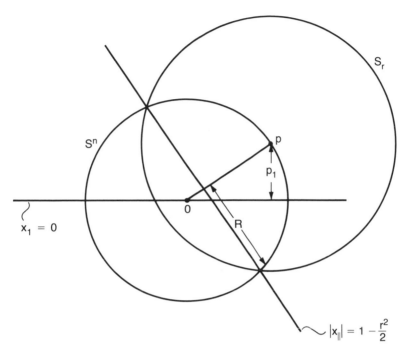

Figure 14.1
A diagram showing S^n and S_r. S^n is the unit sphere centered at the origin and S_r is the radius r sphere centered at p. p and the origin O are labeled. The hyperplane $x_1 = 0$, which forms the decision boundary, is shown. The hyperplane $|x_\parallel| = 1 - \frac{r^2}{2}$ is shown. The intersection of S^n and S_r is an $n - 1$ sphere of radius R lying on this hyperplane.

$l = (1 - r^2/2)p_1/\sqrt{1 - p_1^2}$ from the center of $S'(r)$. Note that $l \sim \varepsilon/\sqrt{n}$ will be small in the case of primary interest $p_1 \sim \varepsilon/\sqrt{n}$.

Now if we have a sphere of radius ρ, the fraction of its area in the band with first component between 0 and d (figure 14.3) is given by:

$$F(d, \rho) \equiv \int_0^{d/\rho} (1 - z^2)^{(n-3)/2}\, dz\, \frac{A_{n-1}}{A_n} \tag{14.1}$$

(for $n \geq 3$, $d \leq \rho$), where $A_n = \dfrac{2\pi^{n/2}}{\Gamma(n/2)}$ is the area of the unit n sphere. (For a derivation of this integral formula see the chapter appendix.) A simple application of Stirling's formula $\Gamma(x) = e^{-x}e^{(x-1/2)\ln(x)}\sqrt{2\pi}\left(1 + \dfrac{1}{12x} + \cdots\right)$

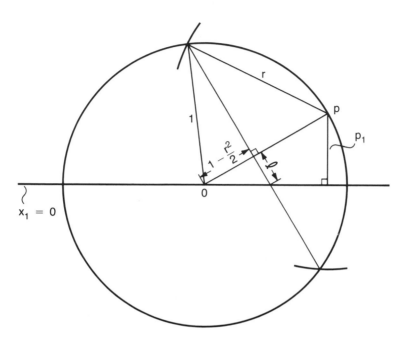

Figure 14.2
The same diagram as figure 14.1, relabeled to clarify the trigonometric calculations. S_r is indicated here by only two arcs.

yields

$$\frac{A_{n-1}}{A_n} = \frac{\sqrt{n}}{\sqrt{2\pi}}\left(1 + O\left(\frac{1}{n}\right)\right).$$

(14.2)

Now the integrand is less than 1, so we have

$$F(d, \rho) < d\frac{\sqrt{n}}{\rho\sqrt{2\pi}}.$$

(14.3)

For $d \leq \varepsilon/\sqrt{n}$, we find that $1 \geq c \equiv \left(1 - \frac{d^2}{\rho^2}\right)^{(n-3)/2} \geq \left(1 - \frac{\varepsilon^2}{\rho^2 n}\right)^{n/2} \sim$

$e^{-\varepsilon^2/2\rho^2} \sim 1$ for large n and small ε and ρ of order 1 (which will be the case of interest). Already for $n = 3$ and $\varepsilon < 1$, we have $c > 1/2$. Thus

$$F(d, \rho) > dc'\frac{\sqrt{n}}{\sqrt{2\pi}\rho}$$

(14.4)

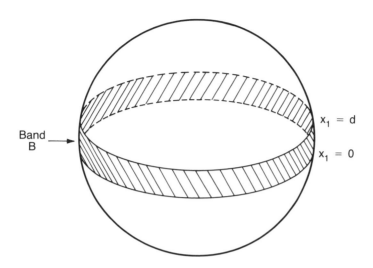

Figure 14.3
The band B is the region on the sphere between the planes $x_1 = 0$ and $x_1 = d$. $F(d, p)$ is the fraction of the area of the whole sphere (of radius ρ) which is contained in B.

where $c' = c(1 + O(1/n))$ is a constant that can be lower bounded very close to 1.

We will use our bounds on $F(d, \rho)$ in several ways. First, observe from equation 14.3 that $F(p_1, 1) \le \dfrac{p_1 \sqrt{n}}{\sqrt{2\pi}} < \varepsilon/2$ for $p_1 = \varepsilon/\sqrt{n}$. Thus, the measure on S^n of points further from the separating plane than $\varepsilon/\sqrt{n}$ is in fact greater than $1 - \varepsilon$.

Next, choose r_0 as a radius such that a fraction α of the sphere S^n is contained within a sphere of radius r_0 from p, for some fixed fraction $\alpha < \frac{1}{2}$. (We will soon take $\alpha = \frac{1}{6}$.) Recall that we have defined $S(r_0)$ as the sphere of radius r_0 centered at p and $S'(r_0)$ as the intersection of the sphere $S(r_0)$ and the unit sphere S^n. We have observed that the $(n - 1)$ sphere $S'(r_0)$ lies in a plane a distance $d_0 = 1 - r_0^2/2$ from the origin. Thus, the condition that $S(r_0)$ contain a fraction (at least) α of the measure is equivalent to the condition that $F(d_0, 1) \le \frac{1}{2} - \alpha$. From equation 4.3, we see we can achieve this if $d_0 \le d' \equiv (\frac{1}{2} - \alpha)\dfrac{\sqrt{2\pi}}{\sqrt{n}}$. We may thus choose $r_0 = \sqrt{2 - 2d'^2}$. We will call enough examples (roughly k/α) so that we have very high confidence that we have k examples in a sphere of radius r_0.

Now (recalling the discussion in the paragraph above equation 14.1) we have $P(r_0, p_1) = \frac{1}{2} + F(l_0, r_0)$ where we have defined $l_0 = l(r_0) = d'p_1/\sqrt{1-p_1^2}$. Substituting for d' and using equation 14.4, we bound:

$$P(r_0, p_1) > \frac{1}{2} + \frac{p_1}{r_0}\left(\frac{1}{2} - \alpha\right). \tag{14.5}$$

Define $LE(q, m, \kappa)$ as the probability of having at most κ successes in m independent Bernoulli trials each with probability of success q and recall (Angluin and Valiant 1979), for $0 \le \beta \le 1$, that

$$LE(q, m, (1 - \beta)mq) \le e^{-\beta^2 mq/2}. \tag{14.6}$$

Then the probability of that we fail to get k examples within a sphere of radius r_0 around p is less than

$$LE(\alpha, M, k) \le e^{-(1-(k/\alpha M))^2(\alpha M/2)} \tag{14.7}$$

for $M > k/\alpha$, which is exponentially small for large M.

Given that we have k examples within radius r_0, the probability that we missclassify p is less than

$$LE\left(\frac{1}{2} + \frac{p_1}{r_0}\left(\frac{1}{2} - \alpha\right), k, k/2\right) \le e^{-(k/4r_0)(p_1^2(1-2\alpha)^2/(r_0+p_1(1-2\alpha)))}. \tag{14.8}$$

The probability of misclassifying p will thus be less than δ for

$$k > \ln(\delta)\frac{4r_0}{p_1^2}\frac{(r_0 + p_1(1 - 2\alpha))}{(1 - 2\alpha)^2}. \tag{14.9}$$

Recalling our requirement that $M > k/\alpha$, we find that $\alpha = 1/6$ will minimize the number of examples we need. If we substitute $\alpha = 1/6$, $p_1 \sim \varepsilon/\sqrt{n}$, $r_0 \sim \sqrt{2}$, we find $k > 18\ln(\delta)\frac{n}{\varepsilon^2}$.

Finally we may put all our estimates together and sacrifice a few factors of 2 to get a rigorous bound on the probability of error. Take $p_1 = \varepsilon/2n$. Only a fraction less than $\varepsilon/2$ of points is closer to the separating hyperplane than this. Take $\delta = \varepsilon/4$. Now for $k \ge 36\ln\left(\frac{\varepsilon}{4}\right)\frac{n}{\varepsilon^2}$ we have probability less than $\varepsilon/4$ of misclassifying any but a fraction $\varepsilon/2$ of the examples, provided we get k examples in a radius r_0, and we see that for $M \ge$

$\max\left(7k, 600\ln\left(\dfrac{\varepsilon}{4}\right)\right)$, the probability is less than $\varepsilon/4$ of failing to get k examples within distance r_0. Now we see that if we call M examples, choose another point at random, and apply k-nearest neighbor, the probability will be less than ε that we fail to correctly classify it. ∎

Theorem 14.1 is stated for halfspaces that go through the center of the sphere, that is, have threshold zero. The more general case of finite threshold can be handled by the following modified algorithm. Call M classified examples, and determine the fraction γ that are positive. Then classify future examples as positive if, of the k closest examples in the database, more than γk are positive; else guess the example is negative. The proof of theorem 14.1 can readily be extended to this generalization.

I believe that a similar theorem would hold for the uniform distribution on the unit ball, the interior of S^n, but the proof would be slightly more involved (due to the appearance of edge effects). It definitely is not true in the distribution-independent framework, however.

My result is tight in the sense that if we use a database of size $M < n^j$ for j any constant, k-nearest neighbor will not achieve ε accuracy for $k \sim O\left(\dfrac{n}{\varepsilon^2}\right)$. Indeed the nearest neighbor to a point p in such a data set is roughly at a distance η such that S_η contains measure n^{-j}. But for such an η, my arguments imply (see figure 14.2 again) that $F(1 - \eta^2/2, 1) < \frac{1}{2} - n^{-j}$. Equation 14.4 then implies that $\eta > \sqrt{2 - \dfrac{\sqrt{2\pi}}{\sqrt{nc'}} - \dfrac{2\sqrt{2\pi}}{n^j c'}}$, or more roughly,

$$\eta \sim \sqrt{2} - n^{-1/2}. \tag{14.10}$$

But then for any point p a distance $\dfrac{\varepsilon}{\sqrt{n}}$ from the separating hyperplane, the probability the nearest point is on the same side of the hyperplane is only greater than one-half by a quantity of order $\dfrac{\varepsilon}{\sqrt{n}}$. In order to get high confidence of correctly classifying this point, we find that we require k of order n/ε^2.[14]

I have not phrased the theorem in the PAC language; that is, I have not proved that I have confidence $1 - \delta$ that the classifier has error less than ε.

Theorem 14.1 bounds the expected error. This translates, of course, into a trivial PAC learning bound that for $k \sim n \ln(\varepsilon^{-1}\delta^{-1})/\varepsilon^2\delta^2$, k-nearest neighbor achieves with confidence $1 - \delta$ accuracy ε, since if there were probability δ of having error greater than ε, the bound on expected error would immediately be violated. This is a much weaker PAC learning result than is possible, however. Since, unfortunately, the arguments of the next section strongly limit the usefulness of the k-nearest neighbor algorithm, I have not been motivated to explore this subject further and exhibit a tighter PAC learning bound.

To put the convergence results we have attained in perspective, recall that a rigorous lower bound of $n/32\varepsilon$ can be given on the number of examples needed for PAC learning a single halfspace in the distribution-independent context (Ehrenfeucht et al. 1988) and $\dfrac{32n}{\varepsilon} \ln \dfrac{32}{\varepsilon}$ examples are known to suffice (Blumer et al. 1987). Nearest neighbor appears to require $\Omega(n\ln(\varepsilon^{-1})/\varepsilon^2)$ examples, which is suboptimal but not horrendous.

Also as far as time performance goes, nearest neighbor is reasonable. For the problem of learning a uniform distribution on S^n for a single halfspace, the perceptron algorithm can be seen to produce a classifier in time $O(n^2/\varepsilon^3)$ (Baum 1989b). Once the classifier is produced, however, a decision can be made on how one expects new examples to be classified in time $O(n)$. Nearest neighbor defines its classifier in time M. However, it takes time roughly $O(Mn\ln(M))$ to classify new examples. This can be accomplished since we can find the distance between two points in time $O(n)$, thus the distance between the candidate (the point to be classified) and each point in our database in time $O(Mn)$, and then we can sort these distances in time $O(\ln(M))$. In this fashion we use time roughly $n^2\varepsilon^{-2}\ln(n)\ln(\varepsilon^{-1})$ to classify examples.[15]

14.5   Learning Unions of Halfspaces

The problem of PAC learning, in time polynomial in n, the class of functions defined by unions (or equivalently intersections) of two halfspaces is a natural challenge. The problem seems simple and has been studied at least since the advent of the perceptron algorithm (Ridgeway 1962). A natural credit assignment problem arises and cannot be avoided in any obvious way (Baum 1989a). My current prejudice is that a union of halfspaces probably cannot be PAC learned in the distribution-independent context. My opinion is that all the functions known to be PAC learnable in time polynomial in dimension are more or less trivial and that nonlearnability, if demonstrated, of such a simple and natural class of functions as unions of halfspaces would hammer shut the coffin of the distribution-independent approach, at least regarding results relevant to natural learning.

On the other hand, I have performed extensive experiments using a simple generalization of the perceptron algorithm to learn unions of half-spaces for the uniform distribution, and the algorithm seems extremely effective and fast in experiments up to $n = 1000$.

Unfortunately, k-nearest neighbor does not appear capable of learning a union of halfspaces, even for the uniform distribution, using a number of

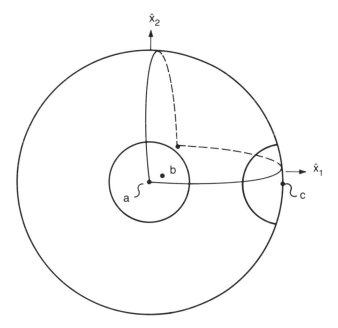

Figure 14.4
The first and second Cartesian coordinate axes $\hat{x}_1$ and $\hat{x}_2$ are shown. Positive examples are those with first and second Cartesian coordinates greater than zero. The decision boundary is shown. The points a and c constitute negative examples. b is a positive example. A sphere around a is shown. One quarter of examples in this sphere will be positive and three quarters negative. A sphere around c is shown. Almost half the examples in this sphere will be positive examples.

examples polynomial in n. The reason is easy to understand. As n gets large, the distance to the nearest neighbor among any polynomial-sized data set grows toward $\sqrt{2}$, as was seen in equation 14.10.

Now consider for definiteness the case of figure 14.4. Our classifying function is: $\vec{x}$ is positive if and only if $x_1 > 0$ and $x_2 > 0$. If we look at a unit ball about the point $a = (0, 0, \vec{y})$, for $\vec{y}$ any unit $n - 2$ component vector, we find that one-quarter of the measure contained in this ball is in the positive region and three-quarters is negative. If we consider the ball about a point $b = \left(\dfrac{\varepsilon}{\sqrt{n}}, \dfrac{\varepsilon}{\sqrt{n}}, \vec{y}' \right)$ for $\vec{y}'$ any $n - 2$ vector of norm $\sqrt{\dfrac{1 - 2\varepsilon^2}{n}}$, then slightly more than one-quarter of the measure will be positive and so, by k-nearest neighbor, we could distinguish a from b as in the previous section and correctly find more than one-quarter of the nearest neighbors are positive, which we might take as an indication that b is in fact a positive example. However, if we consider the ball about point

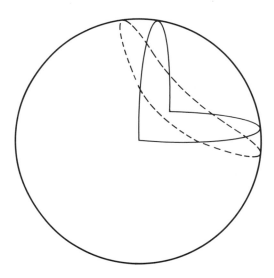

Figure 14.5
For any polynomial number of examples, the decision region formed by k-nearest neighbor cuts off the corners and bows out in the middle of the target hyperplanes. The target region is outlined in a solid lines; the decision region found by k-nearest neighbor is outlined by a dashed line.

$$c = \left(1 - \frac{\varepsilon}{\sqrt{n}}, -\frac{\varepsilon}{n}, \vec{y}\,''\right) \text{ for } \vec{y}\,'' \text{ any } n - 2 \text{ vector of norm } \sqrt{\frac{2\varepsilon}{\sqrt{n}} - \frac{2\varepsilon^2}{n}}, \text{ we}$$

discover that almost half the examples in the ball will be positive, in spite of the fact that c is a negative example. If we classify an example as positive provided more than γk of its k-nearest neighbors are positive, we will misclassify either b or c for any polynomial size k and any threshold γ.

In short, for any polynomial number of examples, the decision region formed by k-nearest neighbor will cut off the corners and bow out in the middle of the target hyperplanes, as in figure 14.5, and will thus not accurately reflect the target function. The information for accurate decisions is locally but not globally available. I have not been able to conceive of any effective way to improve this algorithm and seriously doubt one exists.

This obstruction to the use of k-nearest neighbor transcends the union of halfspace problem. It will persist for any class of functions and distribution that does not have a symmetry forcing $P(r_0, p)$ to be independent of p for any point p on the decision boundary (for some fixed r_0 sufficiently large so that $S(r_0)$ contains some finite fraction of the measure).

14.6 Discussion

We reviewed theorems regarding the number of training examples needed to train feedforward neural networks when valid generalization is desired. The assumption is that training and testing examples are drawn from some fixed but arbitrary distribution on $\Re^n \times \{0, 1\}$. The results are that if M examples can be loaded onto a net with W weights and N nodes, if $M > \Omega\left(\frac{W}{\varepsilon} \log(N)\right)$, then with very high confidence one expects the net generated will misclassify at most a fraction ε of test examples; conversely, any learning algorithm using fewer than $O\left(\frac{W}{\varepsilon}\right)$ examples will be fooled by some distributions and make greater than a fraction ε of errors. These lower and upper bounds are thus tight to within constant and logarithmic factors.

I presented some experimental findings that indicate some possible improvements in these results. The experiment was to generate examples from the uniform distribution and then classify these examples using some particular random neural network chosen as target function. A data set is then generated and loaded by backpropagation onto a second network. Finally, the generalization achieved by this network is measured.

The results seemed to indicate the following heuristic rule holds. If M examples are loaded onto a net with W weights (for $M \gg W$), the net will make a fraction ε of errors on new examples chosen from the same distribution where $\varepsilon = \dfrac{W}{M}$. If true, this improves the theorems in several regards. The logarithmic and constant factors by which the lower and upper bounds (on number of examples needed) seem effectively to all be replaceable by the constant one. The lower bound, which was proved to hold "for some distribution," seems valid as well for the uniform distribution. The lower bound, which was proved to hold only for one-hidden-layer nets, holds as well for multilayer nets. It appears that multilayer nets have a VC dimension roughly equal to their total number of weights.

An interesting open problem is to prove that this heuristic in fact holds, at least in the limit of large random-target nets of the type considered and for uniform input distributions.

We then considered the rate of convergence of the k-nearest neighbor algorithm to yield an ε-accurate classifier when training and test examples are generated according to the uniform distribution on S^n and classified according to simple target functions. For target functions defined by a single halfspace, we found that for appropriately chosen k, convergence is reasonably rapid. Indeed, a set of $M = O\left(\dfrac{n}{\varepsilon^2} \ln \dfrac{1}{\varepsilon}\right)$ examples suffices to yield ε accurate classification for k-nearest neighbor with $k = O\left(\dfrac{n}{\varepsilon^2} \ln \dfrac{1}{\varepsilon}\right)$.

Unfortunately, we found further that when the target function is defined as a union of two halfspaces (and for most other realistic cases), the number of examples needed for accurate classification is exponential in n. Thus the conclusion is essentially negative: k-nearest neighbor will not be an effective algorithm for learning in high dimensions except in very special circumstances.

This bodes ill not only for using nearest-neighbor algorithms to learn but also for memory-based reasoning systems based on associative memories (see, e.g., Waltz 1988; Abu-Mostafa and Psaltis 1987). As the feature dimension gets large, the "nearest" k previous experiences need not be a reasonable guide for future behavior unless the distance metric can be well enough chosen that the distribution is far friendlier than uniform.

The results on generalization by neural networks, both theoretical and experimental, coupled with various successful real-world applications of backpropagation, where far fewer data points were used than we would have predicted, indicate that real-world distributions may be far more trivial than uniform distributions. An important problem, therefore, is to extend learning theory to the regime of simple distributions.

Appendix

I give a brief derivation of equation 14.1 for $F(d, \rho)$ defined as the fraction of the surface of the *n*-sphere of radius ρ centered at the origin, which is between $x_n = 0$ and $x_n = d$, for $d \le \rho$. Recall we have defined the sphere as

$$x_1^2 + x_2^2 + \cdots + x_n^2 = \rho^2. \tag{14A.1}$$

We may define spherical coordinates by

$$x_1 = \rho \cos \theta_{n-1} \cos \theta_{n-2} \ldots \cos \theta_2 \cos \theta_1$$
$$x_2 = \rho \cos \theta_{n-1} \cos \theta_{n-2} \ldots \cos \theta_2 \sin \theta_1$$
$$x_3 = \rho \cos \theta_{n-1} \cos \theta_{n-2} \ldots \sin \theta_2$$

$\ldots$

$$x_{n-1} = \rho \cos \theta_{n-1} \sin \theta_{n-2}$$
$$x_n = \rho \sin \theta_{n-1}$$

Now if we define A_n as the area of the unit *n*-sphere, we have $\rho^{n-1} A_n$ as the area of the *n*-sphere of radius ρ and

$$F(d, \rho) = \frac{1}{A_n} \int_0^{\theta_d} d\theta_{n-1} \int d\theta_{n-2} d\theta_{n-3} \cdots$$
$$\times d\theta_1 (\cos \theta_{n-1})^{n-2} (\cos \theta_{n-2})^{n-3} \ldots \cos \theta_2 \tag{14A.3}$$

where $\rho \sin \theta_d \equiv d$. Recognizing the integral over $d\theta_{n-2} d\theta_{n-3} \ldots d\theta_1$ as the definition of A_{n-1}, we may write this as

$$F(d, \rho) = \frac{1}{A_n} \int_0^{\theta_d} d\theta_{n-1} (\cos \theta_{n-1})^{n-2} A_{n-1} \tag{14A.4}$$

Now defining $z = \sin \theta_{n-1}$ we find $dz = \cos \theta_{n-1} d\theta_{n-1}$ abd $\cos \theta_{n-1} = (1 - z^2)^{1/2}$. Finally

$$F(d, \rho) = \frac{A_{n-1}}{A_n} \int_0^{d/\rho} dz(1 - z^2)^{(n-3)/2} \tag{14A.5}$$

which is equation 14.1.

Notes

1. In fact, the problem, "Given a set of classified examples, are they consistent with classification by a union of two halfspaces?" has been proved NP-complete (Blum and Rivest 1988). Together with results of Pitt and Valiant (1986), this implies that one can not PAC learn a union of two halfspaces using as hypothesis function a union of two halfspaces in polynomial time in the distribution-independent sense (unless P = NP). It is, of course, an open question whether one can learn this class of functions using more general hypothesis functions. See Baum (1989a, 1989c) for more on this point.

2. Also the theorem that one can only learn concept classes of finite Vapnik-Chervonenkis (VC) dimension (Blumer et al. 1987) places severe constraints on the malicious distortion any algorithm can tolerate in the distribution independent framework.

3. Also, in contrast to many learning algorithms previously considered, especially within the computational learning community, the nearest-neighbor algorithm produces a hypothesis function that is not drawn from any evident fixed class of functions.

4. This theorem thus holds in a more general context than PAC learning, which assumes a distribution D on $\Re^n$ and a deterministic classification by some target function.

5. We say an example is loaded if, when we present the example $\vec{x}$ to the input of the net, the output of the net is the correct classification (1 or 0). In the discussion, I have fixed the topology of the net and ask for some choice of weights such that a large fraction of the example set is loaded.

6. These results have recently been generalized to feedforward nets of sigmoid functions (Haussler 1989).

7. For simplicity, in the intuitive explanation, I talk of loading the full set. Similarly the probability A will load a fraction $1 - \varepsilon/2$ of the examples is exponentially small. See Baum and Haussler (1989) for details.

8. More precisely, the theorem is proved by a cross-validation technique (Blumer et al. 1987). One chooses a set of 2m examples and considers all the ways one can use a subset of size m as training set and its complement as testing set. The total number of functions implementable on the whole set is then bounded by $(Ne2m/W)^W$, but the probability is less than $(1 - \varepsilon)^m$ that any one such function fools us—that is, loads the training set but fails on the testing set.

9. More precisely $m_L = \dfrac{2\lfloor k/2 \rfloor n - 1}{32\varepsilon}$ examples. Note $W = k(n + 1)$ for the one hidden layer, one output net considered.

10. Note that these are far from being random functions in some sense. The target functions I use are special in that they are realized by relatively small feedforward networks.

11. This might be attributable simply to random variation. Note that the standard deviation values given should not be taken too seriously; each is based on only five events.

12. Other distortion measures could also be used but will not be considered in this chapter.

13. Note my convention differs from the usual mathematical convention, where S^n is an n-manifold, naturally embedded in $n + 1$ dimensions. By S^2, I mean the circle that can be drawn on a piece of paper.

14. We start at the origin and take k steps of a random walk with probability $\frac{1}{2} + \frac{\varepsilon}{\sqrt{n}}$ of moving right and probability $\frac{1}{2} - \frac{\varepsilon}{\sqrt{n}}$ of moving left. To have confidence that we arrive to the right of the origin, we must have our mean $(k\varepsilon/\sqrt{n})$ greater than our standard deviation (roughly $\sqrt{k}$), or in other words $k > n/\varepsilon^2$.

15. It does not appear that $k - d$ trees would help since the number of matches needed, k, is comparable to the size of the database (Friedman, Bentley, and Finkel 1977).

References

Abu-Mostafa, Y. S., and Psaltis, D. (1987). Optical neural computers. *Scientific American* 256, no. 3, pp. 88–95.

Angluin, D., and Valiant, L. G. (1979). Fast probabilistic algorithms for Hamiltonian circuits and matchings. *Journal of Computer and Systems Sciences* 18, pp. 155–193.

Baum, E. B. (1988). On the capabilities of multilayer perceptrons. *Journal of Complexity* 4, pp. 193–215.

Baum, E. B. (1989a). On learning a union of half spaces. *Journal of Complexity* 5, no. 4.

Baum, E. B. (1989). The perceptron algorithm is fast for non-malicious distributions. Submitted for publication.

Baum, E. B. (1989c). A proposal for more powerful learning algorithms. *Neural Computation* 1, no. 2.

Baum, E. B, and Haussler, D. (1989). What size net gives valid generalization? *Neural Computation* 1, pp. 151–160.

Blum, A., and Rivest, R. L. (1988). Training a 3-node neural network is NP-complete. In *Advances in Neural Information Processing Systems 1*, pp. 494–501. Ed. D. S. Touretzky. San Mateo, CA: Morgan Kaufmann.

Blumer, A., Ehrenfeucht, A., Haussler, D., Warmuth, M. (1987). Learnability and the Vapnik-Chervonenkis Dimensions. Technical Report UCSC-CRL-87-20. University of California–Santa Cruz.

Cover, T. M. (1965). Geometrical and statistical properties of systems of linear inequalities with applications in pattern recognition. *IEEE Trans. Elec. Comput.* EC-14, pp. 326–334.

Cover, T. M. (1968). Rates of convergence of nearest neighbor decision procedures. *Proc. First Annal Hawaii Conference on Systems Theory*, pp. 413–415.

Cover, T. M., and Hart, P. E. (1967). Nearest neighbor pattern classification. *IEEE Trans. Info. Theory*, IT-13, pp. 21–27.

Denker, J. S., Gardner, W. R., Graf, H. P., Henderson, D., Howard, R. E., Hubbard, W., Jackel, L. D., Baird, H. S., and Guyon, I. (1988). Neural network recognizer for hand-written zip code digits. In *Neural Information Processing Systems 1*, pp. 323–331., Ed. D. Touretzky. San Mateo, CA: Morgan Kaufmann.

Duda, R. O., and Hart, P. E. (1973). *Pattern Classification and Scene Analysis*. New York: John Wiley.

Ehrenfeucht, A., Haussler, D., Kearns, M., and Valiant, L. (1988). A general lower bound on the number of examples needed for learning. In *Proceedings of the 1988 Workshop on Computational Learning Theory*, pp. 139–154. Ed. D. Haussler and L. Pitt. San Mateo, CA: Morgan Kauffman.

Friedman, J. H., Bentley, J. L., and Finkel, R. A. (1977). An algorithm for finding best matches in logarithmic expected time. *ACM Trans. on Mathematical Software* 3, no. 3, pp. 200–226.

Haussler, D. (1989). Generalizing the PAC model for neural nets and other learning applications. University of California Santa Cruz Technical Report USCS-CRL-89-30.

Judd, S. (1988). On the complexity of loading shallow networks. *Journal of Complexity* 4, pp. 177–192.

Maass, W. (1993). Neural Nets with Superlinear VC Dimension. *Neural Computation*, forthcoming.

Pitt, L., and Valiant, L. G. (1986). Computational Limits on Learning from Examples. Tech Report TR-05-86. Harvard University.

Ridgeway, W. C. III (1962). An Adaptive Logic System with Generalizing Properties. Tech report 1556-1. Solid State Electronics Laboratory, Stanford University.

Rivest, R., Haussler, D., and Warmuth, M. K. (1989). *Proceedings of the Second Annual Workshop on Computational Learning Theory*. San Mateo, CA: Morgan Kauffman.

Valiant, L. G. (1984). A theory of the learnable. *Comm. ACM* 27, no. 11, pp. 1134–1142.

Waltz, D. L. (1988). The prospects for building truly intelligent machines. *Daedalus* 117, no. 1, pp. 191–212.

IV EXPERIMENTAL

15 Comparing Connectionist and Symbolic Learning Methods

J. R. Quinlan

15.1 Introduction

Numerous papers that have appeared over the past few years compare the performance of a variety of learning algorithms on real and constructed data sets. Such comparisons, uncovering the strengths and weaknesses of algorithms on different tasks, provide valuable data points that help to map and understand the inherent capabilities of the methods. One emerging theme is that these capabilities appear to be task dependent—few researchers would claim that one method is uniformly superior to another.

This chapter focuses on two kinds of learning algorithms: *symbolic* methods, which represent what is learned as (usually propositional) expressions over the given attributes, and *connectionist* methods, where learning consists of adjusting weights in a (usually given) network. In particular, we examine one exemplar of each of these approaches: algorithms that construct decision trees for symbolic methods and, for networks, the use of backpropagation to determine appropriate weights. While it could certainly be argued that there are more powerful methods on both sides, at least these are representative of the two camps. My intention is not so much to provide more empirical data points comparing the approaches but rather to try to characterize some classes of problems that might be expected to be well or ill suited to either approach.

I first summarize highlights of four comparative studies that have included both decision-tree methods and networks trained by backpropagation. After drawing some general conclusions from the reported results, I then consider two extreme characterizations of learning tasks as *sequential* or *parallel*. This leads to the conjecture that decision-tree methods are unsuitable for parallel tasks and that gradient-descent training of networks on sequential tasks is likely to be slow. Both conjectures are illustrated by experiments using two constructed tasks, one of each kind.

15.2 Four Studies

In this section we look at the evidence provided by four recent studies, extracting information relevant to decision trees and networks. This chapter considers only the performance dimension of the two learning meth-

Table 15.1
Results extracted from Weiss and Kapouleas (1989)

	Domain			Network		Decision tree	
	Size	Atts	Classes	Error rate %	Time (secs)	Error rate %	Time (secs)
Iris	150	4	3	3.3		4.7	
Appendicitis	106	8	2	14.2		15.1	
Breast cancer	286	9	2	28.5		22.9	
Thyroid	3772	22	3	1.5	756000	0.6	8.3

ods, as measured by the time required to learn from a training set and the accuracy with which unseen cases are then classified; other important dimensions, such as intelligibility of the learned classifiers or their ability to withstand partial corruption, will be ignored. Similarly, no account will be taken of variations among decision-tree methods and among implementations of backpropagation. Such variations certainly exist, but they are probably much smaller within each group than between the groups.

The first study we will examine is that of Weiss and Kapouleas (1989), in which many learning methods drawn from AI and statistics were applied to four well-known data sets. In the case of the networks, one layer of hidden units was used with the best number of such units determined from experiment. Relevant sections of their results appear in table 15.1. (In this and subsequent tables, some information missing from the published studies has been estimated from my own or other independent experiments, and these estimates have been identified by italicizing them.) The authors conclude: "In every case a [symbolic] solution was found that exceeded the performance of solutions posed using different underlying models.... The neural nets did perform well.... However, overall they were not the best classifiers; they consumed enormous amounts of cpu time; and they were sometimes equalled by simple classifiers." Their statement regarding the computational requirements of backpropagation is illustrated by the last domain: training until no observed improvement required over 8 central processing unit days on a Sun 4/280, while our own experiments show that, for this data set, a decision-tree method requires about 8 seconds on similar hardware.

Dietterich, Hild, and Bakiri (1990) report trials using one large data set containing 20K words, where each letter in each word provides one in-

Table 15.2
Results from Dieterich Wild, and Bakiri (1990)

	Domain			Network		Decision tree	
	Size	Atts	Classes	Error rate %	Time (secs)	Error rate %	Time (secs)
NETtalk (1K wds)	7K?	7 × 29	324	29.3		34.8	
NETtalk (1K wds)	7K?	7 × 29	115?	28.4		29.9	

stance. The task is to map each letter, in the context of the three preceding and three following letters, to a phoneme/stress pair encoded as 26 bits. When testing, each of these output bit vectors is mapped to the nearest of the 324 possible phoneme/stress pairs, or to the nearest pair that occurs in the training set. In these trials, both the phoneme and stress must be correct before the instance is regarded as correctly classified.

Table 15.2 summarizes results using randomly selected 1000-word training and test sets and two different mappings of output vectors to phoneme/stress pairs. Although the differences between the corresponding error rates appear small, they are statistically significant. After performing experiments to test a variety of hypotheses to explain the difference, Dieterich, Hild, and Bakiri conclude, "The third hypothesis—that back-propagation was capturing statistical information by some mechanism (perhaps the continuous output activations)—was demonstrated to be the primary difference between [the decision-tree method] and [back-propagation]."

Shavlik, Mooney, and Towell (1991) used a large collection of data sets to investigate network and decision-tree learning. Table 15.3 shows learning time and error rates in the same format as the other tables. The authors observed that backpropagation is slower to train but generally produces a more accurate classifier, particularly when there are few training instances. With the exception of Audiology, they found that networks were better at dealing with noisy data.

Fisher and McKusick (1989) carried out experiments on two real-world data sets and four artificial domains. Although they do not report detailed results, their trials led them to a number of conclusions, two of which are most relevant to the enterprise of establishing method-task fits. They observe that the type of classifier needed for some domains favors a network approach. For example, *m out of n* descriptions of classes look for at least

Table 15.3
Results from Shavlik, Mooney, and Towell (1991)

	Domain			Network		Decision tree	
				Error rate %	Time (secs)	Error rate %	Time (secs)
	Size	Atts	Classes				
Soybean	289	50	17	5.9	5260	11.0	161
Chess	591	36	2	3.7	34700	3.0	33
Audiology	226	58	24	22.3	19000	24.5	66
Heart disease	303	14	2	19.4	4060	28.8	69
NETtalk (808 wds)	4259	7	115	37.0	168000	35.2	5410
NETtalk 'A'	444	7	18	33.6	234000	36.9	378

m of a possible n conditions to be satisfied; Spackman (1988) notes that such descriptions are common in biomedical domains. While m *out of* n descriptions can be represented naturally in a network, their propositional form requires one disjunct for every way of selecting a subset of size m, making propositional descriptions complex and thus difficult to learn. Second, Fisher and McKusick (1989) follow Hunt (1975) in noting that decision trees usually test one attribute at a time.[1] Noise in the values of the tested attribute will quickly tend to throw such classifiers off the track, leading to higher error rates.

The picture that emerges from these studies is far from clear, but there seem to be two points of general agreement:

1. Backpropagation usually requires a great deal more computation.

2. The predictive accuracy of both approaches is roughly the same, with backpropagation often slightly more accurate (but see Weiss and Kapouleas above).

Both points are consistent with the observation that backpropagation is exploring a larger hypothesis space; it thus takes longer to find a suitable hypothesis, but a better fit is possible. However, these points are in fact "average findings" over several domains, some of which are much more favorable to one or the other approach. In the Soybean trials from table 15.3, for instance, backpropagation required only one order of magnitude more computation than ID3 and produced a noticeably superior classifier. In the NETtalk 'A' trials from the same table, even though the amount of information in the training data was smaller (444 × 7 attribute values as opposed to 289 × 50), backpropagation required three orders of magnitude more time and produced a slightly inferior classifier. For the more voluminous Thyroid data (table 15.1), the time differential grew to five orders of magnitude. Can we identify any characteristics of these tasks that would account for this great disparity of relative performance?

15.3 Parallel and Sequential Classifiers

As Hunt (1975) pointed out, networks and decision trees classify instances in markedly different ways. A network requires the value of each input variable and computes from them a value for each output variable. It is thus a *parallel* classification mechanism since the calculations at one level of the network depend only on results from previous levels and could thus be carried out simultaneously. A decision tree, on the other hand, examines one input variable and, depending on its value, invokes one of a set of subtrees. Each subtree may examine different input variables and, in general, a decision tree only examines some of the input variables before making a classification.

We can think of a spectrum of classification tasks corresponding to this same distinction. At one extreme are *P-type tasks*, where all the input variables are always relevant to the classification. Consider an *n*-dimensional description space and a yes-no concept represented by a general hyperplane decision surface in this space. To decide whether a particular point lies above or below the hyperplane, we must know all its coordinates, not just some of them. At the other extreme are the *S-type tasks*, in which the relevance of a particular input variable depends on the values of other input variables. In a concept such as "red and round, or yellow and hot," the shape of the object is relevant only if it is red and the temperature only if it is yellow.

Although these extremes are caricatures, similarities can be seen in real classification tasks. In sensor fusion problems, for example, a classifier must combine inputs that, individually, are only weakly correlated with class. Neglecting an input would be akin to discarding part of the evidence, a clearly suboptimal procedure. In contrast, deciding whether a particular chess position is checkmate will usually involve only some subset of the pieces on the board, with the whereabouts (or existence) of other pieces having no bearing on the classification.

15.4   Two Conjectures

In these terms, we can now state two conjectures and the reasoning underlying them:

1. Decision-tree methods are unsuitable for P-type problems.

2. Backpropagation will require inordinate amounts of learning time for S-type problems with few zero inputs.

The justification for the first is straightforward. If there are n input variables, all of which must be taken into account in making a classification, a decision tree will attempt to partition the data into at least 2^n mutually exclusive subsets. Unless there are sufficient data to ensure that each of these subsets contains a representative number of training instances, the decision tree will be a poor classifier.

Now consider the use of backpropagation with S-type training data. In a single training event, only a few of the input variables will be relevant to the classification (and this subset will change from event to event). Consider now one of the nonrelevant inputs, input i, say, and let $\{w_{ij}\}$ be the weights on the links connecting this input to the hidden layer. If input i is nonzero, the partial derivative of the error function with respect to w_{ij} will generally be nonzero, and so w_{ij} will be changed. If input i is irrelevant to the class of most of the training instances, these inopportune adjustments will tend to obscure the "sensible" adjustments made when input i *is* relevant. Even if gradients are aggregated over all training events, the information from those instances for which a particular input variable is relevant will be masked by that from (more numerous) instances for which it is not. Put another way, almost all components of the gradient will be irrelevant to the training instance, so gradient descent will resemble a random walk!

It is possible to identify domains in the previous section that have similarities to these P-type and S-type caricatures.[2] The Thyroid data (table 15.1) and the Chess data (table 15.3) are both S-like; the relevance of some attributes depends strongly on the values of other attributes, and the class of each instance depends only on a small subset of the attributes. In both these domains, backpropagation learns slowly. On the other hand, the Heart Disease data (table 15.3) seems to be a kind of weak-fusion task in which little or no information can be discarded without loss of accuracy; on this domain, the decision-tree classifier proves noticeably inferior.

15.5 An Experiment

To provide a clear trial of these conjectures, two artificial data sets were defined. Both have two classes and ten attributes $A_0, A_1, \ldots, A_9$ with continuous values in $[0, 1)$, five of which are always irrelevant to classification.

In the S-type problem, an instance's class is defined by a *1-decision list* (Rivest 1987):

if $A_7 > 0.6$ then class 1, else

if $A_3 > 0.4$ then class 0, else

if $A_2 \leq 0.3$ then class 1, else

if $A_9 \leq 0.7$ then class 0, else

if $A_4 > 0.4$ then class 1, else class 0

in which the relevance of attributes later in the list clearly depends on the values of earlier attributes. For the P-type problem, five prototype points were generated randomly, as follows:

	A_2	A_3	A_4	A_7	A_9
class 0:	.353	.447	.319	.584	.384
	.900	.164	.159	.583	.390
	.299	.076	.405	.663	.003
class 1:	.788	.266	.983	.609	.886
	.338	.387	.644	.532	.652

The class of an instance is then determined by finding the closest prototype point (ignoring the irrelevant attributes) and assigning the instance to the class associated with that point. Clearly, it is impossible to determine the class of an instance without examining *all* the relevant attributes.

For each problem, 1000 instances were generated randomly and classified by the relevant method. The first 500 of these were used as training instances and the remaining 500 reserved as test instances. Both problems were then tackled by representative systems:

• *bp* (McClelland and Rumelhart 1988), adjusting weights after every pattern and using the default learning parameters $\alpha = 0.9$ and $\varepsilon = 0.05$, and

• *C4.5*, a recent version of ID3 (Quinlan 1986, 1990), also using default parameter settings.

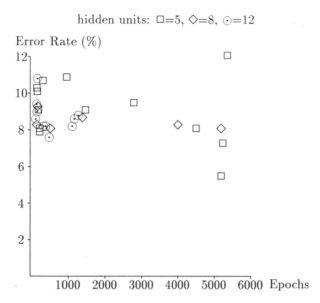

Figure 15.1
S-type: network accuracy on unseens versus training epochs

All trials were run on a DECstation 3100.

For the S-type problem, it is simple to design a network with five hidden units that will correctly classify all instances. To allow for alternative solutions, however, several training runs were completed for each of 5, 8, and 12 hidden units. Figure 15.1 plots, at various stages in these trials, the number of passes through the training instances, or *epochs*, against error rate of the network on the unseen test set. The time required for each epoch varied from about 0.3 to 0.65 seconds on the DECstation. Each training run was stopped after about 5000 epochs (approximately 40 minutes). As the figure shows, it seems likely that the network would need a great deal more training before it was able to classify unseen cases with near-perfect accuracy. In comparison, C4.5 found a decision tree in 1.8 seconds. This tree, shown in figure 15.2, has an error rate of 0.6% on the unseen test cases and differs from the true decision list only in that the thresholds are not exact. (This result also serves as a counterexample to Shavlik, Mooney, and Towell's [1991] conjecture that, for continuous-valued data, network classifiers are more accurate than decision trees.)

A7 > 0.595 : 1
A7 ≤ 0.595 :
    A3 > 0.391 : 0
    A3 ≤ 0.391 :
        A2 ≤ 0.296 : 1
        A2 > 0.296 :
            A9 ≤ 0.689 : 0
            A9 > 0.689 :
                A4 ≤ 0.407 : 0
                A4 > 0.407 : 1

Figure 15.2
S-type problem: decision tree

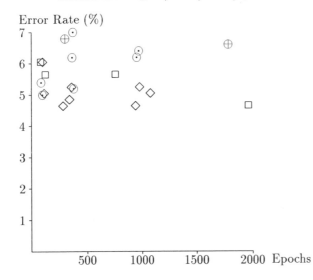

Figure 15.3
P-type: network accuracy on unseens versus training epochs

```
A4 ≤ 0.58 :
│   A9 ≤ 0.529 : 0
│   A9 > 0.529 :
│   │   A4 ≤ 0.265 : 0
│   │   A4 > 0.265 :
│   │   │   A5 > 0.893 : 0
│   │   │   A5 ≤ 0.893 :
│   │   │   │   A9 > 0.745 : 1
│   │   │   │   A9 ≤ 0.745 :
│   │   │   │   │   A4 > 0.507 : 1
│   │   │   │   │   A4 ≤ 0.507 :
│   │   │   │   │   │   A3 > 0.573 : 0
│   │   │   │   │   │   A3 ≤ 0.573 :
│   │   │   │   │   │   │   A2 ≤ 0.461 : 1
│   │   │   │   │   │   │   A2 > 0.461 : 0
A4 > 0.58 :
│   A9 ≤ 0.12 : 0
│   A9 > 0.12 :
│   │   A9 > 0.262 : 1
│   │   A9 ≤ 0.262 :
│   │   │   A4 ≤ 0.87 : 0
│   │   │   A4 > 0.87 : 1
```

Figure 15.4
P-type problem: decision tree

A different picture emerges on the P-type problem. As before, several network training runs were conducted using different numbers of hidden units, as set out in figure 15.3. The network achieved a 95% accuracy rate within a few dozen epochs, although it did not thereafter improve rapidly. C4.5 required 3.7 seconds to construct the decision tree that appears in figure 15.4. This tree, which correctly classifies 90.8% of the test instances, incorporates a test on an irrelevant attribute (A_5) and will never examine all relevant attributes when classifying an instance. C4.5 would require a great deal more data to match the classification accuracy that the network achieves relatively quickly.

15.6 Conclusion

It might well be argued that artificial data sets always vindicate their designer's convictions. The two problems discussed above, however, are very similar indeed: they have the same number of attributes of the same type, with the same irrelevant attributes in each case, and with approximately equal proportions of the two classes. Yet these problems produced quite different learning outcomes from the two learning methods.

The first conjecture advanced here, that P-type problems are ill suited to decision-tree methods, can be seen as a special case of the minimum-description-length principle (Rissanen 1983). For problems of this type, an exact representation of a classifier as a decision tree is complex, since each attribute must be tested along each path. We would therefore expect that large numbers of data would be required to substantiate this complexity.

The second conjecture, that S-type problems with few zero inputs will prove difficult for backpropagation, applies equally well to any method of adjusting weights by gradient descent. The reasoning behind this conjecture relies more on intuition than the justification for the first, although the phenomenon has been observed on other small, artificial tasks and with one different network learning system.

Finally, the welcome explosion in the number of well-conducted comparison studies is providing a wealth of data on how learning systems behave on different tasks. One of the most rewarding enterprises for the next few years will be to extract from these data some understanding of problem types and their relationship to classes of learning algorithms.

Notes

1. There are decision-tree methods that test several attributes together; see, for example, Utgoff and Brodley (1991).

2. Bud Frawley of GTE Laboratories suggested, tongue in cheek, that I should develop a measure of a task's P-ness or S-ness.

References

Dietterich, T. D., Hild, H., and Bakiri, G. A comparative study of ID3 and backpropagation for English text-to-speech mapping. *Proceedings of the Seventh International Conference on Machine Learning*, Austin, June 1990.

Fisher, D. H., and McKusick, K. B. An empirical comparison of ID3 and backpropagation. *Proceedings of the Eleventh International Joint Conference on Artificial Intelligence*, Detroit, August 1989.

Hunt, E. B. *Artificial Intelligence*. New York: Academic Press, 1975.

McClelland, J. L., and Rumelhart, D. E. *Explorations in Parallel Distributed Processing*. Cambridge, MA: MIT Press, 1988.

Quinlan, J. R. Induction of decision trees. *Machine Learning 1*, 1 (April 1986), pp. 81–106.

Quinlan, J. R. Decision trees and decisionmaking. *IEEE Transactions on Systems, Man, and Cybernetics 20*, 2 (March 1990), pp. 339–346.

Rissanen, J. A universal prior for integers and estimation by minimum description length. *Annals of Statistics 11*, 2 (1983), pp. 416–431.

Shavlik, J. W., Mooney, R. J., and Towell, G. G. Symbolic and neural learning algorithms: An experimental comparison. *Machine Learning 6*, 2 (March 1991), pp. 111–144.

Rivest, R. L. Learning decision lists. *Machine Learning 2*, 3 (November 1987), pp. 229–246.

Spackman, K. A. Learning categorical decision criteria in biomedical domains. *Proceedings of the Fifth International Conference on Machine Learning*, Ann Arbor, June 1988.

Utgoff, P. E., and Brodley, C. E. Linear machine decision trees. Technical Report 91-10. Department of Computer Science, University of Massachusetts Amherst, 1991.

Weiss, S. M., and Kapouleas, I. An empirical comparison of pattern recognition, neural nets, and machine learning classification methods. *Proceedings of the Eleventh International Joint Conference on Artificial Intelligence*, Detroit, August 1989.

16 Weight Elimination and Effective Network Size

Andreas S. Weigend and David E. Rumelhart

16.1 Introduction

Connectionist networks, also called brain-style computation or artificial neural networks, are ensembles of interconnected, usually nonlinear, units. The values of the connections between the units are estimated by a learning algorithm. This approach differs from traditional statistics by both the ubiquitous use of nonlinearities and the sheer number of parameters.

Connectionist networks were first applied to time-series prediction by Lapedes and Farber (1987). Whereas many researchers in the dynamical systems community deal only with noise-free, computer-generated time series, we focus on noisy, real-world data of limited record length. In this case, the problem of overfitting can become serious.

A priori, it is not clear what network size is required to solve a given problem. If the network is too small, it will not be flexible enough to emulate the dynamics of the system that produced the time series ("underfitting"). If it is too large, the excess freedom will allow the network to fit not only the signal but also the noise ("overfitting"). Both too-small and too-large networks thus give poor predictions in the presence of noise.

The key idea of weight elimination is to add a penalty term accounting for network complexity to the usual cost function. The trade-off between performance and complexity is reflected in the sum of a performance and a complexity term. There is a u shaped minimum between the extremes of having a too-simple network that produces horrendous errors and a network with small errors on the training data that has enormous complexity. This sum is minimized through error backpropagation.

16.1.1 Architecture

Figure 16.1 shows the architecture (the pattern of connectivity or topology) of a feedforward network with one hidden layer. (For the time series we analyzed, one hidden layer sufficed.) The abbreviation d-n-1 denotes the following network:

- The d *input units* are given the past values $x_{t-1}, \ldots, x_{t-d}$ of the time series $\{x_t\}$.
- The input units are fully connected to n *nonlinear hidden units*.
- All hidden units are connected to a linear *output unit*.

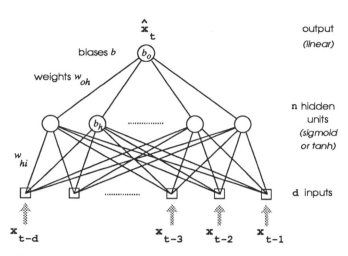

Figure 16.1
Architecture of a simple feedforward network

- Output and hidden units have adjustable *biases b*.
- The *weights* can be positive, negative, or zero.

The nonlinearities are located in the activation function (or transfer function) of the hidden units. The output (or response) of a hidden unit is called its *activation*. It is a composition of two operators: an affine mapping, followed by a nonlinear transformation. First, the inputs into a hidden unit h are linearly combined, and a bias b_h (or offset) is added,

$$\xi_h = \sum_{i=1}^{d} w_{hi} x_i + b_h = \vec{w}_h \cdot \vec{x} + b_h.$$

x_i stands for x_{t-i}, the value of input i, and w_{hi} is the weight between input unit i and hidden unit h.

Before turning to the second step, we give a geometric interpretation of ξ_h. A hidden unit only responds to $\vec{w}_h \cdot \vec{x}$, the projection of the input vector $\vec{x} = (x_1, x_2, \ldots, x_d)$ onto the weight vector $\vec{w}_h = (w_{h1}, w_{h2}, \ldots, w_{hd})$. Changes in the input that are orthogonal to the direction of the weight vector have no effect on the activation of the hidden unit. The "equi-activation surfaces" (on which a hidden unit's activation is constant) are hyperplanes orthogonal to the direction of $\vec{w}_h$. The parameters of a hidden unit h can be characterized by

- a direction, $\vec{w}_h/\|\vec{w}_h\|$,
- a scale parameter, $\|\vec{w}_h\|$, and
- a location parameter, $b_h/\|\vec{w}_h\|$.

The symbol $\|\cdot\|$ denotes the (Euclidean) length of the vector.

The second step can be viewed as "piping" ξ_h through a nonlinear *activation function*. We here choose *sigmoid* (or logistic) units whose activations S_h are given by

$$S_h = S(\xi_h) = \frac{1}{1 + e^{-a\xi_h}} = \frac{1}{2}\left(1 + \tanh\frac{a}{2}\xi_h\right).$$

The gain a can be absorbed into weights and biases without loss of generality and is set to unity. The sigmoid performs a smooth mapping $(+\infty, -\infty) \rightarrow (0, 1)$.

The output of the network yields the prediction $\hat{x}_t$ as a weighted sum of the activations of the hidden units. To summarize, such a network globally superimposes nonlinear functions to produce an output that can be viewed as a surface above the $(x_1, x_2, \ldots, x_d)$-plane of the inputs.

Viewed from the perspective of statistics, the network estimates the *conditional mean*,

$$E[p(x_t|x_{t-1}, x_{t-2}, \ldots, x_{t-d}, \text{parameters})],$$

where p is the probability of an output value x_t for a given input vector. Note that this probability distribution p of the model, given inputs and parameters, is not to be confused with the probability distribution of the observed output given the predicted output, that is, the error model. Whereas the prior assumptions about measurement noise and model misspecification are reflected in a usually simple error model (we here assume the errors to be Gaussian distributed), the conditional mean depends on the data and can be fairly complicated.

16.1.2 Evaluation

To evaluate and compare the predictive power of different algorithms, we use the *normalized mean squared error* (or *average relative variance*[1]) of a set $\mathscr{S}$, NMSE($\mathscr{S}$), defined as

$$\frac{\sum_{k \in \mathscr{S}}(\text{target}_k - \text{prediction}_k)^2}{\sum_{k \in \mathscr{S}}(\text{target}_k - \text{mean})^2} = \frac{1}{\hat{\sigma}^2}\frac{1}{N}\sum_{k \in \mathscr{S}}(x_k - \hat{x}_k)^2. \tag{16.1}$$

The sum extends over the set $\mathscr{S}$ of pairs of the actual values (or targets, x_k) and predicted values ($\hat{x}_k$). The averaging (division by N, the number of data points in a set $\mathscr{S}$) makes the measure independent of the size of the set. The normalization (division by $\hat{\sigma}^2$, the estimated variance of the data) removes the dependence on the dynamic range of the data.

This quantity corresponds to the fraction of the squared error of the data that is not "explained" by the network, compared to simply predicting the mean of the data set. The symbol $\mathscr{S}$ in equation 16.1 indicates the data set used to compute the errors:

• Training set. This part of the data is used to estimate the parameters. The *fitting error* (or *approximation error* or *in-sample performance*) describes the fidelity to the data. If the model also needs to be determined, this set is further split into two sets. The first set, still called *training set*, is used for direct parameter estimation. The second set is referred to as *cross-validation set* and is used to determine the stopping point of the training process.[2]

• Prediction set. A certain part of the available data is strictly kept apart and only used to quote the expected performance in the future as *prediction error* or *out-of-sample performance*.

Ultimately, we are interested in good performance for future predictions. Can we simply use the performance on the training set as an estimate of the predictive performance? Do we really need to set some data apart as prediction set?

It is well known that the in-sample performance can be a poor estimate of the out-of-sample performance, particularly in the presence of noise. For linear regression, it is sometimes possible to correct for the usually overoptimistic estimate. An example is to multiply the fitting error with $(N + k)/(N - k)$, where N is the number of data points and k is the number of parameters of the model (Akaike 1970). It is not at all clear to what degree such approximations hold for nonlinear models, such as connectionist networks.

Now, even if we decided to ignore the issue of nonlinearities completely, what value should we use for k? Although the number of *available* parameters of the network is fixed, the number of *effective* parameters increases during training. Although all parameters are already present at the beginning of the training process, the number of parameters that are effective for solving the task is zero since they were just randomly initialized. We show in section 16.3.1 how the number of effective parameters increases during training. This focus on learning is different from the typical assumption in statistics that the parameters are fully estimated at the time of model selection.

Up to now, we have ignored the question of how to determine the values of the weights and biases. In the next section, we turn to this question of parameter estimation and also to the problem of mcdel selection in the presence of noise.

16.2   Learning

16.2.1   Backpropagation

We use the error backpropagation algorithm to train the network: the parameters are changed by gradient descent on the cost surface over the weights and biases. On the whole, the problem of building a network that readily memorizes a set of training data has proved easier than expected. However, the problem of good generallzation has proved more difficult.

16.2.2   Generalization

Connectionist networks are in essence statistical devices for inductive inference. There is a trade-off between two goals. On the one hand, we want such devices to be as general as possible so that they can learn a broad range of problems. This recommends large and flexible networks. On the other hand, the true measure of an inductive device is not how well it performs on the training examples but how it performs on cases it has not yet seen—that is, its out-of-sample performance.

Too many weights of high precision make it easy for a network to fit the noise of the training data. In this case, when the network picks out the idiosyncrasies of the training sample, the generalization to new cases is poor. This *overfitting problem* is familiar in inductive inference, such as polynomial curve fitting. In the extreme, the polynomial fits the training points exactly and merely interpolates between them.

There are several potential solutions to this problem. We focus here on the so-called minimal network strategy. The underlying hypothesis is: if several networks fit the data almost equally well, the simplest one will on the average provide the best generalization. Evaluating this hypothesis requires some way of measuring simplicity and a search procedure for finding the desired network.

The complexity of an algorithm can be measured by the length of its minimal description in some language. The old but vague intuition of Occam's razor—or dream—can be formalized as the *minimum description length criterion*: Given some data, the most probable model is the model that minimizes the sum

description length(data given model) + description length(model).

This sum represents the trade-off between residual error and model complexity. The goal is to find a network that has the lowest complexity while fitting the data adequately. The complexity of a network is dominated by the number of bits needed to encode the weights. It is roughly proportional to the number of weights times the number of bits per weight. We focus here on the procedure of weight elimination that tries to find a network with the smallest number of weights.

In section 16.3.1, we compare weight elimination to *cross-validation*; in that case, the cost function consists only of the error term. Overfitting is prevented by stopping the training early, before the error reaches its asymptotic minimum. This leads to a network with fewer effective parameters than the total number of weights and biases.

16.2.3 Weight Elimination

In 1987, Rumelhart proposed several methods for finding minimal networks within the framework of backpropagation learning. A natural description of the complexity of a network uses quantities such as the size of the weights, the number of connections, the number of hidden units, the number of layers of hidden units, or the symmetries of the network. We focus on the method of weight elimination that considers the size of the weights and the number of weights and interpret the complexity term as a prior distribution of the weights.

Method   The idea is indeed simple in conception: add to the error a term that counts the number of parameters. We are looking for a differentiable function that is zero for zero weights and approaches a constant for large weights. We choose

$$\frac{w_i^2/w_0^2}{1 + w_i^2/w_0^2}.$$

w_0 is the scale for the weights. The subscript i in w_i simply enumerates the weights. The sum extends over all connections $\mathscr{C}$. Note that the biases do not enter the cost function: all offsets are a priori equally probable. (In the framework developed below, this corresponds to a noninformative prior; the probability density for the location parameter is flat.)

The performance term depends on the model for measurement errors. Since we assume that the errors are Gaussian distributed, the complete cost function is given by

$$\sum_{k \in \mathscr{T}} (\text{target}_k - \text{output}_k)^2 + \lambda \sum_{i \in \mathscr{C}} \frac{w_i^2/w_0^2}{1 + w_i^2/w_0^2}. \tag{16.2}$$

The first term, summed over the set of training examples $\mathscr{T}$, measures the performance of the network. The second term measures the size of the network. λ represents the relative importance of the complexity term with respect to the performance term.

The learning rule is to change the weights and biases according to the gradient of the *entire* cost function, continuously doing justice to the trade-off between error and complexity. This is different from the methods mentioned in section 16.1.2, which consider a set of fixed models, estimate the parameters for each of them, and then compare between the models.

The complexity cost is shown in figure 16.2 as function of w_i/w_0. For $|w_i| \gg w_0$, the cost of a weight approaches unity (times λ). This justifies the interpretation of the complexity term as a counter of significantly sized weights. For $|w_i| \ll w_0$, the cost is close to zero. "Large" and "small" are defined with respect to the scale w_0. It is a free parameter of the weight elimination procedure. In our experience, choosing w_0 of order unity is

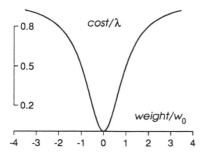

Figure 16.2
Complexity cost (in units of λ) of a weight as function of the size of the weight (in units of w_o)

good for activations of order unity. The effects of the choice for w_0 are discussed further below.

λ is dynamically adjusted in training. This dynamic increase, described in detail in Weigend et al. (1992), is related to the concept of iterated training as opposed to one-shot parameter estimation. At the beginning of the training, the weights are not useful yet, since they were just initialized randomly. Any significant cost for complexity would devour the whole network. Hence, λ starts at zero. The usual subsequent increase corresponds to attaching more importance to the complexity term or, from the perspective developed in the next section, to sharpening the peak around zero of the prior distribution of the probability density function of the weights.

Interpretation as Prior Probability   In a Bayesian framework, the complexity cost can be viewed as the negative logarithm of the prior probability of a weight. In figure 16.3, we show the prior probability density function from which single weights of size w_i are drawn,

$$\text{prior} \propto \left[\exp\left(-\frac{w_i^2/w_0^2}{1 + w_i^2/w_0^2} \right) \right]^{\lambda}.$$

It is a mixture of a flat distribution and a bump around zero. Relevant weights are drawn from the flat distribution. Weights that are merely the result of noise are drawn from the bump centered on zero; they are expected to be small.

So far, we have described only our choice of the prior for a single weight. How do we get to the whole network? Assuming that the weights can be

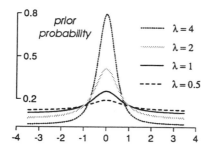

Figure 16.3
Prior probability of a weight as function of the size of the weight (in units of w_o), plotted for different values of λ

treated as independent, we simply sum over the connections in equation 16.2.

Ridge Regresssion as Special Case   We here discuss the relationship of our method of weight *elimination* to weight *decay*, proposed by Hinton and by Le Cun in 1987. In weight decay, a small percentage of the weight is subtracted at each weight update,

$$\Delta w_i = \text{(weight change due to error backprop.)} - \alpha w_i.$$

This can be viewed as an exponential decay of the weight. It corresponds to a quadratic complexity cost ($\propto w_i^2$), known in the statistics community as *ridge regression*. It is contained in the weight elimination scheme as the special case of large w_0. Weight decay always prefers networks with many small weights. Weight elimination prefers few large weights over many medium-sized weights in the region where it saturates. The scale parameter w_0 allows us to express a preference for many small weights (w_0 large) versus a few large weights (w_0 small). Depending on the dynamic range and the number of the units of the preceding layer, w_0 might be given different values for different layers of the network.

Expressing the cost of a weight as a prior can make it easier to interpret distributions that are not intuitive when viewed as penalty costs. Nowlan (1991) proposes a mixture of a few Gaussians as prior. This prior assumes that networks with weights around a few centers are more likely than networks with weights of many different values; see also Nowlan and Hinton (1992).

We now apply these methods to time-series prediction.

16.3   Sunspots

The sunspot series has served as a benchmark in the statistics literature. Within the paradigm of autoregression, different models differ in the specific choice of the primitives for the surface above the input space. In the simplest case, a single hyperplane approximates the data points. Such a *linear autoregressive model* is a linear superposition of past values.

The evaluation of the network model, however, is carried out by comparison to a *nonlinear* model, the *threshold autoregressive model* (TAR) by Tong and Lim (1980) (see also Tong 1990). It has served as a benchmark for Subba Rao and Gabr (1984), for Priestley (1988), for Lewis and Stevens (1991), for Stokbro (1991), and for others.

The TAR model is globally nonlinear: it consists of two local linear autoregressive models. Tong and Lim found optimal performance for input dimension $d = 12$. They used yearly sunspot data from 1700 through 1920 for training and the data from 1921 to 1979 to evaluate the predictions.

To make the comparison between network and TAR performance as close as possible, we use their exact data for training and evaluation, their choice of the input dimension, their error model, and their evaluation criterion.

16.3.1 Learning the Series

In this section we analyze the in-sample learning behavior of the networks—first with a cross-validation set (needed to determine a stopping point when there is no complexity term in the cost function) and then with weight elimination. The out-of-sample performance will be analyzed in section 16.3.2.

Internal Validation (Early Stopping) The learning of the sunspot series of a 12-8-1 network is shown in figure 16.4 as a function of epochs. An epoch is one iteration of gradient descent in which the network sees each point from the training set once. Training with standard backpropagation (no weight elimination) is displayed in the left panel. (The panel on the right-hand side is discussed below.)

The success in mastering the training set is indicated by the monotonic decrease of the lowest curve, indicating the *in-sample performance* (or *fitting error*). To get a feeling for the nonstationarity of the time series, the prediction set was split in two parts, 1921–1955 and 1956–1979. On both prediction sets, the error first decreases but then starts to increase: the network begins to use its resources to fit the noise of the training set. It starts to pick out properties that are specific to the training set but not present in the prediction sets. This is an indication of overfitting.

When should the training should be stopped? Since prediction sets should not be used for this decision, a validation set is required to determine the end of the training process. To get a feeling for the effect of the sampling error by picking a specific training set–validation set combination, we investigated several training set–validation set pairs.

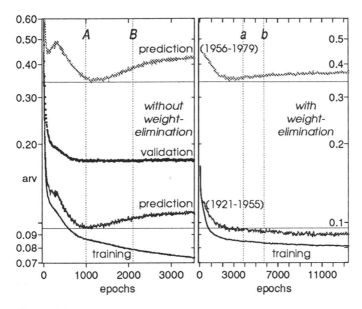

Figure 16.4
Learning curves of a 12-8-1 network. The average relative single-step prediction variances are given for the training sets, and early and late prediction sets (as well as for the cross-validation set for the network trained without weight-elimination on the left side). The vertical lines (A, B, a, b) indicate different stopping points. The average relative variance is normalized by the variance of the entire record, $\sigma^2 = 1535$

The validation sets consisted of 22 years chosen at random from the time before 1920. Those points were removed in the corresponding training sets, reducing their size by 10 percent. The variations in performance due to different pairs of training and validation sets are larger than the variations due to different sets of random initial weights.[3] In the example given in figure 16.4, the validation set error approaches an asymptotic value. Since it does not increase, it is not entirely clear which set of weights should be taken. We thus compare in section 16.3.2 the performance for two stopping points, A and B.

Some of the problems with early stopping through cross-validation are that (1) a part of the available training data cannot be used directly for parameter estimation, (2) the monitored validation set error often shows multiple minima as a function of training time (even in the simple linear case analyzed by Baldi and Chauvin 1991), (3) the specific solution at the stopping points depends strongly on the specific pair of training set and validation set, and (4) the results are sensitive to the initial parameters.

Before comparing cross-validation with weight elimination, we turn in the next section to how the effective number of parameters changes with training. We first focus on the activations of the hidden units, then on the weights between inputs and hidden units.

Effective Dimension of Hidden Units   Still within the framework of standard backpropagation, we analyze the change of the effective dimension of the hidden unit space during training by computing the spectrum of the eigenvalues of the covariance matrix of the hidden unit activations. The covariance C_{ij} corresponds to the two-point correlation between the activations of the two hidden units i and j, computed over the training set,

$$C_{ij} = \mathbf{E}[(S_i - \bar{S}_i)(S_j - \bar{S}_j)],$$

where $\bar{S}_i = \mathbf{E}[S_i]$ is the mean activation of hidden unit i, taken over the set of training points. Since the covariance matrix is symmetric, $C_{ij} = C_{ji}$, its eigenvalues are real.

Linear correlation is appropriate, since the output linearly combines the hidden unit activations. The number of significantly sized eigenvalues is a measure of the effective dimension of the hidden unit space. It can be viewed as the effective rank of the covariance matrix. For linear networks, Baldi and Hornik (in press) use similar concepts.

Figure 16.5 shows the eigenvalue spectrum as a function of training time.[4] The eigenvalues correspond to the variances captured by the corresponding eigenvectors. In the figure, we plot the square root of the eigenvalues. They correspond to the standard deviations "explained" by the corresponding principal components. The figure shows that *gradient descent extracts one component after another*. This provides some justification for the whole strategy of oversized networks and early stopping; the dimension of the hidden unit space starts essentially at zero and then increases in training. The goal is to stop at just the right dimension.

So far, we have focused on eigenvalues derived from hidden unit *activations*. We now turn to eigenvalues derived from *weights*. We analyze the singular value decomposition of the weight matrix between inputs and hidden units. We decompose the 12×8 weight matrix (inputs $\times$ hidden units) into two orthogonal matrices and one diagonal matrix and display the square root of the eigenvalues of that diagonal matrix in figure 16.6. At

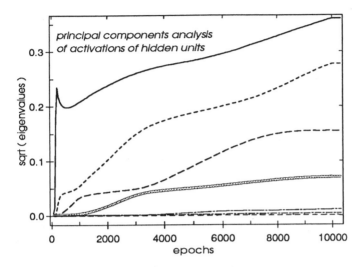

Figure 16.5
Eigenvalue spectrum of the covariance matrix of the hidden unit activations. The double line represents the fourth largest eigenvalue

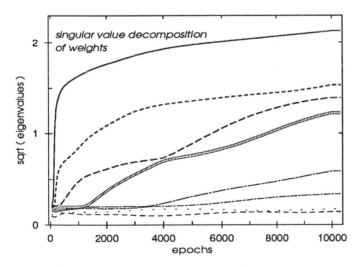

Figure 16.6
Eigenvalue spectrum of the singular value-decomposed matrix of weights between input and hidden units

the beginning of the training, the eigenvalues just reflect the initialization of the weights.[5] As training proceeds, the dimension spanned by the weight space increases.

Both figures 16.5 and 16.6 contain information only from the training set. We now compare this information with the performance on the prediction set. In the run used for the eigenvalue calculations, the out-of-sample error reached its minimum around epoch 1000. At that point in training, the hidden units span an effectively three-dimensional space. Extracting the fourth and subsequent eigenvalues hence corresponds to overfitting.

In the next section, we turn to training with weight elimination. Interestingly, weight elimination yields networks with three hidden units. This agreement between the effective dimension of hidden units at the onset of overfitting and the number of hidden units after weight elimination is encouraging.

Weight Elimination   As in backpropagation without weight elimination, we start with a network sufficiently large for the task. The training curve for backpropagation with weight elimination is shown in the right panel of figure 16.4. Significant overfitting is avoided, even for training times four times as long. Since the entire training set is used, we are relieved of the uncertainty of a specific choice for a validation set. But we still have to decide when the asymptotic state is reached. The performance of two solutions (*a* and *b*) is compared in section 16.3.2. It turns out that the exact stopping point is not important. In the first 5000 epochs, the procedure eliminated the weights between the output unit and five of the eight hidden units. Only three hidden units survived.

Weights from inputs to dead hidden units have no effect on the output. Since there is no reason for the network to pay a price for these weights, they subsequently also get eliminated. For time-series prediction, weight elimination acts as hidden unit elimination.

We analyzed the specific solution of the network that was stopped at point *b* and subsequently trained with a very small learning rate for a few epochs. The main contribution to the first hidden unit comes from x_{t-9}, to the second hidden unit from x_{t-2}, and to the third hidden unit from x_{t-1}. In contrast to the output weights, only very few of the weights from the input units to the active hidden units disappeared. (The weights and biases of the network are given in Weigend et al. 1990).

Predictions are obtained by adding the values of these three hidden units. The main encoding is performed by the nonlinear projection from the twelve-dimensional input space onto the three-dimensional hidden unit space.

16.3.2 Predictions and Comparisons

So far, we have concentrated on the *learning* behavior of the network. Just obtaining a small network, however, is not an end in itself; the ultimate goal is to *predict* future values. In this section, we assess the predictive power of the network and compare it to other approaches. We first analyze single-step predictions and then turn to multistep predictions.

Single-Step Prediction The term *single-step prediction* (or *one-step-ahead prediction*) is used when all input units, are given the actual values of the time series (as opposed to the predicted values). To assess the single-step prediction performance, we use the normalized mean squared error defined in equation 16.1.

The weight-eliminated network gives

$$\text{NMSE(train)} = 0.082, \quad \text{NMSE(predict)}_{1921-1955} = 0.086.$$

The corresponding values for the TAR model are

$$\text{NMSE(train)} = 0.097, \quad \text{NMSE(predict)}_{1921-1955} = 0.097.$$

Comparing these numbers, we see that the single-step predictions of the network and the benchmark model are comparable. Despite this similarity, significant differences will appear for predictions further than one step into the future.

Multistep Prediction There are two ways to predict further than one step into the future. We first present the results of iterated single-step predictions and subsequently turn to direct multistep predictions. Most of the analysis so far applies to regression in general. Iterated predictions, however, are specific to time series.

In *iterated single-step* predictions, the predicted output is fed back as input for the next prediction, and all other input units are shifted back one unit. Hence, the inputs consist of *predicted* values as opposed to observations of the original time series. The predicted value for time t, obtained after I iterations, is denoted by $\hat{x}_{t,I}$.

The prediction error will not only depend on I but also on the time $(t - I)$ when the iteration was started. We wish to obtain a performance measure as a function of the number of iterations I that averages over the starting times. Since we want to exploit fully the standard prediction set range for the sunspot data from $t_{\text{BEGIN}} = 1921$ to $t_{\text{END}} = 1955$, we compute for each I the average

$$\frac{1}{\sigma^2} \frac{1}{t_{\text{END}} - (t_{\text{BEGIN}} - 1 + I)} \sum_{t_{\text{BEGIN}} - 1 + I}^{t_{\text{END}}} (x_t - \hat{x}_{t,I})^2.$$

This (average relative) prediction variance after I iterations is shown in figure 16.7. To indicate the spread of network performances, we give several network solution. The letters A, B, a, b refer to the different stopping points, shown in figure 16.4. The differences between the different network solutions are not significant.

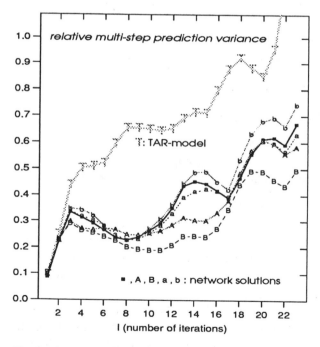

Figure 16.7
Relative prediction error after I iterations for the sunspot series. Gray T's give the performance of the TAR model. Black squares show the performance of the weight-eliminated network with three hidden units. The other curves indicate the performance of the network solutions from figure 16.4

An alternative to this multistep prediction by iterated single-step prediction is *direct multistep* prediction: the network is trained to predict directly several steps ahead. On the sunspot data set, the prediction error for direct multistep prediction was worse than the error for iterated single-step prediction; direct predictions require a more complex network.

In summary, although we took extreme care not to gain any unfair advantage over Tong and Lim (1980) (by taking the same input dimension, using identical data sets, minimizing the same sum of squared errors, etc.), the multistep predictions were found to be significantly better: on average, the iterated prediction variances of the network were about half the iterated prediction variances of the TAR model. This concludes the comparison with the benchmark model.[6]

Subba Rao and Gabr (1984) apply a *bilinear model*[7] to the sunspot data and find an improvement of about 15% over the TAR model, both for single-step and iterated predictions. On predictions further than one step into the future, the networks outperform the bilinear model on average by 35% in mean squared error.

Stokbro (1991) uses a *weighted linear predictor* (WLP). In a WLP, each primitive is the product of a first-order polynomial and a normalized Gaussian radial basis function. The predictor is the linear superposition of these primitives. Stokbro compares WLP with the network solution on the 1921–1946 prediction set given in Weigend, Huberman, and Rumelhart (1990). For one and two iterations, both methods have similar errors. When iterated more than twice, the network outperforms the WLP model.

Recently, Lewis and Stevens (1991) applied *multivariate adaptive regression splines* (MARS) by Friedman (1991) to the sunspot series. We find that the performance of MARS is very similar to the performance of the network. Given that the primitives of both schemes (sigmoids and splines) are smooth, and given that both approaches employ a regularization scheme that penalizes complexity, the similar performance is not astonishing but rather encouraging.

16.3.3 Varying the Input Dimension

Up to now, all predictions were based on information of the preceding 12 years. What happens if we vary the input dimension? When the number of input units is reduced, we expect the error to increase, at least at some stage. But when the number of input units is increased, two effects compete. On the one hand, more information becomes available, possibly

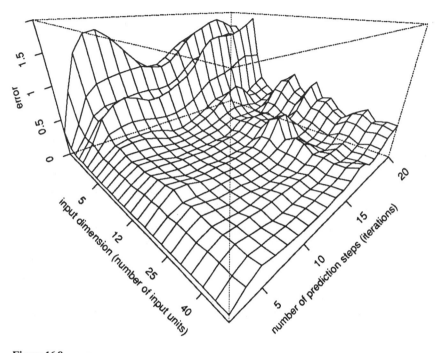

Figure 16.8
Prediction error for sunspots as function of the number of inputs and forecasting time

allowing for better predictions. On the other hand, the higher the input dimension is, the more sparsely distributed the training data are. Will the networks be robust if more input units than necessary are present?

The prediction error for iterated single-step predictions (for the 1921–1955 set) is shown in figure 16.8 as surface above the number of inputs and the prediction time into the future. Networks with one input unit of lag one already manage to capture two-thirds of the single-step variance, reducing it to 0.33. The solution is practically linear with an offset. Networks with two input units reduce the normalized mean squared error to 0.17. They begin to use the available nonlinearities. With increasing number of input units, the error reaches a roughly constant value. The performance does not degrade with input dimension several times larger than necessary; the networks ignore irrelevant information.

To summarize, we use a procedure called weight elimination that addresses the related problems of network size and overfitting by dynamically eliminating weights during training. In this chapter, we focus on the time series of yearly sunspot averages from the year 1700 onward. On iterated predictions into the future, the network performance turns out to be very similar to MARS and significantly better than other models.

We close with two references to further examples of networks for time-series prediction. In Weigend, Huberman, and Rumelhart (1990), we analyze a time series from a computational ecosystem and show that connectionist networks can predict the utilization of the resources of the ecosystem for hundreds of steps into the future. And in Weigend Huberman, Rumelhart (1992), we apply networks to the prediction of the notoriously noisy foreign exchange rates and show that the key to a solution there is selection of the relevant variables through weight elimination.

Acknowledgments

The original formulation of weight elimination benefited from conversations with Paul Smolensky. We also thank Jerry Friedman, Steve Hanson, Mike Mozer, and Art Owen for discussions.

Notes

1. In this chapter, the term *variance* refers to sums of squared errors. In the statistics community, there also exists a narrower meaning, as in bias-variance trade-off. We use the term *variance* to denote the sum of both the squared bias and the variance in the narrower sense. Incidentally, in the connectionist community, the term *bias* simply denotes an additive constant to the input of a unit.

2. Our use of the term *cross-validation* differs from repeated leave-k-out procedures in that we use only one cross-validation set. Since our emphasis is on the *training* process, we use the validation set to monitor the progress during training.

3. We chose the years for the validation sets randomly. An improvement might be to consider only random splits where the first and second moments (mean and variance) of the validation set match the training set. Another idea is first to train, stop, and save several networks on different training-validation pairs and then combine their individual predictions. The combination is done by freezing the weights and biases of the subnets and letting only the few new combination weights adapt to the entire training set.

4. The activations of the eight hidden units for each ot the 209 points of the training set were recorded after every 50 epochs of training with learning rate 0.03. The overshooting of the largest principal component disappears if the hidden unit activations are multiplied with their corresponding output weights prior to computing the covariance matrix.

5. We started the training with weights drawn from a uniform distribution over the interval $[-0.03, 0.03]$, corresponding to almost linear hidden units.

6. The discrepancy between a negligible difference in single-step prediction accuracy and a factor of two for iterated predictions is interesting. A conjecture (from a discussion with Jerry Friedman) is the following: Consider the single-step squared error decomposed into a squared bias and a variance. In this note—in contrast to the rest of the chapter—the

term *variance* refers to the spread of network solutions (Geman, Bienenstock, and Doursat 1992). Since a network is a more flexible model than a TAR model, the bias of the network is smaller than the bias of TAR. If iterating amplifies the squared bias more than the variance, the observed effect is explained.

7. In addition to linear autoregression (terms proportional to x_{t-i}), Subba Rao and Gabr (1984) allow terms proportional to the forecasting errors ε_{t-j} as well as terms proportional to the product $x_{t-k}\varepsilon_{t-l}$ (bilinear interactions). In the framework of connectionist networks, arbitrary interactions between lagged inputs x_{t-k} and past prediction errors ε_{t-l} are modeled by enhancing the usual input with a set of units representing ε_{t-l}. Such a network can learn to extract possibly nonlinear responses to outside shocks.

References

Akaike, Hirotugo. Statistical predictor identification. *Ann. Institute of Statistical Mathematics*, 22:203–217, 1970.

Baldi, Pierre, and Chauvin, Yves. Temporal evolution of generalization during learning in linear networks. *Neural Computation*, 3:589–603, 1991.

Baldi, Pierre, and Hornik, Kurt. Back-propagation and unsupervised learning in linear networks. In Chauvin, Y., and Rumelhart, D. E., editors, *Theory, Architectures and Applications*. Lawrence Erlbaum, (in press).

Friedman, Jerome H. Multivariate adaptive regression splines. *Annals of Statistics*, 19:1–141, 1991.

Geman, Stuart, Bienenstock, Elie, and Doursat, René. Neural networks and the bias/variance dilemma. *Neural Computation*, 4:1–58, 1992.

Lapedes, Alan S., and Farber, Robert M. Nonlinear signal processing using neural networks: Prediction and system modelling. Technical Report LA-UR-87-2662. Los Alamos National Laboratory, 1987.

Lewis, Peter A. W., and Stevens, J. G. Nonlinear modeling of time series using multivariate adaptive regression splines (MARS). *Journal of the American Statistical Association*, 86:864–877, 1991.

Nowlan, Steven J. Soft Competitive Adaptation. Neural Network Learning Algorithms Based on Fitting Statistical Mixtures. Ph.D. dissertation, Carnegie Mellon University, 1991.

Priestley, Maurice B. *Non-linear and Non-stationary Time Series Analysis*. Academic Press, 1988.

Stokbro, Kurt. Predicting chaos with weighted maps. Technical Report 91/10 S. Nordita, Copenhagen, 1991.

Subba Rao, T., and Gabr, M. M. *An Introduction to Bispectral Analysis and Bilinear Time Series Models*. Lecture Notes in Statistics, no. 24. Springer, 1984.

Tong, Howell. *Non-linear Time Series: A Dynamical System Approach*. Oxford University Press, 1990.

Tong, Howell, and Lim, K. S. Threshold autoregression, limit cycles and cyclical data. *Journal of the Royal Statistical Society B*, 42:245–292, 1980.

Weigend, Andreas S., Huberman, Bernardo A., and Rumelhart, David E. Predicting the future: A connectionist approach. *International Journal of Neural Systems*, 1:193–209, 1990.

Weigend, Andreas S., Huberman, Bernardo A., and Rumelhart, David E. Predicting sunspots and exchange rates with connectionist networks. In Casdagli, M., and Eubank, S., editors, *Nonlinear Modeling and Forecasting,* pp. 395–432. Addison-Wesley, 1992.

17 Simulation Results for a New Two-armed Bandit Heuristic

Ronald L. Rivest and Yiqun Yin

17.1 Introduction

Bandit problems were first introduced by Robbins [10] in 1952. The name derives from an imagined slot machine with $k \geq 2$ arms. When an arm is pulled, the player wins a random reward according to an unknown probability distribution π_j. The player's problem is to choose a sequence of pulls on the k arms, depending on the results of previous trials, so as to maximize the long-run total reward. In general, we consider the problem of sampling $x_1, x_2, \ldots$ sequentially from k statistical populations (arms, medical treatments, etc.) specified by density functions $f(x, \theta_j)$ with respect to some measure v, where $f(\cdot, \cdot)$ is known and the θ_j's are unknown parameters belonging to some set Θ. We assume that the average reward

$$\mu(\theta) = \int_{-\infty}^{\infty} xf(x, \theta)\, dv(x) \tag{1}$$

is well defined for all $\theta \in \Theta$. The goal is to maximize, in some sense, the expected value of the sum

$$S_n = x_1 + x_2 + \cdots + x_n \tag{2}$$

as $n \to \infty$. There have been several different approaches to this problem based on different formulations of optimality.

In 1985 Lai and Robbins [6] constructed a class of asymptotically efficient strategies (also called "adaptive allocation rules"), and many works in recent years are based on their results. An adaptive allocation rule ϕ for a k-armed bandit problem is a sequence of random variables $\phi_1, \phi_2, \ldots$ taking values in the set $\{1, 2, \ldots, k\}$. We will give a brief survey of their algorithms in section 17.2.

Another approach is to consider for large fixed n (finite horizon) the Bayes problem of maximizing

$$\int_{\Theta} E_\theta S_n\, dH(\theta), \tag{3}$$

where $H(\theta)$ is a prior distribution on Θ^k, and where $\theta = (\theta_1, \theta_2, \ldots, \theta_k)$ gives the parameters defining the probability distribution for the rewards of each arm. Berry and Fristedt [1] studied the dynamic programming equations for the Bayes optimal solution analytically and obtained several interesting results about the Bayes optimal rules with respect to general priors. However, Bayes rules are usually described only implicitly by the dynamic programming equations, and they are usually difficult to compute numerically.

Besides the bandit problem we discussed above, there is also a class of "discounted multiarmed bandit problems," in which a discount factor of β, for some $0 < \beta < 1$, is introduced. Here we consider the problem of maximizing the expected value of the series

$$\sum_{i=1}^{\infty} \beta^{i-1} x_i. \tag{4}$$

Major advances in this problem were made by Gittins and Jones (see [3] for a survey of their work); their strategies are usually called "Gittins index rules." These rules have been shown to be optimal for the discounted problem.

In another point of view, the classical bandit problem can also be viewed as a learning process, in which we make decisions according to what we have learned in the past. Narendra and Thathachar [9] used "learning automata" as a framework for attacking this problem. Their basic idea is to update the probabilities of pulling each arm at every stage, based on the previous results. Most of these schemes were shown to be ε-optimal, which means that for every ε there exists a learning automaton that can achieve an asymptotic average reward rate that is within ε of optimality. Because learning automata have limited number of states, one cannot expect optimal performance from them.

17.2 Asymptotically Efficient Adaptive Allocation Rules

Let

$$\mu^*(\theta) = \max_{1 \le j \le k} \mu(\theta_j) = \mu(\theta^*) \tag{5}$$

for some $\theta^* \in \{\theta_1, \theta_2, \ldots, \theta_k\}$. Robbins [10] formulated a notion of asymptotic optimality as obtaining

$$\lim_{n \to \infty} n^{-1} E_\theta S_n = \mu^*(\theta) \quad \text{for all} \quad \theta \in \Theta^k. \tag{6}$$

For the case $k = 2$, he also introduced a class of simple allocation rules that attains (6). A natural question is how to make the rule so that $n^{-1} E_\theta S_n$ approaches $\mu^*(\theta)$ as quickly as possible.

Lai and Robbins [6] introduced the concept of "regret" as

$$R_n(\theta) = n\mu^*(\theta) - E_\theta S_n = \sum_{j:\mu(\theta_j)<\mu^*(\theta)} (\mu^*(\theta) - \mu(\theta_j))E_\theta T_n(j) \tag{7}$$

where $T_n(j)$ is the total number of observations from π_j up to stage n. Therefore, maximizing $E_\theta S_n$ is equivalent to minimizing the regret $R_n(\theta)$. Their main theoretical result is that for every reasonably good allocation rule (one that satisfies $R_n(\theta) = o(n^a)$ for every $a > 0$ for every fixed θ), we also have

$$\liminf_{n\to\infty} \frac{R_n(\theta)}{\ln n} \geq \sum_{j:\mu(\theta_j)<\mu^*(\theta)} \frac{(\mu^*(\theta) - \mu(\theta_j))}{I(\theta_j, \theta^*)} \tag{8}$$

for all $\theta \in \Theta^k$, where

$$I(\theta, \lambda) = \int_{-\infty}^{\infty} \{\ln[f(x, \theta)/f(x, \lambda)]\} f(x, \theta) \, dv(x) \tag{9}$$

is the Kullback-Leibler information number which gives a measure of the difference between two density functions. Moreover, a class of allocation rules that asymptotically attains this theoretical lower bound is constructed.

For $j = 1, 2, \ldots, k$, let $Y_{j1}, Y_{j2}, \ldots, Y_{jT_n(j)}$ denote the successive observations from π_j. Define

$$\hat{\mu}_n(j) = \frac{Y_{j1} + Y_{j2} + \cdots + Y_{jT_n(j)}}{T_n(j)}$$

as the estimated sample mean, and define a certain upper confidence bound for the mean of each population π_j as

$$U_n(j) = g_{n, T_n(j)}(Y_{j1}, \ldots, Y_{jT_n(j)}). \tag{10}$$

Define $j_n \in \{1, 2, \ldots, k\}$ such that

$$\hat{\mu}_n(j_n) = \max\{\hat{\mu}_n(j) : T_n(j) \geq \delta n\}. \tag{11}$$

At stage $n + 1$, then, where $j = (n + 1) \bmod k$, we select arm j only if

$$\hat{\mu}_n(j_n) \leq U_n(j); \tag{12}$$

otherwise we select arm j_n. Lai and Robbins proved that this rule satisfies the equation

$$E_\theta(T_n(j)) \sim \frac{\ln n}{I(\theta_j, \theta^*)} \tag{13}$$

for every j such that $\mu(\theta_j) < \mu(\theta^*)$.

For normal, Bernoulli, Poisson, and double exponential populations, they expressed the upper confidence bound as

$$U_n(j) = \inf\{\lambda \geq \hat{\mu}_n(j) : I(\hat{\mu}_n(j), \lambda) \geq a_{ni}\}, \tag{14}$$

where a_{ni} ($n = 1, 2, \ldots, i = 1, 2, \ldots, n$) are positive constants satsifying certain conditions. For example, in the case of a two-armed Bernoulli bandit a_{ni} can be chosen as $(\ln n)/i$.

17.3   A New Heuristic Algorithm

In this section we propose a simple heuristic algorithm for the bandit problem, which seems to have (empirically) better performance than the algorithm of Lai and Robbins [6] discussed in the previous section.

As before, let $Y_{j1}, Y_{j2}, \ldots, Y_{jT_n(j)}$ denote the successive observations from π_j up to stage n. We define $\hat{\mu}_n(j)$ as the estimated sample mean (as above), and define $\hat{\sigma}_n(j)$ as the estimated standard deviation of the sample mean, for $j = 1, 2, \ldots, k$. The new allocation rule is the following:

At stage $n + 1$, we associate a random variable $Z_n(j)$ with each arm j, where $Z_n(j)$ has a normal distribution with mean $\hat{\mu}_n(j)$ and standard deviation $\hat{\sigma}_n(j)$. We then sample from population j_n, where

$$Z_n(j_n) = \max\{Z_n(1), Z_n(2), \ldots, Z_n(k)\}.$$

We call this new heuristic the "Z-heuristic." The $Z_n(j)$ variables are intended to reflect the learner's uncertainty about the true values for $\theta(j)$.

We now apply both the Lai and Robbins algorithm and our new heuristic to construct allocation rules for normal and Bernoulli populations. The simulation results are given in the next section.

17.4   Experimental Results

We considered the bandit problem for two kinds of arms: Bernoulli variables and normal variables. In both case the parameter θ was equal to the expected reward. For the Bernoulli arms with parameter θ a reward of value 1 was received with probability θ, and a reward of value 0 was received with probability $(1 - \theta)$. For the normal arms the mean reward was θ, and the variance was equal to 1.

We implemented the Lai and Robbins algorithm and the Z-heuristic and ran these algorithms for $n = 10^7$ trials for $k = 2$ and four sets of probabilities:

$\theta = (0.1, 0.9)$,

$\theta = (0.46, 0.54)$,

$\theta = (0.496, 0.504)$, and

$\theta = (0.4996, 0.5004)$.

We also calculated for these experiments the theoretical bound from equation (13). Because this formula behaved poorly for small values of n, we also calculated the value of the heuristic formula

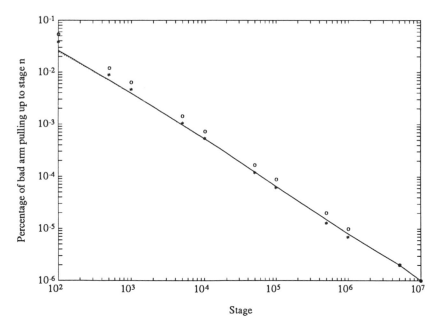

Figure 17.1
Two Bernoulli arms: $\theta = (0.1, 0.9)$

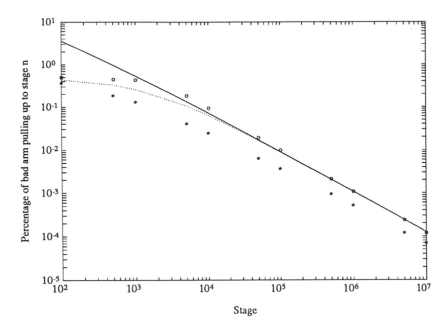

Figure 17.2
Two Bernoulli arms: $\theta = (0.46, 0.54)$.

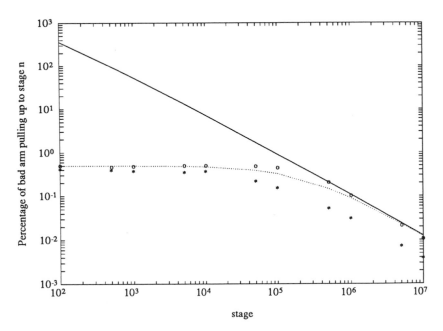

Figure 17.3
Two Bernoulli arms: $\theta = (0.496, 0.504)$

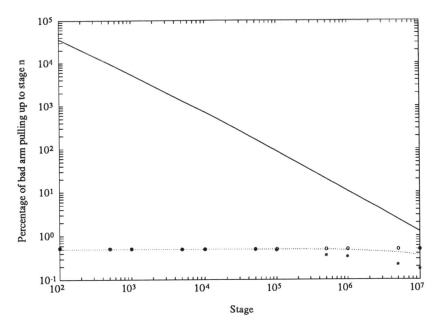

Figure 17.4
Two Bernoulli arms: $\theta = (0.4996, 0.5004)$

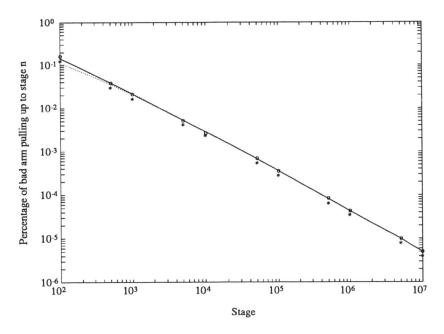

Figure 17.5
Two normal arms: $\theta = (0.1, 0.9)$

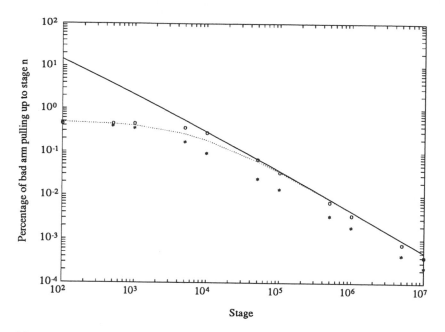

Figure 17.6
Two normal arms: $\theta = (0.46, 0.54)$

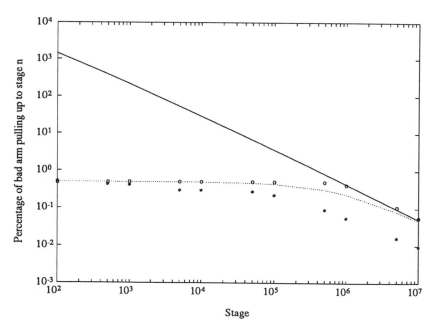

Figure 17.7
Two normal arms: $\theta = (0.496, 0.504)$

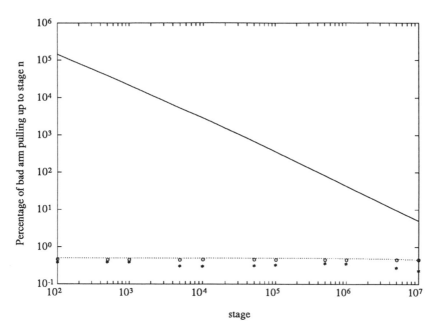

Figure 17.8
Two normal arms: $\theta = (0.4996, 0.5004)$

$$E_\theta(T_n(j)) \sim \frac{\ln n}{I(\theta_1, \theta_2) + \dfrac{2 \ln n}{n}} \tag{15}$$

(which is approximately $n/2$ for small n, but approaches the Lai and Robbins bound asymptotically).

The results are plotted in figures 17.1–17.8. In each case, the Lai and Robbins bound is plotted as a heavy line, and formula (15) is plotted as a dotted line. The performance of the Lai and Robbins algorithm is plotted as o's, and the Z-heuristic is plotted as $*$'s.

We see that the Z-heuristic performs much better than the Lai and Robbins algorithm for the experiments we tried. We conjecture that the Z-heuristic is asymptotically optimal, and we are working to prove this conjecture.

Notes

Supported by NSF grant CCR-8914428, ARO grant DAAL03-86-K-0171, and the Siemens Corporation.

References

[1] Berry, D. A., and Fristedt, B. *Bandit Problems-Sequential Allocation of Experiments.* Chapman and Hall, New York, 1985.

[2] Chang, Fu, and Tze Leung Lai. Optimal stopping and dynamic allocation. *Advances in Applied Probability* 19:829–853, 1987.

[3] Gittins, J. C. *Multi-armed Bandit Allocation Indices.* John Wiley and Sons, New York, 1989.

[4] Lai, T. L. Asymptotic solutions of bandit problems. In W. Fleming and P. L. Lions, editors, *Stochastic Differential Systems, Stochastic Control Theory and Applications.* Springer-Verlag, Berlin, 1988.

[5] Lai, T. L., and Herbert Robbins. Optimal sequential sampling from two populations. *Proceedings National Academy Science USA* 81:1284–1286, 1984.

[6] Lai, T. L., and Herbert Robbins. Asymptotically efficient adaptive allocation rules. *Advances in Applied Mathematics* 6:4–22, 1985.

[7] Lai, Tze Leung. Adaptive treatment allocation and the multi-armed bandit problem. *Annals of Statistics* 15 (3): 1091–1114, 1987.

[8] Lai, Tze Leung, and Zhiliang Ying. Open bandit processes and optimal scheduling of queueing networks. *Advances in Applied Probability* 20:447–472, 1988.

[9] Narendra, Kumpati S., and Mandayam A. L. Thathachar. *Learning Automata—An Introduction.* Prentice-Hall, New York, 1989.

[10] Robbins, H. Some aspects of the sequential design of experiments. *Bulletin American Mathematical Society* 55:527–535, 1952.

[11] Tsitsiklis, John N. A lemma on the multiarmed bandit problem. *IEEE Transactions on Automatic Control,* AC-31 (6), 1986.

[12] Whittle, Peter. *Optimization Over Time,* Vol. 2. John Wiley and Sons, New York, 1983.

18 Hard Questions about Easy Tasks: Issues from Learning to Play Games

Susan L. Epstein

As AI produces more powerful and successful expert systems (Guha and Lenat, 1990; Ginsberg, Weiss, and Politakis 1988; Rokey and Grenander 1990), the tasks end users set for them become ever more ambitious. In many areas it is no longer enough to provide computer systems that perform as well as humans; users want computer systems that *outperform* people. When a task has well-defined standards, such as not spilling the paint on a car production line or machining a piece within a specific tolerance, evaluation of the expert system's performance is a well-defined mathematical computation. It is not difficult, at least in theory, to hold such systems to quantifiable standards that people cannot attain.

People also excel, however, at behaviors for which there are no known absolute standards of perfection. For example, although there are many excellent human chess players, no one knows whether the game should be a win for black, a win for white, or a draw. Thus one could produce an expert program to play chess and have no absolute standard for it. The program could defeat all other chess programs, draw with the human world champion, and yet we would not know if it modeled the best chess play possible. Another example is intelligent robotic agents that function in environments hostile to people: in extreme temperatures, under water, on another planet. Not only are these difficult tasks, but we have no standards for excellence at them.

For such behaviors, it may be unreasonable to expect any expert system to spring forth in perfection. Human experts are not born; people *learn* their expertise. Expert systems could also construct their expertise incrementally, from their experience in the problem domain. Just as people begin with rudimentary hardware and software facilities, it is reasonable to provide such a learning expert system with initial powers and knowledge. The identification, implementation, and balance of this start-up information with the extraction of useful data from experience are the central concerns of this research.

A learning expert system for a single problem may be uneconomical, because its development time is so much greater than the hand-coded, nonlearning, problem-specific solution. To learn about its domain, an expert system must have some prior knowledge: the nature of the domain, what it is to learn, and how it is to learn it. The more domain-specific advice we deny such a program, the more it must be endowed with world knowledge or commonsense. CYC (Lenat and Feigenbaum 1991), for example, requires an enormous fund of knowledge before it can embark on discovery.

The approach described here takes a middle road; given general prior knowledge for a set of related problem classes (a *skill*), it develops expertise at them. There are several good reasons for considering such learning in a skill domain. First, the significant development cost for a learning expert system in the context of a single problem is amortized across multiple problems. Second, a skill reduces the identification of necessary world knowledge to a task of manageable size. Third, learning in a skill domain more closely models human experts, who are competent at a variety of related problems and whose performance gracefully degrades rather than collapses in an unfamiliar environment. Fourth, the perspective on the task provided by a variety of related problems should help the designer identify the important commonalities among them, called here a *weak theory* for the domain. Finally, an expert system that learns in a skill domain may contribute to human knowledge by the application of known, relevant principles to situations that people have not encountered or have not recognized.

People learn in a skill domain from expert information, expert observation, and attempted performance. *Expert information* is identifiable general problem-solving knowledge and decision-making principles. Such knowledge is introduced first when one studies to become an expert; it is given. *Expert observation* is the ability to watch an external, detailed, varied model of performance and to extract and remember the salient portions of its behavior. This is the key to apprenticeship; most human experts train this way and continue to improve throughout their professional lives from such study. *Attempted performance* is the learner's repeated efforts to produce behavior that replicates the outcome the learner has observed the model achieve. Ultimately, it is not enough to be instructed and observe; human experts learn from their own problem-solving experiences.

HOYLE is a program that learns in a skill domain from expert information, expert observation, and attempted performance. It has a weak theory for the domain of all two-person perfect-information games. This weak theory details what a game is, how one plays a game, what decision principles may be relevant, and what is worth remembering. Given any game definition, HOYLE can immediately play that game correctly—make rule-abiding moves—because it has sufficient expert information. The program learns to play in competition against an external model; HOYLE observes an expert while it attempts to perform like one. As it plays, the program analyzes its experience and learns to play the game better. Gradually HOYLE becomes an expert at the game and often learns to play it perfectly.

Although this chapter cites some experiences with HOYLE, its context is far broader than game playing. The program itself serves primarily as an example; it highlights problems with broad repercussions, particularly for robotics. The first section describes the problem domain and the task in which these questions arose, with an overview of HOYLE's architecture and weak theory. The second section raises some hard questions drawn from development experience, questions likely to be overlooked in the first ambitious throes of designing an expert system that learns in a skill domain. The second section also provides preliminary working answers to these questions and warns about the scope of those answers. The final section discusses why these are hard questions and what further work they suggest.

18.1   A Game-Playing Program

Consider the ancient African game of achi, played by two participants on a board like the one in figure 18.1. One participant has four black stones; the other has four white stones. The object of the game is to place three stones of the same color on a straight line, vertically, horizontally, or

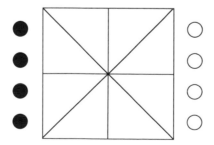

Figure 18.1
The ancient African game of achi. The initial board position is shown.

diagonally. Participants take turns placing their stones on any unoccupied intersection point of two or more lines on the board. There are nine such points; once all four of your stones are on the board, you move by relocating one of your stones to the single remaining unoccupied intersection point. Achi came from a book on games (Bell 1969), with no indication of what it would mean to be an expert at it. Would an achi expert always win if given the opportunity to go first? or second? Does an achi expert always open in the center? in a corner? Is there a typical scenario for achi when played by two experts?

HOYLE is a program that learns to play games like achi. Its test bed is an anthropological collection of seven games from two sources (Bell 1969; Zaslavsky 1982). These games were selected because they span a broad variety of cultures and therefore probably capture some aspects of game playing that people find particularly intriguing. Every test-bed game has two participants: *Player* (the one who moves first) and *Opponent*. Each game is relatively simple; it has rules that are easy to understand, and one complete playing experience (*contest*) at it should end in less than a half-hour. Some of the games are cyclic, several have identifiable *stages* (opening, middle game, endgame), and at least one has a problem space (*game graph*) of more than a billion possible states, each of which describes where the pieces appear on the board and whose turn it is. A brief description of each game appears in the chapter appendix. HOYLE's goal is to learn to play each game as well as possible.

Absolute expertise is when one performs perfectly. It can be derived either from exhaustive search in the problem space or from a complete and correct mathematical theory for the problem space. In HOYLE's domain, absolute expertise is demonstrated by perfect play: against any opponent and from any position, an absolute expert (*perfect player*) should make the best possible move. Perfect play can be simulated by either exhaustive minimax search of the game graph (Nilsson 1980) or a complete and correct mathematical theory for the properties of the game (for example, Berlekamp, Conway, and Guy 1982). For most interesting games, however, the game graph is too large to search exhaustively, and few games have known mathematical solutions. Thus, a cybernetic perfect player is rarely possible.

When exhaustive search is intractable and there is no complete and correct theory for the domain, the human heuristic alternative is *relative expertise* (or simply *expertise*)—performance better than that of most other people. In particular, a game-playing expert manifests that expertise by consistently achieving a better contest *outcome* (win, draw, loss—in that order) more regularly than most other players. Thus far, the programs that simulate expertise do so only for a single game. Examples include programs that play checkers (Samuel 1963, 1967; Schaeffer et al. 1991), backgammon (Berliner 1980; Tesauro and Sejnowski 1989), chess (Berliner 1989; Hsu et al. 1990), Othello (Lee and Mahajan 1990), and Go (Chen 1989; Kierulf, Chen, and Nievergelt 1990). They rely primarily on search heuristics, large knowledge bases, and pattern classification.

HOYLE differs from most other game-playing programs in three ways. First, it can play any two-person perfect-information, finite board game, one where all information is disclosed and equally available to two participants. Given the definition of a game, HOYLE plays according to the provided rules against a human or programmed participant. Second, it is limitedly rational; it does not employ the correct, exhaustive search algorithm for perfect play but relies on its weak theory instead. Third, it learns; its playing behavior is transformed by its experience. Learning occurs during and after a sequence of contests (*tournament*) of a single game. HOYLE acquires *useful knowledge* about each game, information that is meaningful to its human mentors and may enable it to play as an expert would. The remainder of this section describes HOYLE's weak theory, its move selection process, and its useful knowledge.

18.1.1   The Weak Theory

HOYLE's weak theory has four major components: the game frame, the game-playing algorithm, the game library, and the Advisors. A game is defined to HOYLE as a set of values and functions that describe its board, playing pieces, and rules. This is called *boxtop information*, because commercial games typically list this information on the inside of the top of the cardboard box in which they are packaged. The *game frame* formats the boxtop information: the name of the game, names of the tokens for Player and Opponent, a description of the initial board, and functions to provide directions, accept and filter a submitted move, display the current state, effect a move, generate legal moves, detect the end of a contest, and calculate the winner or loser. HOYLE's version of the boxtop information for achi appears in table 18.1.

The *game-playing algorithm* is a procedure that, with access to the appropriate game frame, plays, referees, and moderates any game in the

Table 18.1
The instantiated game frame for achi

Name: *achi*
Token for Player: *Black*
Token for Opponent: *White*
Initial-board: (*NIL NIL NIL NIL NIL NIL NIL NIL NIL*)
Directions for user: *directions-achi*
Move input reader: *reader-achi*
Move filter: *legalp-achi*
Display function for current state: *display-achi*
Move effector: *effector-achi*
Legal move generator: *generator-achi*
Predicate to detect end of contest: *endp-achi*
Predicate to calculate winner: *winp-achi*
Predicate to calculate loser: *lossp-achi*

Note: Four variables and nine functions completely define the game.

domain. A pseudocode version of the game-playing algorithm appears in table 18.2. Once a game is chosen and defined, the game-playing algorithm plays a sequence of contests. At the beginning of a contest, the participants decide who will go first and set up the board. Then, until the contest ends, they take turns making legal moves. The game-playing algorithm verifies that moves are legal. If it is the program's turn to move, the algorithm resigns if it cannot move, and takes the default move if only one is available. When there is more than one move, the game-playing algorithm selects one according to principles described below. At the end of the contest, the algorithm calculates the outcome and records it, along with all the moves in the *contest history*. Finally, the algorithm calls the learning procedures that analyze each contest in the *postmortem* after the contest ends.

The *game library* is a frame whose slot names focus attention on the useful knowledge to be learned. Useful knowledge is gathered or calculated by heuristic procedures. It is not necessarily correct, or even regularly applicable, but the weak theory assumes it will be relevant (i.e., should be recognized and remembered). Some slots represent strategic questions, such as, "Which participant, if any, has the advantage in this game?" and "Which territory is key?" Other slots cache selected tactical information, such as moves a non-HOYLE expert has been observed to make in a particular situation. The game library slots appear in table 18.3

Table 18.2
A pseudocode version of HOYLE's game-playing algorithm

Select a game
Initialize the game frame
For some number of contests   *tournament length or leave unspecified*
   Determine the identities of Player and Opponent
   Initialize the board
   Do while the contest is not over
      If it is the keyboard's turn   *non-HOYLE mover*
        then do until a legal move is input
          request a move
      else   generate all legal moves   *HOYLE to move*
          case:
          there are no legal moves: resign
          there is exactly one legal move: make it
          there is more than one legal move: consult the Advisors to select one
   Record the most recent move in the contest's history
Announce the result of the contest   *winner or draw?*
Conduct a postmortem on the contest

Note: This algorithm is used to play any game.

Table 18.3
The game library

Contest traces: *description of participants, outcome, and all move sequences for selected contests*
Openings: *selected initial move sequences and their contest outcomes*
Expert moves: *selected state-move pairs*

Significant win states: *states that guarantee a win for a specified participant with perfect play*
Significant loss states: *states that guarantee a loss for a specified participant despite perfect play*

Player has won: *whether the first participant has ever won a contest*
Opponent has won: *whether the second participant has ever won a contest*
Key territory: *positions valuable to occupy*
Mediation method: *tier 3 control structures that support expert play*
Role winner: *the participant believed to have the advantage, if any*
Relevant forks: *known applicable forks*

Note: Slots focus attention on what is to be learned. Each slot has a learning procedure associated with it.

with a brief description of their contents. Terminology in table 18.3 is further defined in section 18.1.3.

An *Advisor* is a game-independent, heuristic procedure that recommends and advises against legal moves during play. There are 15 Advisors, each with its own narrow perspective on how to select good moves and avoid bad ones. An Advisor expresses its opinion as a *comment*, a 3-tuple consisting of the Advisor's name, the move it references, and a *strength*, an integer from 0 (adamant opposition) to 10 (insistent support). An Advisor may make any number of comments on a game state, and many Advisors use information from the game library when they construct their comments. Some Advisors are always correct, but most of them are only plausible reasoners.

Brief descriptions of the individual Advisors appear in table 18.4. Each one epitomizes a simplistic view of reality. During play, HOYLE consults

Table 18.4
HOYLE's Advisors

Advisor	Rationale
Tier 1	
Wiser	Makes the correct move if the current state is remembered as a certain win.
Sadder	Resigns if the current state is remembered as a certain loss.
Victory	Takes the winning move from the current state.
Don't Lose	Eliminates any move that will result in an immediate loss.
Tier 2	
Panic	Blocks a winning move the nonmover would have if it were now her turn. If all such winning moves for the nonmover cannot be blocked by a single move, resigns.
Shortsight	Advises for and against moves based on a two-ply lookahead.
Enough Rope	If it were the nonmover's turn now and she would have a losing move, avoids blocking it, i.e., leaves her the opportunity to err.
Tier 3	
Pitchfork	Advances offensive forks and destroys defensive ones.
Candide	Formulates and advances naive offensive plans.
Worried	Observes and destroys naive offensive plans for the other participant.
Greedy	Proposes moves that advance more than one plan to win.
Open	Recommends previously observed expert openings.
Anthropomorph	Moves as a winning or drawing expert once did.
Not Again	Avoids moving as a losing HOYLE once did.
Cyber	Moves as a winning or drawing HOYLE once did.

Note: Each represents a narrow, game-independant perspective on how to select a good move.

its Advisors to avoid extensive forward search into the game graph. The Advisors variously rely on memory and incremental learning, supplemented by two-ply lookahead, the null move heuristic, and knowledge of fork offense and defense (Epstein 1990). Each Advisor is restricted to the same limited computation time in which to construct its comments.

It is important to note what HOYLE does not have or do. There are no game-specific features, such as corner or edge, and no state evaluation function to approximate and compare the worth of alternative states. There is no abstraction language with concepts like subgoal or gambit. The program does not communicate with or query its expert model; HOYLE's is a silent apprenticeship. Finally, HOYLE does not learn its weak theory. The slots in the game frame and the game library are fixed and can only be instantiated by the prespecified procedures associated with them. The Advisors are also fixed, and new Advisors are not learned.

The weak theory is primitive, deliberately so. It is intended to capture only the minimal knowledge that an expert might have—generally applicable information that should be valid but not particularly powerful. One of the challenges for learning in a skill domain is to identify the strongest possible weak theory, one that focuses attention appropriately and provides good decision-making principles in a problem-independent manner.

18.1.2 Move Selection

When it is HOYLE's turn to move in a contest, the game-playing algorithm references the appropriate game frame and calls the legal move generator on the current state. The legal moves from the current state are forwarded to the Advisors for comments. If, for example, it is HOYLE's turn in the tic-tac-toe game state of figure 18.2, where Player (X's) is the mover, the Advisors are provided with a list of all the legal moves: 2, 6, 7, 8, and 9. Panic would insist that a move in position 6 is the only way to prevent a win by Opponent in the second row. Worried would suggest moves in position 2 and position 8 to prevent an eventual loss in the second column after two turns, and moves in positions 7, 8, and 9 to prevent an eventual loss in the third row. The strength of Worried's comments about the the second column would be greater than those about the third row because the former respond to a more immediate threat. Victory would insist on a move in position 2 to win immediately in the first row.

To play any game HOYLE must resolve conflicts across its Advisors, which are essentially competing heuristics. The Advisors are grouped into

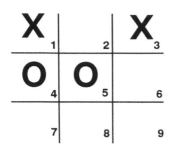

Figure 18.2
A game state from tic-tac-toe. The Advisors do not agree on the next move.

three priority classes called *tiers*; they are grouped by tier in table 18.4. One tier at a time, the Advisors post their comments on a blackboard. By the strength of its negative comment, an Advisor may eliminate certain legal moves from consideration. By the strength of its positive comment, an Advisor may force the selection of a move. If a tier is able, through this combination of recommendation and rejection, to select a unique move, no subsequent tier is consulted; otherwise the restricted move set is forwarded to the next tier. In the example of figure 18.2, this hierarchical consultation system would have registered Victory's insistence on a move into position 2 in tier 1 and never would have given either tier 2's Panic or tier 3's Worried the opportunity to comment.

Each tier has its own control structure. The control structure for tier 1 (Wiser, Sadder, Victory, and Don't Lose) and tier 2 (Panic, Shortsight, and Enough Rope) is prespecified and fixed. It gives certain Advisors priority and/or absolute authority in move selection. The control structure for tier 3 (all the other Advisors) is learned. In the third tier, the Advisors take particularly narrow views and are prone to substantial disagreement. For example, Candide formulates winning positions for the mover without ever considering that the other participant will attempt to interfere with them or win itself in the meantime, while Worried does the same for the nonmover. The thesis is that some synergy among these shortsighted, simplistic reasons will result in the selection of a move that supports expert long-range behavior—that good immediate rationales also support long-term perspectives.

In the third tier, the comments of all the Advisors are combined in a process called *voting*. There are four fundamental ways to vote, each a domain-independent method derived from voting procedures within political structures. Method 1 tallies the comment strengths for each move and selects the move with the highest score. Each of the other voting procedures deliberately discards information from method 1 in an attempt to avoid unintentional bias. Method 2 first smooths the comments' strengths to "yes," "no," or "don't care" and then tallies by move and selects the most preferred. This technique is intended to alleviate any bias introduced in the numerical strengths assigned by the Advisors. Method 3 considers only the single strongest positive or negative comment from each Advisor and tallies the comment strengths to select the strongest move. This approach is intended to alleviate any bias introduced by multiple comments from the same Advisor. Finally, method 4 both considers only the single strongest comment from each Advisor and smooths the comment strengths. Method 4 represents the most substantial information loss and would be expected to be the least sensitive to the Advisors' comments. In the event of a tie under any method, one of the top-scoring moves is selected at random.

18.1.3   Learning Useful Knowledge

What HOYLE knows in advance, before it ever plays any contest at a new game, is its weak theory for games in general and the new game's definition. The weak theory states how a game is defined, how to play games, what good rationales for move selection are, what is important about a game, and how to learn that useful knowledge. Thus, the program begins as a legitimate participant, equivalent to an intelligent human novice.

What HOYLE learns is useful knowledge, that is, slot values in the game library. Once HOYLE acquires enough useful knowledge and applies it during play, the program should simulate expert performance. How HOYLE learns is determined by what it is learning; each game library slot for useful knowledge has its own learning algorithm. There is no uniformity required of these learning algorithms; they may employ any method, including inductive inference and explanation-based learning. After a contest or a tournament, the execution of a slot's learning procedure calculates and stores one or more values for the slot. When HOYLE learns is determined by the slot. Some slot values, such as significant states, can change after a single contest; others, such as role winner, summarize or record experience from a tournament or a set of tournaments.

HOYLE does not remember every detail of its playing experience. HOYLE's memory is selective; it does not record every contest it plays or every move the other participant makes. Any experience stored in the first three slots of table 18.3 is selected by the heuristic procedure associated with its respective slot. Nor is the program restricted to its play experience; it analyzes each individual contest in the postmortem to identify and then test certain states encountered during play. Such a state is judged *significant* if it is equivalent to a nondraw leaf in the game graph; every alternative from it results in a win for the same participant. These *significant states* summarize the result of a resource-bounded, breadth-first search. Their examination and storage is a deliberately limited version of retrograde analysis and transposition tables (Slate and Atkin 1977), one that uses play experience to focus its search.

Useful knowledge slots may have default values and are open to recomputation. The mediation method slot, for example, defaults to method 1; HOYLE can learn to play expertly without learning how to resolve conflicts. No slot value is ever assumed to be fixed; HOYLE is always willing to revise its beliefs about a game.

18.2   The Questions and Some Responses to Them

HOYLE begins with the knowledge to play each game in its test bed legally and learns to play expertly, usually perfectly. The data provided here were generated with a version of HOYLE that had no knowledge of symmetry. The absence of symmetry was deliberate; the resultant combinatoric explosions highlight difficulties that might otherwise go unnoticed. The answers provided are HOYLE's current working resolutions of these questions. The caveats immediately following each answer are reminders that no simplistic resolution is likely to suffice.

Question 1:   Given a competitive domain in which to learn, what should be the nature of the opposition?

When a program learns from expert observation, the nature of the expert is extremely important. In particular, a program that learns under a weak theory is necessarily dependent upon and guided by its expert model in a variety of ways. HOYLE, for example, learns during tournaments against another participant. The program effectively apprentices itself to this other participant, to gain a head start with some portion of its presumably expert knowledge. The postmortem is specifically directed to the portion of the game graph highlighted by the other participant's decisions; significant states and openings are learned there. The Advisor Anthropomorph applies the useful knowledge on expert moves and contest histories to imitate the other participant, who may be a human at the keyboard, a separate *model program*, or a copy of HOYLE itself.

The nature of its opposition is crucial to HOYLE's developing expertise. Recall that expertise entails performing better than most other players, not just a single trainer. Even if it were computationally feasible, a perfect-player model program is probably unwise. Perfect opposition, human or programmed, may not prepare the learning program to produce imperfect, but still acceptable, solutions. In particular, a program that learns against a perfect player is unlikely to encounter portions of the search space that are reached only by error. If the learning program later encounters participants other than the model program against which it learned, it may not know how to play against them. The less difficult, but still challenging, variations that appear may be so far outside the learning program's experience that it fails miserably, despite reliable performance against the original, more proficient model program. Even a novice may, with some fortuitous distraction, confound an expert; experience only against a perfect model would not prepare a learning program for such confusion.

If a perfect model program is impractical and/or too narrow, what about a random one? Empirical tests with HOYLE have shown that a random model program, by the construction of unlikely experience, slows the achievement of expert performance to an unacceptable degree. Even a single mistake by the model can slow learning drastically. Certainly at some point HOYLE must be able to compete successfully against experts that make errors, but learning against random opposition is tedious and uneconomical.

Answer: HOYLE's working solution to this question is a separate, handcrafted, stochastic model program for each game, one that offers a broad spectrum of high-quality opposition. For tic-tac-toe, for example, the model program opens approximately half the time in the center, and the remainder in a randomly selected corner. This provides HOYLE with a flexible, but not overly distracting, learning environment.

For most of the games, learning speed and effectiveness have been observed against random opposition, perfect opposition, human opposition,

HOYLE itself, and model programs. The effort required to understand each game and build each model program appears to be well spent; HOYLE's learning is faster with an error-free, intelligent opposition and more thorough with a varied opposition. Although computational learning theory suggests that a good model program has a distribution of examples as close as possible to the real world, these results indicate that HOYLE learns to play better faster when it learns without the errors rampant in human competition. Thus HOYLE's real world is not people but the most important parts of the game graph.

Caveat: HOYLE's model programs are difficult to build. Each of them has developed cyclically; HOYLE learns to defeat what was believed to be a model program for high-quality expert play, and then the programmer revises and strengthens the model. On every iteration, HOYLE learns faster and more thoroughly, and the programmer's understanding of the game improves. In a peculiar turnabout, the model program ultimately may represent the best human understanding of expertise, understanding developed from imitation of the learning expert program and from competition against it.

Question 2:   What does it mean to have learned to perform expertly?

How, for example, would you be able to tell that you had learned to play achi well? Expert performance does not necessarily mean winning, because that might depend on the nature of the game. Perhaps two perfect players always draw at achi, or perhaps going first or second offers a considerable advantage. Even if one knew how an achi contest should end when the participants play perfectly, recall that the goal is expert performance, not perfection. If you played your first contest at achi and drew, or even won, you probably would not claim, "Okay, I know how to play this game," get up, and walk away. The criterion should stipulate that good performance is consistent—that is, that learning is reliable.

Answer: HOYLE uses a *behavioral standard*, a requirement that the program achieve *expert outcome* (the outcome an expert would) on some number n of consecutive trials. Figure 18.3 shows three *performance curves* for tic-tac-toe; each plots the cumulative number of contests won or drawn (expert outcome) against the cumulative number of contests played during a 20-contest tournament against the model tic-tac-toe program. The top

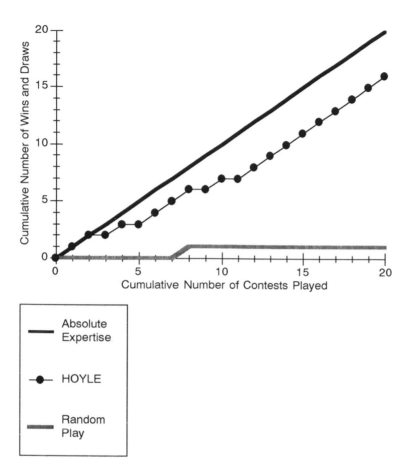

Figure 18.3
Learning tic-tac-toe in a 20-contest tournament. The cumulative number of contests where expert outcome is realized against a model program is plotted against the cumulative number of contests played.

curve shows how the model would perform against itself, the bottom curve shows how a random player performed against the model, and the middle curve shows how HOYLE performed against the model program. While HOYLE's performance curve parallels the model's, the program is simulating expertise. The behavioral standard requires that the program's performance curve parallel the model program's for *n* consecutive contests. In figure 18.3, HOYLE's performance curve begins to parallel the model program's consistently after 11 contests.

Caveat: Any finite behavior pattern can be deceptive, even a long-range one. Prediction of future behavior from historical data on an ill-understood model is notoriously untrustworthy. In a competitive domain, where the model deliberately attempts to outwit any prediction, reliance on good past performance may not be enough.

Question 3:   Is a behavioral standard sufficient to learn to perform expertly?

When apprenticed to the kind of nondeterministic model program advocated here, learning is also nondeterministic. An expert program that learns from such a model program will acquire useful knowledge that varies in quantity and content from one run to the next. For example, HOYLE's Advisors find corner openings in tic-tac-toe more difficult to contend with than center openings. How long it takes HOYLE to meet its behavioral standard is directly related to how early and how often in the tournament the model program happens to confront HOYLE with corner openings. Thus, a behavioral standard does not really reflect what the program is able do, only what it has learned to do with what it has experienced. In addition, learning time will vary; it should be computed and averaged across a set of runs.

A more difficult problem arose when HOYLE appeared to have learned lose tic-tac-toe, a game with a known mathematical solution (Cohen 1972) whose straightforward representation is beyond the game-specific library's expressive ability. Although the program cannot explicitly represent how to play perfect lose tic-tac-toe, it can learn a control strategy to manifest that knowledge implicitly. The role of Player in this game requires particular care. In some tournaments for lose tic-tac-toe, HOYLE met the behavioral standard and stopped after 20, 50, even 100 contests with the claim that it had learned the game. Because there are so many distinct early-move sequences, however, a careful observer of the tournament could defeat the program after it had claimed to have learned to play expertly. The observer needed only to present a sequence of early moves that the program had never seen and could not deal with correctly.

HOYLE's learning was *incomplete*, even though it had met the behavioral standard. Certainly, HOYLE could be trained to play lose tic-tac-toe perfectly if an expert presented all possible early-move sequences. Although, without knowledge of symmetry, such perfect training requires almost 200 contests, there is no guarantee that 200 contests played against a nondeterministic model program, even 200 consecutive contests where the program achieves expert outcome, will teach HOYLE everything it needs to know to play perfectly. Although computational learning theory states that a behavioral standard is more reliable when the distribution of examples is closer to the distribution from the real world, a behavioral standard in a varied and randomly generated experience set can offer no guarantee.

The appropriate value of n represents how long the learning program is required to perform expertly. For a particular problem class, the appropriate value of n that guarantees sufficiently broad experience against a nondeterministic model is unknown. Thus, even a program that meets the criterion may not have acquired adequate expertise. A novice who plays poorly may unintentionally lead the program into a part of the game graph where it has no experience and may be particularly vulnerable. (This is what good players often label "beginner's luck.") Of greater concern is that, after the program appears to have learned according to the behavioral standard, clever new opposition may lead the program into some challenging part of the search space where it may fail.

Greg Gupton's Othello program (1989) may have been a victim of such variety. The program used an evaluation function developed with a genetic algorithm that trained on a suite of 10 master-level contests taken from an American publication on Othello. It placed fourth in the North American Othello Championship, a tournament environment where time, and therefore computational speed, is crucial. Among the programs at the tournament that were implemented on a personal computer, Gupton's finished highest. Several months later, however, at the First Computer Olympiad in Europe, most of the Othello programs were on equally small and slow machines, and Gupton's program finished thirteenth in a field of 15. Gupton suspects that his evaluation function plays a peculiarly American variety of Othello and that it should have been retrained on another suite to develop a different evaluation function for its European opposition.

Turing (1963) included a question about the correct move for a very simple chess position in his description of a test for an intelligent machine. Play indistinguishable from not particularly expert human performance would meet the Turing test, since Turing was willing, even eager, to tolerate fallibility. We believe that the most recent version of HOYLE with knowledge of symmetry (Epstein 1992) meets the Turing test; it is difficult to distinguish its playing behavior during and after learning from that of a person, even one who is a good game player. Human observers often impute motives and discovery plans to HOYLE when they watch it learn, despite the absence of any such exploration in the code. If Turing's examiner were to query more deeply, however, the reader is referred to question 9.

Answer: HOYLE's current resolution of the learning evaluation problem is to demand, in addition to behavioral consistency, that the program achieve some *stability of knowledge*. This means that transformations of useful knowledge settle to some basic low level of activity. When the program repeatedly achieves expert-contest outcomes and encounters little new useful knowledge, the learner has established an equilibrium with its learning environment.

Caveat: One way to develop stability of knowledge is to vary the learning environment deliberately, as the model programs vary their opposition. A model, however, can only provide challenges that its human designers anticipate. A model can offer no guarantee in a problem space that people do not fully understand. And even if HOYLE learns against a model that is an exhaustive paradigm of perfect play, it might still not be able to deal correctly with errors.

Question 4:   Given a set of control strategies, which is the best for learning a problem class?

To develop a good control strategy for a specific problem class, an expert program might begin with several alternatives drawn from its general problem-solving knowledge and select among them. A program that learns from experience, without analogy to other problem classes, must find some way to choose among these control strategies. Some strategies might never learn in a specified problem class; some strategies might learn in the same problem class faster than others.

HOYLE's four voting methods for tier 3, for example, determine how the Advisors' advice should be combined there. Table 18.5 shows how many contests it took for HOYLE to learn its five two-dimensional games against the model program. HOYLE applied the same behavioral standard ($n = 10$) with each of the four methods on five runs for each game, 100 tournaments in all. Each entry in the table represents the average tournament length for a specific game and method across five runs; the

Table 18.5
HOYLE learns to play games under different control strategies

Method	Tic-tac-toe	Lose tic-tac-toe	Achi	Pong hau k'i	Tsoro yematatu
1	24.2 (4.5)	206.0 (19.5)	10.0 (0.0)	10.0 (0.0)	10.0 (0.0)
2	38.2 (5.5)	256.4 (24.5)	10.0 (0.0)	10.0 (0.0)	10.0 (0.0)
3	50.2 (16.3)	273.2 (46.9)	17.6 (5.2)	10.0 (0.0)	10.0 (0.0)
4	48.6 (20.2)	275.6 (29.3)	17.6 (3.7)	10.0 (0.0)	10.0 (0.0)
Average	40.38	252.8	13.8	10.0	10.0

Note: Entries represent the average number of contests, across five trials, played until the program is able to meet a behavioral standard of $n = 10$.

number in parentheses is the standard deviation of those tournament lengths. For example, table 18.5 indicates that under method 1 HOYLE had to play 24.2 contests on average against the tic-tac-toe model program to draw 10 consecutive times and that there was a standard deviation of 4.5 contests across the five runs used to calculate that average. If HOYLE can be said to learn pong hau k'i and tsoro yematatu, that learning comes immediately, from the application of memory and prior knowledge of the domain to the rules of the game.

Answer: HOYLE's empirical results indicate that the fastest control strategy for learning in this test bed is method 1. In the three games in which HOYLE needs to learn, the difference in learning speed between method 1 and the others is statistically significant at the 99% confidence level. There is, however, no clear ordering of the methods by speed after method 1.

Caveat: Although these trials varied in the number of contests before HOYLE claimed to have learned a game, speed and thoroughness had no clear correlation. Table 18.6 shows how many significant win states HOYLE cached during the same runs that generated the data in table 18.5. Each entry in the table represents an average result across five runs. For example, on average under method 1, table 18.6 indicates that HOYLE learned 3.4 significant win states against the tic-tac-toe model program, with a standard deviation of 0.4 across the five runs. In the three games where HOYLE needs to learn, the difference in number of states cached between method 1 and the others is statistically significant at the 99% confidence level. Results for significant loss states and for expert moves are similar. A method that achieved expertise more quickly,

Table 18.6
HOYLE learns to play games under different control strategies

Method	Tic-tac-toe	Lose tic-tac-toe	Achi	Pong hau k'i	Tsoro yematatu
1	3.4 (0.4)	92.4 (19.5)	0.0 (0.0)	0.0 (0.0)	0.0 (0.0)
2	6.6 (1.2)	110.4 (4.4)	0.0 (0.0)	0.0 (0.0)	0.0 (0.0)
3	8.8 (3.6)	129.8 (26.6)	2.0 (1.7)	0.0 (0.0)	0.0 (0.0)
4	9.2 (4.2)	134.2 (15.0)	1.8 (0.8)	0.0 (0.0)	0.0 (0.0)

Note: Entries represent the average number of significant win states, across five trials, played until the program is able to meet a behavioral standard of $n = 10$.

like method 1, may have risked fewer variations and therefore have accumulated a smaller amount of useful knowledge. A method that achieved expertise more slowly, like method 3, may have digressed into portions of the search space an expert need never consider. The difference in number of significant win states identified between method 1 and the others is significant at the 99% confidence level. Whether all those data are crucial to expert play is unclear, but how much HOYLE caches is clearly related to the breadth of experience it has had due to a specific method. Because learning is nondeterministic, strategy comparisons must be approximate.

Question 5:   What does it mean for one problem class to be more difficult to learn than another?

It may be argued that one problem class is more difficult to learn than another if it takes the expert program longer to master it. Longer may be measured as more practice at the problem class until the behavioral standard is met or as more time elapses. In table 18.5, for example, lose tic-tac-toe is clearly the most difficult of these games if measured by average number of contests played until the behavioral standard is met. Based on computation time, however, achi was more difficult for HOYLE, because the average achi contest required roughly four times as many moves as the average lose tic-tac-toe contest, as well as greater deliberation time on each move. Most people encountering these two games for the first time expect achi, probably because it is cyclic and has an unfamiliar name, to be more complex. Eventually, however, most people formulate a simple set of achi production rules that enable them to draw consistently. After learning to play the two for a while, people consider achi easier.

Alternatively, it might be argued that an expert program makes more mistakes while learning a more difficult problem class. Mistakes during learning can be categorized either as recoverable errors, where an expert could still succeed at the practice problem, or irrecoverable ones, where no expert could succeed after such an error. The distinction between the two is important, for, depending upon the domain, a designer may be willing to tolerate many recoverable errors but few irrecoverable errors in an expert program that learns. Without an absolute standard of perfection, however, the distinction between them must be left to the model program. Unless the model program is of very high quality, error rate seems an untrustworthy standard.

A third alternative is to presume that the problem class with the larger or more complex search space will be more difficult to master. The results described above dispute this as a comparative standard. The lose tic-tac-toe game graph contains 5478 nodes. The achi game graph has two sections: the first section is a tree of 5240 nodes; the second is a cyclic graph attached to every leaf from the first section. Each cyclic graph has the same 630 nodes and a branching factor of four from every node. Despite the size and complexity of the achi graph, HOYLE consistently caches a smaller amount of useful knowledge about it (table 18.6) and achieves reliable expert performance at it in fewer contests (table 18.5). Problem difficulty is not so dependent on search space size as one might expect.

A final possibility is to define difficulty in terms of computational complexity. For HOYLE, since the resources devoted to control strategy are minimal, computational complexity would measure the resources consumed by the Advisors to construct their comments. Because each Advisor has a resource limit, complexity would be measured as the fraction of the available time consumed during decision making. If this measurement is taken during learning, such complexity gauges how ignorant the program is at that moment—that is, how hard it is for it to select a move given its limited useful knowledge. If this measurement is taken after learning, such complexity gauges how efficiently the program retrieves useful knowledge and makes decisions after learning, rather than how difficult it was to acquire that useful knowledge in the first place. Thus, computational complexity is an inappropriate standard here.

Answer: HOYLE compares problem difficulty across a variety of likely learning strategies. The average across methods, in time or number of contests, until HOYLE meets the behavioral standard reflects how hard it is for the program to learn the game. To the extent that these numbers

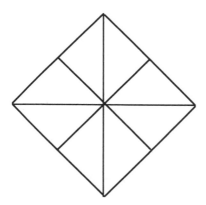

Figure 18.4
The initial board state for the game of foo

corroborate human behavior, HOYLE may be said to simulate human game learning.

People, with their fallible memories, may have more difficulty than HOYLE in learning games that demand much pattern recognition. HOYLE, without knowledge of abstraction or analogy, may have more difficulty than people in learning games where such high-level procedures may be brought to bear. Consider, for example, the game of foo, played on the board in figure 18.4. In foo, Player has five yellow markers and Opponent four green markers. Initially the board is empty, and a turn consists of placing a marker on the intersection of two or more lines. There are nine such positions. The first one to place three of the same color markers on the same straight line wins. There are eight such winning lines. Play ends in a draw when all positions are occupied. Most people readily detect the isomorphism between the foo board and the tic-tac-toe board and begin to play foo at the same level at which they already play tic-tac-toe. HOYLE's learned expertise in tic-tac-toe, however, would have no impact at all on the speed with which it would learn foo.

Caveat: An important reason that HOYLE has more difficulty learning lose tic-tac-toe than learning the other games in its test bed may be that it has no useful knowledge representation for "move symmetrically through the center with respect to Opponent's most recent move." Thus, how diffi-cult a problem class is to learn may be a function not only of the problem space's size and complexity but also of the adequacy and extensibility of the program's representation language for useful knowledge.

Question 6:   How does real-world training affect learning?

Expert systems are designed to function in the real world. If an expert system learns, that learning should be in the real world when affordable, and otherwise in an excellent simulation of it. This question is not directed at the order in which HOYLE experiences different states during learning. Presumably a tournament with a strong model program and a sufficiently high behavioral standard will expose the learner to a broad spectrum of important training instances. The concern here is with the variation that comes from imitation of an imperfect opposition. Question 1 argued for an error-free model program as a rich developmental training ground. Eventually, however, the learning expert system is to function in the real world and must encounter error. Some words of caution are appropriate here for the overly optimistic developer.

Answer: HOYLE's real-world training is dramatically affected by noise and by model inaccuracy. An error-ridden environment slows learning dramatically. For example, early in one lose tic-tac-toe contest a human expert mistyped a move and confirmed it, thereby subverting HOYLE's error-protection mechanisms. Against a perfect player, this mistake should have been fatal, but it was early in the learning tournament; HOYLE knew so little about the game that the person went on to win anyway. As a result, HOYLE regarded the human's error as an example of expert behavior and lost half of the next 30-odd contests, attempting to win by repeating the error. Eventually, the program determined that the move was indeed incorrect and abandoned it, but that single error occupied approximately 15% of HOYLE's total learning effort for the game. This experience was the original motivation for the development of HOYLE's model programs; it made clear how difficult it is to learn with a fallible model.

Lack of understanding of the domain by the developer can also slow both program development and learning. One cannot rely on the expert program's ability to learn to cover lack of knowledge about what the program is supposed to learn; the better the model program is, the better the results are. For example, achi came from an anthropology book. It was quite apparent to us, after playing it a bit, that it was not possible to fork at achi. When, one day, HOYLE claimed to have forked the model program, we spent hours searching for the responsible bug in the code. There was none. After we revised the model program so that it too could fork, HOYLE's learning speed and playing performance for achi improved dramatically.

Given the ambitious nature of the tasks proposed for these systems, some lack of understanding of the domain by the developer is probably inevitable. At that point, the expert program should be harnessed to construct a better environment in which to learn. For example, Qubic© is a version of tic-tac-toe played on a three-dimensional board consisting of four parallel four-by-four grids. The object of Qubic is to place four in a row, column, or diagonal. There are 76 ways to win at Qubic and more than a billion nodes in its game graph; it is an interesting game, generally acknowledged to lie on the border between simple games and the challenging ones, like checkers and chess. The computer-generated proof that Qubic is a win for Player (Patashnik 1980) consists of one contest path through the game graph; it does not offer adequate information to construct a model program for the game. HOYLE was trained, therefore, against an expert human who had developed a complex fork for the game. After a single contest, one of HOYLE's Advisors was able to learn this fork, guard against it, and even use it against the expert (Epstein 1990). After that, HOYLE went on to win 9 of the next 12 contests and draw the other 3; it played too well. The obvious response to this is to have HOYLE play itself when it exceeds expectations. Once chess programs are able to defeat the best humans, they too will have to learn against each other. In a competitive domain, it is relatively easy to have the expert program perturb its learning environment. Once a learning program understands its domain better than people do, it should direct its own study of the problem space.

Caveat: There is some knowledge that the real-world training postulated here with an expert model program can never impart. Lose tic-tac-toe is a case in point. There is only one correct opening move in this game; against a perfect participant, every other opening is a certain loss. By definition, no expert model program for lose tic-tac-toe would ever execute any but the single opening, since the others do not offer high-quality play. The manner in which the weak openings must be defeated, however, is neither intuitive nor clearly related to the way contests with the correct opening proceed. HOYLE may never observe or risk the wrong openings and thus may never learn the correct responses to them. HOYLE will not become an absolute expert at lose tic-tac-toe unless it has the opportunity to observe the expert model's performance against *less* able competitors than HOYLE. Unless a learning program has some knowledge-seeking goal that transcends mere simulation of visible expertise, some knowledge will be reserved to people.

Question 7: Is a good control strategy for learning also a good control strategy for performance after learning?

The goal is to produce a program that not only learns well but also performs well. The strategy for learning in a skill domain may be different from the strategy for performing there; once the program has extracted useful knowledge from a series of learning experiences and has learned to perform very well in the problem class under one control strategy, another control strategy might then execute for that problem class at least as effectively and more efficiently than the one under which learning took place.

This issue was examined in the following experiment. With a behavioral standard of $n = 10$, HOYLE learned the five two-dimensional games against a model program (the *learning phase*); learning was then turned off while two copies of the program, using different tier 3 voting methods, played tournaments of 100 contests against each other (the *testing phase*). Because these tournaments were intended to measure postlearning performance, both versions shared common useful knowledge acquired during the first experiment but left unchanged by experience in the second experiment. Since there are four basic voting methods, six tournaments covered all possible pairings. Data from one such tournament for tic-tac-toe appear in table 18.7. Each row in the table describes a tournament where the copy of HOYLE for Player uses First Method to select its moves and the copy for Opponent uses Second Method. The first row indicates that method 1 and method 2 played perfectly against each other; every contest resulted in a draw. Subsequent rows, however, indicate that some methods, such as 1 and 3, were able to defeat each other, after HOYLE claimed to have learned a game that is known to be a draw when played perfectly by both participants.

Forcing two methods to compete against each other after they have learned to play well is equivalent to bringing in new expert opposition on

Table 18.7
A tic-tac-toe tournament among four versions of HOYLE

First method	Second method	Player wins	Draws	Player loses
1	2	0	100	0
1	3	2	92	6
1	4	4	95	1
2	3	3	94	3
2	4	1	97	2
3	4	4	93	3

Note: Every pair of control strategy methods played 100 contests against each other after learning was believed to be complete.

which to test them. As table 18.7 shows, a strategy that had met the behavioral standard in the learning phase could be proved not yet expert in the testing phase. Some methods were able to outplay others regularly in these tournaments. Inspection of the traces reveals that such uneven play is caused by methods whose decisions force the exploration of previously unencountered regions of the search space. In its learning phase against the model program in tic-tac-toe, for example, method 1 encountered openings only in the center or in a corner. When confronted in the testing phase by another method in this experiment that opened in a side square, method 1 lost.

Methods that are as good for playing as for learning should continue to achieve expert outcomes in these tournaments. For pong hau k'i and tsoro yematatu, this was the case; all 600 contests in the testing phase for each game were draws. In slightly more than 95% of the tic-tac-toe contests, the methods that had claimed to have learned the game were able to reach an appropriate outcome, i.e., to draw. For achi, however, this figure declined to 74% and for lose tic-tac-toe to 17%. No method for achi or lose tic-tac-toe was clearly superior to the others; the methods lost with almost even regularity. The explanation is not that HOYLE had failed to learn but that it had failed to learn enough. The new opposition exploited HOYLE's incomplete learning by forcing the exploration of less promising regions of the game graph that the model program had avoided, like the side square opening in tic-tac-toe. Although such an opening should still result in a draw, it deflects play into an area of the game graph where good moves are relatively rare (Berlekamp, Conway, and Guy 1982). More experience was required to play well, experience that HOYLE still did not have after it had met the behavioral standard.

The results just cited were somewhat exacerbated by the fact that learning was turned off during these tournaments. The various versions of HOYLE were repeatedly confounded by weaker playing that they would, under normal circumstances, have quickly learned to combat. There are, however, many real-world domains where one might be able to develop an expert system by permitting it to learn in the laboratory but be forced to deploy a nonlearning version. Such situations could confront similar failures.

Answer: An experiment designed to compare the efficacy of HOYLE's various playing strategies highlighted incomplete learning instead. Such repeated evidence of incomplete learning engendered HOYLE's conservative stance on the transition between a learning strategy and a playing strategy. The program does not revise its control strategy until after it has learned to play well, first against the model program and then against various strategic versions of itself. Readiness to revise the control strategy is evaluated both on stability of useful knowledge and a behavioral standard, but the learning algorithms are never turned off; HOYLE never behaves as if it has finished learning to play a game. This is a departure from, for example, Samuel's checker playing program, with its different strategies for learning and playing. When HOYLE judges that it knows enough, it interleaves learning with the strategy revision techniques described below.

Caveat: A good strategy for learning can be expected to be a good strategy for performance after learning only if the learning was reasonably complete. Otherwise, the time to switch from a good strategy for learning to a good strategy for performing may never come.

Question 8:   How can the relative importance of expert principles be harnessed to improve performance?

Because expert principles are extracted from human experience, there is no reason to expect that they provide nonredundant information, that they include all necessary methods, or even that they are correct. Each principle should be evaluated within the context of a particular problem class. Some principles may be irrelevant; they may never participate in the execution of a problem class. Other principles may be *significant*; they may consistently agree with and participate in decisions that result in expert performance. The entire set of principles is generally applicable and therefore weak; one way to strengthen performance is to identify the relevant and significant ones for a particular problem class and use that information to customize the control structure.

The relative importance of expert principles in HOYLE's skill domain is problem dependent; each of the tier 3 Advisors is more useful in some games than in others. For example, some games, such as lose tic-tac-toe, should be played defensively; others, like pong hau k'i, should be played offensively. For HOYLE's tier 3 Advisors, relevance and significance are calculated retrospectively, from experience. A tier 3 Advisor is defined to be *relevant* to a particular game if it has ever made a comment during the learning of that game. A relevant Advisor's significance is defined as the number of comments it made that agreed with the move actually selected in contests where HOYLE achieved an expert outcome. The Advisors are ranked on their significance, and the three highest (or more, if there were ties) are judged the most significant. The following results are for HOYLE's eight tier 3 Advisors. When HOYLE learned the five games in table 18.5 against their respective model programs with a behavioral standard of $n = 10$ contests, every Advisor was applicable to at least two games, and every game used at least four Advisors for successful performance, even after learning. No two of these games had the same set of most significant Advisors, a measure of the diversity of the test-bed. In two games, all the Advisors were relevant; the other games had four, five, and seven relevant Advisors.

Answer: Although postlearning performance is not guaranteed expert if learning was incomplete, there are some simple methods that can refine control strategy relatively safely. HOYLE's working solution for any given game is to ignore its irrelevant Advisors and emphasize its significant ones. While HOYLE learns to play a game against the model program and various strategic versions of itself, it calculates the game's relevant and significant tier 3 Advisors. After learning, it constructs a variation on each of the voting methods with which it was able to learn the game. A *variation* is a modified version of a tier 3 voting method with the irrelevant Advisors eliminated and the comment weights of the most significant Advisors doubled. The useful knowledge is retained while each variation is then tested against the model program in another tournament, during which HOYLE continues to learn. Elimination of irrelevant Advisors provides an expected substantial computational speed-up, since each Advisor has its own time allotment.

In tests on the five two-dimensional games, doubling of the comment weights appears to have had no significant postlearning impact on play performance against the expert system. Method 4 should be the most susceptible to reduced effectiveness under variation, because it already loses substantial information when it restricts each Advisor to a single comment and smooths comment strengths before voting. Only in lose tic-tac-toe did the variation on method 4 play less well, either because the game is difficult or because it was only partially learned. There is only one correct opening move in lose tic-tac-toe, and the model program never plays any other, but traces indicate that under the method 4 variation, HOYLE attempts a variety of unusual openings that necessarily lead to its defeat.

Emphasis on the most significant Advisors is risky. Although doubling the comment weights of the three most significant Advisors rarely degrades playing ability, it has never been observed to improve it. It is also incorrect to calculate relevance and significance only once, and then rely upon those values. During learning, some Advisors, such as Anthropomorph, may be particularly useful. After learning, once the postmortem has acquired enough useful information, any need for those same Advisors may have been compiled out. Against a set of participants, relevance and significance also may fluctuate with the playing environment. HOYLE therefore recomputes significance dynamically, at the beginning of each tournament. This periodic reevaluation simulates a kind of self-awareness that reflects both learning progress and competitive experience.

Caveat: As the program's experience base changes, the relevant and significant Advisors for a game may change too. As treated here, irrelevant Advisors, once eliminated, have no further opportunity to prove their value in a given problem class. Some long-range power could be sacrificed in a shortsighted reach for efficiency.

Question 9: Is expert performance enough for an expert system?

A human's expertise is usually judged only on relative performance, without any standards for the description and sharing of knowledge. This may certify as expert one who can perform in the problem class but cannot explain her behavior to others, a state of affairs with which expert systems developers are all too well acquainted. Programs, however, are held to a higher standard. If people are to trust cybernetic experts, the former must be satisfied that the latter reason correctly. For a program to be accepted as an expert, it must not only perform well but also make explicit the knowledge that supports its performance. Thus, some level of transparency that reveals humanlike reasoning is demanded of an expert system.

Particularly when learning is likely to be incomplete, an expert program needs to summarize and communicate what it learns to the skeptical and/ or supportive humans who observe, use, and learn from it. Everyone who watches HOYLE learn immediately asks, "What did it know before it started, and what did it learn?" Expert game players always ask to see the game library before and after learning.

Finally, the role of conceptual explanation in expertise is unclear, even among people. One school of thought (Brooks 1991) argues that the creation and description of concepts is secondary to intelligent behavior, that low-level reactions to the environment pyramid to produce high-level performance, and that concepts are merely a convenient, post facto shorthand for communication. Others (Kirsh 1991) believe that concepts and their representation are crucial to the development of intelligent behavior and that learning depends upon them.

Answer: HOYLE not only plays expertly but also displays its learned knowledge declaratively and applies it in a variety of procedures. If learned useful knowledge is interesting to expert players, it should be important to HOYLE too. HOYLE's game library slots are based on questions experienced game players ask about a game. These slots represent useful abstractions and terminology that game-playing experts use to communicate with each other. Planned research work includes additional useful knowledge slots and further application of their values by HOYLE's current and projected Advisors.

Caveat: A deeper difficulty is the display of understanding. A person who understands a game is able to discourse on it, to respond to questions about it, and to deal with it well in a variety of situations—in other words, to apply knowledge appropriately. Even with a broad knowledge base, as Lenat and Feigenbaum (1991) admit, meaning ultimately bottoms out; that is, at any fixed level of abstraction, representation has a limit. Despite its limited domain, HOYLE could eventually fail the Turing test. A question like, "What is the primary subgoal of a participant in this game?" has no slot in HOYLE's game library and is not readily deducible from it. Were such a question included in the Turing test, the program would not respond as well as a person.

18.3   Conclusion

Even in HOYLE's relatively simple test bed, significant and difficult issues arise. The questions raised here are hard because skill domains, by definition, have no accessible perfect theory. Humans may be such poor models for these domains, or perfect performance may be so ill defined, that people may not even be able to recognize when a program has achieved its goal. Instead, designers are forced to use a heuristic standard that judges relative performance for skill domains in a nondeterministic learning environment. Such a standard is itself both nondeterministic and subjective. If computer scientists aspire to have machines outperform people in domains they do not fully comprehend, consistency must be an important criterion. Consistency includes both the achievement of performance goals across a long sequence of trials and the relative stability of acquired useful knowledge.

In a competitive domain, the learning environment should support progress in stages. Initially the opposition should be as error free as possible but offer a variety of high-quality behavior for imitation. Once the learning program achieves apparent mastery, the environment should incorporate a low error level within a highly competitive framework. One way to achieve such an environment is to introduce a variety of human competitors; another is to have the learning program compete with variations of itself. The latter also offers an opportunity to experiment with the learning program's control strategy.

When an expert system learns to perform in a problem class by developing and refining a control strategy, such performance must be strictly relative; strategies must also be compared with each other. This is particularly important once the program becomes more skilled than any human. Work like HOYLE highlights the importance of the study of alternative control strategies and of programs that can modify their own strategies, and evaluate those modifications, on manageable tasks.

Human expertise is developed gradually, on a sequence of increasingly difficult problem classes. Complexity in a competitive environment is best evaluated by the duration of the learning period, measured in computational time or in number of experiences. Learning in a dynamic environment, however, requires continual reevaluation by the program of its own behavior, a kind of mechanized self-awareness. As they expose the learning program to different challenges, new experiences and new competitors may provide it with new useful knowledge and require different responses. New problem classes may raise different issues and demand the support of a more sophisticated weak theory.

As HOYLE's playing skill meets the Turing test, the expansion of the test bed to more difficult games will make greater demands upon the program's weak theory. HOYLE is learning 14 additional games whose expert outcome is unknown and directing the refinement of their model programs with its successes against them. In this sense, one expert learning program has become not only an expert apprentice but also an expert colleague.

Acknowledgments

This work was supported in part by NSF 9001936 and PSC-CUNY 666397. I thank Hans Berliner, Doug Fisher, and Virginia Teller for their thoughtful critiques and support in the development and presentation of this material. Michael Georgopoulos and Kouros Esfahany provided expert-level programming support.

Appendix: The Test-bed Games

• **Tic-tac-toe** is played on a 3 × 3 grid. Player has five X's and Opponent four O's. Initially the board is empty. A turn consists of placing one marker in any empty square. The first participant to place three of the same markers in a row, vertically, horizontally, or diagonally, wins. There are eight such winning lines. Play ends in a draw when there are no more empty squares. Tic-tac-toe is a draw game when played perfectly by both participants. There are 5478 distinct nodes in the game tree.

• **Lose tic-tac-toe** is played on a 3 × 3 grid. Player has five X's and Opponent four O's. Initially the board is empty. A turn consists of placing one marker in any empty square. The first participant to place three of the same markers in a row, vertically, horizontally, or diagonally, loses. There

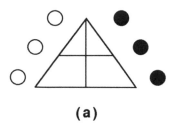 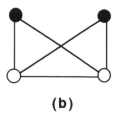

(a)   **(b)**

Figure 18.5
The game boards for (*a*) tsoro yematatu and (*b*) pong hau k'i

are eight such losing lines. Play ends in a draw when there are no more empty squares. Lose tic-tac-toe is a draw game when played perfectly by both participants. There are 5478 distinct nodes in the game tree.

• **Tsoro yematatu** is played on the board of figure 18.5a. Player has three black markers and Opponent three white ones. Initially the board is empty, and a turn consists of placing one marker on the intersection of two or more lines. There are seven such positions. Once all three of a participant's markers are on the board, a turn consists of moving one of those markers to the single empty position. The first participant to place three of the same markers in a row on any of the five lines wins. Play ends in a draw when it cycles through the same state often enough. Tsoro yematatu is a draw game when played perfectly by both participants. The game graph consists of 855 distinct nodes in a tree for the first stage; each leaf from the first stage then has a cyclic graph through 140 nodes with branching factor three from every node.

• **Pong hau k'i** is played on the board of figure 18.5b. Player has two black markers and Opponent two white ones. The initial state of the board is shown. A marker may lie on any intersection of two or more lines. There are five such positions. A move slides one marker to an adjacent position along a line without going through a third position or over another marker. The first participant unable to move loses. Play ends in a draw when it cycles through the same state often enough. Pong hau k'i is a draw game when played perfectly by both participants. There are 30 nodes in the game graph.

• **Achi** is played on the board in figure 18.1. Player has four black markers and Opponent four white ones. Initially the board is empty, and a turn consists of placing one marker on the intersection of two or more lines.

There are nine such positions. Once all four of a participant's markers are on the board, a turn consists of moving one of them to the single empty position. The first participant to place three of the same markers in a row, vertically, horizontally, or diagonally, wins. There are eight such winning lines. Play ends in a draw when it cycles through the same state often enough. Achi is a draw game when played perfectly by both participants. The game graph consists of 5240 distinct nodes in a tree for the first stage; each leaf from the first stage then has a cyclic graph through 630 nodes with branching factor four from every node.

- **Three-dimensional tic-tac-toe** is played on a 3 × 3 × 3 grid. Player has 14 X's and Opponent 13 O's. Initially the board is empty. A turn consists of placing one marker in any empty square. The first participant to place three of the same markers in a row, vertically, horizontally, or diagonally, wins. There are 49 such winning lines. Play ends in a draw when there are no more empty squares. Three-dimensional tic-tac-toe is a win for Player when played perfectly by both participants.

- **Qubic** is played on a 4 × 4 × 4 grid. Player has 32 X's and Opponent 32 O's. Initially the board is empty. A turn consists of placing one marker in any empty square. The first participant to place four of the same markers in a row, vertically, horizontally, or diagonally, wins. There are 76 such winning lines. Play ends in a draw when there are no more empty squares. Qubic is a win for Player when played perfectly by both participants.

References

Bell, R. C. 1969. *Board and Table Games from Many Civilizations*. London: Oxford University Press.

Berlekamp, E. R., Conway, J. H., and Guy, R. K. 1982. *Winning Ways for Your Mathematical Plays*. 2 vols. London: Academic Press.

Berliner, H. J. 1980. Backgammon Computer Program Beats World Champion. *Artificial Intelligence* 14 (2): 205–220.

Berliner, H., and Ebeling, C. 1989. Pattern Knowledge and Search: The SUPREM Architecture. *Artificial Intelligence* 38 (2): 161–198.

Brooks, R. A. 1991. Intelligence without Representation. *Artificial Intelligence* 47 (1–3): 139–160.

Chen, K. 1989. Group Identification in Computer Go. In *Heuristic Programming in Artificial Intelligence—The First Computer Olympiad*, pp. 195–210 Ed. D. Levy and D. Beal. New York: John Wiley.

Cohen, D. I. A. 1972. The Solution of a Simple Game. *Mathematics Magazine* 45 (4): 213–216.

Epstein, S. L. 1990. Learning Plans for Competitive Domains. In *Proceedings of the Seventh International Conference on Machine Learning*, pp. 190–197. Ed. B. W. Porter and R. J. Mooney. San Mateo, Calif.: Morgan Kaufmann.

Epstein, S. L. Prior Knowledge Strengthens Learning to Control Search in Weak Theory Domains. *International Journal of Intelligent Systems* 7:547–586.

Ginsberg, A., Weiss, S. M., and Politakis, P. 1988. Automatic Knowledge Base Refinement for Classification Systems. *Artificial Intelligence* 35 (2): 197–226.

Guha, R. V., and Lenat, D. B. 1990. Cyc: A Midterm Report. *AI Magazine* 11 (3): 32–59.

Gupton, G. 1989. Genetic Learning Algorithm Applied to the Game of Othello. In *Heuristic Programming in Artificial Intelligence—The First Computer Olympiad*, pp. 241–254. Ed. D. Levy and D. Beal. New York: John Wiley.

Hsu, F.-h., Anantharaman, T. S., Campbell, M. S., and Nowatzyk, A. 1990. Deep Thought. In *Computers, Chess, and Cognition*, pp. 55–78. Ed. T. Marsland and J. Schaeffer. New York: Springer-Verlag.

Kierulf, A., Chen, K., and Nievergelt, J. 1990. Smart Game Board and Go Explorer: A Study in Software and Knowledge Engineering. *Communications of the ACM* 33 (2): 152–166.

Kirsh, D. 1991. Today, the Earwig, Tomorrow Man? *Artificial Intelligence* 47 (1–3): 161–184.

Lee, K. F., and Mahajan, S. 1990. The Development of a World Class Othello Program. *Artificial Intelligence* 43 (1): 21–36.

Lenat, D. B., and Feigenbaum, E. A. 1991. On the Thresholds of Knowledge. *Artificial Intelligence* 47 (1–3): 185–250.

Nilsson, N. J. 1980. *Principles of Artificial Intelligence*. Palo Alto: Tioga Publishing.

Patashnik, O. 1980. Qubic: $4 \times 4 \times 4$ Tic-Tac-Toe. *Mathematics Magazine*. 53:202–216.

Rokey, M., and Grenander, S. 1990. Planning for Space Telerobotics: The Remote Mission Specialist. *IEEE Expert* 5 (3): 8–15.

Samuel, A. L. 1963. Some Studies in Machine Learning Using the Game of Checkers. In *Computers and Thought*, pp. 71–105. Ed. E. A. Feigenbaum and J. Feldman. New York: McGraw-Hill.

Samuel, A. L. 1967. Some Studies in Machine Learning Using the Game of Checkers. II—Recent Progress. *IBM Journal of Research and Development* 11 (6): 601–617.

Schaeffer, J., Culberson, J., Treloar, N., Knight, B., Lu, P., and Szafron, D. 1991. Reviving the Game of Checkers. In *Heuristic Programming in Artificial Intelligence 2—The Second Computer Olympiad*, pp. 119–136. Ed. D. N. L. Levy and D. F. Beal. Chichester, England: Ellis Horwood.

Slate, D. J., and Atkin, L. R. 1977. CHESS 4.5—The Northwestern University Chess Program. In *Chess Skill in Man and Machine*. Ed. P. Frey. Berlin: Springer.

Tesauro, G., and Sejnowski, T. J. 1989. A Parallel Network That Learns to Play Backgammon. *Artificial Intelligence* 39 (3): 357–390.

Turing, A. 1963. Computing Machinery and Intelligence. In *Computers and Thought*, Ed. E. A. Feigenbaum. New York: McGraw-Hill.

Zaslavsky, C. 1982. *Tic Tac Toe and Other Three-in-a-Row Games, from Ancient Egypt to the Modern Computer*. New York: Crowell.

19 Experiments on the Transfer of Knowledge between Neural Networks

Lorien Y. Pratt

19.1 Introduction

Backpropagation neural networks (Rumelhart, Hinton, and Williams 1987) have been compared to decision trees and statistical techniques for classifier induction in a number of recent papers (Weiss and Kulikowski 1991; Shavlik, Mooney, and Towell 1991; Atlas et al. 1990a, 1990b, 1990c; Cole et al. 1990; Dietterich, Hild, and Bakiri 1990; Fisher and McKusick 1989; Weiss and Kapouleas 1989; Mooney et al. 1989; also see chapter XX to this book). Although these studies describe some problems for which neural networks achieve superior performance to other methods, they also show fairly consistently that longer training times are required. Furthermore, Judd (1988) has shown that neural network learning is NP-complete.

There are at least two general approaches to speeding up neural network learning. One is to explore improvements to the backpropagation algorithm that allow quicker determination of network weights based on the training data alone (cf. the conjugate gradient algorithm of Barnard and Cole 1989). A complementary approach is to *bias* learning by using knowledge that supplements the training data.[1]

Many recent research efforts can be viewed as falling into this latter category. Knowledge can be injected at a number of different points into backpropagation networks. These entry points include:

• Network topology (cf. Lang 1990; Towell, Shavlik, and Noordewier 1990).

• Input unit values (preprocessing).

• Node-activation functions (cf. Moody and Darken 1989).

• Objective function (Hanson and Pratt 1989; Lang 1990).

• Target unit values (postprocessing).

• Training data order (cf. Kruschke 1990).

• Initial network weights (Towell, Shavlik, and Noordewier 1990).

• Learning parameters η, α (many studies, where these parameters are chosen based on their success on previous problems).

Understanding of the classification domain and experience with networks for related tasks are usually used to determine values for each of these choices.[2]

To the extent that mechanisms are available to store and copy the knowledge about a task domain from which these choices are derived, that knowledge can be reused when appropriate, potentially saving training time for future projects. Automated procedures for converting this information to one or more of the above backpropagation entry points are also helpful. For example, Maclin and Shavlik (chapter 9 in this book) assume that relevant knowledge is available in the form of a propositional domain theory and show an algorithm for converting it into a network topology and initial weights.

Unfortunately, formalized knowledge about neural network task domains is not often available. An alternative is simply to use the weights generated by a backpropagation network trained on one task to bias learning on a related task. This approach is complementary to Shavlik's, since it can deal with information that is infeasible to express symbolically and since it, too, uses the initial network weights as an entry point. We call this process network *transfer*: given a *source* network for a related problem, how can its weights be converted to the initial weights of a new *target* network learning task in order to bias further learning?

The study of transfer in neural networks also has a broader scope, incorporating the question of how information from learned decision trees (Quinlan 1986) can be utilized by neural networks. In both formalisms, it is possible to represent the basic decision-making unit as a linear separation of feature space. Therefore, learned information is interchangeable; distinctions made by decision trees can be used in neural networks, and vice versa. Several studies have recognized the strong representational similarities between the two formalisms (Utgoff 1990; Shavlik, Mooney, and Towell 1991; Sankar and Mammone 1990; Dietterich, Hild, and Bakiri 1990). The study of network transfer has the potential to exploit this relationship to improve learning speed and/or network performance.

Figure 19.1 illustrates the transfer problem, along with its relationship to the extraction of rules from neural networks, insertion of rules into networks, and the utilization of learned decision trees.

19.1.1   Types of Source/Target Relationships in Transfer

We distinguish between two general classes of relationships between source and target networks:

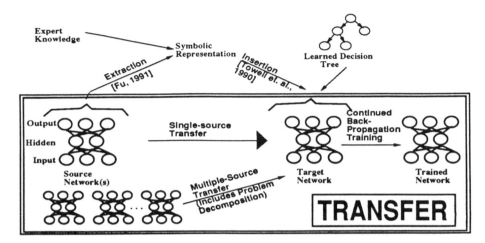

Figure 19.1
A general framework for network transfer

Related problem: The source network learns a problem that is related to the target. For example, a speech-recognition network might be trained on speakers with only an American accent and its results transferred to a network for recognizing speech from a population of British speakers. In this case, source and target networks have no specific topological relationship (although in practice they often have the same input and output units). Since intermediate features may be shared between related problems, utilizing source network weights in target training may speed up learning. Note that here, learned weights represent complete, but probably partially incorrect, knowledge.

Subnetwork → target network: The source network is trained on some subset of the target network task. For example, a source network might handle only vowel-sound recognition, and the target network would recognize all phonemes. There is usually a clear correspondence between source and target network nodes, and the target network training data is a superset of that in the source network. Note that weights represent partial, but largely correct, knowledge.

Our focus here is on transfer from subnetworks; related problem transfer is explored in Pratt (1993).

There are two possible formulations of the subnetwork → target network transfer problem:

1. We are given a trained subnetwork, to utilize as we choose as part of a larger network.

2. We are given a large network learning task, which has not been pre-trained. We may then choose to decompose the task, training smaller networks for subtasks before joining them to solve the larger task.

The experiments reported here bear on both of these approaches. The second approach is motivated by many empirical studies (Tesauro 1987), which indicate that neural network training is particularly slow for large networks. Therefore, breaking a larger problem into pieces may speed up the learning process. The idea of problem decomposition has also been widely studied for AI problems (Simon 1981).

19.1.2 Types of Subnetworks

We can distinguish between two general classes of source subnetworks, corresponding to *horizontal* and *vertical* decompositions of the target network. In horizontal decomposition, subnetworks are determined by dividing the network between layers (figure 19.2). In vertical decomposition, subnetworks span multiple layers and may represent subproblems for subsets of the output classes (figure 19.3).

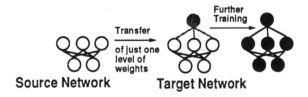

Figure 19.2
Horizontal decomposition

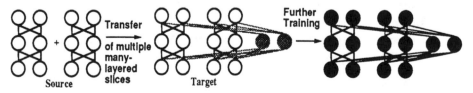

Figure 19.3
Vertical decomposition

19.1.3   Overview

In section 19.2, I present a pilot study that explores the utilization of weights for a single layer of a fabricated network. The focus for this study is on how transferred weights can best be retained during continued back-propagation training. This study illustrates the importance of the weight magnitudes that define hyperplane decision regions that are transferred from the source network (horizontal decomposition). When magnitudes are set too low, transferred decision regions lose their position and, hence, any benefit of transferred information. When magnitudes are set too high, errorful transferred decision regions are not free to change position. Properly set weight magnitudes lead to faster learning on the target task.

In sections 19.3 and 19.4, I describe two studies on more complex tasks that demonstrate transfer from multiple vertically decomposed source networks. Section 19.3 explores transfer in a vowel-sound-recognition task. It shows that learning speed, including subnetwork training time, is substantially faster than when networks are trained without decomposition and that the improvement in learning speed is statistically significant. Section 19.4 shows that this idea scales to a very large and difficult speech-recognition problem; I demonstrate an order-of-magnitude speedup on this task. These latter two studies are based very strongly on the work of Waibel, Sawai, and Shikano (1989); they can be viewed as validations of their problem decomposition methodology on networks with different architectures and for different tasks.

This chapter expands upon, and includes portions of, work previously presented in Pratt and Kamm (1991) and Pratt, Mostow, and Kamm (1991).

19.2   Pilot Study: Weight Magnitudes and Network Initialization

In this section, I present results of a study that explores the dynamics of networks that have had some of their weights preset nonrandomly. The goal was to understand how the magnitudes of preset weights interact with their initial positions and the training data during backpropagation learning. I first present a method for interpreting backpropagation network weights in terms of hyperplane decision regions. I then show conditions on these decision regions for solving the task represented by a set of training data. Finally, I present conditions and results of experiments that explore how networks preset when some of these conditions hold behave during backpropagation training.

19.2.1   Understanding Network Weights in Terms of Hyperplane Decision Regions

Consider a single-hidden-layer network that is fully connected in the input-to-hidden (IH) and hidden-to-output (HO) layers and trained for a classification task. Each output unit represents a different class. Let the input to unit j be $I_j = \sum_i y_i w_{ij}$, where y_i is the activation of incoming unit i, and w_{ij} is the weight between units i and j. To determine unit j's activation, we can view I_j as being passed through the threshold function:

$$\text{activation } a_j = \begin{cases} 1 & \text{if } I_j > 0 \\ 0 & \text{if } I_j \leq 0 \end{cases}$$

This activation function is a simplification of the sigmoid: $a_j = \dfrac{1}{1 + e^{(-I_j)}}$, which is the activation function used in backpropagation networks. For large I_j, the sigmoid function is close to 1; it is near 0 for small I_j. For intermediate I_j, the sigmoid may produce a real-valued number between 0 and 1, whereas the threshold activation function will always output strictly 0 or 1. When weights on connections incoming to a neuron are large in absolute magnitude, $|I_j|$ will tend to be large, so the threshold activation function approximates a sigmoid better than when $|I_j|$ is smaller. The consequence of viewing activation functions as thresholds is that it may appear that more hidden units are necessary to solve a problem than are strictly required (see Sontag 1989).

Consider a space of n dimensions, where n is the number of input units. As shown for $n = 2$ in figure 19.4, training data define points in this space, which can be labeled by corresponding target values. Weights leading from input units to a particular hidden unit, along with the hidden-unit bias, determine a hyperplane-bounded decision region in this space. For $n = 2$, the hyperplane is a line. Input vectors on one side of the hyperplane cause a hidden-unit activation of 0; vectors on the other side cause an activation of 1.

One condition for a trained network is that IH hyperplanes separate the training data such that no decision region contains training data items with different target values. If this was not the case, then the two input vectors for those different targets would cause the same hidden-unit acti-

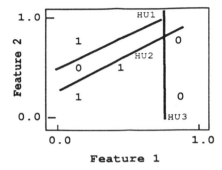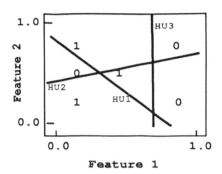

Figure 19.4
Two examples of IH hyperplane sets that separate training data in a small network

vations, resulting in identical output unit activations, which is clearly not the goal of training.

Another condition on a trained network is that IH hyperplanes are placed such that there is a correct configuration of HO hyperplanes possible (i.e., hidden-layer activations are linearly separable).

Since obtaining IH hyperplanes that separate training data items for different targets by IH hyperplanes is one goal of learning, it is reasonable to expect that presetting IH weights to produce such hyperplanes will lead to faster learning. I performed a series of experiments, described in section 19.2.3, to test this hypothesis.

19.2.2   How Weight Magnitudes Affect Training After Transfer

One complication of simply initializing IH weights with separating hyperplanes is that hyperplane positions determine only the ratio of weights that connect to a hidden unit; they do not also determine weight magnitudes, which can be varied arbitrarily while retaining the same weight ratios. Therefore I also studied the effect of varying the magnitudes of weights from subnetworks to attempt to understand the effect that they have on further training.

We can predict this effect to an extent by examining the input-to-hidden weight update equation used by backpropagation (Rumelhart, Hinton, and Williams 1987):

$$\Delta w_{ij} = \underbrace{\eta y_j (1 - y_j)}_{(1)} \underbrace{\sum_k \underbrace{\delta_k w_{jk}}_{(3)} x_i}_{(2)} \tag{19.1}$$

Here, j indexes hidden units, i indexes input units, k indexes output units, x_i is the activation of input unit i, y_j is the activation of hidden unit j, and w_{ij} is the the weight from unit i to unit j. δ_k is a weighted error from the hidden-to-output layer. Δw_{ij} is the modification to each weight calculated on each backpropagation pass.

Term 19.2 is largest for values of y_j near .5, smaller for values close to 0 or 1. Its effect is to force faster weight changes when the hidden unit activation is near .5.

Term (2) has two effects. First, along with the other terms in this equation, it contributes to determining the magnitude of Δw_{ij}. δ_k is the error associated with output unit k, as calculated in the HO layer. It is weighted by the connecting weight w_{jk} and the result is summed over all output units. A large term (2) leads to a large change in a weight, resulting in a smaller Δw_{ij}. Second, term (2) determines the sign of Δw_{ij}. A positive term (2) leads to a larger Δw_{ij}, leading eventually to larger output activations, which brings actual and target output values closer.

Term (3) makes individual weight changes in proportion to the magnitude of the input unit's activation.

There are two reasons to believe that, based on this equation alone, larger weight magnitudes will lead to smaller Δw_{ij}. First, large weight magnitudes tend to lead to large input values, which, after processing through the sigmoidal (or threshold), lead to hidden-unit activations y_j uhich are close to 0 (for large-magnitude negative inputs) or 1 (for large-magnitude positive inputs). Either value leads to smaller values of term (1). Second, this equation does not directly include a factor that scales Δw_{ij} relative to w_{ij}. Therefore, larger weight magnitudes will have smaller relative changes.

Although these input-to-hidden equation factors are not the only ones affecting the rate of hyperplane movement (error from the output layer and input activations are also factors), we do expect that, all other things being equal, large weight magnitudes lead to slower hyperplane movement, which is desirable for correct transferred weights. I now describe a series of experiments that validate this hypothesis, as well as the fact that such weights do retain some degree of flexibility.

19.2.3 Conditions and Results

All networks studied had a 2-3-1 (two input units, three hidden units, one output unit) topology. They were trained on a small set of hand-chosen training data that were not linearly separable and that contained six patterns (figure 19.4). Each training data target was either 0 or 1. A manual search for values of η and α (10 pairs tried, on networks with random initial weights) resulted in locally optimal values of $\eta = 1.5$, $\alpha = .9$, which were used for all experiments. Standard backpropagation (Rumelhart, Hinton, and Williams 1987) was used, with a sigmoidal activation function, training after every pattern presentation, and training data presented sequentially.

A number of experiments were performed, summarized in table 19.1. Experiments fell into the following five categories:

1. Random low-magnitude initial weights (experiment 1): In the control experiment, 30 networks were initialized with random weights in the

Table 19.1
Conditions and results for the pilot study

Exp #, IH source	IH avg. mag.	HO avg. mag.	# converging	Mean epochs to converge	Sig. diff. from #1?
1: Random	.25	.25	28	528	—
2: Preset	.25	.25	26	501	N
3: Preset	2.5	.00625	26	228	Y
4: Preset	5.0	.00625	23	151	Y
5: Preset	2.5	.25	29	173	Y
6: Preset	2.5	2.5	22	425	N
7: Preset	.25	.00625	29	438	N
8: 0.6-perturbed	2.5	.00625	24	199	Y
9: Centroid	.25	.25	28	591	N
10: Centroid	1.25	.00625	30	859	Y
11: Centroid	2.5	.00625	20	898	Y
12: Random	2.5	.00625	23	329	N

Note: Each row of this table shows results from a set of 30 trials (each with different random initial weights) of the conditions shown. Column 2 shows the average magnitude for the weights obtained from successfully trained subnetworks. Column 3 shows various average magnitudes for random initial weights in the hidden-to-output layer. Every network was trained for 2000 epochs. Convergence time was measured as the number of epochs of training before the total squared error over all patterns dropped below 0.1. Column 4 shows the number of networks converging, out of a possible 30. Column 5 shows the mean number of epochs required for the networks that did converge to do so. Finally, each condition was compared to the control condition (experiment 1), to determine if the list of convergence times was significantly different, according to a one-sided t-test. Column 6 indicates whether the result was significant ($p < 0.01$).

range: $[-0.5, 0.5]$ (average IH, HO magnitudes of 0.25); 28 trials converged to a solution. As shown, the mean time to converge for the 28 networks was 528 epochs.

2. Preset separating IH weights (experiments 2–7): 30 networks were trained to convergence (nonconverging networks were omitted by changing initial weight sets), and their separating IH weights were extracted and used to initialize a new set of 30 networks (not all of which converged). IH and HO magnitudes were rescaled in a variety of ways, as shown.

3. Perturbed (experiment 8): The same weights as in the previous experiments were used, but each IH weight was modified to be $w = w + rw$, where r was a uniform random variable in $[-0.6, 0.6]$. This produced hyperplanes that did not separate training data completely but were in the proximity of effective final positions.

4. Centroid initialization (experiments 9–11): To test the generality of the idea of placing hyperplanes near training data (without necessarily being near a separating configuration), IH hyperplanes were initialized to pass through the training data centroid (median value of each input dimension).

5. Random high-magnitude initial weights (experiment 12): This experiment verified that the speedup found with high weight magnitudes was due to both their positions and their magnitudes instead of just their magnitudes. As shown, the high-magnitude random networks did not converge significantly faster ($df = 44$) than low-magnitude initialized networks.

Additional tests found no significant differences in learning times between experiments (3, 4), (3, 8), and (4, 8).

19.2.4   Discussion

These results yield several observations that can be used as hypotheses for investigation of more complex tasks:

• Learning was faster in networks with preset IH weights than when they were randomly initialized. In experiments 3, 4, 5, and 8, learning speed was significantly faster ($p < .0001$, $df = 50, 44, 46, 54$) than when weights were initialized randomly.[3]

• Learning was faster in networks with preset IH weights specifying near-correct hyperplane positions than when IH weights were randomly initialized. This was shown in experiment 8, where perturbed networks

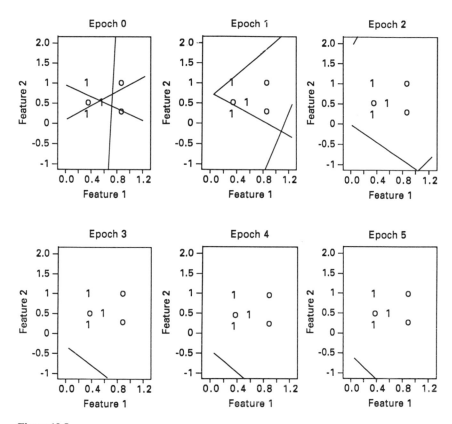

Figure 19.5
Hyperplanes during a typical run of experiment 2. Although they are present in correct position, low magnitudes make them quickly move out of position

trained significantly faster ($p < .0001$, $df = 46$) than randomly initialized networks.

• Surprisingly, correctly preset IH hyperplanes moved out of position. This happened when IH magnitudes were too low, as in experiment 2. Hyperplanes were observed to diverge rapidly in early epochs, losing their preset positions (figure 19.5).

• Raising IH weight magnitudes made hyperplanes more retentive. In experiment 4, hyperplanes moved out of position to a much smaller degree than in experiment 2 (figure 19.6). The mean number of training data patterns crossed by moving hyperplanes during learning was 24.6 in ex-

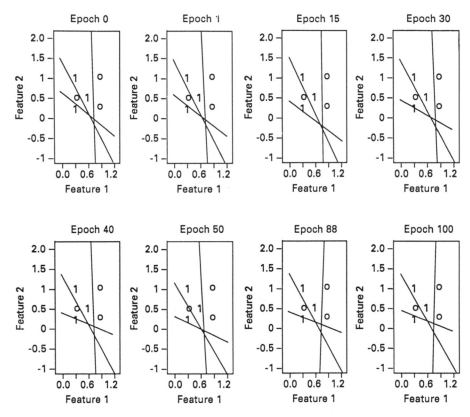

Figure 19.6
Hyperplanes during a typical run of experiment 4. Preset hyperplanes retain their positions
and learning is much faster

periment 4, compared to 36.4 for experiment 2. The difference was significant, with $p < 0.01$, $df = 58$.

- Fastest learning was obtained when **IH** weights were preset in the correct positions and weight magnitudes were raised to make them retentive.
This was shown in experiment 4.

- Networks with preset hyperplanes tended not to converge as often. This
was shown by experiments 2–5 and 8 (figure 19.7).

- A scheme for initializing hyperplanes in the proximity of their final positions did not work. Experiments 9–11 explored how examination of train-

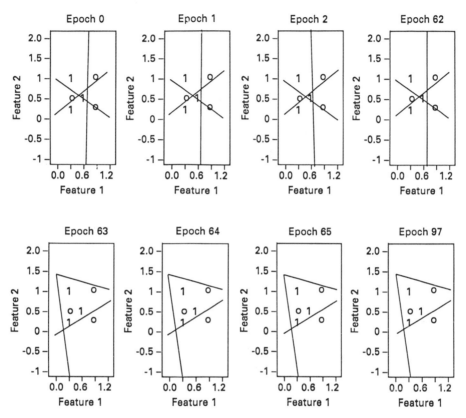

Figure 19.7
Hyperplanes showing what can go wrong in experiment 4. Preset hyperplanes suddenly jump out of position and do not recover

ing data for initial weight placements, not transferred weights, can speed up learning.

• Relative magnitudes between IH and HO layer affects learning speed but not as much as absolute IH magnitude. Experiments 2 and 6 have the same relative IH and HO magnitudes, but experiment 2 converged more often. Experiments 3 and 5 have very different IH:HO magnitude ratios, but both show significant speedup over the random condition. However, HO magnitudes are important. Experiment 6 shows that if they are set too high, convergence can be affected; only 22 of 30 runs converged, and the ones that did were not faster than the random case.

An additional small experiment was performed to explore the sensitivity of these results to the learning rate (η). In this study, η was set much lower, to 0.1 (instead of 0.5), with the same momentum value of 0.9. Ten networks were run for a variety of conditions. We found that randomly initialized networks took around 7000 epochs to converge, both preset and preset perturbed networks took around 4000 epochs, and preset raised-magnitude networks required 1000 epochs. Although convergence times were in general much longer than when $\eta = 0.5$, these results are similar to those of the more rigorous study.

Recall that the study described in this section is exploratory, meant to give some insight into network dynamics. It does not test some important aspects of network biasing through initial weights. Therefore, the above points await validation through more systematic experiments, evaluation on real-world-sized tasks (it is hoped with more than two input units) and those in which generalization performance on unseen data can be measured.

19.3   Problem Decomposition in a Vowel-Recognition Task

In the previous section, I showed that hyperplanes initialized near correct positions may move more quickly into those positions, thus speeding up learning. Here I extend those results to a more complex task. I demonstrate a technique for presetting network weights that produces faster learning, even taking into account the time to learn the values of preset weights. This is because the original problem is vertically decomposed into subproblems, allowing for the reduction of search combinatorics. In this and the next section I borrow a decomposition technique introduced by Waibel, Sawai, and Shikano (1989), who showed improved learning speed and performance in networks for spoken consonant recognition (see also Waibel et al. 1987; Waibel 1989; and Hataoka and Waibel 1989).

19.3.1   Motivation for Problem Decomposition

It has often been observed that small backpropagation networks train quickly, but large ones seem to require exponentially longer time (Tesauro 1987; Tesauro and Janssens 1988). One solution to this problem is to train only small networks. Many real-world problems can be readily decomposed into smaller subproblems. Smaller networks can be trained on these subproblems and then combined later into larger networks to solve the original problem. Depending on the degree of subproblem independence, this can lead to enormous improvements in training time.

If we let n be the number of weights in a network and let p be the number of possible values for each weight, then there are p^n different possible states for the network. Measuring worst-case training time as that required to search each state, an exhaustive search of all of network states would require examination of $O(p^n)$ different weight assignments.

If we are given information about a domain that says that the solution to weights $1 \cdots \frac{n}{2}$ is independent of the solution to weights $\frac{n}{2} + 1 \cdots n$, then it is not necessary to consider all combinations of solutions to the two subproblems. This information can reduce the search to $O(2 \times p^{n/2})$, which is substantially smaller. For example, in even a very small, low-precision network with $n = 6$, $p = 10$, the difference is 1 million weight vectors to be searched versus 2000.

19.3.2   Conditions

We trained a network to recognize the 11 steady-state vowels of British English using a training set of LPC-derived log area ratios, using data from Robinson (1989), which contains more details on signal preprocessing. I also rescaled this data, which originally fell between -5.211 and 5.074, to be restricted to the range $[0, 1]$. The network had 10 input units and 11 output units, each representing a vowel sound. Training was on 528 vowels pronounced by four male and four female speakers, and the test set was 462 vowels from four male and three female speakers not included in that set. All training used standard backpropagation, with weights updated after every training pattern, and patterns presented in the same order every epoch.

Four nondecomposed networks were trained, each with 26 hidden units (583 weights). We used training parameters $\eta = 0.3$, $\alpha = 0.9$, which were chosen as causing the fastest learning over five epochs of each of 10 parameter pairs tried.

We also studied the performance of networks in which IH and HO hyperplanes were preset through problem decomposition. We used parameters $\eta = 0.6$, $\alpha = 0.8$, which were chosen because they led to fast learning in previously trained nondecomposed networks. The decom-

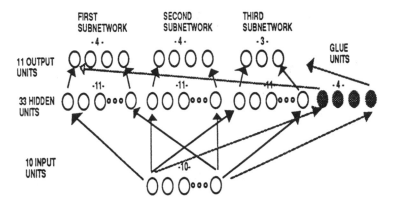

Figure 19.8
A vowel-sound-recognition network has been decomposed into three smaller subnetworks,
following the above topology. They are trained separately and then joined into the larger
network by training "glue" units. Arrows delimit regions of full connectivity. Numbers indicate unit counts

posed architecture used is illustrated in figure 19.8. Decomposed networks
had 567 weights.

The training methodology borrowed from Waibel, Sawai, and Shikano
(1989) for decomposed networks was used. It contains these steps:

1. Subnetwork training: Divide network into subsets; train each individually.

2. Glue training: Combine subnetworks into a larger network using additional "glue" units. These are trained while subnetwork weights are frozen.

3. Fine tuning: All weights are modified during further training.

Although this methodology may be useful in some problems, there are
a couple of reasons to question whether it will always improve network
performance. First, for fine tuning to be useful, it would seem to require
that, as in experiment 8 of the previous section, subnetwork training develops a set of roughly positioned hyperplanes, and fine-tuning moves them
into place. This will not necessarily happen in all decomposed networks;
there may be local minima that are optimal for subproblems but are not
near an optimum solution for the full problem. Also, generalization tests
(Morgan and Bourlard 1990) indicate that performance can be degraded
in a network that overfits its data, so a careful methodology is necessary
to obtain the best subnetworks, as well as the best combined network.

I sought to test whether problem decomposition was useful in decreasing training time on the vowel-recognition task. Five different decomposed networks were trained using the above procedure. Each trial used different initial random subnetwork and glue weights; they were then compared to the four nondecomposed networks. Each subnetwork was trained on all input vectors in the training set, with all-zero target vectors for irrelevant input patterns. An input pattern was considered irrelevant to a particular subnetwork if its target label was not in the set of four or three vowels for which that subnetwork was responsible. We used an "oversized" network training technique (Weigend, Sawai, and Shikano 1990) to control for overfitting: subnetwork training, glue training, and fine tuning were continued until the performance on the test set ceased to improve. We performed t-tests of significance on the learning time and performance difference between the two populations of decomposed and nondecomposed networks.

19.3.3 Measurement of Backpropagation Learning Time When Some Weights Are Fixed during Training

Backpropagation network learning time is usually reported as the number of epochs required for training. However, for accurate comparison of learning times between nondecomposed networks and those for which glue training is performed, a more precise measure is required. This is because during glue training, many network weights remain fixed, requiring fewer calculations on the backpropagation pass of the algorithm. We considered several measures of training time, including counting the number of weight updates in the network. Unfortunately, this measure inaccurately favors learning with fixed weights, because it does not count calculations spent during the feedforward pass, when all weight values are used.

A more accurate measure of learning time is to calculate explicitly the number of arithmetic operations performed by the learning algorithm. By examining the equations used by backpropagation to calculate node activations and weight updates, we derived a measure of the number of operations (addition, subtraction, multiplication, division, exponentiation) executed in an epoch. This measure was then used to compare network learning times.

Let I, H, and O be the number of input, hidden, and output units, respectively. Let f_H be the number of units in the fan-in to a hidden unit, f_O

Table 19.2

		mult/div/exp	add/sub	
Feedforward	For all H	f_H	$f_H - 1$	Calculate input
		2	1	Sigmoid
	For all O	f_O	$f_O - 1$	Calculation input
		2	1	Sigmoid
Backpropagation	For all O	2	2	Calculate δ's
		$2f_O$		Calculate Δw_{ij}
			f_O	Modify weights
	For all H	2	1	Calculate δ's
		g_H	$g_H - 1$	Calculate $\sum_k$
		$2f_H$		Calculate Δw_{ij}
			f_H	Modify weights

be the fan-in to each output unit, and g_H be the fan-out from a hidden unit. Examination of the standard backpropagation feedforward and weight update equations yields table 19.2, which shows the number of arithmetic operations required.[4] Using this table, we can calculate the number of operations required for each of the subnetworks. One useful result is that a fully connected feedforward network takes $H(5f_H + 4 + 2g_H) + O(6 + 5f_O)$ operations per training pattern.

Note that the operations used here are only those that are fundamental to the learning algorithm. Different implementations of backpropagation will have varying amounts of overhead for the feedforward and back-propagation passes. Thus, the measure reported here will not necessarily correspond to actual machine time.

19.3.4 Results

Performance: No significant difference in test set score was found between performance of the decomposed and nondecomposed networks ($p > 0.01$, $df = 7$). Performance scores, in percentage correct on the test data, were 53, 58, 55, 56, 55 for the decomposed and 58, 61, 59, 54 for the non-decomposed networks.

Learning speed: Decomposed networks learned faster than nondecomposed networks. The mean decomposed time was 40% of the mean non-decomposed time (learning significantly faster with $p < .001$, $df = 7$). Using the measure of number of arithmetic operations during learning described above, the mean decomposed learning time was 1.348×10^9 operations (3096 epochs). In units of 10^8 operations, the decomposed networks required 17.5, 21.5, 9.22, 18.81, and 16.12 operations. The nondecomposed networks required 30.9, 30.9, 38.6, and 34.8×10^8 operations. Fine tuning: For one arbitrarily chosen set of trained subnetwork weights, four different networks were trained, starting with different random glue weights. Generalization scores were calculated every 10 epochs. The best scores observed were 47, 35, 43, and 52. These are markedly *lower* than the scores at the end of glue training. Substituting further glue training for fine tuning did not cause such a drop in performance (nor did performance improve substantially).

Note that this study extends the results of Waibel, Sawai, and Shikano (1989) in that it uses a network with one hidden layer instead of two. It also uses different training data than their consonant-recognition task. Under these different conditions, our experiments also show improved learning speed from problem decomposition. We have also explored the utility of a three-step problem decomposition methodology and found, in contrast to the previous work, that the third step, called fine tuning," may not always be useful. Finally, we have established that the network training time speedup over nondecomposed networks is statistically significant.

In the following section, we explore a further modification of the problem decomposition model. As in the vowel-recognition task, a network is decomposed into subnetworks that are trained separately. However, we also decompose the set of input units.

19.4   Problem Decomposition in a Large Speech Recognition Problem

In this section, we describe an application of the results of the previous two sections to a large acoustic-phonetic mapping problem. We demonstrate an order-of-magnitude speedup in training time for this task.

This work was done as part of the Bellcore AP-net project (Kamm and Singhal 1990). The general goal of the AP-net project is to develop a system for large-vocabulary, speaker-independent recognition of continuous speech. This task is divided into three stages, illustrated in figure 19.9 The input to stage 1 is an acoustic waveform, processed to generate a spectrotemporal representation. This is used as input to a feedforward neural network. The role of the network is to produce an output activa-

Recognized Words or Sentences

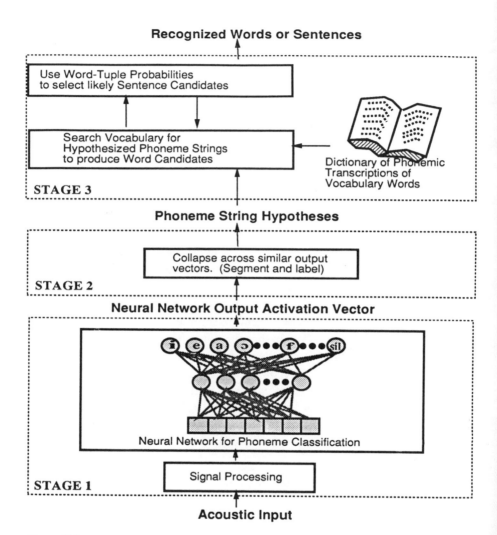

Figure 19.9
Speech recognition using AP-net

tion for each of 46 "phoneme" classes. The network generates a vector of output activations every 5 ms. The role of stage 2 is to collapse network activations for the 5-ms frames into a string of phonemes. Stage 3 might then recognize a word or sentence by incorporating constraints from phoneme dictionaries and word-tuple probabilities into the output of stage 2.

Section 19.4.1 describes the use of a neural network for stage 1 of the AP-net task. We describe a previous study of this problem, whose performance serves as a benchmark for comparison with decomposed networks. Section 19.4.1 also describes the signal preprocessing and specialized training procedure used for all AP-net networks. Section 19.4.2 describes how AP-net was decomposed. Section 19.4.3 discusses how network performance was measured. Experimental results are given in section 19.4.4.

19.4.1   Previous Work: Nondecomposed AP-net Networks

Networks with Varying Input Durations   In a previous experiment designed to study the effect of network input span on phoneme classification performance (Kamm and Singhal 1990), three AP-net networks were trained. The first network derived its input from seven contiguous 5-ms frames of speech, providing information spanning 35 ms of speech. Each speech frame was represented by 21 input units, yielding $7 \times 21 = 147$ total input units. The second network also received input from seven frames of speech, but these were obtained from every other 5-ms segment of the input signal, yielding an input duration spanning 65 ms. The third network skipped three 5-ms frames between inputs, yielding a 125-ms input duration. All three networks had 30 hidden units and 46 output units, each corresponding to a phoneme class. Their architectures are shown in figure 19.10.

Signal Preprocessing   The training set for these experiments was a portion of the DARPA acoustic-phonetic (A-P) corpus (Fisher et al. 1987; also called the TI-MIT corpus), which contains recordings of continuous utterances from 630 speakers, along with transcriptions specifying the phonemes uttered. This corpus is used extensively in phoneme-recognition research.

A subset of the DARPA A-P corpus consisting of 200 sentences spoken by 10 male and 10 female speakers was used for training. Testing was performed on a disjoint 200-sentence set. Input to the network was a spectrotemporal representation consisting of the scaled outputs of 21

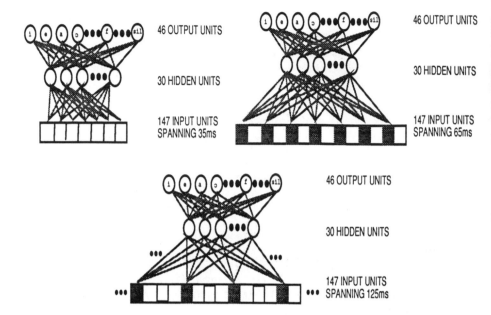

Figure 19.10
Three AP-net networks with different input spans

overlapping bandpass filters (with center frequencies from ≈ 140 Hz to ≈ 7000 Hz and 1-Bark[5] spacing) sampled at seven 5-ms time steps. Network input thus consisted of seven sets of 21 values. This input was obtained from 10-ms frames of speech, using a 5-ms frame shift. This process yielded 108,983 patterns in the training set and 112,970 patterns in the testing set. Every network had 46 output units, each corresponding to a phoneme class.

Training Procedure For training, the target vector for each training pattern identified the phoneme that occurred during the center of the seven input frames. The output unit corresponding to this phoneme received a target activation of 0.9; all other output units received target activations of 0.1. A modified version of the backpropagation algorithm (Rumelhart, Hinton, and Williams 1987) was used for training. The two changes to the learning algorithm were to scale the learning rate on each output unit relative to the frequency of occurrence of its corresponding phoneme class and to disable training of certain output units whenever the training pattern contained a phoneme transition, in order to avoid ambiguous training examples. These two modifications are described in more detail in Kamm and Singhal (1990).

The networks were trained using backpropagation parameters η (learning rate) = 0.1 and α (momentum) = 0.1. These parameters were chosen as the best out of a group of four parameter pairs tried; that is, using these values, squared error decreased monotonically and most rapidly over the first few training epochs. The same parameters were used for all three networks, each of which was trained for 300 epochs.

Test Results   After training, the weights were fixed and the networks were tested on the disjoint 200-sentence set. Using the top-three normalized average hit-rate measure (see section 19.4.3), the best performance for the test sentences was obtained by the 125-ms network, with an average hit rate of 61.7% and an average false-positive rate of 3.1%. In the current study, we use this performance score as a benchmark for comparison with the network trained using the problem-decomposition methodology.

19.4.2   Problem Decomposition in AP-net

The Decomposed AP-net Architecture   The problem-decomposition methodology introduced in section 19.3 can be applied to networks with different topologies. The networks in Waibel, Sawai, and Shikano (1989) had two layers of hidden units, while those in section 19.3 had only a single hidden layer. In both cases, subnetworks used connections from all input units; decomposition was achieved by dividing the output units into nonoverlapping subsets.

For AP-net, we maintained the multiple input spans used in the nondecomposed AP-net experiments (see section 19.4.1). The use of multiple input spans can be viewed as decomposing the problem in terms of the input units. The problem was further decomposed by assigning the output units so that different subnets included different (but overlapping) subsets of output classes. The results reported by Kamm and Singhal (1990) showed that the 35-ms and 65-ms monolithic networks had much higher performance for phonemes with short average duration than for the longest phonemes (diphthongs). Based on this finding, we decomposed the problem on the output units so that the two subnetworks with short-duration input spans "specialized" on subsets of phonemes with short and intermediate average durations. To assign phoneme classes to subnetworks, we analyzed a portion of the DARPA A-P corpus to determine the distribution of durations for each phoneme class. Phonemes that were usually of short duration were included as output classes for the first network; short and midlength phoneme classes formed the output classes for the second network; and all phonemes classes were included in the third network. A phoneme class was included in the 35-ms network if more than 10% of the utterances of any phoneme in that class were under 25 ms long. A phoneme class was chosen for the 65-ms network if more than 50% of the utterances of any phoneme in that class were under 65 ms long. The resulting assignment of phoneme classes to subnetworks follows:

Subnet	Input span	Phoneme classes
1	35 ms	sil k t ax p dx dh d g b
2	65 ms	sil l n ix r z k m t ax p dx y v dh ng d ch g jh b
3	125 ms	sil s iy ae l n ix ih ao r aa ay z ey eh er sh ow k axr ah w m f t ux ax p dx y oy aw v uw dh ng d hh ch g th jh b hv uh zh

The decomposed AP-net topology is shown in figure 19.11.

Note that, in contrast to the networks described by Waibe, Sawai, and Shikano (1989), where longer-duration phonemes are recognized by a sec-

Subnet#	Input span	Phoneme classes
1	35ms	sil k t ax p dx dh d g b
2	65ms	sil l n ix r z k m t ax p dx y v dh ng d ch g jh b
3	125ms	sil s iy ae l n ix ih ao r aa ay z ey eh er sh ow k axr ah w m f t ux ax p dx y oy aw v uw dh ng d hh ch g th jh b hv uh zh

The decomposed AP-net topology is shown in Figure 11.

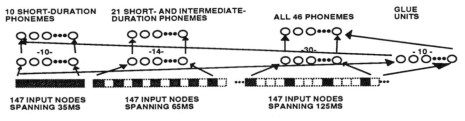

10 SHORT-DURATION PHONEMES   **21 SHORT- AND INTERMEDIATE-DURATION PHONEMES**   **ALL 46 PHONEMES**   **GLUE UNITS**

-10-   -14-   -30-   -10-

147 INPUT NODES SPANNING 35MS   **147 INPUT NODES SPANNING 65MS**   **147 INPUT NODES SPANNING 125MS**

Figure 19.11
The AP-net decomposed network architecture

ond hidden layer, AP-net accomplishes this same end with a single hidden layer and multiple input spans.

Training Methodology   Subnetwork training, glue training, and fine tuning were performed as described in section 19.3, using a custom-built simulator, written in Fortran, running on an Alliant FX80 computer.

The subnetwork training data was the same 200-sentence set used to train the networks described in section 19.4.1. We performed a rough search for satisfactory training parameters (η, α) for each subnetwork, for glue training, and for fine tuning by running a few training epochs and choosing the parameters that generated the lowest error score.

Subnetworks were trained until there was no substantial improvement in performance over time on the testing data. Weights from subnetwork epochs with the best score were used to initialize those subnets in the full decomposed network. Glue training was then performed, and when the performance score leveled out, fine tuning was performed.

Using the topology in figure 19.11, we first achieved a performance score of 56% average hit rate (AHR). Using fewer hidden units than shown in figure 19.11, network performance did not exceed 51% normalized average hit rate. Since this was no better than the previous AP-net system (section 19.4.1), we sought to improve this score. We began by increasing subnetwork hidden-unit and glue-unit counts to the values shown. This raised performance score to 56%. An analysis of errors in this network showed that subnetworks were firing on phonemes for which they were not trained. We determined that this was caused by an aspect of the back-propagation modification mentioned in section 19.4.1: learning rate scaling factors for nontarget units were on average 100 times smaller than those for target units. Thus, output units were not being trained quickly enough not to fire when their corresponding phoneme class was not the target. By multiplying the scaling factor for nontarget phonemes by 100, we were able both to alleviate this problem and to increase the subnetwork hit rate score by several percentage points, which led to an increase in the overall network score, to 62.4% AHR, as discussed in more detail below.

19.4.3   Measurement of AP-net Network Performance

As discussed by Kamm and Singhal (1990), determining an appropriate performance measure for AP-net is not a straightforward process. The values reported in that paper included the top-three AHR and top-three average false alarm (AFA). The top-three hit rate for each output class was defined as the number of test patterns where the output unit corresponding to the target class had one of the three highest activations (over all output classes), divided by the number of patterns where that class was the target. The top-three AHR was the average of the top-three hit rate for the 46 phoneme classes. The top-three false alarm rate for output class i was computed as the number of patterns where the target phoneme is not in class i, the output unit corresponding to class i has one of the three highest activations, and the output unit corresponding to the target phoneme does *not* have one of the three highest activations, divided by the total number of patterns where the target phoneme is *not* in class i. The top-three AFA was defined to be the average of the false alarm rates for the 46 output classes.

It is important to be able to compare the performance of the AP-net network against those of other methods for performing the same task. A recent hidden Markov model (HMM) phoneme-recognition system (Lee and Hon 1989) had a 46% error rate on the DARPA A-P corpus, measured as the number of phonemes chosen incorrectly. AP-net generates an output activation vector for each successive 5-ms *frame* of speech (based on 35 ms, 65 ms, or 125 ms of context information). Phoneme durations typically exceed 5 ms, so, in order to compare AP-net to HMM systems, its activation vectors must be converted to phoneme strings.

It should be possible to obtain a measure of AP-net performance that suggests the score that will be obtained after output activation vectors are converted into phoneme hypothesis strings by some postprocessing method in stage 2 (recall figure 19.9). Because optimal postprocessing strategies are not yet developed, the top-three score was used as a performance measure, on the assumption that providing information about the top-three phoneme-class candidates to the postprocessing step would yield higher phoneme-recognition performance than providing only information about the top candidate. However, the top-three AHR and AFA measures used by Kamm and Singhal do not take into account the relative frequency of occurrence of the different phoneme classes in the corpus. To provide a performance estimate that reflects the distribution of phonemes, we calculated a *normalized* top-three AHR and AFA score by computing a weighted average of phoneme hit rates. Specifically, the proportion of each phoneme in the corpus (or in the subnetwork phoneme set) is multiplied by each hit rate and false alarm score, and the result is summed.

These normalized averaged scores are generally about 5% higher than the scores reported in Kamm and Singhal (1990), reflecting the fact that these networks tended to have higher performance on the more frequently occurring phoneme classes.[6]

19.4.4 Results

Table 19.3 summarizes the conditions used to train networks in this study. For comparison, conditions for the highest-performance nondecomposed network are also shown. As can be seen, three subnetworks were trained; then glue training was performed, followed by fine tuning. The second column shows the number of parameter pairs (η, α) explored. The η and α values shown in the third and fourth columns were selected for training the network. The number of operations per pattern (column six) was calculated as described in section 19.3.3. The total operation count was obtained by multiplying the operations per pattern by the number of patterns (108,983) times the number of epochs used for training.

The resulting performance scores of each of the decomposed networks (as tested on the 200-sentence test set, containing 112,970 patterns), along with the scores for the 125-ms nondecomposed network, are shown in table 19.4.

The top-three normalized AHR and normalized AFA measures are calculated as described in section 19.4.3. Unnormalized AHR and AFA measures are shown for purposes of comparison. If we measure overall performance as the top-three normalized AHR minus the top-three nor-

Table 19.3
Training operations

Network	Parameter pairs tried	η	α	Epochs	Operations per pattern	Total operations
Previous 125-ms Non-decomposed AP-net	4	.1	.10	300	32486	10.62×10^{11}
Decomposed subnetworks						
35ms subnet	6	2.5	.10	7	8250	$.06 \times 10^{11}$
65ms subnet	5	1.2	.20	3	12705	$.04 \times 10^{11}$
125ms subnet	7	3.0	.01	10	32486	$.35 \times 10^{11}$
Full decomposed AP-net						
glue training	2	2.0	.50	9	46485	$.46 \times 10^{11}$
fine tuning	1	2.0	.50	2	88199	$.19 \times 10^{11}$
Total						1.10×10^{11}

Table 19.4
Classification performance

Network	top-3 normalized AHR	top-3 normalized AFA	top-3 AHR	top-3 AFA
Previous 125-ms nondecomposed AP-net	**61.7**	3.1	55.6	2.5
Decomposed subnetworks				
35ms subnet	70.1	7.4	69.0	2.1
65ms subnet	65.2	5.8	62.0	2.4
125ms subnet	33.1	4.3	33.0	4.4
Full decomposed AP-net				
after glue training	56.5	4.0	45.0	3.1
after fine tuning	**62.4**	3.5	55.6	2.5

malized AFA, then the final network (after glue training and fine tuning) achieved essentially equivalent performance to the 125-ms nondecomposed network, but in only $\dfrac{1.1 \times 10^{11}}{10.62 \times 10^{11}} \approx 10\%$ of the operations. The 10.62×10^{11} operations required about 10 days of processing on an Alliant six-way FX80; this was reduced to about a day of processing through problem decomposition, representing a substantial savings in training time.

Figure 19.12 shows the performance of the individual phonemes in the trained network.

We also performed tests on an independent set of 850 sentences that were not in either the training set or the test set used for cross-validation. Results are shown in table 19.5. According to this measure of performance, if we use the normalized scores again as a criterion, after fine tuning, the modular network achieved superior performance in, again, about a tenth of the training time.

19.4.5 AP-net Discussion

Given the magnitude of the difference between learning times of the nondecomposed versus the decomposed network and given the fact that problem decomposition has shown significant learning speed improvement in more controlled studies, it is probable that the savings can be at least partially attributed to the problem-decomposition methodology. However, there are a couple of other differences between the nondecomposed

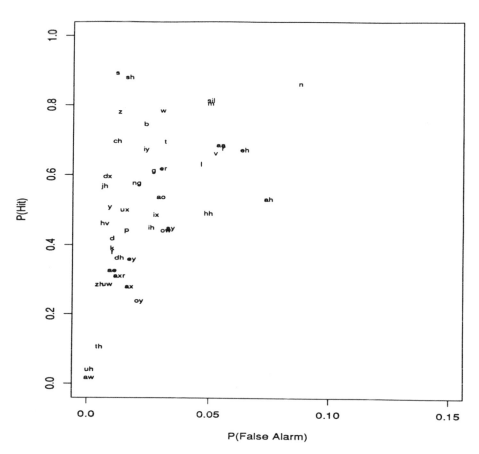

Figure 19.12
Performance of various phonemes on best network trained, showing top-3 AHR and top-3 AFA for each

Table 19.5
Results of AP-net testing on a data set not used for training or cross-validation

Network	top-3 top-3 AHR	top-3 top-3 AFA	top-3 AHR	top-3 AFA	Total Op's
125ms AP-net (after 300 epochs)	62.6	2.7	57.4	2.4	10.6×10^{11}
Decomposed network after fine tuning (as above)	65.7	2.7	57.0	2.3	1.1×10^{11}

and decomposed AP-net experiments that could not be thoroughly controlled for, due to the very large size of this network.

First, the decomposed network had many more weights than the nondecomposed AP-net. The larger number of weights might make modeling the training data a simpler task, and, as a consequence, might result in a bias toward higher performance for the decomposed network. It is possible that the speedier training time we observed was due to a larger number of weights instead of to the decomposition methodology. Whether a decomposed network would learn faster than a nondecomposed network when the number of weights in the two networks is approximately equal remains to be tested. As discussed in section 19.4.2, we raised the weight counts as a possible solution to low performance scores after training. This was done before we modified the subnetwork training algorithm to reduce false-positive responses. Whether a decomposed network trained on the modified algorithm would learn faster than a network with the same number of weights, but not trained using decomposition, remains to be tested.

Second, we performed a more extensive search in η and α space than Kamm and Singhal (1990), resulting in generally higher learning rates and training times of only a few epochs. The range of learning rates explored in the current study included higher rates than those explored by Kamm and Singhal, so it is difficult to determine whether the learning speedup (in terms of arithmetic operations) is attributable to problem decomposition or learning rate. To address this issue, we also trained nondecomposed 125-ms networks for approximately the same number of operations as the decomposed net, using the learning parameters used for the 125-ms subnetwork and the original parameters for the nondecomposed network. On the 200-sentence test set, these networks had normalized AHAs of 47.3% and 46.3% and normalized AFAs of 5.9% and 5.1%, respectively. This performance is markedly poorer than performance of the decomposed network, supporting the hypothesis that the problem decomposition strategy was a primary contributor to the learning speedup.

The problem-decomposition strategy facilitated the more thorough search for learning parameters, since it allowed the use of different parameters for training the different subnetworks. In many empirical studies utilizing the backpropagation algorithm, it is difficult to control for the η and α parameters. Often, they are held constant over all experimental conditions. However, since optimal parameter values are often training-set dependent, this constraint can result in misleading comparisons if η and α are chosen optimally for one network but not another. Our experience in this project supports the fact that the careful selection of network training parameters is critical for successful training (and performance) (see also Kolen and Pollack 1990). For one particular set of parameters, glue training achieved 25% AHR on the training data after three epochs, while for another set of parameters, glue training achieved 48% AHR after three epochs. The run that started at 25% never exceeded a 40% score, even after many training runs. Because of the need to control for this variation, one possible future direction for this work is to explore algorithms that automatically and adaptively determine the values of these parameters (Atlas et al. 1990b; Barnard and Cole 1989; Brent 1990; Chan and Fallside 1987).

In comparison to the study described in the previous section, here it is clear that fine tuning did improve network performance considerably. This may have been because subnetwork training for the previous vowel-recognition network was stopped just before overfitting began, and so further fine tuning caused networks to begin to overfit their data. Here, it was not as clear that the network had begun overfitting by the time that fine tuning was started, perhaps because of the greater complexity of the problem to be learned.

19.5 Discussion

The vowel- and phoneme-recognition problem decomposition experiments demonstrated some of the same major findings as the less complex pilot study, despite fundamental differences in the nature of the task decomposition among the studies. (Recall that problem decomposition in the pilot study involved presetting the IH weights only—horizontal decomposition—but problem decomposition for the more complex speech-recognition problems used vertical decomposition.) In all three studies, time to convergence was shorter when some of the weights in the network were preset to nonrandom values than when all weights were set to random initial values. Furthermore, when the preset weights had relatively high magnitudes, the networks were able to retain hyperplane positions defined by the weights during subsequent training.

Note that by considering transfer of partially correct weights, we are addressing a more complex issue than if multiple network weight sets were simply glued together in a decomposed network at run time. We have explored how backpropagation learning uses both error-free and errorful preset weight subsets.

19.5.1 Open Questions and Future Directions

These experiments leave many open questions for further research, including the following:

• More systematic studies of backpropagation dynamics on complex tasks should be done to explore further the pilot study hypotheses. In particular, it would be helpful to develop some principled weight magnitude determination strategy.

• Only a single train/test set split was used to verify that the vowel-recognition network achieved equivalent performance for the decomposed and nondecomposed conditions. This is not a reliable estimate of the true error rate of this system: a more rigorous analysis, perhaps using a leaving-one-out strategy (Weiss and Kulikowski 1991), should be performed to verify these results.

• We used an oversized network training scheme for the vowel-recognition task, stopping training just before a degrading generalization score indicated overfitting. More work is necessary to establish how this methodology can best be combined with problem decomposition. In particular, the problems with fine tuning may be due to the fact that subnetworks were trained until they were just on the verge of overfitting, and fine tuning resulted in poor performance because it overfit the data. Also, although the difference was not significant, we did see slightly degraded performance in the decomposed network, indicating a potential problem in the use of this technique.

• The speedup observed in decomposed versus nondecomposed networks might be due not to the decomposed training methodology but to the constrained topology used to train networks. We have performed some preliminary experiments on nondecomposed networks with similar topologies to the decomposed network for the AP-net task, but trained in a single session. Training times remain slow, indicating that training subnetworks separately has its own advantages.

• It is interesting that weight magnitudes from prior training worked so well in the problem-decomposition tasks, without magnitude rescaling.

This may have been due to the high network weights generated by subnetwork training. For example, the average subnetwork weight magnitude in the vowel study was 15.5, which is large compared to the average magnitude of random initial weights, which was 0.25. For substantially different source and target network tasks, careful magnitude tuning may be necessary. Furthermore, for a technique like that described in Towell, Shavlik, and Noordewier (1990), which uses weight sets obtained by means other than prior network training, more attention to weight magnitudes may be helpful in dealing with potentially incorrect initial weights.

• The network decomposition on the vowel-recognition task was chosen arbitrarily. It is important to characterize the nature of decompositions for which speedup occurs. Careful analysis of subproblem interactions should aid in this endeavor. Also, further experiments with different arbitrary decompositions should indicate sensitivity to particular decompositions. In particular, it would be useful to investigate whether different learning dynamics occur when networks are decomposed vertically or horizontally. The choice of network decomposition on the phoneme-recognition task was more principled. It should also be fruitful to explore automated methods for guiding problem decomposition using domain knowledge. Automatic methods for determining decompositions that only use information within the training data have also been recently explored (Nowlan 1990).

• When training data are impoverished (noisy, incorrect, or partial), it may be possible to achieve a performance improvement by using transferred weights. Although this question has been explored in related contexts (Towel, Shavlik, and Noordewier 1990; Waibel, Sawai, and Shikano 1989), an important open issue is whether direct network transfer produces significant performance improvement over randomly initialized networks.

• Note that transfer (as well as the other techniques shown in figure 19.1) determines a set of initial weights, which are then used for further training. The model of transfer used here decouples initial weight determination from learning. Therefore, the learning algorithm can probably be changed (for example, to conjugate gradient; Barnard and Cole 1989) without changes to the transfer process. A study should be performed to verify that transfer remains effective with this and other learning algorithms.

- Further explorations of hyperplane movement dynamics on more complex tasks would aid our understanding of how best to bias networks after transfer. Although hyperplanes are more difficult to visualize for high-dimensional tasks, it is still possible to obtain statistics such as speed of hyperplane movement across feature space and the epochs during training when *they cross training examples.*

- Many other studies are possible by relaxing the assumptions made in the experiments reported here. Potential extensions include multiple hidden-layer networks, networks for regression instead of classification tasks, and transfer in networks with more structured topologies.

- Finally, our most active area of current research explores transfer between networks trained on different but related populations of training data, for source and target networks with the same topology. For example, speaker-dependent training may be speeded up by transferring weights from a network trained on multiple speakers. The effectiveness of transfer has been evaluated under conditions of different relationships between source and target training data (i.e., superset → subset, subset → superset, disjoint but related populations, etc.). This research is reported by Pratt (1993), which shows substantial learning speed improvement via transfer.

19.6 Summary

We have addressed the question of how information stored in one neural network may be transferred to another network for a different task. We explored the behavior of backpropagation when some weights in a network are preset and studied the effect of using weights from pretrained subnets on learning time for a larger network. The results demonstrated that the relative magnitudes of the preset weights (compared to the untrained weights) are important for retaining the locations of pretrained hyperplanes during subsequent learning. We also showed that learning time can be reduced by a factor of 10 using these task-decomposition techniques. Techniques like those described here should facilitate the construction of complex networks that address real-world problems.

Acknowledgments

The research program reported here has benefitted substantially from the participation of Candace Kamm, who collaborated on the AP-net project.

She and Jack Mostow also helped considerably with this paper's preparation. Thanks also to John Smith, Geoff Towell, Michiel Noordewier, Haym Hirsh, David Ackley, Dan Kahn, Sharad Singhal, Vincent Sgro, and Diane Zimmerman, who provided helpful comments on previous drafts.

Notes

This work was performed in part while the author was supported by a research assistantship from Siemens, Inc. Partial support was also provided by DOE DE-FG02-91ER61129, through subcontract 097P753 from the University of Wisconsin and by Bellcore.

1. In this chapter, I use the term *knowledge* in a more general sense than may be expected by AI researchers; I define it as any source of information that can be utilized to speed up network training. Knowledge may or may not be expressed in a logical formalism (Langley 1989).

2. Note that I do not give the corresponding list for the sorts of information that can be *extracted* from a network, like the weights (which we use), size of data set used to train the source, number of epochs used to train source, and centroid of source classes.

3. In order to perform a fair significance test in comparisons with randomly initialized networks, when only some subset $k < 28$ of networks converged, the $(30 - k)$ largest times were removed. For experiment 9, the two worst centroid-initialized scores were removed, since networks in experiment 7 converged more often than the random case.

4. This table omits calculations required to incorporate momentum (α) into weight updates.

5. Barks rescale frequency to reflect equal intervals along the basilar membrane in the cochlea. The scaling is also approximately linearly related to pitch perception. See Schroeder, Atal, and Hall (1979).

6. Note that this strategy does not normalize phonemes in terms of their frame-wise occurrence in the corpus, which would result in inappropriate emphasis on the longer-duration phonemes.

References

Atlas, L. E., J. Connor, D. Park, A. Lippman, R. Cole, M. El-Sharkawi, R. J. Marks, Y. Muthusamy, and M. Rudnick. A performance comparison of trained multi-layer perceptrons and trained classification trees. In *IEEE International Conference on Systems, Man, and Cybernetics*, Cambridge, Massachusetts, November 14–17, 1990a.

Atlas, Les, Ronald Cole, Yeshwant Muthasamy, Alan Lippman, Jerome Connor, Dong Park, Mohamed El-Sharkawi, and Robert J. Marks II. A performance comparison of trained multi-layer perceptrons and trained classification trees. In D. S. Touretzky, editor, *Advances in Neural Information Processing Systems 2*, pp. 622–629. San Mateo, CA; Morgan Kaufmann, Morgan 1990b.

Atlas, Les, Ronald Cole, Yeshwant Muthusamy, A. Lippman, Jerome Connor, D. Park, M. El-Sharkawi, and Robert J. Marks II. Performance comparisons between backpropagation networks and classification trees on three real-world applications. *Proceedings of the IEEE*, 78 (10): 1614–1619. October 1990c.

Barnard, Etienne, and Ronald A. Cole. A neural-net training program based on conjugate-gradient optimization. Technical Report CSE 89-014. Oregon Graduate Center, July 1989.

Brent, Richard P. Fast training algorithms for multi-layer neural nets. Technical Report NA-90-03, Numerical Analysis Project. Computer Science Department, Stanford University, March 1990.

Chan, L.-W., and F. Fallside. An adaptive training algorithm for back propagation networks. *Computer Speech and Language*, 2:205–218, 1987.

Cole, R. A., Y. K. Muthusamy, L. Atlas, T. Leen, and M. Rudnick. Speaker-independent vovel recognition: Comparison of backpropagation and trained classification trees. In *Proceedings of the Twenty-third Annual Hawaii International Conference on System Sciences, Kailua-Kona, Hawaii, January 2–5*, pp. 132–141. 1990.

Dieterich, Tom G., Hermann Hild, and Ghulum Bakiri. A comparative study of ID3 and backpropagation for English text-to-speech mapping. Technical Report (unnumbered). Department of Computer Science, Oregon State University, 1990.

Fisher, Douglas H., and Kathleen B. McKusick. An empirical comparison of ID3 and backpropagation. In *Proceedings of the Eleventh International Joint Conference on Artificial Intelligence*, pp. 788–793, Detroit, August 1989.

Fisher, W. M., V. Zue, J. Bernstein, and D. Pallett. An acoustic-phonetic data base. *Journal of the Acoustical Society of America*. 81 (1): S92, Spring 1987.

Fu, LiMin. Rule learning by searching on adapted nets. In *Proceedings of the Ninth National Conference on Artificial Intelligence (AAAI-91)*, pp. 590–595, Anaheim, CA, 1991.

Hanson, Stephen José, and Lorien Y. Pratt. Comparing biases for minimal network construction with back-propagation. In D. S. Touretzky, editor, *Advances in Neural Information Processing Systems 1*, pp. 177–185. San Mateo, CA: Morgan Kaufmann, 1989.

Hataoka, Nobuo, and Alex H. Waibel. Speaker-independent phoneme recognition on TIMIT database using integated time-delay neural networks (TDNNs). Technical Report CIU-CS-89-190. Carnegie-Mellon University, November 1989.

Judd, Stephen. Learning in neural networks. In *Proceedings of the 1988 Workshop on Computational Learning Theory*, pp. 2–8. San Mateo, CA: Morgan Kaufmann, 1988.

Kamm, C. A., and S. Singhal. Effect of neural network input span on phoneme classification. In *Proceedings of the International Joint Conference on Neural Networks, 1990*, volume 1, pp. 195–200. San Diego, 1990.

Kolen, John F., and Jordan Pollack. Scenes from exclusive-or: Back propagation is sensitive to initial conditions. In *Proceedings of the Twelfth Annual Conference of the Cognitive Science Society*, p. 868, Cambridge, MA, July 1990.

Kruschke, John K. ALCOVE: A connectionist model of category learning. Technical Report 19. Indiana University Cognitive Science Department, June 1990.

Lang, Kevin. Variable resolution learning techniques for speech recognition. In D. S. Touretzky, editor, *Advances in Neural Information Processing Systems 2*. San Mateo, CA: Morgan Kaufmann, 1990.

Langley, Pat. Unifying themes in empirical and explanation-based learning. In *Proceedings of the Sixth International Workshop on Machine Learning, Cornell University*, pp. 2–4, Ithaca, NY, June 1989.

Lee, Kai-fu, and Hsiao-wuen Hon. Speaker-independent phone recognition using Hidden Markov Models. *IEEE Transactions on Acoustics, Speech, and Signal Processing*, 37 (11): 1641–1648, November 1989.

Moody, John, and Christian J. Darken. Fast learning in networks of locally-tuned processing units. *Neural Computation*, 1:281–294, 1989.

Mooney, Raymond J., J. W. Shavlik, G. G. Towell, and A. Gove. An experimental comparison of symbolic and connectionist learning algorithms. In *Proceedings of the Eleventh International Joint Conference on Artificial Intelligence*, pp. 775–780, August 1989.

Morgan, N., and H. Bourlard. Generalization and parameter estimation in feedforward nets: Some experiments. In D. S. Touretzky, editor, *Advances in Neural Information Processing Systems 2*, pp. 630–637. San Mateo, CA: Morgan Kaufmann, 1990.

Nowlan, Steven J. Competing experts: An experimental investigation of associative mixture models. Technical Report CRG-TR-90-5. Carnegie-Mellon University, 1990.

Pratt, Lorien Y., and Candace A. Kamm. Improving a phoneme classification neural network through problem decomposition. In *Proceedings of the International Joint Conference on Neural Networks (IJCNN-91)*, pp. 821–826, Seattle, July 1991.

Pratt, Lorien Y., Jack Mostow, and Candace A. Kamm. Direct transfer of learned information among neural networks. In *Proceedings of the Ninth National Conference on Artificial Intelligence (AAAI-91)*, pp. 584–589. Anaheim CA, 1991.

Pratt, Lorien Y. Discriminability-based transfer between neural networks, 1993. In C. L. Giles, S. J. Hanson, and J. D. Cowan, editors, *Advances in Neural Information Processing Systems 5*, pp. 204–211. San Mateo, CA: Morgan Kaufmann 1993.

Quinlan, J. R. Induction of decision trees. *Machine Learning*, 1:81–106, 1986.

Quinlan, J. R. Comparing connectionist and symbolic learning methods. In *Computational Learning Theory and Natural Learning Systems, Constraints and Prospects*. Cambridge: MIT Press, 1992.

Robinson, Anthony John. Dynamic Error Propagation Networks. PhD. dissertation, Cambridge University, June 1989.

Rumelhart, D. E., G. E. Hinton, and R. J. Williams. Learning internal representations by error propagation. In David E. Rumelhart and James L. McClelland, editors, *Parallel Distributed Processing: Explorations in the Microstructure of Cognition*, volume 1, pp. 318–362. Cambridge, MA: Bradford Books, 1987.

Sankar, A., and R. J. Mammone. A fast learning algorithm for tree neural networks. 1990 Conference on Information Sciences and Systems, Princeton, NJ, March 1990.

Schroeder, M. R., B. S. Atal, and J. L. Hall. Optimizing digital speech codes by exploiting masking properties of the human ear. *Journal of the Acoustical Society of America* 66:1647–1652, 1979.

Shavlik, Jude. Integrating explanatory and neural approaches to machine learning. In *Computational Learning Theory and Natural Learning Systems, Constraints and Prospects*. Cambridge, MA: MIT Press.

Shavlik, J. W., R. J. Mooney, and G. G. Towell. Symbolic and neural net learning algorithms: An experimental comparison. *Machine Learning*, 6 (2): 111–143, 1991.

Simon, H. *The Sciences of the Artificial* (2nd ed.). Cambridge, MA: MIT Press, 1981.

Sontag, Eduardo. Sigmoids distinguish more efficiently than heavisides. *Neural Computation*, 1:470–472, 1989.

Tesauro, Gerald. Scaling relationships in back-propagation learning: Dependence on training set size. *Complex Systems*, 1:367–372, 1987.

Tesauro, Gerald, and Robert Janssens. Scaling relationships in back-propagation learning: Dependence on predicate order. Technical Report CCSR-88-1, Center for Complex Systems Research, University of Illinois at Urbana-Champaign, February 1988.

Towell, Geoffrey G., Jude W. Shavlik, and Michiel O. Noordewier. Refinement of approximate domain theories by knowledge-based neural networks. In *Proceedings of AAAI-90*, pp. 861–866. San Mateo, CA: Morgan Kaufmann, July 1990.

Utgoff, Paul E. Perceptron trees: A case study in hybrid concept representations. *Connection Science*, 1 (4), 1990.

Waibel, Alexander. Modular construction of time-delay neural networks for speech recognition. *Neural Computation*, 1:39–46, 1989.

Waibel, Alexander, T. Hanazawa, Geoff Hinton, Kiyohiro Shikano, and Kevin Lang. Phoneme recognition using time-delay neural networks. Technical Report TR-I-0006. ATR Interpreting Telephony Research Laboratories, Japan, October 1987.

Waibel, Alexander, Hidefumi Sawai, and Kiyohiro Shikano. Modularity and scaling in large phonemic neural networks. *IEEE Transactions on Acoustics, Speech, and Signal Processing*, 37 (12): 1888–1898, December 1989.

Watrous, Raymond. Context-modulated discrimination of similar vowels using second-order connectionist networks. Technical Report CRG-TR-89-5. University of Toronto, Connectionist Research Group, December 1989.

Weigend, Andreas S., Bernardo A. Huberman, and David E. Rumelhart. Predicting the future: A connectionist approach. *International Journal of Neural Systems*, 1:193–209, 1990.

Weiss, Sholom M., and Ioannis Kapouleas. An empirical comparison of pattern recognition, neural nets, and machine learning classification methods. In *Proceedings of the International Joint Conference on Artificial Intelligence*, pp. 781–787, Detroit, 1989.

Weiss, Sholom M., and Casimir A. Kulikowski. *Computer Systems that Learn*. San Mateo, CA: Morgan Kaufmann. 1991.

Contributors

Ranan B. Banerji
Department of Mathematics and
Computer Science
Saint Joseph's University

Eric B. Baum
NEC Research Institute

William W. Cohen
AT&T Bell Laboratories

Diane J. Cook
Computer Science Engineering
University of Texas at Arlington

George Drastal
Siemens Corporate Research

Susan L. Epstein
Department of Computer Science
Hunter College, CUNY

Haym Hirsh
Department of Computer Science
Rutgers University

Stephen Judd
Siemens Corporate Research

Marek Karpinski
Department of Computer Science
University of Bonn

Michael J. Kearns
AT&T Bell Laboratories

Wolfgang Maass
IIPG
Technische Universitaet Graz

Richard Maclin
Computer Sciences Department
University of Wisconsin at
Madison

Daniel N. Osherson
IDIAP

Lorien Y. Pratt
Department of Mathematical and
Computer Sciences
Colorado School of Mines

J. R. Quinlan
Basser Department of Computer
Science
University of Sydney

Harish Ragavan
Beckman Institute
University of Illinois

Larry Rendell
Beckman Institute
University of Illinois

Ronald L. Rivest
Laboratory for Computer Science
Massachusetts Institute of
Technology

David E. Rumelhart
Department of Psychology
Stanford University

Robert E. Schapire
AT&T Bell Laboratories

Raj Seshu
University of Denver
Department of Mathematics and
Computer Science

Jude W. Shavlik
Computer Sciences Department
University of Wisconsin at
Madison

Michael Stob
Department of Mathematics
Calvin College

György Turán
Automata Theory Research Group
JATE, Hungarian Academy of
Sciences

Andreas Weigend
Xerox PARC

Scott Weinstein
University of Pennsylvania

Thorsten Werther
Department of Computer Science
University of Bonn

Yiqun Yin
Laboratory for Computer Science
Massachusetts Institute of
Technology

Index